D1409710

THE
YEARBOOK OF ENGLISH STUDIES
VOLUME 7
1977

FUTURE VOLUMES

From Volume VIII (1978) onwards the *Yearbook of English Studies* will contain several changes of format and content. Part of it will continue to serve as an additional outlet for essays and reviews submitted to the English Editors of the *Modern Language Review*, on the literature and language of English-speaking countries. But a substantial portion of each *Yearbook* will from now on consist of specially commissioned articles on a broad topic or theme, and of articles and reviews submitted to the Editors which happen to have a bearing on that particular *Yearbook*'s topic or theme. It is hoped in this way to limit the proportion of more narrowly specialist material in the *Yearbook* in order to give each volume a greater centrality of interest and a wider readership. The first two volumes (VIII and IX) will be concerned respectively with American Literature and with Theatrical Literature.

To coincide with this change of content, certain changes of format are being introduced. The volumes will be set in a larger and more spacious type than before, and there will be a new style of soft-cover binding.

Contributions submitted to the *Modern Language Review* or the *Yearbook* will continue to be considered for both publications interchangeably. Manuscripts and copies of books for review should be sent to the Editors, *Modern Language Review* and *Yearbook of English Studies*, Department of English, University of Warwick, Coventry CV4 7AL, England.

The Yearbook

of

English Studies

Edited by

G. K. HUNTER and C. J. RAWSON

Assistant Editor

JENNY MEZCIEMS

VOLUME 7

1977

Modern Humanities Research Association

The Yearbook of English Studies

is published by

THE MODERN HUMANITIES RESEARCH ASSOCIATION

and may be ordered from

The Honorary Treasurer, MHRA

King's College, Strand, London WC2R 2LS, England

Editorial Address

The Department of English, The University of Warwick, Coventry CV4 7AL

Advisory Panel

MALCOLM BRADBURY	R. L. SMALLWOOD
J. L. BRADLEY	J. B. TRAPP
PHILIP EDWARDS	R. S. WOOF
PAT ROGERS	ROSEMARY WOOLF
LARZER ZIFF	

160519

© MODERN HUMANITIES RESEARCH ASSOCIATION 1977

This publication is copyright under the Berne Convention and the International Copyright Convention. All rights reserved. Apart from any copying under the UK Copyright Act 1956, part 1, section 7, whereby a single copy of an article may be supplied, under certain conditions, for the purpose of research or private study, by a library of a class prescribed by the UK Board of Trade Regulations (Statutory Instruments, 1957, No. 868), no part of this publication may be reproduced, stored in a retrieval system or transmitted in any form without the prior permission of the copyright owners. Permission is not required to copy abstracts of papers or articles on condition that a full reference to the source is shown.

Multiple copying of the contents of the publication without permission is always illegal.

ISBN 0 900547 45 6

Printed in Great Britain by

W. S. MANEY AND SON LTD   LEEDS LS9 7DL   ENGLAND

Contents

ARTICLES (continued)

REVIEWS

REVIEWS (continued)

REVIEWS (continued)

REVIEWS (continued)

Exemplum and Refrain: The Meaning of *Deor*

JEROME MANDEL

Clemson University

Although *Deor* has long been the object of scholarly investigation, most writers on the poem have concerned themselves with the meaning of particular words and especially with the identification of the proper names in the catalogue of misfortunes which occupies more than half the poem. I want to forego for the moment the problems of literal meaning and examine the poem's overall signification as this is revealed in the relation between the exempla and the refrain, paying particular attention to the referents of *þæs* and *þisses*.[1] While I am not quite willing to accept *Deor* as 'a very sophisticated version of a charm',[2] I do agree with Bloomfield that the *þisses* of the refrain refers to some general human concern outside the poem itself and not to Deor's individual misfortune which he describes at the end of the poem. Indeed, I am convinced that *Deor* is designed not to console but to teach.

The five exempla and Deor's experience at the court of the Heodenings, while in themselves unique, epitomize a kind of misfortune with general if not universal relevance. The opening exempla are most obviously unified in that each reflects adversity, and so contributes in part to the tone of the poem. But the poet also carefully and more philosophically unifies the exempla by imbuing misery, regardless of its specific occurrence, with essentially the same characteristics: (1) misery has a physical and a spiritual aspect (it affects the body and the mind) and (2) misery involves isolation or separation of one kind or another. The poet reinforces that unity by appealing to what the audience knows as true: knowledge, the 'we have heard' formula, appears as a leit-motif in the poem and (by creating a context of 'that which is known') helps to establish the validity of the poet's Christian message. With the exception of the Welund and Beadohild passages (which, since even we know about them, may have been so well known that the 'we have heard' formula would have been gratuitous), the poet emphasizes the

---

[1] The most commonly accepted reading is that *Deor* is a personal lament concerned with the misfortune and afflictions that befall men in this world and suggesting that these sorrows pass in time. See Stanley B. Greenfield, 'The Old English Elegies', in *Continuations and Beginnings*, edited by E. G. Stanley (London, 1966), pp. 160–3, for the most modern statement of this view. Other attempts to make aesthetic sense of the whole poem are F. Norman, '*Deor*: A Criticism and an Interpretation', *MLR*, 32 (1937), 374–81 (restated in 'Problems in the Dating of *Deor* and its Allusions', in *Franciplegius*, edited by Jess B. Bessinger, Jr and Robert P. Creed (New York, 1965), p. 209, and compare Kemp Malone, 'On Deor 14–17', *MP*, 40 (1942–3), 1–18 (p. 2); P. J. Frankis, '*Deor* and *Wulf and Eadwacer*: Some Conjectures', *Medium Ævum*, 31 (1962), 161–75; Morton W. Bloomfield, 'The Form of *Deor*', *PMLA*, 79 (1964), 534–41; and Norman Eliason, 'Two Old English Scop Poems', *PMLA*, 81 (1966), 185–92, reiterated in greater detail in '*Deor* — A Begging Poem?', in *Medieval Literature and Civilization*, edited by D. A. Pearsall and R. A. Waldron (London, 1969), pp. 55–61. None has achieved wide acceptance. For a conflation of critical attitudes and review of scholarship see Jerome Mandel, *Studies in the Structure of Old English Poetry* (unpublished dissertation, Ohio State University, 1966). For a pleasant analysis of critical assumptions about the poem and the ways in which they mislead critics and misfocus conclusions, see Neil D. Isaacs, *Structural Principles in Old English Poetry* (Knoxville, 1968), pp. 107–14.

[2] Bloomfield, p. 534.

audience's awareness of the afflictions suffered by Maeðhild (*We . . . gefrugnon*, l. 14), Ðeodric (*þæt wæs monegum cuð*, l. 19b), and Eormanric (*We geascodan*, l. 21a); and he closes the poem with an intimate revelation of his own (or his persona's) affliction, albeit fictionalized.[1] Thus surrounded by what the audience knows and accepts as true, the moral (which is only part of what the whole poem teaches), that God gives to some and witholds from others, gains in validity.

But there may be another reason for this emphasis upon what the audience knows to be true. If the *þisses* of the refrain is supposed to refer to a specific misfortune suffered by a listener similar to the generic misfortune described in the exempla, then the listener can acknowledge his own misfortune more readily once he recognizes it as similar to one that is publicly known and widely understood, the common knowledge of all the listeners. So, in each exemplum I intend to discuss the referents of *þæs* and *þisses* as well as isolation or separation, working through grammar to universal relevance in order to discover the poem's unity and meaning.

Although the allusion to Welund may generate the whole familiar story in the mind of the listener, the *Deor* poet concentrates on one small point in the story: Welund's physical affliction and his isolation (most probably on the small island). The poet emphasizes Welund's isolation by the contrastive collocation of *gesiþþe* and *sorge ond longaþ* in l. 3, a justaposition that implies the separation of a man from society characteristic of the exile,[2] and the poet emphasizes Welund's knowledge and experience of misfortune: *Welund . . . wræces cunnade* (l. 1), *earfoþa dreag* (l. 2b), and *wean oft onfond* (l. 4b). The audience is told five times in the first four lines nothing more than that Welund suffered misery, troubles, sorrow, severe misery, and woe; an unconscionable five-fold iteration unless it is supposed to establish that the referent of *þæs* in the refrain is the misfortune described in the exemplum. The precise nature of Welund's *wræces*, *earfoþa*, and *wean* distinguishes his misfortune from that of the others who follow. Although there is some indication that Welund was troubled in spirit (e.g., *sorge* and *longaþ* and perhaps *anhydig*), his primary misery is of the flesh, his misfortune physical.[3] Precisely which of the many possible misfortunes attributable to Welund is meant by this emphasis finds definition toward the end: Welund experienced woe when Nið had hamstrung him. However one understands *seonobende*, as fetters made of sinew or as hamstringing, the result is the same: a physical limitation, an affliction of the body. It is this to which *þæs* in the refrain refers and which finally passes. Clearly, *þæs* in line 7 cannot refer to the fact that Welund was hamstrung. If it did, how then could we understand that it *ofereode*? His severed tendon was not re-knit. It is the physical

[1] Whether or not 'Deor' is the actual name of the *scop* who sings the song (which seems unlikely) or the adopted persona of the *scop*, and whether or not the events he relates concerning his departure from the court of the Heodenings are true (which seems unlikely) or fictionalized are not relevant here. The point is that the story is supposed to be accepted by the listeners as true. And it is possible, of course, that there is a grain of truth in it. The poet says that at the time of his misfortune among the Heodenings his name *was* (past tense) Deor (*Me wæs Deor noma*, l. 37b). And if we agree that 'the *Deor* poet was presumably a priest or monk' (Kemp Malone, 'The Tale of Geat and Mæðhild', *ES*, 19 (1937), 193–9 (p. 198)), he could well be referring to his experience prior to entering orders. It is well known that a change of name often accompanied a change in state of life. The practice, of great antiquity, continues in religious orders in the west to this day.

[2] So also Frankis, p. 168, and A. C. Bouman, *Patterns in Old English and Old Icelandic Literature* (Leiden, 1962), p. 102.

[3] But compare L. Whitbread, 'A Medieval English Metaphor', *PQ*, 17 (1938), 365–70 (pp. 367–8), who implicitly looks upon Weland's sufferings as more mental than physical.

misery, the limitation and imprisonment caused by hamstringing, not the hamstringing itself, to which *þæs* refers and which *ofereode*.

By saying *þisses swa mæg*, the poet implies that whatever similar or related misfortune a listener suffers can also pass away. The Welund exemplum has specific relevance to any member of the audience who has been maimed or wounded. As I understand Anglo-Saxon society and history, that would include most of the audience (and may indicate one reason why the poet began with Welund and physical affliction).[1] The audience is told that Welund's suffering, the limitation of the flesh, and the isolation which followed inevitably from his hamstringing, passed away; anyone in the audience who has also been cut or maimed or bruised must realize that his suffering, the result of a wound, may also pass away. I am not convinced that it is important to know just how the misfortune passed away. *Þæs ofereode* emphasizes the fact that something passed away, changed, not how it passed away. To concern oneself with the question of 'how' is to introduce the notion of retribution into the poem which, to my mind, exists neither in the exemplum nor the refrain; nor is it implicit in the relation between exemplum and refrain.

The kind of misfortune that the poet describes for Welund is quite different from that which the poet characterizes by the example of Beadohild. Welund's affliction is essentially of the flesh; Beadohild's misery is of the mind and spirit. The exemplum begins with a contrast that locates the affliction in her mind: although the death of her brothers is a great misfortune, it is not so grievous *on sefan* (l. 9a) as the fact that she is pregnant by the slayer of her brothers. The poet focuses on the mind and spirit, the cognitive rather than the physical: *on sefan* in line 9a, her realization that she was pregnant (*ongieten hæfde* | *þæt heo eacen wæs*, ll. 10b–11a), and her inability to think resolutely (*æfre ne meahte* | *þriste geþencan*, ll. 11b–12a). Just as there was a spiritual aspect to Welund's physical suffering, there is a physical dimension to Beadohild's spiritual suffering; she is, after all, pregnant, and we know from other sources that she did not arrive at this state in the most pleasant of ways. Like Welund, Beadohild is cut off and alone. Welund's isolation is physical; Beadohild suffers an isolation in spirit. Her misery stems from a classic medieval dilemma: she is bearing the child of the man who slew her brothers. Her awareness of the condition and the irresoluteness of her thinking on the problem suggest a secret that isolates her from normal human concourse. The poet shows this by his emphasis upon the mental anguish to which the *þaes* of the refrain refers. *Þaes* cannot refer to the causes of her unhappiness (the fact that Welund raped her and left her pregnant, the death of her brothers) because they in fact did not pass away. What did pass away was the result, her subsequent unhappiness and specifically her suffering of spirit, her inability to think resolutely what to do. Any listener who suffers in a way similar to *this* (*þisses* in the refrain) — that is, who has a secret problem that torments his mind — should be made aware that whether or not the problem is relieved, the torment it causes can pass away.

---

[1] See F. L. Attenborough, *The Laws of the Earliest English Kings* (Cambridge, 1922), especially pp. 5–17. Of ninety items of law preserved in a late manuscript and said to be those of Æthelberht of Kent set down in the time of Augustine, almost half are devoted exclusively to the penalties that must be paid if various parts of the body are cut, damaged, disfigured, pierced, broken, lacerated, bruised, or destroyed.

Precisely what the poet had in mind when he referred to the tale of Geat and Mæðhild (as the lady is now commonly known) has eluded several generations of scholars. What was true for Lawrence about sixty years ago, unfortunately, is still true for us. 'In the present state of our knowledge, no one can dogmatize about [Mæð] 'Hild' and 'Geat' — the passage is too brief, too corrupt and too allusive.'[1] What distinguishes the exemplum of Mæðhild (and Geat) from the others is that it concerns love characterized here as a *sorglufu* (l. 16a). Since something (perhaps either Mæðhild's *monge* or Geat's *frige*) relevant to this love became boundless or overpowering (*wurdon grundlease*, l. 15). we may fairly assume that the event referred to in the exemplum is significant and important enough to characterize this particular kind of misfortune for an audience familiar with the tale. Like those of Beadohild and Welund, this misfortune seems to affect both the mind and the body; either Mæðhild or Geat or both are so affected by their *sorglufu* that it deprived them (or him or her) of all sleep. I suspect, although of course it is impossible to prove, that there is the connotation of isolation in these lines, the separation of the lovers one from the other[2] or, equally possible, the separation of the lovers from others by virtue of their *sorglufu* (which would, in this case, be a secret love affair as, perhaps, between lovers from warring tribes). But this is mostly, in the nature of the case, speculation. The causes of the misery are not important. The effect of the causes is *sorglufu*, the referent of *þæs*; it is the effect which passes away. Anyone listening to the poem in the eighth century (or later) might well recognize his own misfortune reflected in the story of Geat and Mæðhild and realize that, since the *sorglufu* of Mæðhild and Geat passed away, his own *sorglufu* can also pass away.

Whether the Ðeodric of *Deor* ll. 18–19 is Ðeodric the Frank as Professor Malone argues[3] or, as is more commonly believed, Ðeodric the Ostrogoth ought not to concern us overmuch here. The lines are so indirect and allusive that it is impossible for us to know what the poet was referring to. What precisely is the referent of *þæs*? Given the precedent established by the Welund exemplum, that *þæs* refers to some kind of misery or misfortune, how then are we to understand that the passage refers to woe which subsequently passed away: (1) is Ðeodric's possession of Mæringaburg meant to indicate a tyrannical rule and therefore woe for the people; or (2) is the woe Ðeodric's because he ruled Mæringaburg for thirty years and then his rule came to an end;[4] or (3) is the thirty year period that Ðeodric ruled the Mærings meant to indicate thirty years of exile during which he was separated from his own people (not the Mærings) although he was at the same time

---

[1] W. W. Lawrence, 'The Song of Deor', *MP*, 9 (1911–12), 23–45 (p. 40). Almost everyone who has written on the poem has been forced to deal with this crux. The most interesting of the various suggestions are offered by Lawrence (above); Frederick Tupper, Jr, 'The Song of Deor', *MP*, 9 (1911–12), 265–7, and 'The Third Strophe of "Deor"', *Anglia*, 37 (1913), 118–23; Malone's edition (London, 1933; third edition 1961), and several articles: 'Mæðhild', *ELH*, 3 (1936), 253–6; 'The Tale of Geat and Mæðhild', *ES*, 19 (1937), 193–9; and 'On Deor 14–17', *MP*, 40 (1942–3), 1–18. Chief among those who object to Malone's reading are F. Norman, '*Deor*: A Criticism and an Interpretation', *MLR*, 32 (1937), 374–81, and '*Deor* and Modern Scandinavian Ballads', *London Medieval Studies*, 1 (1938), 165–78; L. Whitbread, 'The Third Section of *Deor*', *MP*, 38 (1941), 371–84; and Norman Eliason, 'The Story of Geat and Mæðhild in *Deor*', *SP*, 62 (1965), 495–509.

[2] F. Norman, 'Problems in the Dating of *Deor* . . .', p. 209, also assumes 'some trouble with her clan, and [that] Geat was an exile'.

[3] See Malone's edition, pp. 9–13. Morton Bloomfield, p. 536, n. 17, provides a brief though adequate summary of the problem.

[4] Margaret Ashdown, 'Notes on Two Passages of Old English Verse', *RES*, 5 (1929), 324–7.

ruling the Mærings? We cannot know whether Đeodric was meant to represent a good or a bad king. I am inclined to understand Đeodric as a good king in exile, separated from his rightful people. In this reading, which I want to emphasize is tentative, Đeodric characterizes a particular kind of affliction, that of a good man suffering in his separation from his rightful place in society. The exemplum should appeal, I suggest, to the exile in the audience, the one most clearly separated from what he feels to be his proper place in society. As with the other exempla, the important thing is not how Đeodric came to be in exile nor how he overcame that misfortune. We are only told, if I read the exemplum correctly, that Đeodric was in exile or separated from his people for a long time (thirty years, during which he ruled a town not his by right) and that his misery, specifically the misery of exile, came to an end. Any man who suffers similarly can recognize his misfortune in that of Đeodric (*þæt wæs monegum cuþ*) and realize that the end of his own exile is also possible (*þisses swa mæg*).

Most critics insist that in the next section of *Deor* the poet departs from his usual method and does not represent the central figure, Eormanric, as one who has out-lived misfortune. But, it seems to me, the point of this exemplum is not that Eorman-ric oppressed his people nor that the Goths outlived misfortune, but rather that the relationship between Eormanric and many of his warriors (*secg monig*, l. 24a) epitomizes a particular kind of misfortune which, in time, can pass away. This misfortune involves a separation of the king from his people; they are not in accord as they ought to be in a well run kingdom. Rather, the poet carefully juxtaposes and contrasts what the warriors can expect from their lord (*wean on wenan*, in expectation of evil, l. 25a) and what they wish for their lord (*wyscte geneahhe* | *þæt þæs cynerices ofercumen wære*, wished constantly that that kingdom would be over-come, l. 25b–26). By focusing on the retainers' awareness of their isolation from their ruler, the poet shows how the tyranny of a bad king can create a situation of misery, yet another kind of affliction which his listeners can recognize and see, possibly, as similar to their own.[1]

As I read the poem, *þæs* in the refrain refers not to Eormanric's cruel thought or savagery, nor to his retainers' sorrow or their resultant wish that he be overthrown, but to the situation defined by these causally related attitudes. If *þæs* refers to the warriors' wish (they eventually ceased to wish that the king be overthrown), then the exemplum is pointless and irrelevant. If *þæs* refers to the warriors' sufferings, and alternatively if *þæs* refers to a lord of cruel disposition characterized by Eormanric, then the relation between *þæs* and *þisses* is insulting to the audience and therefore dangerous for the poet-performer. That is, if *þæs* refers to the warriors' sufferings or the lord's cruelty, then the performer places himself in danger by implying, with *þisses*, that the members of his audience are made miserable by their lord or that the lord is cruel. It seems to me that the only way *þæs* can refer to the exemplum and keep the parts of the exemplum in their proper relationship is if it refers to the

---

[1] This particular misfortune, the separation of ruler and ruled, reflects a political occurrence of some frequency in Anglo-Saxon England. In 757, for example, Æthelbald of Mercia, after ruling forty-one years and with just cause earning the title royal tyrant, was murdered by his bodyguard. The story, and others like it, is recorded by Sir Frank Stenton, *Anglo Saxon England* (Oxford, 1965), p. 204, who comments: 'A king of this type could easily become involved in feuds which override the loyalty of the retainer to his chief'. I think the Eormanric exemplum refers to a situation of this kind which it recognizes as an affliction that can be overcome.

situation which the exemplum as a whole defines: the misery of political oppression. Eormanric is cruel: his savagery creates a situation in which his retainers are in constant fear, oppressed, expecting the worst, wishing to be free of that fear; this is a miserable situation. It is a situation which passed away. Then what does *þisses* in the refrain refer to? I don't believe a *scop* would have had the temerity to imply that his present audience is composed of a ruler who terrorizes his following and a band of retainers who wish for their lord's overthrow. But I do believe in a *scop* appealing to members of his audience who have been driven into exile by a situation similar to that which he presents in the Eormanric exemplum. The exemplum is meant to be relevant to exiles in the poet's audience, people from outside the court of the performance. They can most easily recognize that *þisses* does not by comparison implicate the retainers in the audience or condemn the lord in whose court the poem is sung. They recognize in the relation between Eormanric and his men the political situation of a distant court from which they are exiled.

If both the Ðeodric and Eormanric exempla do indeed have specific relevance to exiles in the audience, they do so in entirely different ways. They epitomize opposite kinds of misfortune associated with exile, but, like the exempla of Welund and Beadohild, they complement each other. The Ðeodric exemplum emphasizes the fact of exile, and the point of the refrain is that exile, no matter how comfortable, is a misery which can pass away. The cause of exile, the condition of exile, and the overcoming of exile are not to the point. Exile itself is misery. Ðeodric's passed away; so can that of any exile who hears the poem. But the Eormanric exemplum emphasizes the cause of exile: a particularly repressive political situation. Any man driven into exile can know through the exemplum of Eormanric and his men that the situation does indeed pass away. As in the other exempla, these two are characterized by isolation: the physical separation of a king from his rightful people (Ðeodric) and the separation in spirit of a king and his people (Eormanric).

After these five exempla the poet moves to a general consideration of misfortune. In doing so, he follows a characteristic Anglo-Saxon pattern of moving from the personal to the general, a process which recognizes a universal principle operating in individual experience. The shift occurs quite easily, since the general passage begins with a sitting *sorgcearig* (sorrowful one, l. 28a) who may well reflect the *secg monig* who sat *sorgum gebunden* (l. 24) in the immediately preceding exemplum. One sits bound by sorrows and yet expects more; the other thinks that he has enough, an endless portion of sorrows, and discovers how to understand them in a way that may make them more bearable.

> Siteð sorgcearig,   sælum bidæled,
> on sefan sweorceð,   sylfum þinceð
> þæt sy endeleas   earfoða dæl.
> Mæg ðonne geþencan,   þæt geond þas woruld
> witig dryhten   wendeþ geneahhe,
> eorle monegum   are gesceawað,
> wislicne blæd,   sumum weana dæl.[1]
>
>   (l. 28)

These lines emphatically sound the theme of the poem, which is reflected in the important contrastive collocation of *sorgcearig* and *sælum* in l. 28. It is the theme

[1] My text is that of Krapp and Dobbie, *The Anglo Saxon Poetic Records*, III, *The Exeter Book* (New York, 1936).

reflected also by the refrain, as we understand it to this point, that no matter how steeped in sorrow a man might be, suffering can pass away because mighty God changes things frequently throughout this world (ll. 31b–32). Indeed, these general remarks echo the refrain in structure as well: like the refrain, these lines are composed of two parts, one of which looks upon past and present misery (ll. 28–30), the other of which takes an ameliorative and future view of these miseries (ll. 31–4), indicating that they can pass away.

The five exempla with which the poem begins identify some of the kinds of adversity that the Lord can make to pass away: physical (Welund) and spiritual (Beadohild) affliction, sorrow that can come from love (Mæðhild), the sorrow of exile or of a good king separated from his people (Ðeodric), and the sorrow of an oppressive political situation (Eormanric). The poet, however, does more than offer Stoic consolation. The ameliorative thrust of the general consideration of misfortune (that is, ll. 31–4) is based on two different claims: first, that God changes things, and second, that God allows to some a portion of honour and to others a portion of woe. Taken together, these claims enlarge the poem's theme: good as well as misery can pass away. In juxtaposing honour (are . . . wislicne blæd, ll. 33b–34a) and woe (weana dæl, l. 34b) which God shows to men, the poet implicitly acknowledges the transitoriness of both good and ill in this world. Good, as well as sorrow, is transient, subject to the vagaries of fortune and the will of God. By pointing specifically at this world (þas woruld, l. 31b), the poet introduces a cosmic dimension to his poem: all things can pass away. And this is what the poem teaches.

In the concluding lines of the poem the speaker seems to offer himself and his own experience as the epitome of a kind of sorrow that can affect all men, and by making public his past adversity, he permits those in his audience who have suffered a similar setback to recognize their misfortune in his.

> Þæt ic bi me sylfum   secgan wille,
> þæt ic hwile waes   Heodeninga scop,
> dryhtne dyre.   Me wæs Deor noma.
> Ahte ic fela wintra   folgað tilne,
> holdne hlaford,   oþþæt Heorrenda nu,
> leoðcræftig monn   londryht geþah,
> þæt me eorla hleo   ær gesealde.
>   Þæs ofereode,   þisses swa mæg.

(l. 35)

Several considerations indicate that the Deor exemplum is not to be taken literally, that the exemplum does not, in fact, characterize the misfortune of a scop who lost his job. Most important is the juxtaposition of the Deor exemplum and the general comments on adversity. When the speaker says Þæt ic bi me sylfum secgan wille (I can say this about myself) immediately after saying that God changes things, grants honour to some, woe to others, he proffers what appears to be his own experience as evidence of the universal principle he has articulated in the previous lines. The Deor exemplum shows honour, a portion of woe, and God changing things.

To what, then, do þæs and þisses in the final refrain refer? If we apply to this refrain the same criteria that we have applied throughout, then þæs refers to Deor's misfortune and þisses to a misfortune similar to that of Deor suffered by any member of the audience. But surely we are not to suppose the poet's audience filled with unemployed scops. Rather, Deor's particular misfortune, like those in the other exempla, is a metaphor, the incarnation of the general in the particular. Deor's misfortune represents a kind of misfortune, perhaps no more specific than 'something important lost or taken away'. So imprecise a loss becomes true misfortune when active agents are introduced: a competitor and a lord, a person in power, who can reward and take away. We are not told whether Heorrenda, regardless of his reputation, is better than Deor or not; we are only told that he is skilled in song and that he now possesses what Deor formerly possessed. The final exemplum has specific relevance to any man who has suffered a loss with or without justice. This is rather too quiet a way to end the poem and, in fact, the poem ends quite differently.

The Deor exemplum differs fundamentally from the other exempla in the poem. Coming after the general remarks on adversity, both the exemplum and the refrain are cast in new light. The Deor exemplum, more precisely and specifically than any of the others, reflects the poet's comments on adversity and honour. The opening five exempla emphasize adversity which is characterized by reference to particular people, those to whom God has shown a portion of woes (*weana dæl*, l. 34b). But in the Deor exemplum, the poet, by contrasting the rising fortunes of Heorrenda with the falling fortunes of Deor, shows both those to whom God gives honour (Heorrenda) and those to whom God shows a portion of woes (Deor). And in doing so, the poet complicates the referents of *þaes* and *þisses* in the concluding refrain. In the previous exempla, *þæs* has always referred to the particular kind of misfortune characterized in the exempla, and *þisses* has referred, in my reading of the poem, to any similar misfortune suffered by a listener. But the poet has shown us that good and ill are in the hands of God, who can make each pass away (l. 32). Thus, the *þæs* of the final refrain can refer as easily to Heorrenda's good fortune as it can to Deor's ill fortune.[1]

The possible referents of *þæs* and *þisses* in the final refrain become four:

(1)   that (good fortune of Heorrenda) passed away; this (good fortune similar to that of Heorrenda) can also pass away;

(2)   that (good fortune of Heorrenda) passed away; this (misfortune similar to that of Deor) can also pass away;

(3)   that (misfortune of Deor) passed away; this (good fortune similar to that of Heorrenda) can also pass away;

(4)   that (misfortune of Deor) passed away; this (misfortune similar to that of Deor) can also pass away.

I would prefer to dismiss the second and third of these possibilities because they require the disjuncture of *þæs* and *þisses*: one referring to good, the other to ill fortune. It certainly would be more neat to a modern sensibility if *þæs* and *þisses* would refer to the same kind of misfortune as they have, apparently heretofore. Unfortunately, it is impossible to dismiss them. If we permit only the first and last of the possibilities above, then *þæs* and *þisses* refer either both to good or both to ill fortune. But in the final refrain one cannot choose between them. To insist that both must refer to some ill fortune because in the previous exempla they have referred exclusively to misfortune is to deny the general reflection on adversity and the structure of the Deor exemplum which, uniquely among the exempla, presents

[1] While this possibility has been seen by others (e.g. Neil Isaacs, p. 113) it has been developed only by Murray R. Markland, 'Boethius, Alfred, and Deor', *MP*, 66 (1968), 1–4, who continues to see *þisses* as referring to 'the poet's current misery' (p. 4).

good fortune as a clear and possible referent. To insist that both must refer to good fortune is to deny the general reflection on adversity, the use of the refrain in the previous exempla, and the structure of the Deor exemplum. If one cannot choose on logical or aesthetic grounds between the first and last possibilities, then one must allow them both, accept the ambiguity, and understand both good and ill fortune as the dual referents of *þæs* and *þisses* in the final refrain. The effect of understanding the referents in this way is to allow the second and third possibilities that I would have liked to dismiss. That is, if one accepts the possibility of dual referents for *þæs* and *þisses*, then one must also allow the possibility that *þæs* and *þisses* refer to different kinds of fortune. This is entirely in keeping with the argument of the general reflection on adversity which insists that good and ill are in the hands of God. But it also places a new burden on the refrain as it has been previously employed; from the point of view of the end of the poem (that is, to listeners who have heard the poem before), it is quite possible that throughout the poem the *þæs* of the refrain refers to misfortune in the historic past while *þisses* refers to good fortune in the present world: that (misfortune of the past) passed away; this (good fortune — the pleasures of monastery or king's court, the very singing of the poem) can likewise pass away.[1]

While I have tried to identify the precise referents of *þæs* and *þisses* with twentieth-century tools, I am not certain that they should be identified at all: the poem is restricted by doing so. The point of the poem is carried in the refrain which says only that something passed away and that something else can also do so. In one sense the refrain is the poem, the exempla merely flesh, the incarnation of idea in specific form (and therefore limiting). Thus, it makes no difference what one understands as the precise referents of *þæs* and *þisses* (good fortune, misfortune, physical pain, sorrows of the mind, love, exile, political oppression) since the only thing important about them all is that, whatever they are, they pass away.

Deor does far more than catalogue the adversity suffered by others. There is, in the poem, a sliding scale of complexity and meaning, of purpose and teaching that fascinates and compels. Like all great poems, *Deor* is designed to appeal to its audience on a primal level, that of one's first experience with the poem, where the poem's sufficient point is that misery passes. It is also designed to appeal in quite another way to the reflective portion of the audience, already familiar with the poem and more intent on its meaning, which discovers that the poem's necessary point is that everything passes. The poem is remarkable for the way in which it involves the listener, asking him to recognize first his own suffering in terms of the suffering of others and then his own life and world in terms of a principle of change. *Deor* insists, explicitly, that God controls good and evil and can change them; and, by showing how good and evil can change with the will of God, the poet implicitly emphasizes, in a cosmic vision characteristic of much Anglo-Saxon poetry, the transience of this world. If *Deor* teaches anything, it teaches that everything, not just misfortune, changes in the kingdom of earth.

[1] I agree whole-heartedly, but for different reasons, with F. Norman, 'Problems in the Dating of Deor . . .', p. 209, that 'the last verse is an integral and essential part of the whole structure and the real reason why the poem was composed at all'. To which he adds: 'Therefore it is far more likely that the Kehrreim is invented for the very last verse and that then all the other heroic examples of misfortune outlived were collected' (p. 212, n. 5). For Norman, the Deor exemplum and refrain best articulate the poem's purpose, to reveal the poet as beggar; to my mind, they are the *sine qua non* of the poet's teaching, without which the poem's point would be much diminished. Without the Deor exemplum and refrain, the poem's point is that suffering passes; with them, the point is that everything in the world passes.

Alcuin and Old English Poetry

W. F. BOLTON

Rutgers University

Quid Hinieldus cum Christo? Alcuin's question contains the only four words of pre-Conquest Anglo-Latin that most students of Old English poetry ever read, and even their mentors may go no further in their study of Alcuin than the decent few paragraphs that most literary histories accord him.[1] As a result, student and mentor alike risk both a serious misreading of the famous rhetorical question and total neglect of the contributions that a study of Alcuin can make to their understanding of Old English poetry. In general those contributions are his witness to the affinities between the vernacular literature and contemporary Latin writing; for our purposes, it may be convenient to group them under the headings 'concepts', 'phrases', and 'topoi'.[2] The first heading includes similarities of thought that involve no particular verbal parallels. The second, by contrast, includes particularities of diction, *loci paralleli*, that span the two languages. And the third refers to situations or ideas that developed a characteristic expression, an associated diction of conventional rhetorical shape and lexical content (I avoid saying 'formula' simply because that word is so often modified by 'oral', while what we have here is distinctly literate and literary).

A review of Alcuin's witness to the concepts and diction of *Beowulf* in any detail would fill a book; the same for the remainder of Old English poetry would fill another. I am in the process of completing the book on Alcuin and *Beowulf*, but rather than attempt another on the remaining verse I offer here some inceptive and illustrative remarks on what Alcuin has to tell us about the literary and intellectual background of six well known and frequently studied Old English poems: *The Wanderer*, *The Seafarer*, *The Dream of the Rood*, *The Husband's Message*, *The Battle of Maldon*, and *Genesis B*. I quote the text of Alcuin from the best available editions, but often enough this is no better than Migne's nineteenth-century reprint of Frobenius's eighteenth-century edition, a text that omits the famous question about Ingeld from its version of Alcuin's letter to Hygbald of Lindisfarne; the identification of Hinieldus with Ingeld was not, consequently, made prior to Jänicke in 1872.[3] How much, then, we can learn from further study of Alcuin may in part be

---

[1] *Monumenta Germaniae Historica*, Epistolae IV, 2, edited by E. Dümmler (Berlin, 1895), p. 183, l. 22; hereafter cited as *Epistolae* and quoted without editorial marks. Latin quotations in this paper are normalized according to the standard of Lewis and Short's *Latin Dictionary*. On Alcuin's letters, see also Wolfgang Edelstein, *Eruditio und sapientia . . . Untersuchungen zu Alcuins Briefen*, Freiburger Studien zu Politik und Soziologie (Freiburg im Breisgau, 1965).

[2] See W. F. Bolton, 'Pre-Conquest Anglo-Latin: Perspectives and Prospects', *Comparative Literature*, 23 (1971), 151–66.

[3] *Patrologia Latina*, edited by J.-P. Migne, 221 vols (Paris, 1844–91), c. 243; hereafter cited as *P.L.* and quoted without editorial marks; Oskar Jänicke, 'Zur deutschen Heldensage', *Zeitschrift für deutsches Alterthum*, 15 (1872), 310–32, especially 313–14. See also Michael D. Cherniss, *Ingeld and Christ: Heroic Concepts and Values in Old English Christian Poetry* (The Hague and Paris, 1972), and Robert Levine, 'Ingeld and Christ: A Medieval Problem', *Viator*, 2 (1971), 105–28.

limited by the editions we have to work with. But even on the basis of what is available, much is to be learned from a study of his pages.

Alcuin can, in one sense, be thought of as standing in relation to his own age much as Shakespeare stood to his: he was representative of it, but to a superlative degree.[1] (The *Beowulf* poet, by contrast, despite Alcuin's apparent reference to other poetry on the Ingeld theme, seems to have been quite singular.) Alcuin was a near contemporary of the *Beowulf* poet, as the date of Alcuin's birth and of the poem's composition are now reckoned: he was born about 735 and lived the first half-century of his life as a Northumbrian, most of it in the cathedral school at York where he was successively student, master, and head. It seems that he did next to no writing during this period. But in 782, when he was about fifty, when the active life of many an eighth-century Englishman was long over, he answered a call from Charlemagne to join the Frankish court and establish a programme of education for it. Until the end of his life, as the testimony of his letters and poems shows, he continued to regard himself as an Englishman, albeit in exile; to refer to books he knew only from his English reading; to write to English friends with a special tone of mutuality; and to allude to his predecessors in the tradition of Anglo-Latin literature, particularly Bede. But, despite rare and brief returns to England, he lived out the rest of his life as a subject of Charlemagne, first as court humanist and later as Abbot of Tours from 796 until his death in 804. It was during his 'Carolingian' period that almost all of his writing was done, writing that includes not only the letters and poems but educational treatises and textbooks, doctrinal tracts and writing against the Adoptionist heresy, exegesis, hagiography, liturgy and logic, all (and there is a great deal of it) embodying the best education that the Northumbrian successors of Bede could provide, illuminated by the continental travel and court employments that Bede never knew. The volume, the variety, and the erudition of Alcuin's writing make it an especially useful source for the student of Old English poetry alert to its affinities with the larger Latin literature of the same time and place.

I

'Hige sceal þe heardra,   heorte þe cenre,
mod sceal þe mare,   þe ure mægen lytlað.'[2]

(*Maldon*, l. 312)

These famous lines have struck many readers as a sublime expression of the heroic ethic. Actually they contrast two ethics, and point a conclusion about the values taught by adversity that is not at all exclusive to the heroic ethic and may well be opposed to it. Alcuin uses words such as *anima*, *sapientia*, *prudentia mentis*, and *prudens animo*, to express the Old English *hige*, *heorte*, and *mod* of the speech, and his

[1] Recent books about Alcuin include Eleanor Shipley Duckett, *Alcuin, Friend of Charlemagne: His World and His Work* (New York, 1951, reprinted with expanded bibliography 1965); Arthur Kleinclausz, *Alcuin*, Annales de l'Université de Lyon, Séries 3 (lettres), fasc. 13 (Paris, 1948); and G. Ellard, *Master Alcuin, Liturgist: A Partner of our Piety* (Chicago, 1956). A chapter of Volume II of my *History of Anglo-Latin Literature, 597–1066* (in preparation, with C. A. Ladd), will be devoted to Alcuin.
[2] *The Battle of Maldon*, edited by E. V. Gordon (London, 1937); hereafter cited as *Maldon*.

allusions to St Paul and St Jerome give Byrhtwold's lines a didactic thrust not often recognized in critical interpretations:

Infirmitas corporis tui te fortem faciat in anima; et cum apostolo: 'Quando infirmior, tunc fortior' [II Corinthians, 12. 10]. Castigatio corporis profectus sit animae. (*Epistolae*, 167.29; compare 236.9–10, 259.32)

Mihique, fracto corpore, solatio est sententia sancti Hieronimi, qui ait in epistola ad Nepotianum: 'Omnes paene virtutes corporis mutantur in senibus et, crescente sola sapientia, decrescunt cetera'. (*Epistolae*, 178.4)

> Corporis exsuperat vires prudentia mentis.
> Vir prudens animo est melior, quam fortis in armis.
> (*Carmina*, LXII. 9. 117)[1]

Dr Swanton refers to the pseudo-Alcuinian *Liber de divinis officiis* (of the tenth century) for illustration of the 'essentially cosmic conceptions' of *The Dream of the Rood*, lines 4–9:

> Þuhte me þæt ic gesawe   syllicre treow
> on lyft lædan,   leohte bewunden,
> beama beorhtost.   Eall þæt beacen wæs
> begoten mid golde;   gimmas stodon
> fægere æt foldan sceatum,   swylce þær fife wæron
> uppe on þam eaxlegespanne.[2]

The authentically Alcuinian *Commentaria in S. Johannis Evangelium*[3] not only illustrates the same point, but gives it the tropological meaning necessary to link this detail of the iconography of the Cross with the moral situation of the Dreamer. (The passage, like much of the work, is drawn directly from St Augustine; in common with many other such derivative passages in the writing of Alcuin, it gains particular relevance for the study of Old English poetry because its incorporation here is evidence for its prominent presence in Anglo-Saxon literary culture.)

Lata est [crux] quippe in transverso ligno, quo extenduntur pendentis manus, et significat opera bona in latitudine caritatis; longa est a transverso ligno usque ad terram, ubi dorsum et pedes figuntur, et significat perseverantiam in longitudine temporis, usque ad finem; alta est in cacumine, quod a transverso ligno sursum rursus extenditur, et significat supernum finem quo cuncta opera referuntur, quoniam cuncta quae latitudine ac longitudine bene ac perseveranter fiunt, propter altitudinem divinorum facienda sunt praemiorum; profunda est in ea parte, qua in terra figitur: ibi quippe occulta est, nec videri potest, sed cuncta ejus apparentia et eminentia inde consurgunt; sicut bona nostra de profunditate gratiae Dei, quae comprehendi ac dijudicari non potest, universa procedunt. (*Johannis*, 983)

Swanton also refers to Alcuin's letter to Odwin *De baptismi caerimoniis* in *P.L.*, CI. 613; a better text is in *Epistolae*, 202–3. The lines Swanton was discussing are *The*

---

[1] *Monumenta Germaniae Historica*, Poetae latini aevi Carolini I, edited by E. Dümmler (Berlin, 1880); hereafter cited as *Carmina* and quoted without editorial marks. For the attribution to Alcuin see A. Streib, 'Wer ist der Verfasser der Praecepta vivendi?', *Münchener Museum für Philologie des Mittelalters und der Renaissance*, 2 (1913), 343–64, and M. Boas, *Alcuin und Cato* (Leiden, 1937). Both verses reflect Wisdom, 6.1: 'Melior est sapientia quam vires, et vir prudens quam fortis'.

[2] *The Dream of the Rood*, edited by Michael Swanton (Manchester and New York, 1970), p. 51; hereafter cited as *Dream of the Rood* and quoted without vowel quantity markings. For the denial of Alcuin's authorship, see J. J. Ryan, 'Pseudo-Alcuin's *Liber de divinis officiis* and the *Liber "Dominus vobiscum"* of St. Peter Damiani', *Mediaeval Studies*, 14 (1952), 159–63.

[3] *P.L.*, C. 743–1008; hereafter cited as *Johannis*. See also Friedrich Weichert, 'Alkuin als Exeget', (unpublished dissertation, University of Münster, 1949).

Dream of the Rood 117–18, lines that complete a series of observations on the paradox that Christ ensured life for the faithful by His death, and that the instrument of His agony is now the agency of their safety:

> 'Dead he þær byrigde;   hwæðere eft Dryhten aras
> mid his miclan mihte   mannum to helpe.'

> '. . . se ðe for Dryhtnes naman   deaðes wolde
> biteres onbyrigan,   swa he ær on ðam beame dyde.'

> 'Ne þearf ðær þonne ænig   unforht wesan
> þe him ær in breostum bereð   beacna selest.'
> *(Dream of the Rood, ll. 101–2, 113–14, 117–18)*

For this paradox, which had in any case more than sacramental connotations, Alcuin's poetry on the Cross conveys a more complete and relevant version than does the letter to Odwin:

> Vexillum sublimae crucis venerare, fidelis,
>   Qua qui se munit, tristia non metuit.
> Crux benedicta nitet, dominus qua carne pependit,
>   Atque suo clausit funere mortis iter.
> Hic auctor vitae mortem moriendo peremit,
>   Vulneribus sanans vulnera nostra suis.
> *(Carmina,* cxiv.1.1; compare cix.10. 1–7)

Alcuin also provides excellent testimony to the curency in Anglo-Saxon civilization of two ideas that I previously identified in more remote sources as underlying motifs in *The Dream of the Rood*. The first of these was that the 'engel' of line 9b, 'Beheoldon þær engel Dryhtnes ealle', was the Cross or Christ Himself, and hence that scribal corruption in the line as we have it need not be assumed.[1] In his commentary on *Genesis*,[2] Alcuin wrote 'Aut enim angeli nomine Dominus Christus significatus est, qui sine dubio Deus est, et manifeste a propheta dictus est, *magni consilii angelus*. Aut quia Deus erat in angelo; et ex persona Dei angelus loquebatur, sicut in prophetis etiam fieri solet' *(Genesin,* 546). The second point is that *The Dream of the Rood* employs paradox as a structural principle, contrasting the simultaneous degradation and glory of the Cross and relating it to the moral progress of the Dreamer.[3] The most important lines in the employment of this principle are

> 'Nu ðu miht gehyran,   hæleð min se leofa,
> þæt ic bealu-wara weorc   gebiden hæbbe,
> sarra sorga.   Is nu sæl cumen
> þæt me weorðiað   wide ond side
> menn ofer moldan   ond eall þeos mære gesceaft,
> gebiddaþ him to þyssum beacne.   On me Bearn Godes
> þrowode hwile.   Forþan ic þrymfæst nu
> hlifige under heofenum,   ond ic hælan mæg
> æghwylcne anra   þara þe him bið egesa to me.

---

[1] W. F. Bolton, '*The Dream of the Rood* 9b: "Engel" = Nuntius?', *N & Q*, 213 (1968), 165–6.
[2] *Interrogationes et responsiones in Genesin, P.L.*, c. 516–66; hereafter cited as *Genesin*.
[3] W. F. Bolton, 'Tatwine's *De Cruce Christi* and *The Dream of the Rood*', *Archiv*, 200 (1963), 344–6. See also H. B. Meyer, '*Crux, decus es mundi*: Alkuins Kreuz- und Osterfrömmigkeit', in *Paschatis sollemnia*: Festschrift für J. A. Jungmann, edited by B. Fischer and J. Wagner (Freiburg im Breisgau, 1959), pp. 96–107.

> Iu ic wæs geworden   wita heardost,
> leodum laðost,   ærþan ic him lifes weg
> rihtne gerymde,   reordberendum.'
>
> (*Dream of the Rood*, l. 78; see also ll. 117-18, quoted above)

Alcuin, in his commentary on John derived from Augustine, gives quite a specific account of the paradox from a viewpoint culturally close to that of the poet:

Nullum genus mortis intolerabilius fuit cruce, propter longos cruciatus: sed nihil nunc gloriosius quam signum crucis portare in fronte. (*Johannis*, 857)

Exaltationem quippe dicit passionis, non glorificationis; crucis, non caeli, nam ibi exaltatus est, quando pependit in ligno; sed illa exaltatio, humiliatio fuit. Tunc enim factus est Patri oboediens usque ad mortem, mortem autem crucis. Propter quod exaltavit illum Deus. Altera exaltatio fuit, quando elevatus est in crucem; altera dum ascendit in caelum. (*Johannis*, 865)

Alcuin provides analogues for commonplaces in other Old English poems. One such is the need to obtain heavenly rewards by earthly efforts, as *The Seafarer* puts it:

> For þon biþ eorla gehwam   æftercweþendra
> lof lifgendra   lastworda betst,
> þæt he gewyrce,   ær he on weg scyle,
> fremum on foldan   wið feonda niþ,
> deorum dædum   deofle togeanes,
> þæt hine ælda bearn   æfter hergen,
> ond his lof siþþan   lifge mid englum
> awa to ealdre,   ecan lifes blæd,
> dream mid dugeþum.[1]
>
> (*Seafarer*, l. 72)

Cogita, quod transitoria sunt haec omnia, quae in hoc saeculo habemus, et quia necessarium est unicuique hominum aeternam sibi per temporalia benefacta promereri gloriam. (*Epistolae*, 74.22; compare *Epistolae* 313.13-14, quoted below)

Another is the uncertainty of worldly events and of human foresight of them, with the consequent implication that human wisdom should take as its object, amid the mutability of the earth, the eternal work of the Lord. *The Wanderer* poet writes

> Forþon ne mæg wearþan wis   wer ær he age
> wintra dæl in woruldrice.
>
> Ongietan sceal gleaw hæle   hu gæstlic bið
> þonne eall þisse worulde wela   weste stondeð . . .
>
> Se þonne þisne wealsteal   wise geþohte
> ond þis deorce life   deope geondþenceð
> frod in ferðe,   feor oft gemon
> wælsleahta worn . . .
>
> Swa cwæð snottor on mode;   gesæt him sundor æt rune.[2]
>
> (*Wanderer*, ll. 64-65a, 73-4, 88-91a, 111)

---

[1] *The Seafarer*, edited by I. L. Gordon (London, 1960); hereafter cited as *Seafarer*. Compare also *Seafarer*, 97-102 with *Epistolae*, 182.8-11 on the futility of precious metals and gems before the Eternal Judge.

[2] *The Wanderer*, edited by R. F. Leslie (Manchester, 1966); hereafter cited as *Wanderer* and quoted without vowel quantity markings.

Alcuin has a similar view of what are essentially cognitive concerns: 'Incerta est humanae prudentiae saecularibus providentia rebus. Hoc solum de futuris considerantem non fallat, quod caritas in praeceptis Dei hujus vitae temporibus peragit.' (*Epistolae*, 182.41). I take 'de futuris considerans' to express 'snottor on mode ... æt rune'; the future is *rune* precisely because 'the foresight of human wisdom is uncertain in worldly affairs'.

Professor J. E. Cross has shown that the theme of the decay of the world in its last age is a traditional one. It makes its appearance often in Old English verse, not least in a number of passages in *The Wanderer*:[1]

<blockquote>
Swa þes middangeard
ealra dogra gehwam   dreoseð ond fealleþ.
</blockquote>

<blockquote>
... swa nu missenlice   geond þisne middangeard
winde biwaune   weallas stondaþ,
hrime bihrorene,   hryðge þa ederas.
Woriað þa winsalo,   waldend licgað
dreame bidrorene;   duguþ eal gecrong
wlonc bi wealle.
</blockquote>

<blockquote>
Yþde swa þisne eardgeard   ælda Scyppend
oþþæt burgwara   breahtma lease
eald enta geweorc   idlu stodon.
</blockquote>

<blockquote>
Stondeð nu on laste   leofre duguþe
weal wundrum heah   wyrmlicum fah.
</blockquote>

(Wanderer, ll. 62b–63, 75–80a, 85–7, 97–8)

To the Latin sources that Cross gives for the development of this theme should be added these passages from Alcuin:

Praeterit enim figura hujus mundi; et omnia caduca sunt, quae hic videntur vel habentur. Hoc solum de suo labore potest homo secum affere, quod in eleemosynis vel bonis operibus gerit. (*Epistolae*, 44.29)

... in hoc ruinoso cadentis saeculi fine (*Epistolae*, 437.6)

Felix equidem Atravata civitas, tam excellenti munita patrono! Etsi murorum ruinis vilescat, illius tamen meritorum nobilitate clarescit.[2]

The last passage is especially noteworthy, for it pointedly distinguishes between the physical decay of the noble city and its walls on one hand, and the permanence of its saintly patron's merits on the other.

Professor Cross has also written of the *sum* series in *The Wanderer*,

<blockquote>
Sume wig fornom,
ferede in forðwege;   sumne fugel oþbær
ofer heanne holm;   sumne se hara wulf
deaðe gedælde;   sumne dreorighleor
in eorðscræfe   eorl gehydde,
</blockquote>

(Wanderer, l. 80b)

---

[1] J. E. Cross, 'Aspects of Microcosm and Macrocosm in Old English Literature', *Comparative Literature*, 14 (1962), 1–22.

[2] *Vita sancti Vedasti Atrabatensis*, edited by B. Krusch, *Monumenta Germaniae Historica*, Scriptores rerum Merovingicarum III (Hannover, 1896), p. 424, ll. 26–8; compare Hebrews 8. 13, quoted by Alcuin in *P.L.*, c. 1070.

that in common with some other employments of the rhetorical figure *repetitio*, it was

used to reiterate the dogma of the resurrection of the body, whose ultimate scriptural source was Apocalypse xx.13. The catalogue had been used in a remarkably consistent way by a number of Christian apologists who had, from time to time, to defend the dogma against heretics and unbelievers ... The list, reflecting, as it does, an objection to the dogma of resurrection, would demand in the Christian listeners' minds the only answer.[1]

Among the apologists that Cross cited was Augustine, but the passage in question, from *De civitate Dei* xx. 20, was available to the *Wanderer* poet in Alcuin's slightly different version much closer to hand: 'Absit hoc a fide nostra dubitare, ut resuscitanda corpora vitaeque reddenda, non possint omnipotentia creatoris omnia revocari, quae vel bestia, vel ignis absumpsit, vel in pulverem cineremque collapsa, vel in humorem resoluta, vel in auras sunt exaltata.[2]

Professor Peter Clemoes has cited Alcuin's *De animae ratione* as one instance of the *mens absentia cogitans* that appears in *The Wanderer* (ll. 29b–57) and *The Seafarer* (ll. 58–64a). Other instances from Alcuin's writings should be added to the one he cites.[3]

Sed aliud est migrare corpore, aliud corde: migrat corpore, qui motu corporis mutat locum; migrat corde, qui motu cordis mutat affectum. (*Johannis*, 850)

Vox dolentis et miseriam suam plangentis, quod diu in peregrinatione hujus mortalitatis incolatus ejus prolongetur. Incola vero est qui terram alienam colit ... Corpus locis, et anima affectibus peregrinatur.[4]

The wandering spirit is, in a manner, an insubstantial surrogate for a letter:

Cearo bið geniwad
þam þe sendan sceal　　swiþe geneahhe
ofer waþema gebind　　werigne sefan.

(*Wanderer*, l. 55b)

For þon nu min hyge hweorfeð　　ofer hreþerlocan,
min modsefa　　mid mereflode,
ofer hwæles eþel　　hweorfeð wide,
eorþan sceatas ...

(*Seafarer*, l. 58)

Letters are frequently personified in Alcuin's writings, where they provide a stable messenger between the isolated writer and his former companions, one that contrasts with the instability of the persona depicted in *The Wanderer* and *The Seafarer*. Alcuin appears to have been the 'ghost writer' for Charlemagne in one such verse letter:

---

[1] J. E. Cross, *Latin Themes in Old English Poetry* (Lund, 1962), p. 6, with reference to his paper 'On *The Wanderer* lines 80–84: A Study of a Figure and a Theme', *Vetenskaps-Societetens i Lund Årsbok* (1958–9), 77–110.

[2] *De fide sanctae et individuae Trinitatis*, *P.L.*, ci. 52. It was on the basis of this work that Albert S. Cook attempted to fix 'The Date of the Old English Elene', *Anglia*, 15 (1892–3), 9–20, believing Cynewulf to have used Alcuin as a source; but Cook was refuted by C. F. Brown, 'Cynewulf and Alcuin', *PMLA*, 18 (1903), 308–34, who showed that both Anglo-Saxon writers were orthodox in their reliance on, *inter alia*, Augustine.

[2] Peter Clemoes, '*Mens absentia cogitans* in *The Seafarer* and *The Wanderer*', in *Medieval Literature and Civilization: Studies in Memory of G. N. Garmonsway*, edited by D. A. Pearsall and R. A. Waldron (London, 1969), pp. 62–77.

[4] *Expositio in psalmos graduales*, *P.L.*, c. 620.

Curre per Ausoniae, non segnis epistola, campos . . .
Hinc celer egrediens facili, mea carta, volatu
Per silvas, colles, valles quoque praepete cursu
Alma deo cari Benedicti tecta require.[1]

Alcuin's description of the soul that Professor Clemoes cited ran, in part, '[mens] tantae celeritatis [est], ut uno temporis puncto caelum collustret, et si velit, maria pervolet, terras et urbes peragret'. The language of Alcuin's poem clearly recalls that of his treatise on the soul in this particular.

II

In the matter of poetic diction Alcuin also provides a parallel for a term like *hreþerloca* (*Seafarer*, l. 58) in his kenning-like replies to Pippin, which include 'P. Quid est corpus? — A. Domicilium animae.' The same work also throws light on the notions of the ship as habitation that underlie *The Seafarer*, lines 4b–8a,

> [ic] hæbbe
> gecunnad in ceole   cearselda fela,
> atol yþa gewealc,   þær mec oft bigeat
> nearo nihtwaco   æt nacan stefnan,
> þonne he be clifum cnossað.

'Navis est domus erratica, ubilibet hospitium, viator sine vestigiis, vicinus harenae.'[2] And Alcuin shows that in the passage where *The Seafarer* most resembles *The Wanderer*, both poems were participating in phraseology shared by Anglo-Latin writers as well:

> Nap nihtscua,   norþan sniwde,
> hrim hrusan bond,   hægl feol on eorþan,
> corna caldast.
>
> *(Seafarer*, l. 31)

> . . . nipeð nihtscua   norþan onsendeð
> hreo hæglfare   hæleþum on andan.
>
> *(Wanderer*, l. 104; compare *Beowulf*, ll. 547–8)

> Nix etenim ningit, cernite, grando ruit.
>
> *(Carmina*, LV.8.2)

> Nix ruit e caelo, gelidus simul ingruit imber.
>
> *(Carmina*, XL.1; compare *Aeneid*, XII.284)

> Nox ruit hibernis algida flatibus.
>
> (Bede, *Historia abbatum*, II.14)

---

[1] *Die Gedichte des Paulus Diaconus*, edited by K. Neff (Munich, 1908), pp. 140–1, ll. 10, 17–19. For the attribution to Alcuin, see Luitpold Wallach, *Alcuin and Charlemagne: Studies in Carolingian History and Literature* (Ithaca, New York, 1959), p. 209. See also A. Blaschka, 'Der Topos scribendo solari: Briefschreiben als Trost', *Wissenschaftliche Zeitschrift der Martin Luther Universität Halle-Wittenberg*, 5 (1956), 637–8, and A. Fiske, 'Alcuin and Mystical Friendship', *Studi medievali*, third series, 2 (1961), 551–75.

[2] *Disputatio Pippini cum Albino*, edited by W. Suchier, Illinois Studies in Language and Literature, Volume 24, No. 2 (Urbana, 1939), pp. 138, 140. For the 'kennings', see T. Gardner, 'The Old English Kenning: A Characteristic Feature of Germanic Poetical Diction?', *Modern Philology*, 67 (1969), 109–17, and H. Reuschel, 'Kenningar bei Alkuin: Zur *Disputatio Pippini cum Albino*, *Beiträge zur Geschichte der deutschen Sprache und Literatur*, 62 (1938), 143–55.

The similarities range from the naturalistic detail of the freezing rain to the literary detail of alliteration on *n*.

Alcuin demonstrates as well that the assumptions of Byrhtnoþ's 'hicgan to handum and to hige godum' (*Maldon*, l. 4) were common property: 'Per cor cogitatio, et per brachium designatur operatio'.[1] In the same poem, the last surviving line appears to be no more than a necessity occasioned by the historical narrative, for of the two men on the English side named Godric, only one proves loyal: 'Næs þæt na se Godric þe ða guðe forbeah' (*Maldon*, l. 325). But Alcuin shows that the necessity, and with it the diction, were commonplaces: 'Iste est Judas cujus epistola legitur in ecclesiis Christi, non ille traditor' (*Johannis*, 937). Even that apparently most 'ethnic' of gestures, 'wand wacne æsc', 'æscholt asceoc', 'daroð acwehte', 'æsc acwehte' (*Maldon*, ll. 43, 230, 255, 310), finds a parallel in Alcuin's poem of consolation to the monks of Lindisfarne after its devastation by the Vikings, 'Dextera, quae gladios, quae fortia tela vibrabat' (*Carmina*, IX.107), there to suggest the transience of youth and strength.

Two further matters of diction may conclude this section. It is well known that the comparative adjective in line 4 of *The Dream of the Rood*, 'Þuhte me þæt ic gesawe syllicre treow', is unusual. Cook suggested that a line might have been omitted, comparing *Elene*, line 74. Others would supply a negative (*ic ne*, or *ne syllicre*), comparing usage in *Andreas*, lines, 471, 499 and *Elene*, lines 73–4. Most recent editors, however, follow Klaeber in simply assuming an absolute use of the comparative: 'the most wonderful, very wonderful'.[2]

But research on the *locus desperatus* should not ignore Alcuin's evidence that Anglo-Saxon England, on the basis of ancient authority, saw the usage as admissible: 'Invenitur et comparativus pro positivo poni, ut Virgil: " . . . comites senioris Acestae" [*Aeneid*, v.301], pro *senis*. Est quando minus positivo singulari significat, et nulli comparetur, ut Virgil: "tristior et lacrimis oculos suffusa nitentis" [*Aeneid*, I.228] *Tristior* hic ex parte significat *tristem*'.[3]

In his edition of *Genesis B*, Timmer found the use of Old English *leoht* in the sense 'world' to be one 'only illustrated by examples from [the] L[ater] G[enesis], no doubt taken over from OS. *lioht* which may have the meaning "life, world" '. The instance he is discussing is line 310b, 'forþon he heo on wyrse leoht', with further reference to line 850; lines 392, 394, and 401 should also be compared. But Alcuin makes it clear that the usage was one known to him as an Anglo-Saxon, and available for use in Latin as well as Old English and Old Saxon: 'Hoc est opus tuum in hac praesenti luce; haec est merces tua in aeterna gloria' (*Epistolae*, 313.13–14)[4]

---

[1] *Compendium in Canticum Canticorum*, P.L., c. 662, on Canticles, 8.6. (Students of *The Battle of Brunanburh* will find parallels for the 'rout of the enemy' passages in Alcuin's *Carmina*, I. 257–64, 543–52.)

[2] Swanton, p. 100.

[3] *Grammatica*, P.L., CI. 860, slightly re-punctuated and with correction of the Virgilian verses (which, in the *P.L.* edition, read 'comites senioris Acestæ' and 'tristior atque oculos lacrymis suffusa nitentes', the latter wrongly identified as *Aeneid*, I.322). See also W. Schmitz, *Alcuins Ars Grammatica*, Wissenschaftliche Beilage zum Jahresberichte des Städtischen Progymnasiums zu Ratingen (Ratingen, 1908), and H. W. Fortgens, 'De paedagoog Alcuin en zijn *Ars Grammatica*', *Tijdschrift voor Geschiedenis*, 60 (1947), 57–65.

[4] *The Later Genesis*, edited by B. J. Timmer (revised edition, Oxford, 1954), p. 34; hereafter cited as *Genesis B* with slight re-punctuation; compare *Epistolae*, 347.12–13. Professor Alan S. C. Ross does not believe that *lumen* occurs in this sense ('OE. "leoht" "world" ', *N & Q*, 22 (1975), 196).

III

It is, however, in the area of 'concomitant diction', the phraseology that literary tradition provided for particular conceptual frameworks and narrative situations, that Alcuin's writing is most revealing; for what it reveals is a common insular tradition that provided the diction for Old English and Latin literature alike when they touched on similar concepts or situations. It is not perhaps altogether surprising that such should be the case when the theme was religious, and the vocabulary, even the rhetorical redundancy, might be expected in passages such as these:

> Uton we hycgan   hwær we ham agen,
> ond þonne geþencan   hu we þider cumen;
> ond we þonne eac tilien   þæt we to moten
> in þa ecan   eadignesse . . .
>
>   (*Seafarer*, l. 117)

O quam felix est aeterna beatitudo . . . Ad hanc nos festinare oportet, ut illam intrare mereamur . . . tanto avidius totis viribus tendamus ad illam, quanto beatius illam habere poterit qui intrat. (*Epistolae*, 425.16)

We might expect such similarity even where a whole sequence of thoughts was reproduced:

>   . . . ic synnum fah,
> forwunded mid wommum.
>
>   . . . ic wene me
> daga gehwylce   hwænne me Dryhtnes rod . . .
> on þysson lænan   life gefetige
> ond me þonne gebringe   þær is blis micel . . .
>
> Ac hie þonne forhtiað,   ond fea þencaþ
> hwæt hie to Criste   cweðan onginnen.
>   (*Dream of the Rood*, ll. 13b–14, 135b–39, 115–16)

Nam ego, plurimis hujus saeculi jaculis vulneratus, diem trepido animo expecto, quo duci ad judicium vocer ignorans, quid habeam respondere judici meo Jesu Christo . . .

                                  (*Epistolae*, 421.4)

We need to beware, however, of a double standard that accepts as unremarkable close parallels between Old English poetry and its contemporary Latin literature on religious themes, while passages of no obvious spiritual import are held to be distinctive of the true (that is, the extra-ecclesiastical) vernacular voice. Alcuin, who never held a pen or read a page save as an ecclesiastic, would have found in the lines

> greteð gliwstafum,   georne geondsceawað
> secga geseldan —   swimmað oft onweg
> fleotendra ferð —   no þær fela bringeð
> cuðra cwidegiedda,
>
>   (*Wanderer*, l. 52; compare l. 38a)

an echo of his own words to absent friends,

Ecce totus praeteriit annus, quo nec litterarum consolatio oculis advenit, nec salutationis officium auribus insonuit. (*Epistolae*, 39.5; compare 34.29–31)

Quia invida terrarum longinquitas mutuae confabulationis prohibet dulcedinem. (*Epistolae*, 148.33; compare 140.19–20)

In such passages he remarked on the 'litterarum consolatio', the 'mutuae confabulationis dulcedor', the 'salutationis officium', and the barrier that 'terrarum longinquitas' poses, in a manner that recalls the emphasis the *The Wanderer* likewise lays on the verbalization of friendship.

So too the words of the seafarer,

> Calde geþrungen
> wæron mine fet,   forste gebunden
> caldum clommum . . .
>
> (*Seafarer*, l. 8b)

are a metaphorical version of Satan's more literal (but still, from the poet's point of view, imaginary) words.

> . . . licgað me ymbe   irenbenda,
> rideð racentan sal.   Ic eom rices leas,
> habbað me swa hearde   helleclommas
> fæste befangen . . .
>   Me habbað hringa gespong,
> sliðhearda sal,   siðes amyrred,
> afyrred me min feðe.   Fet synt gebundene,
> handa gehæfte;   synt þissa heldora
> wegas forworhte,   swa ic mid wihte ne mæg
> of þissum lioðobendum.   Licgað me ymbe
> heardes irenes   hate geslægene
> grindlas greate,   mid þy me God hafað
> gehæfted be þam healse.
>
> (*Genesis B*, l. 371)

Alcuin recognizes both the literal and the metaphorical versions of this phraseology, participates in it, and contributes to it, when he writes 'Nam nos ambos, ut recognosco, quaedam necessitatis catena constringit et libero cursu voluntatis castra intrare non permittit. Nec est qui compedes rumpere valeat, nisi qui inferni ferrea claustra contrivit'. (*Epistolae*, 141.25)

The presence of yet another topos, it seems, is signalled by the appearance of the cuckoo in *The Husband's Message*: the context is the coming of Spring, the message of summons, the song of the cuckoo. In *The Seafarer* the coming of Spring is described at greater length in terms of the beauty of town and field, and the Spring itself is the messenger even at the same time as it tempts the traveller to remain ashore (as the *lifgende monn* might do in *The Husband's Message*).

> Heht nu sylfa þe
> lustum læran   þæt þu lagu drefde,
> siþþan þu gehyrde   on hliþes oran
> galan geomorne   geac on bearwe.
> Ne laet þuþec siþþan   siþes getwæfan
> lade gelettan,   lifgendne monn.
>   Ongin mere secan,   mæwes eþel;
> onsite sænacan,   þæt þu suð heonan
> ofer merelade   monnan findest,
> þær se þeoden is   þin on wenum.[1]
>
> Bearwas blostmum nimað,   byrig fægriað,
> wongas wlitigað,   woruld onetteð;

---

[1] *Three Old English Elegies*, edited by R. F. Leslie (Manchester, 1961), lines 20b–29, quoted here with vowel quantity and editorial markings omitted.

ealle þa gemoniað   modes fusne
sefan to siþe   þam þe swa þenceð
on flodwegas   feor gewitan.
Swylce geac monað   geomran reorde;
singeð sumeres weard,   sorge beodeð
bitter' in breosthord.

(*Seafarer*, l. 48)

This collocation of events and images evoked as a 'striking parallel' in Sweet's *Reader*, a story of nineteenth-century Russian convict life: when the cuckoo heralded the coming of Spring the inmates knew it was warm enough to attempt escape.[1] Alcuin can offer closer parallels:

Nunc cuculus ramis etiam resonavit in altis;
Florea versicolor pariet nunc germina tellus.
Vinea bachiferas trudit de palmite gemmas,
Suscitat et vario nostras modulamine mentes
Indefessa satis rutilis luscinia ruscis.
Et sol signiferi medium transcendit in orbem,
Et Phoebus vicit tenebrarum regna refulgens;
Atque natans ad vos pelagi trans æquora magni
Albini patris deportat carta salutem,
Moenibus Euboricae habitans tu sacra juventus.
Fas idcirco, reor, . . .
Carminibusque sacris naves implere Fresonum.

(*Carmina*, LIX.I.; compare *Epistolae*, 370.10)

Non castella, domus, urbes, nec florida rura
Deteneant stupidam spatio nec unius horae,
Sed fuge, rumpe mora, propera, percurre volando:
Incolomes sanos gaudentes atque vigentes
Invenies utinam nostros gratanter amicos.

(*Carmina*, IV.68.; compare *Aeneid*, IV.569)[2]

The elements of form and content that the passages from *The Husband's Message* and *The Seafarer* have in common with each other, they also have in common with one or both of the passages from Alcuin's poems: the song of the cuckoo, the coming of Spring and the growing beauty of town and country-side, the message of invitation, the call to put to sea, the warning against allowing any force to detain the addressee of the call, especially the beauty of the land. Some of these elements are transparently figurative ('Carminibusque sacris naves implere', for example); it seems that the topos is sufficiently stable for portions of it to bear extended meanings.

Another passage of Alcuin's explains some of the lines in *The Seafarer* descriptive of old age:

Ne mæg him þonne se flæschoma,   þonne him þæt
   feorg losað,
ne swete forswelgan   ne sar gefelan
ne hond onhreran   ne mid hyge þencan.

(*Seafarer*, l. 94)

---

[1] *Sweet's Anglo-Saxon Reader in Prose and Verse*, revised by C. T. Onions (fourteenth edition, Oxford, 1959), page 221. The note does not appear in the fifteenth edition, revised by Professor Dorothy Whitelock (Oxford, 1967).

[2] See, on Alcuin's *Carmina*, LVII, Peter Dale Scott, 'Alcuin's *Versus de Cuculo*: The Vision of Pastoral Friendship', *Studies in Philology*, 62 (1965), 510–30; W. Bulst, 'Alchuuines *Ecloga de cuculo*', *Zeitschrift für deutsches Altertum und deutsche Literatur*, 86 (1955), 193–6.

The *hond* and *hyge*, to be sure, are a pair like *swete* and *sar*; we have already noticed Alcuin's remark on the subject in connexion with *The Battle of Maldon*. But Alcuin also shows that the collocation of 'ne swete forswelgan' with 'ne hond onhreran' is similarly pointed:

> Qui olim strato laetus recubabat in ostro,
>   Vix panno veteri frigida membra tegit.
> Longa dies oculos atra caligine claudit,
>   Solivagos athomos quae numerare solet.
> Dextera, quae gladios, quae fortia tela vibrabat,
>   Nunc tremit atque ori porrigit aegre cibos . . .
>   Nec cognoscit homo propria membra senex . . .
> Sic ventura dies mentes mutabit et artus,
>   Atque utinam melior proficiat meritis!
>   (*Carmina*, IX.103–8, 114, 117–18; compare XXIII.29–30)

The passage contains two of Alcuin's frequent Virgilianisms (compare 'stratoque super discumbitur ostro' and 'caligine turbidus atra' [*Aeneid* 1.700; XI.876]); Alcuin was, in his way, both a repository and a medium of transmission of much Virgilian and other classical lore for his Anglo-Saxon and Frankish contemporaries.[1]

Alcuin is a figure in whom literary tradition and dogmatic orthodoxy were singularly convergent. In his writings modern scholarship can find abundant material for the explication of Old English poetry, and for the illustration of the relationship between the vernacular and the Latin literature of Anglo-Saxon England.

---

[1] See O. F. Long, 'The Attitude of Alcuin toward Vergil', in *Studies in Honor of Basil L. Gildersleeve* (Baltimore, 1902), 377–86, and E. M. Sanford, 'Alcuin and the Classics', *Classical Journal*, 20 (1925), 526–33.

A New Edition of the B text of *Piers Plowman*

DAVID C. FOWLER

University of Washington

For the past twenty-five years Professors George Kane and E. Talbot Donaldson have been at work on the new B text of *Piers Plowman*, and now at last it has appeared.[1] To the uninitiated this might seem a long time to spend editing a fourteenth-century English alliterative poem of some 7300 lines, but in fact the task before them was a complicated one. *Piers Plowman* exists in three distinct versions customarily designated A, B, and C, and it was necessary for the editors to consider the readings of all three texts while in the process of establishing B. How this was done they explain in a 220-page introduction consisting of five sections.

Section I (pp. 1–15) describes fifteen manuscripts and Crowley's early printed edition used in establishing the text, plus two other manuscripts which for good and sufficient reason are not included in the corpus of variants. Section II (pp. 16–69) attempts to classify the manuscripts, that is, to describe their relationships on the basis of shared unoriginal readings. Section III (pp. 70–97) sets forth the editors' important working hypothesis, namely that the archetypal text of the B version (the form of the text that lies behind the extant manuscripts, but not the author's original) is seriously and demonstrably corrupt. Section IV (pp. 98–127), entitled 'The C–Reviser's B Manuscript', seeks to show that, contrary to previous opinion, the manuscript of B used by the poet to make the C version was also extensively corrupted by errors scribal in origin. The importance of knowing the truth of this matter will be obvious once it is remembered that the C version is being used extensively by the editors to establish their edition of B. Finally, in a long Section V (pp. 128–220), the procedure for editing the B text is described in detail. Following an appendix (pp. 221 ff.) of unoriginal lines in the B manuscripts, the remainder of the book (pp. 227–681) consists of the B text in its entirety with full variant readings from the manuscripts provided on the bottom half of each page. The book, in all of its complexity, has a formidable appearance; and its contents have been deployed and printed with a remarkable precision and accuracy.[2]

To review such a book and get at the heart of the matter in a few pages obviously requires some principle of selection. I shall concentrate first on Sections III and IV of

---

[1] *'Piers Plowman': The B Version. Will's Visions of Piers Plowman, Do-well, Do-better and Do-best. An Edition in the Form of Trinity College Cambridge MS B.15.17, Corrected and Restored from the Known Evidence, with Variant Readings.* By George Kane and E. Talbot Donaldson. London: Athlone Press. 1975. x + 681 pp. £20.00.

[2] There are amazingly few errors considering the volume and complexity of the materials presented. I noted the following: p. 101, line 7 in second block of references, for '*Sepcies* A (ix.17)' read '*Sepcies* A (ix.16 α)'; p. 385, among variants for line 34, for 'þe]' read 'þe (2)]'; p. 467, line 28 of text, last word, add close quote after 'slepe'; p. 668, among variants for line 151, for 'all Cr³' read 'al] Cr³'. What I would classify as doubtful punctuation occurs in the following lines: Prologue, 107–10, II.36–9, III.332, VIII.76, XII.272–6, XX.93–6. In at least one instance the punctuation represents an improvement over previous editions: XX.189.

the introduction and then, instead of dealing directly with the long final Section (v), I shall devote the remaining space to analysis of consecutive examples from the text itself, whereby I trust my evaluation of the editors' procedures set forth in Section v will be evident. This however involves using only a small selection from a large body of evidence, and I shall try to avoid the appearance of arbitrariness by setting forth, in an appendix at the end of this review, a formal classification of the emendations in the text (more than 2600 of them).

Section III of the introduction makes the case for archetypal corruption of the B text. The editors find some six hundred readings which they identify as scribal and unoriginal and this leads them to the following conclusion (pp. 96–7):

> The unanimity or general agreement with which the **B** manuscripts attest the readings of their exclusive common ancestor conceals a history in the archetypal **B** tradition of very extensive scribal substitution ... at the expense of compression, pregnancy, technical excellence, and in the end, of the poetry. This seems to us clear to the limit of certainty possible in textual criticism.

From this statement it might at first appear that the editors have indeed ventured beyond the limits of textual criticism in seeking to identify and correct examples of the lack of compression, pregnancy, technical excellence, and, indeed, poetry, especially when it is often necessary for them to proceed against the unanimous evidence of the manuscripts themselves. But I believe they would want a reviewer to make the point that they are not simply engaged in making a series of subjective judgements. They have had the unique experience of becoming thoroughly, almost oppressively familiar with scribal practices in the *Piers Plowman* manuscripts of all versions, and as literary scholars understandably feel that they can tell a hawk from a handsaw; a line of Langland's poetry from a scribal platitude. To this I would add further that there is nothing inherently implausible in the suggestion that the B archetype is corrupt. The question finally therefore is whether in fact the editors are correct in the radical degree of corruption which they find in B and which they deem it necessary to correct in this new edition.

But before facing this question we must take note of a further complication dealt with in Section IV of the introduction: namely that the archetypal C text, despite the high regard in which it has been held by *Piers Plowman* scholars from R. W. Chambers onwards, is also corrupt. In this case, moreover, the corruption is not simply of the archetype, as in the case of B, but of the author's own text of B used in making the revision which we call C. This explains why the editors feel it necessary at times to emend their text even when the overwhelming evidence of both the B and C manuscripts speak against it. Again I would say that the situation they envisage (an author revising from a corrupt manuscript of his own poem) is perfectly possible. Whether this is in fact the case is a matter we may consider in more concrete terms below in an analysis of actual emendations that the editors resort to in light of their hypothesis.

At this point let me simply state my reaction to the editors' theory of corruption of the B archetype and the text used to make C. The evidence they present is massive (it took me two months just to read through it) but my feeling is that it is not finally persuasive. I state this conclusion reluctantly because, as the editors themselves point out, 'the strong presumption of the corruptness of the archetypal text of the **B** version of *Piers Plowman* is a main instrument for its editors' (p. 97). They have taken a position that might even be described as heroic. The reviewer must either grant their hypothesis and accept this new text (for undoubtedly it is radically new) or else deny the validity of a project that has taken a quarter of a century to complete. In the following critique I shall be trying to avoid the horns of this dilemma.

But if, as I think, the editors are wrong in their belief concerning extensive corruption in the B and C texts, what could possibly have led them to such a conclusion, and to such a massive accumulation of evidence in support of it? All other considerations aside, I believe the fundamental error occurred when they decided that the versification (particularly of the B archetype) was extensively corrupted. They felt that they had found over four hundred instances of this (see below, at end of this review, Appendix, v), and indeed numerically this would make a strong case. The delicate question of whether a given alliterative line is metrically defective can perhaps be argued for or against, but I noticed one thing about their metrical emendations which suggests to me that they are wrong in correcting a line which does not conform to their definition of Langland's alliterative practice (pp. 131 ff).

The first half of the B text, from the Prologue to the end of Passus x, consists (in round numbers) of some 3300 lines. Of these, 2200 are lines inherited from the A text, and the other 1100 lines were newly composed when the revision was made. Looking at some 160 cases of metrical emendation in that part of B which corresponds to A (Appendix, va), we discover that, even accepting all of the editors' emendations as correct, only thirty-five A lines carried over into B required emendation to normalize the alliteration. On the other hand, some 125 new B lines had to be emended, in the editor's opinion. Actually I found only eight instances that really seemed to illustrate genuine corruption of alliteration of A lines in B: IV.15; VI.210; IX.32, 123; X.48, 128, 207, 353. But even if all thirty-five cases are regarded as genuine, including one A line hypothetically inserted in B (I.112) and then emended to correct its alliteration, the proportions are remarkable:

Out of 2200 A lines in B, 35 are emended to restore alliteration.

Out of 1100 new B lines, 125 are emended to restore alliteration.

This is surely not what we ought to expect from a corrupt archetype. There is no reason to suppose that copyists at work on the B text could so systematically spoil the alliteration of new B lines while by some method or other carefully preserving the alliteration of the A lines carried over into B. I therefore conclude that what Professors Kane and Donaldson regard as metrically defective lines in the B text represent for the most part simply the alliteration of the B poet, which does not in fact conform to their definition of Langland's poetic practice. The B poet learned much while writing the B text, producing many lines which were metrically irregular at first, and then returning to them later (in the C text) to polish and improve the alliteration. This is no new observation.

To sum up: the editors looked at the A text, saw a full and consistent system of alliteration, found this to be lacking in B, and concluded that the failure of A's metrical system to be preserved in the B text must be attributed to a defective archetype. The relation of this conclusion to their assumption of single authorship (p. 70) scarcely needs to be pointed out. But the consequences in editing are dire, and it is to these that we must now turn.

In the following examples I use Kane's edition of the A text (1960), and for B and C I cite Walter W. Skeat's edition published by the Early English Text

Society (1869, 1873) to show by comparison the nature of the emendations made by Professors Kane and Donaldson (*K–D*).

1.98–103

> *Skeat* B: And þat is þe *professioun* appertly • þat appendeth for kny3tes,
> And nou3t to fasten a fryday • in fyue score wynter;
> But holden wiþ him & with hir • þat wolden al treuthe,
> And neuer leue hem for loue • ne for lacchyng of syluer.
> For Dauid in his dayes • dubbed kni3tes,
> And did hem swere on here swerde • to serue trewthe eu*er*e;

> *K–D*: [For Dauid in his dayes dubbed kny3tes,
> Dide hem sweren on hir swerd to s*er*uen truþe eu*er*e.
> [That] is [þe] *profession* apertli þat apendeþ to kny3tes,
> And nau3t to fasten o friday in fyue score wynter,
> But holden wiþ hym and w*ith* here þat [asken þe] truþe,
> And neu*er*e leue hem for loue ne lachhynge of [yiftes];]

As the half-brackets indicate, the editors have restored the original order of the A text (1.96–101) by putting the lines on David and the sword back at the beginning of the passage where they belong. Their explanation for the scribal error here is I believe entirely correct: 'Eyeskip (*kny3tes* 98, 100) with subsequent insertion of omitted matter' (p. 84). But I choose this example because it illustrates an important problem in the editing of the B text which the editors have not dealt with satisfactorily. In some cases (like this one) they simply restore the reading of the A text: as in v.94–5 (explained p. 126, n. 64); and in viii.62–3 (explained as eyeskip, p. 99). In other cases they either ignore the problem completely or make minor repairs: iv.75 (ignored, see A iv.61); v.115–18, where 116 is a scribal variation on A v.97, reappearing in its restored form as 118; vi.9–20, where they exclude a line after vi.17 as evincing an 'elementary interest in food' (p. 193), but fail to deal with the scribal features of vi.9–20 at all (see A vii.9–22); vi.179–82, where they exclude another line for its interest in food (occurring after vi.182 (p. 193)), though on these somewhat dubious grounds they should also have excluded vi.181–2, whereas they completely ignore the scribal nature of the disruption in this passage (see A vii.164–70). Why they ignore the scribal phenomena in these cases I am at a loss to explain, since they devote considerable space in their introduction to instances where scribal influence is much less evident than here.

But the charge of inconsistency pales by comparison with the other criticism that must be made, namely that the editors never really face the question of the state of the A text used in making the B revision (see pp. 205, 210 f.). When I first looked at their introduction I was struck by the fact that while there is a whole section devoted to the corruption of the B archetype, and a slightly longer section discussing the C reviser's B manuscript, there is no section entitled 'The B Reviser's A Manuscript' which is surely a crucial question in the editing of *Piers Plowman*. This matter requires more attention than the editors have been willing to give to it. Perhaps they were uncertain about the answer and preferred to say as little as possible: I do not know. Should scribal disruptions of the type listed above be corrected in an edition of the B text? If they are simply corruptions of the B archetype, and not of the A text used in making B, the answer of course is yes. But if these disruptions were in the orginal of A used by the B reviser, then it would seem (and here is my basic criticism of their handling of these particular cases) that the passages should not be restored to the reading of A, since the editors would then be producing a text that never existed on land or sea. This I fear, to a very large extent, is exactly what they have done.

II.91 (*Skeat* II.90)

> *Skeat* B: And in wedes and in wisshynges · and with ydel thouȝtes
>
> *K–D*: And in we[n]es and in wisshynges and wiþ ydel þouȝtes

In this B line expanding on the lordship of lechery, no manuscript reads *wenes*; the readings are *wenyngis* F, *wendys* H, *wedes* WHmCr¹GYOC²CLM, *weddes* Cr²³, and *wedynges* R. Like most of the B manuscripts, the C text also reads *wedes* but, as the editors elsewhere point out, coincident variation is a common phenomenon in *Piers Plowman* manuscripts. Here is the comment on *wenes* (p. 186):

At II.91 *wenyngis* (actions 'of thinking, supposing, expecting, etc.'), *wedes* and *wedynges* have no senses appropriate to the content of lechery, and for *wendys* there seems to be no lexical attestation. There is, however, a word resembling all variants in shape: *wenes* (NED s.v. *Ween* sb. 2, 'expectation, hope') which could with a particular sexual application have generated severally *wedes* and *wenyngis*] *wedynges* as easier homœographs.

This is a perceptive emendation, and in all fairness it should be pointed out that among many cases that are acceptable in accordance with the normal canons of textual criticism (see my Appendix, II) there are a few speculative but plausible corrections: III.222; XI.106; XV.73; XVI.20 (see Skeat), 161; and an ingenious solution of XX.366.

IV.162 (A IV.138; C V.157)

> *Kane* A: And seide it so loude þat soþnesse it herde
>
> *Skeat* B: And seide it so heiȝe · þat al þe halle it herde
>
> *Skeat* C: And cryed vp-on conscience · þe kynge hit myghte yhure
>
> *K–D*:   And seid[e] it so [loude] þat [soþnesse] it herde

Skeat's B text has the backing of all the manuscripts, yet though all the evidence suggests that this line is successively revised in B and C, the editors restore the A reading on the grounds that the change to *heiȝe* is characteristic 'alliterative smoothing' (p. 88), and *al þe halle* is 'more emphatic' and 'probably records scribal response to the sense and feeling of the poem' (p. 87). This one simple example is representative of a very large class of unwarranted emendations that have the effect of harmonizing the B text with the A text (Appendix, IVa). What is the editor of C to do? Cancel his entire line and restore the A reading also?

v.76 (A v.59; *Skeat* B v.77; C VII.64)

> *Kane* A: And carfulliche his cope [comsiþ] he to shewe
>
> *Skeat* B: And carfullich *mea culpa* · he comsed to shewe
>
> *Skeat* C: And cried '*mea culpa*' · corsynge alle hus enemys
>
> *K–D*:   And carefully [his coupe] he comse[þ] to shewe

Here is one of those numerous cases where the A manuscripts disagree and the B manuscripts are practically unanimous in support of a still different reading (as in Skeat's B text). The problem in A is illustrated by the fact that the other modern edition of the A text (Knott–Fowler, 1952) has for this line 'And carfulliche his gilt begynneth to shewe'. The variants for *cope* in A are as follows: *cope* TH², *synnes* Ch, *coupe* DUEN, *compte* R, *counte* A, *wilis* M, *coulpe* W, *Culpe* K, *gylt* JL, *gultus* VH. I am willing to be persuaded that Professor Kane is right in his reconstruction of A v.59; but there is no evidence whatsoever that the A manuscript used by the reviser in composing the B text had any such reading. Yet I take it that the editor's restoration in B v.76, against all the evidence of the B manuscripts (and the C text as well), means that they are operating on the theory that the author's original B text had the same reading as Professor Kane's version of the line in A, despite their opinion (p. 98, n. 2) that there is some evidence that the author 'used a scribal copy of **A** for his revision to **B**'.

v.101–4 (*Skeat* v.100–3)

> *Skeat* B: And when I mete him in market • þat I moste hate
> I hailse hym hendeliche • as I his frende were;
> For he is douȝtier þan I • I dar do non other.
> Ac hadde I maystrye and myȝte • god wote my wille!

> K–D: Whan I met[t]e hym in Market þat I moost hate[de]
> I hailse[d] hym hendely as I his frend were:
> He is douȝtier þan I; I dar [noon harm doon hym],
> Ac hadde I maistrie and myȝt [I wolde murþere hym for euere].

The emendations in these lines are a restoration of the A text form of the passage (A v.81–4) contrary to all the B manuscripts, but justified by the editors on the grounds of 'scribal suppression of the violent statement' (p. 88). I am convinced that this goes well beyond the limits of editing or, if I must accept their definition of its limits, then I have to say that in my opinion this type of emendation (one of many in their text) raises doubts whether the editors have, as they term it, 'familiarity with the content of the poem, and a historically correct understanding of its whole structure of meaning' (p. 131). One of the main purposes in the B poet's revision of the A text was to moderate its angry, revolutionary tone, and the evidences of this are quite visible to anyone making a careful comparison of the two versions. And this holds whether or not one agrees with my opinion that the B version was not completed until after the Peasants Revolt of 1381, following which a hypersensitivity concerning violent statements is readily understandable. Now on this particular point it is quite appropriate that the editors and I be of a different opinion. But it is wrong of them to enshrine their point of view, against all the manuscript evidence, in a seemingly scientific edition of the poem.

Nor is the issue here merely a matter of opinion. Practically every category of what they call scribal censorship can be illustrated in the undoubted work of the B poet retained in their own edition. Thus B's recasting of A v.71–2 in B v.121–2 is an example of what the editors sometimes call 'genteel censorship' (p. 88), and so forth. A rather amazing case is their interpretation of what B does with A's direct address to chaste but avaricious chaplains (A 1.169–71; B 1.195–7). In part the passage is dealt with in fragments: 1.195 bodies **B**: body **A** (1.169) is cited as an instance of scribal variation toward an easier reading (p. 85); 1.195 Manye . . .

hem . . . hire **B**: ȝe . . . ȝow . . . ȝour **A** (1.169) is attributed to a scribal response to the sense and feeling of the poem producing a more emphatic (?) reading (p. 87); and 1.197 hem **B**: ȝow **A** (1.171) is explained as 'smoothing after substitution in 195' (p. 88). Let me just say in passing that the large blocks of evidence of this kind (pp. 78–82, 84–95, 99–103, 112–13, 134, 143–52, 154–8, 167–9, 172–3) should have been done away with in favour of analysis of organic units or passages where a single corruption (eyeskip for example) or a motive for the change (like censorship) may explain a multitude of little changes in a passage. The blocks of variants are impressive in appearance but not very meaningful for understanding why many of the changes actually occur. And I would have thought the organic analysis of these passages more in keeping with the editorial philosophy set forth so persuasively in the introduction to Professor Kane's edition of the A version.

But to return to the passage under consideration, the denunciation of avaricious chaplains: it *is* treated as a unit in another part of the introduction where the editors are showing corruption in the C reviser's B manuscript (pp. 104–5):

In 1.195, 196 **B** archetypally read *Manye curatours kepen hem clene of hire bodies* | *Thei ben acombred wiþ coueitise* where **A**'s text (1.169, 170) makes an abrupt and forceful transition to the preacher's direct accusation, *ȝe curatours þat kepe ȝow clene of ȝour body* and continues in the second person. **B**'s variation is scribal: the archetypal substitution of the third person, probably inattentive and unconscious, was induced by the surrounding context, and the more emphatic *Manye curatours* of 195 specifically echoes *Manye Chapeleyns* of 190. This weakly repetitive line offended the **C** poet; his revision took the form of omitting it altogether. The scribal character of the **B** manuscript that was before him is indicated by his retention of archetypal **B**'s third person pronouns *thei* and *hem* (**C** 1.191, 192).

On the contrary, the passage in B is a deliberate toning down of the angry denunciation of priests by the reviser, himself a priest, who is not only sensitive for that reason but because he is aware of an audience of potentially hostile colleagues ('They wol be wrooþ for I write þus' xv.489), whose sympathy he does not wish to lose. That is why changes like this occur in the B revision, and they are not attributable to scribes. For an example preserved in the K–D B text compare A viii.16–17 with B vii.15 (episcopal correction of the priesthood).

v.210 (*Skeat* v.212)

> *Skeat* B: To broche hem with a [pak-]nedle · and plaited hem togyderes

> K–D: [P]roche[d] hem wiþ a paknedle and playte hem togideres

The emendation of *broche* to *Proched*, I take it, brings the text into line with the editors' conclusions concerning the poet's metrical practice (p. 133): 'He did not, we find, rhyme [b] with [p]'.

vi.187–90 (A vii.175–6; *Skeat* B vi.190–3; C ix.183–7)

> *Kane* A: [A]n he[p] of heremites henten hem spadis
> And doluen drit & dung to ditte out hung*er*.

> *Skeat* B: An heep of heremites · henten hem spades,
> And ketten here copes · and courtpies hem made,
> And wenten as werkemen · with spades and with schoueles,
> And doluen and dykeden · to dryue aweye hunger.

> *Skeat* C: An hep of eremites · henten hem spades,
> Spitten and spradde donge · in despit of hunger.

> Thei coruen here copes • and courtepies hem made,
> And wenten as workmen • to weden and mowen;
> Al for drede of here deþ • suche dyntes ȝaf [hunger.]

K–D: An heep of heremytes henten hem spades
> And kitten hir copes and courtepies hem maked
> And wente as werkmen [to wedynge] and [mowynge]
> And doluen [drit] and [dung] to [ditte out] hunger.

Parts of this passage are classified under different headings, vi.190 *dryue away* B: *ditte out* A (vii.176) as an 'easier reading' (p. 85), vi.190 *and dikeden* B: *drit & dung* A (vii.176) as 'genteel censorship' (p. 88), and vi.189 *to wedynge and mowynge*] C viii.186 (*Skeat* ix.186); *wiþ spades and (wiþ) shoueles* > *aabb | to swynkyn abowtyn* > *aaxy (sense adjusted to following line)* as an example of 'sophistication' in B observable when compared with the reading of C (p. 152). But the time that it takes to locate these scattered references to the passage in question is scarcely justified by the inadequate picture that results from putting them together. In fact what the editors have done is to emend vi.189, presumably because of what they regard as deficient alliteration, by harmonizing it with C ix.186 (there being no such line in A); and they have emended vi.190, because of alleged genteel censorship, by harmonizing it with the A text (vii.176). These emendations are I suppose theoretically possible, but it seems to me that the editors move with suspicious ease from one text to the other, here emending by recourse to A, there by recourse to C, with no real indication of how this all bears on the 'whole structure of meaning' of the passage. Much more perceptive is the analysis of Mabel Day, who many years ago in the pages of *Modern Language Review* presented a study of the revisions of *Piers Plowman*, including this very passage, which has not received the attention it deserves.[1] In this article Miss Day adopted a classic multiple authorship position which I cannot espouse, being currently convinced that dual authorship (A/BC) offers the best hypothesis, but her interpretation of the hermit passage quoted above seems considerably more persuasive than the somewhat fragmented conclusions of Professors Kane and Donaldson.

vii.90–5 (*Skeat* vii.89–94)

K–D: For [þei] lyue in no loue ne no lawe holde.
> [Thei] wedde [no] womman þat [þei] wiþ deele
> But as wilde bestes *with* wehee worþen vppe and werchen,
> And bryngen forþ barnes þat bastardes men calleþ.
> Or [his] bak or [his] boon [þei] brekeþ in his youþe
> And goon [and] faiten *with* [hire] fauntes for *eu*eremoore after.

There is no need to quote other versions of this description of beggars, for it is clear at a glance that the main purpose of the emendations is to change the second person pronouns found in the B archetype to the third person of the A text (A viii.72–7). Since I have already criticized the editors for changing third person pronouns back to the second person (1.195–6), it might seem perverse to rebuke them now for the opposite type of emendation, but I have no choice. For whereas the A poet addresses 'ȝe curatours' (1.169) and 'ȝow renkes þat riche ben on erþe'

---

[1] 'The Revisions of *Piers Plowman*', *MLR*, 23 (1928), 1–27, especially pp. 2 f. R. W. Chambers and J. H. G. Grattan wrote a reply, 'The Text of *Piers Plowman*', published in *MLR*, 26 (1931), 1–51 which, however, did not disprove her basic thesis.

(VIII.165) in declamatory fashion, almost as if he has given up trying to engage their sympathies in his poem, he does not use this manner in addressing these beggars, for whatever reason. While on the other hand the B poet usually employs the pronouns in the opposite fashion, reserving his hortatory second person pronouns for beggars, about whom he has much more to say, eventually, in the B and C versions.

VII.125 (A VIII.107; *Skeat* B VII.120)

Kane A: And beloure þat I [be]louȝ er þeiȝ liflode me faile

Skeat B: And wepen whan I shulde slepe · þough whete bred me faille

K-D: And wepen whan I sholde [werche] þouȝ whete breed me faille

No manuscript of *Piers Plowman* here reads *werche*, but the editors confidently restore it according to the following rationale (p. 193):

At VII.125 archetypal *slepe* must be unoriginal: the meaning developed in 122–4 and continued in the second half of 125 requires in its place an original verb denoting 'labour'. This should, moreover, be set in contrast with the stave *wepen*; it will therefore have been alliterating *werche* rather than *swynke* or *trauaille* or *laboure*. Its corruption by rhyming inducement of preceding *slepen* [read *wepen*?] or by the suggestion of *lacrime . . . nocte* is easy to assume.

A glance at the passage involved shows that B VII.122–7 corresponds closely to A VIII.104–9, with very few differences except for the line in question. The meaning developed in A does indeed stress labour; but this does not prohibit the B reviser from changing this to an emphasis on ascetic practices, a tendency quite evident throughout the B text almost to the point of naivete, as when the hungry are advised to solace themselves by reading the lives of the saints (VII.87). The *lacrime . . . nocte* (VII.128α) is not a mere trap for the unwary scribe; it is a model which the B poet wishes the plowman to emulate, a subtle difference in characterization which the A poet (if he ever laid eyes on this revision) would never have approved. Skeat's paraphrase, with its untroubled acceptance of the differences between the two versions, has the ring of common sense: 'And I will weep when I should sleep, though wheaten bread fail me (in consequence of my watching)' [b]; 'and I will look loweringly upon that whereon I formerly smiled, ere my life fail' [a] (*Parallel Texts*, II, 127).

VIII.87 (*Skeat* VIII.86)

Skeat B: And helpeth alle men · after þat hem nedeth

K-D: [Whiles he haþ ouȝt of his owene he helpeþ þer nede is]

Here the editors simply reject the B line that stands in the B manuscripts and replace it with the equivalent line from A (IX.78), on the following grounds (p. 109): 'The inferior doctrine of **B**'s line (compare VII.76 ff.) suggests an unoriginality confirmed in **C** (X.84) *And helpeth alle men of þat he may spare*, which returns to the sense of **A**. But the shape of **C**'s line indicates that this sense was reimposed on the archetypally corrupted **B** line.' Even if the doctrinal differences are really present, they do not justify such wholesale revamping of the text. In fact A commends selfless but discriminating generosity, B reiterates the idea adding a tinge of paternalism, and C urges a similar generosity qualified by a concern for one's own sustenance. There is no return to the sense of A. But the main point is that there is no justification for this kind of harmonization of the A and B texts (Appendix, IVa).

IX.93 (*Skeat* IX.90)

> *Skeat* B: He is worse þan Iudas • þat ȝiueth a iaper siluer
>
> *K–D*:   He is [Iugged wiþ] Iudas þat ȝyueþ a Iaper siluer

The manuscripts read as in Skeat's text; Professors Kane and Donaldson justify their emendation on the following grounds (p. 196): 'At IX.93 *Iugged wiþ*] *wors þan* the stave-sound can only be [dʒ]; the lost sense and language are indicated by 87 above; the substitution was for greater emphasis.' No doubt the emendation was prompted by their conviction that 'the stave-sound can only be [dʒ]'. But the passage as a whole in which this line appears is one of those agonized responses by the B poet to Dame Study's searing denunciation of those who spurn the poor crying at the gate (A XI.45). It is evident that this touched a nerve, for lines echoing that part of the A text recur frequently in B. 'Allas þat a cristene creature shal be vnkynde til anoþer!' (B IX.86) expresses well the high emotion of this passage, and the line in question here continues it. If he were told that 'He is worse þan Iudas' does not alliterate I suspect the author's answer would be, 'It may not alliterate, but it's true!'. It is, moreover, a direct translation of the following Latin: *Proditor est prelatus cum Iuda* (IX.94a). One should not change a line just to make the author's words fit the text he is citing; but caution is surely advisable in emending if the manuscripts uniformly attest a reading which translates the Latin quoted.

x.58 (*Skeat* x.57)

> *Skeat* B: And gnawen god with þe gorge • whan her gutte is fulle
>
> *K–D*:   And gnawen god [in] þe gorge whanne hir guttes fullen

Here the problem is not so much the emendation itself, which is confirmed by the A text (XI.44), but the rationale given in support of it (p. 103): 'The appallingly graphic representation of blasphemy, *gnawen god in þe gorge*, 'bite God persistently in the throat', was either missed or rejected as outrageous, and a more colourless expression substituted; but *gnawen wiþ þe gorge* is actually nonsense.' They then criticize the corresponding definition of *gnauen* in the *Middle English Dictionary* because the editors do not interpret the line this way. No one, so far as I am aware, has ever proposed such a novel interpretation of the line, and I find it hard to believe that the idea will ever be generally accepted. The point of Dame Study's satire is directed against the greedy self-indulgence of those 'kete' men who 'dryuele at hir deys' 'at mete in hir murþe' and have God 'muche in hire mouþ'. She even reiterates unmistakably (B x.67), 'God is muche in þe gorge of þise grete maistres'. There can surely be no doubt about her meaning.

x.399, 400 (*Skeat* B x.394; C XII.226, 232)

> *Skeat* B: At here moste myschief • whan þei shal lyf lete
>
> *Skeat* C: Ac me were leuere, by oure lorde • a lippe of godes grace (226)
> At here moste meschef • mercy were þe beste (232)
>
> *K–D*:   [Ac] at hire mooste meschief [mercy were þe beste]
> Whan þei shal lif lete [a lippe of goddes grace]

Let Professors Kane and Donaldson describe in their own words what they have done here (pp. 182–3):

At x.399, 400 the **B** archetype reads a single line. The suggestion of its scribal alliteration *aabb* that it may be two original first half-lines run together is confirmed by **C** xi.230 [=*Skeat* C xii.232], which we take to be also the unrevised original B form of 399. We find the second half-line for 400 in **C** xi.224 [=*Skeat* C xii.226] which, from the echo (*lif lete > leuere*) which so often characterizes revised lines, is its equivalent. Corruption here probably in the second archetypal phase, will have been by attraction between the complementary meanings of 399a and 400a.

In order to appreciate the effect of these emendations, we must pause to remind ourselves what the context for them is. In A, the dreamer has launched into his closing meditation (A xi.258–313), and is now setting forth his ironical conclusion that Solomon and Aristotle, despite all their wisdom, are in hell. From this he draws the 'moral' (A xi.276–8):

> And ʒif I shal werke be here werkis to wynne me heuene,
> And for here werkis & here wyt wende to pyne,
> Þanne wrouʒt I vnwisly wiþ alle þe wyt þat I lere.

Looking at Skeat's B text, we find that the reviser reproduces these three lines almost without change (*Skeat* B x.387–9), and then adds a long passage of his own relating to wise but ungodly clerks in his own day (*Skeat* B x.390–413). God grant that the clergy, who are the carpenters of Holy Church, do not for their worldliness suffer the fate of the carpenters who built Noah's ark! The particular part of this addition we need to focus on is its opening (*Skeat* B x.390–4):

> Ac of fele witty in feith · litel ferly I haue,
> Þough her goste be vn*gra*ciouse · god for to plese.
> For many men on þis molde · more sette here hertis
> In good þan in god · for-þi hem grace failleth,
> At here moste myschief · whan þei shal lyf lete.

I see nothing wrong with these lines as they stand, articulating as they do a concern expressed repeatedly in the B text (Passus xv passim) over lack of spirituality in the clergy. But for the sake of argument let us, with the editors, cast a suspicious eye on the last line quoted, with its unusual alliteration (*aabb*). What do we find in the C text?

When he undertook his revision, the poet made new and interesting use of this passage. He incorporated it into a long speech of Recklessness (*Skeat* C xii.195–309), originally a minor figure who spoke only a few lines (*Skeat* B xi.33–40), but who is now given the words of the dreamer's meditation cast in a new dramatic form (*Skeat* C xii.224–34):

> Ac ich countresegge þe nat, clergie · ne þy connynge, scripture;
> That ho so doþ by ʒoure doctrine · dop wel, ich leyue.
> Ac me were leuere, by oure lorde · a lippe of godes grace
> Than al þe kynde witt þat ʒe can boþe · and connynge of ʒoure bokes.
> (B 390) For of fele witty in faith · litel ferly ich haue,
> (B 391) Thauh here gost be vngraciouse · god for to plese.
> (B 392) For meny men of þis molde · setten more here herte
> (B 393) In worldliche good þan in god · for-þy grace hem failleþ.
> (B 394) At here moste meschef · mercy were þe beste;
> And mercy of mercy · needes mot aryse,
> As holy writ wittnesseþ · godes word in the godspelle.

Here the authorship question is not involved; we are dealing with B and C only, which we can agree were the work of one man. But surely a simple comparison shows that the editors have mistakenly taken a new C line from the dramatization of Recklessness (*Skeat* C XII.226) and used it to restore the B line (*Skeat* B X.394), while at the end of the C passage quoted we see the reason for the author's changes: he wished to soften the hint of damnation in B, and turn it into an exhortation, urging the worldly clergy to show mercy, even if only as a form of enlightened self interest (*Skeat* C XII.232–4). Hence there is no basis whatever for the emendations, once we understand the rationale of the change made by the poet in revision to C, a change which, as Skeat observes (*Parallel Texts*, II. 158) 'necessitated several modifications of the wording'.

MANUSCRIPTS R AND F

Now we come to the B continuation, that part of the poem which is an original work of the B poet, and this is perhaps the best time to consider a problem which the editors had to confront, namely the significance for the B text of manuscripts R and F. In their classification of the manuscripts (Section II, pp. 16–69) they identify two main genetic groups, one being RF and the other all the remaining manuscripts of B. From their evidence, which is very full, I would judge this classification to be correct. They then go on, however (pp. 63–9), in an examination of RF passages, to conclude that the major differences between RF and the other manuscripts (including in this many long passages) are scribal in nature, despite their own earlier views to the contrary (p. 64 and n. 101). Surely Skeat was right in saying that R 'represents . . . a copy of the B-text with all the latest additions' (B text, p. 411). The editors try to show that where (for example) the RF group has long passages not in WHmCrGYOC²CBmBoCotLMS, the latter group has lost them through corruption via the usual scribal errors such as eyeskip, attraction of alliteration, etc. Less commonly RF omits long passages which are explained in the same way. I do not find these explanations at all convincing, and am at a loss to explain their change of opinion. Was it that the editors felt RF must be *either* a genetic group *or* a group formed by virtue of shared authorial revisions? But surely RF is *both*. This means that in any given case of RF additions or omissions a separate decision must be made. Without trying to deal with every case, it seems to me that the following are certainly later revisions of the B text in manuscripts R and F:

XI.160–70: an aside to men of Holy Church containing additional arguments in support of the salvation of the righteous heathen.

XI.383–93: a further exhortation by Reason on behalf of patience and restraint in the rebuking of others.

XII.116–25: more biblical examples to reinforce the analogy between the ark of the covenant and priests of the Church; no man should lay a hand on them by way of criticism of learning, whatever shortcomings individual clerics may have.

XIII.399–408: addition of gluttony to the sins on Haukyn's coat.

XIII.436–53: an exhortation to the rich to serve the poor at table rather than jesters; and to include a learned man to expound the gospel, and the blind or bedridden as evidence of the host's charity. These are 'God's minstrels' and are to be preferred to the japers and janglers being denounced in the original B passage

(XIII.421–35, 454–6), which is itself another of the B poet's numerous responses to the biting satire delivered by Dame Study (A XI.5–92).

XIV.228–38: in this case it would appear that two lines (228–9) are omitted for scribal reasons by the remaining B manuscripts (repetition of 'And if' in 227, 230) and are preserved only in RF; but lines 230–8 constitute a revision like XIII.399–408 above, adding gluttony to the list of sins that are unable to get the better of the poor.

XV.244–8: allows that charity was formerly to be found dwelling with archbishops and bishops, who now are guilty of avarice.

XV.511–28: an insertion on martyrs, including St Thomas à Becket, and a probable allusion to the assassination in 1381 of Simon Sudbury, Archbishop of Canterbury. This is a particularly obvious case, since the RF passage interrupts the flow of the surrounding denunciation of bishops, and it is well to note that the emendation occurring where the regular B text resumes ([And nauȝt to] xv.529) is essential to effect a transition back to the sentence that breaks off at xv.510. The inserted words come, of course, from RF.

XIX–XX: these two passus are said to contain no revision, but I think this is not entirely true. As far as the group RF is concerned, possible cases of deliberate change may be found in xx.27 and xx.126–30 (especially 127, 130); the editors seem to regard these as scribal aberrations restorable from RF.

XI.339–40 (*Skeat* B XI.330–1; C XIV.147–8)

> *Skeat* B: Males drowen hem to males · a mornynges bi hem-self,
> And in euenynges also · ȝe[de] males fro femeles.

> *Skeat* C: Maules drowen hem to maules · on morwenynge by hem-self,
> And femeles to femeles · *herdeyed and drow.   [*ferdide T]

> *K–D*: Males drowen hem to males [al mornyng] by hemselue,
> And [femelles to femelles ferded and drowe].

These lines occur in the dreamer's vision of the creation, explaining how reason governed the behaviour of all the animals. I cannot believe that the emendations here are correct, but the ingenuity of the editor's explanation is itself worthy of note (p. 160):

> XI.339 C XIII.147 most **B** and all **C** manuscripts read *a-/on/in/and morwenynge(s)* which, in the context of the seasonal mating of animals, is absurd: a single **B** manuscript reads *all mornynge*. Referring to the ancient notion *post coitum est omne animal triste*, this variant appears the probable original as both meaningful and by its difficulty likely to have generated a homœograph.

XIII.37–41

> *K–D*: Conscience called after mete and þanne cam Scripture
> And serued hem þus soone of sondry metes manye,
> Of Austyn, of Ambrose, of [alle] þe foure Euaungelistes:
> *Edentes & bibentes que apud eos sunt.*
> Ac þis maister [of þise men] no maner flessh [eet],
> Ac [he eet] mete of moore cost, mortrews and potages.

There is no need to quote Skeat's text here; *of þise men* simply replaces *ne his man* in Skeat (and the manuscripts), and the following changes merely adjust here and there to accommodate the new singular subject (*maister*). The editors explain (pp. 179–80):

At xiii.40 (after various dishes, Austin, Ambrose, the evangelists, were set before the friar theologian) archetypal **B** reads that neither *þis maister ne his man* ate meat of any kind, but dined on more expensive foods. The passage is suspect because no companion has been mentioned; because it is not Langland's dramatic practice to introduce unfunctional personages; and because declining to eat meat would be uncharacteristic of a glutton. The revised **C** line (xv.45) [= *Skeat* C xvi.46], *of this mete þat mayster myhte nat wel shewe* ('chew'), points to the violent allegorical figure we have reconstructed as the original **B** reading. Its corruption will have been by revulsion, whether conscious or unconscious, from even the suggestion of cannibalism.

I am not sure what they mean by saying that declining to eat meat would be uncharacteristic of a glutton, since the point is that the gluttonous doctor simply preferred to launch immediately into the rich and costly foods, scorning the healthier diet offered by the evangelists and the church fathers. If the master's man is introduced suddenly or without purpose here, then the same would have to be said of 'his felawe' in xiii.94 (*Skeat* C xvi.102) and perhaps also in xx.349.

xiv.23-4

> *K-D:*   Shal neuere [myx] bymolen it, ne moþe after biten it,
> Ne fend ne fals man defoulen it in þi lyue.

Conscience promises Haukyn the active man that if he completes the process of contrition, confession, and satisfaction his coat, which has been stained with the seven sins, will become whole and clean. The single emendation here is *myx* replacing the archetypal *myst*, and it is justified as follows (p. 194): 'At xiv.23 archetypal *myst*, 'water vapour' is inappropriate as a substance unlikely to stain or spot (*bymolen*) Haukyn's coat; the original must have been *myx*, 'filth', for which *myst* is either a visual error or a homœograph induced by subconscious censorship.' The editors apparently have not been confronted with the problem of mildew, but those of us less fortunate must surely argue that moisture is a full and sufficient cause for spotted clothes. In any case is it not true that these lines echo the gospel? *But lay up for yourselves treasures in heaven, where neither moth nor rust doth corrupt, and where thieves do not break through nor steal* (Matthew 6. 20). All the elements of the verse are in the two lines quoted, including the thieves (*Ne fend ne fals man*), though of course the idea of rust (Vulgate *aerugo*) must take a different form (*bymolen*) when applied to a coat.

xiv.225-6 (*Skeat* B xiv.224-5)

> *Skeat* B: If wratthe wrastel with þe pore · he hath þe worse ende;
> For if þey bothe pleyne · þe pore is but fieble.

> *K-D:*   If wraþe wrastle wiþ þe poore he haþ þe worse ende
> [For] if þei pleyne [þe feblere is þe poore].

The emendation in line 226b goes against the evidence of both the B and C texts, and is entirely unjustified, like the large number of other cases of emending to produce regular alliterative patterns (Appendix, v). I only mention it here because the line contains one word which conceivably ought to be emended (or at least mentioned in a footnote), and that is *pleyne*. The idea of the poor man engaging in a wrestling match with the sins is amusingly developed further, with a kind of Cornish zeal for the game, in the adjacent passage devoted to covetousness (xiv.239-44), where the word *layk* (line 244) provides the clue for correcting *pleyne* to read *pleyen* (as in some manuscripts of the C text, *Skeat* C xvii.68).

xiv.307 (*Skeat* B xiv.303; C xvii.142)

> *Skeat* B: And euere þe lasse þat he bereth • þe hardyer he is of herte
>
> *Skeat* C: And euere þe lasse þat eny lyf ledeþ • the lyghter hus herte is þere
>
> *K–D*:   And euer þe lasse þat he [lede], þe [liȝter] he is of herte

This is just a clear, simple case of unwarranted emending to produce regular alliteration. In reality the poet wrote the line as it stands in B, and then returned to it for precisely the purpose of regularizing the metre: the result appears as C xvii.142. Then Professors Kane and Donaldson give us still a third form, actually a mixture of B and C. Particularly unfortunate is the impression this gives, when multiplied hundreds of times (Appendix, v), of a poet who goes along making little changes in wording for no particular reason. The way the editors have restored the B line leaves no motive for the slightly different form of the line that appears in C, whereas before the change was understandable as a revision to improve alliteration.

xv.504–69 (*Skeat* B xv.532–60, 495–531)

As the corresponding line numbers from Skeat indicate, the editors are of the opinion that a displacement has occurred in the B archetype, which is also preserved in C (*Skeat* xviii.194–282), thus constituting additional evidence in support of their thesis that the C version was based on a corrupt copy of B. Their explanation of how this occurred is too long to quote here, but I commend it to the reader for its logic, ingenuity, and honesty in argument (pp. 176–9). Nevertheless I must say that the application of logic to a poet's order of presentation is a precarious business. When is a discourse 'interrupted for no apparent homiletic or dramatic purpose or effect' (p. 176)? After considering their evidence, I still prefer the archetypal order of this passage, which summarizes readily as follows (*Skeat* B xv.483–571):

What pope or prelate now performs Christ's command, *Go ye into all the world, and preach the gospel to every creature*? Prelates now reverence the cross on the coin, and glory in the red noble rather than in the cross of Christ. Secular lords would be doing the church a service should they take their possessions from them! Why don't these prelates who take pride in their honorary titles (Bishop of Bethlehem, Babylon, etc.) go forth and preach the gospel to their heathen charges in these areas?

How the editors can consider the passage hard to follow or lacking in forcefulness (p. 177) I cannot understand. That it might be 'bad composition' (p. 178) I emphatically deny.

xvii.94 (*Skeat* B xvii.92; C xx.82)

> *Skeat* B: May no medicine on molde • þe man to hele brynge
>
> *Skeat* C: Ne medecine vnder molde • þe man to hele brynge
>
> *K–D*:   May no medicyne [vnder mone] þe man to heele brynge

In this case I might have been inclined to read *vnder molde* in B, since it has the support of RF and the C text, and might be an instance of RF revision which the editors usually adopt. Here is their argument for making still another emendation (pp. 111–12):

In xvii.94 archetypal **B** read *May no medicyne vnder molde þe man to heele brynge* (*on molde* records sophisticating further variation by one genetic group). This is contextually not meaningful. The 'medicine' is to be Christ's redeeming blood, and thereafter the sacraments of confession and communion. The obvious original meaning, restorable on the suggestion of *vnder*, is *vnder mone*, 'sublunary, earthly, subject to decay', which we have adopted. The **C** text here (xix.84) reproduces the corrupt reading of the **B** archetype.

There is truth in this, but the medicine referred to is all medicines *other than* that which Christ will bring, and so we are left with the simple question: would the poet refer to medicine as being 'under the earth'? Before deciding that he would not, it might be well to consult some standard medieval reference such as the medical and mineral sections (Books vii and xvi) of Bartholomæus Anglicus, *De Proprietatibus Rerum* (now handily available in the translation of John Trevisa, *On the Properties of Things* (Oxford, 1975)). Referring to medicine as *vnder molde* could be a way of saying the most remote or inaccessible medicines of all.

xviii.53 (*Skeat* B xviii.53; C xxi.53)

   Skeat B: And bede hym drynke his deth-yuel • his dayes were ydone

   Skeat C: And [beden] hym drynke, hus deþ to lette • and hus dayes lengthen

   K–D: And beden hym drynken his deeþ [to lette and] hise daies [lengþe]

Here B is made to conform with the C text, because the editors regard the archetypal reading of B as scribal, being 'more emphatic' (p. 91) than C. On the other hand Skeat observes: 'There is a most remarkable variation here; in the B-text, Christ is said to be asked to drink, to *shorten* his life; in the C text, to *lengthen* it' (*Parallel Texts*, ii, 251). Remarkable indeed. Scribes do not do this sort of thing; the author himself is responsible for the change, representing as it does a crux in interpretation of the passion narrative.

xviii.109

   K–D: Whan crist cam hir kyngdom þe crowne sholde [lese]:
            Cum veniat sanctus sanctorum cessabit unxio vestra.

Skeat has *cesse*; the editors adopt the reading of RF, *lese*. The C text does not support RF, but instead reads 'When crist with crois ouercam • ʒoure kyngdom shal to-cleue' (*Skeat* C xxi.114). It may be that all three variants represent not scribal activity but authorial uncertainty about the application of the prophecy in Daniel 9. 24–6. Does Daniel refer to the cessation of the line of anointed Jewish rulers (*cesse*)? the loss of their messiah to the gentiles (*lese*)? the destruction of Jerusalem by Titus and Vespasian (*to-cleue*)?

xix.442 (*Skeat* xix.439)

   Skeat B: And god amende þe pope • þat pileth holykirke

   K–D: And [Piers] amende þe pope, þat pileþ holy kirke

All B manuscripts and the C text of course support Skeat's reading. The editors discuss conjectural emendations, which they regard 'as possible rather than likely or confident restorations because, resting on less information, they involve a larger speculative element' (p. 207). Under this heading they discuss the present case (p. 208):

The line lacks a stave on [p]; if *god* was original the line might have read *god haue pite on*, or *pardon*, or *make parfit* or *punisshe*, or even *preie god amende þe pope*. But from consideration of the identity of the speaker and the suggestion of 426 ff., it seems to us more probable that Piers, *Emperour of al þe world* in an ideal universal Christendom, is the likelier agency invoked. While these indications are strong our decision nevertheless is arbitrary.

The gradations of confidence set forth by the editors in their discussion of conjectural emendation is new in my experience. It carries with it the virtue of honesty, but it leaves me wondering how they got themselves into the position of making, by their own definition, arbitrary emendations. I can only suppose that their belief in the radical, widespread corruption of the B archetype has lulled them into a more relaxed attitude toward these matters than they should have permitted themselves.

Going through this new edition of the B version of *Piers Plowman* and re-enacting the decisions of its editors has been an arduous but stimulating experience. Clearly I am convinced that in large part it is a text that never existed in the fourteenth century. Nevertheless it scrupulously provides us with full and accurate information on the readings of the manuscripts, and the opinions of its editors are a constant challenge to the reader. The danger, of course, is that not every reader of this edition may be inclined to scrutinize the process by which the text has been established, and particularly if the edition were to be published in a simplified form without the full apparatus, something which I trust Professors Kane and Donaldson will not sanction. In its present form, however, with the editors' corrections clearly identified, this new B text could become a strong stimulus in the continuing quest for understanding of this fascinating and difficult poem. But is has not rendered obsolete, and it cannot replace, the edition of Walter W. Skeat.

APPENDIX

CLASSIFICATION OF EMENDATIONS IN THE KANE–DONALDSON EDITION OF THE B VERSION OF *PIERS PLOWMAN*

1. Emendations of their base manuscript (W) which bring it into agreement with Skeat's edition of the B-text. (638 cases)

Prologue, 24, 25, 27, 29, 39, 69, 105, 110, 149, 162, 163, 170, 186, 188, 189, 204, 212, 231. **I.**6, 23, 31, 37–8, 50, 58, 68, 106, 124, 125, 126, 130, 132, 147, 170, 172, 183. **II.**27a, 57, 61, 100, 104, 105, 112, 147, 148, 186, 187, 217, 225. **III.**57, 82, 101, 105, 108, 112, 117, 142, 217, 225, 254a, 280, 283, 335. **IV.**24, 28, 52, 54, 67, 75, 103, 128, 175, 189. **V.**41, 49, 67, 69, 89, 93, 149, 154, 164, 168, 169, 179, 205, 251, 269a, 273a, 279, 281a, 283a, 297, 298, 305, 324, 343, 367, 381, 382, 403, 416, 430, 437, 441, 486a, 487, 506, 518, 550, 568, 577, 584, 592, 598, 603a, 605, 606, 609, 618, 629, 635. **VI.**43, 70, 72, 77, 124, 127, 146, 147, 174, 182, 220, 226, 228, 299, 324, 331. **VII.**2, 77a, 83a, 89, 99, 144, 158, 194. **VIII.**29, 52, 59, 64, 130, 131. **IX.**11, 47, 57, 77, 88, 96, 103, 105, 120, 127, 129, 147, 148, 163, 164, 184, 209. **X.**4, 27, 28, 33, 34, 90, 103, 119, 120, 135, 158, 167, 177, 178, 180, 195, 213, 215, 222, 243, 245, 252a, 266a, 267, 268a, 270a, 276, 293, 297–308, 321, 325, 335, 359a, 363, 364, 374, 386, 402, 410, 417–19, 422, 436a, 439, 440, 441, 442, 444, 450a, 456, 462, 466, 467, 480. **XI.**10, 20, 61, 80, 81a, 82, 100, 103, 131–2, 136, 151, 160–70, 181, 186, 196, 220, 255a, 257, 259, 274a, 300, 311, 315, 316, 324, 333, 349, 360, 380, 382, 383–93, 414, 421, 429–31. **XII.**2, 9, 17, 21, 47, 54, 55–7, 61, 76, 78, 82, 90, 103, 116–25, 125, 131, 135, 137, 138, 140, 146, 151–2, 154, 155, 163, 164, 187, 188, 192, 198, 199, 205, 210, 213, 213a, 228, 237, 249, 277. **XIII.**9, 10, 19, 29, 36, 39, 44, 50, 81, 93, 94, 98, 105, 134, 136, 142, 155, 159, 162, 164–71, 178, 193, 204, 205, 220, 225, 229, 240, 245, 254a, 256, 259, 266, 269, 282–3, 285, 292–8, 300, 322, 328, 330a, 333, 334, 348, 351, 354, 355, 367, 372, 373, 377, 382, 383, 393, 394, 399–408, 411, 412, 416, 418, 428, 430, 433, 436–53, 456, 459. **XIV.**32, 75, 79, 90, 102, 126, 127, 142, 146, 160,

4

161, 168, 179, 183, 185, 187, 189, 195, 197, 211, 212, 213a, 220, 222, 228–38, 241, 242, 248, 252, 268, 276, 289, 303a, 311, 322, 328. **XV.**8, 15, 25, 36, 38, 39, 45, 46, 62, 65, 82, 94, 96, 99, 101, 107, 133, 142, 143, 144, 152, 156, 177, 187, 206, 209, 223, 232, 244–8, 251, 303–4, 308, 329, 331, 365, 374, 375, 387, 397, 399, 401, 411, 414, 418, 425, 429, 431a, 432, 434, 456, 470, 472–85, 486, 490a, 497, 503, 511–28, 540, 556, 573–6, 578, 601, 605, 610. **XVI.**8, 11, 16, 22, 25a, 30, 54, 60, 73, 83, 86, 87, 99a, 110a, 112, 120a, 131, 159, 166, 175, 178, 186, 204, 205, 219, 241, 248. **XVII.**5, 22, 27, 42, 70, 71, 106, 108, 114a, 124, 135, 143, 152, 156, 162, 167, 168, 169, 176, 178, 186–7, 200a, 201, 213, 218, 234, 244, 251, 260, 281, 285, 289, 300, 308, 313–14, 322, 352. **XVIII.**10, 30, 41, 74, 75, 104, 105, 117, 148, 166, 191, 200, 204, 209, 217, 221, 222, 225, 234, 240, 250, 259, 267, 268, 272, 277, 298, 300, 313–14, 330, 331, 338, 348, 363, 373, 389, 406, 408b, 417, 420, 421a, 423, 427, 428, 431. **XIX.**8, 15, 34, 36, 38, 40, 65, 68, 78, 89, 96, 114, 124, 146, 153, 169, 173, 181a, 186, 188, 215, 245, 246, 254, 262, 278, 290, 311, 326, 347, 353, 376, 379, 386, 425, 428, 441, 467. **XX.**24, 51, 55, 64, 65, 83, 95, 102, 105, 114, 136, 144, 147, 149, 162, 170, 171, 179, 181, 190, 217, 234, 235, 255, 256a, 260–3, 295, 301, 305, 310, 343, 367.

ii. Emendations that go beyond Skeat but seem justifiable on various grounds. (429 cases)

Prologue, 71, 179, 185. **I.**36, 37, 43, 73, 79, 88, 112–13, 136, 142, 152, 165, 171, 174, 177, 182, 186, 187, 188, 200, 206, 209. **II.**1, 3, 5, 8, 9, 22, 47, 91, 101, 113, 117, 120, 124, 128, 131, 133, 138, 145, 176, 180, 181, 183, 198, 200, 203–7, 212, 222, 224, 229, 231, 233, 238. **III.**3, 6, 30, 48, 87, 114, 118, 124, 125, 132, 141, 145, 147, 150, 151, 160, 179, 183, 210, 211, 214, 216, 222, 235, 281, 284, 289, 295, 301, 321, 322. **IV.**1, 4, 10, 32, 47, 63, 79, 94, 104, 105, 109, 110, 117, 132, 136, 145. **V.**15, 19, 29, 34, 35, 47, 61, 74, 99, 188, 190, 195, 197, 212, 215, 216, 217, 219, 223, 225, 307, 309, 312–13, 315, 320, 326, 327, 329, 337, 350, 356, 357, 358, 362, 407, 419, 444, 450, 462, 465, 470, 472, 473, 482, 500, 501, 504, 514, 526, 542, 552, 572, 573, 575, 576, 583, 584, 588, 597, 599, 610, 612, 613, 617, 630. **VI.**2, 30, 34, 67, 74, 84, 88, 92, 95, 113, 115, 119, 120, 128, 152, 175, 179, 185, 198, 200, 205, 207, 215, 221, 272, 279, 281, 285, 306, 312, 313, 319, 320, 323, 326. **VII.**1, 16, 24, 34, 49, 65, 106, 111, 117, 133, 143a, 145, 148, 173, 179–80, 191. **VIII.**11, 12, 24, 27, 30, 31, 70, 72, 74, 84, 111, 128. **IX.**3, 4, 7, 9, 17, 22, 56, 137, 175, 195. **X.**9, 54, 71, 72, 79–80, 88, 131, 132, 136, 175, 176, 383, 384, 397, 428. **XI.**7, 58a, 106, 109, 110, 197, 198, 201, 209, 267, 331. **XII.**59, 104, 195, 214, 219–22. **XIII.**51, 103, 104, 228, 349, 360, 363, 390, 425, 454. **XIV.**183, 204, 205, 217, 294, 312. **XV.**63a, 73, 116, 135, 162a, 188, 193, 207, 338, 396, 461, 529, 530, 531, 532, 586, 588, 592, 604. **XVI.**50, 77, 93, 119, 123, 136, 140, 142, 161, 211, 220, 250, 262, 275. **XVII.**1, 9, 11, 12, 17, 88, 105, 143, 168, 173, 183, 198, 206, 209, 283, 293, 303, 306, 329, 331, 341a. **XVIII.**6–9, 28, 87, 96, 101, 151, 157, 159, 262, 266, 270, 275, 359, 375. **XIX.**43, 56–9, 64, 73, 75, 77, 90, 94, 117, 118, 130, 145, 152, 172a, 179, 189, 208, 216, 236–7, 249, 273, 274, 275, 283, 284, 314–15, 330, 334, 336, 394, 415, 422, 430, 446, 453, 463. **XX.**6, 8, 10, 27, 37, 38, 39, 42, 62, 63, 67, 78, 93, 104, 119, 138, 141, 183, 191, 198, 208, 210, 211, 218, 221, 249, 253, 263, 277, 284, 291, 320, 336, 350, 356, 366, 382.

iii. Emendations for which justification is insufficient. (273 cases)

Prologue, 177, 180, 221, 222, 228, 229. **I.**4, 16, 31a, 57. **II.**35, 40, 107, 122, 130, 140, 153, 156, 230. **III.**49, 107, 198, 260, 264–5, 327, 342, 350. **IV.**41, 150. **V.**37, 42, 165, 235, 243, 274, 275, 374, 376, 413, 447, 522, 631. **VI.**133, 158. **VII.**42, 90, 91, 94, 95. **IX.**39, 59, 89, 113, 115, 124, 125a, 149, 155a, 181, 193. **X.**11, 84, 95, 204, 204a, 209, 244, 270, 281, 292, 310, 385, 406, 461, 479. **XI.**9, 41, 49, 60, 79, 83, 103, 127, 150, 158, 184, 217, 255, 278, 301, 302, 326, 328, 339, 378, 396, 410, 411, 420. **XII.**7, 23, 42, 66, 88, 133, 161, 226, 229, 230, 233, 261, 273, 276, 285, 293. **XIII.**3, 18, 30, 46, 53–4, 80, 121, 131, 132, 140, 145, 152, 163a, 213, 227, 249a, 270, 271, 278, 289, 311, 358, 366, 409, 410. **XIV.**21, 22, 23, 28, 74, 80, 81, 86, 141, 171, 190, 196, 198, 202, 207, 216, 255, 273, 275, 277, 283, 286–7, 292–3, 307a–9, 316. **XV.**16–17, 41, 109, 139, 195, 198, 255, 275, 289, 318, 346, 356, 361, 366, 376, 390, 460, 501, 504–69, 505, 571, 581. **XVI.**9, 17, 38, 43, 66, 78, 122, 147, 182, 201, 214, 219a, 245, 251. **XVII.**4, 16, 18, 26, 35, 59, 76, 89, 94, 97, 116, 171, 225, 269, 272, 324, 340. **XVIII.**51, 76, 86, 100, 109, 123, 242, 315a, 317–18, 343, 414, 421, 424. **XIX.**47, 76, 149, 159, 162, 164, 174, 183, 184–5, 197, 205, 213, 298, 301, 302, 303, 348, 380, 387, 399, 400, 407, 408, 412, 448, 457, 470. **XX.**25, 36, 60, 120, 125, 151, 215, 219, 236, 273, 283, 290, 292, 342, 375.

IV. Unjustified emendations which have the effect of harmonizing the B text with one of the other versions.

a. Harmonized with the A text. (684 cases)

Prologue, 2, 8, 13, 20, 22, 26, 31, 34, 36, 37, 38, 41, 42, 44, 45, 48, 57, 59, 62, 64, 67, 72, 73, 76, 77, 80, 81, 82, 84, 86, 213, 214, 217, 224. **I.**1, 8, 24, 25, 41, 44, 45, 48, 49, 51, 59, 60, 63, 64, 69, 70, 76, 77, 78, 80, 81, 85, 89, 91, 92, 98–103, 99, 100, 102, 103, 104, 105, 107, 108, 109, 175, 176, 185, 191, 195, 196, 197, 198, 199, 202. **II.**6, 10, 20, 45, 54, 72, 74, 75, 89, 116, 134, 135, 136, 137, 139, 141, 152, 158, 160, 163, 164, 166, 184, 185, 190, 191, 193, 201, 202, 204–5, 213, 223, 227. **III.**2, 5, 8, 11, 12, 14, 15, 19, 28, 31, 32, 36, 37, 38, 39, 41, 42, 46, 51, 63, 64, 67, 69, 78, 79, 84, 86, 90, 94, 95, 97, 98, 99, 102, 104, 106, 109, 115, 117, 122, 123, 126, 128, 130, 131, 136, 137, 140, 148, 149, 154, 158, 162, 165, 168, 180, 182, 194, 204, 209, 215, 219, 223–4, 224, 226, 232, 233, 234, 246, 250, 254, 278, 290, 293. **IV.**7, 14, 20, 21, 22, 29, 31, 44, 46, 53, 56, 57, 58, 64, 66, 76, 80, 86, 90, 95, 96, 98, 99, 101, 102, 106, 107, 108, 111, 118, 130, 131, 135, 137, 140, 141, 142, 146, 162, 183, 184, 186, 190, 192, 193, 195. **V.**2, 7, 10, 17, 21, 26, 27, 31, 44, 56, 70, 71, 72, 76, 78, 79, 81, 83, 94–5, 96, 97, 98, 99, 101, 102, 103, 104, 105, 106, 107, 108, 109, 110, 111, 112, 113, 114, 115, 117, 118, 119, 120, 126, 127, 128, 129, 199, 200, 208, 211, 213, 214, 220, 299, 303, 304, 317, 321, 325, 328, 331, 333, 334, 342, 345, 348, 349, 353, 363, 445, 448, 458, 460, 515, 525, 527, 530, 531, 532, 533, 536, 540, 541, 545, 555, 557, 559, 560, 565, 567, 570, 578, 585, 591, 596, 621, 623, 625, 627, 628, 632, 634. **VI.**9, 16, 19, 20, 21, 23, 24, 25, 26, 28, 31, 32, 33, 37, 38, 39, 41, 42, 44, 45, 50, 51, 53, 56, 58, 59, 60, 61, 65, 76, 87, 89, 90, 93, 94, 97, 103, 104, 105, 108, 109, 114, 116, 122, 131, 137, 138, 145, 153, 154, 156, 157, 167, 170, 173, 178, 183, 186, 190, 197, 203, 204, 206, 209, 216, 218, 219, 223–4, 231, 232, 236, 237, 238, 239, 241, 242, 243, 244, 247, 248, 249, 253, 258, 262, 264, 266, 267, 268, 269, 270, 273, 275, 276–7, 278, 283, 286, 288, 289, 290, 291, 292, 296, 298, 301, 302, 303, 304, 308, 310, 317, 318, 325. **VII.**4, 6, 10, 17, 19, 26, 27, 28, 30, 31, 32, 52, 59, 61, 63, 64, 67, 69, 97, 98, 103, 105, 108, 118, 119, 123, 127, 129, 130, 132, 134, 138, 139, 140, 146, 151, 159, 160, 163, 164, 175, 177, 178, 181, 182, 185, 186, 187, 189, 192, 195, 196, 198, 199, 202, 203. **VIII.**18, 20a, 22, 23, 32, 34, 36, 37, 39, 40, 41, 42, 43, 44, 45, 46, 47, 48–50, 53, 57, 62–3, 66, 69, 75, 76, 77, 78, 80, 81, 82, 83, 85, 86, 87, 88, 89, 90, 92, 94, 95, 97, 98, 100, 101, 102, 103, 104–5, 106, 108, 109, 110, 112–13, 116, 118, 119, 122, 125, 129. **IX.**24, 26, 31, 33, 34, 49, 50, 51, 52, 54, 68–70, 127, 130, 132, 133, 138, 141, 142, 145, 160, 161, 162, 167, 169–71, 168, 170, 172, 178, 179, 190, 192, 198, 199, 201, 207, 208. **X.**2, 3, 5, 13, 17, 18, 19, 20, 21, 36, 37, 47, 49, 55, 56, 58, 61, 62, 69, 70, 107, 110, 118, 126, 127, 129, 137, 138, 140, 141, 142, 143, 147, 150, 151, 154, 155, 156, 157, 159, 160, 161, 165, 166, 172, 174, 183, 187, 191, 202, 203, 212, 214, 216, 217–18, 221, 225, 226, 228, 229, 230, 234–5, 236, 300, 302, 303, 311, 337, 338, 339, 340, 341, 349, 350, 352, 354, 356, 375, 376, 382, 391, 392, 421, 424, 427, 431, 448–9, 464.

b. Harmonized with the C text. (236 cases)

Prologue, 109, 148, 150, 166, 171, 175, 182, 189–97, 193, 198, 200, 205, **I.**11, 153, 154. **II.**12, 88, 90, 93. **III.**62, 67, 69, 113. **IV.**37, 38–9. **V.**32, 87, 178, 181, 182, 183, 193, 194, 289, 291, 369, 386, 387, 391, 393, 405, 409, 427, 477, 478, 479, 480, 483, 484, 486, 494, 513. **VI.**49, 64, 145, 155, 201. **VII.**30, 31, 57, 58, 84, 96, 152. **VIII.**14, 67. **IX.**183. **X.**78, 87. **XI.**2, 5, 8, 56, 59, 84, 105, 121, 129, 130, 133, 141, 142, 148, 149, 203, 204a, 205, 239, 242, 253, 263, 264, 292, 293, 305, 338, 340, 342, 357, 363, 371, 403, 412, 436. **XII.**173, 178, 183–4, 193, 201, 209, 211, 280, 284, 290. **XIII.**2, 40, 41, 45, 95, 96, 100, 113, 119, 222, 233, 326, 329, 330, 345, 374, 386, 423, 427, 455. **XIV.**46, 56, 57, 58, 118, 131a, 213, 215, 315, 319–20. **XV.**18, 78, 92, 98, 100, 102, 157, 358, 382, 513, 547, 550, 553, 555, 612. **XVI.**115, 157, 273. **XVII.**142, 144, 152a, 184, 203, 211, 237, 267–8, 299, 311, 320. **XVIII.**14, 24, 40, 53, 83, 95, 97, 106, 147, 149, 161–2, 179, 198, 252, 253, 254, 284, 315, 376, 382, 393. **XIX.**62, 148, 154, 182, 230, 238, 241, 271, 280, 292, 308, 335, 343, 357, 362, 363, 429, 437, 464. **XX.**14, 34, 54, 87, 106, 126, 127, 130, 140, 163, 212, 228, 256, 261, 300, 308, 313, 337, 355, 360, 363, 365, 381.

V. The unacceptable practice of emending to produce regular alliterative patterns.

a. First half of B text, Prologue and Passus I–x. (160 cases)

Prologue, 103, 117, 122, 143, 159, 201, 206. **I.**112, 118, 121, 122, 123, 160. **II.**27, 36, 43, 84, 143. **III.**71, 75, 177, 229, 241, 255, 292, 296, 298, 303, 316, 319, 334, 341, 344, 345, 346, 351.

IV.15, 23, 36, 91, 158, 159, 168, 194. **V.**9, 23, 38, 52, 84, 130, 151–2, 167, 173, 176, 185, 191, 196, 210, 239, 254, 260–1, 267, 271, 276, 283, 286, 377, 399, 404, 411, 414, 439, 440, 491, 496, 508, 512, 534, 535, 554. **VI.**123, 148, 150, 162–3, 180, 181, 189, 210, 282, 327. **VII.**7, 35, 40, 46, 50, 60, 70, 71, 123, 125. **IX.**15, 16, 23, 27, 32, 40, 42–3, 73, 79, 90, 93, 98, 101, 110, 123, 157, 166, 182, 185, 191, 194, 202, 203–4. **X.**46, 48, 51, 91, 109, 128, 134, 189, 193, 207, 227, 248, 252, 257, 278, 279, 280, 285, 290, 307, 313, 316, 319, 320, 327, 329, 330, 353, 373, 399–400, 429, 432, 452, 453, 470, 473, 478.

b. The B-Continuation, Passus xi–xx. (256 cases)

XI.14, 52, 53, 67, 70, 81, 96, 134, 180, 182, 185, 233, 240, 241, 283, 291, 325, 344, 353–4, 356, 372, 373, 374, 398, 399, 408, 409, 422, 432, 434, 437, 440, 441. **XII.**4, 6, 22, 24, 40, 60, 81, 89, 91, 95, 101, 119, 127, 129, 130, 162, 194, 204, 240–3, 262, 263, 268, 291. **XIII.**8, 16, 25, 35, 47, 48, 82, 85, 86, 106, 117, 128, 139, 174, 194, 196, 211, 253, 254, 325, 340, 375. **XIV.**7, 8, 9, 46, 47, 48, 49, 50, 62, 78, 82, 96, 99, 124, 125, 223, 226, 253, 260, 267, 270, 271, 274, 278, 284–5, 301–3, 307, 314. **XV.**63, 70, 72, 76, 84, 106, 111, 114, 115, 117, 119, 121–2, 123, 126–7, 138, 140, 163–4, 201, 213, 224, 231, 234, 237, 243, 244, 268, 269, 295, 307, 312, 313, 314, 321, 324, 353, 378–9, 394, 395, 419, 422, 445, 451, 471, 492, 523, 546, 548, 551, 552, 566. **XVI.**33, 71, 108–10, 121, 150, 158, 192, 193, 202, 231, 267. **XVII.**3, 7, 33, 54, 73, 77, 79–80, 82, 90, 92, 103, 118, 155, 166, 217, 227, 247, 281–2, 296–7, 301, 330. **XVIII.**2, 46, 48, 54, 71, 82, 113, 119, 131, 152–3, 155, 160, 170, 180, 194, 223, 239, 282, 283, 295, 296, 299, 307, 309, 342, 350, 374, 378, 391, 401, 405. **XIX.**60, 97, 101, 140, 180, 212, 229, 235, 240, 243, 251, 253, 270, 316, 321, 345, 368, 369, 375, 409, 426, 442, 477, 478, 479. **XX.**19, 70, 109, 155, 292, 307, 326, 354, 372, 376, 377, 379.

Natural and Rational Love in Medieval Literature

GERALD MORGAN

Trinity College, Dublin

Alas, Love, I would thou couldst as well defend
thyself as thou canst offend others (Sidney)

I

It is sometimes the case that our understanding of literature is inhibited by the very greatness of the scholars that have sought to explain it to us. An eminent example is to be found in the field of medieval love poetry, for no question is more vexed than that of courtly love. Most of us will have been introduced to the subject in the following manner:

> Every one has heard of courtly love, and every one knows that it appears quite suddenly at the end of the eleventh century in Languedoc . . . The sentiment, of course, is love, but love of a highly specialized sort, whose characteristics may be enumerated as Humility, Courtesy, Adultery, and the Religion of Love.[1]

C. S. Lewis was not the kind of scholar to conceal his opinions beneath a display of professional caution; the impact of *The Allegory of Love* would no doubt have been less had he done so. But now we can see that there is after all a need for caution. Professor Donaldson, indeed, has told us that what Lewis has to offer is not so much scholarship as myth.[2] We may perhaps agree that there are some mythical elements in Lewis's account; the emotion of love, for instance, is not an invention of the Middle Ages but a universal phenomenon.[3] Our present difficulties arise, however, from the contrary consideration; there is much sound learning and often justice in what Lewis has to say about medieval conceptions of love. The basic objection to the account that he gives of courtly love (as Professor Donaldson himself observes) is that in it he attempts too much.[4] The various treatments of love in medieval courtly literature cannot be constrained in the way that he proposes.

The use of the term 'courtly' establishes a link between Provençal lyric poetry of the early twelfth century, Northern French romance of the late twelfth century (Chrétien de Troyes), *Le Roman de la rose* of the mid-thirteenth century (Guillaume de Lorris and Jean de Meun), Italian literature of the early fourteenth century (Dante), and English literature of the late fourteenth century (the work of the *Gawain* poet, Chaucer, and Gower), and of course extends well beyond the confines of the medieval period itself. The fact is beyond dispute that all this poetry is the product of a specifically court culture; an illumination in MS Corpus Christi College, Cambridge 61, for example, depicts Chaucer reading his *Troilus* at the

---

[1] C. S. Lewis, *The Allegory of Love* (London, 1936), p. 2.
[2] E. T. Donaldson, 'The Myth of Courtly Love', *Speaking of Chaucer* (London, 1970), pp. 154–63.
[3] On this point see P. Dronke, *Medieval Latin and the Rise of European Love-Lyric*, 2 vols, second edition (Oxford, 1968), I, xvi–xvii and 1–56.
[4] Donaldson, pp. 155–6.

court of Richard II. This common courtly environment gives to medieval literature an appearance of unity, and is especially striking from a modern point of view.[1] But it is only an appearance; the essential ambiguity of the phrase 'courtly love' arises from the second of its two terms.

Even in present day usage we can recognize that different meanings attach themselves to the single word *love*: (i) the settled affections within the family, for example, of parents for child or of brother for sister (*OED* s.v. *love*, sb. 1). (ii) the love of God for his creatures, or of the creature for his Creator (*OED* 2). (iii) the love of a young man for a young lady (*OED* 4). In the modern language *love* does service equally for these different conceptions, although we can isolate the second by using the word *charity*. Now *love* is as ambiguous in the medieval language as it is in the modern. We need at least to distinguish between two radically different conceptions: (i) *fin' amors*: love itself is ethically normative. This is the illicit love that is described by Lewis and which is characteristic of the Provençal lyric poets; the phrase *fin' amors* is indeed that used by the Provençal poets themselves. (ii) *amour courtois*: love is merely an aspect of *courtoisie*, that is, of the chivalric ethic. This is the lawful love that is compatible with Christian marriage.[2]

In order to understand the difference between these conceptions of love we need to turn to the Aristotelian and Scholastic psychological system in terms of which they are later defined. Aristotle was a biologist and empiricist, and his observation of the created world led him to classify all living organisms in a hierarchy of being on the basis of the powers of soul possessed by them. Thus, in ascending order:

(i) vegetative soul: its object is the individual body united to a soul. It is the source of nutrition, growth, and reproduction (plants).

(ii) sensitive soul: its object is every sensible body. To the principle of nutrition, growth, and reproduction is added that of sensation (animals).

(iii) rational soul: its object is being itself. To the principles of nutrition, etc. and sensation is added that of intellect (man).[3]

Thus the higher order possesses the principle of the lower and an additional differentiating principle of its own. It is important to note that Aristotle and those scholastic thinkers who follow his teaching insist upon the unity of the rational soul (see *ST*, 1a 76.3 *corp.*). Man is conceived as a unity who combines in his being the powers of nutrition, etc., sensation, and intellect. He is not to be supposed as possessing three souls. This point is crucial to the analysis of love in medieval literature.

Both the sensitive and rational souls presuppose activity in relation to an external object, and in this respect St Thomas (following Aristotle) distinguishes two kinds of power (or faculty):

(i) cognitive, that is, the acquisition of knowledge.

(ii) appetitive, that is, the impulse to act which follows from that acquisition of knowledge (see *ST* 1a 78.1 *corp.*).

These are operative at both the sensitive and rational levels.

---

[1] On this subject see G. Mathew, *The Court of Richard II* (London, 1968).

[2] See M. Lazar, *Amour courtois et 'fin'amors' dans la littérature du xiie siècle* (Paris, 1964), pp. 21–46.

[3] See Aquinas, *Summa Theologiae*, 1a 78.1. Reference is throughout to the edition of T. Gilby and others (London, 1964—), hereafter cited as *ST*.

A *The Sensitive Soul*

(i) cognition: the cognitive act of the sensitive soul is sensation, that is, an impression received by the senses from the outside world, for example, colour (greenness) by the sense of sight, sound (loudness) by the sense of hearing, etc.

(ii) appetition: the sensation gives rise to a reaction, that is, a judgement as to whether the object of the senses is good or bad for one, accompanied by a feeling of pain or pleasure. This in turn prompts a movement or impulse towards that judged by the sense as good and away from that judged by the sense as bad. This movement (that is, the impulse to act and not the act itself) is called emotion (as the etymology of the word might suggest); the scholastic word (emphasizing rather the bodily change that is suffered) is passion.

B *The Rational Soul*

(i) cognition: the faculty of rational cognition is known as the intellect. St Thomas (*ST*, 1a 79.8 *corp.*) distinguishes between two characteristic activities of the intellect:

1. understanding or simple apprehension, that is, the operation by which the intellect grasps intuitively a self-evident truth. The scholastic word for this activity is *intelligentia*.

2. reasoning, that is, a discursive process whereby the intellect passes from two or several propositions (premises) to another proposition (conclusion). This is *ratio*, properly so called.

(ii) appetition: the faculty of rational appetition is known as the will (*voluntas*).

This analytical procedure may lead us to forget the necessary interrelationship of these activities in the behaviour of the single human being. But the fact of interrelationship is not neglected by St Thomas, despite the intricacy of his discussion. Thus we need to bear in mind that the Aristotelian scheme is hierarchical (that is, the rational faculties are superior to the sensitive faculties) and that man is a unity (so that a movement of the sensitive soul is necessarily transmitted to the rational soul which controls it). The movement of the sensitive soul is spontaneous and necessary; the movement of the rational soul is deliberate and free.

In this way Scholasticism accounts for the spontaneity of our emotions and the freedom of our will. Human behaviour is not determined by an emotional response, for we are free as rational creatures to accept or reject the movement of the senses. This is necessary because the good as apprehended by the senses does not always correspond with the good as apprehended by the intellect. To take a pertinent example: an object of beauty (a beautiful woman, say) elicits a movement of the sensitive soul towards it, since our natures are ordered towards the good. This is the emotion or passion. If we find, for example, that the woman is married we can reject her as a legitimate object of desire. This is an act of will. As moral creatures we are free to act or not to act; the arbiter of conduct is our will and not our emotions.[1]

---

[1] See *ST*, 1a 2ae 1.1 *corp.* and 1a 2ae 10.2. *corp.* Compare the speech of Raison in *Le Roman de la rose*, ll. 4351–8; reference is to the edition of E. Langlois, Société des Anciens Textes Français, 5 vols (Paris, 1914–24), cited hereafter as *RR*.

II

The most lucid account of the nature of love by a medieval poet is that given by Dante in the *Purgatorio* (17. 91–105 and 18. 19–75). Here Dante draws a distinction between natural love and rational love:

> 'Nè creator nè creatura mai,'
> cominciò el 'figliuol, fu sanza amore,
> o naturale o d'animo; e tu 'l sai . . .'
>
> (*Purgatorio*, 17. 91)[1]

In so doing he introduces to us an opposition between natural and voluntary activity that is fundamental to the thought of St Thomas. This opposition is not between that which does not act for an end and that which does, for Aristotle has established the purposiveness of Nature (*Physica*, 196b 21). The Christian philosopher recognizes that all things that have being have it by virtue of the operation of Providence, and that it is this Providence which supplies an end for all created being (*ST*, 1a 22.2 *corp.*). The distinction between natural and voluntary activity, therefore, has to be seen within the framework of a providential order.

Natural love thus describes the ordering (or determination) of the created world to the good. It explains the purposiveness of Nature, but it is a purposiveness supplied by an external cause, and not one based on knowledge. A favourite analogy of St Thomas is that of the arrow directed to its target by the archer (see *ST*, 1a 2.3 *corp.* and 1a 2ae 1.2 *corp.*). It is this natural love that causes a stone to seek the earth, or flame to move upwards. It is to be noted that the natural love is a conviction of the whole being of man (whose unity, as we have seen, St Thomas is on all occasions concerned to stress) and not merely in relation to his vegetative and sensitive functions. St Thomas is very clear on this point: 'amor naturalis non solum est in viribus animae vegetativae, sed in omnibus potentiis animae, et etiam in omnibus partibus corporis, et universaliter in omnibus rebus' (*ST*, 1a 2ae 26.1 ad. 3). Thus the intellect and will of man by virtue of his nature are ordered to the good; the intellect necessarily apprehends universal truth or first principles and the will necessarily desires the universal good (see *ST*, 1a 2ae 10.1 *corp.*). So Dante can say:

> Però, là onde vegna lo intelletto
> delle prime notizie, omo non sape,
> e de' primi appetibili l'affetto,
> che sono in voi, sì come studio in ape
> di far lo mele; e questa prima voglia
> merto di lode o di biasmo non cape
>
> (*Purgatorio*, 18. 55)

The ordering of intellect and will to the good might seem to contradict the assertion of man's freedom. But it is also fundamental to the teaching of St Thomas (as indeed a requirement of Revelation) that an authentic human act (*actus humanus*) is one for which he is responsible. The freedom of the will rests upon the fact that in this life the universal good is not proposed to it, for the universal good the will must inevitably seek (*ST*, 1a 2ae 10.2 *corp.*). The present objects of the will are no more than so many particular goods, which it is free to pursue or not to

---

[1] Reference is to the edition of J. D. Sinclair, *The Divine Comedy of Dante Alighieri*, 3 vols (London, 1971).

pursue (*ST*, 1a 2ae 10.1 ad. 3), for the particular good can be viewed by the intellect from two aspects, either in terms of its approximation to the universal good or in terms of its deficiency in comparison with the universal good (*ST*, 1a 2ae 13.6 *corp.*). The will has free choice, then, not of the end but of the means to the end (*ST*, 1a 2ae 13.5 *corp.*).

The opposition of natural and rational love holds good in terms of the events of this world, although the two loves are unified in the scheme of the divine creation as a whole. In practice, therefore, it is likely that the natural love will be associated with the activities of the vegetative and sensitive soul:

Et ideo proprium est naturae rationalis ut tendat in finem quasi se agens vel ducens ad finem, naturae vero irrationalis quasi ab alio acta vel ducta, sive in finem apprehensum, sicut bruta animalia, sive in finem non apprehensum, sicut ea quae omnino cognitione carent. (*ST*, 1a 2ae 1.2 *corp.*)

So Dante describes a movement of the sensitive soul (a passion) and refers to it as natural (*Purgatorio*, 18. 19–27).

If we are to place a value upon the love that is represented by a medieval poet we need to establish whether it is an act or a passion that is being described. A passion is neither good nor bad in itself, but may often be represented as good or bad. One reason is that for the Christian the whole of created being is good; love seen from the persepective of the divine providence can legitimately, therefore, be said to be good. Dante says of it that it is 'sempre sanza errore' (*Purgatorio*, xvii, 94). Another is that love is seen in relation to the exercise of reason, as being properly or defectively governed by it, and therefore in a secondary manner may be described as either good or bad (*ST*, 1a 2ae 24.1 *corp.* and ad. 3). Since the reason commonly fails to exert due control love is therefore felt by some to be the source of evil (*ST* 1a 2ae 26.3 ad. 3). This is effectively how Raison first of all defines love in *Le Roman de la rose* (ll. 4377 ff.).

An act of will is by definition an act for which man is responsible. The rational love, therefore, is good or bad in so far as it is in or out of accord with the right judgements of the intellect. The criterion of the intellect is that which is in accord with man's ultimate good or supernatural end, that is, union with the divine will (see *Purgatorio*, 17. 97).

III

There remain yet further distinctions to make. St Thomas distinguishes between two aspects of love, which he calls love of friendship and love of desire (the latter not to be confused with desire itself). Love of friendship is love of a thing for the sake of the thing itself, whereas love of desire is love of a thing for something other than its self, for example, of wine for its sweetness (*ST*, 1a 2ae 26.4 *corp.*). It is in these terms that Raison subsequently distinguishes for the young lover true and false loves (see *RR*, ll. 4685 ff. and 4769 ff.). The love of friendship is defined in terms of a connaturality of the individual wills (ll. 4685–92); the false love is characterized by the love of men not for themselves but for their goods (ll. 4769–82).

A distinction must now be drawn between love and desire, that is, between two passions. Love is the most fundamental of all the passions, and indeed the very source of human behaviour (*ST*, 1a 2ae 27.4). It is the sense of affinity or fitness between the subject and an object; the words that St Thomas habitually uses to describe it are *coaptatio*, *complacentia*, and *connaturalitas*. It is, therefore, a passion in the strictest sense, for it refers essentially to the receptivity of the subject to the impact made upon it by a desirable object (*ST*, 1a 2ae 26.2 *corp.*). Desire is the movement towards the object that stems from a sense of affinity with it and a realization of its absence; that is, desire is not love but an effect of love (*ST*, 1a 2ae 30.2. ad. 1 and 2). The relationship of love to desire, then, is that of inclination to movement.

This distinction remains for the most part unobserved in medieval love poetry. Love is presented to us in its most persistent guise as a conflict between contrary forces; the rhetorical figure that is best fitted to its expression is the oxymoron. Raison's first description of love to the young lover in *Le Roman de la rose* is no more than an extended series of oxymorons:

> Amour ce est pais haïneuse,
> Amour c'est haïne amoureuse;
> C'est leiautez la desleiaus,
> C'est la desleiautez leiaus;
> C'est peeur toute asseüree,
> Esperance desesperee;
> C'est raison toute forsenable,
> C'est forsenerie raisnable . . .
>
> (*RR*, l. 4293)

This is the 'dredful joye' that so baffles the dreamer in *The Parliament of Fowls* (3). What is being described is not love, properly speaking, but desire. The sense of affinity of a subject with an object can hardly be accompanied by a feeling of pain. The combination of pain and pleasure in desire can, however, be readily understood, the pleasure arising from the desirability of the object, the pain from the absence of attainment.

It will be apparent, therefore, that in the discussion of love a definition of terms is essential. St Thomas examines the lexical range of *amor*, *dilectio*, *amicitia*, and *caritas* in the *Summa Theologiae* (1a 2ae 26.3). The following are the distinctions that emerge:

(i) *amor* has the widest range, and can be used both for the act and the passion.

(ii) *dilectio*, since implying choice (*electio*), is restricted to the act of will, whether good or bad.

(iii) *amicitia* refers to a disposition of the soul brought about by successive acts.

(iv) *caritas* can apply to an act or passion on the one hand (as emphasizing the special value of love) or to a disposition of the soul on the other.

Dante is at one with St Thomas in using *amor* in this wide sense, but talks of the act of will that arises from a movement of the sensitive soul as *disire* (*Purgatorio*, 18. 31). We have already observed the process whereby such desire can come to be thought of exclusively as a sinful act of will, that is, lust. This is the word that is applied to the behaviour of Aurelius (and with at least an implication of its modern sense, I think) towards the end of *The Franklin's Tale* (*F*, 1522).

IV

In the best medieval poetry the analysis of love is a matter of very considerable moral subtlety. The reader (or auditor) who is to appreciate it most fully needs to be constantly alert to the potential ambiguity of the central term *love* and to be aware of its casuistical exploitation. A good example of the casuistry of love is provided by the narrator in *Troilus and Criseyde* (1. 232–59). He attempts to win his audience to the cause of love by developing what appears to be an impeccable syllogism:

(i) Love is a law of our nature that cannot be resisted (1. 236–8).

(ii) Love is good and a source of good (1. 246–52).

(iii) Love should therefore be wholeheartedly accepted (1. 253–6).

Now this conclusion is false, because it involves an illicit shift in the meaning of love (from the natural love to the rational). We are reminded again of Dante:

> Or ti puote apparer quant'è nascosa
> la veritate alla gente ch'avvera
> ciascun amore in sè laudabil cosa,
> però che forse appar la sua matera
> sempre esser buona; ma non ciascun segno
> è buono, ancor che buona sia la cera
>
> (Purgatorio, 18. 34)

It is a point that we can take easily enough in the context of the *Troilus*, for the partisanship of the narrator is apparent from the beginning of the poem. Moreover, in his representation of the course of love in the soul of Troilus Chaucer is careful to distinguish between a movement of the sensitive soul (1. 267–322) and the accompanying act of will (1. 358–92).

The process of falling in love is described in terms which make it clear that initially we are concerned with a physiological process; it is the sight of Criseyde (that is, a sense impression, 1. 272–3) that causes the heart of Troilus to unfold (that is, a movement of the sensitive appetite, 1. 278–80).[1] It is worth noting that Chaucer himself is responsible for drawing attention to this physiological process, since lines 274–80 constitute an addition to his principal source (the *Filostrato* of Boccaccio). He is also responsible for the development of this idea at lines 295–8, where he describes the external object as imprinting itself upon the soul of Troilus:

> And of hire look in him ther gan to quyken
> So gret desir and such affeccioun,
> That in his hertes botme gan to stiken
> Of hir his fixe and depe impressioun.

The use of *impressioun* (1. 298) suggests the image of the soul as wax and the object as the stamp, which was commonly employed to describe this process.[2] In the

---

[1] The heart is here viewed as the seat of the emotions and particularly of love; see *OED* s.v. *heart*, sb. 9 and 10, *MED* s.v. *herte* n. 3a (a) and (b). The system of thought that is presupposed is Platonic. It is true that Plato himself locates the spirited part of the soul in the heart and the appetitive below the diaphragm; see *Republic*, 435E–441C; *Timaeus*, 69C–72D. Plotinus, however, tends in practice to identify the spirited and the appetitive parts of the soul, and it is presumably syncretism of this kind that leads to the heart being regarded as the seat of the emotions in general; see *Enneads*, I. 1, passim, IV. 3, 23 and 28, and IV. 4, 20 and 28, and R. S. Peters, *Brett's History of Psychology*, revised edition (London and New York, 1962), pp. 208–14. It is interesting to note that St Thomas sets out the Platonic tripartite scheme of the soul as follows: 'Plato posuit diversas animas esse in corpore uno, etiam secundum organa distinctas, quibus diversa opera vitae attribuebat, dicens vim nutritivam esse in hepate, concupiscibilem in corde, cognoscitivam in cerebro' (*ST*, 1a 76.3. *corp.*). The Platonic distinction between the spirited and appetitive parts of the soul still finds a place in the Scholastic synthesis in the classification of the emotions into the irascible and concupiscible (see *ST*, 1a 81.2. *corp.*).

[2] See Chaucer's *Boece*, v, metrum 4, ll. 1–19 and Dante, *Purgatorio*, 18. 38–9 (quoted in the text).

following stanza Chaucer introduces the idea of love entering Troilus's heart by means of the fine rays that issue from Criseyde's eyes ('subtile stremes', 1. 305). The conception of love entering the heart through the eye was, of course, a common-place.[1] It was held, however, to be not merely a poetic conceit but also a physio-logical fact; that is, an effluence passed from the eyes of the lady through those of the lover into his heart. Hence one can appreciate the peculiar appropriateness of the allegory of the God of Love and his arrows in *Le Roman de la rose* (see ll. 1681 ff.).

Thus there can be no doubt that what Chaucer describes in *Troilus and Criseyde*, 1. 267–308 is the progress of natural love in the soul of Troilus, that is, in effect, a movement of the sensitive soul, a law of his physical being.

Movements of the sensitive soul must necessarily engage the rational soul, and here man is free to accept or reject the object of the sensitive appetite. In lines 365–92 Chaucer describes the rational acceptance by Troilus of his love for Criseyde, that is, he embraces his desire with his whole mind (1. 365).[2] He argues that service of Criseyde cannot be wasted since she is so good (1. 372–4) and that his love, even if made public, would be a source of praise and exaltation and not of shame (1. 374–6). The concessive clause ('Al were it wist') suggests an awareness on Troilus's part of a moral ambiguity; this impression is confirmed by his sub-sequent determination to keep the love secret (1. 380–85; compare 11. 29–42).

There can be no doubt here also that what is described is a fully rational love, freely accepted by Troilus himself (1. 379 and 391–2).

In the *Canticus Troili* that follows (1. 400–20)[3] Chaucer reveals to us the impli-cations of this rational acceptance. The song expresses the paradoxical nature of the love (or rather, desire), and thus employs the familiar figure of oxymoron: 'O quike deth, O swete harm so queynte' (1. 411). It is a song, however, that is formally addressed to God (1. 400), and in this way Chaucer alerts us to the necessary imper-fection of the human love that Troilus describes. Moreover, the pregnant question that Troilus is made to ask: 'If love be good, from whennes cometh my woo?' (1. 402) has a force that goes beyond his immediate circumstances to |the human predicament in general, for it points to the need at one and the same time to recognize the value of human love and its insufficiency. Troilus, however, acknow-ledges that the intensity of this paradox in his own experience stems from his act of

---

[1] Compare, for example, *The Knight's Tale*, A 1096–7.

[2] The mind is here viewed as the seat of the distinctively rational activities of man; see *OED* s.v. *mind*, sb[1]. 18. Dante uses *animo* to refer to the rational soul apprehended as a unity in the orthodox Scholastic manner (*Purg.*, 18. 19–33). But he also uses it in a more restricted sense in drawing the crucial distinction between natural and rational love (*Purg.*, 17. 93). What Dante understands by *animo* here is clarified by his definition of *mente* itself in the *Convivio*, III.2.10–16: 'Lo loco nel quale dico esso ragionare sì è la mente; ma per dire che sia la mente, non si prende di ciò più intendimento che di prima, e però è da vedere che questa mente propriamente significa . . . E quella anima che tutte queste potenze comprende, [e] è perfettissima di tutte l'altre, è l'anima umana, la quale con la nobilitade de la potenza ultima, cioè ragione, participa de la divina natura a guisa di sempiterna intelligenzia . . . In questa nobilissima parte de l'anima sono più vertudi, sì come dice lo Filosofo massimamente nel sesto de l'[Etica]; dove dice che in essa è una vertù che si chiama scientifica, e una che si chiama ragionativa, o vero consigliativa: e con quest[e] sono certe vertudi — sì come in quello medesimo luogo Aristotile dice — sì come la vertù inventiva e giudicativa. E tutte queste nobilissime vertudi, e l'altre che sono in quella eccellentissima potenza, sì chiama insieme con questo vocabulo del quale si volea sapere che fosse, cioè mente. Per che è manifesto che per mente s'intende questa ultima e nobilissima parte de l'anima.' Reference is to G. Busnelli and G. Vandelli, *Il Convivio*, second edition (Florence, 1964).

[3] Chaucer is here rendering Petrarch's Sonnet 88.

consent (1. 411–13). But he goes on to commit himself wholeheartedly to the God of Love (1. 421–34). Chaucer stresses (to a degree that Boccaccio does not) the completeness of Troilus's surrender to love. Troilus does not regret but rejoices in his love for Criseyde, however paradoxical (and hence imperfect) it might be: 'Yow thanke I, lord, that han me brought to this' (1. 424). As a result of this acceptance love binds itself in Troilus more securely (1. 435–55).

It will be apparent from this account that the tragedy of Troilus is not at all the product of a universal determinism. Rather Chaucer has shown to us in the figure of Troilus the conscious and complete acceptance of a purely earthly ideal of love, and has made us aware of its insufficiency. It will be apparent too that the movement of love in the soul of Troilus can be presented without distortion in terms of the scholastic account given by Dante in the *Purgatorio* (xviii, 19–39). Chaucer gives concrete imaginative expression to that which Dante presents in a more philosophical manner. Since scholasticism does not localize parts of the soul (became of its insistence upon the soul's unity), Dante does not specify where in man the senses are located. In describing love as entering the heart through the eyes Chaucer is drawing upon a literary tradition going back to *Le Roman de la rose*, a tradition, however, that seems to have been based upon a neo-Platonic system of thought.

V

The kind of casuistry that is displayed by the narrator in *Troilus and Criseyde* is at the very centre of *fin' amors*, for as we have seen it involves the claim that love itself is ethically normative. The fundamental principle of *fin' amors* is that love is sovereign and irresistible. Thus in *Le Roman de la rose* Amor is presented to us allegorically as a god to whom the young man has no option but to submit (*RR*, ll. 865 ff. and 1681 ff.). Arcite explains it to us in *The Knight's Tale* in the following terms:

> Love is a gretter lawe, by my pan,
> Than may be yeve to any erthely man;
> And therfore positif lawe and swich decree
> Is broken al day for love in ech degree.
> A man moot nedes love, maugree his heed.
> He may nat fleen it, thogh he sholde be deed,
> Al be she mayde, or wydwe, or elles wyf
>
> (A, 1165)

From Arcite's speech we can see why it is that adultery is a common element in the elaboration of *fin' amors*; it is an inevitable corollary of the principle of the irresistibility of love. We need not therefore seek to explain it in social terms as Lewis does in *The Allegory of Love* (p. 13). The evidence that he adduces (for example, of arranged marriages) is in any case unconvincing. A writer such as Chrétien de Troyes insists again and again on the essential freedom of the marriage bond.[1] In his own representation of the married love of Arveragus and Dorigen, Chaucer (or his Franklin narrator on this occasion a distinction without a difference) underlines this conception:

---

[1] See, for example, *Le Chevalier de la charrete*, ll. 5993–6006 and 6047–56, and *Le Chevalier au lion*, ll. 3866–75 and 4112–24.

> Love is a thyng as any spirit free.
> Wommen, of kynde, desiren libertee,
> And nat to been constreyned as a thral;
> And so doon men, if I sooth seyen shal
>
> (F, 767)

The great medieval poets, then, are clear in their apprehension of moral issues, and see that the moral analysis that supports *fin' amors* is defective. *Fin' amors* conceals (whether deliberately or otherwise) an illicit shift from the sensitive to the rational levels. It presupposes that a law of our senses (a passion, emotion) governs our whole being as rational creatures. Such poets as Chrétien are committed to the view that it is man's reason and not his emotion that is the true arbiter of conduct. Lewis's account (which we can see to be essentially an account of *fin' amors*) is especially unfortunate as a gloss to late fourteenth century English poetry. In the last resort (although only in the last resort) Sir Gawain opts for chastity rather than courtesy when he is forced to chose between them (so far is he from contemplating adultery):

> For þat prynces of pris depresed hym so þikke,
> Nurned hym so neʒe þe þred, þat nede hym bihoued
> Oþer lach þer hir luf, oþer lodly refuse.
> He cared for his cortaysye, lest craþayn he were,
> And more for his meschef ʒ if he schulde make synne,
> And be traytor to þat tolke þat þat telde aʒt
>
> (l. 1770)[1]

The Franklin's Tale in its expression of a loving relationship within marriage is true to the same tradition of the representation of love in courtly literature. This is the central English tradition and it leads directly on to Sidney and Spenser. Indeed there is no more fitting conclusion to our analysis than the judgement by which Euarchus sets aside love as a possible defence of the behaviour of Pyrocles and Musidorus:

If that unbridled desire which is entitled love might purge such a sickness as this, surely we should have many loving excuses of hateful mischiefs. Nay rather, no mischief should be committed that should not be veiled under the name of love. For as well he that steals might allege the love of money, he that murders the love of revenge, he that rebels the love of greatness, as the adulterer the love of a woman; since they do in all speech affirm they love that which an ill-governed passion maketh them to follow. But love may have no such privilege. That sweet and heavenly uniting of the minds, which properly is called love, hath no other knot but virtue; and therefore if it be a right love, it can never slide into any action that is not virtuous. (*Arcadia*, 406/30–407/5)[2]

---

[1] Reference is to J. R. R. Tolkien and E. V. Gordon, *Sir Gawain and the Green Knight*, second edition, revised by N. Davis (Oxford, 1967).

[2] Reference is to J. Robertson, *Sir Philip Sidney: The Countess of Pembroke's Arcadia* (Oxford, 1973).

Chaucer's *Termes*

J. D. BURNLEY
University of Sheffield

I

Chaucer's earliest critics were appreciative of his work in ways which, we can well imagine, he would himself have approved. The parting dedication of *Troilus and Criseyde* to Gower and Strode accords well with the assessment of his work made by his contemporary, Thomas Usk, who refers to him as 'the noble philosophical poete in English'. Nor would Chaucer, we may suppose, despite his misunderstanding with the God of Love in the Prologue to *The Legend of Good Women*, wish to repudiate his reputation as a poet of love; even though, *in extremis*, he may have felt it necessary to reaffirm his belief in a more orthodox Christian morality. On the themes for which he was renowned, contemporary critics, modern academic criticism, and the poet himself would probably be in agreement; hence another contemporary, Eustace Deschamps, may state most economically for us the consensus for a learned poet:

> O Socratès plains de philosophie,
> Seneque en meurs et Auglus en pratique,
> Ovides grans en ta poëterie,
> Briés en parler, saiges en rethorique,
> Aigles treshaulz, qui par ta theorique
> Enlumines le regne d'Eneas.[1]

Yet one aspect of Chaucer's reputation in the century following his death would not lead to such general accord, for he was also praised as a linguistic innovator, a consummate craftsman in the skills of verbal manipulation, and a master of diction. Here, the modern scholar, disregarding the limits imposed upon his own vision by linguistic evolution, would be likely to accuse these early admirers of seeing their master through eyes deceived by a current obsession with lexical embellishment; and Dunbar's praise of Chaucer's 'fresh anamalit termes celicall' may well seem adequate justification for his view. But evaluative phrases of this nature do not specify precisely the grounds of admiration; nor indeed do all the early critics who praise Chaucer's diction emphasize the aureate splendour of his verse by the use of such extravagant language. The critical imprecision of these writers sometimes leads to apparent disagreement: Hawes, in 1503 or 1504, states that 'he was expert | In eloquent terms subtle and couert', whilst Skelton, a year or two later, in *Phyllyp Sparowe*, insists on the relative simplicity of Chaucer's diction. But such apparent

---

[1] The quotation is from *Geoffrey Chaucer*, edited by J. A. Burrow, Penguin Critical Anthologies (Harmondsworth, 1969), p. 26. For this, and other early references to Chaucer's work, see C. F. E. Spurgeon, *Five Hundred Years of Chaucer Criticism and Allusion*, 3 vols (Cambridge, 1925). *Pratique*, *theorique*, and *moeurs* are three major branches of *philosophie*. In this division, the first may refer to Chaucer's skill as a philosopher of government, as well as his mastery of the *trivium*. *Theorique* refers to his knowledge of the *quadrivium*. All quotations are from F. N. Robinson, *The Works of Geoffrey Chaucer*, second edition (London, 1957).

differences should not be pressed too hard and, if we set aside the natural conten-
tiousness of Skelton, the comparison he gives of the styles and subject matter of
Gower, Lydgate, and Chaucer is in itself worthy of deeper consideration. It arises
from the desire of a young noblewoman to write an elegy for a pet bird. She
expresses concern that she cannot find adequate literary language (she refers to
termes, line 783) to suit the occasion, and this deficiency leads her to a brief review of
the work of the three acknowledged masters of English composition. Gower and
Lydgate are swiftly dispensed with: the former is valuable for his content, but his
language is dated; the latter is a great craftsman, but his themes are unclear,
because of his over-elaborate diction, which is now becoming unfashionable.
Chaucer, like Gower, seems to be considered somewhat archaic in his language;
yet he is wholeheartedly praised, both for his content and his execution, and the
emendation of his verse, to make it accord with existing language and taste, is
decried. Of his style, Skelton says:

> His Englysh well alowed
> (So as it is enprowed),
> For as it is enployd,
> There is no Englysh voyd,
> At those dayes moch commended;
> . . . .
> His termes were not darke,
> But plesaunt, easy, and playne;
> Ne worde he wrote in vayne.
>
> *(Phyllyp Sparowe*, 792–803)

In its insistence on the simplicity of Chaucer's vocabulary Skelton's assessment is in
implicit contrast with that of many other writers, but it is also more discriminating
than they, for Skelton distinguishes clearly between lexical resources and their
employment. Chaucer's verse is admirable for the obvious care in verbal composition which it exhibits, its resultant economy of expression, its *brevitas*.[1] Indeed,
Skelton ascribes to Chaucer that stylistic virtue which he, himself, had awarded
the Clerk and exhibited in his *Tale*:

> Noght o word spak he moore than was neede,
> And that was seyd in forme and reverence,
> And short and quyk and ful of hy sentence.
>
> (A 304)

The implication is of a spare, but conceptually weighty style, in which each word,
by its choice and combination, is given its fullest complement of meaning.

In this context, the choice by Skelton's young noblewoman of the word *termes*
(line 783), to indicate her linguistic insufficiency, is an interesting one, since something other than reference to the general word stock of the language is here
implied. These *termes* are those words and phrases which in combination would have
a special appropriateness for expressing the sentiments of the literary form of elegy.
It is, of course, traditionally the function of eloquence effectively to represent the
feelings of the speaker, and the power of elegant speech, which was to be derived

---

[1] Skelton's praise of Chaucer's diction is reminiscent of Cicero's definition of *brevitas*: 'Brevitas est,
cum nisi necessarium nullum assumitur verbum'. *De Inventione*, 1.22.32, edited and translated by
H. M. Hubbell, Loeb Classical Library (London, 1949). Both conciseness and elevation are admired
in Chaucer by the anonymous *Book of Courtesy* and by Caxton (Spurgeon, I, 57 and 62).

from a grounding in the *trivium*, had long been a mark of courtliness.[1] Yet the failure of Jane Scrope to find suitable *termes* in English is not intended as a slight to her wit, so much as a compliment to her femininity. The elegy is a learned genre, and womanly eloquence, according to Chaucer himself, should be free of the affectation of recondite terms, plain, and filled with good sense (C 50 ff.). Thus, rather than adopt monstrously inappropriate English diction, Jane turns to Latin. But it is clear that, in the opinion of many fifteenth-century writers, Chaucer would have possessed the learning, and could have discovered the *termes*, to answer to this situation; for his contribution to the expressive range of English is an achievement for which he is repeatedly praised.

Indeed, when Chaucer uses the word *termes*, he is employing a recent introduction to the language, deriving through Old French from the scholastic Latin *terminus*, where it was used to signify a piece of natural language severely delimited in sense, and of non-figurative use. This precise, technical sense had already been broadened in the usage of Chaucer's time but if we examine his employment of it we shall find that connotations of a restricted or defined usage are still present in most occurrences of the word. *Termes* may be unfamiliar words, or quotations from a second language substituted in discourse, but they are most commonly utterances felt to be words or phrases characteristic of the usage of certain professional groups, social types or categories, or of particular areas of intellectual endeavour. The outstanding feature of most of Chaucer's uses of the word is this sense of distinctness from the language of every day. A great many of Chaucer's references to *termes* are to the languages associated with the scientific exposition of his time: he refers to the *termes* of natural science (*physik*, *Troilus and Criseyde*, II.1038), to the *termes* of alchemy (G 752), astrology (F 1266), medicine (C 311), the *termes* of rhetoric and the schools (E 16), and the Latin *termes* of theology and the law (A 639; B¹ 1189). As words and phrases proper to these specific fields of discourse, all such would be included within the embracing reference of *termes of philosophie* (HF 857). *Termes*, however, may be distinguished not only by their use in technical areas of this kind, but also by their frequent use in defined literary situations, where we should recognize in them the skills of traditional diction. Thus, the 'craft of fyn lovynge' has its *loves termes*, mentioned in *Troilus and Criseyde* (II.1067), and exemplified in *The Book of the Duchess*:

> My suffisaunce, my lust, my lyf,
> Myn hap, myn hele, and al my blesse,
> My worldes welfare, and my goddesse.
>
> (1038)

Finally, *termes* may belong to the distinguishable language habits of different social classes (A 3917), to the 'brode' or 'faire' speech of the churl or the courtier. It is clear from all this that Chaucer's use of the word *termes* shares with that of Skelton the requirement that they are words, or senses of words, distinguished by their

---

[1] John of Salisbury, *Metalogicon*, I. 7 in J.-P. Migne, *Patrologia Latina*, 221 vols (Paris, 1844–91), CXCIX: 'What is eloquence but the faculty of fittingly saying what the mind wants to express?'. The skill in *wel-seyinge*, which Lydgate ascribed to Chaucer, is represented in Old French by the phrase *bien parler*. Jean d'Harens, in the prologue to his translation of *De Inventione* and *Ad Herennium*, completed in Acre in 1282, leaves us in no doubt of the interdependence of the arts of the *trivium* in attaining eloquence: 'et ensi sont necessaires cestes III sciences a bien parler, et sont ausi come entrelacées'. Edited by L. DeLisle, *Notices et Extraits*, 36 (Paris, 1899), p. 217.

appropriateness in particular functions and situations: they represent the intuitive categorization of lexical resources by use.

II

We may now begin to consider, firstly in terms of modern linguistic concepts, and subsequently according to contemporary linguistic and stylistic assumptions, the significance of Chaucer's use of the word *termes* for the judgements made by early writers upon his style. In connexion with the first of these intentions it is noteworthy that, in the sense outlined above, the word *termes* occurs in the singular only once in the entire works of Chaucer, and that this is the fixed adverbial phrase *speken in terme*. We may leave the meaning of this phrase to emerge in the course of later discussion, for our account of the use of the word *termes* has already led us to a formulation of the familiar and related concepts of *register* and *collocation*.[1] Any language has, within the pattern of its usages, certain words and phrases which are distinguished by specialized or technical use. These are supplemented by an even larger group which have senses similarly appropriate to such fields of discourse. But although the registerial affinities of words and phrases in the first group are obvious as a result of their restricted occurrence, the affinities of the second group need not be at all clear when they are found out of context.[2] Thus, the modern English word *operation*, appearing by itself, can be assigned to no particular register; but when in collocation with others words and phrases from the same register; *surgeon*, *table*, *scalpel*, *anaesthetic*, or when used in the situational context of a hospital, we perceive an affinity between the words, and allot them to the register of surgery. Similarly in Chaucer's language, the form *grace* occurring alone, because of its imprecision in sense, is unassignable to any particular register, but when it occurs in the context of *hap*, the collocation specifies the sense, and at once asserts that both belong to the same philosophical register: they become *termes of philosophie*, referring specifically to the Boethian discussion of chance and predestination. In examples of this kind, it is the co-occurrence, the collocation of *termes* (hence the ubiquitous plural) which identifies them as members of a particular register. By contrast, the Host's denial of his ability to *speken in terme* (C 311) prefaces an assembly of words peculiar to the restricted language of medicine, which are instantly recognizable as such outside any context.

Although neither the notion of register, nor the relationships between registers, are rigorously definable, the perception of characteristic uses of linguistic material, of which registers are composed, does seem to represent an aspect of the competence of any speaker who is reasonably familiar with a language within its cultural context. It is well within his power to state with considerable accuracy the customary field of discourse to which particular groups of words and phrases may belong. Thus, we may see that Chaucer's use of the word *termes* coincides closely with more

---

[1] M. A. K. Halliday, Angus McIntosh, and Peter Strevens, *The Linguistic Sciences and Language Teaching* (London, 1964), pp. 87 ff. The language habits of socially distinct groups are often called *codes* by sociolinguists. For the sake of clarity, in the present paper, which deals exclusively with lexis, I shall use only the term *register*.

[2] T. F. Mitchell, 'The Language of Buying and Selling in Cyrenaica: A Situational Statement', *Hespéris*, 44 (1957), 31–71 (pp. 39–40).

modern ideas of register and collocation, including both the first group of words, which are restricted to specific discourses, and the second group which are so assigned in particular senses, revealed by their collocations. Although both are stylistically important, our primary interest in the present paper will be with this second group, where assignment to a register depends upon the collocation of lexical material in relation to a broad situation of use, and where Chaucer's application of the word *termes* depends upon the frequent mutual occurrence of the words within a particular area of intellectual interest or social activity.

Since the same words and phrases may be assigned to more than one register, when a categorization of lexical items is attempted, registers are rarely distinct. Moreover, when considered from the point of view of the relations between fields of discourse, groups of usages become related to each other in ways determined by extralinguistic connexions in the culture to which the language belongs. Just as the register of *physik* is included within that of *philosophie*, as a result of the categorization of the medieval sciences, so social registers are differentiated according to the hierarchical nature of medieval society, so that certain linguistic usages are characteristic of the churl, whilst others are appropriate to the aristocrat. Socially distinct registers may intersect registers proper to a more general human situation, like that of love. Hence, in Chaucer's works, we can find a distinction between the language of the love affairs of the upper classes and that to be found among the lower classes. In courtly verse, the lovers refer to each other by a series of *loves termes*, which are characteristically prefixed by possessive pronouns: *his hertes lif, his lust, his sorwes leche, his blisse*. A number of other, more diverse phrases, may also be assigned to this register: *herte trewe, lady grace, stonden in grace, guerdoun, die giltelees, aspre peynes smerte, me recommaunde unto youre grace*. Many of these also belong to other registers, most notably that of feudal justice and the last, at least, is further specifiable as an epistolary commendation; yet, in collocation, they can all be said to belong to the register of aristocratic love. In contrast, *The Miller's Tale* and *The Tale of Sir Thopas* give us some notion of the love language of the lower orders: *oore, love-longyng, suete bird, bright in bower, under goore, make, weilawei, hende, lemman, comen . . . his care*.

III

The categorization of vocabulary into registers, although impossible to achieve with absolute rigour, is an attempt on the part of linguists to state theoretically an aspect of the intuitive grasp of his language possessed by any member of a linguistic community, whether in fourteenth-century England or the present day. The principles behind it are much more readily apprehended than those underlying the abstractions of grammatical structure, and Chaucer's use of the word *termes* implies that he had an intuitive appreciation of them; but direct evidence that this extended to a conscious awareness is very scanty. We can do little more than infer an answer to this problem from the concerns of the schools in the arts of logic, grammar, and rhetoric, where an examination of the linguistic ideas available reveals the most profitable area of inquiry to be that portion of rhetoric which was devoted to style and diction, *elocutio*. Yet the most interesting of the ideas which we must invoke seems not to be limited by the schematization of knowledge imposed by the schools, but rather to be a widespread and generally accepted philosophical notion common to the three liberal arts, and therefore unprofitable to assign to any particular source.

Before he begins to recall the tales told by each individual pilgrim on the road to Canterbury, Chaucer warns that he will recite them in the words of their original teller, and begs his audience's indulgence if some of them should be ungentle in language. He pretends to give their actual words, to 'speke hir wordes *proprely*', for it is a commonplace principle of fictional composition that the language must be appropriate to the circumstances and the personality depicted. Thus, the Miller does not restrain his language or content, and goes on to tell a tale fitting for a churl (A 3169, 3917). These principles of composition accord well with the opinion of the humanist, John of Salisbury (*Metalogicon*, I. 17), that the aim of the art of poetry is to strive to create a credible representation of reality. Such an aim had also been that of the oratory of the Roman courts of law, from whence much medieval literary theory descended, and where an impression of verisimilitude was necessary for a case to succeed. The method enjoined was to seek out distinctive characteristics (*proprietates*) of whatever one wished to re-create before the judges and to ensure that each was reconcilable with the other in building up an argument, so that every aspect of the total creation corresponded with others in producing something acceptable as natural. The numerous quotations from Horace employed by rhetoricians in expounding these ideas indicate the debt they owed to the *Ars Poetica*, but in the organization of the rhetorics these ideas are not presented as an integrated theory of composition but rather as a series of hints.[1] The idea of decorum is still inchoate, and awaits development by later centuries.

The notion of *proprietas*, however, was a vital one to any educated man in the fourteenth century. The word had an enormously wide range of use, and was familiar to the medieval schools as one of the five predicables of scholastic logic (*genus, species, differentia, proprietas, accidentia*), deriving most directly for them from Porphyry's *Isagoge*. As part of the technique of definition and categorization, *proprietas* occurs with slightly different senses in each of the three linguistic arts. With relation to literary composition it could provide the *locus* for the expansion of an argument or, by following the *proprietates* of persons and things to be dealt with, it furnished the norms on which the theory of three levels of style depended (*Documentum*, II. 3. 145–61). It formed the basis of Matthieu de Vendôme's theory of description (*Ars Versificatoria*, I. xli–v), where he concentrates upon the *proprietates* of the individuals he wishes to describe, intending by this means to produce a similitude to life which will be easily and directly available to the imagination of his reader. Such an argument is used by Thomas Waleys in favour of the directness of apprehension associated with figurative language, which can be produced by the expedient of finding similar *proprietates* in apparently dissimilar objects.[2] At the level of diction the application of the adjective *propria* to words often implies what Gower calls *congruete*; the maintenance of logical acceptability between the meanings

---

[1] As in Geoffroi de Vinsauf, *Documentum de Arte Versificandi*, IV. 155, and Matthieu de Vendôme, *Ars Versificatoria*, IV. 38; both in E. Faral, *Les arts poétiques du xiie et du xiiie siècle* (Paris, 1924).

[2] Thomas Waleys, *De Modo Componendi Sermones*, in Th.-M. Charland, *Artes Praedicandi* (Paris and Ottawa, 1936), pp. 396–7. The value of a knowledge of the *proprietates* of things is commended for its use in finding *similitudines*. Such a method of instruction is considered peculiarly effective since it approximates to the current theory of perception *per conversionem ad phantasmata*.

of grammatically related words.[1] Handbooks from Isidore onwards warn against the associated vice of *acyrologia*. Even more common is the distinction between *verga propria* and *translata*, which answers to a conviction that words had an originally appropriate sense, so that other senses and uses were 'transferred' or figurative.

In discussing diction, Cicero, the supposed perfector of Greek rhetoric, is frequently invoked as an authority, though the ideas ascribed to him are usually those which were commonplace in the Roman schools. Throughout the middle ages the *Rhetorica ad Herennium* was ascribed to Cicero, and it is in this popular work that we encounter a sense of *propria* somewhat different from either the lexico-grammatical implications of *acyrologia* or the questions of referential meaning associated with the contrast with *translata*. The author states that the hallmark of a good style is its possession of three qualities: 'elegantiam, conpositionem, digni-tatem'. The last is achieved by the use of rhetorical figures, the second by the cultivation of a mellifluous diction, and the first by correct grammar and clarity of expression. Clarity 'conparatur duabus rebus, usitatis verbis et propriis. Usitata sunt ea quae versantur in consuetudine cotidiana; propria, quae eius rei verba sunt aut esse possunt qua de loquemur'.[2] The ready intelligibility of a style is seen to be a function of everyday usage; and *proprietas* is here concerned with usage rather than with grammar or semantics. More strikingly, Chirius Fortunatianus, arguing that *copia* and *bonitas* in lexical resources are among the foundations of good style, advises that *copia* is to be achieved by a wide and varied reading 'ut a peritis multa discamus, quae sint aut propria aut comitiorum aut artium vel studiorum, ut nauticae, rusticae rei et de iure civili'.[3] *Bonitas* is to be achieved by the omission of colloquialisms, archaisms, exclusively poetic, and obscure words. Provincialisms 'quae propria sunt quarundam gentium, sicut Hispani non cubitum vocant, sed Graeco nomine ancona', are also be to avoided;[4] yet, if archaisms are *propria* in a particular context, Cicero himself is said to have sanctioned their use. For some special applications technical uses of familiar words are advised, and Fortunatianus gives an example in the form of a question and answer: 'In elocutione proprietas tantum verborum captanda est an et significatio? ita, ut dictatorem dictum dicas, flaminem proditum, Vestae virginem captam'.[5]

As we have seen, the notion of *proprietas* transcended the division of the *trivium*, and was concerned in a general way with the analysis and classification of the natural world, whose artful reflection was the concern of poetry. It is not a large

[1] *Confessio Amantis*, VII.1531, in *The English Works of John Gower*, edited by G. C. Macaulay, 2 vols, E.E.T.S., Extra Series, 81, 82 (London, 1900–1).

[2] Clarity . . . 'is achieved by two means, the use of current terms and of proper terms. Current terms are such as are habitually used in everyday speech. Proper terms are such as are, or can be, the designations specially characteristic of the subject of our discourse'. *Rhetorica ad Herennium*, VI. xii. 17, edited and translated by Harry Caplan, Loeb Classical Library (London, 1954).

[3] 'That we may learn from experienced men many words which are proper to either public meetings, or the arts or studies, as to sailing, agriculture, or the law'. C. Fortunatianus, *Artis Rhetoricae Libri Tres*, in *Rhetores Latini Minores*, edited by C. F. Halm (Leipzig, 1863), p. 122. Fortunatianus's rhetoric, which was recommended by Cassiodorus, became a popular handbook in the medieval schools. It drew additional prestige from its association with the pseudo-Augustinian *De Rhetorica*. P. Abelson, *The Seven Liberal Arts* (New York, 1965), pp. 55–6.

[4] 'Which are proper to particular peoples, just as the Spanish do not say *cubitus*, but call it by the Greek name *ancona*' (Halm, p. 123).

[5] 'In diction, must the propriety of the words be captured as well as the meaning? Yes, so that you may speak of the dictator being nominated (*dictum*), the priest ordained (*proditum*), the Vestal virgin selected (*captam*)' (Halm, p. 124).

step, at any point in its long history, for the application of the concept of *proprietas* to become narrowed to the appropriacy of certain linguistic forms to particular human groups, types, or interests: this is what we find in Fortunatianus's remarks on style, and less explicitly in the *Rhetorica ad Herennium*. Such a theoretical position differs little from the modern concept of register, except in point of view. Whilst register implies the categorization of the contents of the vocabulary by reference to stipulated fields of discourse, the notion of *proprietas* in usage implies a knowledge of the distinctive features of the use of vocabulary items, with the aim of generating a clear and lifelike representation of a particular object, person, or discourse. In the former, the aim is lexical classification; in the latter, the employment of the bases of this classification for the purposes of elegant composition. They are, in fact, two views of a single mutual relationship which exists between some groups of collocations (*termes*) and the field of discourse in which they habitually collocate. Although we cannot state for certain that Chaucer had a conscious grasp of any theory parallel to that of modern linguists in this respect, we may add to our inferences from his poetic techniques the assurance that, had he felt the need to externalize his intuitive grasp of the proprieties of usage, the conceptual apparatus required was close at hand. We are certainly safe in suggesting the corollary of this: that its very availability to Chaucer may have served to sharpen a natural sensitivity to usage which is necessary in any good poet.

IV

When we turn to his poetry, Chaucer's usage shows that, at whatever level, he was well aware of the particular appropriateness of certain linguistic forms to certain areas of discussion or modes of discourse, and Pandarus's adaptation of Horace's *Ars Poetica* to give advice on the composition of a letter indicates his awareness of the potential effect of the collocation of *termes* from different registers. It is striking that Chaucer, as well as stating the usually accepted sense of Horace's analogy ('hold of thi matere | The forme alwey, and do that it be lik'), makes a specific reference to incongruity of diction deriving from the use of *termes* from different registers:

> Ne jompre ek no discordant thyng yfeere,
> As thus, to usen termes of phisik
> In loves termes; hold of thi matere
> The forme alwey, and do that it be lik;
> For if a peyntour wolde peynte a pyk
> With asses feet, and hede it as an ape
> It cordeth naught, so nere it but a jape.

(*Troilus and Criseyde*, ii.1037)

A deliberate breach of the rules of congruity, as enjoined by the teaching of *elocutio*, may be merely comic, as when, at the beginning of *Sir Thopas*, there is a wide discrepancy on the scale of social registers between the calls for attention and the address to the audience. The manoeuvre is instantly recognizable as an exaggeration of the typical social flattery directed at the audience in the popular romance: 'Now holde youre mouth, *par charitee*, | Bothe knyght and lady free, | And herkneth to my spelle;' (B² 2081-83). The disastrous collapse from high style at the beginning of the second part of *The Squire's Tale* is comparable. The mixture of registers could also be merely chaotic, as in Pandarus's example; but it could be used with artistic control, by means of which, within the confines of one particular discourse, allusion to another conceptual area might be contrived by the intrusion of words from a distinct register. The comic and ironic effect, in *The Miller's Tale*, of the terms of affection of the popular lyric together with the affectation of courtly sensibility in a rustic setting, has been well demonstrated by E. T. Donaldson, so that we may be justified in ignoring this outstanding example to begin by a consideration of the technique applied more simply.[1]

In his *De Civitate Dei*, IV. 4, St Augustine employs a doctrinal method common in moralistic literature and which, descending as it does from the Cynico-Stoic moral tradition, was ancient even in his day: the attention of the audience is directed to an individual whose position on the social scale is different from that which he occupies on the scale of moral integrity. Augustine's version of this is noteworthy in that he demonstrates a moral identity between two individuals underlying a linguistic distinction dependent upon social status. Alexander, a powerful emperor, wreaks destruction, and is compared with a pirate leader who performs similar deeds, but at a humbler social level. Morally, they are equivalent in their lack of justice, but social differences ensure that their conditions of life are differently designated by linguistic custom as *imperator* and *latro*.

We may now recall that Deschamps compared Chaucer with Seneca for the worth of his moral writings, and that his notion of *gentillesse* (Boethian *nobilitas*) is greatly influenced by the tendency of thought which we have just noticed. It is, therefore, hardly surprising to find Chaucer drawing from this stream of thought and combining it with the deliberate mis-registration of *termes* for moral effect. Any sense of surprise is further diminished by the fact that Augustine himself had sanctioned linguistic improprieties in the cause of spiritual teaching, and indeed, the reconciliation by argument of unsuitable collocations is recommended as a means of expanding the divisions of the theme of a sermon by Thomas Waleys in his *De Modo Componendi Sermones*, written in the second quarter of the fourteenth century.[2] Thus the Manciple declares, according to established rhetorical precept, that the word must be suited to the deed. A word should appear in the company of other *termes* from the register in which they are all commonly used, and they should be used with application to their customary field of discourse. The Manciple's evocation of rhetorical theory comes in the context of a classical fable dealing not merely with noblemen but with a god, for whom the stylistic context is suitably elevated. More strikingly, it immediately follows a shocking breach of propriety in which the narrator has told how Phebus's wife has sent for her lemman:

> Hir lemman? Certes, this is a knavyssh speche!
> Foryeveth it me, and that I yow biseche.
>
> (H 205)

He has foreseen the outrage of his audience at such mis-registration and is ready with the paradoxical excuse that the word is, indeed, appropriate, but in a less

---

[1] E. T. Donaldson, 'The Idiom of Popular Poetry in *The Miller's Tale*', *English Institute Essays, 1950*, edited by A. S. Downer (New York, 1951), reprinted in *Speaking of Chaucer* (London, 1970), pp. 13–29.
[2] St Augustine, in *De Doctrina Christiana*, II. 13. 19–20, defends the literal translation of the Scriptures into Latin, even though the purity of the language might suffer, by the principle that the exact sense of the original must be preserved. Thomas Waleys in Th.-M. Charland, p. 399, states that a particular division of the theme may be dilated: 'ex apparenti improprietate locutionis, dum conatur praedicator locutionem hujusmodi ad proprietatem reducere'.

obvious respect than that allowed by the requirements of stylistic propriety, which
are here based exclusively upon the conventions of social appropriateness. The
audience's attention is now directed away from the social register, of which they are
necessarily most aware in a courtly fable, to contemplation of the moral circumstances. Here, despite the habitual linguistic distinction maintained in social registers, the action and morality of individuals of whatever level of society will be
identically judged:

> Ther nys no difference, trewely,
> Bitwixe a wyf that is of heigh degree,
> If of hir body dishonest she bee,
> And a povre wenche, oother than this —
> If it so be they werke bothe amys —
> But that the gentile, in estaat above,
> She shal be cleped his lady, as in love;
> And for that oother is a povre womman,
> She shal be cleped his wenche or his lemman.
>
> (H 212)

In the judgement of moral philosophy, concerned only with their actions, there is
no difference in kind between the two classes of women, yet usage ensures that the
words by which they are designated imply an estimate of their worth in terms of
connotations drawn from the social registers to which the words belong.[1]

Psychologically, the effect of the intrusion into a particular discourse of words
from a widely different register is one of linguistic shock; for one's expectancies,
which have become attuned to the collocation of *termes* from a recognizable register,
and to one set of proprieties, are suddenly disrupted. The reaction of an audience
may be very like that described by Professor McIntosh when discussing lexically
anomalous sentences: the hearer is forced back upon his own resources to find
circumstances or situation which will explain the deviation and make it acceptably
meaningful.[2] In the technique described above, the moralistic writer is ready with
the answer the moment he has provoked his audience to the question. But the poet
need not be so conscientious, for the power of *termes* to make allusion outside the
immediate field of discourse to another in which they have a special propriety, if
they are not directly exploited by explicatory argument, has great value for him and
for an alert audience who shares his language and cultural background. Although
the allusions of some uses of *termes* may be difficult for the modern audience to grasp
they form a technique by which Chaucer lends conceptual density to an admittedly
economical style.

In some uses their effect may be localized; an allusion serving the purpose of
elaborating the conceptual texture of the diction in a way common in courtly
speech, perhaps giving a sense of vehemence and earnestness but remaining
essentially undeveloped. Thus, in *The Book of the Duchess*, the Man in Black

---

[1] Compare the Parson's phrase *thral of synne* which, like Troilus as the subject of Love, derives from
Stoic notions of subjection to the passions. Chaucer's handling of the material in *The Manciple's Tale*
is based upon scholastic techniques of the definition of the *species*, in which *proprietates* are associated
with *differentiae*. The latter are features which serve to separate the *species* from the *genus*: 'ut cum
quaeritur quid inter regem sit et tyrannum, adiecta differentia, quid uterque definitur, ut "rex modes-
tus et temperatus, tyrannus vero crudelis" '. Isidore, *Etymologiarum*, I. 31, edited by W. M. Lindsay
(Oxford, 1911).
[2] Angus McIntosh, 'Patterns and Ranges', in Angus McIntosh and M. A. K. Halliday, *Patterns of
Language* (London, 1966), pp. 183–99.

corrects his own careless expression in a way not utterly different from that of the
Manciple:

> I wolde ever, withoute drede,
> Have loved hir, for I moste nede.
> 'Nede!' nay, trewely, I gabbe now;
> Noght 'nede', and I wol tellen how,
> For of good wille myn herte hyt wolde.
>
> (1073)

The alteration from the facile 'moste nede' to the collocation of *nede* and *wille*
represents both a shift in the sense of *nede* and a transformation of the seriousness of
commitment to Blanche. With the collocation, and especially the contrast made
between them, *nede* and *wille* become *termes* with the function of allusion to the
continuing Boethian discussion of Free Will and Necessity. The mourner was not
destined to love Blanche, but chose to do so, and he soon tells us (1115) that he
does not intend to repent this deliberate choice as a sin; technically, a misdirection of
the will. Thus, from the trivial motivation of conventional love reflections, a weighty
allusion to questions of choice, sin, and justification emerges. The revelation of
termes gives stature to the relationship, gravity to the loss, and relates the situation to
the philosophical themes which perturb more than one of Chaucer's lovers.

In some applications, however, this allusive technique may be part of a larger
scheme within the same poem, perhaps of characterization and motive, as in *Troilus
and Criseyde*. Here, as we have seen, Pandarus has skills in eloquence. But, besides his
knowledge of the Horatian canons of style, he is a skilled rhetorical practitioner,
employing eloquence for its original purpose of persuasion. At the beginining of
Book II he sets out on his errand on Troilus's behalf with the narrator's invocation
of Janus, god of doorways but also symbol of rhetorical ambiguity, as his support.
After an initial and apparently inconsequential conversation with his niece, during
which he manages to implant the idea of Troilus as a second Hector in her mind, he
returns to the good fortune which he claims has befallen her and to which he had
referred at his entrance. Before beginning to tell the 'thyng to doon yow pleye',
which he had promised earlier, he commences to assert his integrity in a stanza cast
in high style (232–8). Criseyde answers him soberly enough, but is unsettled by his
change in style and begs him to 'Lat be to me youre fremde manere speche' and to
speak freely and familiarly, as her uncle. Pandarus's reply is an accumulation of the
termes of rhetorical theory, in which he denies his intention of using the persuasive
power of rhetoric upon one already well disposed to him. Some men, he says, employ
'subtyl art' in the composition of their narratives, which are nevertheless told with a
particular end in view:

> And sithen th'ende is every tales strengthe,
> And this matere is so bihovely,
> What sholde I peynte or drawen it on lengthe
> To yow, that ben my frend so feythfully?
>
> (II.260)

Here, the worde *ende* is somewhat ambiguous: the actual closing stages of a
composition may be important, but they are important because they reveal the
dénouement of the plot or the purpose of the narrative. Here, Pandarus is saying that
the point or purpose of the recitation is what matters, and the subject matter (*matere*)
of his tale is so important that he will have no need to ornament it with the colours

of rhetoric (*peynte*: Latin *pingere*) or to expand it (*amplificatio*). He then considers his audience and, adapting his technique to her requirements, privately decides not to 'make a proces' (a resolution which he repeats aloud a little later) or adopt complex arguments. But he launches into a persuasive speech replete with the rhetoric of *fine amour* and the arguments of the preacher. Once more Criseyde is aware of his eloquence and replies with an emotive outburst and a battery of rhetorical questions, amidst which is the accusation of the deceptive use of rhetorical skill:

> Is al this paynted proces seyd, allas!
> Right for this fyn?[1]
>
> (II.424)

Pandarus's reply is an even more impassioned protestation of good faith, which shakes Criseyde's feeble resolution and, indeed, awakens her interest in Troilus, for as Pandarus is about to storm out she restrains him in a shocking lapse of stylistic propriety:

> And up he sterte, and on his way he raughte,
> Til she agayn hym by the lappe kaughte.
>
> (II.447)

The outraged rhetoric of both is betrayed by this action, and their conscious use of rhetorical *termes* weighs skill against sincerity in our judgement of their motives. Pandarus attempts to manipulate his niece by his eloquence: Criseyde, echoing his word *proces*, recognizes the fact, indulging herself with accusations of treachery. After this, it is not difficult to believe that Criseyde finds Pandarus's threat of suicide a convenient excuse for reasonably complying to an extent, uncertain even to her, with his requests.

Important as the use of the collocation of *termes* is in the elaboration of the personalities and natures of Pandarus and Criseyde in this short scene, it is relatively restricted by comparison with the strategy adopted in the poem as a whole, where the use of *termes* does much to orientate the themes of the work.

The psychology of St Thomas Aquinas, which has a strong claim, in its generality, to be considered as the standard psychology of the period, identified the tendency to sin as a misdirection of the affections of the will. Thus, the identical impulse which ought to lead man to salvation when it is fixed upon God can lead to damnation when it is fixed upon the world. Such, at its baldest, is the moral psychology underlying *Troilus and Criseyde*, and such a framework naturally furnishes the outline of a series of ironic parallels in which the ideal path of salvation exists as an allusive paradigm, a direct contrast with a less happy progress. The constant comparison, which is not always a contrast, of earthly and spiritual love is a ubiquitous feature of medieval poetry, and is reflected in its language, where great difficulty may be experienced in separating the two registers. In the fourteenth century, especially, the informal comparison between feudal loyalty, and both human and divine love, as a result of which all three had shared a common vocabulary from early times, becomes elaborated and institutionalized by the poets of Northern France and England. Under the influence of the *Roman de la Rose*,

---

[1] The account of the ambiguity of this phrase given by Professor Empson in *Seven Types of Ambiguity* (Harmondsworth, 1961), p. 62 is quite unacceptable. His contention that there is an allusion to the law courts depends upon a deliberate metanalysis of the word *peynted*, and fails to acknowledge its rhetorical reference. In this connexion see J. D. Burnley, 'Chaucer's Art of Verbal Allusion: Two Notes', *Neophilologus*, 56 (1972), 93–9 (pp. 93–4).

love is apotheosized and demands a theology and a liturgy of his own. Chaucer, nurtured by a familiarity with the *Roman de la Rose* and the line of *dits amoureux* deriving from it, is one of the earliest English poets to provide love with a deity and a cult, and he does this most extensively in *Troilus and Criseyde*. It is in this connexion that we find the most ambitious deployment of *termes* to underpin the contrast between divine and human love which is implicit in the poem.

As if to introduce the theme of the poem, the technique commences in Book I and is intimately interwoven with its narrative development, re-echoing at intervals throughout the poem. Book I is the book of Troilus's *despeir*; the word is to be found at least half a dozen times in the course of the narration. In itself this is not important, since the word is common in discussions of love, and its opposition to *grace* is insufficient to justify the assumption of the existence of an ironic allusion to the technical, theological register; for both the words and their relationship were interchangeable in register when Chaucer wrote. Yet scattered throughout the book are uses of other words whose register is difficult to ascertain or whose registerial affinity is more decidedly religious than secular: *repente, converte, ordre*. The stream of religious allusion originates at line fifteen, with the narrator's misappropriation of a title of the Pope, in which the word *Love* is substituted for the word *God*. Such references reach a concentration shortly after Troilus's first sight of Criseyde. It is made abundantly clear that Troilus is sensuously affected by Criseyde's appearance: *horses lawe* and the *lawe of kynde* are paralleled, and we are told that Troilus became the helpless *subgit* of the passion of love, which has been kindled by the *depe impressioun* made upon his senses by Criseyde.[1] Referring to the change in Troilus's heart the narrator exclaims: 'Blissed be Love, that kan thus folk converte!' (1.308). This last word had, at this period, a specifically religious sense and had meant, in Medieval Latin, the act of turning from the secular to the monastic life.[2] Within ten lines of his 'conversion', we find Troilus repenting his mockery of lovers and referring to them in *termes* proper to a religious community: 'In feith, youre ordre is ruled in good wise!' (1.336). The references to despair and grace, to a *guerdon* greater than deserts, to the *observaunces* of lovers, continue throughout the book. Before long, Troilus gives the consent of his reason to the tendency of the will stimulated by the appearance of Criseyde and, like the Man in Black, he shows no inclination to repent (1.391–2). The narrative climax of the book is reached with the scene in which Troilus at last confesses his attachment to Pandarus; a scene which also represents the climax of the more or less covert stream of allusion. Pandarus announces that he has a good analogy with Troilus's condition in mind, and this turns out to be a clarification of the allusions made up to this point. Troilus is told that Love has converted him from wickedness, and that this repentance will lead to him becoming the noblest pillar of his order. A detailed parallel is made with the experience of the most zealous supports of the Church; men who, like St Paul, are converted from being persecutors to become the greatest defenders of the faith. The notion of conversion to a regular order of lovers, which is

---

[1] Mrs I. Gordon discusses the change in Troilus from the moral point of view in *The Double Sorrow of Troilus* (Oxford, 1970), pp. 64–73. She argues that the reference to Bayard and *horses lawe* is intended to imply the blindness of passion unmoderated by reason. Such an allusion is likely, since the Stoic idea of the *subgit* of passion is present, and Bayard is explicitly associated with rational blindness in *The Canon's Yeoman's Tale*, G 1413 as well as in *Confessio Amantis*, VI.1280.

[2] C. Du Cange, *Glossarium Mediae et Infimae Latinitatis*, s.v. *conversio*.

parallel to the re-dedication of the Christian spirit, is now established in a way
which will ensure its endurance throughout the poem. The key words appear from
time to time: Criseyde becomes 'able to converte' (II.903), and there are references
to love's saints, to being in bliss, and Cupid is called an immortal god. But the final
development of the technique does not come until Book IV, when the lovers are to
be separated. Criseyde is ready for a further conversion:

> And, Troilus, my clothes everychon
> Shul blake ben in tokenyng, herte swete,
> That I am as out of this world agon,
> That wont was yow to setten in quiete;
> And of myn ordre, ay til deth me mete,
> The observaunce evere, in youre absence,
> Shal sorwe ben, compleynt, and abstinence.
>
> (IV.778)

A new order is envisaged of sorrowing lovers whose clothes are black in mourning,
like those of a nun; Criseyde is turning from the world, becoming a *conversa* in this
order to await her death in asceticism. The allusion to conversion in its technical
sense, and the reference to black clothes, strikes us with sudden force, for in the very
line after the introduction of the notion of conversion in Book I, Criseyde is identified as 'She, this in blak . . .' (I.309). A series of connexions are now made, for we
also remember her words to her uncle, when previously she appeared in her own
fancy as a recluse who ought to pass her days reading saints lives rather than
dancing; she had, in fact, just turned from reading the *Romance of Thebes*. The
effect of these connexions is to throw into ironic contrast the behaviour of Criseyde
and her own dreams of herself, and since on that previous occasion her widow's
habit did not signify withdrawal we know that she will never keep faith with
Troilus now. Against the sphere of allusion created by this masterly use of *termes* and
figures Criseyde, who is subject to the *love of kynde*, suddenly appears more morally
fragile than ever before, carrying within her the unattainable aspirations to stability
but certain to fall far short of the ideal. Attractive as she is, and blissful as the affair
has been, the evocation of the orders of celestial lovers places it inescapably inside
the structure of orthodox theology, where it appears as no more than one of the
passing things of earth. Hence, the use of *termes* and associated figures orientates the
whole moral theme of the poem, preparing for, though certainly not justifying to
us, the violent repudiation of earthly affection which fills the epilogue.

V

Chaucer's earliest critics were economical in analysis of their master and extravagant in his praise. They praised his skill with *termes*, both in the range and elaboration of his vocabulary and in the skill which he exhibited in its poetic arrangement,
but they neglected to explain in detail, or exemplify precisely, what it was they so
admired. In this discussion of the use of *termes* by Chaucer, I have tried to indicate
what the use of the word *termes* may signify and to suggest that Chaucer was
conscious of and could exploit for poetic effect, a notion of propriety in diction
which greatly exceeds in range and complexity the familiar, but yet imperfectly
defined, concept of the three levels of style. Three main examples have been given
of this technique in practice, and they are all examples in which the art is employed

to ends which amply justify Chaucer's medieval reputation as a learned poet of morality, philosophy, and love. Indeed, the use of *termes* is not restricted to a mere rhetorical embellishment, nor to a passing pun, but is often an organic part of the poem in which it appears. As a technique it is frequently difficult to unravel from the texture of other allusive or ironic devices with which it combines, without failing to do critical justice to the part it plays in the total effect of the work. This is especially true of Chaucer's mature work, as I hope to have demonstrated in an earlier paper on the employment of the technique in *The Merchant's Tale*.[1] Yet, though Chaucer's use of *termes* covers a range of effect from the simple pun or word play to the emergence of an elaborate figurative pattern, the basic technique where certain words gain power from use, context, and collocation, remains the same, and perhaps forms the basis of the brevity and eloquence, that skill in *termes*, for which his early admirers revered him.

[1] J. D. Burnley, 'The Morality of *The Merchant's Tale*', *YES*, 6 (1976), 16–25.

The *Troilus* Frontispiece and Chaucer's Audience

DEREK PEARSALL

University of York

The assumptions that literary scholars make about the nature of Chaucer's audience have a powerful and often unadmitted influence on the way in which they read his poetry. It is important therefore that these assumptions, which are difficult to substantiate and which yet are a necessary preliminary in the processes of historical criticism, should be clearly recognized and constantly re-examined. It is the purpose of this paper to examine again the famous frontispiece (fol. 1b) in Corpus Christi College, Cambridge, MS 61 of *Troilus and Criseyde*,[1] and to consider the ways in which such a picture can justifiably be interpreted in relation to questions about the nature of Chaucer's audience. It is a splendid picture, and a brilliant scene, with gorgeously costumed king, queen, and nobles in elegant postures of attention and inattention as Chaucer, clad in seemly sober hue, reads from his latest poem; a reading graced, we may deduce, by his own gifts for dramatic delivery, for shafts of wit and irony, for sly winks and meaningful asides, and enlivened by the quick responses of an alert, subtle, and discriminating aristocratic audience.

The potency of this picture in creating or helping to create an image of Chaucer the 'court-poet' is undeniable. Its effect in colouring assumptions about the nature of Chaucer's audience is well illustrated by Nevill Coghill, in his association of Chaucer's use of the 'Possessive Demonstrative' (*This Troilus*, etc.) with the frontispiece:

It is only one of Chaucer's many stratagems and subterfuges in relation to his audience, as he stood exposed before them in the pulpit in which we see him in the Corpus Christi manuscript of *Troilus and Criseyde*. Before such listeners how delicate a tact was needed! ... It can be dangerous to lecture a king. If we reflect that *Troilus and Criseyde* was completed towards 1385, when Richard II and his newly-married wife, Anne of Bohemia, were both nineteen years old, and seated there before him, we can appreciate the directness of the personal address to them in the lines, 'O yonge, fresshe folkes, he or she ... ' It is not surprising that Chaucer came to adopt the ambush of a double-*persona* when he came to write *The Canterbury Tales*.[2]

The association of Chaucer, as 'court-poet', with the immediate entourage of king and higher nobility, and the extension of this association into a generalization about Chaucer's audience, are perhaps the more questionable products of what may be called 'the frontispiece theory'.

The fact is, however, that this famous picture has a by no means unambiguous relation even to the poem with which it is associated. It is presumed that the manuscript, which is of the early fifteenth century, was once owned by Anne Nevill, Duchess of Buckingham, since her name appears in a note added to *Troilus*

---

[1] Frequently reproduced, most recently and conveniently as frontispiece and cover illustration to both volumes of P. M. Kean, *Chaucer and the Making of English Poetry* (London, 1972).

[2] 'Chaucer's narrative art in *The Canterbury Tales*', in *Chaucer and Chaucerians*, edited by D. S. Brewer (London, 1966), pp. 135–6.

and Criseyde, IV.581 ('neuer foryeteth: Anne neuyll'), and her identity is proved by another note in the manuscript mentioning the name 'Knyvett', with which family she has a connexion through her daughter.[1] Anne Nevill was the daughter of Ralph, Earl of Westmorland, and Joan Beaufort, legitimized daughter of John of Gaunt by Katharine Swynford, and the Beaufort connexion has been used to suggest that the Corpus MS is a transcription of a family copy made in the 1380s, that is, at the time the poem was written, and that the frontispiece is likewise a copy of a historically authentic 'scene' in the original. This, of course, is the purest speculation, and it is not in any way supported by the fact that the Corpus MS, in addition to the frontispiece, contains spaces for a further ninety-four miniatures. Brusendorff's deduction that this presupposes an exemplar in which the pictures were present is quite unnecessary,[2] since such blanks, or pictures partially completed, often appear in illustrated manuscripts, whether prepared as a commercial speculation or with specific customers in mind, and simply reflect the uncertain state of an expensive and complex market. Once the pressure to 'authenticate' the picture is removed, its inclusion can be seen simply as reflecting the judgement of the manuscript's editor, publisher, or buyer that such a picture would be stylish and appropriate. There is no reason to deny that the picture is intended to be associated with the text, nor that it is intended to create the impression of a real occasion, perhaps even with some attempt at portraiture.[3] As a picture, and as a publisher's venture, it is on this reading a clever and obviously successful variation on the presentation picture (the standard method of indicating 'publication' and claiming patronage in manuscript frontispieces) as if to imply that this is how Chaucer 'presented' his poem to his audience. The fact that the manuscript's publisher chose to foster this implication is of course a reminder that Chaucer makes no such claim, nor can it be made for his poem by anyone else, since the poem is dedicated to Gower and Strode.

There is no need to multiply examples of presentation pictures at this period, except perhaps to mention that some of the more elaborate French specimens show a well developed art of portraiture, as in the two copies of Pierre Salmon's *Réponses à Charles VI* (Bibliothèque Nationale MS fr. 23279 and Geneva, Bibliothèque publique et universitaire, MS fr. 165) or *Le livre des merveilles* (Bibliothèque Nationale MS fr. 2810), all from the Boucicaut workshop, and all discussed by Millard Meiss.[4] It is important to note, however, that Meiss is prepared to identify

---

[1] For accounts of the MS, and discussion of the frontispiece, see M. R. James, *Descriptive Catalogue of the Manuscripts in the Library of Corpus Christi College, Cambridge*, 2 vols (Cambridge, 1912), I, 126–7; *Troilus and Criseyde*, edited by R. K. Root (Princeton, 1926; reprinted 1945), p. liii; A. Brusendorff, *The Chaucer Tradition* (Copenhagen, 1925; reprinted Gloucester, Massachusetts, 1965), pp. 19–23; Margaret Galway, 'The *Troilus* Frontispiece', *MLR*, 44 (1949), 161–77; George Williams, 'The *Troilus and Criseyde* Frontispiece again', *MLR*, 57 (1962), 173–8.
[2] Brusendorff, p. 23, followed by Galway, p. 161.
[3] The picture of Chaucer bears some resemblance to the Hoccleve portraits and a closer resemblance to the initial portrait in BM MS Lansdowne 851: see Brusendorff, pp. 18–20 (Brusendorff refers to Lansdowne 699: this is a mistake); also J. Mitchell, *Thomas Hoccleve* (Urbana, Illinois, 1968), pp. 110–15, and M. H. Spielmann, *The Portraits of Geoffrey Chaucer* (London, 1900). There are eight Chaucer portraits in MSS, others cut out, and an exceptionally strong tradition, therefore, of Chaucer portraiture; it is quite possible that the frontispiece painter had an exemplar. Of the others represented in the miniature, perhaps Richard, Anne, and Gaunt might be thought to be recognizable.
[4] *French Painting in the Time of Jean de Berry: The Boucicaut Master* (London, 1968), figs. 67, 69, 70, 72, 98. In the companion volume, *The Late Fourteenth Century and the Patronage of the Duke*, 2 vols (London, 1967), Meiss discusses sixty-six portraits of Jean de Berry, pp. 68–94.

only the outstanding members of these presentation groups, such as Berry, Burgundy, and Anjou, those whose identity is signalled in clearly defined ways, usually heraldic, and evidently regards the remainder as not intended to be identified. Furthermore, these presentation pictures, as can be deduced from various kinds of evidence (such as the existence of variant forms of the same picture, the presence of historically impossible juxtapositions of figures, and the hopes of 'presentation' that were not fulfilled), are not representations of 'real' scenes. It is quite clear that a professional art historian would regard the attempt by literary scholars to identify all the figures in the *Troilus* frontispiece, identifications unsupported by evidence of heraldic arms, badges, insignia, characteristic dress or attributes, as speculation of the wildest kind.[1] Nor is such speculation necessary, for once the situation is seen in terms of patterns of manuscript production and demand, and the pressure towards historical authentication removed, the picture can be recognized as fully explicable from within the poem. In other words, it represents as a reality the myth of delivery that Chaucer cultivates so assiduously in the poem,[2] with his references to 'al this compaignye' of lovers 'in this place'.[3]

Even as a representation of a mythical reading the picture is, at the very least, highly stylized. The scene is portrayed out of doors, presumably so as to accommodate some of the latest fashions of French and Italian landscape painting,[4] and the terms of reference given to the painter are of the broadest kind. Patricia Kean attempts to recognize this in entitling the reproductions of the picture in *Chaucer and the Making of English Poetry* 'The Poet reading to an Audience' instead of 'Chaucer reading to the Court of Richard II', the usual title, but it must be admitted that the book from which 'the Poet' is supposed to be 'reading' is not at all obvious in the picture. It is, in fact, not there, and has only been supplied by modern interpretation. What the painter has represented, understandably enough, since it is the only

[1] 'Much pleasant speculation may be indulged in', as Brusendorff says (p. 22); see the articles cited above by Galway and Williams for some examples. One is reluctant to abandon all the ingenuity that Margaret Galway expends on the picture, her theory, for instance, that the background of the picture represents scenes from the earlier life of the court personages in the foreground. Such a theory, however, has no bearing on the question of the reality of the picture's portrayal of Chaucer's audience. Other possibilities for these enigmatic background scenes, equally irrelevant to the present argument, are that they represent the return of the company to the castle; or that they represent episodes from the story of *Troilus* (as the presentation picture of Bersuire's translation of Livy, Bibliothèque Nationale MS fr. 259, fol. 15, shows scenes of Romulus and Remus in the background: Meiss, *Boucicaut Master*, fig. 431); or that they are merely decorative in-filling.

[2] 'It [the frontispiece] might itself even be a product of the poem's power to create the sense of a listening group' (D. Brewer, 'Troilus and Criseyde', p. 196, in the Sphere *History of Literature in the English Language*, Volume I: *The Middle Ages*, edited by W. F. Bolton (London, 1970), pp. 195–228).

[3] *Troilus*, I. 450; II. 30 (Chaucer is quoted from the second edition of F. N. Robinson (Cambridge, Massachusetts, 1957)). For a more sophisticated literary interpretation of the myth of delivery, one can turn to essays by Brewer, already cited, by G. Shepherd, in *Chaucer and Chaucerians*, pp. 65–87, and by D. Mehl, in *Chaucer and Middle English Studies in Honour of R. H. Robbins*, edited by B. Rowland (London, 1974), pp. 173–89, and an important book by R. M. Durling, *The Figure of the Poet in Renaissance Epic* (Cambridge, Massachusetts, 1965), Chapter 2.

[4] See M. Rickert, *Painting in Britain: The Middle Ages*, Pelican History of Art (Harmondsworth, 1954; second edition, 1965), p. 176; G. Mathew, *The Court of Richard II* (London, 1968), p. 205. Stylistically, the picture is extremely complex. Francis Wormald, in his paper on 'The Wilton Diptych', *Journal of the Warburg and Courtauld Institutes*, 17 (1954), 191–203, suggests a connexion with the paintings of the months in the Torre dell' Aquila at Trento (p. 195).

PLATE I

Corpus Christi College Cambridge MS 61. Chaucer's *Troilus and Criseyde*
fol. 1b.   The author and his audience

Reproduced by permission of the Master and Fellows of Corpus Christi College, Cambridge

PLATE II

British Library MS Royal 20.C.vii. *Chroniques de France*
fol. 47.   Preaching a crusade

Reproduced by permission of the British Library Board

PLATE III

British Library MS Royal 20.C.vii. *Chroniques de France*
fol. 76b.   The archbishop of Rouen preaching a crusade

Reproduced by permission of the British Library Board

PLATE IV

British Library MS Royal 8.G.iii. Petrus de Aureolis. *Compendium super Bibliam*
fol. 2.   The author preaching to an audience

Reproduced by permission of the British Library Board

iconography available for such a picture,[1] is a preacher.[2] Pictures of a similar kind, showing a figure in a pulpit, gesturing with one hand, and addressing an audience of richly clad nobles, not all of them apparently listening (this is due to the need to present at least some of the audience, for the viewer's sake, in frontal poses), are not difficult to find. Mostly they show the audience drawn up to one side,[3] but occasionally the audience surrounds the speaker, in the manner of the *Troilus* picture,[4] and a particular resemblance may be claimed, on grounds of composition, for the portrait of the author preaching to an audience in the *Compendium super Bibliam* of Petrus de Aureolis, Archbishop of Aix in the early fourteenth century.[5] In addition to the resemblances of general foreground composition,[6] of figure grouping and posture, and of such details as the location and angle of the pulpit, this picture is of course also a model as to function for the *Troilus* frontispiece, since it serves both as author-portrait and as 'presentation' picture.[7] Stylistically, furthermore, the picture has many points of contact with the *Troilus* frontispiece, and both

[1] Meiss, speaking of the new subjects, especially secular subjects, demanded of late fourteenth-century painters, says: 'The less specific the instructions given to the illustrator the more he tended to tell the new stories with groups of figures from his repertory that seemed to suit' (*French Painting in the Time of Jean de Berry: The Late Fourteenth Century*, p. 15).

[2] The iconography of 'the poet' or author is barely developed at this time. Some Italian MSS of the fourteenth century show him as a solitary figure writing in or reading from a book, e.g. Petrarch, in Fitzwilliam Museum, Cambridge, MS McLean 173, fols. 1, 51; Guido della Colonna, in BM MS Add. 15477, fol. 1. Such pictures are evidently related to the iconography of 'the teacher', who is familiarly represented reading at a lectern to students who themselves are usually following their books or writing notes, e.g. Azzo in Bodley MS Canon. Misc. 416, fol. 1, Aristotle in Bodley MS Douce 319, fol. 86, both Italian MSS of the fourteenth century (see *Illuminated Manuscripts in the Bodleian Library Oxford*, edited by O. Pächt and J. J. G. Alexander, 3 vols (Oxford, 1966–73), plate 10, no. 107, and plate 14, no. 154); also the frequent pictures of Solomon as teacher in the *Bible Historiale*, e.g. BM MS Royal 19.D.v., fols, 1, 13b, 19, 26b. It is only in the fifteenth century that more sophisticated author-portraits begin to appear, such as the picture of Vegetius, at a lectern, reading to the Emperor and his court, who are seated on benches, like a lecture audience, in Bodley MS Laud lat. 56 (French, early 15th century), fol. 1, or the striking picture of Boccaccio, seated outside an enclosed garden, writing down the conversation going on inside, in Bodley MS Douce 213 (French, mid-15th century), fol. 1. See Pächt and Alexander, plate 51, no. 660, and plate 55, no. 717.

[3] There is a good example in an early fifteenth-century French MS of the French metrical history of the *Deposition and Death of Richard II* (edited by J. Webb, *Archaeologia*, 20, 1824, 1–423, where the miniatures are reproduced as engravings), BM MS Harley 1319, where fol. 12 shows Archbishop Arundel preaching Henry's cause. The development of such pictures can be traced through the many simpler versions of preaching scenes which occur in MSS of the French *Bible Historiale* (e.g. BM MS Royal 19.D.v., English, first half of 14th century, fol. 99, Jeremiah preaching, fol. 131b, Joel; MS Royal 19.D.ii, French, c. 1350, fols. 487b, 492, 495b, 497b, 499b, 500b, all representing Paul preaching; MS Royal 17.E.vii, French, 1357, fol. 217b, in vol. II, representing an apostle preaching; MS Royal 15.D.iii, French, early 15th century, fols. 496, 497b, 498b, 503, all of Paul), of Gregory's *Dialogues* (e.g. MS Royal 20.D.v., French/English, c. 1400, fols. 31b, 118b, Christ preaching), of the *Golden Legend* (e.g. MS Royal 19.B.xvii, French, 1382, fols. 63b, 220b, 277b, of a bishop, St Bernard, and St Francis respectively), and, among secular works, of the *Chroniques de France*, where the preaching of a crusade is frequently illustrated in the conventional manner (e.g. MS Royal 16.G.vi, French, second quarter of the 14th century, fol. 436b; MS Royal 20.C.vii, French, late 14th century, fol. 47). It is interesting to watch, in these scenes, the development of grouping, poses, portraiture, diagonal placing of pulpit, outdoor scenery, and characteristic hand gestures.

[4] A striking example, and an index to the iconographic origins of the *Troilus* picture, is a miniature of the archbishop of Rouen preaching a crusade in a late fourteenth-century French MS of the *Chroniques de France*, BM MS Royal 20.C.vii, fol. 76b.

[5] BM MS Royal 8.G.iii (English, early 15th century), fol. 2: see Sir George F. Warner and J. P. Gibson, *British Museum: Catalogue of Western Manuscripts in the Old Royal and King's Collections*, 4 vols (1921), I. 274. There is a reproduction of the picture in vol. IV, plate 62.

[6] The background is quite dissimilar, and shows God enthroned on a mountain: the mountain may, however, have provided the hint for the vertically stepped background of the *Troilus* picture.

[7] Compare the use of a preacher for the initial miniature in a French MS, c. 1400, of Deguileville's *Pélerinage de la vie humaine*, Bodley MS Douce 300, fol. 1.

paintings are associated with early fifteenth-century English ateliers influenced by Herman Scheerre.[1] It would not be wise to declare the Petrus de Aureolis picture a model for the *Troilus* frontispiece, but the existence of such a parallel at least tends to confirm the interpretation of the latter on aesthetic rather than on historical grounds.

If it be argued that the manuscript's editor or the miniature painter is perfectly justified in drawing evidence from the poem as to the poem's audience or original audience, it would be necessary to remember how inherently fallible if not deliberately misleading such evidence commonly is, from the *scop* of *Beowulf* to the ale-swilling minstrel of *Havelok* or *Winner and Waster*. And if it be argued further that the tone of the comments concerning the audience in the poem, and the whole sophistication of its address, is such as to presuppose a highly sophisticated audience, then one would have to remark that the immediate circle of king and nobility is not the only place for such sophistication to be found, except in the mind of a publisher conscious of the appeal of such a claim.[2]

There is no evidence to prove that Chaucer did not give command performances at court, nor that the *Troilus* frontispiece is not a partial record of the memory of such a performance. Such evidence is not, in the nature of things, likely to be forthcoming: all I have argued for is the difficulty of using the frontispiece as evidence for what has often been treated as an obvious deduction. One might add to the negative evidence the omission of any explicit record of such a command performance, surely a momentous event, in the text of the poem, in any manuscript of the poem, or in any royal or household document. Indeed, the absence of any presentation copy of any of Chaucer's poems, or of any manuscript with a presentation picture (except the mutation of such a picture in Corpus 61) or patronal portrait, seems a strange gap in the evidence we might expect to have, especially in comparison with the frequency of such copies and such pictures among the manuscripts of Lydgate and Hoccleve.[3] Such comparisons are conventionally countered by the argument that Chaucer's relations with the royal court were too intimate for such a formal commemoration to be appropriate. J. Norton-Smith, who posits a close personal involvement of poet and queen, as patroness and muse, in the Prologue to the *Legend of Good Women*, deals with the absence of evidence in this way:

Its [the poem's] precise personal origin in the medieval system of patronage disappears without a trace . . . The documentation for an informed view of this artistic situation simply does not exist, nor does it seem that the period troubled itself to provide any useful record of it.[4]

---

[1] See C. L. Kuhn, 'Herman Scheerre and English Illumination in the Fifteenth Century'. *Art Bulletin*, 22 (1940), 138–56 (p. 155).

[2] The work of Mary Giffin, *Studies on Chaucer and his Audience* (Hull, Quebec, 1956), recognizes the variety of Chaucer's audiences (p. 20) and has some lavish speculations on their nature, but the dominant sense of audience is that of the *Troilus* frontispiece, with which the book begins (p. 17), and the equation of 'courtly' and 'sophisticated' is readily made.

[3] There are Lydgate presentation pictures in BM MSS Harley 2278, Harley 4826, and Cotton Augustus A.iv, in Trinity College, Cambridge, MS 1283 (0.5.2), and in the Crawford-Rylands MS of the *Troy Book* (see D. Pearsall, *John Lydgate* (London, 1970), pp. 33, 47, 76–7), and pictures showing the presentation of Hoccleve's *Regement of Princes* to Henry V in BM MSS Royal 17.D.vi and Arundel 38. The absence of any presentation copy or picture for Gower's *Confessio Amantis* raises questions, likewise, about the reality of Richard II's role as 'patron' of the first version: see the Prologue to the *Confessio Amantis* (*Works*, edited by G. C. Macaulay, 4 vols (Oxford, 1899–1902)), lines 51–3, first recension copies only.

[4] *Geoffrey Chaucer* (London, 1974), pp. 65–6.

One would have to remark that relations of poet and patron, in earlier Anglo-Norman poetry, in contemporary French poetry, in early fifteenth-century English poetry, where such relations exist, are fully documented.

It is no part of the argument here to deny that Chaucer, in addition to having his work copied for sale or circulation, may often have been in the habit of reading his poetry aloud to a listening audience, though there seems no reason to suppose that this listening audience was always or ever that of the *Troilus* frontispiece. Nor is it possible to deny that certain of his poems, namely the *Book of the Duchess*, the *Legend of Good Women*, the *Complaint to his Purse*, and *Lak of Stedfastnesse*, have explicit connexions with the inner court circle of royal family and higher nobility.[1] The existence of such connexions, however, in conjunction with the evidence of the frontispiece, has been allowed to dominate overmuch the image of Chaucer's audience. It has led furthermore to distortions in the interpretation of other kinds of evidence. It is probably true that Richard's was the first English-speaking court since the Conquest, but the process by which English supplanted French must have been a gradual one. The *Life of the Black Prince* in French verse by the herald of Sir John Chandos was composed in 1385 and was evidently addressed to an English audience,[2] while even after 1400 Gower saw fit to dedicate the *Cinkante Balades* and *Traitié pour essampler les amantz marietz* to Henry IV, 'por desporter vo noble Court roial'.[3] It is, in fact, the tenacity of French, eventually and inevitably to be superseded as it was, that needs stressing.[4] Its decline only begins to accelerate after the Deposition. Such a delicately balanced situation, in which Gower can regard writing in English in the late 1380s as a radically new departure,[5] must obviously affect the view we have of the immediacy and extent of Chaucer's access to the inner and presumably most conservative court circle. Much more has been made too of Richard's own qualifications as a patron of letters than the facts would seem to warrant.[6] It is an innocent assumption on the part of literary scholars that associates literary activity at the court necessarily with the person of the king. We might do well to look beyond the entourage of king and nobility for Chaucer's audience, to the multitude of household knights and officials, career diplomats and civil servants, who constitute the 'court' in its wider sense, that is, the national administration and its metropolitan milieu. It is here that we find men (Clifford,

---

[1] Court occasions deduced for many others of Chaucer's poems rest upon the ingenuity of modern scholars or upon Shirley's gossip.

[2] The poem is edited by M. K. Pope and E. C. Lodge (Oxford, 1910). There is no evidence that the poem was received at court: the brief references to Richard (lines 1599, 2097, 4135–50) would presumably have been expanded in such a case.

[3] *Works*, I, 337 (line 27). The significance of this dedication is not diminished if the composition of these poems is assigned to an earlier date in Gower's poetic career. For dating, see J. H. Fisher, *John Gower, Moral Philosopher and Friend of Chaucer* (New York, 1964), pp. 71–88.

[4] This is especially true in view of the interpretation conventionally given to some familiar pieces of evidence, such as the statute of 1362 that pleadings in the courts of common law should in future be in English. This statute, often cited as a clear indication of change, was neither influential nor symptomatic: it was inoperative in the lower courts, where English would naturally have been the language of most participants in any case, while in the higher courts, where French was firmly established as the language of professional pleaders, it was ineffectual. See G. E. Woodbine, 'The Language of English Law', *Speculum*, 18 (1943), 395–436.

[5] 'And for that fewe men endite | In oure englissh, I thenke make | A bok for Engelondes sake' (*Confessio Amantis*, Prologue 22–4).

[6] For a sceptical discussion, see R. S. Loomis, 'The Library of Richard II', *Studies in Language, Literature and Culture of the Middle Ages and Later*, edited by E. Bagby Atwood and A. A. Hill (Austin, Texas, 1969), pp. 173–8.

Clanvowe, Scogan, Hoccleve, Usk, Gower, Strode) whose known interests and known association with Chaucer make them apt candidates for a 'Chaucer circle'.

The existence among Chaucer's audience of a 'familiar group' of the kind I have outlined above has long been recognized.[1] The purpose of this paper has been to bring this group into greater prominence by subordinating to it the claims of the royal 'court' as more narrowly conceived by literary scholars, and more specifically to confront and question one important piece of evidence that has been allowed to substantiate those claims.

[1] See, for example, D. Brewer, *Chaucer in his Time* (London, 1963), p. 200. See further K. B. McFarlane, *Lancastrian Kings and Lollard Knights* (Oxford, 1972), pp. 139–226, and D. W. Robertson, *Chaucer's London* (New York, 1968), pp. 179–222.

Gabriel Harvey, 'Pasquill', Spenser's Lost *Dreames*, and *The Faerie Queene*

TIMOTHY COOK

University of Ulster

The purpose of this article is to re-examine the remarks made by Gabriel Harvey on Spenser's lost *Dreames*[1] and to present new evidence which may have some bearing on their nature and their relationship to *The Faerie Queene*.

The question of the lost *Dreames* is, of course, fully discussed in Volume Eight of the Variorum Edition of Spenser.[2] Most commentators cited there are inclined to identify them with one or other of the sets of vision poems in the *Complaints*. However, two of the sets are translations, one of them from Petrarch, and in his comments Harvey specifically praises the *Dreames* for their 'invention', comparing them moreover with the very Petrarch work translated. We are left, then, with the only set which is entirely Spenser's own, the *Visions of the Worlds Vanitie*. That this work too cannot be identified with the *Dreames* seems clear from Spenser's own postscript to the first of his letters to Harvey: 'I take best my *Dreames* shoulde come forth alone being growen by means of the Glosse (running continually in the maner of a Paraphrase) full as great as my *Calendar*' (*Poetical Works*, p. 612). Simple mathematical calculations will show that the *Visions of the Worlds Vanitie* would require, to make up a volume the same size as the *Shepheardes Calender*, a commentary three or four times the length of the one in the earlier work.[3] Even E.K. would have found it difficult to expatiate on the *Visions of the Worlds Vanitie* at that length!

It seems we must look elsewhere for clues as to the nature of the *Dreames*, and Harvey's comments in particular deserve further investigation. As Spenserians will remember, he found that the *Dreames* savoured 'of that singular extraordinarie veine of invention which I have admired only in Lucian, Petrarch, Aretine, Pasquill and all the most delicate and fine conceited Greeks and Italians'. Nevertheless he still agrees with the divine who preferred 'St. John's Revelation before all the veriest Mætaphysicall visions and jollyest conceited Dreames or Extasies that ever were devised by one or other'.

Now Harvey's list of four names is, in this context, both intriguing and revealing. Of the writers mentioned all are associated with *extended* fantasy of some kind, varying from the satirical to the visionary-religious; Lucian takes us far away from

---

[1] The third of the *Three Proper and Wittie Familiar Letters* published by Bynneman (London, 1580). Reprinted in Spenser's *Poetical Works*, edited by J. C. Smith and E. de Selincourt (Oxford, 1970; reprint of 1912 edition), p. 628.

[2] *The Works of Edmund Spenser*, edited by E. Greenlaw and others, 11 vols (Baltimore, 1932 onwards). Hereafter referred to as *Variorum*. The most important articles cited are those of P. M. Buck in *PMLA*, 23 (1908), 80–99 and Helen E. Sandison in *PMLA*, 25 (1910), 134–51.

[3] My estimates of volume size are based on the Spenser Society facsimile of the 1579 edition of the *Shepheardes Calender*, with an introduction by H. O. Sommer (Manchester, 1890), and assume a similar format for the *Dreames*.

the real world, whether we are visiting his version of Hades, sitting in judgement on personified philosophies, or sharing his Edward Lear-like adventures in the *Vera Historia*; Petrarch expresses himself through extended visions in a vocabulary of the imagination of a very different kind in the *Trionfi*; Aretino, while using the device of the extended dream occasionally, as in his jocular 'Parnaso in Sogno' (*Lettere*, 1.281) is especially noted for yet another type of departure from reality in his *Ragionamenti*, where the exploits of his nuns, married women, and courtesans surely achieve the ultimate in his chosen field of invention.[1]

However, for our present purposes it is the fourth member of the quartet, Pasquill, whose presence in the list is most interesting. For it seems clear from the context that Harvey is not here using the name as it is generally used in one form or another as a term covering all the writers of pasquinades (of whom Aretino was of course himself one) since Cardinal Carafa in 1501 first instituted the practice of allowing satirical writings to be attached on a particular day of the year to a mutilated statue on the Campidoglio, but that he is referring to a specific borrower of the name, the Italian Protestant humanist Celio Secondo Curione, who in 1544 published in Basle a collection of pasquinades.[2] It was thanks to him that in the words of R. and F. Silenzi 'un altro Pasquino, per uno strano fenomeno di sdoppiamento veniva rapito di notte tempo dal piedestallo di Parione e, trascinato a Basilea, una delle roccaforti del protestantesimo, iniziava quasi subito una serie di dispute teologiche'.[3]

Among the satirical verses and other pieces in Latin, German, and Italian published in this anonymous volume are some polemical dialogues of Curione's own, including his *Pasquillus Ecstaticus*, and some of these, with additions, were brought out in a new volume under the author's name in the same year.[4] The subsequent popularity of the *Ecstaticus* is attested by its later translation into Italian by Curione's associate, Bernardino Ochino, as *Pasquino in Estasi*, into French as *Les Visions de Pasquille*, and into English as *Pasquine in a Traunce*.[5] If we consider the context of Harvey's mention of Pasquill, the form of the name as he gives it, and his use of the word 'Extasies' a little later on, it seems very likely that it is to this work, in one or other of its Latin editions, that he is implicitly referring. Likelihood becomes near certainty when we discover from two mentions of his name in the *Ciceronianus* that Harvey knew and admired Curione's work as a commentator on Cicero.[6] Moreover he definitely possessed a copy of Livy with emendations by Curione.[7] It would have been extraordinary if Harvey had not known of the other

---

[1] For Harvey's knowledge of the *Lettere* see E. M. Relle, 'Some New Marginalia and Poems of Gabriel Harvey', *RES*, New Series, 23 (1972), 401–16 (p. 414).

[2] *Pasquillorum Tomi Duo. Quorum primo versibus ac rhythmis, altero soluta oratione continentur . . .* (Eleutheropoli [Basle], 1544). Referred to hereafter as *Pasquillorum*.

[3] *Cinquecento Pasquinate*, edited, with an historical introduction, by R. and F. Silenzi (Milan, 1932), p. 40. See also, for the history of the pasquinade in the early Cinquecento, D. Gnoli, *Le Origini di Maestro Pasquino* (Rome, 1890).

[4] *Caelii Secundi Curionis Pasquillus Ecstaticus una cum aliis etiam pariter sanctis et lepidis dialogis* (Ioannes Oporinus, Basle, 1544?).

[5] *Pasquino in Estasi* (Rome, 1545?); *Les Visions de Pasquille. Le jugement d'iceluy ou Pasquille prisonnier* (no place of publication given, 1547); *Pasquine in a Traunce. A Christian and learned Dialogue contayning wonderful and most strange newes out of Heaven, Purgatorie and Hell . . .* Turned but lately out of the Italian into this tongue, by W. P. (Wylliam Seres) (London, 1566). A second edition of the English translation was published by Thomas East in 1584.

[6] *Ciceronianus*, edited by H. S. Wilson (Lincoln, Nebraska, 1945), pp. 90, 94.

[7] See Virginia F. Stern, 'Gabriel Harvey's Biblioteca', *Renaissance Quarterly*, 25 (1972), 1–62 (p. 38).

activities of a man famed throughout the Europe of his day for his championship of the Lutheran cause,[1] especially when we take into account Harvey's own admiration for Luther, amply demonstrated in his marginalia.[2]

So much for the probability of Curione's being the 'Pasquill' to whom Harvey refers. However, the trail does not stop there, for when we investigate further the English translation of the *Pasquillus Ecstaticus* we find that the translator, whose name is given on the title-page as W.P., is tentatively identified by Pollard and Redgrave with that William Phiston who in 1580 dedicated a translation of some sermons by Bernardino Ochino (himself, as we have seen, a translator and associate of Curione) to Archbishop Grindal.[3] If this identification is correct (and considering the nature of the other works translated by him the identification is not very doubtful) it seems at least possible that Spenser, who in 1579 was secretary to Bishop Young, Grindal's former chaplain and protégé and was probably in London for some months in 1580 before his first journey to Ireland,[4] knew Phiston as a fellow admirer of Grindal's and as an active translator of moral and religious works in Italian and French, and was aware of his work on this translation.

Since the *Pasquillus Ecstaticus* will be unfamiliar to most of the readers of this article, a summary of it may be helpful. It is in fact a prose dialogue between Pasquill (to use Harvey's form of the name) and his fellow statue Marforius in which the former describes a visionary experience he has just had. Impelled by doubts about the official Catholic version of the after-life, doubts inspired by his contemplation of the orderly processes of change in the world as controlled by God through nature, which he describes in a memorable passage (*Pasquillorum*, pp. 430 ff.) slightly reminiscent of the end of Spenser's *Mutabilitie Cantos*, he had decided to go and see Heaven for himself, and had first set about studying the techniques used by the friars for provoking visions. He gives an hilarious account of these (pp. 446-8) which owes a certain amount to Lucian's description of Menippus's preparations for his visit to Hades. After performing the appropriate rites he had attained a state of trance and was immediately visited by Hieruschatanael, the angel of true and sacred visions, who revealed that there were in fact two heavens; the Pope's and Christ's. The rest of the dialogue in the earlier version deals with Pasquill's tour of the first of these heavens, the false Papal one, and ends with his vision of the true one.

The descriptions of the heavens draw their imagery, as one would expect, largely from Revelation and Dante and are interspersed with long passages in which the two statues discuss points relevant to the vision, with Pasquill educating Marforius step by step in Protestantism. The chief target of Pasquill's argument is the Mary cult: the Catholic version of Mary is described three times; first towards the beginning where she is compared with heathen goddesses and unfavourably contrasted with the humble Mary 'ancilla Domini' of the Gospels, secondly when

---

[1] For evidence of Curione's contemporary importance see P. Tacchi Venturi, *Storia della Compagnia di Gesu in Italia*, 2 vols (Milan 1910–53), I, 441 and note. *Pasquine in a Traunce* was mentioned during the defence pleas of those implicated in the Marprelate affair; see Edward Arber, *Introductory Sketch to the Marprelate Controversy* (London, 1880), p. 97.

[2] See *Gabriel Harvey's Marginalia*, edited by G. C. Moore Smith (Stratford-upon-Avon, 1913), pp. 119, 121.

[3] See *Short Title Catalogue of Books Printed in England, 1475–1640* (London, 1969), entry 6130, and M. C. Scott, *Elizabethan Translations from the Italian* (Boston, 1916), pp. 257, 261.

[4] See I. Gollancz, 'Spenseriana', *Proceedings of the British Academy* (1907–8), 99–105.

she appears as the lofty enthroned queen at the heart of the Papal heaven, and finally where, towards the end, she is contrasted with Sponsa Christi, the Church, the true Bride of Christ as seen by Pasquill in a vision of the Holy City closely paralleling that of St John. However, many other topics are covered, notably the 'simplicitas' of the informed believer, defined as 'candor et synceritas [sic] animi' (as opposed both to the 'duplicitas' said by Pasquill to be characteristic of the hierarchy and to the ignorance of the laity),[1] the cult of virginity, the existence of Purgatory, and the adulation of the saints. The discussion is vigorous and often entertainingly irreverent as when Marforius comments on his friend's description of the angels flying in and out of the Papal heaven 'Tu ne mihi columbarium potius quam coelum depingis Pasquille?'.[2]

What may however be of more interest to Spenser scholars, in view of the suggestion made years ago by Josephine Bennett that Book I of *The Faerie Queene* may contain material originally in the *Dreames*,[3] is that, in this Revelation-based tract apparently linked by Harvey with that lost work, there are a number of passages that call the early part of Spenser's masterpiece to mind. For instance, Pasquill's description of the Papal heaven, though basically Dantesque, shares with the House of Pride such features as the high walls, the porter,[4] and the ruinous foundations, in addition to the enthroned queen (named in Curione 'Beata Virgo') mentioned above, thus providing us with an earlier example of the use of these mainly Court of Love details in an anti-Catholic work. Of the central palace, compared in its costliness with St Peter's, Rome, and in its 'fashion' to the Colosseum 'all covered over' and therefore 'exceeding darke', we are told that its 'Pillers were laden with little painted tables and with vows and with Golde and with Silver' while the queen who sat at its heart in a high seat was 'of a duskish colour' and had 'at her back the Sonne and at her feete the Moone'. The sun's beams, however, are not at liberty and cannot therefore 'lighten' the place because the sun itself is 'compassed about with a Payre of Beads' identified by Pasquill as the Rosary (*Pasquine in a Traunce*, fol. 66v. onwards).

The manner in which Curione here adapts to his anti-Catholic purpose St John's portrayal of the 'Woman clothed with the Sun' in Revelation XII is a good example of his 'invention', and it is easy to see why Harvey, if he came across an enthroned queen derived from Revelation and used for similar purposes in the *Dreames*, should be reminded of the *Pasquillus Ecstaticus*. Interestingly enough, though, the closest of Spenser's lofty ladies to this one is not Lucifera or Duessa in Book I but Philotime in Book II, in her room which was

> . . . large and wide,
> As it some Gyeld or solemne Temple weare:
> Many great golden pillours did vpbeare
> The massy roofe, and riches huge sustayne,

---

[1] *Pasquillorum*, p. 439. This discussion is actually part of the preamble to the vision.

[2] *Pasquillorum*, p. 454. I find it difficult to agree with the judgement of R. and F. Silenzi (*Cinquecento Pasquinate*, p. 52) that 'Pasquino, in funzione di propugnatore delle nuove idee, non riesce ad essere divertente'.

[3] See *The Evolution of The Faerie Queene* (Chicago, 1942), p. 123.

[4] Curione's porter, the 'orthodox' St Peter, is, however, distinctly unwelcoming to the sceptical Pasquill, and has, with his age and his rusty keys, more in common with Ignaro than with Malvenu. See *The Faerie Queene*, I. 8.30 onwards and *Pasquine in a Traunce*, fol. 74r., though I would not wish to make too much of these parallels.

And euery *pillour decked* was full deare
With crownes and Diademes, and titles vaine,

(II.7.43. The italics are mine)

a passage which looks as though it could be a modification by Spenser of Curione's ecclesiastical setting to serve the purposes of his own attack on secular vanities.

Pasquill goes on to describe the Rosary as 'that with the which the Paternosters or rather the Ave Maries are given by tale to God rather to the Devil, that which every foolish woman caryeth in her hande . . . that which is paynted alwayes in the hande of Ipocrisie'. It is only a short creative step from this to Corceca with her beads, her Paternosters, and her Aves and to Archimago strowing 'an *Aue-Mary* after and before.[1] Conventional though these descriptions may seem, Archimago is actually called 'Hypocrisie', Spenser's only use of the word, in the Argument to Book 1, Canto 1, shortly before that line about him occurs, while Corceca, as her name tells us, is Spiritual Blindness, the most damning form of foolishness.

However, it is in an earlier passage of the *Pasquillus Ecstaticus*, while Pasquill and his angelic guide are visiting the martyrs' region of the Papal heaven, that perhaps the most interesting possible link with Spenser may be found. Here two saints are singled out for special discussion.[2] The first is St Christopher, the fictitious Catholic version of whom Pasquill tells Marforius he saw as a 'monstrous giant' in that heaven. He also refers to the tree that he 'stays himself by' in church paintings. The conversation then turns to St George, and the angel explains to Pasquill the true significance of his legend, as follows (I give it in Curione's more elegant original Latin):

Dicebat hic, Cappadociam mundum significare, in quo passim magno illi draconi, id est diabolo servimus: quos ad unum usque deglutivit, ut nihil restituerit nisi illa unica regis filia quo nomine ecclesia Sponsa Christi in sacris denotatur. Quae cum & ipsa periclitarentur adfuisse Christum ceu strenuum militem qui, occisa dracone, filiam regis liveravit.' (*Pasquillorum*, p. 483)

Mrs Bennett, writing on Book 1 of *The Faerie Queene*, was uncertain where Spenser might have come across the identification of St George with Christ.[3] Here is a work by a Protestant writer, available in English since 1566, which may provide the answer. Furthermore, could not the fictitious St Christopher ridiculed earlier have given him the idea of setting against the representative of the True Faith that other 'monstrous giant', Orgoglio, whose 'stalking steps are stayde | Vpon a snaggy Oke' as a fitting champion of Catholicism?[4]

---

[1] *Faerie Queene*, 1.3.35 and 1.3.13. The *Variorum* Commentary does not, in fact, list sources or parallels for these characters.

[2] *Pasquine in a Traunce*, fol. 46v.

[3] *The Evolution of The Faerie Queene*, p. 110.

[4] See *Faerie Queene*, 1.7.8. and 1.7.10. Such verbal coincidences strengthen my belief that, while Harvey knew the *Pasquillus Ecstaticus* in its Latin version, Spenser was familiar with Phiston's translation. It is perhaps worth noting here that Phiston's introduction includes a description of the Pope as a pedlar reminiscent of the (Catholic) fox's disguise in *The Shepheardes Calender* ('Maye', ll. 238 onwards). For Orgoglio two major sources are generally acknowledged: the giant slain by King Arthur in Malory's *Morte d'Arthur*, Book v, Chapter 5, found in other Arthurian writers as well (see J. E. Hankins, *Source and Meaning in Spenser's Allegory* (Oxford, 1971), p. 126 and note) and the Classical Typhon (see, for example, S. R. K. Heninger Jr, 'The Orgoglio Episode in *The Faerie Queene*', ELH, 26 (1959), 171–87). However, the Arthurian giant wields a very ordinary club and the Classical Typhon of the classical sources is a hundred headed fire-breather, though other features of the myth undoubtedly influenced Spenser.

To conclude, it seems likely that Gabriel Harvey was indeed reminded by the lost *Dreames* of the *Pasquillus Ecstaticus*, a work which has interesting possible links with the early part of *The Faerie Queene*, not all attributable to their common source in Revelation. Is it not at least possible that Spenser not only knew Curione's tract but was prompted by it to use Revelation as the basis for a didactic fiction of his own attacking Catholicism? If that were the case, and if the earlier work did help to suggest the Red Cross Knight to him, then Curione's opposition of the 'Beata Virgo' of Mariolatry to Mary the lowly handmaid of the Lord and to the Church as Spouse of Christ, taken together with the discussion of 'simplicitas' and 'duplicitas' referred to above, may also have given him a starting point for his own Una-Duessa antithesis.[1] Finally, what Harvey read in the *Dreames*, the evidence here considered would suggest, could have been material from Book 1 in an earlier version, as Mrs Bennett thought, very probably in the form of an extended vision.

[1] Pasquill discusses the nature of the true, humble Mary at the beginning of the *Ecstaticus*, then shows us his false Mary enthroned, and finally contrasts her, this time with Sponsa Christi, in his Revelation-based vision of the Holy City and Christ's marriage. Spenser begins with Una on her lowly ass, goes on to show us the enthroned Duessa, and ends with Red Cross's marriage to Una, having previously shown us the Holy City without Christ's marriage, to avoid duplication. Hankins (pp. 99–119) gives an excellent account of the various allegorical interpretations of Duessa and the place of Revelation in Book 1.

Shakerley Marmion Dramatist: Declared an Outlaw in 1624?

ALLAN P. GREEN

Sea Girt, New Jersey

There is a notable gap in our knowledge of Marmion's career between, roughly, 1624 and 1629. On 11 July of the latter year, a criminal indictment was brought against him by the Middlesex Grand Jury, charging the dramatist-to-be with having assaulted one Edward Moore in 'the highway of St. Giles's-in-the-Fields co. Midd.' and having given him 'on the left part of his head a serious wound of which he has languished from the said 11th July to the day of the taking of this inquisition, to wit, 1 September' [1629].[1]

W. W. Greg, who examined the records of the case, which are preserved at the Guildhall Library, noted that Marmion apparently did not appear, thus forfeiting his bail, posted at forty pounds. The dramatist's father put up twenty pounds of the bail money and one Richard Browne a like amount. The Bill of 1 September 1629, Greg noted, is marked 'extra' in the margin, which he tells us means still at large.[2]

In the Middlesex indictment, Marmion is described as 'late of the said parish [that is, St Giles's] gentleman' and he may have been resident in that parish, a notoriously disreputable one, for some time. It need only be noted in passing that his three known plays reveal a considerable familiarity with the low life of the London suburbs. However, the point that I wish to make is that on the basis of new evidence, it is unlikely that the Middlesex criminal indictment was an isolated incident, for Marmion may already have been an outlaw as early as 1624.

A rapid summary of the few known facts about Marmion, barring those of birth and early education, will serve to prelude the new criminal charge. For these facts we are almost entirely dependent on Anthony à Wood, who informs us, in the augmented life of Marmion published in the second edition of the *Athenae Oxonienses* of 1721, that the dramatist became 'a Gent. Com. of *Wadham* Coll. [Oxford] in 1617'.[3] There is no record of his admittance at this date, but Wood's statement is in all likelihood based on the fact that Marmion's caution money was received on 28 April 1616.[4] Upon matriculation from Wadham College, he subscribed to the Thirty-Nine Articles on 16 February 1621, spelling his name 'Shakerly Marmion' in a graceful Italian hand.[5] His B.A. is dated 1 March 1622 and his M.A. 7 July 1624.[6] The editor of *The Registers of Wadham College*, R. B. Gardiner, tells us that

[1] *Middlesex County Records*, edited by J. C. Jeaffreson, Middlesex County Record Society, 4 vols (London, 1887–1902), III, 27.
[2] *The Soddered Citizen*, edited by J. H. P. Pafford, with an introduction by W. W. Greg, Malone Society Reprints (Oxford, 1936), p. xii.
[3] Anthony à Wood, *Athenae Oxonienses*, second edition, 2 vols (London, 1721), II, 626.
[4] *Registers of Wadham College, Oxford*, edited by R. B. Gardiner, 2 parts (London, 1889), Part I (1613–1719), p. 48.
[5] The signature is photographically reproduced in *The Soddered Citizen*, p. [xxxviii].
[6] *Registers of Wadham College*, I, 48.

Marmion occupied the Bottom Chamber under the Chaplain's from October 1622 until July 1624 and, as M.A., the Founder's Chamber until July of 1625.[1] Whether, in the light of the new criminal charge, he was in residence so late as July of 1625 may be questioned. It is known, however, that in order to provide accommodation for the Parliament that convened at Oxford in August 1625, the University dismissed its students before the end of July.

To date nothing is known of Marmion after his departure from Oxford, placed by Gardiner, as noted, in the summer of 1625, and the criminal charge of July 1629. Since fairly continuous records of play licensing and play and verse publication account for the period from December 1631, when *Holland's Leaguer* was performed by the Prince's Company at Salisbury Court (in the Prologue Marmion describes himself as one of the 'new poets' writing for this fledgling company), to 1638, when his tribute to Jonson, entitled 'A Funerall sacrifice, to the sacred memory of his thrice honoured Father BEN, IOHNSON' appeared in *Ionsonus Virbius*, the period of Marmion's soldiering in Holland may safely be dated between 1625 and 1629. In a recent contribution to *Notes & Queries*, I offered new evidence which established the exact dates of Sir Sigismund Ziszan's service in the United Provinces as from 16 February 1626 until 27 September 1626 and three and a half months, probably immediately following, in the service of the King of Denmark. If Wood is correct in his statement, first made in the second edition of the *Athenae Oxenienses*, that Marmion served in the Low Countries under Ziszan, then this gives us the exact dates of Marmion's foreign military service.

This chronology would place Marmion back in London at the beginning of 1627, or with perhaps a scant year or so to establish himself as one of the Sons of Ben, a distinction he clearly boasts of in his poem to Jonson, and to participate in those convivial gatherings at the Devil Tavern, presided over by Jonson, doubtless 'the boon Delphic god' alluded to by Careless in *A Fine Companion* (II.4).[2] A difficulty here is that it is not known exactly how incapacitating Jonson's stroke of 1628 was, although Herford and Simpson surmise that it confined him to his chamber for the rest of his life.[3] Of course, it is also possible that Marmion may have won Jonson's friendship before going overseas in February of 1626. Whatever the circumstances of his life in the blank years 1625 to 1626 after leaving Oxford, it is more than likely that he was leading a disreputable life in London.

A complete check of the indexes of the courts of Common Pleas, King's Bench, and Chancery for the entire period 1620 to 1639, has turned up the following Chancery case, dated 14 June 1624 and indexed 'Spencer Potts v. Shakerley Marmion': 'The sheriff has returned that the defendant is not to be found upon the Act [that is, for his production]. Therefore a Commission Rebel is directed to Richard Pangbourne, Edward Bethell, Richard Henning, Henry Picksley, Walter Robinson, and Edward Fryers to attach [that is, arrest] the defendant.'[4] It is unfortunate that nothing further can be found concerning this indictment, which

[1] *Registers of Wadham College, Oxford*, p. v.
[2] *The Dramatic Works of Shackerley Marmion*, edited by James Maidment and W. H. Logan (Edinburgh, 1874; reprinted by Benjamin Blom (New York, 1967)), p. 138.
[3] *Ben Jonson*, edited by C. H. Herford and P. Simpson, 11 vols (Oxford, 1925–52), I, 91–2, 213–14.
[4] Public Record Office, Index to Chancery Decrees and Orders, C33/145. There is no Bill or Answer in the Series C2 or C3.

shows the dramatist to have been declared a rebel some three weeks before the date of his Oxford M.A.

A difficulty peculiar to Marmion biography lies in the fact that both the dramatist and his father shared the same Christian name. Might the indictment just cited refer to Shakerley Marmion the elder? The available evidence suggests not. Every instance of the name Shakerley Marmion was, of course, noted in the indexes. It appears only four times during the period and three of these notices are clearly to the father. That the sheriff's report just given pertains to the son will become evident upon examination of the other cases.

We have seen that in the Middlesex assault case of 1629 the elder Shakerley provided half of the bail money for his son. To date, this is the last evidence of the father. In 1615 he had sold the manor of Aynho, Northamptonshire, to Sir Richard Cartwright in order to pay his debts and to purchase a lease of the Rectory Manor at Adderbury, in Oxfordshire.[1] Information concerning the elder Shakerley's marriage, tenancy of the manor of Aynho, and the trust agreement he was obliged to enter into in order to complete the sale of the manor to Cartwright and to provide for his wife and children, is to be found in the Aynho Estate Documents, which are preserved at the Northamptonshire Record Office, and need not concern us here.

Suffice it to say that by 1615 the father's economic fortunes were at a low ebb; however, he was able to send his elder son to Oxford. Of the dramatist's younger brother Richard it might be noted that there is no record of his attending either university. Richard was a London goldsmith by 1636 with a shop in West Cheap ward.[2] Whatever the economic condition of the family might have been, new evidence of the elder Shakerley from Common Pleas reveals him to have been living as late as 1638, or almost a decade after any previous notice of him. It is very likely, therefore, that the Shakerley Marmion buried at St Margaret's, Westminster in 1642 is the dramatist's father.[3] This also tends to support Wood's placing the dramatist's death in 1639, upon his return from the expedition against the Scottish Covenanters. The dramatist, Wood tells us, 'was obscurely buried in the Church of S. *Bartholm.* near *Smithfield* in *London*'.[4] The registers of both St Bartholomew-the-Great and St Bartholomew-the-Less are extant, but neither records the burial of a Shakerley Marmion. However, the dramatist's mother is very likely the 'Mary the wife of Shakerley Marmian' who was buried at St Bartholomew-the-Great in 1632.[5] If so, the dramatist's parents were buried apart, which may hint at some estrangement in life.

The new evidence, consisting of three cases from Common Pleas, shows the elder Shakerley to have been in economic difficulties later in life. The first is a case of 1626 and concerns the attempted recovery by one John Harman, Esq. of a debt of forty pounds owed to him by 'Shakerley Marmion lately of London gentleman alias Shakerley Marmion of Atterbury Oxon. gentleman'.[6] Though summoned

[1] *Victoria County History, Oxford*, edited by Mary D. Lobel and Alan Crossley, 10 vols, Volume 9 (Oxford, 1969), 16.
[2] *Inhabitants of London, 1638*, edited by T. C. Dale, 2 vols (London, 1931), II, 60.
[3] A. M. Burke, *Memorials of St Margaret's, Westminster* (London, 1914), p. 642.
[4] *Athenae Oxonienses*, II, 626.
[5] Guildhall Library MS 6777/1, p. 166, column 2.
[6] P.R.O., Common Pleas 40/2184, Trinity Term, 1626.

Shakerley did not appear and Harman was granted execution together with thirty-five shillings damages. In the second Common Pleas case 'Shackerley Marmion Esq and Anthony Wayneman gentleman' entered a plea to have payment of forty pounds which they said was owed to them and unjustly detained by one 'William Stevens lately of Dedington in Oxon. vintner'.[1] This loan was made on 14 February 1626 at Deddington, Oxfordshire, which suggests that Shakerley was probably still holding a lease of the Rectory Manor at Adderbury at that time. Shakerley and Wayneman said that they had suffered damages amounting to ten pounds by Stevens's refusal to pay them the forty pounds according to the terms of the bond, which was produced in court. Stevens's attorney, one James Chesterman, told the court that his master Stevens had given him no answer to this charge. The court determined that Stevens should pay the debt together with forty shillings damages.

The third Common Pleas case, dated Trinity Term 1638, reveals that 'Shakerley Marmyon of London Esquire alias Shakerley Marmion of Cliston [that is, Clifton] in Oxon'. was summoned by one Robert Russell to answer for payment of twenty-six pounds.[2] Russell said, through his attorney Henry Kemp, that 'Shakerley on 22 October 1624 in London in the parish of St. Mary le Bow Cheap Ward by a certain bill obligatory sealed with Shakerley's seal and produced in this court acknowledged that he owed Robert £13 14/- payable to Robert £5 14/- on the first day of Hillary term called Candelmass next after the date of the bill and £8 the residue on the first day in Easter term next following and Shakerley well and truly obliged himself to make this payment by the said bill of £26'. Shakerley appeared in the person of his attorney Thomas Jordan, who informed the court that he had received no answer from his master. The court adjudged that Russell should recover from Shakerley twenty-six pounds payable according to the terms of the bill as well as thirty shillings damages.

It is this last Common Pleas case that shows that the dramatist's father was living as late as 1638, when he was in his sixty-third year. More interestingly, it reveals that in October 1624 he was a resident of the parish of St Mary-le-Bow, Cheap Ward, the same ward in which his younger son Richard had a goldsmith's shop *circa* 1636. Now the dramatist, it will be recalled from the Chancery case noted earlier, was an outlaw in June of 1624, or but four months before the above notice of Shakerley Marmion of London and Clifton, Oxfordshire. Can it be doubted that the sheriff's report refers to anyone other than the dramatist? The evidence is all but conclusive: it seems highly probable that in June of 1624, Marmion, with a commission rebel issued for his arrest, was hiding in the obscurity of those suburban lanes and alleys he alludes to so frequently and knowledgeably in his plays.

In view of this new criminal indictment of 1624, which throws an ominous light on Marmion's life during the obscure years following his departure from Oxford, and before his going overseas to serve under Ziszan in February 1627, what are we to make of the motives of Wood's informant, the unidentified Mr Charles Wilkinson, to whom in 1691 Wood wrote in search of new information about the dramatist?[3] That informant, it may be surmised, was intent on giving only those facts which might redound to the family's credit and he is the likely source of the intelligence

---

[1] P.R.O., Common Pleas 40/2215, Hilary Term, 1628.
[2] P.R.O., Common Pleas 40/2421, Trinity Term, 1638.
[3] *The Life and Times of Anthony Wood*, edited by Andrew Clark, 5 vols (Oxford, 1891-5), III, 349.

that in former times the Marmions had held the coronation service of King's Champion and that the dramatist had been a valued friend of Sir John Suckling. The Royalist implications of these additions to the life of the dramatist would doubtless have appealed to the vanity of the Marmion family, as they would have to Wood; moreover, it is hard to believe that Wood's informant would have been ignorant of the facts of a criminal nature bearing on the dramatist that have come to light since Wood wrote. Those facts tend to confirm the persistent, if vague, idea of the scapegrace heir with no certain direction, who alternated between the Muses and Mars.

Absalom and Achitophel: a Patron's Name or a Patriot's?

HANNAH BUCHAN

University of Glasgow

In *Milton and the Miltonic Dryden* Mrs Anne Ferry has demonstrated the value of a study of Dryden's adaptations of Miltonic language. Such adaptations, she tells us, 'in ironic parodies, serious imitations, and allusive comparisons, by calling the reader's attention to parallels between the satire and *Paradise Lost*, create a context in which *Absalom amd Achitophel* may be richly understood' (p. 41). One passage in the later poem where a closer study of allusive comparison may add to the richness of our understanding occurs at lines 179–91. These have been something of a textual crux, which it may be possible to clear up by showing the differing relevance of the textual variants to the whole context provided by *Paradise Lost*. Apart from the textual question, the variants are interesting in their own right, in their contribution to meaning. It also may not be too much to say that in them we see the process of adaptation actually taking place.

The accepted reading of line 179, in the description of Achitophel, who 'Usurp'd a Patriott's All-attoning Name' was not settled until the second edition, when the line was not only revised in itself, but had added to it a new passage twelve lines long:

> So easie still it proves in Factious Times,
> With publick Zeal to cancel private Crimes:
> How safe is Treason, and how sacred ill,
> Where none can sin against the Peoples Will:
> Where Crouds can wink; and no offence be known,
> Since in anothers guilt they find their own.
> Yet, Fame deserv'd, no Enemy can grudge;
> The Statesman we abhor, but praise the Judge.
> In *Israels* Courts ne'r sat an *Abbethdin*
> With more discerning Eyes, or Hands more clean:
> Unbrib'd, unsought, the Wretched to redress;
> Swift of Dispatch, and easie of Access.

The addition of this passage may be one sign of Dryden's attempt to clarify or reinforce the implications of line 179, and the variant readings of the line itself may point to hesitations as to the choice of language which would best embody such implications and allow of such expansion. Certainly the history of this line has been thought difficult. Noyes expressed his wonder how Dryden could have supposed the first form of the line (which reads 'Patron's' as against 'Patriott's') to make sense, how a patron's name could be *All-attoning*. He also felt that the omission of the additional passage 'occasions an abrupt and awkward transition' (to ll. 192–3: 'O, had he been content to serve the Crown | With vertues only proper to the Gown'). Swedenborg is interested in Noyes's suggestion that the twelve lines were in Dryden's original manuscript and then omitted to deepen the satire on Shaftesbury. He speculates on how Dryden might have come to change the copy (possibly the king objected to the passage) and how it could have been changed while in the hands of the printer. But the answer to both of Noyes's difficulties could be much less speculative and a good deal simpler if we notice the Miltonic resonance that several of the words in line 179 as originally printed had for Dryden.

In all issues of the first edition the first word of line 179 was 'Assum'd'. The alteration to 'Usurp'd', as Professor Kinsley has said, is to a stronger word, and clearly it suggests more sharply that it is a king's authority which is Achitopel's true objective, an authority to which he has no right. But in making the change Dryden was making a choice, and in fact we seem to see him in the act of choosing between two Miltonic words and choosing with a particular reference in mind. Both words occur frequently in *Paradise Lost*, as one might imagine, and separately. But they occur together in the reference to Nimrod in Book xII, lines 65–6, where he tries to introduce tyranny, 'assuming | Authority usurpt, from God not giv'n'. Dryden comes down in the end in favour of 'Usurp'd'. Yet however well 'Usurp'd' suits Achitophel in general, the object of the verb, 'A Patriott's Name', in the line as it stands, is not anything specifically associated with kings. But 'a Patron's Name', the reading of the first issue of the first edition, could be. In Marlowe's *Edward II*, for example, Isabella reproaches the king for his neglect of duty with the words 'Patron shouldest thou be —' (Act IV, Scene 2). Yet one can see too the attractions of 'Assum'd', for in Achitophel's case, as in Nimrod's, it can bear the straightforward sense it has of 'taking something upon oneself', but also its sense of 'simulating', 'assuming a false role'. This hypocrisy of Achitophel's is not quite implied by 'usurp'd' and is the feature dwelt on in the first half of the added passage, as if the point needed to be made more explicitly.

In the first issue of the first edition, then, the name is a patron's. The issue has some clear misprints ('cuold' for 'could', 'Kold' for 'Bold', 'Kody' for 'Body') and in the second issue these obvious errors are corrected. But 'Patron's' has also been altered, to 'Patriott's', as if it too were an error. In the third issue 'could', 'Bold', and 'Body' are correctly printed. 'Patron's' reappears. In issue four, we are back again to 'Patriott's'. Throughout the history of these issues it has been assumed by Macdonald, in his bibliography of Dryden, and by Dryden's editors, Noyes (with some doubt) and Kinsley, that 'Patriott's' is the true, original reading, and thus that in the third issue, though all the clear misprints have been corrected, 'Patron's' does not also represent a correction, back to an original reading, but the return of an original error, from issue one. Swedenborg thinks Dryden has been undecided. This seems the more likely case, that the third issue does represent Dryden's original intention, though he may eventually, as in the case of the first word in the line, 'Assum'd', have chosen to alter it. He could have done this for much the same reason as in that case, that the sense of his original word was finally elaborated in the additional passage, in the second half, as the second sense of 'Assum'd' had been in the first. So he had less need of 'patron'.

The full couplet with its variants reads 'Then seiz'd with Fear, yet still affecting Fame, | Usurp'd [Assum'd] a Patriott's [Patron's] All-attoning Name'. The first line has Miltonic echoes of a not particularly interesting kind, with little resonance. Words are simply taken from Milton and undergo little transformation in their new context. As Achitophel momentarily feared he had gone too far, so amazement 'seiz'd' the rebel angels to see Satan recoil from Abdiel's stroke (vi.198) and again when the angels of God plucked up mountains to overwhelm them (vi.647). On the first day of battle when they were 'with pale fear surpris'd, | Then first with fear surpris'd' (VI.393–4) Satan encouraged them with prospects not merely of liberty, 'but what we more affect, | Honour, Dominion, Glory and renown' (VI.421–2). The next line however is more interesting. If we do not assume that 'Patron's' is a simple misprint, but that there has been a hesitation between it and 'Patriott's', 'Patron's' then becomes a verbal echo of Milton of a resonant kind. The additional passage tells us that Achitophel fulfilled his role of Lord Chancellor, the presiding judge in the court of Chancery, admirably, 'Unbribed' unsought, the Wretched to redress'. In other words he was a true 'patron', in the now obsolete sense of a defender or protector of someone in a court of law. What praise is given him in the additional passage is whole-heartedly warm and generous. The regret, too, that the passage expresses is whole-hearted in tone, suggesting the pity of it, as there is pity in Satan's case, in that Satan and Achitophel both have great gifts which rightly used could have made them a power for good. Achitophel could have been a true patron to the whole community, not simply to the wretched in court. Instead, in the world of politics, he may be justly accused of being a false patron or champion, in a wider sense, the sense in which Gabriel accuses Satan of being a 'sly hypocrite, who now wouldst seem | Patron of Liberty' (IV.957–8). To take the word from this context in Milton partly removes the difficulty which Noyes felt of understanding how a patron's name could be all-attoning. To set up as a champion of public liberty, 'public reason just', as Satan put it, might as easily atone for a multitude of sins, 'With publick Zeal to cancel private Crimes', as setting up for a patriot. Moreover, if we recall *Paradise Lost* once more, Milton tells us that no 'Patron or Intercessor' appeared in Heaven on man's behalf until Christ offered himself (III.219). 'Patron' is here clearly being used in the sense of a legal protector or defender, and Milton goes on to tell us (III.234) that man himself was unable to bring any 'Atonement'. Therefore Christ offered himself. Here clearly is the source of what puzzled Noyes, the association of a patron with atonement. The seventeenth century took a legalistic view of the atonement. The word itself occurs only four times in Milton's work and only once in his poetry, here, where atonement is pre-eminently what distinguishes man's patron or intercessor. The word 'usurp'd' now is also seen to become more fully appropriate to 'patron'. Man's champion was Christ the King. In *Absalom and Achitophel* the community's true defender is the King David, and Achitophel not only assumes but usurps the authority of the regal, and legal, defender of the realm. At the same time it should be said that leaders of faction often professed to be patriots, uniting a disunited country, and the original meaning of 'atone' was to make at one or unite. If we bear this in mind the heterogeneity of the mob which Achitophel heads makes any such claim ludicrous.

Patron or patriot, either name can be given to Achitophel now only in irony and this is so much so that Dryden might well hesitate between them. The sins for which, masquerading as patron of liberty, Achitophel makes atonement are his own, chiefly the exploitation of the people and the rebellion against true authority (though the people also sin) for his own ends, and the atonement he makes is a false one, a blanket cover for these sins. He makes up for them by pretending to champion the people. But he is no true intercessor or reconciler. The first reading, 'Patron's', makes these implications clear, if we have *Paradise Lost* in mind, as does the additional passage. What the use of the phrase 'Patron's All-attoning name' rather than 'Patriott's All-attoning name' also makes as clear, by implication from the *Paradise Lost* situation, as the additional passage does, is that, had he been willing to fulfil faithfully those duties to the community required of him by his gifts and his place, he could have played a role nearer to that of Christ than Satan, under the God-like king, as well in his policital life as in the law courts. One of the subtleties of Dryden's use of *Paradise Lost* is that his characters slide imperceptibly in and out of Miltonic roles; the king, for example, being now God, now Christ; Absalom being now Adam, now a false Christ and now, most destructively of all, an Eve. This last implication is the hardest blow which Absalom in his pride could be dealt.

If we allow that 'Patron's' may not be a misprint but the correct original meaning the question arises why, there having been a hesitation between the two words, 'Patriott's' was the final choice. Possibly 'Patron' in the sense of 'legal defender' or 'champion' was already becoming obsolete, superseded by the modern sense of 'supporter or encourager of projects, especially artistic ones'. This sense was of course prominent in Dryden's day and patrons were important people. Barzillai who contrasts in the poem with Achitophel is a patron in this sense as well as a true patron or defender of liberty, though the word itself is not used of him. Then, too, 'patriot' at this time was associated with faction, as we see in the first line of the additional passage or in line 973. It frequently had ironic overtones, as in the king's crisp gloss on its 'modern sense': 'One that would by law supplant his Prince' (l. 966). Or there is his impatient 'Never was Patriot yet, but was a Fool' (l. 968); 'Patriot' is becoming disreputable. Instead of keeping a word of subtle meaning, but by now perhaps liable to puzzling misinterpretation, Dryden may eventually have chosen, or even allowed to creep in, a simpler one, with suitably derogatory and ironic suggestions, while making the sense of his original word 'Patron's' (like the full meaning of his original word 'Assum'd') explicit, without irony, in the body of the additional passage. Having settled for 'patriot' and so lost the kingly associations of 'patron' as 'defender of his people', he may then have transferred them to the verb, changing 'Assum'd' to 'Usurp'd'. This might indicate that the third issue of the first edition prints the line in its original form correctly in all respects, but that the reading we accept today was his final choice. It might also suggest that the additional passage was not, as Noyes conjectured it might have been, in Dryden's original text, and then omitted to deepen the satire on Shaftesbury. As for the abrupt and awkward transition which he felt its absence occasioned, if we look at 'Patron's' in the legal senses and in the contexts suggested, then a transition from it to the couplet immediately following the passage ('Oh, had he been content to serve the Crown, | With Vertues onely proper to the Gown', ll. 201–2), is completely natural, much more so than if the original word had been 'Patriott's', for patriots have no connexion with gowns or law-courts. It looks therefore all but certain that 'Patron's' was an original reading, later altered, and the twelve lines an addition to the original poem, when Dryden was debating the choice of 'Patron's' or 'Patriott's'.

But the hesitation over the choice, if we agree with Swedenborg that that is what it is, makes line 179 a tiny instance of Dryden's minute knowledge of *Paradise Lost*, and, with the additional passage, of his subtle and thoughtful use of it. We seem to catch him in the very act of exploring his Miltonic language and the opportunities that it here offers him. Reluctant to lose a meaning, anxious to include all choices, he extends simultaneously his own and our richness of understanding. One asks oneself how many of his readers had his kind of knowledge and could appreciate the full profundities it gave to *Absalom and Achitophel*. Perhaps only a handful. A less detailed knowledge could make Dryden's general points, though it is strange that Dr Johnson, a scholar and editor, who was near enough to Dryden's time to have heard of the great run on the poem when it first appeared, never mentions its connexions with *Paradise Lost*. The biblical allegory may well have obscured what would still be the less well known one. For a full appreciation of that, Dryden may have relied only on a small number of close and discerning readers of Milton. But one point he must have hoped to make clear through his Miltonic adaptations. Any reader of Milton must appreciate his reverence for law. It is of course God's law and not man's or the king's that he venerates. Dryden can be more adroit than scrupulous in drawing his parallels with the characters and themes from *Paradise Lost* and he does not make these distinctions. One of his chief purposes is to uphold the king in his insistence, made explicit in his closing speech, on the necessity of law and obedience to law. This has throughout been one of the controlling themes of the poem, and it is provided by the adaptation of *Paradise Lost*. The additional passage is nicely integrated into this main theme. It does not simply enumerate a man's bad points and offset them with what can be said in his favour. It is far more precise and apposite than that. The impression is given of a balanced judgement, passed on a man who is both politician and judge. When he administers the law he is fair to all men. So law is not a matter only of political issues, for men in the public eye. It is shown in operation, in the courts of the land, where in the hands of the good judge it can protect the rights even of the poorest, even in a country seemingly bent on making money, as is, ironically and sadly, this particular judge himself in his private capacity. It might well have occurred to Dryden to make more of this, through the extended portrait of Achitophel the patron or judge, than could be made by the simple word 'patron' alone, especially as in one role he did not assume or usurp the title but had a true claim to it, while his claim to be a patriot was completely false. So Dryden chooses 'patriott's'. What Achitophel the judge upholds, divine indifferent law, Achitophel the politician would destroy, and later of course we see the politician using what is clearly a gift for forensic eloquence to pervert Absalom, an almost pitiably less intelligent man, to whom his father the king properly both is and is not indifferent.

'The Entire Works of Clarinda': Unpublished Juvenile Verse by Lady Mary Wortley Montagu

ISOBEL GRUNDY

Queen Mary College, London

The common reader feels a strong interest in the earliest literary attempts of future writers, leading to varying degrees of regret for Pope's *Alcander*, Fanny Burney's 'Elegies, Odes, Plays, Songs, Stories, Farces, — nay, Tragedies and Epic Poems' burned on her fifteenth birthday, and those love-letters composed for ladies by the thirteen-year-old Samuel Richardson.[1] Where very early efforts survive, they may throw light not so much on the budding of literary identity, for the earlier and later style may differ widely, but on early influences, the grown writer's point of departure. Pope's Horatian 'Ode on Solitude', written at the age of twelve though revised later, is more like Cowley's translations than like his own later imitations of Horace.[2]

Lady Mary Pierrepont, born the year after Pope, lived to make her slighter mark beside his in the world of Augustan letters as Lady Mary Wortley Montagu. To the end of her life she kept two albums of her work composed between the ages of twelve and sixteen, during the period 1701–5.[3] They tell a remarkable story about the far from Augustan patterns of poetry available at this time to an ambitious girl.

This period, infertile in poetry, has been called 'the desert of early eighteenth-century verse'.[4] Dryden had died in 1700; the *Miscellany* connected with his name continued sporadically until its introduction of Pope to the public in 1709. Lady Mary might be regarded as lucky in that the list of poets publishing during this decade (Halifax, Garth, Prior, Granville, Congreve, Addison) coincided closely with that of the circle of friends of her father, the Earl of Kingston, as well as that of the first readers of Pope's pastorals in manuscript.[5] The child Lady Mary must have admired these men. She appealed to Congreve for help with her scholarly studies, later recalling that 'the smallest error could not 'scape his sight'.[6] She composed verse compliments to Halifax and Garth on poems of theirs. Her father, a younger brother of Oldham's patron and himself an early reader of Pope, had introduced his daughter at the age of eight as a toast of the Kit-Cat Club.[7]

---

[1] Joyce Hemlow, *The History of Fanny Burney* (Oxford, 1958), p. 1; Richardson, *Selected Letters*, edited by J. Carroll (Oxford, 1964), p. 231.

[2] *The Twickenham Edition of the Poems of Alexander Pope*, edited by John Butt, 11 vols (London 1939–69), VI, 3–4; cited hereafter as *Twickenham*.

[3] Now Volumes 250 and 251, Harrowby Manuscripts Trust, Sandon Hall, Stafford, used by kind permission of Lord Harrowby, and hereafter referred to as H MS 250 and 251. (Folio numbers in H MS 250 are editorial.) The contents are discussed by Robert Halsband in his *Life of Lady Mary Wortley Montagu* (Oxford, 1956), pp. 5–7.

[4] Elizabeth Handasyde, *Granville the Polite* (Oxford, 1933), p. 125.

[5] George Sherburn, *The Early Career of Alexander Pope* (Oxford, 1956), pp. 52–3.

[6] Joseph Spence, *Observations, Anecdotes, and Characters of Books and Men . . .*, edited by J. M. Osborn, 2 vols (Oxford, 1966), I, 304; Lady Mary, 'To the Memory of Mr. Congreve', *Essays and Poems and 'Simplicity', a Comedy*, edited by R. Halsband and I. Grundy (Oxford, 1977), p. 246.

[7] *Essays and Poems*, p. 9.

The petting of the wits remained a treasured memory, but it is unlikely that Lady Mary dared to approach any of them as literary mentors. Her father 'did not think himselfe oblig'd to be very attentive to his children's Education'. A story that she shared lessons from her brother's tutors was probably, her grand-daughter thought, unfounded.[1] An aura of secrecy and even furtiveness hangs about her adolescent devotion to 'poetry my dear my darling choice' (making her pray 'Uncensured let mee Numbers write'), as about her Latin studies of 'five or six hours a day . . . whilst everybody else thought I was reading nothing but novels and romances'.[2] Perhaps she, or her father, knew Locke's dictum that any 'Poetick Vein' in children should be 'stifled, and suppressed, as much as may be' by their parents.[3]

Though not suppressed, her poetic vein found no encouragement or mature criticism. Boys at school had their Latin and English verses worked over by demanding masters; Pope received from Sir William Trumbull 'guidance through something like a decade [which] might well have replaced the formal training of the university', and revised his manuscript pastorals 'upon ye Objections' of 'an astonishing list' of connoisseurs of poetry.[4] Lady Mary began and ended her poetic career as a careless writer who revised haphazardly. According to her grand-daughter 'she had the gift of writing freely in the first words that presented themselves',[5] a gift less valuable for poetry than for letters and for her now vanished journal. Pope knew well that 'no one qualification is so likely to make a good writer, as the power of rejecting his own thoughts; and it must be this (if any thing) that can give . . . a chance to be one'.[6] Lady Mary was of course socially a successor to those gentlemen who would sooner not have written at all than written with labour. Nevertheless one may regret her lack, before she met and collaborated with Pope and Gay, of somebody to inculcate the habit of polishing. It is harder to regret the interestingly old-fashioned tone of her early poems.

The first of her two juvenile collections, a folio bound in contemporary vellum (H MS 250), is entitled 'Poems Novells Letters Songs etc. Dedicated to the Fair Hands of the Beauteous Hermensilda by her Most Obedient Strephon'. In smaller script, perhaps at a later date, Lady Mary added 'made at the age of 14. Anno Domini, 1704'. The volume contains an epistolary prose romance, fifteen neatly copied poems, three more which are so blotted, torn, or scribbled over as to be more or less illegible,[7] twenty stubs where pages have been cut out, and four leaves bearing lists of characters from French and English plays and romances, recorded probably for the sake of their high-sounding names, some of which Lady Mary, or 'Strephon', borrowed. The poems have mostly been given titles, if only 'Poem'. The margins of the excised pages suggest that some contained prose, some probably verse, and the last more lists.

Another list, from the outer vellum cover, may serve as sample: 'Melecinda, F. Pierrepont, Silvianetta, Clarinda, Florice, Arpasia, Orinda, Hermensilde,

---

[1] *Essays and Poems*, pp. 9, 77; *The Complete Letters of Lady Mary Wortley Montague*, edited by Robert Halsband, 3 vols (Oxford, 1965-7), III, 25-6.
[2] H MS 250, ff. 5, 13; Spence, I, 303.
[3] *Some Thoughts Concerning Education* (London, 1693), p. 207.
[4] Sherburn, pp. 42, 52-3.
[5] *Essays and Poems*, pp. 21-2.
[6] Preface to his *Works*, 1717; *Twickenham*, I, 8.
[7] An inoffensive poem entitled 'The Country' (f. 15) is obliterated with scribbling; the words written over appear to include 'folle, sotte je suis', 'I Write soe very silly' and 'A Foole'.

Leonora, Belvidera, Emillia, Aminta, Lucinda, Artemisa.' The odd one out is Lady Mary's sister Frances, later Countess of Mar. The romance names may have been used for friends; Lady Mary took 'Clarinda' as her *nom de plume* in her next album. The real name of another person, her early companion Sarah Chiswell,[1] occurs separately on this cover. Lady Mary is less likely to have been addressing the poet Katherine Philips (1631–64) than some other person called after her, when she praised 'Orinda' as a contemporary in terms resembling those of Katherine Philips's own verse (H MS 251, f. 25), offering 'Pure and uninterrested' friendship and the homage of a 'Virgin muse', in contrast with the selfish 'dross attends on vulgar Loves'. In using the name 'Ardelia' she apparently intended no reference to the future Lady Winchilsea (1661–1720), whose poems she later owned in print and manuscript copies. She linked 'Belvidera' with a real place, the River Severn, and gave the name 'Hermensilde', variously spelt and taken probably from La Calprenède's romance *Herménégilde* (1643), to an actual girl named Jane Smith.[2] Other jottings on the cover include 'Thoresby [country seat of her father] October the 19th 1705' and drawings of spades, hearts, etc., which accord better with the court world of her later eclogues than with the pastoral one of her juvenilia.

This album, incomplete as it is, tells a good deal about Lady Mary's attitude to her writing. She assumes for her whole literary enterprise the role of the pastoral poet Strephon, and some poems are written as if by him. But the fourteen-year-old scribbling girl now and then peers out from behind her mask: in the lists and jottings, certain poems, and the 'Preface' on the verso of Strephon's title-page. This reads:

I Question not but here is very manny faults but if any reasonable Person considers 3 thing[s] they wou'd forgive them,
   1 I am a Woman
   2 without any advantage of Education
   3 all these was writ at the age of 14.[3]

Though she lacked education and called herself 'A Virgin muse untaught by rules of art', she did not lack literary models. She retells a story from Ovid, claims she has 'Paraphras'd' (very loosely indeed) the first idyll of Moschus, and praises Lord Halifax for *his* praise of the charms of Lady Sunderland (ff. 1–4). These poems reflect the glamour of the barely glimpsed worlds of antiquity and of contemporary high society. Most of the other poems sing the praises of country retirement, of which Lady Mary did have experience (ff. 13, 15–17). She treats this theme in various ways: lyrical first-person outbursts beginning 'Give mee my God, some close obscure retreat' or 'Here I all calm, without a wish I sit'; generalized meditations:

> Happy and only Happy hee
> Who from toiling Business Free,
> From Lawsuits and from Love
> Can to A Country Seat remove;

---

[1] *Letters*, I, 114, n.4; II, 67.
[2] A generation later, around 1733, Lady Mary's daughter, the future Countess of Bute, filled an album with verses in which her relatives and friends figure as 'Melantha', 'Evadne', 'Timandra', etc. (Wharncliffe MS 506, Sheffield Central Library). Lady Bute also made the only known copy of a poem from her mother's juvenile albums (Portland MS xx.1, Longleat).
[3] In all quotations from MS I have followed Lady Mary's spelling, made a very few alterations to her punctuation and capitalization (inserting capitals at the beginning of lines, for instance), expanded ampersands and lowered raised letters.

and narratives of how 'I' or Strephon or Belvidera retreated from town to country and was thankful.

Lady Mary may not have held these sentiments in real life, though she was born into the country house milieu celebrated by seventeenth-century poets. She must have written most of these poems at Thoresby, a magnificent mansion in the Dukeries, built about 1683, with a lake ('murmuring streams' are joined in the poems with 'silver floods') and a long-established park on the edge of Sherwood Forest (one poem talks of 'Trees my only Confidantes . . . Aged Monarchs of the Groves'; two others mention 'this Lovely silent wood'). Her verse, however, paints a selective picture. Perpetual spring reigns until she suddenly looks at nature with an unideal eye, when it gives way to cold and floods. Her grandiose Thoresby surroundings do not prevent her from writing

> No Gaudy sights I see, no Palaces
> But Humble shrubs[1] and Cottages,
> The Seats of Virtue and of Happiness.

She apparently recalled one of these poems, 'My Wish', in Constantinople in 1718, when she wrote her best example of this genre, into which she allowed no hint of her occasional boredom with her rural sanctuary to intrude.[2] At Constantinople she contrasted her meditative self with the vizier and his noisy train; here she often brings in the unhappy rich and great as foil for the happy poet or lover. At twenty-one she was to wish romantically to be a farmer's daughter;[3] most of her juvenile verse mentions only to deplore the conditions of town life: 'the Toils of State', drudgery, ambition, and corruption naïvely symbolized by 'Costly Viands', 'dear Ragou's', and 'Fricacees'.

Despite their touches of personal experience, these poems are as essentially literary as the imitations of Moschus and Ovid, presided over by Horace or his many English disciples. 'The influence of Horace is apt to be subtle and indefinite . . . In the writings of the preceding century, he had already been so frequently put to use that many of his teachings were handed on to the eighteenth century as traditions of English literature, rather than as something distinctively Horatian.'[4] Lady Mary's husband, Edward Wortley Montagu, was to expound Virgil and Horace to her, and in 1717 she was said to know them both by heart. She would have shared Wortley's opinion that Cowley 'excell'd all of his own time in learning as well as wit', as well as that of a modern critic who finds him 'in temper . . . supremely Horatian'.[5] She took his Pindaric Odes as model for her irregular verses 'To Truth' (an early poem surviving not in the albums but in copies revised in later years).[6] As an adult she wrote correct couplets or regular stanzas; as a girl she freely followed Cowley in introducing irregularly longer or shorter lines.

---

[1] Compare Cowley's 'plebeian underwood' ('Of Solitude', *The English Writings of Abraham Cowley*, edited by A. R. Waller, 2 vols (Cambridge, 1905–6), II, 395). Lady Mary's title 'My Wish' derives from his 'The Wish'.

[2] *Essays and Poems*, pp. 206, 209; *Letters*, I, 366.

[3] *Letters*, I, 61.

[4] Caroline Goad, *Horace in the English Literature of the Eighteenth Century* (New Haven, 1918), p. 5.

[5] *Letters*, I, 9, 268, n. 1; Douglas Bush, *English Literature in the Earlier Seventeenth Century* (Oxford, second edition, 1962), p. 165.

[6] *Essays and Poems*, p. 178.

The rural poems include some of her weakest: landscape is never particularized beyond murmuring groves and verdant meads; she cannot compete with the nightingale as 'artless Soneteir'. But in one of the group, 'Bagatelle',[1] choice of simple and restraining form has produced a success:

> By the silver Severn's Flood
> Near a lofty, verdant wood
> The beauteous Belvidera stood.
>
> She saw the beauties of the spring,
> She heard the Little Linnets sing,
> She heard the River's murmuring.
>
> She saw the Flowers all gay and Fair,
> The Zephyrs softly mov'd her hair
> And Fan'd her with a gentle Air.
>
> She saw the sporting Lambs did play,
> She saw the Meads all fresh and gay,
> She saw the beauties of the blooming May.
>
> She saw — what she had never seen before,
> Seeing these charms she smiled and swore
> She'd never see th'inconstant Town no more.

Connected with the rural poems are two of more explicitly religious moralizing, again in the seventeenth-century manner, which contrast 'triffleing Transitory Things' with the world beyond death (H MS 250, ff. 13–15; 251, ff. 14–15). The young girl quotes from St Matthew's gospel about moths and rust (6.19–20), vividly expresses fear of judgement, names Milton, Cowley, and Waller as poets who will lose their tribute of reverence beyond the grave, and tries her hand as a preacher: 'Speak, Usurer, what will thy Bags Avail'. She can define the future state only by negatives:

> There is no Lamentations heard
> Of Kings Depos'd, or Armies fear'd,
> No freind betray'd complains,
> Etternall silence all around remains.

Lady Mary conjures the awesomeness of death with some skill:

> What's death, that at the name Wee are Dismay'd,
> Why shrinks my soul, and why am I affraid?
> Trembling wee stand, and when wee plunge wee fear,
> And goe to unknown worlds wee know not where,
> Amazing thought, yet thither I must goe,
> There is the Period — Period — No!
> There's Strange, Dark, unknown worlds below.

This foreshadows a poem she wrote in 1736 on the fear and fascination of death, beginning 'With toilsome steps I pass through Life's dull Road'.[2] In the mature poem she echoes Dryden to poignant effect; here his influence has caused the passage quoted to end in the inanity of 'There is what no man knows, and all men fear, |

---

[1] H MS 250, f. 17; 251, f. 15. *OED*'s first use of this word to denote 'a piece of verse or music in light style' (in its example 'amatory and pastoral') dates from 1827.
[2] *Essays and Poems*, pp. 290–91.

There is I know not what, I know not where'.[1] The next section opens with equally unfortunate briskness: 'Well, all must Dye and t'is in Vain | To spend my life in Cries and fruitlessly Complain.' She can already strike the required pose, but she cannot hold it.

An entirely different style characterizes two poems (H MS 250, ff. 2–3) which Lady Mary later incorporated at key points in a long verse and prose romance, 'The Adventurer'. As separate pieces she entitled them 'Invitation' and 'Recanting'. The first, on a page torn so that less than half of the poem remains, opens 'Come all you Lovers, hither [fly]'; in its revised setting it becomes an inscription 'in Azure' on the altar in the temple of Love. The second is a lover's speech rejecting his perjured mistress, which echoes another famous passage from Dryden ('How I lov'd, | Witness ye Dayes and Nights, and all your hours')[2] and employs a stylized Renaissance eroticism ('No more your Breasts like Snowy Hills appear').

Since these two poems mix 'Love and wit' and one of them is defaced, they (if not other pieces more thoroughly defaced or cut out) may hold the explanation of the circumstances behind two poems which renounce poetry. In these Lady Mary seems to be speaking in her own voice rather than Strephon's. The first runs:

> T'was folly made mee fondly write
> (For what [have] I to doe with Love and wit?)
> I own I tre[s]pass'd wickedly in Rhime
> But oh my Punishment exceeds my crime,
> My Folies tho' on parchment writt
> I soon might burn and then forget
> But if I Now both burn and blot
> (By mee) the[y] cannot bee forgot.

This sounds like a response to some actual provocation. Lady Mary had already copied out the prose 'Adventures of Indamora' and left a blank space following the introductory 'To the Reader' (f. 5), when she went back and copied in two of the only three untitled pieces in the volume: that just quoted, and a longer one, contemplative and disillusioned, which begins

> Look round (my soul) and if you can
> Point out — who is a happy man,
> The man who never did for ought complain.
> This 15 year I've search't the world in vain
> But all on every side I see
> Nothing but sighs and endless misery.

This poem, interesting as Lady Mary's first excursion into satire, firmly contradicts the ideas of those on country retirement. After her vain fifteen-year search, she now finds that nobody is happy but a figure familiar to us from the Restoration stage:

> Quite without reason — half without a Soul,
> A Noisy fashionable flasshy fool
> Who lives and talks and moves without a thought,
> A Senseless apish self admireing sot.

She then adapts the scheme of Horace's First Satire of the First Book, where each group of men envies the others; but she makes each group deride the rest.

---

[1] Based on the famous passage in *Aureng-Zebe*, Act IV (Dryden, *Dramatic Works*, edited by M. Summers, 6 vols (London, 1931–2), IV, 128.
[2] *All for Love*, Act II (*Dramatic Works*, IV, 212).

The Soldeir proud of rags and scars
(The Honnourable profit of the wars)
Laughs at the fop who painted has beheld
Battels hee durst not look on in the feild.
　　The Statesman smiles to see the poet's ode
Extoll his gouty Lordship as a god
When all hee gets is but a gracious Nod.
　　The poet waiting at the great man's door
Haughty in rags and proudly poor
Disdains the ignorant rich . . .

and honours the poverty of Samuel Butler. This might seem to suggest that each group *is* content with its own lot; but Lady Mary argues the vanity of each group's pretensions, her own with the rest: 'And poetry my dear my darling choice | Is all chimera, fancied joys.' The conclusion, like those of the poems on death, turns towards 'Heaven's unknown and unimmagin'd bliss', and does so more effectively for following on an attempt at worldliness.

Apparently soon afterwards she started another folio album (H MS 251, leather-bound). She transcribed her prose romance and six poems from the earlier volume with revisions, and incorporated the two love poems in a new prose and verse romance. She dropped her two classical imitations and the compliment to Halifax, although the new collection included more of both these kinds among its twenty-one new poems. The last pages of the volume remained blank, except for a smudged statement, 'Made when Cloe was but 12 years old'. The handwriting of these words (if they are Lady Mary's) is more childish than that of the poems; they must have had a separate *raison d'être*, probably as heading for something never transcribed. The title-page, set out as if printed, makes a handsome appearance. Lady Mary had given up the persona of Strephon; she first wrote 'Clarindae' and presumably intended 'Opera', but changed her mind and Englished the title as 'The Entire Works / of Clarinda. / London.'

The volume opens with the long new romance, 'The Adventurer', modelled on Aphra Behn's *Voyage to the Isle of Love*. Then come '2 espistles [sic] in imitation of Ovid', rural-retirement and meditative poems (mostly transcribed from the earlier album), a great variety of classical imitations and love poetry, and a compliment to Samuel Garth on a yet unpublished poem of his, calling him Machaon after his own hero and comparing him to Waller.[1] Like a geological deposit, the poems show a layer of each influence from Lady Mary's already extensive reading. From the previous century Aphra Behn, La Calprenède's romances, John Sheffield Duke of Buckingham, and Granville have left their mark, besides Cowley, Dryden, and possibly Rochester.[2] There is a full-dress imitation of Virgil, but it is Ovid who dominates this volume. The apparent shift of emphasis from the Horatian may be simply the result of Lady Mary's having destroyed parts of the earlier collection, perhaps because of the risqué nature of the Ovidian material.

Lady Mary's statements are inconsistent about the amount of Latin she knew when she wrote these poems. In her later days she told Joseph Spence that she began

---

[1] F. 25; Garth, 'To the Lady Louisa Lenos', printed in *Ovid's Epistles*, 1725.
[2] As an adult Lady Mary voiced disapproval of Rochester, but echoed him in her verse (*Letters*, III, 9; *Essays and Poems*, pp. 232, 233).

it at thirteen and mastered it in two years, which would be the years of her juvenilia.[1] Letters that passed between her and her future husband (through his sister) in 1709, about four years after the last of the early poems, suggest that her Latin studies were still in their infancy; but less than a year later she submitted to Bishop Burnet a translation of Epictetus's *Enchiridion*, done from Latin, with a covering letter quoting in the same language from Erasmus.[2] In the same year (1710) she drafted a fictionalized autobiography telling how she impressed 'Sebastian' (Edward Wortley Montagu) at their first meeting with her understanding of 'allmost any' Latin author, but also describing Sebastian's pleasure in explaining passages to her.[3]

On the whole it seems likely that she continued in a state of imperfect knowledge for longer than she told Spence. (Her studies may have flagged when she entered fashionable society and revived after her meeting with Wortley.) The deprecatory tone of her letters to Anne Wortley suggests that she sought to charm her suitor by appeals for help rather than to dazzle him as the autobiography reports. She was probably learning Latin when she wrote her early verse, but had not yet acquired the competence evident in her translation of Epictetus.

Lady Mary told Spence that her admiration for Ovid's *Metamorphoses* (in translation) 'was one of the chief reasons that set me upon the thoughts of stealing the Latin language'.[4] Translations were doubtless available in her father's library long before she herself owned a wide range of Ovid's works in Latin, French, and English, including *Metamorphoses* in each.[5] Although the first poem in her earliest album, and two more in her second, retold *Metamorphoses* stories, her verse was less responsive to the mythological narratives of that work than to the psychological self-dramatizations of the *Heroides*, which she later owned in French and English. She caught more of the visual richness of the *Metamorphoses* in her romance 'The Adventurer' than in poems based on Ovid's tales, which (like the Moschus paraphrase, her only avowed use of a Greek source) lack any obvious connexion with either the original or any known version. She made Latona flee through Lycia before the birth of her children instead of, like Ovid, afterwards (H MS 250, f. 1; *Metamorphoses*, VI, 337). Though she entitled her poem on the death of Adonis 'From Ovid's Metamorphoses', she wrote (like Bion) of Venus being scratched by brambles and of roses springing from her blood, where Ovid wrote of Adonis's blood producing anemones or windflowers, and she concluded with an apparently original conceit about the rose as special friend to beauty.[6] Only her accounts of 'The Golden Age' and of the return of Justice to heaven, which had become more or less common property, remained fairly close to Ovid (ff. 13–14, 25–6; *Metamorphoses*, I).

She already knew the *Heroides*, in some form, well. Her first juvenile album carefully listed the personages in 'O[vid's] espistles'. At only '12 years of Age', as the title claims, she wrote or drafted an epistle called 'Julia to Ovid', which (like

---

[1] Spence, 1, 304.
[2] *Letters*, 1, 6, 8–9, 43, 46.
[3] *Essays and Poems*, pp. 78, 79.
[4] Spence, 1, 303.
[5] 'Catalogue [of] Lady Mary Wortley's books Packed up to be Sent Abroad July 1739', Wharncliffe MS 135, Sheffield Central Library.
[6] H MS 251, f. 12; *Metamorphoses*, X, 720–39; Thomas Stanley's translation of Bion with *Poems* (London, 1651), p. 33.

'To Truth') pleased her enough for her to polish and keep it: this, besides referring confidently to the *Ars Amatoria* and *Amores*, copied the tone and subject matter of the *Heroides*, wittily setting the poet in the position of one of his own characters.[1] In her use of Ovid, Lady Mary was one of the last exemplars of 'the potency of the tradition which romanticized classical figures and stories in a way that no reading of the classics could "correct" '.[2] The heroic epistles were popular, having been 'Translated by Several Hands' in 1680 with a preface by Dryden, mocked the same year in *The Wits Paraphras'd: or, Paraphrase upon Paraphrase. In a Burlesque on the Several late Translations of Ovids Epistles* and in Alexander Radcliffe's *Ovid Travestie*, and imitated in David Crawfurd's *Ovidius Britannicus* and John Oldmixon's *Amores Britannici* (both published in 1703, the latter an up-dating of Michael Drayton's *England's Heroicall Epistles*, 1597, which Lady Mary later owned). Ovid's *Heroides* include letters written from men as well as from women, and treat many different love situations besides parting; Lady Mary was most attracted by the theme of the forsaken woman, as were other imitators such as Pope.[3] She turned to the *Heroides* for the '2 espistles' already mentioned (complaints against their lovers by Cleopatra and by Alexander's queen Statira),[4] for other non-historical epistles, and for passages in 'The Adventurer'. Her love-lyrics betray more generalized Ovidian influence. A poem entitled 'An Imitation of Ovid's Epistles' shows a martial and indignant spirit such as none of Ovid's heroines can match.

Love in these poems is the classical god-inspired madness highly romanticized, unrelated to any social system, and doomed to end in tears, parting, and frequently death. Openings are rhetorical ('Ha! is it true my Alexander fled', 'Is't possible — is Caesar prov'd ingrate?', 'No Hermenesilde'); endings often forecast the heroine's death for love. This heroine sees herself in pathetic terms ('I (oh fool)', 'I in tears half Dead', 'A credulous maid all easie to believe') and her lover as worthless yet still desirable ('Dear perjur'd King', 'my Dear unkind', 'his dear Deludeing Toungue'); she seeks with authentic Ovidian masochism to extract the maximum pathos from her state. The conventional apparatus of sighs and tears, doubts and fears, tormenting thoughts and troubled breasts, laments for lost innocence and lost beauty, is all mobilized to batter the reader's sensibilities. Rhetorical devices include question, exclamation, and repetition. The last makes for heavier emotional emphasis, as in

> Yet know my Alexander, know that I
> Without you cannot Live — but I Can dye,
> And Dye I will rather then share your heart;

or, with an interruption to screw the tension still further,

> Here Lies a Queen —
> (Oh Virgins, may her fate your warning prove!)
> A Queen who was undone and died for Love.

---

[1] *Essays and Poems*, pp. 176–7.
[2] Douglas Bush, *Mythology and The Renaissance Tradition in English Poetry* (Minneapolis, 1957), p. 80.
[3] For his debt to Ovid see *Twickenham*, II, 293–303, 356–7; R. A. Brower, *Alexander Pope: The Poetry of Allusion* (Oxford, 1959), pp. 63–84.
[4] H MS 251, ff. 11–12, each prefixed by a brief 'Argument' in the manner of Drayton. Lady Mary based her Cleopatra not on Dryden or Shakespeare but on the romance of that name by La Calprenède, which she wrongly attributed to 'Mr de Scudrey'; Statira had also been treated as a heroine of romance by La Calprenède, and of tragedy by Nathaniel Lee.

This style had been naturalized for English imitators of the *Heroides* by the first of them, Michael Drayton, in such passages as

> You blusht, I blusht; your Cheeke pale, pale was mine,
> My Red, thy Red, my Whiteness answer'd thine;
> You sigh'd, I sigh'd, we both one Passion prove,
> But thy sigh is for Hate, my sigh for Love.

These laboriously symmetrical lines are compressed into an antithetical couplet in Oldmixon's more modern version.[1] Meanwhile the ornate style had become more flexible in Dryden's plays, whose characters were the first Lady Mary made lists of. Despite Dryden's superior versification, his victims use the same diction, the same repetition of broken phrases, as Lady Mary's:

> Ah turn your Sight to me, my dearest Lord!
> Can you not one, one parting look afford?
> Ev'n so unkind in death? but 'tis in vain;
> I lose my breath, and to the Winds complain . . .
> I can, I can forgive: is that a task
> To love, like mine? Are you so good to ask?
> One kiss — Oh 'tis too great a blessing this;
> I would not live to violate the bliss.[2]

Given a knack of writing freely, the style was not very difficult to copy.

In maturity Lady Mary continued to draw on the Ovidian tradition: in her eclogues, in epistles with real-life dramatized settings (where love clashes with prosaic social and economic conditions instead of with heroic duty), and in her love poems.[3] Even in youth her interest in the literary treatment of love became linked with that in the social predicament of women, represented here by 'An Imitation of Ovid's Epistles' (H MS 251, f. 30). The female speaker tells her lover he *is* unkind to leave her for battle, and asks 'Why has the cruel Power Confined | To this weak clay my Warlike mind?'. She contrasts a woman's actual powerlessness with the power that poetic language attributes to her. Literary images appear in contexts which deny their traditional currency: 'darts' are real weapons of war, and military glory opposes 'the boasted Glories of my Eyes'. The heroine's vision of 'Acts, worthy of my Soul and of my Love' (like death in battle to save her lover) fades before the realization that 'By Love alone I'm doom'd to dye for you'. She then wavers, renounces her 'courage', and suggests an ideal of 'soft moments' and 'peaceful joys' in opposition to 'Blood and Danger'. Having shown that the rhetorical apparatus is false as applied to love, Lady Mary suggests that it is equally false as applied to war: martial 'Triumphs' and 'Conquests' are made to carry a hint of the frivolous social variety. Both glories are alike vain; the two conventions undermine each other. Her complex material, however, defeats her: the last four lines waver again towards the unattainable and questionable life of action, so that the poem's total effect is blurred. But its unresolved tensions produce some finely ironical lines, including the last, 'And I can kill with nothing but my Eyes'.

---

[1] 'King John to Matilda', Drayton, *Englands Heroicall Epistles*, 1597: *Works*, edited by J. W. Hebel, 5 vols (Oxford, 1961), II, 147; Oldmixon, *Amores Britannici* (London, 1703), p. 25. Lady Mary owned a copy of Drayton's poems in 1739 (Wharncliffe MS 135).

[2] *Aureng-Zebe*, Act v (*Dramatic Works*, IV, 153–4).

[3] *Essays and Poems*, pp. 221, 227, 230, 270; see I. M. Grundy, 'Ovid and Eighteenth-Century Divorce', *RES*, new series 23 (1972), pp. 417–28.

Wortley Montagu was to mention Virgil to his wife as 'Your own Poet' in 1710.[1]
Her rhetoric of love, now and later, owed much to the opening of the *Aeneid*, Book IV,
but probably in 1704-5 she had read Virgil, like Ovid, mainly at second hand. Her
'Tenth Eclogue of Virgil Imitated' (ff. 28-9), which is remarkable among her
juvenilia for maintaining a high level of smoothness and competence through 74
lines, apparently never appeals back from the translators she knew (Stafford and
Sir William Temple) to the Latin original.[2] She shows some independence of
invention, and when she adapts does so with sensitivity, often loosening and
expanding: where Temple has

> But yet *Arcadians* is my grief allay'd,
> To think that in these Woods, and Hills, & Plains,
> When I am silent in the Grave, your Swains
> Shall sing my Loves . . .

Lady Mary writes

> Arcadian maids, my sorrows are allaid
> To think, when I shall in my grave be laid
> You shall (with pitying tears) my hopeless Loves
> Sing, to these Hills, and Rocks, and Echoing Groves.

Her choice of this eclogue was presumably influenced by its Ovidian subject matter;
but her version is visually richer than her epistles, tranquil not hysterical in tone,
euphoniously flowing not staccato and repetitious. She makes interesting changes to
Virgil, substituting a forsaken girl and 'cruel faithless Swain' for the forsaken
shepherd and false mistress, and giving the girl a magnanimous wish that her
swain may prove 'Successful, tho' 'tis in another Love'. Mention of the 'shineing
court | Where all the vain and painted Nymphs resort' as a third alternative to
either 'war's alarms' or pastoral 'downy hours' gives a touch of the contemporary.
Self-expression and literary precedent were not mutually exclusive for Lady Mary:
when in 1716 she wrote the last of her eclogues, 'Satturday', to relieve, as she said,
her own feelings about the ruin of her beauty by smallpox, she turned to Virgil
again and drew heavily on her own early imitation.[3]

Most of her juvenile poems observe firmly marked though complex literary conventions, which are on the whole incompatible with such ingredients of Lady Mary's
mature verse as topical content and social satire: but here and there in the albums these
ingredients begin to emerge. Many poems could equally well have been suggested
by an actual or fictional occasion. The subject of 'An Imitation of Ovid's Epistles'
(a lover off to war) must have been commonly met with among her contemporaries
in these years of Marlborough's campaigns; it is just as common in romance. In
'Irresolution' (f. 28) Damon sends his mistress, the narrator, a note while she is
'with Fair Chloris in the Eastern Grove', a location either on an actual estate or in
some projected romantic story. This poem employs realistic detail: 'the Friendly
Maid | Oppen'd the Note and bid me, boldly read'. Lady Mary may perhaps be
attempting a sketch from life in 'To Policrite' (f. 24), a courtier and man of pleasure
who frequents ruelles, visiting days, assemblies, and the theatre; 'Noe Ball in Town,

---

[1] *Letters*, I, 268, n. 1.
[2] Published in *Virgil's Eclogues* with the first volume of Dryden's *Miscellany*, 1684 (re-numbered
pages 80-92).
[3] *Essays and Poems*, p. 201.

but you they first invite, | And constant at St James' every night.' It is almost
certain that Hermensilde, 'Attendant on the best of Queens' in London, to whom
Lady Mary addressed H MS 250 and a group of poems in H MS 251, was her early
friend Jane Smith (d. 1730), daughter to the Speaker of the House of Commons for
1705–8, who became Maid of Honour to Queen Anne during that time.[1]

Of more interest than the identity of Policrite and Hermensilde are the differing
attitudes of the poems addressed to them. (Lady Mary's letters of about five years
later vary similarly as she extolls the pleasure of retirement to her lover, while to less
serious-minded female friends she complains bitterly of its tedium.) The speaker of
'To Policrite' sorrows for his absence, but does not repine because she much prefers
'my charming Solitude . . . My happy safe retreat, my darling Choice' to the great
world where he shines. The Hermensilde poems, on the contrary, appear in a
sequence in which various unpoetic feelings seem to be struggling into poetic utter-
ance. In the first of these, 'Adeiu [sic] to Vanity' (f. 26), 'poor Clarinda' describes
her love in terms different from those of the Ovidian epistles, more moralistic and
less romantic ('doatingly', 'unpardonable', 'fond disease'), which recall 'wickedly'
and 'crime' in 'T'was folly made mee fondly write'. The heroine has been rejected
not because her lover is faithless but because

> I want a bright Actractive [sic] form,
> I want the very power to Charm
> And all those graces requisite to move
> The Soul to a degree of Love.

Her 'faithfull Glass' contradicts Vanity and shows her as unlovable. The idea is
more characteristic of the self-conscious adolescent than of any poetic tradition
known to Lady Mary. Unrequited love has ceased to be a sign of sensibility to be
indulged in and become a 'foible' to be controlled and vanquished.

Next comes 'The Dispair' (f. 27), the first poem addressed to Hermensilde. It has
much in common (flames, tears, perjury, plaints) with the earlier historical epistles,
and its conclusion would fit any of them nicely. There is, however, a significant
difference: the moral values attached to town and country have been reversed.
Retirement to 'some silent Grove' has become an unwilling business associated with
retreat to the grave; urban 'Circles, parks, and walks and plays' are no longer
condemned but regretted as 'the deversions of my happier days'. Next (before
'Irresolution'), 'The Excuse' bids an elegant farewell to the 'Rural Deities' which
love for Damon has ousted as 'my muse's constant theam'.

> Forgive me charming Shade
> And thou Oh Sacred Grove
> Where oft I've sat and Read
> Sad Tragick tales of Love . . .
>
> Forgive [me] if you doe not Charm
> With the same softness as before.

Damon receives different literary treatment from previous heroes; here love
conflicts with pastoral preoccupations instead of, as in 'To Policrite', reinforcing
them.

---

[1] John Chamberlayne, *Angliæ Notitia*, 1704; *Magnæ Britanniæ Notitia*, 1708; *Letters*, I, 250, n. 2.

After 'Irresolution' Lady Mary transcribed her rendering of Virgil's tenth eclogue. She followed this with the first of two poems 'To Hermenesilde' (ff. 29–30), which is unlike any part of Ovid except perhaps the *Tristia*. Its opening lines conjure a different world from that of Virgil's eclogue: 'While Here I stay condemn'd to desart feilds, | Denied the pleasures that dear London yeilds . . .'. The charming shades have become 'Bleak northern Groves, and Drowned Plains'; the shepherds have metamorphosed into 'Aukard Swains | Or country 'Squires yet more dull then they'. As in 'The Dispair', the writer has been deserted, but she now complains as friend not as lover: though Hermensilde is described as a love goddess in the courtly tradition, the execution done by her eyes does not hinder the love between her and the writer, who blames not her but 'Fortune' (possibly in the guise of her appointment, or her father's) for her desertion, although she does blame Hermensilde for failing to answer her letters. She envies her friend's triumphs among beaux and poets, and feels the loss of her no more keenly than that of 'the Town'. The pastoral outlook has been temporarily discarded for the metropolitan, the friends resembling a pair of heroines in contemporary comedy as much as Katherine Philips's *précieuses*.

Lady Mary's poetic methods did not, however, develop steadily: the second 'To Hermenesilde' (f. 31) reverts to Ovidian type: one of the most forceful of that type indeed, embracing surges of contradictory emotions without sense of strain. Love, not friendship, is its burden; it echoes Dryden's *Troilus*; the defiant note in its early lines ('Back I return you all your broken vows') is as extreme as the self-abasement at the end ('Love and Submission is in every line'). It makes no mention of town or countryside, but in the next two poems (ff. 31–2, titles obliterated) Clarinda eloquently calls 'sighing Winds', 'pitying Air', oak trees, and echoes to witness Hermensilde's betrayal. Rural deities are back in power, and love inseparable in verse from its pastoral props.

The longest work in the albums, 'The Adventurer' (H MS 251, ff. 1–10), unites the traditions of romance and pastoral, both forms of escape literature 'meant for the young'.[1] Following its model, Aphra Behn's *Voyage to the Isle of Love* (1684), it blends elements dating back to the Renaissance with others from the French romances which Lady Mary read with delight.[2] In form it is an account of his experiences addressed by the Adventurer, who shares Lady Mary's earliest *nom de plume* of Strephon, to his friend Lucidor. The epistolary frame provides a perfunctory introduction and conclusion, but Strephon comes to life through his narrated encounters, not his relationship with Lucidor. He experiences love in three forms: he truly loves Calista, who however loves another and ultimately kills herself in a manner worthy of Ovid or Restoration tragedy; he is falsely loved and jilted by the fickle and mercenary Marrillia; he proves unable to make up his mind between Ardelia and Helvidia, devotees of 'Coquetrish'.

The prose and verse sections of this work resemble the categories of recitative and aria in contemporary opera, or blank verse and song in Dryden's *King Arthur* (1691), or couplets and lyrics in Aphra Behn's romance.[3] The verse passages employ a

---

[1] G. A. Highet, *The Classical Tradition* (London, 1949; reprinted 1967), p. 165.
[2] *Essays and Poems*, p. 11.
[3] Pastoral opera had already grown out of pastoral drama and masque to became an established form (Highet, p. 175).

variety of stanza forms besides heroic couplets. Lady Mary tends to use prose for narrative and verse for emotional outpourings, but it is difficult to classify situations for which she chooses couplets or stanzas. Couplets are used for Calista's 'paper' which first reveals her feelings to Strephon, but alternately rhyming quatrains for her speech which he then overhears.

The proportion of prose to verse changes after about two-thirds of the work, during which short linking passages of prose (often mere stage directions or changes of scene) alternate with fairly brief passages in verse (none more than 23 lines). This pattern is broken by 'The Complaint' (originally 'Recanting'), Strephon's formal 62-line renunciation of Marrillia, which is Ovidian in structure and rhetoric though not epistolary in form. Written at first as a separate poem, it fits perfectly into its place in 'The Adventurer'; its self-sufficient development disrupts the rapid flow of verse punctuated with prose, and marks Lady Mary's switch from the pathetic to the comic mode. After two prose sentences and two couplets she settles into long unbroken alternate passages of prose and verse, which accelerate movement and favour narrative rather than drama.

'The Adventurer', alone among her juvenilia, is rich in visual detail and imagery. Lines like 'Budding Roses Strow the perfum'd Grownd', however unconvincing as description of natural scenes, vividly suggest French rococo paintings (called in the final number of the *Spectator* 'Gay, Janty, Fluttering Pictures'), where the blossoms have been scattered with affected carelessness. For Strephon's first sight of Calista she provides a tableau, 'The Description':

> The Sun had scarse retir'd to Thetis' Bed,
> Throu' all the Trees the Wanton Zephyr plaid,
> Under a shady Beech Calista Lay
> To sheild her face from the hot scorching Day,
> On Flowers the Lovely Charmer sleeping Laid
> Pillows of Roses did support her head,
> A Careless Vail was cast upon her Breast
> Which Little envy'd Zephyrs Kiss't.
> The Wanton Gods the thin Loose Gause did move
> Discovering whole charming Worlds of Love,
> Amaz'd, confus'd, I wondring stood and Gaz'd,
> (Who at such Beauties cou'd bee unamaz'd)
> But t'was not Long that I unmov'd did stand,
> I Kneel't, and now grown bolder, Kiss't her hand.

A parallel passage marks his first sight of her after she has rejected him and fallen hopelessly in love with Hephestion:

At last I found the Lovely Maid Asleep, not on a Bed of Flowers as heretofore when she and I was Free,

> But in a solitary Dismal Grove
> Where Philomell still sings Sad tales of Love,
> Where on each tree Young Mourning Doves
> Lament in Murmurs their unhappy Loves,
> No Fruit, or Flowers, move Delight,
> Here Dwells a gloom that almost equalls Night.
> T'was in that mournfull region of Dispair
> I saw my Lovely Cruel Fair,
> Throu' her clos'd eyes some Pearly drops did steal
> Which on her Naked riseing Bosom fell,
> Her Bosom which still seem'd with sighs to swell.

These recall a whole line of paintings of popular classical subjects, many from Ovid (Actæon watching Diana bathing, Danæ receiving the shower of gold, Ariadne deserted by Theseus), as well as Dryden's 'Cymon and Iphigenia' (lines 86–106) and similar passages in Aphra Behn.[1] In *The Faerie Queene* also, heroines (both real and in pictures) are frequently discoverd asleep, as Leda is in Book VI (x. 10 ff.). Douglas Bush calls Spenser's works 'an endless gallery of mythological paintings'.[2] Lady Mary may have read Spenser or only those influenced by him; she had certainly seen pictures and prints of such subjects in her father's house and library. If 'The Adventurer' forms a gallery, its central picture is the prose description of Love's temple (with its altar 'not enrich'd with Gemns or Gold but all inlaid with hearts', where Cupid 'with his Golden pointed Arrow . . . Seems to Derect your Eyes' to the 'Invitation' transcribed from Lady Mary's earlier album) which follows the baroque symbolic tradition exemplified by Mrs Behn's 'Love in fantastic triumph sat'.

'The Adventurer' is an allegory, as such unique among Lady Mary's early pieces, but like others among them it prepares for later work. It demonstrates the roots of eighteenth-century satiric personification in the earlier form descending from the Middle Ages. Its allegory uses places, characters, and technical terms deriving from the code of courtly love, like Declaration (a significant step in each of the first two courtships, in their response to which the heroines reveal their nature).[3] Allegorical places include the isle of love itself, fallaciously beautiful, 'Little Provinces call'd Billets-doux', the 'Large Castle' of marriage, inhabited by 'Discord, Strife, and Uneasyness', and true love as 'the Ruines of a Famous old Palace' now 'wholly abandon'd'. Strephon first sees Calista 'near too near' but not in True Love, which explains the unhappy outcome of the affair. The altar and temple of Love draw pilgrims from groves and from the deserts of Dispair and Remembrance but not from 'the wood of Coquetrish'. In the earlier adventures the hero ceremonially sacrifices his heart on Love's altar; coquetry makes no such demand.

Besides the non-allegorical Strephon and heroines, Lady Mary's characters include qualities personified in two different manners. Jealousie ('Her hair all Snakes, her drink is Lovers' Tears') ultimately derives from the appearance of Envy in set pieces of the seven deadly sins (like *The Faerie Queene*, II.7.22, where the allegorical figure is male). Reason, dramatic not decorative, is at first, as in 'Reason perswaded mee', hardly personified at all; later he acquires definition as 'the Venerable Guide', is addressed in the language used by contemporary tragic heroes to their confidants, and appears at turning points in the action and tries, generally in vain, to modify or influence Love.

In the third adventure, romance begins to give way to social comedy. The 'wood of Coquetrish' represents the real world of London life, not learnt from books but from the distant observation of a girl still in the schoolroom. 'Dutchesse here Gallops in hackney Coach', lovers not only write songs but make 'Balls and

---

[1] *A Voyage to the Isle of Love* (*The Works of Aphra Behn*, edited by M. Summers, 6 vols (London, 1915), VI, 232, 234, etc.).

[2] *Mythology and the Renaissance Tradition*, p. 86.

[3] This formal diction lends weight to Lady Mary's use of the word when, in her courtship letters to Wortley, she apologizes for her own immodesty in resorting to 'declaration', a proceeding unthinkable on the female side in a romance such as this one (1711, *Letters*, I, 73, 96).

magnificent treats'. The phrases strike freshly: not pastoral formulations but would-be worldly ones, not prolix like Lady Mary's early verse but succinct like her letters throughout her life. Ardelia and Helvidia are depicted in a new way: not introspectively but from the viewpoint of an observer or letter writer reporting the vagaries of her acquaintance. After Strephon betrays each of them, their probable courses of action are presented not from their emotional angle but from his strategic one. The reader is not asked to identify with either of them, nor (at this stage) with Strephon. If the blonde Ardelia, 'soft and tender and believeing', recalls the classic Ovidian heroine, the brunette Helvidia, witty and affected with 'peirceing eyes', suggests Lady Mary herself. She is not therefore, however, exempt from satire: 'how imposible to deceive her unless she contributed to it her self (as Ladies of her humour Generally doe').

Strephon's changed behaviour is explicitly contrasted with the past: he makes multiple Declarations 'not as before with fears and tremblings, downcast Looks and Sighs, but Gay and Laughing'.

> To each I swore, that she had all my breast
> (Yet still I Lov'd the present best) . . .
> When Absent both, I sigh't for Neither.

He resembles, in fact, the deplorable Marrillia before him; yet he enjoys 'perpetuall pleasure', until the comedy incident of his absent-mindedly sending to each lady the 'little billet' intended for the other. After they discover his duplicity, he reverts from his easy tone to the language of romantic suffering, 'Oh racking thought . . . oh tortureing Pain', now used for the purpose of irony. Such suffering ought, as before, to go together with fidelity, whereas Strephon now feels no guilt, and is sure he could win back either lady by renouncing the other. His anguish arises from nothing more than inability to choose between them: a burlesque situation, as Gay later understood. Here Lady Mary's mannered, pastoral-romance style reaches its zenith. The element of intentional self-parody is fairly clear from the diction of the farewell to 'the Little Coquet Cupid' which concludes 'The Adventurer', but the style is a hard one to burlesque, and Lady Mary's intention would perhaps not be certain without help from the context (the fickle Strephon abandoning two faithful girls who certainly do not scorn him):

> No more! I'le never, Never will again
> For a frail, faithless, ficil, maid complain,
> But to the fair perfidious I'le return
> Hatred for hatred, Scorn for Scorn.

In fine my Lucidor I Left the charming Isle, and here ended all that you desire to know.

Most of the poems which follow this in H MS 251 still use language appropriate to 'the charming Isle'; the last piece in the volume represents Lady Mary's own more restrained farewell:

> Oh Love! in Prospect, full of soft Delight,
> All o're Enchanting, at a Distant Sight.
> Immagination paints thee ever gay,
> And Smileing Pleasures in our Fancys play.
> Charm'd with the dear Delusion we go on
> Nor find the Folly, till we are undone.

Her next surviving verse, from a letter of February 1712, has a topical bite foreign
to her pastoral albums: 'Of Noble Maids, how wretched is the Fate! | Ruin'd with
Jointures, curs'd by an Estate . . .'.[1] She had not yet made the acquaintance of
Pope, but at some point in the intervening years she had left the seventeenth century
behind her.

[1] *Letters*, I, 116.

Political Characterization in *Gulliver's Travels*

J. A. DOWNIE

University College of North Wales, Bangor

From the time of its publication onwards *Gulliver's Travels* has been subjected to severe political analysis, and attempts have been made, with varying degrees of ingenuity, to find consistent political characterization and a foolproof political allegory. Sir Charles Firth's lecture on the political significance of *Gulliver's Travels* has been superseded in more recent years by Arthur Case's explanation of political allusions, especially in *A Voyage to Lilliput*.[1] Despite their inherent historical inaccuracy and subsequent attempts to elucidate Swift's meaning in terms of the little language he used in his *Journal to Stella*, and his undoubted fondness for nonsense words, Case's views have gained some currency and remain unchallenged. Irvin Ehrenpreis has said that 'there is not a great deal to alter in his foundations', though he did make the important distinction between the actual events of 1708–15 and Swift's own highly personalized and distorted image of them.[2] While Case admits that the 'burden of proof lies on the shoulders of anyone who argues that the political allegory is consistent' in *Gulliver's Travels*, these admirable sentiments make no significant contribution to his subsequent efforts to convince the reader of the rightness of his argument in favour of a fairly strict political characterization, and too often we are obliged to be content with a platitudinous: 'It is hardly necessary to labor the significance of the rest of the allegory'.[3] No one has questioned the identification of Flimnap as Walpole, the representation of the Orders of the Garter, the Bath, and the Thistle by the three coloured silks, the references to the Big-Endians and the Little-Endians, the high-heels and the low-heels. But the problems of pinpointing a consistent allegory remain, and considerable difficulty obscures the characterization of Skyresh Bolgolam, of Reldresal, and of Lord Munodi in *A Voyage to Laputa*. Can such characters be identified with any certainty, and were they, indeed, meant to represent particular men? Is the answer not merely one of reconciling the general satire of *Gulliver's Travels* with a desire to narrow down Swift's design? Is there not a tendency to attribute a specific aim to the darts with which he was liberally showering the contemporary political scene when the real issue is more concerned with policies and measures, and not men?

---

[1] C. H. Firth, 'The Political Significance of *Gulliver's Travels*', *Proceedings of the British Academy* (1919–1920), 237–59; Arthur E. Case, *Four Essays on Gulliver's Travels* (Princeton, New Jersey, 1950), pp. 70–96.

[2] Irvin Ehrenpreis, 'The Origins of *Gulliver's Travels*', *PMLA*, 72 (1957), 880–99 (p. 881). A gauge of the currency of Case's conclusions is the fact that they have been reprinted in full in both *Discussions of Jonathan Swift*, edited by John Traugott (Boston, Massachusetts, 1962), pp. 105–20, and *Jonathan Swift: A Critical Anthology*, edited by Denis Donoghue (Harmondsworth, 1971), pp. 317–42. I should like to thank Professor Pat Rogers for his advice during the preparation of this article. He is not responsible for the conclusions reached, but his suggestions prevented a number of omissions.

[3] Case, pp. 70, 89. Subsequent page references are given in the text within parentheses.

I

The careers of Oxford and Bolingbroke, writes Case, 'undoubtedly contribute incidents to Gulliver's career'. 'Consistency can be obtained', he assumes, not unreasonably, 'by supposing that Gulliver's career in Lilliput represents the joint political fortunes of Oxford and Bolingbroke during the latter half of Queen Anne's reign' (p. 70). Certainly it is likely that when Gulliver is housed in 'an ancient Temple, esteemed to be the largest in the whole Kingdom', Oxford's two years in the Tower of London from 1715 to 1717 are meant to spring to mind, the presumed deaths of the Princes in the Tower being analogous with the 'unnatural Murder' which had 'polluted' the Temple 'some Years before'.[1] At the other end of the book, Gulliver's flight to Blefuscu to escape the rumoured punishment about to break upon him can be readily explained as an allusion to Bolingbroke's premature departure for France and the court of James III at St Germain soon after the accession of George I. Both the unsavoury means of putting out the fire in the royal apartments, and the unorthodox capture of the Blefuscan fleet which put an end to the war with as little ceremony as possible can be taken, quite correctly, as the ministry's determined effort to end the War of the Spanish Succession as soon as was practicable after 1710. So far so good, and there are countless other incidents which bear close scrutiny in this way. It is only when one forsakes the general for the particular that difficulties occur.

Case was attempting something new when he claimed that from the vantage point of the later chapters of *A Voyage to Lilliput* 'it is possible to extract a number of probable allusions to events of the years 1708–1710'. He felt that there *was* an allegory here, one, moreover, which was 'exactly coincidental with Gulliver's residence in Lilliput and Blefuscu', stemming from Harley's fall in 1708 and leading up to his reinstatement at the head of the incoming ministry in 1710 (p. 70). Unfortunately a close examination of Case's historical parallels does not stand up. Harley's ouster did not, on its own, secure control of the cabinet for the whigs, who were not 'led by Godolphin and Marlborough'. Gulliver may have been 'pictured as having been caught off guard' when washed up on the Lilliputian sands, but Harley was anything but a docile sacrifice to whig arrogance in February 1708, and he almost succeeded, to the utter amazement of observers, in separating Marlborough from Godolphin, and in securing the Lord Treasurer's dismissal. Swift accounted it 'the greatest piece of court skill that has been acted these many years'.[2] Case feels that Harley, at this time, was 'contemplating violence against his enemies': his subsequent decision to persuade Queen Anne to allow him to resign (for that was what happened) was, according to Case, based on the assumption that 'submission [was] the more prudent course'. Referring to his later treatment of the whigs, Case would have Harley regard this submission 'as a tacit promise binding him in honor not to injure his captors even when it lies within his

---

[1] *Gulliver's Travels*, p. 27 (quotations follow Herbert Davis's edition in *The Prose Works of Jonathan Swift*, 14 vols (Oxford, 1939–68), Volume XI (1941; revised 1959). Subsequent page references are included in the text where appropriate within parentheses). The 'temple' and the 'unnatural Murder' have, of course, also been taken as references to the execution of Charles I in Westminster Hall, and this is perhaps a measure of the ambiguity of Swift's alleged allegories.

[2] *The Correspondence of Jonathan Swift*, edited by Harold Williams, 5 vols (Oxford, 1963–5), I, 71: Swift to Archbishop King, 12 February 1707–8. For Harley's fall, see G. S. Holmes and W. A. Speck, 'The Fall of Harley in 1708 Reconsidered', *EHR*, 79 (1965), 673–98.

power to do so'. This, then, is Case's interpretation of the Ministerial Revolution of 1710, and fundamentally ahistorical reasoning permits him to equate Gulliver's actions on his release from his bonds with the character of the tory political recovery. 'It is hardly necessary', he writes, 'to point out the parallel between this conduct and that of the Tory leaders towards the Whigs' (p. 70).

Such an interpretation of Gulliver's initial situation on the shore of Lilliput is a prime illustration of the dire straits into which literal, or in this case superliteral, readings of *A Voyage to Lilliput* can lead us. Founded on a radical misunderstanding of the structure of the Goldolphin ministry in 1708 and the circumstances surrounding Harley's fall from office, Case neither provides a moderately adequate account of the true history of political events in England from 1708 to 1710, nor attempts to put forward an effective argument to show that Swift viewed Harley's resignation and ultimate reinstatement at the head of the incoming moderate tory administration in this way. Further, when assuming that the committee appointed to draw up an inventory of Gulliver's possessions 'stands for the investigation by a committee of Whig lords, of . . . William Gregg' (a clerk in Harley's office who had been found guilty of treasonable correspondence with France), Case alleges that Gulliver's own words on the subject are probably a conscious reflection of Harley's innocence. His behaviour in 1708 is, in Case's view, paralleled by Gulliver's conduct when asked to surrender his possessions. Gulliver, confident in his own behaviour towards his tormentors, stares the Lilliputian King steadfastly in the eye, disregarding the troops who were prepared to resist any hostile action of their adversary. To say this was strained would be classic understatement. There is nothing in my reading of the story of Gulliver's first experiences in Lilliput to assign to it particular events in the political history of 1708 to 1710. Wherever and whenever Swift is wishing to call to mind actual political happenings in reference to Oxford and Bolingbroke he limits his design to general allusions, and he concerns himself with the Oxford ministry's struggle for peace from 1710 onwards. Any other interpretation abuses both history and Swift's own image of the Ministerial Revolution.

The problem of topicality in *Gulliver's Travels* is paramount. Was Swift referring specifically to the political events of the second half of the reign of Queen Anne? Or, as seems more likely, was he more concerned with the situation in the years around 1720? Recently Pat Rogers and J. M. Treadwell have independently argued the case for placing *A Voyage to Laputa* firmly in the context of the South Sea Bubble.[1] The parallels to be found in *A Voyage to Lilliput* seem a little earlier, and they relate, I feel, to the impeachments of Oxford and Bolingbroke. Gulliver's release, if meant to be taken allegorically at all, corresponds with Oxford's release from the Tower in 1717. Case would have it represent 'a series of political developments which culminated early in 1711' (p. 72). This interpretation assumes, as other commentators have done, that Skyresh Bolgolam characterizes the Earl of Nottingham. For this to seem feasible, however, Case has telescoped the four years of the Oxford ministry. 'Almost from the time of his accession to the chancellorship [in August 1710]', writes Case, Oxford 'had begun to lose the personal, though not the political favor of the Queen'. Emphasizing Oxford's fondness for the bottle as

[1] Pat Rogers, 'Gulliver and the Engineers', *MLR*, 70 (1975), 260–70; J. M. Treadwell, 'Jonathan Swift: the Satirist as Projector', *Texas Studies in Literature and Language*, 17 (1975), 439–60.

the prime cause of his downfall, Case maintains that 'Queen Anne dispensed with Oxford's services and vowed never to make use of them again' (pp. 75–6). In fact the process of disintegration which eventually resulted in Oxford's dismissal began only in November 1713 with the death of his favourite daughter. In August 1713 he routed Bolingbroke 'in the corridors of Kensington and Whitehall', whilst his son succeeded in finalizing a marriage alliance with the richest heiress in England, Lady Harriet Holles, daughter of his late ally, the Duke of Newcastle.[1] In the autumn his power was as great as it had ever been. His fall resulted only from his fatal error in asking for the Dukedom to be conferred on his son and his subsequent demoralization on his daughter's death, which precipitated an uncharacteristic lack of self-control and led to his appearing before the Queen drunk, disorientated, and utterly unfit for business in the course of 1714. Reluctantly, Queen Anne received his white staff of office *four days* before her own demise. One looks in vain for evidence to support Case's statement that 'Anne had shown her displeasure at Oxford's personal behavior toward her as early as 1712' (p. 89). As Geoffrey Holmes observes, 'the first real breach in the unique relationship which Oxford had enjoyed with Queen Anne from 1706' was when he asked for the Dukedom for his son.[2] It is surely not Queen Anne to whom Swift is referring in the episode of the fire in the royal palace. The Queen of Lilliput's refusal to utilize those rooms polluted by Gulliver's urine is meant to parallel not Anne's attitude to the Peace of Utrecht, but the attitude of the Hanoverians. Queen Anne was pleased with the outcome of the War of the Spanish Succession. She approved all the negotiations. Oxford's conduct in relation to the war was not the reason for his disgrace. The tory ministry had burst into office on the crest of a tidal wave of war weariness. There is no evidence to endorse Case's mistaken belief that Oxford and Bolingbroke 'could not negotiate openly with France . . . because the war was still generally popular' (pp. 74–5). It most certainly was not. Only the whigs and financiers, the stockjobbers whom Swift so loved to hate, were in favour of continuing the war to the bitter end. The majority of the political nation nourished naturally tory sentiments, and they were heartily sick of the war.[3]

In concluding the presentation of his analysis of *A Voyage to Lilliput* and its close association with the events of 1708–1715, Case writes: 'The strongest arguments in favor of this interpretation . . . are its consistency and the exactness with which it follows the chronology of the events which it symbolizes. Single incidents are often open to more than one explanation: a series carries conviction in proportion to its length' (p. 79). I believe that my illustration of the dangers of trying to dress Swift's satire in too well-tailored a garb has shown not only that Case's analysis of *A Voyage to Lilliput* is erroneous, but that it is downright unhistorical. Swift could hardly have misinterpreted so wildly events in which he was himself concerned. The allegory in *A Voyage to Lilliput* is a general one, centring on the peace concluded by the Oxford ministry, and the subsequent impeachments of those who had had

---

[1] See Geoffrey Holmes, 'Harley, St John and the Death of the Tory Party', in *Britain after the Glorious Revolution 1689–1714*, edited by Holmes (London, 1969), p. 225.

[2] Holmes, pp. 225–6. Harley bitterly regretted his 'never enough to be lamented folly in mentioning to her Majesty the titles'. HMC *Portland*, v, 466.

[3] Ehrenpreis also points out Case's mistaken implications in relating the episode of the fire to Oxford's difficulties with Queen Anne, but he believes that 'references to Bolingbroke (rather than Oxford) control the fable'. Ehrenpreis, pp. 881–3.

a hand in its architecture. Gulliver is a complex figure representing sometimes Oxford, sometimes Bolingbroke, and, no doubt, occasionally Swift himself. And this strange creature, Gulliver/Oxford/Bolingbroke/Swift, was, in certain instances, meant to symbolize the fate of all three real men on the accession of George I.[1]

II

Turning to the actual Lilliputian characters described by Swift, one is struck almost immediately by their inexactitude. Skyresh Bolgolam and Flimnap draw up articles of impeachment against Gulliver 'in Conjunction with . . . *Limtoc* the General, *Lalcon* the Chamberlain, and *Balmuff* the grand Justiciary' (p. 68). If these officials were designed to symbolize their real counterparts in 1714 on the accession of George I, then Marlborough, Shrewsbury, and Cowper must, as Case suggests, be the men pointed at, though the identification of the second of these, 'a mild man who took no active part in the attack on the defeated ministry', is, he admits, 'a little doubtful', and the substitution of Devonshire, the Lord Steward, is advocated (p. 77).[2] In fact in my view the names coined are meant to personify not the particular holder of the office, but the office itself. H. D. Kelling, solving Swift's alleged language game to his own satisfaction, transcribes *Limtoc* as *milles-cottes*, which he took as a passing reference to Marlborough's avarice.[3] Perhaps so, but a more satisfactory persona for the Duke is the character usually identified with Nottingham, Skyresh Bolgolam himself.

The history of the identification of Nottingham as Skyresh Bolgolam is distinguished, but unconvincing. Based on Swift's reference to his 'morose and sour Complection' (p. 42), conjuring up the contemporary nickname habitually applied to Nottingham, that of 'Dismal', successive commentators have participated in some amazing mental gymnastics to find data in *A Voyage to Lilliput* to support their conclusions. Swift was none too friendly with Nottingham, but Nottingham was never in the Admiralty during the period in question, while Bolgolam was Lord High Admiral of Lilliput. References to the period when Nottingham did act as first Lord of the Admiralty, from 1680 to 1684, seem forced, and so do similar ones relating to his interest in naval affairs in the first half of the 1690s. How are these to be reconciled with Swift's categorical statement that Bolgolam was 'very much in his Master's Confidence, and a Person well versed in Affairs' (p. 42)? Nottingham was Lord President of the Council under George I, but only until the aftermath of the Fifteen rebellion. On 29 February 1716 he was dismissed. All attempts to label Nottingham as a whig are vain. He was a High Tory. He gained office as a result of his apostasy in December 1711 when he led the motion in the Lords for a

---

[1] The imagery of impeachment plays a vital role in *A Voyage to Lilliput*. Edward Rosenheim Jr makes out a good case for the Atterbury trial figuring in the satire of the first book. ('Swift and the Atterbury Case', in *The Augustan Milieu: Essays presented to Louis A. Landa*, edited by H. K. Miller, Eric Rothstein, and G. S. Rousseau (Oxford, 1970), pp. 174–204). While I am sure that the affair was, like the Bubble and Wood's halfpence, always in the back of Swift's mind while he was writing *Gulliver's Travels*, I still feel that the first book is concerned primarily with the impeachments of Oxford and Bolingbroke, though of course the Atterbury case provided added incentive to his satire.

Still on the theme of impeachments, W. A. Speck, using the dates actually supplied by Swift for Gulliver's sojourn in Lilliput, suggests that there might be a reference here to the impeachment of the whig leaders in 1701, an event which precipitated Swift's *Discourse of the Contests and Dissensions . . . in Athens and Rome*, his first political tract. See W. A. Speck, *Swift* (London, 1969), p. 112.

[2] In fact Shrewsbury had been an integral part of the Oxford administration.

[3] H. D. Kelling, 'Some Significant Names in *Gullivers Travels*', *SP*, 48 (1951), 761–8 (p. 765).

declaration of 'No Peace without Spain' as a ruse to secure whig approval of an Occasional Conformity bill. 'On [Harley's] rise to power as Chancellor of the Exchequer', writes Case, with typical disregard of his dates, 'Nottingham proposed in the House of Lords an amendment to the royal address . . . an open attempt to restrict the powers of the new Tory administration'. According to Case, 'Harley and St John felt it prudent not to oppose this amendment, and it was consequently carried' (pp. 72–3). It is to this, he feels, that Gulliver is referring when given the conditions on which he is to receive his liberty: 'I SWORE and subscribed to these Articles with great Chearfulness and Content, although some of them were not so honourable as I could have wished; which proceeded wholly from the Malice of *Skyresh Bolgolam* the High Admiral: Whereupon my Chains were immediately unlocked, and I was at full Liberty' (p. 44). Once again Case is abusing history. It was then almost eighteen months since the Oxford ministry had come to power, and any deleterious effects of Nottingham's motion were overcome by the creation of twelve peers to secure a government majority in the Lords.[1] Gulliver is here alluding not to Nottingham's motion, but to the conditions upon which Oxford was released from the Tower in 1717. He was forbidden the court by the express order of George I: compare this with the second condition offered Gulliver, that 'He shall not presume to come into our Metropolis, without our express Order' (p. 43). Nottingham, even if he had ever held any influence in the councils of George I, did so no longer after 1715, and Firth's characterization of him as Bolgolam depends on the false assumption that Swift began writing *A Voyage to Lilliput* in 1714.

In many ways it is possible to view Bolgolam as a symbol for those whigs who were enemies of Oxford, Bolingbroke, and Swift in the last years of Anne's reign, and who threatened to wreak vengeance under the Hanoverians. Certainly I feel no doubt that Swift is concerned with the years 1714 to 1717 during the Lilliput sequence, and the varied misfortunes of his two comrades-in-arms and himself on Anne's death. But there are reasons for Swift's assuming that Marlborough would resent most bitterly the treatment meted out to him by the Oxford ministry, for in many ways the captain-general had suffered most at its hands. 'The duke of Marlborough says, There is nothing he now desires so much as to contrive some way how to soften Dr Swift', Stella was told in 1712, 'he is mistaken; for those things that have been hardest against him were not written by me . . . although I love him not'.[2] Is this perhaps the same irony, conscious or unconscious, that prompted Gulliver to stress that Bolgolam 'was pleased, without any Provocation, to be my mortal Enemy' (p. 42)? Swift *had* been hard on Marlborough, and he could well have presumed that the Duke was the figurehead behind all subsequent moves against Oxford during the impeachments. Misers are traditionally portrayed as 'sour' and 'morose'. It is a much smaller step to admiral from captain-general than from Lord President of the Council.

In 1951, analysing Swift's language in *Gulliver's Travels*, H. D. Kelling came to the conclusion that *bol* was French for mouthful, and that *gola* equated the Spanish or Italian for gluttony. Together, then, *Bolgolam* was meant to suggest greed, and

---

[1] For Swift's views on the creation of the twelve peers, see *Journal to Stella*, edited by Harold Williams, 2 vols (Oxford, 1948), II, 451.
[2] *Journal*, II, 460: 8 January 1712.

Marlborough's avarice was proverbial among contemporaries. It is curious that two years later Paul Odell Clark tried to explain the names used in *Gulliver's Travels* by examining Swift's inordinate fondness for language games. He criticized Kelling's method, yet in the formula he himself concocted, based on the little language, Bolgolam also translated into Marlborough.[1] This, in itself, proves nothing, of course, but when taken in conjunction with other reasons for characterizing Marlborough, rather than Nottingham, as Skyresh Bolgolam, there seems some basis for shortening the odds in the Duke's favour. There is no real evidence to suggest that Nottingham was especially hostile to his fellow tories on the accession of George I, while Swift could well have imagined Marlborough expressing extreme resentment against his apparent persecutors. Swift's own writings in the cause of peace had indirectly censured Marlborough's conduct, and had minimized his part in the victory over France. Is this not what Gulliver's friend meant when he assured him that Bolgolam's 'Hatred', whatever its original cause, had been 'much encreased' by the unorthodox victory over the Blefuscans (pp. 67–8)? Certainly one of the main criticisms of Marlborough's generalship was that he had deliberately prolonged the war for his own ends. It is interesting to note that one of Swift's most biting satirical passages parallels this strategy:

so unmeasurable is the Ambition of Princes, that he seemed to think of nothing less than reducing the whole Empire of *Blefuscu* into a Province, and governing it by a Viceroy; of destroying the *Big-Endian* Exiles, and compelling that People to break the smaller End of their Eggs; by which he would remain sole Monarch of the whole World. (p. 53)

Marlborough springs irresistibly to mind in such a context, and Gulliver's fatal error was in persuading the King not to proceed with his plans, in much the same way that the Oxford ministry had curtailed the overbearing influence of Marlborough and his associates and had put an end to the war.

Case succeeds in confusing the characterization of Marlborough by assigning to him, somewhat improbably, the role of adviser to Gulliver when the Lilliputian privy council or cabinet is secretly planning punitive action (pp. 76–7). The mind boggles at his reasons for assuming that the Duke could adequately fill the description of 'a considerable Person at Court (to whom I had been very serviceable at a time when he lay under the highest Displeasure of his Imperial Majesty)' (p. 67). When had Swift, Bolingbroke, or Oxford defended or assisted Marlborough while he was vulnerable to attack either under Queen Anne, or, even less probably, under George I? The problem of identifying Swift's (or Gulliver's) secret ally, however, is great, and perhaps is tied in with the last remaining candidate for characterization in *A Voyage to Lilliput*, the secretary Reldresal. It is generally agreed that there are two possible aspirants for this distinguished position as Swift's real-life friend: Townshend or Carteret, although Stanhope has been put forward without much conviction. Carteret is Firth's choice, the most plausible evidence in favour of the characterization being his obligation to issue a proclamation offering a reward of three hundred pounds for the discovery of the author of the *Drapier's Letters*. Assuming that Carteret was uneasy about this, it is possible, as Firth suggests, that this relates to Reldresal's lenity in advocating not Gulliver's execution, but merely his blinding.[2] Yet Swift is surely being ironical in playing

---

[1] Kelling, pp. 733–4; Paul Odell Clark, 'A *Gulliver* Dictionary', *SP*, 50 (1953), 592–624 (pp. 604–5).
[2] Firth, pp. 245–6.

up Reldresal's supposed friendship to such an extent. According to Gulliver's adviser, he 'always approved himself your true Friend', but when called upon by the King to express his opinion on the case, he 'justified the good Thoughts you have of him'. He 'allowed [Gulliver's] Crimes to be great', and acknowledged his friendship with the accused, which was 'so well known to the World', but nonetheless offered this solution:

That if his Majesty, in Consideration of your Services, and pursuant to his own merciful Disposition, would please to spare your Life, and only give order to put out both your Eyes; he humbly conceived, that by this Expedient, Justice might in some measure be satisfied, and all the World would applaud the *Lenity* of the Emperor, as well as the fair and generous Proceedings of those who have the Honour to be his Counsellors. (p. 70)

Some justice! And Reldresal was clearly some friend to have in need. Case is unconsciously almost as ironical as Swift is consciously so, in basing his belief that Townshend is Reldresal on an unsubstantiated statement that 'the Tory leaders at first regarded [him] as a friend at court after their fall' (p. 78). Yet Townshend surely is the man pointed at when Swift refers to Reldresal as 'the second after the Treasurer'. The special relationship enjoyed by Walpole and Townshend until the late 1720s is too well known to need comment here, and seems to form the basis of Gulliver's observation that 'the rest of the great Officers are much upon a par' (p. 39). Using Swift's little language, Clark also concluded that Reldresal should be translated as Townshend.[1] Firth's contention that Carteret 'stood so high in the King's favour that he might fairly be described as the second man in the Government' is, I feel, stretching a point.[2] Although Townshend as Reldresal still leaves the problem of why Swift should have considered him any sort of ally in the first place (was he merely being ironic to cause problems of identification for contemporaries?), the characterization does fulfil the essential requirements of Gulliver's description. Swift's relations with Carteret have similarly not been unravelled in any detail, though it has been asserted that some sort of contact did exist. In view of this it might not be far wrong to suggest Carteret as his secret adviser. Certainly Swift escaped the consequences of the *Drapier's Letters* despite the reward offered for his discovery. Carteret's attempt to trace the author appears to have been pursued without much enthusiasm.

'For true No-meaning puzzles more than Wit', wrote Pope in the *Epistle to a Lady* (l. 114), when the sentiment was particularly apt in view of attempts to pin down the elusive Timon. Looking at *A Voyage to Lilliput* as a whole one wonders how much of this maxim rubbed off on Swift. In most cases the hints at characterization are vague, and often contradictory, and this appears to have been deliberate. When Swift wished to make his mark he left no reasonable doubt who his target was: when he was hoping merely to tease he drew his alleged parallels with edges that were purposely undefined; a suggestion sufficient to indict Nottingham as Bolgolam here, an ambiguous clue to an obscure historical allegory there. But the effect he tried to give was one of confusion, and it is a measure of his success that such far-fetched readings of *A Voyage to Lilliput* exist.

---

[1] Clark, p. 604.
[2] Firth, p. 246.

III

Recently the topicality of *Gulliver's Travels* has been highlighted by an examination of *A Voyage to Laputa*. Pat Rogers has emphasized the central position of the South Sea Bubble, while J. M. Treadwell correctly takes Case to task for asserting that Munodi's mill was meant to represent the *inauguration* of the South Sea Company in 1711. Gulliver was more than usually exact in his dating of the building of the mill: Treadwell observes that, as Swift was writing in 1726, 'about seven Years ago' refers not to the setting up of the Company but to the Bubble itself, which began to inflate in 1719.[1] This leads us to a secondary consideration; the character of Lord Munodi himself. Case would have Munodi to be not Middleton (Firth's choice), or even Bolingbroke, but Harley, who was responsible for the foundation of the South Sea scheme. This is based on Gulliver's account that Munodi was 'a Person of the first Rank, and had been some Years Governor of *Lagado*; but by a Cabal of Ministers was discharged for Insufficiency' (p. 175). Case translates Munodi as '*mundum odi*' (I hate the world) and sees in this Oxford's retirement from politics after his release from the Tower in 1717.

While it is important to grasp the central position of the Bubble in the satire of *A Voyage to Laputa*, it is possible that Munodi's mill was not meant to represent the South Sea Company at all. Treadwell steers clear of the problem of whether or not Munodi was Harley. I can find little justification in such an identification. The establishment of the South Sea project was not Harley's sole venture in a world in which he was totally unversed, as Case would imply (pp. 87–9). The change of government in 1710 was only effected in the face of whig attempts to destroy the credit of the incoming ministry by precipitating a financial crisis. Harley was one of the few tories who understood the workings of the city, and he had extensive contacts throughout the ranks of the monied men. The establishment of the South Sea Company in 1711 was effectively the linch-pin of the arrangement he had been trying to reach with the financiers, whose proclivities were usually whig.[2] Nor indeed was the South Sea scheme the only one Harley had been involved in, and Swift certainly knew this. In the 1690s the National Land Bank, backed by Harley, almost succeeded in taking over from the whig-orientated Bank of England as the principal source of public credit.[3] Throughout his career Harley was well acquainted with financial problems. He was, after all, Lord Treasurer. Is it likely, then, that Swift would have emphasized that Munodi made only one experiment of this kind? Furthermore Harley was at the height of his power in May 1711 when the negotiations concerning the South Sea Company were in full swing: he was appointed Lord Treasurer, and elevated to the peerage as Earl of Oxford. This hardly tallies with Munodi's revelation that when he agreed to the building of the mill he was 'then not very well with the Court' (p. 178).

In this case I feel Firth's characterization was justified, and that the mill refers not to the Bubble, but to one of Swift's most potent bogeys, Wood's halfpence. As Lord Chancellor of Ireland Middleton had stood out against Wood's patent. He caused Walpole's displeasure and was threatened with dismissal. 'Whatever the

---

[1] Treadwell, p. 454.
[2] See, on this question, B. W. Hill, 'The Change of Government and the "Loss of the City", 1710–1711', *Economic History Review*, 24 (1971), 395–411.
[3] See Dennis Rubini, 'Politics and the Battle for the Banks', *EHR*, 85 (1970), 693–714.

event may be', he wrote to his brother, 'I have the comfort to know that I fall a sacrifice to the opposition I gave to Wood's Halfpence, and I had rather fall for these with my country'.[1] Bearing this hypothesis in mind, let us turn once again to the description of Munodi's mill:

he had a very convenient Mill within Half a Mile of his House, turned by a Current from a large River, and sufficient for his own Family as well as a great Number of his Tenants . . . about seven Years ago, a Club of those Projectors came to him with Proposals to destroy this Mill, and build another on the Side of that Mountain, on the long Ridge whereof a long Canal must be cut for a Repository of Water, to be conveyed up by Pipes and Engines to supply the Mill: Because the Wind and Air upon a Height agitated the Water, and thereby made it fitter for Motion. (pp. 177-8)

The projecting terminology is obviously deliberate, but more significant is the use of the word *mill*. This conjures up images of milled money and the minting process itself. Swift's main complaint in practical terms about Wood's halfpence was that for many years the minting of milled coin had been authorized by the Lord Chancellors of Ireland in sufficient quantities when needed without flooding the market with money. Ensuring by moderate measures that there was no real scarcity of coin, the Lord Chancellor (Munodi) had minted enough money to cater for the requirements of the English population of Ireland (his own family) and the Irish themselves (his tenants). Now, interfering with this happy state of affairs, money was to be minted in England to use in Ireland, and in quantities that threatened to result in an excess of small coins, and this adverse step is surely hinted at when the mill is under discussion.

The supposition that Middleton is Swift's hero Munodi is supported by his advice 'to consult annals and compare dates'. 1723 was the peak of Middleton's opposition to Wood's patent, when he had to give way to Walpole. Two years later the government revoked the earlier decision and cancelled Wood's patent. Is there a parallel here between Middleton's conduct and that of Munodi? If Lagado is meant to symbolize Ireland, then Munodi's governorship could be the Lord Chancellorship. According to Gulliver, Munodi, 'pressed by many of his Friends . . . complyed with the Proposal; and after employing an Hundred Men for two Years, the Work miscarried, the Projectors went off, laying the Blame intirely upon him' (p. 178). Here, apparently, are the two years between 1723 and 1725 during which Wood's patent was operational. Perhaps the allegory is not consistent, but when the mill is under discussion it would appear that Munodi is to be identified as Middleton, and this suggests that Swift was to some extent concentrating on Irish affairs in the much more fragmented *Voyage to Laputa*. There were, then, two main strands to the satire in the third book: one, when projecting is under fire, relates to the whole South Sea Bubble syndrome; the other to Ireland and the symbolic conflict over Wood's halfpence, with which Swift had been preoccupied in the *Drapier's Letters*.

---

[1] 28 December 1723, cited in Firth, pp. 257-8. Clark, p. 614, translates Munodi as Middleton, though of course all his translations may well have been inordinately influenced by the suggestions of Firth and Case. The dangers of playing language games are well illustrated by Marjorie Buckley's article, 'Key to the Language of the Houyhnhnms in *Gulliver's Travels*', in *Fair Liberty Was all His Cry: A Tercentenary Tribute to Jonathan Swift 1667-1745*, edited by A. Norman Jeffares (London, 1967), pp. 270-8. If this is not a parody of work of this genre on the language of *Gulliver's Travels*, and there is no overt indication that it is, then it certainly reads as one.

IV

The most potent and deliberate Swiftian satire on topical politics is made not in *A Voyage to Lilliput*, but in the unduly neglected *Voyage to Brobdingnag*. Gulliver's conversations with the King are the heart of Swift's political satire in *Gulliver's Travels* and they justify the relevance of Augustan satire to modern readers who are quite unfamiliar with contemporary figures and politics. In *A Voyage to Brobdingnag* Swift adopts the old 'Country' maxim of attacking measures not men, and he rehearses 'Country' ideology in opposition to Walpole and all he stood for. Swift's politics have been complicated unnecessarily by his apparent change of party in 1710. W. A. Speck has put forward a convincing argument to show that Swift, like Harley, 'split tickets' on different issues.[1] The complicating factor in the political psychology of both men was their stance on religious matters and their unequivocal support for the Church of England. This ostensibly tory outlook was tempered by an otherwise thoroughgoing 'Country' attitude to politics. 'Country' theory owed much to the doctrines of Harrington, though they were subjected to considerable deliberate distortion to bolster a belief (which, incidentally, Harrington did not share) in an 'ancient constitution'. The essential manifestation of 'Country' theory was a doctrine in which 'the balance of the constitution depended on the complete separation of Parliament and administration': 'It was for the Crown to govern, and for Parliament to exercise a jealous surveillance of government; "corruption" would follow if the Crown discovered any means at all of attaching members of Parliament in the pursuit of its business'.[2] It was precisely Walpole's role as arch-corrupter of parliaments that Swift sought to censure most vehemently. Placemen influenced debates, pensions were given to members of parliament to keep them on the side of the court. Walpole owed his long tenure of office to his success in buying off potential critics of his administration. Even the revival of the Order of the Bath, satirized in *A Voyage to Lilliput*, was to provide 'jobs for the boys' when no more places were available for disposal. To Swift this was anathema. The potent symbol of a standing army, 'a bogey intended for Country gentlemen', was used to portray the various features of a corrupt parliament. Xenophobic Country politicians called for the use of the fleet as the main defensive arm, and reliance on a militia for land warfare.[3] They saw no reason for Britain to interfere in international affairs and preferred a policy of isolation. Somewhat ironically, in view of his rivalry with Harley in the last years of Queen Anne, Bolingbroke, in the 1720s, was attempting to form an opposition party in parliament on the same lines as Harley's 'New Country Party' of the

---

[1] W. A. Speck, 'Swift's Politics', [Dublin] *University Review*, 4 (1967), 53–71 (p. 67).

[2] J. G. A. Pocock, 'Machiavelli, Harrington, and English Political Ideologies in the Eighteenth Century', *William amd Mary Quarterly*, 22 (1965), 549–83 (pp. 571, 577).

[3] See Pocock, p. 563. Ehrenpreis sees much in the King of Brobdingnag's views to 'trace themes back' to the works of Sir William Temple, though he stresses that the King is not a portrait of Temple. In fact the King's views rehearsed 'Country' theory. This is clinched by the exposition of the virtues of a militia over and above a mercenary standing army. 'What if the King of Brobdingnag did dislike armies and had no use for them?', writes Ehrenpreis, 'He nevertheless possessed a militia of two hundred thousand men; and all of Gulliver's apologizing does not convince me that Swift put that army in for any other reason than to enhance the giant king's awfulness at the expense of his coherence' (Ehrenpreis, p. 899). This completely misses the point of the King's emphasis on a militia, the same efficient militia that Harrington admired as the basis of the Roman republic, and not a standing army. My own view is closer to that of Myrddin Jones, 'Swift, Harrington and Corruption in England', *PQ*, 54 (1974), 59–70.

1690s. All malcontents were to be embraced under the convenient blanket of 'Country' ideology to provide effective opposition to Walpole. Swift was in complete accord with this, and it is in this context that the satire of *A Voyage to Brobdingnag* should be examined.

In the second book the personalized wit of the first gives way to an overtly comic but ultimately very serious indictment of Walpole's system of government (which again comes to light in the allegory of Atterbury's arrest and trial on the testimony of government spies in Book III (pp. 191–2)). The most precise formulation, however, occurs in Gulliver's dialogue with the King of Brobdingnag, the consistent feature of which is a desire to belittle Walpole's power by the stress on human insignificance alongside the Brobdingnagians, and the basis for the King's unfavourable opinion of men as 'the most pernicious Race of little odious Vermin that Nature ever suffered to crawl upon the Surface of the Earth' (p. 132) runs through the whole gamut of 'Country' grievances. Dealing first with parliament, Swift's irony is at once apparent in Gulliver's account of the House of Lords, 'the Ornament and Bulwark of the Kingdom'. From the Lords, Swift turns to the Commons, 'all principal Gentlemen, *freely* picked and culled out by the People themselves, for their great Abilities, and Love of their Country' (p. 128). The emphasis on the word *freely* in view of Walpole's blatantly corrupt elections was more than sufficient to serve as a handle for the King of Brobdingnag, in conjunction with Walpole's creation of peers for political reasons:

What Course [he asked] was taken to supply that Assembly, when any noble Family became extinct. What Qualifications were necessary in those who are to be created new Lords: Whether the Humour of the Prince, a Sum of Money to a Court-Lady, or a Prime Minister; or a Design of strengthening a Party opposite to the publick Interest, ever happened to be Motives in those Advancements . . . HE then desired to know, what Arts were practised in electing those whom I called Commoners. Whether, a Stranger with a strong Purse might not influence the vulgar Voters to chuse him before their own Landlord, or the most considerable Gentleman in the Neighbourhood. How it came to pass, that People were so violently bent upon getting into this Assembly, which I allowed to be a great Trouble and Expence, often to the Ruin of their Families, without any Salary or Pension: Because this appeared such an exalted Strain of Virtue and publick Spirit, that his Majesty seemed to doubt it might possibly not be always sincere: And he desired to know, whether such zealous Gentlemen could have any Views of refunding themselves for the Charges and Trouble they were at, by sacrificing the publick Good to the Designs of a weak and vicious Prince, in Conjunction with a corrupted Ministry.

This, in the guise of a simple critique of political standards, was a full-blooded attack on the Walpolean administration. Gulliver proceeded to provoke the King's queries on national debt, on foreign policy, and on the army:

HE fell next upon the Management of our Treasury; and said, he thought my Memory had failed me, because I computed our Taxes at about five or six Millions a Year; and when I came to mention the Issues, he found they sometimes amounted to more than double . . . if what I told him were true, he was still at a Loss how a Kingdom could run out of its Estate like a private Person. He asked me, who were our Creditors? and, where we found Money to pay them? He wondered to hear me talk of such chargeable and extensive Wars; that, certainly we must be a quarrelsome People, or live among very bad Neighbours; and that our Generals must needs be richer than our Kings. He asked, what Business we had out of our own Islands, unless upon the Score of Trade or Treaty, or to defend the Coasts with our Fleet. Above all, he was amazed to hear me talk of a mercenary standing Army in the Midst of Peace, and among a free People. He said, if we were governed by our own Consent in the Persons of our Representatives, he could not imagine of whom we were afraid, or against whom we were to fight; and would hear my Opinion, whether a private Man's House might not better be defended by himself, his Children, and Family; than by half a Dozen Rascals picked up at a Venture in the Streets, for small Wages, who might get an Hundred Times more by cutting their Throats. (pp. 129–31)

Of course it is a truism that Swift was satirizing British politics in *A Voyage to Brobdingnag*, but the allegory is, though concise, the most consistent in the work in its assault on Walpole's political morality and the methods by which he achieved and maintained power. The queries voiced by the King of Brobdingnag amount to a 'Country' manifesto: these were the abuses and anomalies Swift sought to mend. Here Swift's own views are voiced through the vehicle of the King, in competition with no one, and evading the possible confusion of using Gulliver as his medium. When Swift requires his political characterization to be recognized and understood he leaves no room for doubt in the identification. Otherwise he almost certainly meant to tease, playing word games for the edification of an audience of one. Swift's genuine political message figures as a cameo in the more general canvas of *Brobdingnag*: the fact that his most precisely formulated political grievances are aired in this manner may indicate how little we need concern ourselves with disputing the characterization of Limtoc, and free us from the subsequent dangers of historical inaccuracy. I would like to see *Gulliver's Travels* emancipated from arguments over political content, for the sake of the wider social satire. Swift expected that his 'Travells' would 'wonderfully mend the World'.[1] It is the timeless quality of social, not political, satire that makes the work relevant to the modern reader. Taken to its logical conclusion this argument assumes that Bolgolam, Reldresal, Munodi, even Flimnap, become types, symbols, not actual personalities, and that *Gulliver's Travels* is more readily digested in this way.

[1] *Correspondence*, III, 87: Swift to Ford, 14 August 1725.

Hume and Friends, 1756 and 1766:
Two New Letters

J. C. HILSON   JOHN VALDIMIR PRICE

University of Leicester   *University of Edinburgh*

Though his middle years are better documented than any other part of David Hume's life, we still know relatively little about some of the friendships he formed or consolidated during this period. The letters below add to our knowledge of two of the closest of these relationships, with Sir Harry Erskine of Alva, and John 'Fish' Craufurd of Auchenaimes. Both excellently illustrate Hume's statement in the letter to Erskine: 'I desire to live on very easy Terms with my Friends'.

I

The first letter, to Sir Harry Erskine, is Hume's only known letter to him. It was printed in part by John Hill Burton, and reprinted by Greig.[1] According to Hill Burton, the autograph was owned by his father-in-law, Cosmo Innes, the antiquary. This suggests that the autograph was in Scottish hands throughout the nineteenth century; but Greig was unable to locate the original when he published his two volumes of Hume letters in 1932. It was acquired by the National Library of Scotland in 1971.[2]

Sir Henry Erskine was the fifth Baronet of Alva and Cambuskenneth, and second son of Sir John Erskine, the third Baronet (d. 1739). His entire career seems to have been spent in the military, though he represented first Ayr, then Anstruther, in Parliament between 1749 and 1761. Indeed, he was a fairly prominent figure in mid-eighteenth-century political circles as one of the clique of Scotsmen surrounding the Prime Minister, Lord Bute. This relationship brought from Horace Walpole the well-known gibe that Bute 'was too haughty to admit to his familiarity but half a dozen silly authors and flatterers[:] Henry Erskine, a military poet, Home, a tragedy-writing parson'.[3] It was in a military context, however, that Hume probably encountered Sir Harry for the first time. Hume himself explains this in the posthumously published autobiographical sketch, *My Own Life*:

I then received an Invitation from General Stclair to attend him as Secretary to his Expedition, which was at first meant against Canada, but ended in an Incursion on the Coast of France: Next Year, to wit 1747, I received an Invitation from the General to attend him in the same Station in his military Embassy to the Courts of Vienna and Turin. I there wore the Uniform of an Officer; and was introduced at these courts as Aide-de-Camp to the General, along with Sir Harry Erskine and Capt Grant, now General Grant.

---

[1] John Hill Burton, *Life and Correspondence of David Hume*, 2 vols (Edinburgh, 1846), I, 219; *The Letters of David Hume*, edited by J. Y. T. Greig, 2 vols (Oxford, 1932), I, 228–9 (hereafter cited as *HL*). Greig prints only the second paragraph of the letter.

[2] National Library of Scotland, MS Acc. 5371. We are grateful to the Trustees of the Library for their kind permission to publish this letter.

[3] *Horace Walpole Memoirs and Portraits*, edited by Matthew Hodgart (London, 1963), p. 113.

In fact, Hume and Erskine met at least as early as June 1746, in Portsmouth, where preparations were being made for the abortive Canadian expedition mentioned in *My Own Life*.[1] Hume was acting as secretary to General St Clair, and Erskine was deputy quartermaster-general. Interestingly, both men also claimed kin with their general: Hume was distantly related, and Erskine was St Clair's nephew.

The friendship lasted until Erskine's death in 1765. His only surviving letter to Hume, written eleven months before his death, shows the strength of their relationship: in it, Sir Harry expresses his willingness to entrust to Hume the education of his son, with the stipulation that he should not have any 'converse' with John Wilkes.[2]

The letter has not been carefully preserved, and about an inch has been torn away down the entire right-hand margin. This has necessitated some editorial guesswork as to what Hume wrote. Conjectural readings are placed in square brackets. Dates and locations at the end of these letters have been brought forward to the beginning and placed in angular brackets. Otherwise, Hume's spelling and punctuation are retained throughout, except that raised letters are lowered.

<Edinburgh: 20 January 1756>

Dear Sr Harry,

    I had been very anxious for some time, on account of a Rumour,[3] [that the] Ministry intended to take your Commission from you: But receiv'd considerable Ease, on seeing [your] Letter to Edmonstone,[4] where you tell him that the Blow is already struck, & that it has [not hurt] you. It did indeed occur to me, that so singular a way of treating you, wou'd procure you [some] Friends, who, when Power shou'd come to their turn, woud see Justice done you; that it [seems from] the late Promotions that your Brevet of Lieutenant Colonel was entirely to be disreg[arded, &] that to serve longer under such Discouragements was more disagreeable than to lose all your [?Lands] and that at worst, the General, being satisfy'd with your Conduct, wou'd be easily able [to give] you Compensation for your Losses. I hope I am right in these Views or Conjecture[s;] however high an Idea I may have entertain'd of Philosophy in general, or of y[our Aspira]tion towards that noble Acquirement; I shou'd be sorry to find, that the Indifference which you express, proceeded entirely from Philosophy.

  I have been set upon by several to write something, tho' it were only to be inserted in the Magazines, in opposition to this Account, which Voltaire has given

---

[1] Erskine wrote from Portsmouth on 5 June 1746 to a mutual friend, Sir Hew Dalrymple of North Berwick, 'Mr Secretary Hume salutes you'. See J. C. Hilson, 'More Unpublished Letters of David Hume', *Forum for Modern Language Studies*, 6 (1970), 315–26 (p. 317).

[2] Royal Society of Edinburgh Hume MSS, v, 21 (hereafter cited as *RSE*).

[3] The 'Rumour' was that Erskine had been removed from the army list, which was in fact the case in 1756; *DNB* cites his opposition to the use of Hanoverian and Hessian troops as a reason. However, the strictures against him did not endure, and he was restored to his command on the accession of George III in 1760. He eventually rose to the rank of Lieutenant-General.

[4] James Edmonstoune of Newton, an early and lifelong friend of Hume. With Erskine and Hume, he had served on the L'Orient expedition. He began his military career as an Ensign in the 5th Foot in 1739, rising to Lt-Colonel (1st Foot) in 1762. He retired *circa* 1770.

of our Expedition.[1] But my answer still is, that it is not worth while, & that he is so totally mistaken in every Circumstance of that Affair, & indeed of every Affair, that I presume no body will pay [any Atten]tion to him. I hope you are of the same Opinion.

I beg to be remembered to the Doctor.[2] I am sorry to hear that Grant[3] is g[rown out of] all Shape, & yet still retains his Inclination to Foppery: For my Part, I have ceas'd [?caring] since my Belly has swelld so enormously. Alas! that is not an Infirmity, like gre[y hair] to be disguis'd with Powder & Pomatum. We hear that Mrs Murray[4] shines extremely, [& assidu]ously captivates all Hearts, without giving the least Return of her own. I hope, that [Rumours] which have been spred abroad so much to her Disadvantage, are not true. What is [——— do]ing?[5] Is he always as obstinate, & sometimes as much in the wrong, as formerly? [Does your] Dismission from his Majestys Service, ensure us of your Company next Summer? [I] ask you a great many Questions, in order to fill up this Letter of Condoleance or [Consola]tion: But I desire to live on very easy Terms with my Friends. I know you [?are busy]; and I hate to give Trouble. It will be sufficient, if on our Meeting you [respond] to my long Catechism. I am, with great Sincerity

Dear Sir Harry
Your affectionate Friend & humble Servant
David Hume

Edinburgh
20 Jany. 1756

II

The second letter is the earliest (but only by ten days) in Hume's correspondence with John Craufurd of Auchenaimes. Though it is addressed only to 'Dear Jack', the identity of the recipient is clear almost from the first line. Hume followed it ten days later with another letter on the same subject.[6] It constitutes Hume's tenth known letter to Craufurd, Greig having printed four and Klibansky and Mossner five.

---

[1] The work by Voltaire to which Hume alludes is the *History of the War of 1741*, translated into English late in 1755. Voltaire had completed the book several years earlier, but had never published it, only making use of parts of it in other publications. Hume did compose an account of the expedition, usually called 'Descent on the Coast of Britanny' (*RSE*, IX, 12; reprinted in *The Philosophical Works of David Hume*, edited by T. H. Green and T. H. Grose, 4 vols (London, 1874–5), IV, 443–60, and in Hill Burton, II, 441–56). See also E. C. Mossner, *The Life of David Hume* (Edinburgh, 1954), pp. 199–204; and P. H. Meyer, 'Voltaire and Hume's "Descent on the Coast of Britanny"', *Modern Language Notes*, 66 (1951), 429–35.

[2] John Clephane (d. 1758), another member of General St Clair's expedition, and one of Hume's closest friends. After studying medicine at Paris and Leyden, he practised as a physician in Golden Square, London. Alexander Carlyle describes him as 'one of the most sensible, learned and judicious men I ever knew — an admirable classical scholar and a fine historian'. See *The Autobiography of Dr Alexander Carlyle of Inveresk*, edited by John Hill Burton (London and Edinburgh, 1910), p. 362.

[3] James Grant (1720–1806) who served with Hume and Erskine under St Clair, and is mentioned in *My Own Life*.

[4] Possibly the Honourable Miss Helen (Nelly) Murray, sister of Hume's close friend Lord Elibank: she later married Sir John Stuart of Grandtully, one of the principals in the celebrated Douglas Cause.

[5] Unidentified.

[6] Printed with the permission of the current owner. For Hume's second letter to Craufurd, see *New Letters of David Hume*, edited by R. Klibansky and E. C. Mossner (Oxford, 1954), pp. 153–4 (hereafter cited as *NHL*).

John Craufurd of Auchenaimes (d. 1814) was the son of Patrick Craufurd of Auchenaimes (d. 1778). His footman's opinion of him as 'one of the gayest young gentlemen and the greatest gambler that ever belonged to Scotland' seems to have been generally endorsed.[1] He acquired the nickname 'Fish' at Eton on account of his inquisitiveness (his brother James was dubbed 'Flesh' Craufurd). His career shows an almost Boswellian ability and determination to get to know the leading political and literary lights of his day. He was on familiar terms with Lord North, Lord Ossory, the Duke of Grafton, and Lord Chancellor Wedderburn amongst others; and with Voltaire, Horace Walpole, and Mme du Deffand, as the letter below suggests. Sterne spoke of him as a close friend, and Craufurd was instrumental in raising a subscription for Sterne's widow and daughter in 1768: among those from whom he received a contribution was David Hume.[2] Lord Sheffield tells us that Gibbon 'had a particular regard' for Craufurd, and that he was among the last of the historian's friends to see him alive.[3] It is a pity that Boswell seems to have known 'Fish' rather less well than he knew his father, Patrick Craufurd, though there is evidence that young Auchinleck and young Auchenaimes dined together at least once, at Lord Lucan's in 1791:[4] it would be interesting to have a record of what passed between these two inquisitive, hypochondriac rakes.

Craufurd's projection of a rakish persona is clear from his letters to Hume; and it was 'Fish' who sponsored Hume for membership of Almack's, the London gambling club of which he was a founder member.[5] The two men had probably first made each other's acquaintance in Paris between late 1763 and 1766. During this period Hume had received a letter from Sir James MacDonald of Sleat, dated 18 May 1765, stating: 'I send you this by Mr. Crawford, son of Peter Crawford, who I imagine you must know'.[6]

The letter below confirms John MacDonald's observations about Craufurd's gambling proclivities, since this is clearly the 'Weakness' to which Hume alludes towards the end of the first paragraph. The tone of the letter, in which Hume regards an income of eight hundred pounds as adequate so long as Craufurd practises a few economies, is remarkable when we consider that Hume was reported as saying in 1758 that he would give up all expectations in life for thirty pounds a year.[7] Against this must be set his observation in *My Own Life* that by the end of 1747 he was 'Master of near a thousand Pound'. Hume's implied exhortation to Craufurd to give up gambling is diffident to the point of being unmentioned, and in view of the undeniably lean years Hume lived through before the late 1740s, his admonition is remarkably restrained. He had learned how to give advice to a younger man without implying a comparison between their respective situations, and he seems to have been of some assistance in effecting a reconciliation between

[1] John Macdonald, *Memoirs of an Eighteenth-Century Footman*, edited by John Beresford (London, 1927), p. 82. For a full account of Craufurd's career, see Norman Pearson, ' "Fish" Craufurd', *The Nineteenth Century and After*, 75 (1914), 389–401.

[2] *Letters of Laurence Sterne*, edited by L. P. Curtis (Oxford, 1955), pp. 262–3 and 444–5.

[3] *The Miscellaneous Works of Edward Gibbon*, edited by John, Lord Sheffield, Second English edition, 5 vols (London, 1814), I, 422.

[4] *Private Papers of James Boswell from Malahide Castle*, edited by Geoffrey Scott and F. A. Pottle, 18 vols (privately printed: Mt Vernon, 1928–34), XVIII, 101.

[5] *NHL*, p. 155; n. 2.

[6] *Letters of Eminent Persons to David Hume*, edited by John Hill Burton (Edinburgh, 1849), p.54; *RSE*, VI, 23.

[7] *The Diary of Sylas Neville 1767–1788*, edited by Basil Cozens-Hardy (London, 1950), p. 202.

Craufurd and his father, and perhaps in attenuating Craufurd's gambling prodigalities.[1]

It is, however, possible that the moderate tone of this letter was still too strong for Hume's taste, and that he never sent it. The earliest of his other letters to Craufurd is dated 15 November 1766, and begins in much the same manner as this one: 'I was told, dear Jack, by Davie Ross, that your Father had taken out an Inhibition against you . . .'.[2] That letter is unsigned, however, and Hume could have been responding to a letter of Craufurd's written before he had Hume's of 5 November. At any rate this letter confirms that Hume was always prepared to put himself to trouble on Craufurd's behalf. Their friendship lasted until Hume's death in 1776.

Edinburgh: 5 November 1766

Dear Jack,

I was told by Davie Ross[3] t'other day a Measure of your Fathers with regard to you, which, I own, I wou'd blame in the strongest Terms if Decency did not forbid me. Surely, your Faults are very slight in comparison of your good Qualities; and your Behaviour towards him has even been laudable. Among your Faults (for I own you have some) I place a Degree of Spleen and Peevishness; which I regret the most of any, because it renders you unhappy: I dread the Effects which may result from such a Disposition, after the Treatment you have met with. But, my dear Jack, recollect your Good sense; and never from Despair take Revenge on Yourself for the Injuries which others may do you. Your Father, as Mr Ross tells me, is willing to allow you 500 a year, which indeed is too little for a young man who has such Prospects; and considering your way of living, and the Company you frequent, it is impossible you can limit yourself to it. Yet you thought (and the World will think) that if he had allowd you 800, he woud not have been altogether unreasonable, and that you coud with a very little Oeconomy have subsisted on it. I entreat you; form & persist in that plan of Life: When I left you, Fortune had favour'd you; and you was considerably in Cash. Add, from your present Stock, 300 a year to your Allowance: Even, if it were 500 a year, it would not much hurt you: and time will certainly bring you relief, if you remain quiet. Above all things, (I entreat you) but need I finish what I have to say: You conjecture my Meaning; and all Entreaties are vain, if you do not, within yourself, form a determin'd Resolution. But be assur'd, that that Weakness is the only Pretence your Father has for his Conduct, and the only thing that can justify him even in the Eyes of his most partial Friends. Deprive him of that Pretence; and give all your Friends the Satisfaction of being able to justify you in that particular.

But so much for sage Council; which indeed was superfluous. For you knew beforehand the Truth of all I have said. We shall therefore talk of another Subject. It has happend as you foresaw; that I shoud at last, whether I wou'd or not, be oblig'd to give to the Public an Account of this ridiculous Affair between Rousseau

---

[1] *NHL*, p. 155.
[2] *NHL*, p. 153.
[3] David Ross (1727–1805), an Edinburgh lawyer; raised to the Bench as Lord Ankerville, 1776.

and me.[1] D'alembert has made use of the discretionary Power I gave him, and has printed the Narrative you saw, with a Preface, giving an Account of the Necessity which he lay under to do so.[2] The only thing, that displeases me is a Declaration annex'd, which is very disobliging to Horace Walpole: There is also a little Squib thrown at Mde du Duffan if I understand it right.[3] Besides, some obliging things which I said, from my sincere Sentiments, of Mr Walpole, are expung'd, which is a little unaccountable. Is it possible, that a Man of such Parts & Virtues as Dalembert can bear an Ill will to Mr Walpole merely because the latter has a Friendship for a Person whom the former hates? And does Philosophy serve us to so little purpose? Voltaire says you are a Philosopher: and all the World knows Rousseau to be one: Voltaire himself is also one: I say nothing; but the Devil himself will not hinder me from thinking.

I have wrote to Mr Walpole about this Affair of Dalemberts Declaration;[4] and as he makes Profession of being no Philosopher, I doubt not but I shall find him a reasonable Man. I only forgot to mention one thing to Mr Walpole, which I desire you to mention to him, when you see him. It is this: The Duke of Richmond[5] may think it odd, that in a Letter of mine to Rousseau[6] I shoud have promis'd him the Duke's good Offices, tho' I had never spoke to his Grace on the Subject. But my Reason, for trusting to the Duke was, that I knew his great Esteem for Rousseau, and Mr Walpole besides, promisd me, if it was necessary, his good Offices with the Duke, as he had already done with General Conway.[7]

I desire no Politics from you, except an Account of your hopes to succeed in obtaining a Seat next Parliament.[8] I am Dear Jack

Yours sincerely

Edinburgh 5 of Novr   David Hume
1766

---

[1] The famous quarrel between Hume and Rousseau. The work to which Hume alludes is the *Exposé succinct de la contestation qui s'est élevée entre M. Hume et M. Rousseau . . .*, which was published in Paris in October 1766. The English translation appeared in November as *A Concise and Genuine Account of the Dispute between Mr. Hume and Mr. Rousseau.* See Mossner, *Life*, pp. 507–32.

[2] Jean le Rond d'Alembert (1717–83), one of the French *philosophes* most admired by Hume. For d'Alembert's part in the Hume-Rousseau quarrel, see L.-A. Boiteux, 'Le Rôle de d'Alembert dans la Querelle Rousseau-Hume', *Annales de la Société J.-J. Rousseau*, 33 (1950–52), 143–54.

[3] Marie de Vichy-Chamrond (1697–1780), who married in 1718 Jean-Baptiste de la Lande, Marquis du Deffand: French salonnière, and friend and correspondent of Horace Walpole.

[4] See *HL*, II, pp. 100–1.

[5] Charles Lennox, 3rd Duke of Richmond (1735–1806); Secretary of State, Southern Department, May–July 1766. Hume would probably have made his acquaintance in November 1765, when the Duke and his brother arrived in Paris to take over Lord Hertford's Embassy. Hume had become Embassy Secretary to Lord Hertford in September 1763. Richmond and his brother were not so well liked in Paris as Hume and Lord Hertford had been, but it is worth noting that Hume was apparently on good enough terms with Richmond to depend, however slightly, upon his favour.

[6] *HL*, II, 52.

[7] Henry Seymour Conway (1719–95), brother to Francis Seymour Conway, Lord Hertford, and first cousin to Horace Walpole. Secretary of State, Southern Department, 1765–6, and Northern Department, 1766–8, when Hume was his Under-Secretary. He and Lord Hertford both urged publication of the *Concise Account*, and each received one of the ten copies of the French edition which Hume requested of William Strahan: see *HL*, II, 97.

[8] Craufurd was not elected to Parliament until 1774, when he became member for Renfrewshire. Craufurd had asked Baron Mure of Cauldwell to make Hume a voter in Renfrew, but Hume did not vote for him: see *HL*, II, 283–5.

Neither Hume nor anyone else, it seems, was totally successful in reforming Craufurd, and he continued to gamble as long as Hume knew him. One of the last letters Hume wrote was to Craufurd, on 15 June 1776, two months before he died. Hume invites Craufurd to join him in Coventry where his 'only real substantial grievance will be, that in this way of living you will not be able to spend as much a day as a fine gentleman ought to do, but you may lose as much to me in the evening at picket as is proper'.[1] Craufurd was unable to meet him, and Hume was presumably unable to allay Craufurd's professional instinct for gambling with his own appraisal of it as a form of amusement.[2]

[1] *HL*, ii, 327.
[2] Mossner, *Life*, p. 546.

'A Dialogue on Idealities':
An Unpublished Manuscript of
Thomas Love Peacock

NICHOLAS A. JOUKOVSKY

Pennsylvania State University

Among the letters and literary manuscripts of Thomas Love Peacock in the 'Broughton Papers' acquired by the British Museum in 1950, there is an unpublished holograph manuscript entitled 'A Dialogue on Idealities' (Add. MS 47225, ff. 193–207). This is not an entirely new work, as the title might suggest, but a revised and expanded version of the untitled draft (Add. MS 36815, ff. 191–200) published as 'A Dialogue on Friendship after Marriage' in an appendix to the Halliford Edition of Peacock's *Works*.[1] The dialogue, in both versions, is essentially a debate between two married women on the question 'whether a married man or woman may love in a third person the qualities in which the legitimate partner is deficient'. And in both versions a third woman, evidently a mutual acquaintance, appears in the course of the discussion to arbitrate between them. A late work, probably written shortly after *Gryll Grange* (1860), 'A Dialogue on Idealities' is interesting not only as a reflection of Peacock's views on love and marriage but as the only formal dialogue by an author who made extensive use of direct dialogue in his fiction.

Although it is preserved with Peacock's letters to his friend John Cam Hobhouse, Baron Broughton, the manuscript of 'A Dialogue on Idealities' is not mentioned in their extant correspondence, and it may have been presented to Broughton's daughter Charlotte (1831–1914), who was married in 1854 to Dudley Wilmot Carleton, afterwards fourth Baron Dorchester (1822–97).[2] A brief note in Mrs Carleton's hand on the title-page (signed 'C.D.C.' and therefore written before 1875, when she became Lady Dorchester) merely states that the unsigned manuscript was by Peacock and 'given to me', but this would seem to imply that it was given to her by Peacock himself rather than by her father. Peacock had been particularly fond of Lord Broughton's daughters as children, and there is every reason to believe that he remained on familiar terms with 'Chattie' Hobhouse after she reached womanhood. We know, for example, that she occasionally corresponded with him both before and after her marriage, and that at least once, in August 1857, she spent several days with him at Lower Halliford.[3]

---

[1] *The Works of Thomas Love Peacock*, edited by H. F. B. Brett-Smith and C. E. Jones, 10 vols (London, 1924–34), VIII, 447–51. Hereafter cited as *Works*.

[2] These letters are arranged in chronological order in Add. MS 47225. I have thought it sufficient to cite them by date, since the foliation of this unbound manuscript has been revised twice in the last few years, most recently in November 1972.

[3] There are references to their correspondence in Brett-Smith's 'Biographical Introduction' to *Works*, I, clxxix, note, and in Peacock's letters to Lord Broughton of 7 November 1859 and 24 December 1861. Mrs Carleton's visit is described in Peacock's letter to his daughter Mary Ellen of 16 August 1857 (*Works*, VIII, 246).

The Broughton manuscript is a holograph fair copy, consisting of eight double sheets of thin pink octavo notepaper, placed one inside the other to form a single quire of sixteen leaves (measuring $5\frac{1}{4} \times 8\frac{1}{4}$ inches). These have, in turn, been placed inside two extra double sheets of similar, but slightly smaller and darker, paper and pinned together at the fold. The recto of the first leaf bears Peacock's title ('A Dialogue / on / Idealities.') as well as Mrs Carleton's note of ownership ('By / T. L. Peacock / given to me / C.D.C.'). The text, with the title repeated at its head, occupies the rectos of the next fourteen leaves, which are numbered in the upper right-hand corner from 1 to 14. The recto of the final leaf and the versos of all sixteen leaves are blank. Unfortunately the manuscript is not quite complete. A strip approximately two inches wide, possibly containing an authorial note or inscription, has been cut from the bottom of the title leaf, and three passages, amounting to just under nine lines in all, have been neatly cut from folios 9, 11, and 12 of the text. None of the missing passages occurs in the draft, but I have been able to supply one of them, a quotation, from the context. The nature of this quotation ('I take her Body, you her Mind; | Which has the better Bargain?') suggests that the excisions may have been made by someone with a highly developed sense of Victorian prudery. It is hard to think of an equally likely motive for the mutilation of the text, though the bottom of the title leaf may have been cut off for the sake of an autograph.

The fair copy of 'A Dialogue on Idealities' is more than twice as long as the untitled draft, which consists of four separate fragments: (1) an opening, which establishes the two opposing views, and which corresponds fairly closely to the first quarter of the finished work, (2) a brief exchange containing an additional argument, (3) a few lines that appear to be the final portion of another additional argument, and (4) a conclusion, which brings the dialogue to an abrupt end shortly after the entrance of the arbitress, who gives her judgement without having heard the arguments of either side. Since the first and third fragments end in mid-page, and the second is followed by a blank leaf, it seems likely that they were all composed independently. It is not clear whether the additional arguments were written before or after the conclusion, but the order in which they appear in the fair copy, where there is no break between the introductory and concluding portions of the draft, suggests that the latter may have been the case. At any rate Peacock must have realized that his original conclusion was inadequate and decided to extend the dialogue, using the late Middle English romance of *The Knight of Curtesy and the Fair Lady of Faguell* as the basis for further debate. It is evident from the fragmentary state of the draft and from the lack of revision in the fair copy that there must have been at least one other manuscript of the dialogue, an intermediate draft, but only the fragmentary early draft appears to have been found among Peacock's papers.[1]

Although time and place are not specified in either version of the dialogue, the draft evidently has a classical setting, and the fair copy a modern one. The names in the draft (Galatea, Amaryllis, Tityrus, Corydon, Daphnis, and Aegle) all come from the Greek and Latin pastoral tradition, the first five occurring in Theocritus, and all six in Virgil's *Eclogues*. There are no quotations and only two allusions: to

---

[1] The draft was among the Peacock manuscripts purchased by the British Museum from his granddaughter Edith Nicolls Clarke in 1903. See the bibliographical note in *Works*, VIII, 545-6.

'the Greek painter' who 'made one form from many beauties' (Zeuxis of Heraclea, who flourished in the latter part of the fifth century B.C.) and to Amaryllis's visit to Rome, 'where she has found a fashionable amusement which they call "controversies" ' (the declamatory exercises known as *controversiae* became a 'fashionable amusement' among the intelligentsia of Rome in the time of Augustus). In the final version, on the other hand, Peacock not only substitutes Italianate names (Leonora, Isabella, Eugenio, Alphonso, Rodolpho, and Beatrice) but introduces a number of English and French quotations, as well as several new allusions, ranging from a twelfth-century Provençal *tenson* to a nineteenth-century Italian singer. The wealth of quotation and allusion in the final version seems to reflect a subtle change in Peacock's conception of the dialogue. In the draft the principal characters purport to be trying their skill in the manner of the Roman 'controversies', in which 'a question is proposed and there is a trial of skill as to what can be said on both sides'. However, in the fair copy the arbitress is told that they are trying their hands at 'a *tenson* of the twelfth century', a form of poetical debate between rival troubadours that the Reverend Doctor Opimian wishes to revive in the opening chapter of *Gryll Grange*:

The Reverend Doctor Opimian
. . . I do not comprehend how people can find amusement in lectures. I should much prefer a *tenson* of the twelfth century, when two or three masters of the *Gai Saber* discussed questions of love and chivalry.

Miss Gryll
I am afraid, Doctor, our age is too prosy for that sort of thing. We have neither wit enough, nor poetry enough, to furnish the disputants. I can conceive a state of society in which such *tensons* would form a pleasant winter evening amusement: but that state of society is not ours.

The Reverend Doctor Opimian
Well, Miss Gryll, I should like, some winter evening, to challenge you to a *tenson,* and your uncle should be umpire. I think you have wit enough by nature, and I have poetry enough by memory, to supply a fair portion of the requisite materials, without assuming an absolute mastery of the *Gai Saber.*

Miss Gryll
I shall accept the challenge, Doctor. The wit on one side will, I am afraid, be very short-coming; but the poetry on the other will no doubt be abundant. (*Works*, v, 9–10)

If the classical version of the dialogue could be set in the Arcadian world of the pastoral, the modern version would seem to be set in the equally unreal 'state of society' envisioned by Morgana Gryll: one that would be more hospitable to wit and poetry than Victorian England.

Peacock's correspondence with Lord Broughton provides no clue to the date or occasion of 'A Dialogue on Idealities', but it can hardly have been written earlier than 1859, the date of the watermark in the white notepaper of the draft.[1] While little is known about the composition of any of Peacock's later works, the mere record of his publications suggests that he is unlikely to have had much leisure to write the dialogue until after he had finished his 'Memoirs of Percy Bysshe Shelley,

---

[1] The pink notepaper of the fair copy has no watermark, but it is similar, though not identical, to that which Peacock used for his letters to Lord Broughton on 16 August and 9 October 1861 and again on 13 and 27 November 1862. The intervening letters were all written on mourning paper in consequence of the death of his daughter Mary Ellen on 22 October 1861.

Part II' and 'Unpublished Letters of Percy Bysshe Shelley', which appeared in *Fraser's Magazine* for January and March 1860, and *Gryll Grange*, which was serialized in *Fraser's Magazine* from April to December 1860, though it may have been substantially completed before the first instalment was published.[1] The most likely period of composition would appear to be the interval between the completion of *Gryll Grange* some time in 1860 and the onset of his eldest daughter's fatal illness about the beginning of August 1861. Peacock's constant anxiety during Mary Ellen's illness and his severe depression following her death in October apparently suspended his literary activities until after Christmas,[2] but he recovered sufficiently in the following year to produce a 'Supplementary Notice' on Shelley for the March 1862 number of *Fraser's Magazine*, as well as his last little book, *Gl' Ingannati . . . and Aelia Laelia Crispis*, published in August 1862.[3] Peacock's health appears to have declined in the autumn of 1862, and he is not known to have undertaken any further literary work. On the whole, then, it seems most likely that the dialogue was written in 1860 or 1861, though it may have been written as early as 1859 or as late as 1862.

There is no reason to believe that Peacock intended to publish 'A Dialogue on Idealities', either in *Fraser's Magazine* or in the 'Collection of Miscellanies' which he contemplated in 1861.[4] Indeed it seems more likely that he wrote it as an intellectual exercise, if not as a mere 'winter evening amusement'. Some forty years earlier, in April 1818, he had said in a letter to Thomas Jefferson Hogg:

I have been considering the question of marriage and divorce, and have read everything I can get on the subject including that strange tissue of chimæras the Empire of the Nairs. I rather incline still to the orthodox side: but I shall write when I have leisure a dialogue on the subject to get a clearer view of my own notions.[5]

Although he never found the leisure to write this proposed dialogue on marriage and divorce, Peacock evidently found the dialogue a congenial literary form as well as a convenient means of clarifying alternative positions. He may even have recalled this earlier scheme when he came to write 'A Dialogue on Idealities', in which he still rather inclines to 'the orthodox side'. However, the impulse to write the dialogue may have grown out of his recent reconsideration of Shelley's abandonment of his first wife for another young woman who, at least for a time, 'constituted his ideality'. Peacock infuriated many of Shelley's warmer admirers with his vigorous defence of Harriet Shelley in his 'Memoirs of Percy Bysshe Shelley, Part II':

Some of Shelley's friends have spoken and written of Harriet as if to vindicate him it were necessary to disparage her. They might, I think, be content to rest the explanation of his conduct on the ground on which he rested it himself — that he had found in another the intellectual qualities which constituted his ideality of the partner of his life.[6]

[1] See Carl Van Doren, *The Life of Thomas Love Peacock* (London, 1911), pp. 239–40; and Brett-Smith's 'Biographical Introduction' to *Works*, I, cxcvii.

[2] Letters to Lord Broughton of 16 August, 9 October, 21 November, and 24 December 1861.

[3] It was advertised as published in the *Athenaeum* of 16 August 1862 (p. 199) and reviewed in the issue of 6 September 1862 (p. 305).

[4] Letter to Thomas L'Estrange of 11 July 1861 (*Works*, VIII, 253).

[5] *Shelley and His Circle, 1773–1822*, edited by Kenneth Neill Cameron and Donald H. Reiman, 10 vols (Cambridge, Massachusetts, 1961—), VI, 549. Peacock refers to James Henry Lawrence's *The Empire of the Nairs; or, The Rights of Women: An Utopian Romance, in Twelve Books* (1811), a work which influenced Shelley's attack on marriage in *Queen Mab* (1813).

[6] *Works*, VIII, 110–11. *OED* cites this passage as its first and only example of the use of 'ideality' in the sense of an ideal.

The basic question of 'A Dialogue on Idealities' is not raised directly in Peacock's fiction, but there are extended discussions of 'Love and Marriage' in *Melincourt* (1817), Chapter 11 (*Works*, II, 112–21), and of 'The Lottery of Marriage' in *Gryll Grange*, Chapter 12 (*Works*, V, 101–11). The heroines of both tales have ideal conceptions of the qualities they are looking for in a prospective marriage partner. Anthelia Melincourt makes it known to all her suitors that 'the spirit of the age of chivalry, manifested in the forms of modern life, would constitute the only character on which she could fix her affections' (Chapter 8, *Works*, II, 85). And Morgana Gryll speaks of her 'idealities' in discussing her suitors with Algernon Falconer:

> He [Lord Curryfin] so far differs from all my preceding suitors, that in every one of them I found the presence of some quality that displeased me, or the absence of some which would have pleased me: the want, in the one way or the other, of that entire congeniality in taste and feeling, which I think essential to happiness in marriage. He has so strong a desire of pleasing, and such power of acquisition and assimilation, that I think a woman truly attached to him might mould him to her mind. Still, I can scarcely tell why, he does not complete my idealities. They say, Love is his own avenger; and perhaps I shall be punished by finding my idealities realized in one who will not care for me. (Chapter 20, *Works*, V, 207–8)

Unlike the heroines of Peacock's fiction, the two main characters in his dialogue have already made their choice of a partner. Both women are faithful to their husbands, neither of whom has given his wife any serious cause for complaint. But whereas Isabella is satisfied with the reality of her husband Eugenio, Leonora has an ideality which she seeks to complete by enjoying the company of her friend Rodolpho in addition to that of her husband Alphonso. 'Is this right or wrong?' she asks.

'In the questions which have come within my scope', Peacock wrote in a letter to Thomas L'Estrange of 11 July 1861, 'I have endeavoured to be impartial, and to say what could be said on both sides' (*Works*, VIII, 253). It was probably from a desire to clarify the issues involved and to state the case fairly, rather than from timidity, that he decided to leave sex out of the question in 'A Dialogue on Idealities'. Peacock's own point of view would seem to be that of the umpire Beatrice, who concludes, in favour of Isabella, that 'there can be no true happiness in marriage, without unlimited confidence and undivided love'. But the dialogue does not end with a simple victory for the sort of cheerful realism represented by Mr Hilary in *Nightmare Abbey* (1818),[1] for the conclusion clearly reveals the extent to which the 'orthodox' position of Isabella and Beatrice depends upon an idealization of love as well as of the marriage bond. Beatrice does indeed 'recede a little too far from practical life', as Leonora points out; and her admission that theory and practice never quite coincide leaves the whole question up in the air.

Peacock himself had good reason to know the odds against drawing a prize in the lottery of marriage, for his parents appear to have separated when he was three

---

[1] Compare Mr Hilary's response to the disappointed idealism of the Byronic Mr Cypress in *Nightmare Abbey*, Chapter 11: 'Ideal beauty is not the mind's creation: it is real beauty, refined and purified in the mind's alembic, from the alloy which always more or less accompanies it in our mixed and imperfect nature. But still the gold exists in a very ample degree. To expect too much is a disease in the expectant, for which human nature is not responsible . . . To rail against humanity for not being abstract perfection, and against human love for not realising all the splendid visions of the poets of chivalry, is to rail at the summer for not being all sunshine, and at the rose for not being always in bloom.' (*Works*, III, 107–8.)

years old, and his wife had been 'a complete nervous invalid' for a quarter of a century prior to her death in 1851.[1] In his introduction to *Horæ Dramaticæ*, a series of articles that he contributed to *Fraser's Magazine* in 1852–7, he remarks:

Goethe, we think — for we cannot cite chapter and verse — says somewhere something to this effect — that the realities of life present little that is either satisfactory or hopeful; and that the only refuge for a mind, which aspires to better views of society, is in the idealities of the theatre.

Without going to the full extent of this opinion, we may say, that the drama has been the favourite study of this portion of our plurality, and has furnished to us, on many and many occasions, a refuge of light and tranquillity from the storms and darkness of every-day life. (*Works*, x, 3)

The realities of Peacock's later years were much darker than has often been supposed, and there was clearly a strong escapist impulse behind his retreat to his library,[2] as well as his occasional refuge from the realities of life in the idealities of dialogue.

In the text of the dialogue which follows, I have attempted to carry out Peacock's final intentions as indicated in the Broughton manuscript.[3] I have retained his spelling, capitalization, and punctuation, except in a very few cases where the punctuation of the manuscript is obviously defective. My only emendations have been to supply two commas, a period, and a question mark, and to eliminate two inadvertent verbal repetitions. All of these editorial changes and all of Peacock's corrections and revisions in the manuscript are recorded in the textual notes, which are indicated by alphabetical signs. The explanatory notes, indicated numerically, serve to identify quotations and allusions, as well as to show the relationship between the Broughton manuscript and the early draft. I have noted all verbal variants between the fair copy and the corresponding portions of the draft, but I have as a rule ignored the cancellations in the draft, most of which are trivial and none of which are adopted in the fair copy.

1/   A Dialogue on Idealities.

LEONORA   ISABELLA[4]

LEONORA   Well met, Isabella. I have not seen you since you married Eugenio. I hope I may wish you joy of a happy marriage.

ISABELLA   You may indeed, Leonora, and I may thank you for it. I should never have married[5] Eugenio,[a] if you had not forsaken him.[6]

LEONORA   I am told he says, the only kindness I ever showed him was in casting him off, which resulted in his being blessed with you.

---

[1] See Brett-Smith's 'Biographical Introduction' to *Works*, I, xiii–xiv, xx–xxi, clxxix–clxxx.

[2] See Edith Nicolls's 'Biographical Notice' in *The Works of Thomas Love Peacock*, edited by Henry Cole, 3 vols (London, 1875), I, xlix–li.

[3] To save space, however, the speakers' names have been placed in small capitals at the beginning of the first line of each speech. In the manuscript they are centred on the line above the speech and followed by a period, with only the initial letter capitalized and without underlining, unless otherwise indicated in the textual notes.

[4] In the draft, which has no title or heading, Leonora = Galatea, Isabella = Amaryllis, Eugenio = Tityrus, Alphonso = Corydon, Rodolpho = Daphnis, Beatrice = Aegle.

[5] The draft, through an oversight, reads: 'should never have left'.

[6] With the names in the draft, this situation is reminiscent of Virgil, *Eclogues*, I. 27–35, where Tityrus relates that he fell under the spell of Amaryllis after having been forsaken by Galatea.

ISABELLA　If he has said so, it was without malice to you, and simply to express his satisfaction with me. Now, I hope, I may equally congratulate you on the result of your marriage with Alphonso.[1] /2/

LEONORA　Why yes, perhaps. I am happy enough, as this world goes. I think you are my friend. If I thought you would keep my secret, I would tell you something.

ISABELLA　You had better not have a secret. If you have, you had better not trust any one with it.

LEONORA[b]　My dear, I must tell it. The only question is, to whom? I am dying for confidence and sympathy and advice. I had rather tell you than any one. Shall I?

ISABELLA　I do not like having any secrets from my husband.

LEONORA　But this in no way concerns him. I know you will keep it, if you promise.

ISABELLA　Well, for once I will promise.

LEONORA　It is no very great matter, after all. But it might wound Alphonso's self-love. He has many good qualities, but not all that a /3/ man can have. He does not complete my ideality. What I miss in him I find in Rodolpho. Therefore I take pleasure in Rodolpho's company.[2] Is this right or wrong?

ISABELLA　I am not a good judge. I do not find in any other man any qualities that Eugenio wants. No doubt there are many which he has not. But I do not see that he wants them: that I should like him any the better for having them.

LEONORA　You are satisfied with a reality. But I have an ideality, and as the Greek painter made one form from many beauties,[3] so I make one man[4] from a less extensive but not dissimilar combination. I find in Rodolpho some congenialities of thought and feeling and taste, which I do not find in Alphonso. And I like to converse where I find sympathy. I find some in Alphonso, on some[c] subjects, but not on all. I must have sympathy on all. I am clear from all moral error.[5] I rely on my own strength of mind to keep me so. Now, again, is this right or wrong? /4/

ISABELLA　Why, if you press the question, I can only say, wrong. That is my view of the matter. I think married life should be[6] all confidence: and as we must know before-hand that the best of us are not perfect, we should make up our minds before-hand to take the good that falls to our lot, without wishing for that which does not belong to it. I am happier than you are. I am contented and tranquil. You are discontented and feverish.

---

[1] In the draft, 'Daphnis' is altered to 'Corydon'.

[2] The draft adds: 'Tell me your opinion.'

[3] According to Cicero, *De Inventione*, II. I. 1–3, Zeuxis of Heraclea chose five of the most beautiful virgins of Crotona as models for his famous painting of Helen because he did not believe that all the elements of ideal beauty could be found in any individual. Compare *Nightmare Abbey*, Chapter II (Mr Flosky speaking): 'The ideal beauty of the Helen of Zeuxis was the combined medium of the real beauty of the virgins of Crotona.' (*Works*, III, 109.)

[4] The draft reads: 'one perfect man'.

[5] The draft reads: 'moral wrong'.

[6] The draft, through an oversight, omits 'be'.

LEONORA   No: I am contented to be the wife of Alphonso, with the addition of the friendship of Rodolpho.[1]

ISABELLA   I cannot admit the theory. Married love should be one and indivisible. It should not be shared by another, even under the most innocent semblance of affectionate friendship.

LEONORA   But if the husband or the wife does not complete the ideality of a sensitive and[2] imaginative[d] /5/ mind, may not so much as is wanting to complete it be admired, even loved, in another? There is in fact no divided feeling, when the qualities found in the latter have no existence in the former.

ISABELLA   In that case, there is only an imperfect, where in the best theory of marriage there ought to be a perfect, love. We cannot say[3] of any one, that he or she is faultless. There are, in the best, some qualities which we could wish absent, and others which we could wish[4] present: but if the good and the agreeable predominate, that should be sufficient.[5] But here is Beatrice. Let her arbitrate. I will put the question so, that she shall not suppose either of us to be personally concerned in the solution.

BEATRICE   What are you two discussing so earnestly?

ISABELLA   We are trying our hands at a *tenson* of the twelfth century.[6] /6/

BEATRICE   What is the subject?

ISABELLA   We are discussing the love of the Knight of Courtesy and the Lady of Fayel: Whether they were justified in their love, or the Lord of Fayel was justified in his jealousy?[7]

LEONORA   Will you be umpire between us?

BEATRICE[e]   Willingly. But you must first tell me the story: for I am not familiar with it.

ISABELLA   The Knight entered into the service of the Lord of Fayel, and became his bosom friend. The Knight and the Lady conceived great love for each

---

[1] The opening section of the draft ends at this point; the concluding section begins with the next speech, but the next three speeches lack the speakers' names.

[2] The draft reads: 'or'.

[3] The draft reads: 'We can scarcely say.'

[4] The draft omits 'wish'.

[5] The draft proceeds to conclude thus: 'And above all there should be perfect confidence on both sides. But here is Aegle: let her arbitrate[.] /Aegle./ What is it that you two are discussing so earnestly? /Galatea./ Amaryllis has been to Rome where she has found a fashionable amusement which they call "controversies". A question is proposed and there is a trial of skill as to what can be said on both sides. We have been trying our skill in this way on the question whether a married man or woman may love in a third person the qualities in which the legitimate partner is deficient[.] /Amaryllis[.]/ I have said No. /Aegle./ I agree with Amaryllis that there ought to be perfect confidence in marriage.' The Roman *controversiae* were declamatory exercises in which doubtful points of law were debated in terms of imaginary cases. They are best illustrated in the *Controversiae* of the elder Seneca.

[6] A *tenson* was a poetic contest or dialogue, in which rival troubadours supported opposite sides of a question in alternate stanzas. See the discussion of *tensons* in *Gryll Grange*, Chapter 1 (quoted above).

[7] Peacock's account of this famous triangle is based on the late fifteenth-century metrical romance *The Knight of Curtesy and the Fair Lady of Faguell*, which was edited from the unique copy of William Copland's black-letter edition in the Bodleian Library by Joseph Ritson in his *Ancient Engleish Metrical Romanceës*, 3 vols (London, 1802), III, 193–218. Ritson explains in his notes that '*Le chastellain de Couci*, the constable, that is, of *Couci-castle* (so strangely perverted in the present poem to "The knight of *Curtesy*"), and *la dame de Faïel* (Gabrielle de Vergi, or Levergies), here call'd "the lady of Faguell," are celebrateëd loveërs, and the subject of a metrical romance in French of the thirteenth century, stil extant in the national library at Paris' (III, 353–4). The French *Histoire du châtelain de Coucy et de la dame de Fayel*, in which the lovers are by no means chaste, was published by G. A. Crapelet in 1829, but there is no reason to believe that Peacock had read it. Ritson's book is listed in the sale catalogue of Peacock's library (Sotheby, Wilkinson, and Hodge, 11–12 June 1866, lot 528).

other, *en tout bien, tout honneur*.[1] But a servant, who saw them together, made an exaggerated report to the Lord, who sent the Knight on a desperate enterprise, foreseeing that he would not return. The Knight was slain, and dying directed his page to bear his heart to the Lady, wrapped in a lock of her hair, which she had given him. The heart, the hair, and the accompanying message, fell into the hands of the Lord, who caused the heart to be /7/ cooked with an exquisite sauce, and served up to the Lady. When she had eaten it, he told her what it was. The Lady said, that, since she had made herself the tomb of the noblest heart that had ever beaten, nothing else should bear it company.

> That herte shal certayne with me dye,
> I have received thereon the sacrament,
> All erthly[f] fode I here denye,
> For wo and paine my life is spente.
> My husbande, full of crueltè,
> Why have ye done this cursed dede?
> Ye have him slaine, so have ye me,
> The hie God grante to you your mede!
> Than sayd the Lorde, My Lady fayre,
> Forgive me if I have[g] misdone,
> I repent I was not ware
> That ye wolde your herte[h] oppresse so soone.
> The Lady sayd, I you forgive,
> Adieu my Lorde for evermore;
> My time is come, I may not live;
> The Lorde sayd, I am wo therfore.[2]

Now[i] Leonora maintains, that the Knight and the Lady were justified in their pure and innocent love, and that the Lord of Fayel was not justified in his jealousy. I maintain /8/ the contrary, leaving out of the question the cruelty of the revenge. And that is our *tenson*.[j]

LEONORA   I say, if a woman has at once purity of mind and strength of character, she may, without deserving blame and without incurring risk of error, allow herself moral and intellectual sympathy, within those limits in which she does not find it at home.[3]

---

[1] Molière, *Les Fourberies de Scapin*, III.i (Scapin to Zerbinette): 'Il ne prétend à vous qu'en tout bien et en tout honneur' (*Œuvres complètes*, edited by Maurice Rat, 2 vols (Paris, 1956), II, 702). Compare *Gryll Grange*, Chapter 34 (Lord Curryfin speaking of Beaumont and Fletcher's *Lover's Progress*): 'Cleander has a beautiful wife, Calista, and a friend, Lisander. Calista and Lisander love each other, *en tout bien, tout honneur*' (*Works*, V, 355).

[2] *The Knight of Curtesy and the Fair Lady of Faguell*, ll. 461–76 (Ritson, III, 216–17). In transcribing Ritson's text Peacock (1) substitutes 'I here denye' for 'here i denye' and 'Why have ye done' for 'Why have you done', (2) changes the spelling of 'theron', 'sacrament', 'graunte', 'sone', and 'Adew', (3) capitalizes 'i' four times, 'lorde' thrice, and 'lady' twice, (4) omits commas before and after 'my lorde' and substitutes a semicolon for a comma after 'live', and (5) ignores the division of the original into four quatrains.

[3] One of the shorter draft fragments consists of early versions of this speech and the next. This speech is cast in the form of a question: 'But if a woman . . . may she not without blame and without risk allow . . . at home?'.

ISABELLA   I say, No. If she married for love, she found, or supposed she found, in her favoured suitor,[1] the qualities she desired in a husband. If, after marriage, she finds[2] some deficient, she may by degrees find all deficient, if not altogether absent; at least inferior in degree to those which she finds elsewhere. Married love will scarcely survive this trial. Strength of mind has its limits, in love as well as in ambition.

BEATRICE   The first thing that strikes me is, that the Knight and the Lady did not think their love altogether blameless, for they kept it secret.

LEONORA   They thought that the Lord might be jealous, /9/ though his jealousy would be groundless.

ISABELLA   They knew, that the Lord would not believe in the possibility of that sort of love, and I do not see how any one can.

LEONORA   But he himself thought his jealousy[k] ill-founded when they were[l] dead, and most probably would have done so while they were living, if they had had confidence in him.

ISABELLA[m]   He discovered their love, and very naturally thought it not so innocent as it was; and therein his jealousy was well-founded.

LEONORA   But he himself thought it ill-founded, when he knew the truth. She loved in the Knight qualities which did not exist in the Lord. She did him no injury in completing her ideality.

ISABELLA   You suppose that the husband would have been content to say with Ranger:[n]

[*Two indented lines cut from MS*][3]

But I say with Katharine:

> Thy husband is thy lord, thy life, thy keeper,
> Thy head, thy sovereign: one that cares for thee,
> /10/ And for thy maintenance: commits his body
> To painful labour, both by sea and land;
> To watch the night in storms, the day in cold,
> While thou liest warm at home, secure and safe;
> And craves no other tribute at thy hands,
> But love, fair looks, and true obedience:
> Too little payment for so great a debt.[4]

---

[1] The draft reads: 'her favoured lover'.

[2] The draft reads: 'if she afterwards finds'.

[3] There are characters named Ranger in William Wycherley's *Love in a Wood* (1672) and in Benjamin Hoadly's *The Suspicious Husband* (1747), but it is clear from the context that Peacock here quoted the last two lines of Congreve's song 'Tell me no more I am deceived', as read by Ranger (with the substitution of 'Which' for 'Who') in Act 1, Scene 1, of *The Suspicious Husband: A Comedy* (London, 1747), p. 2: '*I take her Body, you her Mind; | Which has the better Bargain?*'. Mary Wollstonecraft also associates these lines with Ranger in a note to *A Vindication of the Rights of Woman* (London, 1792), p. 168: ' "I take her body," says Ranger'.

[4] *The Taming of the Shrew*, v.2.146–54. Shakespeare's eighteenth-century editors almost invariably read 'While' for 'Whilst', but Peacock presumably copied these lines (with only two insignificant changes in punctuation) from Isaac Reed's revision of the Johnson-Steevens edition of *The Plays of William Shakespeare*, 21 vols (London, 1813), IX, 193, the only edition listed in the sale catalogue of his library (lot 562).

LEONORA   No doubt there are some such husbands: but

> Va-t-en voir s'ils viennent, Jean:
> Va-t-en voir s'ils viennent.[1]

What say you to a man, who gambles away his wife's fortune, or squanders it on a mistress?

ISABELLA   I say, I do not care what happens to him. I speak of good husbands, such as was this Lord of Fayel, before he knew the alienation of his wife's affections.

LEONORA   When he thought he had discovered her infidelity. But see how he repented, when he knew the truth.

ISABELLA   I repeat, he⁰ would not have endured it, while they were living. A man who loves his wifeᵖ /11/ would not be content to see her affections given to another, however carefully she might preserve her conjugal purity. This Lord of Fayel must have been only solicitous about his honour: but *Où diable l'honneur va-t-il se nicher?*[2] When a woman has given all the best feelings of her heart to another, I think her husband might say to her, with another old romancer,

> [*Four lines cut from MS*][3]

LEONORA   And I say, with respect to the mind, that is impossible. A woman must see in others qualities which her husband has not, and which she cannotᵠ

---

[1] The refrain of a *chanson populaire* by Antoine Houdar de la Motte (1672–1731), included under the title 'Chanson faite aux eaux de Forges' in *Lettres de monsieur de la Motte, suivies d'un recueil de vers du mesme auteur, pour servir de supplément à ses Œuvres* (n.p., 1754), pp. 242–5. Peacock is more likely to have known the version which appears as 'Les Raretés (Va-t-en voir s'ils viennent, Jean) par Lamotte-Houdart' in H. L. Delloye's collection of *Chants et chansons populaires de la France* (Paris, 1843), première série (no pagination), a work that is listed in the sale catalogue of his library (lot 119). According to a prefatory note by E. T. M. Ourry, 'L'air de *Va-t'en voir s'ils viennent, Jean*, sur lequel il composa cette Chanson, vers l'année 1720, avait déjà popularisé ce refrain dans plus d'une maligne bluette du *Théâtre de la Foire*, et les couplets de Lamotte contribuèrent beaucoup à lui conserver cette popularité dont il jouit encore aujourd'hui'. The song begins:

> On dit qu'il arrive ici
> Une compagnie
> Meilleure que celle-ci
> Et bien mieux choisie:
> Va-t-en voir s'ils viennent, Jean,
> Va-t-en voir s'ils viennent.

Various paragons of virtue are enumerated in the succeeding verses, all of which end with the same refrain. The fifth verse is particularly apposite:

> Une femme et son époux,
> Couple bien fidèle;
> Elle le préfère à tous,
> Et lui n'aime qu'elle.
> Va-t-en voir, etc.

[2] Apparently a commonplace variation on a remark attributed to Molière in Voltaire's *Vie de Molière* (1739): 'Il venait de donner l'aumône à un pauvre; un instant après le pauvre court après lui, et lui dit: "Monsieur, vous n'aviez peut-être pas dessein de me donner un louis d'or, je viens vous le rendre. — Tiens, mon ami, dit Molière, en voilà un autre"; et il s'écria: "Où la vertu va-t-elle se nicher!" ' (*Œuvres complètes de Voltaire*, edited by Louis Moland, 52 vols (Paris, 1877–85), XXIII, 95.) Compare Henry James, 'A Problem' (*Galaxy*, June 1868): ' "*Où diable la jalousie va-t-elle se nicher?*" he cried.' (*The Tales of Henry James*, edited by Maqbool Aziz, 8 vols (Oxford, 1973—), I, 269.)

[3] The excision presumably consisted of, or at least included, a quotation, but I have been unable to guess the identity of this 'old romancer'.

help admiring.[1] If her husband has a voice like a crow, would you prohibit her being charmed by Rubini's singing?[2]

ISABELLA   That is not a case in point. Qualities, which are the object of universal admiration, differ essentially from those which are the charm of confidential intercourse. The singleness and secresy make the wrong, as in the case of the Knight and the Lady. /12/

BEATRICE   In the view of the old romancer, it seems to have been the secresy that caused their calamity.

ISABELLA   The secresy, in such a case, is inevitable. No woman would confide such a secret to her husband. [*Nearly three lines cut from MS*] if the lovers had been both living, and he had known as much as he then knew.

LEONORA   I rest on this: that a woman may, in all honour and purity, love in another qualities which her husband has not, without detracting from her conjugal fidelity.

ISABELLA   And I rest on this: that a woman should not make her election of a husband, till she is satisfied of his possessing, in as great a[r] degree as is compatible with human imperfection, the qualities which make marriage happy.

LEONORA   Suppose her to be mistaken, and to find /13/ that he has not the qualities which she gave him credit for?

ISABELLA   If her mistake is merely negative, she should acquiesce in it. If she finds real vices in the place of supposed virtues, that is a different matter: but it does not belong to the case we are discussing.

LEONORA   I have no more to say. What says Beatrice?

BEATRICE   A husband, who has no vices, who[s] gives his wife no cause of complaint, at least no more than is inseparable from the absolute impossibility of perpetual concord, is deficient in qualities which complete her ideality. Is she, if she finds those qualities in another, justified in giving to that other, for the sake of those qualities, that portion of love, which she would give to her husband if he had them?[t] That, I think, is the question.[u]

LEONORA   That is the question.

BEATRICE   It assumes, what, in the first place, I /14/ cannot admit: that love is divisible.[v] But, in the next place, love is involuntary. If she feels it, she cannot help herself. But she ought to have sufficient self-control to keep the feeling to herself. The moral duty should supersede all other impressions. Above all, there should be no secrets between married persons. Perfect confidence on both sides is the one true antidote to estrangement, mistrust,[w] and jealousy. You may say, there is no example in the world of any such perfect confidence. But you are discussing a moral theory. We may not come fully up to it, but we should make

---

[1] The shortest of the draft fragments is an early version of part of this sentence: 'must see in other men qualities which her husband has not which she would wish him to have and which as he has them not she cannot help liking and admiring in another'.

[2] The Italian tenor Giovanni Battista Rubini (1795–1854) achieved his greatest successes in the operas of Rossini, Bellini, and Donizetti. He was often in London from 1831 to 1843, and Peacock had many opportunities to hear him sing, especially from 1831 to 1834, when he was opera critic for the *Examiner*. In his review of Lord Mount Edgcumbe's *Musical Reminiscences* (*London Review*, April 1835), he describes Rubini as 'the best ... tenor ... perhaps, in the whole musical world' (*Works*, IX, 251). He also refers to him in *Gryll Grange*, Chapter 15 (Miss Ilex speaking): 'Rubini identified the redundancies of ornament with the overflowings of feeling, and the music of Donizetti furnished him most happily with the means of developing this power.' (*Works*, V, 141.)

it our standard, and approach it as nearly as we may. And therefore I say, there can be no true happiness in marriage, without unlimited confidence and undivided love.

LEONORA   So far, then, you decide for Isabella against me. But I doubt, if she will be fully contented with your decision. You recede a little too far from practical life. We appeal to you on the world as it is, and you plant us in Utopia.

BEATRICE   And as far as regards the practical development of moral theory, there, I fear, I must leave you.

a Eugenio] E *written over* T
b LEONORA] *not followed by the customary period.*
c some] *written above deleted* all
d imaginative] *written below the last full line on the page*
e BEATRICE] B *written over* I
f erthly] earthly *with* a *deleted*
g have] have have *MS*
h herte] rte *written over erased* art
i Now] *indented but preceded by a crossed wavy line, presumably indicating that a new paragraph is not intended*
j tenson.] *written above deleted* question
k his jealousy] *interlined with a caret above deleted* it
l were] *follows a deleted letter, apparently an uncompleted* k
m ISABELLA] = Isabella. = *underlined twice and interlined with a caret to indicate change of speaker, though this speech is not otherwise separated from the previous one*
n Ranger] *follows one or two heavily deleted words*
o he] *written over partially deleted* I
p wife] *written below the last full line on the page*
q cannot] c *written over partially deleted* h
r a] a a *MS*
s who] *follows deleted at least* n
t them?] them. *MS*
u question.] question *MS*
v divisible] vi *written over* si
w estrangement, mistrust,] estrangement mistrust *MS*

Trollope, James, and the International Theme

JOHN HALPERIN

University of Southern California

The last novel in Trollope's Palliser series, *The Duke's Children*, was written in 1876 but put away in a desk drawer by the novelist when its predecessor, *The Prime Minister* (1875–6), failed dismally with the reading public. James's *Daisy Miller* appeared in the *Cornhill Magazine* in June–July 1878 and his *An International Episode*, also in the *Cornhill Magazine*, in December 1878–January 1879. One may be reasonably sure that Trollope, a voracious consumer of contemporary fiction and himself a former editor of *Saint Paul's Magazine*, read them both. In June 1878 he sold *The Duke's Children* to *All the Year Round*. It did not begin its run, however, until October 1879, and James read it as he was finishing *The Portrait of a Lady*. Isabel Boncassen, the heroine of *The Duke's Children* and an American, does not appear upon the scene until a third of the way through the novel. Since Trollope had the manuscript of *The Duke's Children* by him during the three years preceding its publication, we cannot rule out the possibility that his portrait of an American in Europe was suggested in part by James's stories, even though Trollope himself had already dealt with the 'international' subject (in much less depth, to be sure) in *He Knew He Was Right* (1868–9) and *The American Senator* (1877). Indeed, there is much in *The Duke's Children* that suggests both *Daisy Miller* and *An International Episode*; and, equally to the point, there is much in *The Portrait of a Lady* that suggests *The Duke's Children*.

On 15 April 1874, just two years before Trollope wrote *The Duke's Children*, Lord Randolph Churchill, third son of the seventh Duke of Marlborough, and Miss Jennie Jerome of New York City were married with much fanfare and publicity at the British Embassy in Paris. The Duchess of Manchester, of an earlier generation but no less removed from the social limelight, was also an American, and there were soon to be other international marriages of this sort, culminating some years later in that of Lord Randolph's nephew, the eighth duke, to Consuela Vanderbilt. Undoubtedly the marriages of the Duke of Manchester and Lord Randolph Churchill were on Trollope's mind when, in *The Duke's Children*, Lord Silverbridge, elder son of the Duke of Omnium, contemplates his desire to marry an American: 'there were certain changes going on in the management of the world which his father did not quite understand . . . Some years ago it might have been improper that an American girl should be elevated to the rank of an English Duchess; but now all that was altered'.[1]

The marriage of Caroline Spalding, an American, to the heir of Lord Peterborough in *He Knew He Was Right* recalls that of the Manchesters and anticipates that of the Silverbridges. When Charles Glascock, the future Lord Peterborough, virtually picks up Caroline Spalding during a trip to Florence, the themes of free

---

[1] *The Duke's Children*, 2 vols (London, 1938), II, 204. All further references to the novel in the text are to this (the Oxford World's Classics) edition.

association with whomever one pleases and of international differences on the subject gain substantial importance, as they were to do later in *Daisy Miller*. American women, Trollope tells us here, talk and move about with the freedom of men; and he comments: 'There is a feeling, however, among pretty women in Europe that such freedom is dangerous, and it is withheld. There is such danger, and more or less of such withholding is expedient; but the American woman does not recognize the danger; and, if she [should withdraw], it is because she is not desirous of the society which is proffered to her'.[1] When Caroline's sister tells her that 'we are not in Boston' and that to have an intimacy with a male acquaintance only recently met 'might be the most horrible thing in the world to do . . . in Florence', Caroline replies: 'Why should that make a difference? Do you mean that one isn't to see one's friends? That must be nonsense' (p. 375). Caroline's uncle, the American minister in Florence, also has doubts about the proprieties involved: 'That their young ladies should walk in public places with unmarried gentlemen is nothing to American fathers and guardians. American young ladies are accustomed to choose their own companions. But the minister was tormented by his doubts as to the ways of Englishmen, and as to the phase in which English habits might most properly exhibit themselves in Italy' (p. 517). Surely the question of whether or not an American girl might properly walk in public in Italy with an unmarried male friend anticipates *Daisy Miller*, published a decade later. A constant supporting element in Trollope's version of the international theme (we find it in *The American Senator* and *The Duke's Children* too) is the American antipathy to English titles which, through association with English aristocrats, is transformed into admiration (Trollope was no enemy of an hereditary aristocracy). Caroline's uncle had made republican speeches at home attacking the idea of aristocracy, but when it seems that his niece may actually marry an aristocrat he changes his tune:

Mr. Spalding was clearly of opinion that, let the value of republican simplicity be what it might, an alliance with the crumbling marbles of Europe would in his niece's circumstances be not inexpedient . . . He had been specially loud against that aristocracy of England which, according to a figure of speech often used by him, was always feeding on the vitals of the people. But now all this was very much changed . . . [At Caroline's wedding] he declared that the republican virtue of the New World had linked itself in a happy alliance with the aristocratic splendour of the Old. (pp. 520, 817, and 824, *passim*)

I would add here, perhaps not irrelevantly, that in the same novel appears 'the republican Browning' and the women's rights enthusiast Wallachia Petrie, a tedious and masculinely assertive woman who is called 'Wally' by her friends, violently opposes the marriage of her friend Caroline, and has more than a suggestion of the lesbian about her. Whether or not she helped to inspire James's treatment of the subject in *The Bostonians* (1886) is a question that might well be asked (and answered elsewhere); in any case, Miss Petrie gives the lie to the assertion that James's novel is the first in English to address itself to this theme.

In *The American Senator*, Gotobed also begins his visit to England predisposed against aristocracy; he too, soon enough, changes his mind. Praising their 'ease of manner', 'grace', and physical appeal, Gotobed decides that 'there is a pleasure in

---

[1] *He Knew He Was Right* (London, 1948), pp. 373–4. All further references to the novel in the text are to this (the Oxford World's Classics) edition.

associating with those of the highest rank', that in being among aristocrats 'he was surrounded by people who claimed and made good their claims to superiority', and that it is 'more easy in this country to sympathise with the rich than with the poor'. Expressing at one point his astonishment over this and other matters to his English friend John Morton, Gotobed is told: 'I suppose . . . the habits of one country are incomprehensible to another'.[1] At the end of the novel Trollope sums up his feelings about the international question in this way: 'when an American comes to us, or a Briton goes to the States . . . the differences which present themselves are so striking that neither can live six months in the country of the other without a holding up of the hands and a torrent of explanations . . . [Nevertheless] we Americans and Englishmen go on writing books about each other, sometimes with bitterness enough, but generally with good final results' (p. 401). James, no doubt, would have written his novels and stories on the international subject with or without such encouragement; the fact remains, for whatever it is worth, that *The American Senator* appeared just a year before *Daisy Miller* and *An International Episode*, and *He Knew He Was Right* a decade earlier.

In *Mr Scarborough's Family*, the great late novel which appeared in 1882-3 (four years after *Daisy Miller* and *An International Episode* and just a year after *The Portrait of a Lady*), Trollope, in his portrayal of Florence Mountjoy, reverts to some of the themes treated in *He Knew He Was Right* (and of course in James's intervening stories). There is nothing 'international' in Florence's engagement and subsequent marriage to Harry Annesley; both are English. But the paramount question at issue in her story is the degree of independence an unmarried woman may have in associating with an unmarried man whom she likes and intends to marry. 'In America', Trollope reminds us here, young ladies 'carry latch-keys, and walk about with young gentlemen as young gentlemen walk about with each other'. Florence's mother complains that her daughter is more American than English in this respect: 'she'll go out in the streets and walk with a young man when all her friends tell her not. Is that her idea of religion?'[2] The 'walking about' business is as central an issue in *He Knew He Was Right* and *Mr Scarborough's Family* as it is in *Daisy Miller*. After all, we think of James as the great comparer of America and Europe; but we perhaps have forgotten that Trollope devoted an entire two-volume work to the international question. Entitled *North America* and published in 1862, this study among other things deals precisely with the kinds of subjects I have mentioned here. Trollope, having spent eight months in America (he went back there again in 1875) and clearly paid much attention to American women, constantly compares them to British women, and speaks often of the 'different laws . . . which govern . . . different societies'. He even devotes several paragraphs to the frequency with which he has seen, with dismay, American 'young girls in the streets . . . alone' at night, coming home from tea parties and other amusements.[3]

Like Caroline Spalding and Isabel Boncassen, Bessie Alden, the heroine of *An International Episode*, is from Boston. Like Isabel, she is proposed to by a future English duke, and like Isabel Archer she turns down her aristocratic suitor, the

[1] *The American Senator* (London, 1878), pp. 146-7, 263, and 267, passim. All further references to the novel in the text are to this (the second English) edition.
[2] *Mr Scarborough's Family* (London, 1946), pp. 451 and 453, in the Oxford World's Classics edition.
[3] *North America*, edited by Robert Mason (Harmondsworth, 1968, abridged), pp. 102 and 42.

first of James's international heroines to do so. She too respects the old-world aristocracy, even lecturing Lord Lambeth at one point on his duties as a nobleman. Lord Lambeth's family, like Lord Silverbridge's, objects to an American marriage: because of this, and also because, like Isabel Archer, Bessie has aspirations that go beyond an easy marriage, she rejects her duke — a reversal of the plot of *The Duke's Children*, though the situation is indeed similar in other respects.

All of this is preface to and context for my main interest here, which is the similarity of Trollope's Isabel to the international heroines of James. Written in 1876 and published in 1879–80, *The Duke's Children*, let us remember, falls in the midst of a flurry of international stories by James, who was still experimenting with his new subject.

Isabel Boncassen, like Mr Spalding and Senator Gotobed, arrives in England prepared to dislike aristocrats. Soon thereafter, though she is not materialistic, Isabel is thrilled by the prospect of marrying a man she can love who also happens to be the heir of a duke: very quickly indeed 'a certain sweetness of the aroma of rank [began] to permeate her republican senses' (I, 315). More to the point, she bears a number of resemblances, beyond her name, to the heroine of *The Portrait of a Lady*. She is intelligent and quick-witted, though she is not intellectual or even overly bright. There is a touch of the snob in her. She is independent, spirited, open to experience, but she is no paragon, and she is never sentimentalized. She is prepared to laugh at English aristocrats but ends up admiring one of them instead. In all of these things she resembles her Jamesian namesake. She, of course, accepts her lord, and will presumably be happy. Isabel Archer lives in a universe less benign; to have accepted *her* lord (Warburton — also the name, incidentally, of the Duke's private secretary in the later Palliser novels) would have been too easy, a closing too prematurely of the door of experience, or so it appears to her.

James seems to me to be responding in part to Trollope in *The Portrait of a Lady*; the patently unhappy ending of his novel declares that such matters are not always so easily or happily resolved. Could he be speaking here directly to the author of *The Duke's Children*? I think it bears repeating that James was reading Trollope's novel in *All the Year Round* as he was finishing *The Portrait of a Lady*; he finished it in July 1880, the same month in which *The Duke's Children* ended its serial run. (*The Portrait of a Lady* then ran from October 1880 to November 1881 in *Macmillan's Magazine* in England and from November 1880 to December 1881 in the *Atlantic Monthly* in America.) Most interesting of all is the fact that the novelists' descriptions of their Isabels often sound strikingly similar. 'She had a very high opinion of herself and was certainly entitled to have it by the undisguised admiration of all that came near her . . . Her brain was firmer than that of most girls.' This, astonishingly enough, is not James, it is Trollope (I, 315–16). A reading of the sixth chapter of *The Portrait of a Lady* will quickly show how alike James's conception of his Isabel is to Trollope's of his. James says of Isabel Archer:

It had been her fortune to possess a finer mind than most of the persons among whom her lot was cast . . . Whether or no she were superior, people were right in admiring her if they thought her so; for it seemed to her often that her mind moved more quickly than theirs . . . Isabel was . . . liable to the sin of self-esteem . . . It often seemed to her that she thought too much about herself.[1]

---

[1] *The Portrait of A Lady*, edited by Leon Edel (Boston, 1963), pp. 52–5, passim. I am quoting here from the Riverside edition.

There is also more in *The Duke's Children* about American ladies 'walking about' in public. Isabel, when she takes a walk with Silverbridge shortly after they have met for the first time, is immediately aware of the problem:

In our country . . . [a] young lady may walk about with a young gentleman just as she might with another young lady; but I [think it is] different here . . . judging by English ways, I believe I am behaving very improperly in walking about with you so long. Ought I not to tell you to go away? . . . I wish to behave well to English eyes . . . when the discrepancies are small, then they have to be attended to. So I shan't walk about with you any more. (I, 268)

Trollope's Isabel, like James's Daisy, has a mind of her own in such matters, however, and soon refuses to be bound by arbitrary conventions: 'the daughter hardly seemed to be under control from the father. She went alone where she liked; talked to those she liked; and did what she liked' (I, 294). Some of her friends admire her sense of freedom, but Trollope himself is not so sure: 'There is . . . a good deal to be said against it. All young ladies cannot be Miss Boncassens, with such an assurance of admirers as to be free from all fears of loneliness' (I, 294). Isabel, like Daisy, is warned about the conventions; Lady Clanfiddle, for example, tells her that 'Americans couldn't be expected to understand English manners', but that on that account they should not be ignored (I, 324). Isabel suspects that 'all conventional rules' of this sort 'are an abomination' (I, 378), but, more than Daisy, she heeds the warning. Nevertheless, she will not be dictated to in love: in America, 'if two young people love each other they go and get married' (II, 71), she tells Silverbridge when he worries about marriage settlements. Like Bessie Alden, she is both more responsive to conventional expectations than Daisy and less stubbornly imperceptive than Isabel Archer. And so, being resident in a universe where marriages between Cinderellas and princes may felicitously be made, she can live happily ever after with her duke. The general situation is similar to those in James's international stories, even if the resolutions are different.

I am not concerned here with the possible real-life counterparts of the two Isabels, though both characters seem derived from actual Platonic affections. (If Isabel Archer is another version of Minny Temple, Isabel Boncassen may be the youthful object of Trollope's well known esteem late in life, Kate Field, also from Boston. Like Caroline Spalding and Isabel Archer, Kate went to Italy as a very young woman. From all accounts she too was 'emotionally ardent and sensually cold'. Kate apparently was imperious in the same pleasant way as Isabel Boncassen is imperious with her admirers. The young man at a loss before a girl of spirit fiercer than his own (Silverbridge) and an older man moved by an emotion not entirely that of a decorous father-in-law (Palliser) represent perhaps two aspects of Trollope's own response to Kate Field.[1] *The Duke's Children*, remember was written at the same time (1876) as the *Autobiography*, which contains Trollope's famous outburst about 'one of the chief pleasures which has graced my later years' and 'a ray of light' encountered in the darkness of his old age.[2] He did not know many American women, after all; there has got to be some of Kate Field in Isabel Boncassen.) However, what matters most here are the literary connexions. If James had, as I think he did have, Trollope's Alice Vavasor (the heroine of *Can You Forgive Her?*, 1864–5) in mind when dealing with the 'thoughtful' woman

[1] See C. P. Snow, *Trollope* (London, 1975), pp. 126, 128.
[2] *An Autobiography* (London, 1961; originally published in 2 vols, 1883), p. 262.

theme in *The Portrait of a Lady*, he may well have had Isabel Boncassen in mind when dealing with the international theme. I suspect he also remembered Caroline Spalding. And it is likely that James's Daisy and his Bessy had some impact upon Trollope's heroine. My concern here is not so much with the question of 'influence' as with the community of interests between the two novelists, with the fact that their themes are often the same themes.

There are, after all, other examples of this sort, not necessarily 'international' in nature yet nonetheless interesting as part of the total picture. One of these is the striking similarity between Trollope's odd little novel *Sir Harry Hotspur of Humblethwaite* (1870) and James's *Washington Square* (1881). In both novels a rich father prevents a marriage between his heiress-daughter and an unprincipled but clever and attractive cousin with whom she is in love. In each case the daughter thinks the would-be lover better than he is; and in each the father tactlessly proves to the daughter that the cousin is only after her money. Each daughter comes to see that the father has been right about the lover, but loves neither the one better nor the other worse for having her eyes opened; the interference in each case destroys for ever the daughter's only chance for happiness. Neither daughter ever marries. The description of the one ('She suffered under a terrible feeling of ill-usage. Why was she, because she was a girl and an heiress, to be debarred from her own happiness? If she were willing to risk herself, why should others interfere?') could easily fit both.[1]

In his essay on Trollope (1883), James said that 'in these matters' (international matters) Trollope did well, though he comments that Isabel Boncassen is more an Englishman's American than an American's.[2] The *Spectator's* reviewer had also suggested that Isabel Boncassen 'is as English as the Duke himself, and not American at all'.[3] Other adverse reactions to Trollope's Isabel have come more recently from the Stebbinses (Trollope, they say, did not understand American girls so well as James and Howells, and should have left the international theme alone), and Pope Hennessy (Isabel Boncassen 'is convincing without being particularly interesting').[4] One of her most 'interesting' properties, however, has been almost totally ignored; the possibility of her having in part inspired James to improve on her, to create a more domestic version of the real thing.

As Polhemus has said, 'A short while after he read Trollope's novel, James portrayed another American lady named Isabel who visits England and wins a proposal from a lord'.[5] True enough, but clearly there is more to say. Trollope and James in the late seventies were writing about many of the same things; and it seems likely that they were responding in some of their fictions to each other and that 'influence', between them, goes in both directions. It appears at times as if a dialogue, an exchange of views, engaged them (it is known that they met one

---

[1] The quotation is from *Sir Harry Hotspur of Humblethwaite* (London, 1928), p. 263.
[2] James's memorial essay was originally published in *Century Magazine* in 1883 and later reprinted in *Partial Portraits* (New York, 1888). My reference here is to the latter, p. 121.
[3] Unsigned notice, *Spectator*, 53 (12 June 1880), 754–5.
[4] See L. P. and R. P. Stebbins, *The Trollopes: The Chronicle of A Writing Family* (New York, 1945), p. 296, and James Pope Hennessy, *Anthony Trollope* (Boston, 1971), p. 352.
[5] See Robert M. Polhemus, *The Changing World of Anthony Trollope* (Berkeley and Los Angeles, 1958), p. 228.

another several times[1]). What may be of most interest here is that, obviously enough, James took from Trollope as much or more than Trollope took from him, despite the fact that such influence as may have occurred has sometimes been assumed to travel in the other direction.

[1] At least twice; once aboard ship travelling from America to England in 1875, and again in 1877 at the home of Lord Houghton. My information is taken from Leon Edel, *Henry James: The Conquest of London 1870–1883* (London, 1962).

Two Emergencies in the Writing of
The Woman in White

JOHN SUTHERLAND

University College, London

Trollope's derogatory comment about Wilkie Collins in his *Autobiography* is well known:

> When I sit down to write a novel I do not at all know, and I do not very much care, how it is to end. Wilkie Collins seems so to construct his that he not only, before writing, plans everything on, down to the minutest detail, from the beginning to the end; but then plots it all back again, to see that there is no piece of necessary dove-tailing which does not dove-tail with absolute accuracy. The construction is most minute and most wonderful. But I can never lose the taste of the construction.[1]

Nowhere is the mechanical perfection of Wilkie Collins's plotting more evident than in the early sections of *The Woman in White*. Collins took immense pains with setting up this story, 'the longest and the most complicated I have ever tried yet'.[2] In the summer of 1859 he took a cottage at Broadstairs (an expense which he could ill afford) and worked away during the sweltering hot months, devising a story of needle sharpness. Even so he could not entirely satisfy himself. After the early numbers were set up in proof for *All the Year Round* he broke them down and rewrote them so as to get an even sharper plot opening.

The reader with detective inclinations will find clues enough in the early sections to the farsightedness of Collins's writing. Pesca's political affiliation, which is the machinery used to engineer the climax, is parenthetically mentioned in the first number; no further reference is made to it until the thirty-eighth number. Similarly farsighted preparation is made for other important plot elements such as Countess Fosco's ten thousand pounds, her husband's strange aversion to Italy, and Anne Catherick's ill health. Arguably the early parts of the story are over-complex and baited. Dickens thought so and lodged an editorial complaint with Collins on 7 January 1860 after the seventh number had just come out:

> I seem to have noticed, here and there, that the great pains you take express themselves a trifle too much, and you know that I always contest your disposition to give an audience credit for nothing, which necessarily involves the forcing of points upon their attention, and which I have always observed them to resent when they find it out — as they always will and do.[3]

Collins, to judge from the subsequent narrative, seems not to have taken too much notice of Dickens's instruction. But the wonder is that when he got into his stride he was actually able to maintain the cat's cradle intricacy of his plot. In what he

[1] *An Autobiography* (London, 1883, reprinted 1950), p. 257.
[2] Letter, 18 August 1859, held in the Pierpont-Morgan Library. I am grateful for permission to quote from correspondence held by the Library.
[3] *The Letters of Charles Dickens*, edited by Walter Dexter, 3 vols (London, 1938), III, 145.

called his 'weekly race'[1] with *All the Year Round* he was, for most of the novel, no more than a week or so ahead of publication deadlines (i.e. a month before magazine day in England so as to get the American sheets off). This may be gathered from occasional comments in letters and from the speed with which he absorbed his own proof corrections into the subsequent manuscript.[2] In Number 49, for example, the manuscript has Laura's maid named 'Susan'. Evidently this was changed in proof to what the printed text has as her name, 'Fanny'. In manuscript Number 50 the maid appears as 'Susan-Fanny' and in Number 51 without any crossing out as 'Fanny'. This sequence of alterations could only occur if the novelist were one number ahead of himself. The dates of composition which Collins himself records on the manuscript (15 August 1859 to 26 July 1860) taken together with the dates of publication (26 November 1859 to 25 August 1860) suggest that after the first third of the novel Collins was obliged to work against the calendar.

It must have been a gruelling year for the novelist. In his letters he reports himself 'horribly fagged' and '*slaving* to break the neck of The Woman in White'.[3] Under this pressure Collins was obliged to rely very heavily on the proof stage for any correction, adjustment, or afterthought improvement. In this respect *All the Year Round* was kinder to the novelist than the thirty-two-page monthly number. He did not have to worry about accommodating 'over-matter'. In the periodical's double-columned format any reasonable over-run could be absorbed and there was never any mutilation of the manuscript copy Collins provided. But in other ways *All the Year Round* with its 'teaspoonful' instalments and its frequency of issue was the epitome of the furnace-like conditions in which the nineteenth-century serialists worked.

In these conditions a writer not entirely clear on where he was going might easily have found himself rushed into an inextricable muddle. To prevent this Collins seems to have relied very much on the blueprint which he had laid down in his mind during the planning stages of the novel at Broadstairs. The manuscript, in fact, is a marvel of spontaneity for a work of such narrative complication. Although there is much scoring out almost all the improvements are those of expression. What we find are mainly minor polishing changes which give a little more suspense, clarity of definition, or perfection of statement. Otherwise Collins seems to have written with the master plan firmly held, guiding him inexorably onwards through the narrative maze to the tremendous denouement.

On two occasions during the narrative progress, however, Collins was shaken out of his rhythm. One of these emergencies he turned to profit with a brilliant improvisation that enhances the story. The second resulted in what remains as the weakest link in the carefully interconnected plot. In what follows it is my intention to examine these two emergencies and their consequences for the novel as a whole.

---

[1] Letter, Pierpont-Morgan Library, dated 'Wednesday' (presumably early summer 1860, since Collins mentions his bargaining with the publishers for the volume publication of *The Woman in White*).

[2] The manuscript of the novel, which is autograph and complete, is held in the Pierpont-Morgan Library. I am grateful for permission to examine and quote from it. The parts of the novel I indicate, as does Collins in the MS, by the *All the Year Round* issue numbers (No. 1 of the novel = No. 31 of the journal).

[3] Letters, Pierpont-Morgan Library, 11 July 1860 and 'Friday', June 1860.

II

In the manuscript preface to *The Woman in White* Collins wrote:

The first chapters (forming the first week's part, and the opening of the second) were re-written, after they had been set up in type . . . The whole of the rest of the MS was written for the press, once, and once only — exactly as it is here preserved. In all cases where there is any important difference between the printed copy and the original manuscript, the additions and alterations (Miss Halcombe's *Dream*, for example, among the number) were made on the spur of the moment, upon the proofs — which I have not preserved.

With reference to the example Collins gives we can elaborate on his account. The Numbers concerned are 46, 47, and 48 (although originally they were intended to have been two only). The stretch of narrative concerned is that which is told through Marian Halcombe's diary and records the opening exchanges in her epic duel with Fosco. Number 46 begins with the diary entry describing Marian and Lauras' evening walk to the boathouse at Blackwater Park. The newly-wed wife confesses the misery of her marriage, and her continuing guilty love for Walter Hartright (who has, of course, gone off on an expedition to Central America to forget *his* love for Laura). As the heroines walk back they hear themselves followed through the dark wood by what seems like a woman. They run in terror back to the house. In the drawing room Fosco makes some sinister small talk before the ladies retire and Marian, by cross-questioning the servants, ascertains that it was none of them who had tracked them in the wood. Number 46, as published, finishes on this point.

The next day Marian receives an expected letter from Mr Kyrle which confirms her suspicions of Sir Percival and the legal document which he wants Laura to sign. Marian arranges to meet the messenger in the grounds; Fosco, however, has followed her and escorts her back to the house where Sir Percival has just come back from some mysterious business. The nervous strain of the cat-and-mouse game begins to tell on Marian. She is exhausted and beginning to sicken; although she does not yet know it the poisonous miasma of Blackwater lake has infected her with typhus. In this state she falls into a disturbed slumber. She dreams vividly of Walter Hartright in the American jungles. She is awoken from this vision by Laura who has found out who it was pursued them last night — 'Anne Catherick.' Number 47, as published, ends on this ejaculation.

The manuscript shows that 46 and 47 were originally meant to have been one Number. They are continuous in the manuscript and 48 is, in fact, renumbered by Collins '47/48'. As it is they make two unusually short Numbers in the periodical. The invariable length of the preceding Numbers in *All the Year Round* is between 12 and 17 columns. Numbers 46 and 47 are eight-and-a-half and seven-and-a-quarter columns respectively, easily the briefest in the whole run of the novel.

The reasons for Collins having to bisect a single Number must be conjectural. It could not have been sickness on his part since he had to perform heroically to carpenter each of the halves into a respectable whole for the journal. Writing the supplementary material must have been harder work than writing a complete new instalment. My guess is that Dickens wanted the extra space for a current affairs article and, uncharacteristically, took from his serial to do so. Normally, of course, the serial, always the first item in *All the Year Round*, was sacrosanct.

For whatever reason Collins at short notice had to improvise, and improvisation meant expansion to bring the numbers up to the minimum length tolerable. In

Number 46 he added in proof the long conversation (in fact more of an inquisition) in which Fosco presses Marian as to where she and Laura have been. At the same time Collins took advantage of the by now hopelessly unjustified proofs to expand considerably Marian's enquiries of the servants whether it was any of them who followed the ladies from the boathouse. Economically the novelist left the proofs of the first half of the Number intact, for which the printer was doubtless grateful.

In the same spirit of economy Collins did not tamper with the first half of Number 47. But the addition he made in the second half of that Number is rather more exciting and less in the nature of routine inflation than what we find in Number 46. In the manuscript Marian falls asleep and is woken soon after by Laura. In the revised, printed version there intervenes the following dream:

The quiet in the house, and the low murmuring hum of summer insects outside the open window, soothed me. My eyes closed of themselves; and I passed gradually into a strange condition, which was not waking — for I knew nothing of what was going on about me; and not sleeping — for I was conscious of my own repose. In this state, my fevered mind broke loose from me, while my weary body was at rest; and in a trance, or day-dream of my fancy — I know not what to call it — I saw Walter Hartright [In her dream she sees him escape death in the jungle from fever, from pigmies' arrows, and from shipwreck. It is, he tells her, all part of the 'Design' leading 'to the unknown Retribution and the inevitable End'] . . . I saw him for the last time. He was kneeling by a tomb of white marble; and the shadow of a veiled woman rose out of the grave beneath, and waited by his side. The unearthly quiet of his face had changed to an unearthly sorrow. But the terrible certainty of his words remained the same. 'Darker and darker', he said; 'farther and farther yet. Death takes the good, the beautiful, and the young — and spares *me*. The Pestilence that wastes, the Arrow that strikes, the Sea that drowns, the Grave that closes over Love and Hope, are steps of my journey, and take me nearer and nearer to the End.'
My heart sank under a dread beyond words, under a grief beyond tears. The darkness closed round the pilgrim at the marble tomb; closed round the veiled woman from the grave; closed round the dreamer who looked on them. I saw and heard no more. (*All the Year Round*, 47 (17 March 1860), 479–80)

Judged by itself this is a brilliant piece of coloratura writing. *The Woman in White* continually hovers on the brink of Gothic supernaturalism, and the visionary dream fits perfectly here. It is possible, too, that Collins was thinking of the memorable stanza which concludes Lyric 56 of Tennyson's *In Memoriam*:

> O life as futile, then, as frail!
> O for thy voice to soothe and bless!
> What hope of answer, or redress?
> Behind the veil, behind the veil.

It is certain, on the other hand, that in the last sentence of the dream he was thinking ahead to the tremendous scene that finishes the second epoch (Number 56) where Walter, believing Laura dead and grieving over her tombstone, encounters a veiled woman:

. . . the veiled woman had possession of me, body and soul. She stopped on one side of the grave. We stood face to face, with the tombstone between us. She was close to the inscription on the side of the pedestal. Her gown touched the black letters.
The voice came nearer, and rose and rose more passionately still. 'Hide your face! don't look at her! Oh, for God's sake, spare him —.'
The woman lifted her veil.
'Sacred to the Memory of Laura, Lady Glyde —.'
Laura, Lady Glyde, was standing by the inscription, and was looking at me over the grave. (*All the Year Round*, 56 (19 May 1860), 128–9)

This dovetails beautifully with the previous dream, and with the first vision of the woman in white. At the same time it emphasizes the main theme of the novel; that in all the apparently impenetrable mystery there lies 'Design'. The increasingly evident purposes of Providence in this design are hinted at (but with no more than hints). The process of the novel is that of a gradual unveiling.

This theme was, of course, introduced with Marian's improvised dream and the visionary Hartright's address to Marian:

I shall come back. The night when I met the lost Woman on the highway, was the night which set my life apart to be the instrument of a Design that is yet unseen. Here, lost in the wilderness, or there, welcomed back in the land of my birth, I am still walking on the dark road which leads me, and you, and the sister of your love and mine, to the unknown Retribution and the inevitable End'. (*All the Year Round*), 47 (17 March 1860), 480)

As well as the encounter over the gravestone Collins exploited the afterthought still further in the 'Brotherhood of the Veil' through which Hartright and Pesca bring about the downfall of Fosco. In the manuscript Collins went on to explain the significance of the society's name: 'the name signifying that, except by superior permission and for matters of life and death, the veil is never lifted between the members, and that they remain, from first to last mysteries to one another'. (This would have come in *All the Year Round*, 68 (11 August 1860), 416.) On second thoughts Collins must have known that this was rubbing the symbolism in rather too hard so he cut out the above and renamed the secret society simply 'The Brotherhood'. Nonetheless the image of the mysterious woman unveiling remains the most powerful and explicatory we can find in the novel.

III

Collins's handling of this emergency may be scored a brilliant success. He showed himself quite capable of masterly improvisation in spite of his notorious propensity for carefully laid and worked out plots. Few novelists can have corrected their proofs so effectively. In the second emergency, however, Collins does not come out quite so well. We can catch him in what seems almost like a fumble and there remains as evidence of it in the printed text of the novel an incongruity which may well worry the most scrupulous and pedantic readers. With other novelists this incongruity might not matter so much; but with Collins, as Trollope noted, we are encouraged to be small minded about such things: 'The author seems always to be warning me to remember that something happened at exactly half-past two o'clock on Tuesday morning; or that a woman disappeared from the road just fifteen yards beyond the fourth milestone.' (*Autobiography*, p. 257)

In the largest sense the second emergency concerns the machinery by which Fosco is defeated. Fosco and Glyde, it will be remembered, intend to murder Anne Catherick (should she not oblige them by dying), pass off her corpse as Lady Glyde's, and return Lady Glyde to the asylum as Anne Catherick. It is a complicated and somewhat unlikely scheme and it is made the more complex for the villains because Anne, who has a weak heart, dies before Laura can be spirited away from Blackwater Park. This creates a dangerous flaw in their plan since if the departure from the country by Laura can be shown to post-date the death certificate then, demonstrably, it would be impossible for her to be Anne Catherick with delusions that she is somebody else.

The possibility of denouement via this chronological discrepancy is raised on a number of occasions in the last third of the novel. Collins evidently intended the reader to be aware of this weak spot; disproof of the villains' machinations by comparison of dates is, we are made to feel, the climax towards which the action is moving. To condition the reader on this point, apparently, Collins added in proof two hundred words of dialogue between Marian and Walter in which he firmly states his resolve to uncover evidence of the inconsistent dates: 'We must persist, to the last, in hunting down the date of Laura's journey. The one weak point in the conspiracy, and probably the one chance of proving that she is a living woman, centre in the discovery of that date.' (*All the Year Round*, 59 (9 June 1860), 197)

Why, one may wonder, did Collins raise the reader's expectation in this way? For in the event the discrepancy of dates turns out to be a gigantic red herring. Hartright can prove nothing on this score despite all his frantic endeavours and the denouement is worked quite otherwise. Hartright goes to Fosco's hideout and blackmails him with the threat of exposure to the Brotherhood. Thus threatened, the Napoleon of crime makes a signed confession. As part of this he gives the name of the cabby who delivered Lady Glyde to London, and the letter from Glyde which proves the impossibility of her being in town on the day she 'died'. But it is merely confirmatory evidence and strikes one as something of an anticlimax after all the pointers we have had.

The more one thinks about this business the stranger it appears; why all this build-up for what turns out, finally, to be a very minor piece of plot machinery? Has Collins deliberately misled the reader into thinking that the end will be brought about by Hartright's detective work turning up the missing evidence? To understand how this puzzle came about it is necessary to reconstruct a crucial part of the narrative, the account of Mrs Michelson in Number 56. It will probably be helpful, once more, to synopsize the narrative here in some detail.

Mrs Michelson, housekeeper and clergyman's widow, is a gullible but incorruptibly honest witness to what took place during her time of service at Blackwater Park. Unfortunately, however, her account suffers from imperfect observation and bias. To our superior knowledge the main events at this period of the narrative are the Count's duping Anne Catherick and Mrs Clements while Marian is disabled with typhus. Fosco has insulted and driven away the local physician Dawson, the servants have been all dismissed, and a mystified Mrs Michelson has been sent on a wild goose chase to Torquay. Blackwater is thus left in the possession of the villainous trio and their hench-woman, Mrs Rubelle. They use their freedom to secrete Marian in a disused part of the house, under the superintendence of Mrs Rubelle. When Laura recovers from her nervous disorder she and the now returned Mrs Michelson are told that Marian has recovered and is now staying with Fosco in St Johns Wood, London. Laura is persuaded by this lie to follow her friend there. What has happened, of course, is that Fosco has Anne Catherick in London and intends to switch her with Laura.

Now this is where the crux occurs. 'Towards five o'clock on the . . . same day'[1] of Laura's departure Mrs Michelson discovers that Marian Halcombe has not left

---

[1] *All the Year Round*, 55 (12 May 1860), 102.

Blackwater at all, but is still convalescent. Indignant beyond words at the deception played upon her she gives notice and then:

I stole back, leaving the sick lady still peacefully asleep, to fetch writing materials from the inhabited part of the house. Returning with them to the bedside immediately I there wrote three notes. One was to Mr. Dawson, begging him to resume his attendance, and telling him that the next day Blackwater Park would have nobody in it but Miss Halcombe and myself. The other two were duplicates addressed to Lady Glyde. In each I told her Ladyship very briefly, what had happened; taking care to preface the statement in consideration for her frail state of health, by mentioning that I was then writing by Miss Halcombe's bed, and that I saw her before me, comfortably asleep. I directed one of these notes to the care of Frederick Fairlie Esquire, and the other to the care of Mrs. Vesey, whose address I had particularly noticed, when I put Lady Glyde's letter into the post. Being ignorant of Count Fosco's address, it was impossible for me to send a third note to his care. I did all I could — it is some comfort to me, now, to know in my own heart and conscience that I did all I could.

I gave the letters, with instructions, to the gardener — a steady man, on whom I could rely. He brought me back word that he had posted the two notes to Lady Glyde in going through the village, and that he had driven round by Mr. Dawson's residence.

This is how the passage was put down in the manuscript. But Collins altered it in proof, so that it appears very differently in the printed version that we have:

I stole back, leaving the sick lady still peacefully asleep, to give the gardener instructions about bringing the doctor. I begged the man, after he had taken Mrs. Rubelle to the station, to drive round by Mr. Dawson's, and leave a message, in my name, asking him to call and see me. I knew he would come on my account, and I knew he would remain when he found Count Fosco had left the house.

In due course of time, the gardener returned, and said that he had driven round by Mr. Dawson's residence, after leaving Mrs. Rubelle at the station. The doctor sent me word that he was poorly in health himself, but that he would call, if possible, the next morning. (*All the Year Round*, 56 (19 May 1860), 123)

Mrs Michelson, at the end of her account, apologizes 'at my own inability to remember the precise day on which Lady Glyde left Blackwater Park for London. I am told that it is of the last importance to ascertain the exact date of that lamentable journey; and I have anxiously taxed my memory to recall it . . . We all know the difficulty, after a lapse of time, of fixing precisely on a past date, unless it has been previously written down' (p. 124). As an added misfortune it appears that Dawson too had 'forgotten' the date on which the gardener came to him with Mrs Michelson's message.

It is not hard to see that Collins was in something of a muddle here. It seems he originally intended the denouement to be sprung by these three posted letters which Mrs Michelson sent off. The date would be 'written down' there in her own hand on the 'same day' that Lady Laura left for London. In 1850 letters would also presumably have two postmarks, one marking the office of despatch and the other the office of delivery. These would clinch matters. Evidence would be lodged with Fairlie, Mrs Vesey, and Dawson, two at least of whom were absolutely reliable.

The disadvantage of this scheme seems to have struck Collins almost immediately; it was too efficient. He still had over a third of his novel to spin out. These letters would not permit the kind of postponement and winding up of suspense he required. It would all be too open-and-shut. Therefore the possibility of proof or disproof was removed with Mrs Michelson's three letters. Unfortunately, however, this did not clear things up very tidily. It is clear that Collins had set up the foregoing narrative for this kind of denouement with the actual anachronism of Anne's death and Laura's arrival. Its possibility could not be removed altogether from the narrative. Moreover the amended version of the plot which tries to leave Mrs Michelson's memory of the day plausibly uncertain has some gaping holes in it. Take for example the Torquay visit; there must surely have been some corroborative evidence from the hotel keepers she spoke to there, or ticket collectors and railway porters, any of whom could have ascertained when she came back to Blackwater. And her return could quite easily be correlated with Laura's departure.

This embarrassing likelihood occurred to Collins. Consequently he removed from the printed text the following sentence which we find, uncrossed-out, in the manuscript: '[Marian] was in a deep sleep at the time, whether naturally or artificially produced she could not say. *Reckoning by her own calculation of days and nights, her removal must have been accomplished on the first evening after I had been sent out of the way to Torquay.* In my absence . . .' (p. 123). It was just this kind of reckoning that Collins had to discourage in the reader. Obscurity and vagueness must shroud the episode to protect its superficial credibility. In the short term the measure worked, but at the cost of a weak link which was very evident in the three-volume issue of the novel. Reviewing the third edition in *The Times*, 30 October 1860, E. S. Dallas made the well known objection about the impossibility of the novel's time scheme (reckoning from Marian's diary Laura must have gone up to London a fortnight later than the narrative asserts her to have done) and went on to point to the no less glaring improbability of the general ignorance of Laura's day of departure and, in particular, Mrs Michelson's convenient loss of memory:

The date might be very easily recovered if the author chose — but he doesn't choose, and he insists, against all probabilities, upon everybody forgetting it. The person who would be most likely to remember it is the housekeeper at Blackwater-park, who pretends to some education, who is the widow of a clergyman, and who writes a pretty long narrative, in which she contrives to remember with wonderful accuracy a great number of minute facts in the precise order of their occurence. On the day in question her mistress leaves Blackwater-park, she herself resigns her situation as housekeeper, and during the day several very remarkable incidents occur, the whole being wound up by the master of the house leaving it in a fury at night. The lady who has such a wonderful memory for everything else cannot remember this day of days, what day of the month, or what day of the week it was.[1]

As we have seen, Collins's first instinct was to leave the date recoverable through Mrs Michelson's letters. Had he kept to his original idea he might have satisfied Dallas, but at the cost of a novel whose end could not be sufficiently postponed for the necessary suspense to gather.

What the time error and Mrs Michelson's improbable vagueness reveal is something of the crisis conditions in which Collins composed the last third of his serial. Its unexpected popularity brought an embarrassingly alert public attention to the weekly development of the plot and a much voiced scepticism that Collins would ever be able to pull everything together. The American correspondent of the *Publishers' Circular*, 1 June 1860, reported:

I see that Mr. Wilkie Collins's *Woman in White* is announced for completion in book form. Will it then really be completed? People here, who have read it in *Harper's Weekly*, have been so excited by it, and so anxious to find out the denouement of the plot, that they have begun to doubt if there can ever be a conclusion to it.

[1] I am grateful to Professor K. J. Fielding for pointing out to me the identity of *The Times*'s reviewer and the general significance of his comments on Collins.

Meanwhile in June and July Collins was complaining of pressure from *All the Year Round*: 'I am *slaving* to break the neck of the Women in White — and get done in five numbers more' he wrote in June, and on 5 July: 'I am *obliged* to end the story in August to avoid running into a new volume [of *All the Year Round*] and with the prospect of *one* double number at least to write'.[1]

If this were not enough the novelist was further harassed by the need to get a complete manuscript to Sampson Low for the three-decker version to be issued, as it normally would be, three weeks before the serial came to an end in the journal. There was obviously some problem about this. The work had been advertised in the *Publishers' Circular* of 2 April 1860 to be 'complete in July'. It was announced as 'immediate' throughout July by Sampson Low. In the event it appeared in volume form around 15 August, only a week or so before it came to its conclusion in *All the Year Round*.

It was under these circumstances that the novelist was forced into the impossibilities and improbabilities which Dallas notes. The wonder is less that we can find them, if we look hard enough, than that they do not protrude to ruin the novel utterly. Even Dallas, after pointing to the error which rendered 'the last volume a mockery, a delusion, and a snare' was generous enough to acknowledge the novel's power to triumph over its own flaws:

What must that novel be which can survive such a blunder? Remember that it is not now published for the first time. It was read from week to week by eager thousands in the pages of *All the Year Round*. In those pages a blunder which renders the whole of the last volume, the climax of the tale, nugatory, escaped the practised eye of Mr. Dickens and his coadjutors, who were blinded, as well they might be, by the strong assertions and earnest style of the narrator. A plot that is worked out of impossibilities, like that of robbing the almanack of a fortnight, may be treated as a jest; but we vote three cheers for the author who is able to practise such a jest with impunity.

---

[1] Letters, Pierpont-Morgan Library, dated 'Friday', June 1860, and 5 July 1860.

Conrad and Cunninghame Graham: A Discussion with Addenda to their Correspondence

CEDRIC WATTS

University of Sussex

'Could you conceive for a moment that I could go on existing if Cunninghame Graham were to die?' (Conrad to Arthur Symons)

As their correspondence shows, Conrad's relationship with Cunninghame Graham, which lasted from 1897 until Conrad's death in 1924, was the warmest and deepest of the friendships made by the Polish exile during his career as a writer, and it was abundantly fruitful in literary consequences. In the first part of this article, I make a survey of those consequences; and in the second part, I augment the record of their correspondence by giving the texts of two unpublished letters.

I

Of R. B. Cunninghame Graham, 1852–1936, 'the Uncrowned King of Scotland', descended from King Robert II; cowboy, cattle rancher, horse dealer; pioneer Socialist; convict; Scottish Nationalist; the model for Saranoff in Shaw's *Arms and the Man*; admired by Engels, flattered by Henry James, blessed by Wyndham Lewis, and celebrated by Jacob Epstein, there has been, strangely and sadly, no biography since 1937, and the memorial inscription proclaiming the 'Master of Life' has vanished from his vandal-battered monument at Dumbarton.[1] Perhaps the first requirement, therefore, in appreciating Graham's effect on Conrad is a leap of imagination in order to recognize that when Graham first approached Conrad it was the latter who was relatively obscure and the former who, with his stormy parliamentary career behind him, was the celebrated and influential public figure: 'a friend at court', as Conrad told Garnett. A further leap is required to recognize the particular kind of influence which Graham, as a sheer living presence, could exert on the imagination of a creative writer: as challenge and provocation, as though to say, 'What fictional characterization can approach in its vividness this flesh-and-blood personality?'. When writing to him, Conrad exclaimed: 'What don't you know! From the outside of a sail to the inside of a prison! When I think of you I feel as tho' I had lived all my life in a dark hole'; 'You seem to know more of all things than I thought it possible for any man to know, since the Renaissance swells'; 'Sometimes I lose all sense of reality in a kind of nightmare effect produced by existence. Then I try to think of you — to wake myself. And it does wake me'.[2] To be flattering was part of the Conradian definition of courtesy;

---

[1] The biographies of Graham are H. F. West's *A Modern Conquistador: Robert Bontine Cunninghame Graham* (London, 1932) and A. F. Tschiffely's *Don Roberto* (London, 1937). Tschiffely's *Tornado Cavalier* (London, 1955) is a shorter adaptation of *Don Roberto*. Laurence Davies and I are at present attempting a critical biography.

[2] The quotations are from my edition, *Joseph Conrad's Letters to R. B. Cunninghame Graham* (London, 1969), referred to hereafter as *Letters*, which provides the evidence for most of the claims about Graham's relationship with Conrad which are made in this article. I have preserved Conrad's orthography.

but these are more than mere flattering hyperboles. The novelist's son, Borys, has told me that even in the last years of Conrad's life a visit from Graham (that athletic, immaculate but exotic visitor, carrying a revolver in a shoulder holster) would always have a rejuvenating, enlivening effect.

It is typical of Graham's perceptiveness and crusading zeal that after reading 'An Outpost of Progress' in the pages of *Cosmopolis*, he had not only written, with enthusiastic praise, to introduce himself to Conrad, but had also proclaimed himself Conrad's 'prophète en titre' and henceforth commended the novelist's works repeatedly in print and in letters to acquaintances; and for years after his friend's death the tributes continued, in memorable essays like 'Inveni Portum' and the prefaces to *Tales of Hearsay* and *Lord Jim*. Characteristically, too, in the early years of their correspondence he had tried to nudge and cajole Conrad towards a commitment to socialism: efforts which elicited a series of predictably pessimistic and sometimes nihilistic replies which stand as laconic commentaries on the bleakest aspects of Conrad's works. 'The fate of a humanity condemned ultimately to perish from cold is not worth troubling about'; 'Life knows us not and we do not know life'; 'There is no morality, no knowledge and no hope'; 'What you want to reform are not institutions — it is human nature. Your faith will never move that mountain' (*Letters*, pp. 65–71).

Nevertheless: 'I am more in sympathy with you than words can express.' Their friendship could easily survive the superficial differences of political opinion, because both men had so much in common. Both were aristocratic adventurers, men of action and travel who had turned to writing after years of taxing labour in far regions; both had strong sympathies with nations lacking autonomy and with colourful but vanishing cultures; and both, consequently, were acute critics of territorial and economic imperialism. In temperament, each was a blend of Don Quixote and Hamlet, of self-sacrificing idealism and pyrrhonistic scepticism; and both, as writers, were keen to exploit oblique, deceptive, and impressionistic narrative methods and to relish the ironies that stem from vivid racial, cultural, and geographical contrasts.

If, on the basis of his correspondence with Graham, we had to predict the effects on Conrad's works of that new friendship, some obvious predictions would be confirmed in the writings of the decade from 1897 to 1907. Political themes predominate: multiple criticisms are made of the methods and premises of the capitalist and the imperialist; pessimistic arguments against socialism, of the kinds rehearsed in the letters, are deployed implicitly and explicitly; and parallels between ancient and modern *conquistadores* become an important source of ironies. South America is chosen as the setting of a major novel; close interest is shown in the tensions between the Quixotic and the introspective elements in human nature; and a prominent motif is that of the 'secret sharer', in which complicity is established between apparently contrasting figures: between, for example, members of the upper classes and revolutionaries or anarchists, between guardians of order and those seeking to subvert it, or between the decent and the corrupt.

The first of Conrad's works to which Graham's presence makes a probable contribution is *Heart of Darkness*, for in this tale Conrad reviewed and developed afresh the themes of 'An Outpost of Progress', that earlier sardonic account of Belgian iniquities in the Congo; and since Graham had been prompted to introduce himself to Conrad by the vigour of the earlier tale's criticism of imperialist hypocrisies and of the complacencies of civilization, his enthusiasm was one of the factors which would have encouraged that imaginative revisiting of the Congo in *Heart of Darkness*. One element absent from 'An Outpost' which is important in the later tale is the use of ironic comparisons of modern European with ancient Roman methods of conquest, and for years Cunninghame Graham, in essays and tales read by Conrad, had been exploiting such comparisons. Thus Graham's controversial and much-reprinted denunciation of British imperialism, 'Bloody Niggers' (which Conrad had read in June 1898), had anticipated Marlow's ruminations in *Heart of Darkness* by its disparagement of 'material and bourgeois Rome . . . conquering the world . . . and by its sheer dead weight of commonplace, filling the office in the old world that now is occupied so worthily by God's own Englishmen' (*The Social-Democrat*, 1 (1897), p. 107). It is not surprising that when the first instalment of *Heart of Darkness* appeared, Conrad remarked to Graham: 'So far the note struck chimes in with your convictions — mais après? There is an après. But I think that if you look a little into the episodes you will find in them the right intention.' (*Letters*, p. 116).

With *Nostromo*, published a few years later, in 1904, Graham has many connexions. During his adventures as a cattle rancher, horse dealer, and cotton merchant in Central and South America, he had been involved in the revolutionary upheavals there: he was an eye witness of the devastation wrought in Paraguay by the campaigns of the dictator Francísco Solano López. In his writings he frequently reminisces about those early experiences, and we know that such reminiscences must have filled many of his conversations with Conrad. On 23 June 1898 Edward Garnett wrote to him: 'Conrad told me you had once assisted at a battle in Paraguay . . . Will your Joss (or that familiar demon that makes you write) not conjure up for you & for us that battle? or won't you expand that sentence of yours about "six women to each man in Paraguay" into a moral sketch on Paraguayan manners[?]' (*Letters*, p. 37).

Between 1897 and 1903, Graham was a particularly close student of South American affairs, and many of his articles and letters to the press make bitter comment on the emergence of the United States as a new imperialist power during this period of the Spanish–American War and of the secession of Panama from Colombia through the intervention of the United States. (The arrival of American warships ensured the Panamanian secession; and, in *Nostromo*, the arrival of the U.S. cruiser *Powhattan* puts an end to the Costaguana–Sulaco war.)

Two of Graham's histories of the Spanish conquest of South America (*A Vanished Arcadia* (1901) and *Hernando de Soto* (1903)) were read and enjoyed by Conrad shortly before and during the writing of *Nostromo*, and he particularly relished the parallels drawn between the *conquistadores* and the present-day imperialists, as well as Graham's sardonic emphasis on the hypocrisy and futility of attempting to found a durable and decent moral order on the basis of 'material interests' and the quest for treasure. Another anticipation of Conrad's themes is provided by Graham's tactical argument that the cruelties inflicted personally by the hardy treasure seekers of the past are almost venial when compared with the devastation wrought relatively impersonally by modern emissaries of 'Progress'. A particularly bitter critic of the United States' territorial ambitions in South America was Graham's friend and correspondent, Don Santiago Pérez Triana, who was later to be prominent at the Hague Peace Conferences. He was introduced by Graham to Conrad and, as Conrad's letter of 31 October 1904 makes clear, became the model on which the characterization of Don José Avellanos was based (*Letters*, pp. 157–8). Another character, Giorgio Viola, was engendered partly by Graham's recollections of his old South American acquaintance, the leonine bar-tender Enrico Clerici, who had served with Garibaldi.[1] As for the character of Don Carlos Gould, there is some plausibility in Norman Sherry's suggestion that this owes something to Don Roberto himself. Professor Sherry cites the physical appearance of both men, the fact that both had early family connexions with South America, and the fact that each had a wife who liked to sketch and who accompanied her husband on exhausting American journeys.[2] We might add that Graham, like Gould, was well known as a proudly equestrian figure (he used to ride on horseback to the House of Commons) and that in 1894 Graham had actually prospected for gold, if not silver, in ancient Spanish mine workings.

Conrad conducted extensive literary research during the writing of *Nostromo*, ransacking volumes of South American memoirs. Working on the assumption that Graham had provided help, Edgar Wright was able to discover one of the major source books for the novel, G. F. Masterman's *Seven Eventful Years in Paraguay*. With minor sources too, used for incidental descriptive detail, a trail leads from Graham to Conrad. For example, among Graham's old notebooks (now in the National Library of Scotland) are notes on a volume by Ramon Páez entitled *Wild Scenes in South America* (1863), and Graham's jottings include passing references to Páez's descriptions of the rey-zamuro vulture and the owl that cries 'ya acabo' ('it is finished'). When Conrad's library was auctioned after his death, *Wild Scenes in South America* was one of the volumes, and anyone who cares to put alongside each other Conrad's and Páez's descriptions of that owl and that vulture will see parallels in phrasing which make it quite clear that *Nostromo* was indebted to Páez's memoirs and, I infer, to Graham's recommendation of them. There are several other parallels which I have noted elsewhere,[3] but for the present it is perhaps sufficient to remark that of all Conrad's acquaintances, Cunninghame Graham was the one person ideally equipped to make available to him, from personal knowledge or from researches, much of that abundance of local detail which helps to make *Nostromo* so convincing a re-creation of South American life.

Similarly, Cunninghame Graham, whose maiden speech in Parliament on 1 February 1887 had assailed 'that society in which capital and luxury made a Heaven for thirty thousand, and a Hell for thirty million',[4] had more first hand experience of the revolutionary, anarchistic, and radical forces in British politics than any other of Conrad's friends. He had been jailed after charging at the police during the Bloody Sunday demonstrations of 1887 (commemorated in William Morris's *News from Nowhere*); had been expelled from France in 1891 after a speech to strikers who had been fired on by the police; had campaigned with Prince Kropotkin among the London dockers and with Morris in the north; had spoken alongside Engels and the assassin Stepniak during the agitation for the eight-hour working

---

[1] *Letters*, p. 38; Norman Sherry, *Conrad's Western World* (London, 1971), pp. 150–52.
[2] Sherry, p. 149.
[3] 'A Minor Source for *Nostromo*', *RES*, 16 (1965), 182–4.
[4] *Hansard*, Third Series, Vol. 310, col. 445.

day; and had represented Britain at the Marxist Congress of the Second International. His numerous articles and reports for socialist journals (the *People's Press*, *Labour Leader*, and others) constantly upbraided pacific moderates among the trade unionists and in the Labour movement at large. 'A general strike! That means a revolution . . . Well, let it come; it cannot come too soon, with butchering Stanleys held in high renown, with cheating and extortion rife amongst us, with sweaters in high places.'[1]

When opposing Graham's socialistic arguments, one of Conrad's most unnerving tactics (as in the following passage from a letter of 1899) was to go even further by adopting a position so anarchic as to anticipate that of the Professor in *The Secret Agent*. 'La société est essentielment criminelle — ou elle n'existerait pas. C'est l'égoisme qui sauve tout . . . Voilà pourquoi je respecte les êxtremes anarchistes. — "Je souhaite l'extermination generale" — Très bien. C'est juste et ce qui est plus c'est clair. On fait des compromis avec des paroles' (*Letters*, p. 117). In a speech to workers in 1890 Graham had said: 'The only crime that is never pardoned or forgiven is poverty. Well, fear is a good lever, too, you know. Having that lever, though, you want a fulcrum . . . Archimedes could have moved the world could he have found a fulcrum. Where is your fulcrum?'. And, as if in echo of this oratory, Conrad's Professor adopts the slogan: 'Madness and despair! Give me that for a lever and I'll move the world.'[2]

Clearly, Graham's presence was one of the most important factors encouraging Conrad to give close attention, in major works like *The Secret Agent* and *Under Western Eyes* as well as in some of the shorter tales, not simply to anarchistic and revolutionary characters but particularly to the seeming paradox of the aristocratic subversive or the elegant revolutionary: to 'Mr. X', for example, that exquisitely fastidious firebrand of 'The Informer' (in *A Set of Six*) whose manner and appearance also give a remarkable physical likeness of Graham. In addition, some of Graham's acquaintances contributed variously to the political works. Sergei Stepniak's career and personality provided a basis for the characterization of Laspara in *Under Western Eyes*, while his novel *The Career of a Nihilist*, which portrays Russian anarchists exiled in Geneva, may have influenced Conrad's choice and presentation of the Genevan setting.[3] In the case of that political fantasy *The Inheritors*, the least unsatisfactory product of Conrad's literary collaborations with Ford Madox Hueffer, the science-fiction elements resulted from Conrad's visit to Graham's physician, Dr John McIntyre, who astounded his guest by giving demonstrations of the powers of the X-ray machine: the rays penetrated matter and flesh, isolating the bones of Conrad's hand, exposing the skeleton of Neil Munro. 'It follows that two universes may exist in the same place and in the same time', concluded Conrad, thus anticipating the novel's explanation of its 'Fourth Dimensionists', who subvert British politics from within.[4] Finally, it should be noted that it was Graham who introduced Max Nordau to Conrad, and the theories about criminal and degenerate psychology postulated by Nordau and his mentor Lombroso may have contributed to the presentation of Kurtz, that 'highly-gifted

[1] *The People's Press* (10 May 1890), p. 6.
[2] Sherry, pp. 431–2, suggests that the slogan derives from Graham's speech.
[3] Watts, 'Stepniak and *Under Western Eyes*', *N & Q*, New Series, 13 (1966), 410–11.
[4] Watts, 'Joseph Conrad, Dr. MacIntyre, and *The Inheritors*', *N & Q*, New Series, 14 (1967), 245–7.

degenerate' of *Heart of Darkness*.[1] They certainly become an explicit and important theme in *The Secret Agent*, in which the principles of physically identifiable criminality or degeneracy are subject to an elaborate game of ironic criticism and mocking endorsement.

The other works of Conrad with which Graham is connected are *The Rescue*, *Typhoon*, and *Tales of Hearsay*. With the first of these, Graham's role was, so to speak, that of porter: he conveyed the cage that saved the novel's heroine from being eaten alive by mosquitoes. Graham happened to be one of the acquaintances of Lady Margaret Brooke, the Dowager Ranee of Sarawak, and when her autobiography (*My Life in Sarawak*) appeared in 1913, he, knowing of Conrad's interest in that region, arranged for her to send him an extra copy to forward to Conrad. Possibly it was receipt of her book that led to the resumption of work on *The Rescue*, whose opening pages contain a clearly identifiable tribute to that first White Rajah of Sarawak, James Brooke, the 'disinterested adventurer' who was in some respects the prototype of Lingard. Certainly, as J. D. Gordan has shown, Conrad made various borrowings from her book, and one of them was the 'Cage', a kind of summer house offering protection from mosquitoes, which, Conrad told the Ranee (in a letter dated 15 July 1920), 'I have transported bodily from your palace at Kuching and transported on board the "Emma" — a great liberty; but I really had to do something to save Mrs Travers from mosquitoes' (*Letters*, p. 210).

For *Typhoon*, Graham seems to have given Conrad the original provocation to begin the actual writing of the book. At the beginning of 1898 Graham was working on the tale 'S.S. *Atlas*', an autobiographical piece describing a stormy transatlantic crossing in a tramp steamer which survived the gales in spite of the intoxication of the Scottish crew and the breaking of its smoke-stack. Graham asked Conrad to confirm the technical accuracy of the description of the ship's ordeal. Conrad's reply (7 January 1898) was long and very informative, with its diagrams and nautical detail; and the tone became more and more enthusiastic as the topic captured Conrad's imagination:

The most dramatic circumstance would be the hellish mess of soot blowing about or washing over the deck. Does the plot hinge on the funnel? You must have a *plot*! If you haven't, every fool reviewer will kick you because there can't be literature without a plot. I am in a state of wild excitement about the stack. Let's know quick what happened in the tramp. A Scotch tramp is a very good tramp. The Engineers tell anecdotes, the mates are grim and over all floats the flavour of an accent that gives a special value to every word pronounced on her deck. You must know I've a soft spot for Scotchmen. (*Letters*, p. 60)

Graham's enquiry seems to have prompted in Conrad a train of reflections about tempest-stricken tramp steamers with Scots crews which would one day result in the writing of *Typhoon*. And when *Typhoon* appeared in 1903 it was dedicated to Graham; and his own copy bears Conrad's inscription, 'To / R. B. Cunninghame Graham / this copy of the book / that was his in / the writing'.

To the posthumous volume, *Tales of Hearsay* (1925), Graham's contribution extended beyond the provision of an eloquent and movingly intimate preface. Richard Curle, the volume's editor, consulted him about the title and the selection of material; and the Graham/Curle correspondence shows that Graham strongly recommended the adoption of the title *Tales of Hearsay* (instead of a suggested

1 Watts, 'Nordau and Kurtz: A Footnote to *Heart of Darkness*', *N & Q*, New Series, 21 (1974), 226–7.

alternative, *The Warrior's Soul*) and urged that a fragment known as 'The Two Sisters' be excluded from the selection. Of this fragment he remarked curtly, in a letter of 8 October 1924, 'A. The discontented artist (Anglice, bloody fool artist) is a worn out theme. B. Spain and the Spanish were an ignis fatuus, to dear Conrad. He understood them as little as I do the Slavs'. The piece that Graham criticized was omitted from *Tales of Hearsay* but was later published as *The Sisters* by Crosby Gaige of New York in 1928. Posterity's judgement of it has been more periphrastic but no less damning than Graham's.

It does a disservice to the relationship between the two men if we do not consider the individual contributions by Cunninghame Graham to Conrad's works; but final emphasis should doubtless fall on the obvious, simple, and essential sustenance provided for Conrad by the unflagging loyalty of an uncompromising 'writer's writer', a man of magnanimous indignations and ideals, whose idealism was the more heroic because of his recognition that, in a world of 'men short-sighted in good and evil' (Conrad's phrase), the ideals most worthy of defence were not necessarily those most likely to prevail. That Cunninghame Graham's monument at Dumbarton has been battered and defaced makes it the more appropriate a memorial to a neglected genius whose writings so often lingered on the theme of forgotten merit. The basic moral structure of Conrad's *Heart of Darkness* and *Nostromo* is provided by St Paul's paradox of the Cretan who says that all Cretans are liars: for both works demonstrate the clear vision which they suggest humans lack; and the paradox is implicit in Cunninghame Graham's whole life, for he strove untiringly on behalf of the world's underdogs while yet writing with sombre pessimism of the impotence of political action when measured against the perennial force of mutability and death.

II

Scholars working on Conrad's correspondence with Graham soon make the melancholy discovery that it seems to have been Conrad's custom to destroy periodically the vast majority of the letters he received. When searching, during the early nineteen-sixties, for Graham's letters to him, I had as little success as Herbert Faulkner West, the biographer who had hunted without avail some thirty years previously. Eventually, through the vigilance of Dr Eloise Knapp Hay, two letters, enthusiastically praising *The Rover*, did come to light; and these, as Dr Hay and I suggested when editing them, probably survived because they were received shortly before Conrad's death, and thus escaped some periodic tidying up.[1] The latest discovery further confirms the theory of 'survival by accident'. Among the papers which at Texas University were audaciously catalogued as 'letters from Cunninghame Graham to J. B. Pinker' I located the third extant letter from Graham to Conrad, which had evidently been forwarded to Pinker and preserved by him. This replies to an unpublished letter from Conrad which happily turned up among the Graham family papers recently and was kindly pointed out to me by Professor John Walker.

These two new items belong to the period when Graham, though sixty-two years old, was serving the War Office as an honorary colonel in South America,

[1] See *Conradiana*, 5 (1973), No. 2, 5–19.

selecting the horses which were needed by the army in Europe during the First World War; a distasteful duty that he was to recall in the essays 'Los Pingos' and 'Bopicuá'. The exchange has a certain ironic poignancy. In 1897 Conrad had hailed with delight Graham's offer of friendly patronage: he recognized, and needed, a helping hand. By 1915 there has been a reversal of roles. The success of *Chance* in the previous year had brought international fame and wealth to Conrad, whereas Graham's work, though still receiving high praise from Edward Garnett and many other reviewers, remained unpopular with the general public. Now it was Conrad's opportunity to offer a helping hand by acting on his friend's behalf in a transaction with the literary agent, J. B. Pinker, which might result in American editions of Graham's tales. The ensuing negotiations, though complicated, were satisfactorily fruitful, for in 1917 no fewer than six collections of the tales were published in New York. Though popular success continued to elude Graham (who had never, in any case, been its most eager suitor), this was not for want of effort by Pinker.

Here are the texts of Conrad's message and Graham's reply. I have preserved the original punctuation and spelling (as in 'musn't' and 'negociation').[1]

Capel House,
Orlestone,
N^r Ashford.
21 Ap. '15

Très cher ami.

This is the business on which I want you to answer me as soon as the dear horses and the charming ladies of the Banda Oriental leave you a moment of leisure:—

A man well known to me by correspondence: A. Knopf partner of the publisher Kennerley in the U S (New York City), has been writing to me with very proper enthusiasm about your work which he has been studying of late, apparently with a view of introducing it to this American public.

He thinks there is a good chance, and he asks me (as your friend) for my assistance in the matter; being obviously under the impression that you are in England.

From a literary point of view there is no doubt that you will find your public there. But this is a business matter mainly. The great thing is that the integrity of your work should be preserved and your interest in it properly secured. It wouldn't do to put yourself in the hands of a publisher unconditionally. You being far away I consulted my good friend and agent Mr Pinker. He thinks that the business is worth going into.

If you want us to start the negociation I would guard the literary side of this transaction while P would do the rest of the necessary diplomacy — tho' indeed the literary side too would be quite safe in his hands, I can assure you. For instance Knopf wants to make up a vol: of *selections* from your stories to begin with; but P at once said that this musn't be allowed (and I fully agree with him) on the ground that it would be literary vandalism — for, each of your volumes has its own special

---

[1] For permission to publish these two letters I am grateful to Admiral Sir Angus Cunninghame Graham, K.B.E., C.B., to the Humanities Research Center of the University of Texas, and to Messrs J. M. Dent & Sons and the Trustees of the Joseph Conrad Estate.

character. From the business point of view it would be a false move too. We think that if anything is done Knopf (or Kennerley) ought to publish a complete vol: under a proper royalty agreement. The selection of the vol: you would perhaps leave to me and P — or you may tell us your wishes in the matter. Anyway pray drop me a line either authorising P to go on (for I am not competent to negociate terms) with the business or telling us to leave it alone. I enclose here Knopf's address in case you should prefer to write to him yourself.[1] This is all for the present. A strictly business letter.

Tout à Vous   J.Conrad.

Fray Bentos
Mayo 19 / 1915

Mi querido Amigo.

Your kind letter just catches me after a very heavy day's work.

I was up by daylight & parting & remising horses for my sixth & last ship by daylight. It is now ten, but I answer at once for I must be off by daylight tomorrow. A thousand thanks.

I leave all to your great kindness, but please make sure of these points.

1. That they *leave nothing out* for fear of the angels.
2. That you yourself choose what is to be published.
3. That my publishers consent is asked for terms. I know you will do all that for me.

Otiosi (as they say in Spanish legal documents). Perhaps you would add to your kindness by writing *a page* of introduction, so that the book should be covered by your aegis.

Otiosi. Pray tell Mr Knopf, *why* I am out here, for I should be pained to think anyone thought I was away travelling when any Englishman should be doing something for the country.

Y no digo mas.

Once more, a thousand thanks.

Je tombe de sommeil . . . can it be that years are telling?

Kindest regards to your wife & love to the boys.

Suyo amigo aff^{mo}
R B Cunninghame Graham

PS I hereby authorize you to entrust Mr Pinker to take in hand the business part of the publication of a volume (not selected sketches but an entire book) in America.

R B Cunninghame Graham

I may be home by the end of June.

---

[1] Pinned to the letter is a card reading 'A. Knopf. c/o / Mitchell Kennerley / Publisher / 32 West Fifty-eighth Street / New York'.

Frances Hodgson Burnett's *The Secret Garden*:
A Possible Source for T. S. Eliot's 'Rose Garden'

CHRISTOPHER HEYWOOD

University of Sheffield

Various literary sources have been suggested for the image of the rose garden which occurs in *Burnt Norton* and in other works by T. S. Eliot. Of these, *Alice in Wonderland* (1865) has the authority of having been suggested by T. S. Eliot himself.[1] Kipling's story *They*, in *Traffics and Discoveries* (1904), which has been suggested by Helen Gardner, offers more persuasive parallels of phrase and theme.[2] Nevertheless, these works contain only general anticipations of the image and are lacking in the detailed ingredients which Eliot assembled in *Burnt Norton* and its later echoes: the roses, the secret door, the bird, the thrush, the menacing and regenerative power of the garden, the vision of children concealed among the leaves, the suppressed laughter, and the sunshine which appears at the moment of resolution. In this article I propose to argue that Frances Hodgson Burnett's *The Secret Garden* was Eliot's principal literary source, and to relate the writing of *Burnt Norton* to the crisis in his life which followed the collapse of his first marriage.

The Secret Garden achieved immediate success upon its simultaneous publication in London and New York in 1911. Recent studies have upheld the claim to classic status of this delightful work, which portrays a process of spiritual desolation, rebirth, and reconciliation.[3] At its climax, this story presents a setting and phrases which closely match Eliot's image in *Burnt Norton*. In his poem, Eliot evokes a speakingly exact picture of the garden at Burnt Norton, a manor house near Chipping Campden in Gloucestershire. His meeting with a companion recalls memories of ghostly presences:

> There they were, dignified, invisible,
> Moving without pressure, over the dead leaves.

A bird warns:

> Go, said the bird, for the leaves were full of children,
> Hidden excitedly, containing laughter.

Eliot's reflection: 'human kind | Cannot bear very much reality' suggests that the children, or the memory of childhood, represent a threat and, more ambiguously, that the dreams of childhood are not realized in adult life. In the resolution at the close of the poem the narrator is reconciled with the past, and the image reappears, this time shorn of its menacing qualities. The 'waste sad time' has become 'ridiculous' and the memories are accepted:

---

[1] See Grover Smith, *T. S. Eliot's Poetry and Plays* (Chicago, 1956), pp. 256, 321.
[2] *The Art of T. S. Eliot* (London, 1949), p. 160.
[3] See Ann Thwaite, *Waiting for the Party* (London, 1974), p. ix. Other studies include: Marghanita Laski, *Mrs Ewing, Mrs Molesworth and Mrs Hodgson Burnett* (London, 1950); and John Rowe Townsend, *Written for Children* (London, 1965).

There rises the hidden laughter
Of children in the foliage
Quick now, here, now, always.

The works by Kipling and 'Lewis Carroll' which have been suggested as possible sources lack detailed correspondences with the cycle of thought and with the details which are presented in Eliot's image. In *Alice in Wonderland*, the story begins beside a river, moves to a claustrophobic interior, and moves out to a 'lovely garden' through a door which has 'a crowd of little animals and birds waiting outside' (Chapter 4). The outdoor settings lack the mystery and reflectiveness of Eliot's portrayal of the garden at Burnt Norton. Carroll relies upon schematic allusion rather than upon sensuous evocation for the setting of his scene, as in: 'the open air' (Chapter 6), 'out under a tree in front of the house' (Chapter 7), and 'A large rose-tree stood near the entrance of the garden: the roses growing on it were white, but there were three gardeners at it, busily painting them red' (Chapter 18). The 'pattering of feet' in *Alice in Wonderland* is heard indoors, on the stairs, and it announces the arrival of the Mouse, not children (Chapter 4). Eliot's phrase 'dead leaves' is anticipated in the concluding paragraphs of Carroll's story (Chapter 12), but the phrase is in everyday use, and whereas Eliot's leaves are stationary underfoot, the leaves in *Alice in Wonderland* are in motion, falling on the heroine and waking her from her dream. The drama which is present in Eliot's image, the suppressed laughter, the leaves with hidden children, the sunlight, and the suggestion that the garden has a redemptive power, are lacking in *Alice in Wonderland*.

The difficulty of accepting Kipling's *They* as a tributary source is less striking. At the moment when Kipling's narrator is mending his car, he is watched by children who are hidden in the wood: 'The wood was so full of noises of summer (though the birds had mated) that I could not at first distinguish these from the tread of small cautious feet stealing across the dead leaves.'[1] To some extent, Kipling's theme anticipates Eliot's. The contrast between a fecund mother's indifference to her offspring, and the love of a blind woman for children she cannot see, or bear, or lose, and also Kipling's conclusion, 'the wisdom of old wives is greater than that of all the Fathers' (pp. 324–5), anticipates Eliot's reflection: 'human kind | Cannot bear very much reality', and matches his epigraph from Heraclitus: 'though the Word governs everything, most people trust in their own wisdom'. Nevertheless, the children in Kipling's story lack the suppressed laughter and excitement of the children invoked in *Burnt Norton*. Also, the garden in Eliot's image differs sharply from Kipling's. The garden behind the house in *They* is entered through a single wooden door which is large enough to admit the narrator's car, and it has azaleas, not roses. The 'patter of feet — quick feet through a room beyond', is heard indoors and not among the leaves. The bird in *Burnt Norton* which leads Eliot and his companion to the garden is not paralleled, and the garden lacks suggestions of regenerative powers.

In contrast to these shadowy and incomplete parallels, more sustained anticipations in Eliot's image can be traced in *The Secret Garden*. In Frances Hodgson Burnett's story, Archibald Craven has lived away from his Yorkshire manor house, Misselthwaite, for the ten years which have succeeded the birth of his son Colin,

---

[1] *Traffics and Discoveries* (London, 1904), p. 313. References are to this edition.

and the death of his wife, Lilias. Both father and son succumb to a nervous, wasting, and debilitating loss of will. Colin becomes an invalid, though no illness is diagnosed, and is moved about in a wheel chair. Archibald leaves his son in the care of a housekeeper, travels abroad, and becomes 'a man who for ten years had kept his mind filled with dark and heart-broken thinking'.[1] The story moves to a climax in which father and son are reconciled to each other and to the paralysing past. Both are restored to health in the rose garden at Misselthwaite. The progress towards Colin's restoration begins when he is joined at Misselthwaite by his orphaned cousin, Mary Lennox, who comes to England for the first time after the death of her parents in India. A robin leads her to the buried key of the rose garden, which becomes the secret playground of the children. The secrecy and the burial of the key to the locked door are the result of Archibald's misgivings over the death of his wife, who had been killed by a falling branch in the rose garden. Together with their rustic friend, Dickon Sowerby, the children discover the secrets of nature in the garden, and Colin finds that he can walk and run as well as Dickon. Mary is apprehensive that their secret playground will be locked away from them, but Dickon reassures her: a missel thrush on its nest has become the symbol of the children's secret, and Dickon says: 'Th'art as safe as a missel thrush' (p.113). In the course of his travels abroad, Archibald experiences a vision in which the voice of Lilias calls him back to Misselthwaite. On his return he finds the children playing, running, and trying to conceal the sounds of their merriment in the garden which he had supposed he would find locked.

Numerous parallels can be traced between this work and Eliot's themes and phrases in the 'rose-garden' image. The passage describing the reunion of father and son at the door of the rose garden at Misselthwaite contains the strongest fore-shadowings of *Burnt Norton*:

The ivy hung thick over the door, the key was buried under the shrubs, no human being had passed that portal for ten lonely years — and yet inside the garden there were sounds. They were the sounds of running, scuffling feet seeming to chase round and round under the trees, they were strange sounds of lowered suppressed voices — exclamations and smothered joyous cries. It seemed actually like the laughter of young things, the uncontrollable laughter of children who were trying not to be heard but who in a moment or so — as their excitement mounted — would burst forth. What in heaven's name was he dreaming of — what in heaven's name did he hear? Was he losing his reason and thinking he heard things which were not for human ears? Was it that the far clear voice had meant?

And then the moment came, the uncontrollable moment when the sounds forgot to hush themselves. The feet ran faster and faster — they were nearing the garden door — there was quick strong young breathing and a wild outbreak of laughing shouts which could not be contained — and the door in the wall was flung wide open, the sheet of ivy swinging back, and a boy burst through it at full speed and, without seeing the outsider, dashed almost into his arms. (pp. 301–2)

In the ensuing reconciliation, Archibald accepts his past life. The psychological threat represented by the garden and by Colin is redeemed. In his phrase 'hidden excitedly, containing laughter', Eliot recaptures the action and phrasing at the climax of *The Secret Garden*: 'uncontrollable laughter . . . as their excitement mounted . . . laughing shouts which could not be contained'. Eliot's reflection, 'Human kind | Cannot bear very much reality', elaborates the alienation between

---

[1] *The Secret Garden* (London, 1911), p. 290. References are to this edition.

father and son in *The Secret Garden*, where Archibald's revulsion against Colin is the result of his son's resemblance to Lilias: Archibald 'could not bear' (p. 296) the resemblance of his son to his dead wife, and until the 'Magic' of the garden and contact with Dickon and his cousin Mary restore him to emotional and physical well-being, Colin 'can't bear people' (p. 191). Eliot's portrayal of the pool and garden at Burnt Norton in touches such as: 'filled with water out of sunlight', 'the surface glittered out of heart of light', and 'white light still and moving', again echoes Frances Hodgson Burnett's phrasing at the approach to the climax of *The Secret Garden*. Archibald Craven is in the Tyrol, seated beside 'sunlit water', listening to the 'laughter' of a stream and 'the stillness' around him. When he hears the voice of his dead wife calling to him, 'It was as if a sweet clear spring had risen until at last it swept the dark water away' (pp. 291–2). The 'bird' and the 'deception of the thrush' in *Burnt Norton* are exactly foreshadowed in the robin which leads Mary to the garden, and the thrush which stands for the children's secret. At the end of *Burnt Norton* Eliot signals his resolution by 'a shaft of sunlight', echoing *The Secret Garden*, where father and son are reunited in 'sunshine' which 'made one feel that one stood in an embowered temple of gold' (p. 303). Eliot's recovery of life and movement is suggested in the double value of the word *quick*, that is, rapid motion and the quality of being alive:

> ... the hidden laughter
> Of children in the foliage
> Quick, now, here now, always.

Similarly, Frances Hodgson Burnett speaks of 'quick strong young breathing' at the climax of her story and, during the development of Mary's interest in the garden, makes use of the northern English form 'wick' (p. 105) in Dickon's speech about the magical life of nature.

In the absence of full documentation of his life and works, any attempt at an elucidation of the importance which *The Secret Garden* may have had for T. S. Eliot must of necessity be provisional. The explanation tentatively offered here is suggested by the outline of Eliot's relationship to Emily Hale which has been given recently in a biographical sketch by T. S. Matthews.[1] Eliot visited the manor house of Burnt Norton and its garden with Emily Hale, during one of the visits to Chipping Campden which followed the breach of his marriage in 1932. Echoes from *The Secret Garden* appear in *Burnt Norton*, written in celebration of the reunion with the companion of his early youth, and reappear as a signature in Eliot's subsequent reinterpretations of the relationship, in *The Family Reunion* and *The Confidential Clerk*. Eliot had signalled to Emily Hale in 1917 by including a portrait of her, *La Figlia che Piange*, among the poems in *Prufrock and other Observations*:

> Her hair over her arms and her arms full of flowers.
> And I wonder how they should have been together!

The impending breach in his by then notoriously wretched marriage to Vivien Haigh-Wood is heralded by Eliot's return to childhood memories in *Animula* and by the reference to childhood scenes in *Marina*, where a possible echo from *The*

---

[1] *Great Tom* (London, 1973), pp. 139–51.

Secret Garden, though less decisive than those in *Burnt Norton*, may have been another signal to Emily Hale:

> Whispers and small laughter between leaves and hurrying feet
> Under sleep, where all the waters meet.

Eliot's position at the reunion with Emily Hale in Chipping Campden was comparable to that of Archibald Craven on his return to Misselthwaite. Eliot's marriage had been in abeyance for over ten years; but in his relationship with Emily Hale he was a Colin, the broken boy in search of a playmate, just as she, a stranger to England and an orphan since early childhood, resembled Mary Lennox. These alternative roles are dramatized in the plays of 1939 and 1954, *The Family Reunion* and *The Confidential Clerk*. In both these works, Eliot reverts to the 'garden' image which had made its first full appearance in *Burnt Norton*. In *The Family Reunion*, Harry re-enacts in melodramatic form the perturbation of Archibald Craven over the death of his wife, but Agatha's revelations precipitate a new phase of thinking, and he sees himself in the role of the restored Colin Craven:

> O my dear, and then you walked through the little door
> And I ran to meet you in the rose-garden.

In Agatha's first reference to the image, the 'black raven' undoubtedly echoes Emily Hale's attitude to Vivien Haigh-Wood at the time of Eliot's first marriage:

> I only looked through the little door
> When the sun was shining on the rose-garden:
> And heard in the distance tiny voices
> And then a black raven flew over.[1]

In *The Confidential Clerk*, Colby and Lucasta relate themselves to each other through their image of a 'secret garden', a phrase for which Agatha's line in *The Family Reunion* is an apt description: 'Here you have found a clue, hidden in the obvious place' (p. 110). In *The Confidential Clerk*, Lucasta says to Colby:

> You have your secret garden; to which you can retire
> And lock the gate behind you

and he half-heartedly concurs:

> I turn the key, and walk through the gate,
> And there I am, alone, in my 'garden'.[2]

In both these plays, Eliot portrays relationships which are based upon his long friendship with Emily Hale, the 'you', as T. S. Matthews persuasively suggests, of *Burnt Norton*:

> Footfalls echo in the memory
> Down the passage which we did not take
> Towards the door we never opened
> Into the rose-garden. My words echo
> Thus, in your mind.

The association of Emily Hale and the garden at Burnt Norton with the passages in Frances Hodgson Burnett's little classic suggests that the reunion in Chipping Campden included a conversation in which themes and characters from *The*

---

[1] *The Family Reunion* (London, 1939), pp. 107–8.
[2] *The Confidential Clerk* (London, 1954), pp. 51–3.

Secret Garden were invoked. In his commentary on *Four Quartets*, Raymond Preston said of *Burnt Norton*: 'It has the vividness and intimacy of a personal experience.'[1] This view can be sustained. Eliot's late poems and the plays written before 1954 sprang from the revival of an early relationship. In this little-explored context, Frances Hodgson Burnett's book appears to have played a part of considerable importance.

[1] *Four Quartets Rehearsed* (London, 1946), p. 12.

Reviews

A Guide to Theses and Dissertations: An Annotated, International Bibliography of Bibliographies. By MICHAEL M. REYNOLDS. Detroit, Michigan: Gale Research. 1975. xiv + 599 pp. $35.00.

Book Review Index: 1969 Cumulation. Volume V; *1974 Cumulation.* Volume X. Edited by GARY C. TARBERT. Detroit, Michigan: Gale Research. 1975. vi + 660 pp. $85.00; vi + 562 pp. $68.00.

Contemporary Authors: A Bio-Bibliographical Guide to Current Authors and Their Works. Volumes 49–52; Volumes 53–56; *Contemporary Authors: Permanent Series.* Volume I. Edited by CLARE D. KINSMAN. Detroit, Michigan: Gale Research. 1975. 602 pp.; 598 + 109 pp.; 697 pp. $38.00 each.

Michael Reynolds's *Guide to Theses and Dissertations* is a compact volume covering an enormous but unevenly tilled field. The compilation is retrospective up to 1973 and lists over 2,000 bibliographies under nineteen basic subject divisions. 'Theses are rarely printed', the introduction reminds us: 'bibliographic control' of potentially useful material 'is fragmentary' at best. This becomes clear when one turns to the subject index. Theses on only fifteen of the world's literary figures, for instance, have apparently been rendered the service of individual bibliographies. One cannot tell whether this is because they are the most popular subjects for research or have simply been lucky in attracting a particular kind of organizing mind (they include Baudelaire, Kafka, D. H. Lawrence, Thoreau, and Vega Carpio). The subject index has entries ranging from the most particular to the most general: Beer, Exceptional Children, Materialism, Theology and Religion, Worms. There is also an index of institutions, and another of Names and Titles. All these help to make the volume very easy to use, perhaps deceptively so, since there is not really enough in the way of cross-referencing. Alighting by chance on 'Modern Humanities Research Association', among 'Names and Titles', I was referred to an item in the section 'Area Studies (France)' which proved to be a bibliography of research on 'linguistics and stylistics; genres; literature movements and tendencies; literature by periods; and writers, characters, and anonymous works'. Yet there is no entry for this work in the subject index under either 'Literature — France' or 'France — Literature'. It would seem that the all-important subject index is compiled by reference solely to titles, not contents. The scope is wide and the coverage international. Annotations are descriptive, not evaluative and, with the emphasis on location, bibliographies not personally examined (apparently very few) are question-marked to invite verification. General bibliographies of theses from single institutions are excluded except in the case of those devoted to particular subjects.

Book Review Index gathers material from six periodic issues covering reviews published over the year. The 1974 volume claims to index all reviews from 228 periodicals (the list of 223 periodicals in the 1969 volume is slightly different), from the scholarly to the popular or specialist, and to include material otherwise unindexed though accessible. The list is obviously selective, as regards both title and subject matter: many an inclusion at once suggests an omission, especially to a reader on this side of the Atlantic. *The Observer* is in, but not the *Sunday Times*; *American Notes and Queries*, but not *Notes and Queries*. *Dance Magazine, Hobbies, Flying,* and *Yachting* are amongst journals representing the specialist fields. For books of interest to academics the omissions matter, since the journals selected may not be those containing the most important reviews. However, the arrangement by author, with a separate entry for each review citation, means that a much reviewed book stands out boldly with perhaps as many as twenty entries. Citations give neither publisher nor price, nor reviewer's name. Allowing for the different frequencies of journal publication and for other kinds of time-lag one might well need to look up the same title in more than one cumulative volume of this index. The 1969 Cumulation appears six years late, but this is apparently by way of filling a gap in the series.

Contemporary Authors binds four volumes at a time in one alphabetical sequence. The two four-volume volumes to hand came out within months of each other, the later one containing the cumulative index for Volumes 1 to 56. This will cut out the tedium of consulting interim cumulations in alternate volumes, although one may still search in vain for any particular one among 'today's active writers' who may have been long active and well known but not yet recorded, or recorded but dead (some entries in the main sequence are merely obituary citations and give no further details). The series evidently aims at exhaustiveness: 'Thousands of the authors covered in *CA* are not included in any similar biographical reference work'. The scope is international and the information detailed, including the occupations of the writer's parents and a guide to the pronunciation of his name if considered difficult ('Nicole' is 'Ni-*cull*', but there is no help with 'Baeuml' or 'Wagn'). Most book titles in foreign languages are translated. A 'Work in Progress' section may well be a useful feature, and I am told that this directory recently proved more useful than any other to an English university library supplying background for the introduction of a visiting American speaker. An extra paragraph, headed 'Sidelights', gives a concluding flourish to many entries, offering 'a comprehensive essay on the writer's achievements, ideas, and goals' in two or three sentences. The effect is often one of breathtakingly ambitious profundity combined with a kind of homeliness, unintentionally funny to read but, I should have thought, superfluous in a serious reference work.

Earlier volumes of *Contemporary Authors* are revised 'about five years later' but the first revision of Volumes 13–16, published 1965–6, appeared in 1975. The ongoing series is now complemented by the arrival of Volume 1 in the *Permanent Series*, which aims to simplify future revision. Sketches of authors previously listed, who at the time of publication of this volume were either deceased or retired and presumed inactive, are here presented in their final form, revised wherever possible with the help of the author himself. Volume 1 is, in fact, made up of sketches taken only from Volumes 9–12 and 13–16 of the main series. Complications arising in the sequence of revision, cumulative indexing, and transference to the *Permanent Series* may perhaps be best described by quotation: 'Occasionally, a revised volume of *CA* and the cumulative index containing *CAP* references for authors transferred from the revised volume will not be available simultaneously. Thus, there will necessarily be periods when the latest sketches for certain inactive authors will not be locatable through the then-current index, or when the sketch will not be available, pending appearance of the next volume in the *Permanent Series*. The editors will work to keep such periods as brief as possible, and will be glad to accept collect telephone calls concerning authors in this interim status.' This seems extremely obliging but might prove expensive. In this work, however, as in many Gale Research publications, an unacknowledged but inevitable bias operates in favour of American material and American readers, in spite of claims to worldwide coverage.

JENNY MEZCIEMS

UNIVERSITY OF WARWICK

English Prose, Prose Fiction, and Criticism to 1660: A Guide to Information Sources. By
    S. K. HENINGER, JR. (American Literature, English Literature, and World
    Literatures in English Information Guide Series, 2) Detroit, Michigan: Gale
    Research. x + 256 pp. $18.00.

This book is part of what is intended as a large series on English Literature. Prose
writings are listed under twelve headings; General, Religious Writings, Historical
Writings, and so on. This kind of subdivision poses fundamental problems for the
bibliographer. He seeks to break down his material into enough categories to be helpful without introducing the need for excessive cross-referencing. Professor Heninger's
solutions are sensible, though I thought the chapter headed 'Essays' included
material that might be sought elsewhere: Julian of Norwich and Margery Kempe
under 'Religious Writings', for instance, and Greene's *Groatsworth of Wit* and
Repentance under 'Ephemeral and Polemical Writings'. Deficiencies in the classification system may be responsible for the omission of certain primary authors,
such as Thomas Morley, Thomas Whythorne, and Robert Laneham. Each section
is prefaced by a brief and, generally speaking, over-simplified descriptive summary.
Comments on selected items also tend to the simplistic, such as the description of
Melbancke's *Philotimus* as 'a euphuistic trifle', and of Robert Armin's *A Nest of
Ninnies* as 'more jests'.

In a work of this scope omissions are inevitable, and it is no doubt understandable that editions and reprints particularly convenient to British readers should be
ignored. Thus, while listing a number of World's Classics volumes, Professor
Heninger misses others, such as A. C. Ward's *A Miscellany of Tracts and Pamphlets*
(1927), which includes Heninger's items numbered 187, 234, 338, 348, 478, and
640; '*The Advancement of Learning*' and '*New Atlantis*' (1906); Janet Hampden's
selection from Hakluyt (1958); and *The Compleat Angler* (1960, with *The Arte of
Angling*). The American as well as the English reader may regret the omission of
reprints of works such as *Rosalynde* and *Pandosto* in Geoffrey Bullough's *Narrative and
Dramatic Sources of Shakespeare*: of the various Shakespeare-orientated selections
from North's translation of Plutarch; of F. P. Wilson's *Shakespearian and Other
Essays*, edited by Helen Gardner (Oxford, 1969; several of the essays are listed in
their original publication); of Geoffrey Shepherd's edition (1957) of the *Ancrene
Wisse*; and of Joan Rees's book (1964) on Samuel Daniel. Scolar Press facsimiles
seem to be entirely ignored. Books published not quite simultaneously in England
and America often raise problems. Heninger chooses normally to give American
date and place, which is probably sensible in view of his generally American
orientation.

On the whole the volume is carefully presented. It is odd to read in successive
entries of Peter Motteux and Peter Le Motteaux. It seems misleading to give the
supposed dates of first publication of Deloney's *Jack of Newbury* (1597), *Thomas of
Reading* (1598), and *The Gentle* [misprinted *Gentile*] *Craft* (1597) without mentioning
that the first surviving editions are dated respectively 1619, 1612, and 1627. The
date of the first edition of McKerrow's *Nashe* should have been given along with
that of the reprint. Proof-reading is good, though Walter R. Davies's book is *Idea*
[not *Ideal*] *and Act in Elizabethan Fiction*. The volume is pleasantly produced, but in
small type and with unjustified lines. The total absence of French accents can only
be regarded as a deplorable illiteracy, whatever the reason for it.

THE SHAKESPEARE INSTITUTE   STANLEY WELLS
Stratford-upon-Avon

An Introduction to English Poetry. By LAURENCE LERNER. London: Edward Arnold.
1975. x + 230 pp. £5.00 (£1.95 paperbound).

Few will demur at Professor Lerner's assumption that the study of poetry should
start with the reading of poems. He has chosen fifteen to show something of the
development of English poetry during the past four centuries and at the same time
to exemplify a fair variety of genres. While his choices repeatedly illustrate his liking
for verse that can compass irony and wit, he has not excluded instances of 'high
seriousness'. But ought he not to have brought in a humorous poem? Burns's
'Tam o' Shanter', perhaps?

The fifteen essays which follow the reprinted texts differ widely in content.
Though Professor Lerner naturally introduces close analysis into each of them, he
rightly judges that whereas one poem needs to be seen in the context of its author's
work generally, a second may more profitably be related to the literary tradition
to which it belongs, and a third will be best understood when read together with
other poems on the same theme. He varies these approaches as is expedient and
supplies relevant information on historical circumstances, theological systems,
poetic kinds and forms, and changing modes of sensibility.

This is a well-conceived enterprise, and Professor Lerner has the knowledge and
experience and the acuteness of literary insight to conduct it successfully. Special
praise must go to his analysis of Herbert's 'The Bunch of Grapes'; to his observations on literary imitation in his essay on Pope; to his illumination of 'Elegiac
Stanzas, suggested by a Picture of Peele Castle' by comparison with other poems
by Wordsworth; to his sensitive guidance of his reader through Wallace Stevens's
'To an Old Philosopher in Rome'; and to his carefully discriminating account of
Auden's 'City without Walls'. At the same time, he does offer some unacceptable
interpretations. How can he speak of a crucial 'disappearance of imagery' (pp. 18,
220) after line 6 of Shakespeare's Sonnet 34 when 'salve', 'heals', 'wound', 'cures',
'physic', and 'grief' all occur in the next three lines? And is it not perverse to
attempt a reading of Milton's 'On his Blindness' without mentioning the parable of
the talents?

The volume contains rather many minor errors, too. For example, Professor
Lerner garbles Dryden's well known judgement on the metaphysicals (p. 44),
he misquotes the opening couplet of *The Vanity of Human Wishes* (p. 101), he allows
a plausible wrong word to stand half way through 'Peter Grimes' (p. 110) and
another at the end of Wordsworth's 'To the Daisy' ('Sweet Flower! belike') (p.
134), and he omits a whole line from what is 'probably the most famous statement of
Wordsworth's pantheism' (p. 140). Practitioners of close analysis should have more
regard for their texts. Nor should they by their example encourage the widespread
delusion that 'flaunt' is a synonym of 'flout' (p. 41). I pass over obvious typographical errors to ask in conclusion whether it would not have been a service to readers
to number the lines in the fifteen reprinted poems. Without such an aid, Professor
Lerner's references by numbers to particular lines in 'Peter Grimes', a 375-line
poem, become wantonly provocative.

In his 'Conclusion' he defends his employment of a variety of patterns for his
essays; but the true justification is the aptness of these patterns to the particular
poems discussed. He says that he has tried to write 'interpretations, with a touch
of evaluation' (p. 221). The aim is a worthy one, and he has carried it out with
considerable success.

UNIVERSITY OF MANCHESTER

† JOHN D. JUMP

The Black Mind: A History of African Literature. By O. R. DATHORNE. Minneapolis: Minnesota University Press; London: Oxford University Press. 1975. 527 pp. £13.00.

This volume, considerably indebted to Janheinz Jahn's *Bibliography* and *History of Neo-African Literature*, as the author acknowledges, goes rather further than the latter in an attempt to appraise a wider range of individual works in a more exacting way. Clearly Mr Dathorne has done a great deal of reading, and he offers rather more than the uncritical praise-songs devoted so often in the past fifteen years to minor or mediocre work which happened to come from an in-continent. The range he covers is very wide, and includes chapters on both oral and written indigenous literature, short sections on African writing in Latin and English from the eighteenth century, surveys of English, French, and, more briefly, Portuguese writing of more recent times in prose, poetry, and drama, and even a short chapter on 'Africa' in the Caribbean.

Despite the size, range, and cost of the book, however, there are some omissions which indicate its limits. The work is after all called *The Black Mind* so that the word 'literature' might be open to a rather more liberal interpretation than that which gives Edward Wilmot Blyden one passing reference and makes none at all to James Africanus Horton. Mary Smith's *Baba of Karo*, an edited translation of a great old lady's orally delivered memoirs, is not considered as literature because 'it is not a novel'. E. Casely-Hayford of Ghana is given some attention but no reference is made to his contemporary, Solomon Attoh-Ahuma, whose essays *The Gold Coast Nation and National Consciousness* are as much 'literature' as Casely-Hayford's *Ethiopia Unbound*. The chapter on ' "Africa" in Caribbean Literature' is included without any reference, even in the bibliography, to Kenneth Ramchand's *The West Indian Novel and its Background*, in which there is a fifty-page chapter devoted to similar issues. Chinua Achebe is dealt with in more detail than most of the novelists in the volume, but the bibliography does not draw attention to what many people consider one of the best studies so far of a particular African writer, David Carroll's book on Achebe.

Much of the space of the volume is, in fact, taken up with summaries of novels and with critical generalizations (some of them sensible and helpful to a reader who is prepared to go to the works discussed, some of them uncomfortably close to classroom notes for freshmen) which raise questions about the function of the book. It often comes close to an examinee's phrasebook, and the question must be asked whether, if it is to be used as a guide to reading, the criticisms are helpful; and, if it is to be used as a substitute for reading, whether the critical judgements have any educational value. At this point I feel that this is not entirely fair to the book, since it is an attempt to offer a comprehensive guide and has the limitations of such attempts. For the serious student, however, either a good bibliographical guide or a close study of a single writer or group of writers would be of more value, and this book seems to encourage slickness in the student. This is sad because the author has clearly worked hard and long at it. But his critical sense emerges as blurred.

For example, he says that the Novel is the 'only literary art form that has been totally imported and imposed over and above development from an indigenous literary pattern'. With the 'Novel' he contrasts 'Poetry' and 'Drama'. Yet it must be clear that the 'Novel' is a term for only one species of 'Narrative' or 'Fiction', and thus differs from the more general terms 'Poetry' and 'Drama'. Anyone who has read or seen the plays and poems of John Pepper Clark or Wole Soyinka will recognize their relation to so-called 'European' art forms: and those acquainted with Tutuola, Fagunwa, or the many African oral epics will see the similarities between these and European fictional art before the novel. The reviewer suggests, for example, a look at Fagunwa alongside late fourteenth-century Icelandic Romances.

The value of the volume is that it offers a wide, though not altogether complete, survey of the literature of Africa: its weakness is that it attempts comprehensiveness and pays for this with superficiality of critical comment.

PAUL EDWARDS

UNIVERSITY OF EDINBURGH

Yesterday's Woman: Domestic Realism in the English Novel. By VINETA COLBY. Princeton, New Jersey: Princeton University Press. 1974. viii + 269 pp. £6.50.

It occurs to me that this would have been a very much better book if Professor Colby had not felt that she had to have a thesis. She sets out to 'explore and illuminate that grey area in the history of the English novel, the first half of the nineteenth century', and this she does very efficiently, employing a wide range of scholarly reference. She draws attention to such forgotten (or unread) documents as Mrs Sherwood's *Diaries*, the Revd Legh Richmond's *The Dairyman's Daughter* (1810) and his *Domestic Portraiture* (1833), as well as Elizabeth Sewell's too-little-known *Autobiography*. The last was published posthumously in 1907 and its first two or three chapters should be included in any Education syllabus as a cheering reminder of how far we have advanced since the 1830s.

But because she does not feel free simply to talk about these books as, say, Gosse or Saintsbury would have done, quite unashamedly, Professor Colby has to show their relevance to the greater works which followed them, to justify her claim for them as 'seedbeds for the flowering of the major Victorian novels'. And once this claim has been made, it is no longer possible simply to savour the works for themselves, to isolate their *virtu*. We have to link Maria Edgeworth's interest in practical education (and 'the education of the heart'), early in the century, with *Hard Times* or *The Ordeal of Richard Feverel*; the Low Church Evangelicalism of Mrs Tonna and the High Church Evangelicalism of Charlotte Yonge with *Scenes of Clerical Life* and *The Mill on the Floss*; the minute realism of the descriptions of Mrs Gore's tales of fashionable life with Thackeray's novels; and the sense of community in Harriet Martineau's *Deerbrook* (1839) with that of *Middlemarch*. Professor Colby is especially interested in minor fiction between 1820 and 1840 (although, in fact, her most substantial and, I think, rewarding chapter is on Maria Edgeworth), for she feels that these novels 'reflect, on a reduced but accurate scale' the major novels which follow.

She does succeed, through her discussion of these novels, in reconstructing the age and atmosphere in which the later and greater novels were shaped, but she is much less successful in convincing the reader that the earlier works were really influential. The whole question of literary influence is a very complicated and difficult one, unless a scene or character is strikingly similar or there are definite textual echoes, or the later writer acknowledges his indebtedness. Certainly the epithet 'influential' as applied, for example, to *Deerbrook* or *Cecil* seems singularly to lack substantiation. For one thing, the background of many of the greater novelists provides quite enough material for them to draw on, without having recourse to stimulus from earlier writers. George Eliot's interest in Evangelical introspection or Dickens's interest in a harrowing childhood can be explained quite simply without reference to either the self-analysis of Guy, in Charlotte Yonge's *Heir of Redcliffe* or Mrs Tonna's memories of her childish miseries in *Personal Recollections*.

Where influences are concerned, Professor Colby is regrettably blind to the very important effect of French novels in the 1830s upon the English literary scene. That decade may indeed have been 'an artistic vacuum' as far as home products were concerned, but French fiction rushed in to fill it, and Balzac, Hugo, and George Sand were devoured and reviewed widely. Their novels were welcomed as supplying a corrective to the artificial and monotonous pictures of society provided by silver-fork fiction. Although Mrs Colby twice quotes G. H. Lewes, she does not comment on the fact that the extracts come from articles on Balzac. She mentions the phrase 'Dutch realism' as one which recurs in nineteenth-century art and literary criticism and feels that the element of homely truthfulness is a distinctive feature of Victorian fiction. Balzac himself uses the phrase in *La Peau de Chagrin* (Chapter 2) and both the *Quarterly Review* in 1836 and the *Westminster Review* in 1838 employ it to describe the impression of Balzac's own writings. If one were to ask whether George Eliot or Thackeray or Charlotte Brontë would have written any differently if they had not read Harriet Martineau or Mrs Gore or Maria Edgeworth, it seems to me that the answer would have to be, not proven. But Thackeray's debt to Balzac is quite another matter. Influences very seldom run in a straight national line, as the debt of French writers to Richardson, Scott, and Byron in preceding decades show. It is possible, I suppose, that George Eliot's sense of community could have been influenced by *Deerbrook*; it is unlikely that she had not read it, although she never refers to it. But her outspoken enthusiasm for George Sand and her response to the French novelist's belief that all existences are 'solidaires les unes des autres' does suggest a less insular formative influence than that of Harriet Martineau.

PATRICIA THOMSON

UNIVERSITY OF SUSSEX

Religion and Modern Literature: Essays in Theory and Criticism. Edited by G. B. TENNY-SON and EDWARD E. ERICSON, JR. Grand Rapids, Michigan: William B. Eerdmans. 1975. 424 pp. $5.95.

One problem in relating literature to religion is knowing exactly what you mean by religion. To define it as some vacuously Arnoldian concern for 'ultimate reality' is not much help, excluding none but the most trenchantly positivist of writers; to give it substantive theological content is uncomfortably precise, shutting out whole stretches of literature. Dr Johnson would have objected to both approaches: the first meant a meddling with sublime matters properly beyond both writer's and critic's ken; the second entailed a tedious literary rehearsal of formulae familiar enough to all. This anthology, as one might expect, bends the stick in the former direction: it has only one strictly theological article, a piece by C. S. Lewis which yokes a tendentious reading of the New Testament to a conservative prejudice against Romantic notions of originality and spontaneity. Otherwise, 'religion' as a concept is allowed a fair amount of elbow-room, despite the fact that, the book's title notwithstanding, it is blandly identified throughout with that variant of it known as Western Christianity.

Religion and Modern Literature, the editors claim, supplies a convenient selection of texts for students pursuing interdisciplinary courses in literature and theology. In fact, it answers another need too: criticism's own need to spin out its dwindling theoretical currency by harnessing itself to adjacent disciplines. These can be fertile couplings, but they stand in danger of being over-institutionalized; and this volume, despite its grave subject matter, has such a packaged feel about it, cramming a large number of disparate texts into its 400 pages in a panoramic survey which risks sacrificing depth to comprehensiveness. Individual essays tend to excessive brevity, tailing off just when you expect them to develop, sometimes too truncated to evolve arguments adequate to the complexities of their theme. The opening pieces by T. S. Eliot and J. Hillis Miller are cases in point: both raise important questions about the relation of literature to belief, but raise them as part of a general theoretical problem into which the specific issue of literature and religious faith tends to become dissolved. That there is some significant relation between literature and faith is an assumption of all the contributors to this first, theoretical section of the volume, naturally enough, since they are almost all Christian critics. But between Hillis Miller's excessively imprecise suggestion that belief is 'not irrelevant' to criticism, and Flannery O'Connor's excessively assertive claim that 'It makes a great difference to his novel whether [the novelist] believes that we are created in God's image, or whether he believes we create God in our own', the theoretical ground underfoot feels somewhat marshy and unmapped. If O'Connor is right, then we want to know exactly how the difference shows itself; and although Frederick Pottle attempts a concrete demonstration, in his claim that Pound's rejection of original sin flaws the art of his Cantos on hell, it seems altogether too convenient to move so quickly from the doctrinal to the aesthetic; equivalent, indeed, to the kind of Marxist criticism (one up from the 'vulgar') which discerns in each ideological error a correlative technical defect. David Daiches's essay in this section is more dialectical: he argues on the one hand that works of fiction always transform the religious ideologies they work from, but also claims, deploying the well-known hypothesis of the 'great fascist novel', that certain sorts of belief simply are corrupt and narrowing enough to prohibit the production of major art.

The book's second part deals with the religious 'backgrounds' of modern literature, and has much of interest to say; but there is something depressingly familiar about its story line. The death of God, collapse of shared values, loss of transcendental significance, alienation of the individual, search for ultimate meaning: this particular plot has been played out on the stage of innumerable Christian critical works, to the point where the very hugeness of its generalities begins to ring rather hollow. The problem with this Christian reading of 'modern man' is that it shares the unhistorical perspective of the very 'existentialism' to which it proposes an answer; both views merge into a contemplative metaphysics in which terms like 'alienation' become metaphorical gestures rather than dissectable categories. The way to concretize these abstractions is, of course, to take them back to the texts themselves, and this the book does in its concluding part. But to which texts? One can, indeed, almost predict them before one checks the contents page: Kafka, Camus, Lawrence, Eliot, Faulkner, Greene, Golding, Beckett, and a few more. It is not only that this part of the book is notably uneven, juxtaposing Cleanth Brooks's excellent piece on Faulkner from *The Hidden God* with some scrappy, threadbare offerings on Conrad, Greene, and Golding. It is also that a certain conformist, perfunctory editorial line seems to have dictated the selection of topics, and so in part to have conditioned what unevennesses there are. Some years ago, a Marxist critical anthology would have started with Dickens, leapt over James, lunged in on Lawrence, edged around Joyce, and collapsed gratefully into the arms of Grassic Gibbon. Nowadays, Marxist criticism is for the most part aware that its methods are best validated, not by literary objects which spontaneously conform to them, but by those which seem not to. It is when we see a symposium on religion and literature addressing itself to an analysis of Gissing, Bennett, Turgenev, and Fitzgerald that we shall begin to know whether 'religious criticism' has something to offer.

TERRY EAGLETON

WADHAM COLLEGE, OXFORD

The Keen Delight: The Christian Poet in the Modern World. By HAROLD L. WEATHERBY.
    Athens, Ohio: The University of Georgia Press. 1975. viii + 167 pp.
    $7.50.

It comes as an agreeable surprise to find a Catholic critic attacking Newman. For,
in England at least, Newman's name has been a treasured point of reference for
those post-Vatican Council liberal Catholic intellectuals who represent the first
wave of enlightened *enbourgeoisement* within a benighted, massively proletarian
church. Newman, with his rigorous yet ecumenical intellect, his 'existential'
emphasis, his engagements with poetry and culture: if he had not lived he would
have had to have been invented. That he was a 'convert' to Catholicism, bringing
to it insights and traditions cultivated on the outside, is itself an ironic index of
the dilemma which modern Catholic intellectuals have inherited. But it is precisely
the 'existential', subjectivist, and anti-intellectual tendencies in Newman's thought
which Mr Weatherby's book is concerned to upbraid. He distinguishes implicitly
between two Catholic traditions: a Platonic and Augustinian lineage which
influenced Scotus and passed by way of Romanticism to Newman and Hopkins;
and the scholastic heritage of Aristotelian Thomism of which, he claims, T. S. Eliot
is the modern exemplar. The first tradition, while undoubtedly preserving the
letter of Catholic orthodoxy, slides dangerously close to an anti-metaphysical
scepticism which slips the thin end of a wedge between intellect and experience; the
second tradition espouses a thoroughly metaphysical theology which unifies faith
and reason.

This is the gravamen of Mr Weatherby's tenacious critique of Newman and his
breed. Infected by a rationalist age, Newman grasps the notion as a mere dilution
of its real referent, elevates a 'primitive' intuitionism over metaphysical certainty,
and surreptitiously downgrades the Thomistic reasonableness of faith. This
theological shift has its poetic analogues: whereas Dante's scholastic sense of the
sacramentality of Nature does no violence to its physical integrity, Hopkins's
Scotist deviations, mediated by the Romantics and Newman, result in a radically
fragmented view of the world which lacks all realized ontological coherence. It is
left to the Eliot of *Four Quartets* to recover a truly metaphysical theology which
transcends such hit-and-miss intuitionism into the very different cognitions of
'authentic mystical experience'.

The Keen Delight, in short, belongs to a groundswell of neo-scholastic reaction
within an excessively 'experiential' contemporary Catholicism, retrieving
conceptual rigour and ontological certitude from the clammy clutches of the
'lived'. (Mr Weatherby, one suspects, is very probably a Latin Mass man.) But one
wonders whether this whole debate between existential progressive and Thomist
traditionalist, as manifest now in Catholic aesthetics as in liturgy and doctrine,
is not itself ripe for transcendence. It is not only that one's faith in Mr Weatherby's
critical judgement is a little sapped by his determination to follow J. Hillis Miller
in attending to what *Four Quartets* say they think about the secular world rather
than what they unintentionally show. It is also that the upshot of the case, in a
final chapter, is a reactionary refurbishing of the mystified aesthetics of Gilson and
Maritain. It is certainly true that Catholicism implies an ontology, and that
Newman sold points to the sceptics; but whether we can simply return to Thomism
is surely problematical. For one effect of the current European cross-breeding of
Nietzsche, Heidegger, and semiotics (a coupling of decadent Romanticisms at
which Mr Weatherby would doubtless shudder) may well be to force Christianity
radically to rethink the whole foundation of its traditional ontology in the light of
fresh concepts of signification and 'substance'. Whether he shudders or not, Mr
Weatherby should at least submit to the persuasive pressure of this pioneering work.

WADHAM COLLEGE, OXFORD   TERRY EAGLETON

Gathering The Winds: Visionary Imagination and Radical Transformation of Self and Society. By ELEANOR WILNER. Baltimore and London: The Johns Hopkins University Press. 1975. viii + 196 pp. £5.80.

The Holocaust and the Literary Imagination. By LAWRENCE L. LANGER. New Haven and London: Yale University Press. 1975. xiv + 300 pp. £6.90.

Both of these books belong to that undercurrent of passional, apocalyptic, Promethean criticism whose swell (for whatever intriguing historical reasons) has recently been increasingly detectable beneath the civilized surface of liberal humanist letters. Mythology and the millennium, the sense of endings and of the unspeakable: what was once the idiosyncratic stamp of a George Steiner or A. Alvarez has spread over the past few years to touch the concerns of such resolutely unmetaphysical critics as Frank Kermode and Denis Donoghue. Crisis against custom, silence against language, Prometheus against Hermes: the liberal democratic decencies are being interrogated even in the literary critical realm.

Eleanor Wilner's study moves in a world of Jung, shamanism, prophecy, and apocalypse, a world in which there exists a transhistorical constant known as the Imagination, which intervenes at points of historical crisis and oppression to resolve conflict by projecting a vision of wholeness. The candidates for critical analysis select themselves, with one exception: there is Blake, naturally, and Yeats, and (the latest canonized prophet) Marx, but there is also, oddly, Thomas Lovell Beddoes, about whom the author is extremely shrewd and perceptive. Blake is approved for evoking a full millennial vision; Yeats (rather surprisingly for such a relentlessly mythologizing critic) reproved for the cold, willed artifice with which he attempts to transcend dualities; and Beddoes's poetic enterprise winds down into a destructive nihilism which is the inverse of vision.

It is the treatment of Marx which gives the game away. The bibliographical entry for him is revealingly juxtaposed with a work on sorcery and witchcraft; Marx was yet another therapeutic 'visionary', a prophetic idealist who believed in social perfection. It is not only that Eleanor Wilner does not see how this well-intentioned caricature denies Marx's struggle to affirm the scientificity of historical materialism against every brand of petty-bourgeois utopianism; it is also that she thereby plays right into the hands of the *status quo* she clearly dislikes. Designating Marx as a passionate prophet is a tediously familiar tactic for taming him. Nobody objects to visionary humanists; it is just proletarian revolutionaries who tend to make one uneasy. Subtle and eloquent though it is, *Gathering the Winds* is finally of a piece with the world it opposes; Hermes and Prometheus are faces of the same reality.

'Holocaust', in Lawrence Langer's study of literature concerned with Nazi genocide, plays a structurally similar role to Eleanor Wilner's 'apocalypse'. Mr Langer has written a detailed, fiercely compassionate account of some of the most powerful texts to have emerged from that historical moment (Nellie Sachs, Ilse Aichinger, Jakov Lind, and Heinrich Böll among others), and some of the harrowing material he presents is enough to consign any reviewer to silence. Indeed it is precisely that problem of the 'aesthetics of atrocity', of how art can shape the unspeakable without brutal complicity with it, which Mr Langer, in the tradition of Theodor Adorno and George Steiner, persistently raises. Yet it is significant that he regards this as a matter of art giving order to 'chaos'. For there was nothing *chaotic* about fascism: nor is there today. Fascism is a coherent political formation which must be analysed and be resisted; and analysis is not aided by a groundswell of visionary idealism, by that generous-minded gesturing into silence which substitutes an impressionistic rhetoric for understanding and action. The holocaust, Mr Langer claims, 'remains the unconquered Everest of our time, its dark mysteries summoning the intrepid literary spirit to mount its unassailable summit'. There are a good too many sentences like that in his book, cloudy, self-indulgent stuff which blurs the very issues his selected authors dramatize so starkly. Verbose claims for the possible value of silence are no more helpful than idealist protests against societies which thrive on precisely that philosophical basis.

TERRY EAGLETON

WADHAM COLLEGE, OXFORD

Style and Vocabulary: Numerical Studies. By C. B. WILLIAMS. With a foreword by RANDOLPH QUIRK. London: Griffin. 1970. xiv + 161 pp. £2.00.

This is a book on the statistics of literary style, written by a biologist. It opens with a brief historical introduction indicating that the writer's main concern is with authorship studies. Then he discusses some general problems, where a certain naivety and arbitrariness show in his attitude to words and language, and then some statistical problems. This section includes notes on typical distributions and sampling, aimed at the layman. A chapter on word length and sentence length sets out ample evidence from the researches of the writer and others to show that authors have characteristic distribution patterns within a general log-normal distribution. There is some discussion of detail, but the uncritical use of simple traditional word classes from here on makes the data difficult to interpret. This layman finds the graphs and tables indistinct, overcrowded, and confusing.

Dr Williams then passes to vocabulary studies. He considers the relation between the number of different words in a writer's vocabulary and the number of repeated usages of these words in a text, and finds that this 'type-token' relation is fairly constant. Next he pursues the effect of sample size on vocabulary distribution, and follows it with a brief chapter on the measurement of diversity, and a few notes on hexameters. The book peters out in scattered examples, mainly reports of the research by Yule, Morton, and others.

There is some food for thought here, but the attempts to account for patterns revealed by statistical analysis are inadequate. For interested laymen there is a fair spread of standard statistical tools to examine, though not always clearly explained. The book is an example of the sort of isolated work that has characterized statistical work on texts in this country, and it is comforting to note that, since Dr Williams's book was published, the Association for Literary and Linguistic Computing has been formed, bringing together many disciplines and approaches. The secretary is Mrs Joan Smith, 6 Sevenoaks Avenue, Heaton Moor, Stockport, Cheshire SK4 AW4.

J. M. SINCLAIR

UNIVERSITY OF BIRMINGHAM

Factors Conditioning Consonant Duration in Consonantal Context: With Special Reference to Initial and Final Consonant Clusters in English. By ANTTI MUTANEN. (Suomalaisen Tiedeakatemian Toimituksia, Annales Academiae Scientiarum Fennicae, sarja B, nide 183) Helsinki: Suomalainen Tiedeakatemia. 1973. 150 pp. 22 Markkaa.

The aim of Dr Mutanen's study is to establish the durational characteristics of consonants in initial and final clusters in English. The bulk of the work is given over to statistical analysis of spectrographic duration-measurements on a corpus of 210 sentences read by each of five 'R.P.' speakers, in the attempt to unravel the separate and joint influences of 'intrinsic' (voice, place, manner), 'contextual', and 'positional' factors. An appendix of well reproduced (if rather small) spectrograms illustrates the segmentation procedures employed. The inventory for examination is ambitiously large; practically all possible initial clusters, and no fewer than 161 final clusters are included. The test sentences are constructed on a four-syllable, two-beat rhythmic pattern (for example, 'He swept the leaves'). One cluster per sentence is measured, the initial clusters being initial in a stressed syllable, the final clusters in absolute final (prepausal) position. An attempt is also made to establish comparative data on single (unclustered) consonant duration. The literature on segment duration and on the phonotactics of English clusters is briefly reviewed.

Workers in the field will recognize that the labour of measurement and analysis behind Dr Mutanen's work is prodigious; it is a matter for regret, then, that major shortcomings (in the design of the work rather than its execution) detract so much from its final usefulness. Possibly on account of the over-inclusive inventory, each cluster examined occurs only once in the list of recorded sentences, so that even the commonest English clusters have been measured only once per speaker and five times in the entire study. On the other hand, the picture has been complicated by measurements on many clusters that could have been omitted without loss (it is, for example, odd to include sequences involving syllabic consonants among 'final clusters'). It would certainly have been better to take fewer items and establish their behaviour more reliably. Four of the five speakers who recorded the corpus have between them forty-two years' residence in Finland: this is scarcely satisfactory if the aim is to examine 'R.P.'. Only two speakers were used in the attempt to establish the (very necessary) normative data on single consonant duration. Again, only one token per speaker was examined, and the account runs to less than six pages.

It is becoming increasingly clear that the prosodic design and meaningfulness of frame sentences can have an overwhelming effect on segment durations. The present sentences, short, rhythmically monotonous, and often verging on meaninglessness ('For what he opts') offer basically unnatural prosodic conditions. In addition, no variation of prosodic conditions has been tried. Dr Mutanen is not the first worker to measure syllable final clusters in pre-pausal position, but it is a mere assumption that the well known pre-pausal lengthening phenomenon interacts in any simple way with the internal time structure of a cluster. The most disappointing feature of the work, however, is the failure to provide either descriptive rules or explanatory models to make sense of the observations. Any addition to our meagre knowledge of consonant duration is to be welcomed (it is a great pity, incidentally, that Dr Mutanen nowhere gives a simple list of his raw measurements) but there is still much scope for the reliable determination of *what* happens in clusters, and still more for the explanation of *why*. Textual errors are exceedingly numerous.

M. G. ASHBY

UNIVERSITY COLLEGE, LONDON

Richard Jordan's Handbook of Middle English Grammar: Phonology. Translated and revised by EUGENE J. CROOK. (Janua Linguarum, Series Practica, 218) The Hague: Mouton. 1974. xxxiv + 331 pp. fl 90.

Professor Crook has made available to English-speaking students who have no German an indispensable book which on its first appearance in 1925 was immediately classed among the standard works on Middle English phonology. The translation is based on three versions of the *Handbuch*: Jordan's original version of 1925, Matthes's revision of 1934, and a third edition by Klaus Dietz in 1968. The additions made in the English text are in square brackets, but the three German versions are not distinguished from one another by any sign.

The translation is not wholly successful. It is sometimes rather more Germanic than English and this kind of order is not infrequent: 'These [*sc.* the forms *hand, land, sand, strand*] pushed back more and more the — now mostly shortened — *o* forms like *hond, lond* (< *hond* / hɔːnd /, *lond* / lɔːnd/ Ch. < OE *hānd*) in EML progressively to the south, in London and the literary language' (p. 233). At this stage in the book the translator has begun to flag, and we find highly unidiomatic and even ungrammatical sentences such as this: 'Also concerning the fifteenth century especially frequent shortening before single final consonants have [*sic*] already been handled in other contexts [*sic*, for 'another context'] (§ 27).' This is followed by another loss of grammar: 'For bibliography especially to be referred to: the grammatical presentation by Dibelius (1901)', etc. (p. [231]).

As in Matthes's revision, no fundamental changes have been made from Jordan's original *Handbuch*. There are a number of additions of new matter which update the book and make it more useful to students today. Modern linguistic terms are necessary (such as 'phoneme', 'allophone', 'obstruents'); but need 'Anmal' appear throughout as 'Remark' instead of the time-hallowed (and rational) 'Note'?

In the first section of the translator's Preface, 'Phonology', after describing Jordan's approach as structuralist, Professor Crook makes what he regards as a necessary attempt to reach 'some accommodation between the statements in this *Handbook of Middle English Grammar* and the theories of modern generative grammar'; he concludes, with some caution, that Jordan's statements 'are not inherently adverse to these theories' (p. viii). After 'Phonology' comes 'Dialectology' and then 'An Aid to Dialect Study', which gives diagrams of Jordan's interpretation of the late OE and early ME sound systems, followed by detail of the vowel phonemes of the ME dialect areas distinguished in the text. The table of abbreviations comes next; complained of as inadequate in the first two editions, it is here six times the size of the original list, and ought to satisfy anybody.

Among the additions to Part I of the text are twenty-one dialect maps, nearly all adapted from Moore, Meech, and Whitehall, *Middle English Dialect Characteristics and Dialect Boundaries*, and Oakden, *Alliterative Poetry in Middle English*. No criticism is made of the validity of these maps, but when their statements differ from Jordan's this is noted.

In the final section of the book, besides an index of words, there are a list of authors, works, and MSS cited (a large number of these were already in Jordan 1925) and a far-flung bibliography of literature cited, ranging from Green's *Short History of the English People* to Chomsky's *Language and Mind*. (Why is Bloomfield's *Language* omitted? It is cited on page vii.) An unusual and unfortunate phenomenon appears in this bibliography, at least in my copy: pages 274 and 275 are largely illegible because page 274 has been printed over a mirror-image of page 273, page 275 over a mirror-image of page 276. There is a similar fault on the lower half of page 283, although only one item is illegible here.

MARGARET 'ESPINASSE

HULL

Standard English und seine geographische Varianten. By DIETER BÄHR. (Uni-Taschenbücher, 160) Munich: Wilhelm Fink. 1974. 333 pp. DM 19.80.

Mr Bähr has set out to write an introduction to the geographical variants of Standard English for German students of English, taking examples from the entire English-speaking world. Even in 333 pages he can offer us no more than a small selection of the available material and the selection has been made with the examination requirements of German students in mind.

The book is well presented: its very detailed list of contents, the chapter layout, and subject index make for easy reference and there are several maps to illustrate isoglosses and the distribution of dialect features. There are separate bibliographies for each of the eight chapters. Together with the copious data presented in the text, they show the student where to find further sources for the historical background and for the close textual study of those languages relevant to this study.

What they fail to indicate are the sources for theoretical discussion of the data, for example the sociolinguistic aspect of sound changes. This is a particularly serious omission in Chapter One, where theoretical terms are described. After a well-illustrated explanation of possible developments within a lexis there are two very skimpy passages on grammatical and phonological change: the work of Peter Trudgill in Norwich and William Labov in New York could usefully have been quoted here, but their names appear neither in the text nor in any of the bibliographies. Other startling omissions are Messrs Mackey, Fishman, Gumperz, and Haugen, although bilingualism is a constantly recurring phenomenon in the 'English-speaking' world, and Mr Bähr's discussion of the role of dialects and the Celtic languages in the British Isles would have been clearer had he introduced their concepts of codes and linguistic repertoires.

These omissions seem the more indefensible when we note the attention given to Stalin's theories of language and the three-page coverage of A. W. Ross's classification of 'U' and 'non-U'. Possibly the latter source has led Mr Bähr to his conclusion that only through a public school type of education can the native English speaker master the Latin-based words in English. This assertion, however, is unsupported by any evidence: there is no mention of Bernstein's 'restricted and elaborated codes', still less of the controversy surrounding these terms. A similar claim that dialects have a 'more limited vocabulary and often simpler grammatical structure', whereas standard languages have 'cleansed themselves of ugly or superfluous local expressions' (p. 36) is again unsupported, perhaps because linguists no longer take this view.

Several of the grammatical sections of the book are very thin. Even a German student learning Standard British English would need to know the main differences, for example, in the use of the past tenses in British and American English. Nor are quotations from literature very acceptable as the sole source for grammatical description.

Despite these reservations one must say that the book provides the student with data not readily available in German, and the author's evident enthusiasm for his subject ensures that the book is interesting to read.

D. CAVANAGH

UNIVERSITY OF BIRMINGHAM

Regionale und soziale Erscheinungsformen des britischen und amerikanischen Englisch. By WOLFGANG VIERECK. (Anglistische Arbeitshefte, 4) Tübingen: Niemeyer. 1975. x + 144 pp. DM 13.80.

This is a workbook (in the American sense) published as a paperback by the illustrious Max Niemeyer Verlag in a recently launched series. It has been reproduced by photolithography direct from typescript, which means that right margins are unjustified. It is, in fact, exceedingly well produced: very pleasant to handle and to read, and with no misprints of any significance. Here and there, unfortunately, the author forgets to keep strictly to square brackets for phonetic and slants for phonemic *Umschriften*, though he duly records these distinctive symbols (p. xii) in his list of abbreviations.

Paragraphs and subparagraphs are numbered decimally, and the book is well organized in six sections: methods of investigation; regional dialects of England; relations between British and American English; historical backgrounds; social dialects of American English; and, finally, Black English, more especially Gullah, the creolized speech of Negroes living on the South Carolina and Georgia coast, whose superstratum is English but whose substrata are (controversially) the autochthonous tongues of West Africa. There then follow twenty maps of the dialect regions of England and the United States, derived, with due acknowledgements, from the works of Ellis, Orton, Kurath, Lowman, Atwood, and McDavid; and, finally, the texts of the eleven tape-recordings which normally accompany this workbook.

It is important to observe that the phrase *des britischen . . . Englisch* in the title means strictly 'of English spoken in England'. Professor Viereck is little concerned with the speech of Wales, Scotland, and Ireland, and he is not at all concerned with the English of Canada, South Africa, and Australasia. Students using this workbook will find no clear statements about the significantly differing regions covered by the works of Alexander John Ellis (1814–90), Joseph Wright (1855–1930), and Harold Orton (1898–1975). In mentioning the forty-two districts of Ellis's *On Early English Pronunciation, Part V* (1889) Professor Viereck does say casually *einschliesslich Schottland*, but he fails to state anything at all about Ellis's now so valuable descriptions of the dialects of Wexford in Ireland and of South Pembrokeshire and the Gower Peninsula in Wales. Moreover, he fails to point out the very considerable differences between the areas covered by Wright and Orton in their dialectal surveys. Wright's *English Dialect Dictionary* (*EDD*, 1898–1905) covered the whole of the British Isles, whereas Orton's *Survey of English Dialects* (*SED*, 1950–61) covered only the forty counties of England as they then were before the Local Government Act of 1972. Today's students should certainly be reminded in a practical textbook of this kind that Orton's Cumberland and Shropshire are now Cumbria and Salop, and that, sad to say, his Rutland and Huntingdon are counties no more.

A keen sociologist, with wide interests in anthropology, Professor Viereck criticizes Orton's *Survey* somewhat adversely on the ground that it disregards distinctions 'between social layers of the population and between older and younger generations'. Orton was, in fact, an eminent authority on class dialect, but he had to keep his published work within practical and manageable bounds. He did just what he set out to do. Professor Viereck, on the other hand, also does well in anticipating attractive developments in the rapidly advancing science of sociolinguistics and in recommending the researches of Basil Bernstein and other sociologists to the close attention of linguists. He rightly welcomes the appearance of recent monographs like Christopher Heath's *A Study of Speech Patterns in the Urban District of Cannock, Staffordshire* (1971) and Peter Trudgill's *The Social Differentiation of English in Norwich* (1974). Above all, he gives prominence to the Urban Language Series inaugurated in America in 1964 with the publication of William Labov's *The Social Stratification of New York City*, supplementing, on the social side, the great regional *Linguistic Atlases* of the United States.

Among the most stimulating and useful features of this workbook are its skilfully devised exercises or *Aufgaben* which will certainly prove to be veritable godsends to hardpressed chairmen of seminars and proseminars. Their primary function is to set students to work on a theme without delay by sending them straight to a precise statement in a work of reference, or even a periodical, from which they can proceed to develop their own ideas. These exercises deal with basic principles, methods of approach, individual attitudes, and controversial viewpoints, as well as with specific questions relating to phonology, morphology, syntax, and semantics. They naturally include numerous references to the workbook's sixteen separate critical bibliographies or *Literaturangaben* which are likewise in every way helpful, accurate, and fully up to date.

Much diligent research has gone into the making of this book, which fulfils its purpose admirably.

SIMEON POTTER

LONDON

The Psychology of Tragic Drama. By PATRICK ROBERTS. (Ideas and Forms in English Literature) London and Boston: Routledge. 1975. x + 234 pp. £5.95.

In one sense this is a most ambitious book. Through studies of individual plays, mining them for Freudian images, Mr Roberts sets out to explore the relationship between the drama and the unconscious. In the process he is offering a view of dramatic history, for Aeschylus, Ibsen, and Eliot are all included. Since his later pages concentrate on presentations of Orestes and Electra he is also examining the individual's knowing use of archtetypes and the effects of the Freudian enlightenment. All this implies a stimulating bond of analysis and theory. Sadly, Mr Roberts seems unaware of his own scope.

The title is misleading. Nowhere is there a serious discussion of what constitutes tragedy or whether archetypes function differently in other cultural forms. A parallel is briefly offered between Fate and psychological conditioning as types of determinism, but this is inadequate outside a narrow range of classic plays. One doubts if Mr Roberts has any definitions to offer; Ionesco and Pinter are included with scant explanation. Adequate modern investigations of catharsis and tragic sacrifice are needed, but Mr Roberts's work lacks that status. Nor will it suffice as a primer, for the grounding in psychology is unsophisticated and prescriptive. While Jung goes unmentioned, Melanie Klein's theories of infant sexuality recur monotonously. There are no references to comparable detailed criticism such as the many essays duplicating Mr Roberts's discussion of the mother image in Pinter's *The Homecoming*. Thus a chance is lost to see if a truly scientific interpretation is possible via Freud, and how the abilities of given critics may blur the findings. Instead, there are quarrels with writers whose 'insecurity' has made them claim that art is autonomous and psychiatry irrelevant. The effect is both polemical and ghostly, for the culprits are mainly Dover Wilson and Stoll and the notes to this opening section mention nothing published in the last decade.

This would matter less if the traditional academic foundations were adequate here. In fact Mr Roberts is often careless. A major chapter is devoted to Weiss's *Marat/Sade* as a study and enactment of 'the force of primitive violence'. It is claimed that Sade destroys Marat's revolutionary arguments and that 'it is hard to believe' that Weiss holds any balance between them. It might be easier to believe if Mr Roberts had mentioned Weiss's repeated argument that his stance is Marxist, that the activist Marat is his virtual spokesman, that sensationalist productions distort the play if they bury the dialectics, and that the English translation omits an epilogue making the polemical point overt. Incidentally, there are five errors in transcription from that text.

The section on Oresteian plays from Aeschylus to Sartre is much the strongest and its aesthetic judgements more pointed. Yet Mr Roberts is so intent on stressing this myth's pathological interest that he must ignore, say, Goethe's performance in his own version of the role ('a union of physical and spiritual beauty') and condemn the choric resolution of *The Eumenides* as 'naive', 'unconvincing', and even indicative of 'conflict' within Aeschylus's own personality. This is the least likeable aspect of Mr Roberts's approach, an assumption that brief disagreements with literary points justify not critical dismissal of the work itself but thumbnail reports on the writer's psyche. So O'Neill's own confession that his prose style was defective cannot stand; instead his work fails to 'arise from the deepest strata of the author's psychic unconscious'. Mr Roberts's studies are neither original enough nor full enough to justify such tones. Finally relapsing into a simplistic hunt for the same old symbols and captioning *Macbeth* as 'one of the supreme expressions in dramatic poetry of the tragedy wrought by parricidal envy', the author leaves one wondering if psychoanalytic criticism is indeed innately reductive. One also wonders why this example was thought worth publishing.

TONY HOWARD

UNIVERSITY OF WARWICK

The Meter and Melody of 'Beowulf'. By THOMAS CABLE. (Illinois Studies in Language and Literature, 64) Urbana, Chicago, and London: University of Chicago Press. 1974. x + 122 pp. £4.10.

Scanning Old English verse has for a long time been harder than reading it; J. C. Pope lists 279 patterns, A. J. Bliss over 130. The competing theories furthermore offer no *a priori* reason why the complication should not be greater if *Beowulf* were longer, or the investigators prepared to take on a larger corpus. At the same time the most skilful readers usually cannot reproduce even their own ideas of scansion when their readings are recorded. All this has prompted several scholars to launch simplifications of one or other of the accepted systems. Dr Cable has chosen instead to try to get past the problems of 'observational adequacy' to those of 'descriptive' or even 'explanatory adequacy'; in other words, he wants to know not just what the rules of verse in *Beowulf* are, but what they are *for* and what sort of principle underlies them.

One of the tools he employs is a readiness to consider not only what *is* in *Beowulf* but what is not. Why does the poet never write a half-line like *In a somer seson*, or *as hit now hat*, or *To be or not to be* — all natural, indeed almost inevitable patterns both rhythmically and syntactically? If Old English verse 'is really the spoken language rather tidied up' (as we are so often complacently reminded), then the absence of these patterns suggests something distinctly strenuous in the tidying. Dr Cable has little patience with such well-meant pedagogical reassurances, and opens his first chapter with a brief destruction of careless if familiar comparisons between Old English and G. M. Hopkins. He goes on to eliminate A. J. Bliss's category of 'light' or one-stress verses, with arguments that appear hard to refute. It is a telling point, for instance, that all 363 examples of Bliss's *a* and *e* categories occur in the first half-line, simply because if they come in the second the alliteration forces one to stress verbs; yet obviously *sægde se þe cuþe* and *secge ic þe to soðe* should be in the same category, not separated. The conclusion leads one into trouble with Kuhn's Law of Particles, but that is not mentioned at any point by Dr Cable; he prefers to bypass old authority for eternal reason.

Four further chapters consider single problems such as anacrusis and clashing stress, in the process realigning two of Sievers's Types (D2, *bad bolgenmod*, is closer to E, *murnende mod*, than to D1, *cwen Hroðgares*), and also educing some basic principles: it is vital to mark intermediate stress, the first of two clashing stresses will be the heavier, a kind of 'temporal resolution' can be accepted in D verses, and so on. Some of these conclusions may seem obvious. In Chapter 5 Dr Cable repeats several times that modern readers would 'normally' or 'intuitively' give heavier stress to the second syllable of *wis welþungen* than to the first, though Tolkien for one (quite intuitively, indeed without argument) said the opposite. But at any rate it is easy to agree that they should not; and the conclusions drawn offer some striking implications.

It is for instance interesting that the *Beowulf* poet never constructs a verse like (my invention) *morðcwealma mare*, though he does have *morðbeala mare*. Dr Cable argues that this is because -*cwealm*-, a long syllable, would take intermediate stress, being more prominent than -*a*-; and that would lead to a five-unit verse: -*beal*-, however, is resolved with -*a*-, and the thesis produced 'fails to qualify for intermediate metrical ictus . . . for -*beala* does not have greater linguistic prominence than . . . *morð*- or *mar*-'. If this argument is rejected, the rejecter is left with the problem of explaining why the *morðcwealma mare* type does not appear; and saying it does not scan only puts the problem off one further stage! If it is accepted, however, one can deduce (and this is a major step in the overall argument) that the important thing about stressed syllables, intermediate or otherwise, is that they should be more linguistically prominent than 'at least one adjacent syllable'.

Material of this kind is presented testingly but clearly all through the first six chapters. In the seventh, having laid his principles out singly, Dr Cable puts them together and argues (a) that Old English verse can be described in terms of patterns of rise and fall (b) that given a four-unit system there are only eight potential patterns (c) that three of these can be excluded by one of the rules already argued (the second of two adjacent stresses cannot be a 'rise') (d) that the five left are the familiar Five Types, except that (as has again already been argued) the orthodox D2 is really a variant of E. The neatness of the book's argument is compelling, as is its final simplicity; especially so is the fact that Dr Cable is prepared to explain the non-existence of patterns instead of simply classifying what turns up. The last stroke is to point out that though three levels of stress are an integral part of the system, human beings (or so experimentalists aver) can, in speech, only recognize two. Does the theory collapse? No: it means that, as we know but forget, the verse was necessarily sung. Dr Cable goes on boldly to make some suggestions as to how: something, again, that most of his predecessors have balked at.

Old English scansion will no doubt remain a contentious subject, but this book surpasses its forerunners in scope and clarity; the use it makes of modern linguistics and musicology is both sane and helpful; and it opens up exciting possibilities of putting melodic flesh on familiar if abstract bones.

T. A. SHIPPEY

ST JOHN'S COLLEGE, OXFORD

'Daniel' and 'Azarias'. Edited by R. T. FARRELL. (Methuen's Old English Library) London: Methuen; New York: Barnes and Noble. 1974. x + 139 pp. £4.50.

Finnsburh: Fragment and Episode. Edited by DONALD K. FRY. (Methuen's Old English Library) London: Methuen; New York: Barnes and Noble. 1974. xvi + 83 pp. £3.00.

In April 1933, Professor A. H. Smith and Professor F. Norman (then respectively Lecturer in English and Reader in German in the University of London) wrote as General Editors in the first volume of Methuen's Old English Library, 'It has often been the complaint of teachers of Old English that the literary materials of the earlier period of literature have been either unavailable in a form suitable for undergraduate use, or incomplete, or inadequately treated. Texts until recently were not always reliable and sometimes represented long traditions of editorial error. The advantages of such a set of texts as this Old English Library will be self-evident to teachers of Old English: the scheme will eventually allow wider scope in the formulation of courses of study, and the separate treatment of each text, however short, is already revealing many new facts both in the establishment of the text and in its interpretation. Besides this, much that has been written on the subject is still widely scattered in the journals, and it is an important part of our work to bring these materials together, often for the first time'.

With the two volumes under review, the series now includes sixteen such editions and two monographs. In retrospect, the contributors appear to have come from a philological pantheon, although not all were so celebrated at the time they made their contribution to the series. And the Old English Library has gone beyond the stated objectives of its original general editors, for the texts that it continues to provide are not only highly suitable volumes *in usu scholarum*, but in many instances have also become the *textus receptus*. For some there are now alternatives, for example in the Manchester Old and Middle English Texts series; but most of the contributions, despite the increments of scholarship in the field, are unlikely to become out of date in any way that occasional reprinting with additional bibliography will not correct.

Professors Smith and Norman also referred, in their original statement, to 'a general scheme of editing so as to secure a fair agreement in the make-up and apparatus of each volume'. This scheme has been generally preserved, although with Mrs Gordon's *Seafarer* (1960) the series abandoned its earlier employment of the letterforms *yogh* and *wynn*. There remain, of course, inconsistencies, some of them to be observed in the two books under review: volume numbers in the bibliography are upper-case boldface in Fry but lower-case standard in Farrell; Mr Fry's bibliography gives city of publication for books, but Mr Farrell's does not; *Archiv* is reckoned an abbreviation by Fry but a complete title by Farrell; Mr Fry translates Old English quotations in his Introduction but Mr Farrell does not; Fry hyphenates Old English compounds in his text but Farrell does not; Farrell italicizes the whole word when any part of it departs from the manuscript reading, but Fry adheres to the more common practice of italicizing only the letters altered.

The volumes under review differ from each other in additional ways. Although both embrace two texts, the two in Fry's volume are short but have been the subject of much study and interpretation; the two in Farrell's volume are in total over six times as long, but relatively little has been written about them: Farrell himself is the author of all but two of the items in his bibliography published since 1956. Farrell's book is more than half again the length of Fry's, and includes subjects that Fry omits completely (such as a section on difficult words) or deals with only very briefly (such as metre, to which Farrell gives five pages while Fry simply states as an editorial principle that he will not emend *metri causa* if the half-line contains 'two strong stresses, at least four syllables, and proper alliteration' (p. xi)). In Fry's book, on the other hand, his résumé of scholarship on the 'story' of Finnsburh comprises some twenty pages of the Introduction, while a total of four and a half are devoted to the manuscripts, language, and date, and another four and a half to the style. The former three subjects are dealt with in terms largely (and admittedly) in debt to Klaeber, and the section on style is hardly less perfunctory: even the editor's own well-known views on formulism and type-scenes are scarcely permitted to intrude. It is, then, Fry's handling of the story that makes up the bulk of his Introduction, and it is most impressive. He first surveys previous opinions with precision, fairness, and clarity, and then introduces his own: pointing out that *unhlitme* (*Beowulf*, 1129), if it means 'without casting of lots' as many now believe, implies 'voluntarily' rather than the opposite, he restores the manuscript reading of line 1130 to *þeah þe he meahte on mere drifan* (edd. *ne meahte*) and suggests that Hengest remained 'with Finn not because of the weather, but by his own choice, by his own design . . . When the truce ends the battle, Hengest and Finn are evenly matched. Instead of sailing home, Hengest waits for the opportune moment to launch a surprise attack on Finn' (p. 22). The argument is genuinely new and genuinely sound, and it represents a real advance in our understanding of the Episode.

Other innovations of the edition represent less dramatic advances, having to do largely with the materials in the glossary and their presentation. And one may perhaps wonder *cui bono*? Fairly full treatments of the historical, linguistic, and critical questions surrounding Finnsburh are available in the standard editions of *Beowulf* to a degree not paralleled for most other texts in this series, which are either not readily available elsewhere or, if available, not so fully treated. The chief contribution of Fry's edition, his new interpretation of the story, has appeared as an article (*Chaucer Review*, 9 (1974), 1–14). The edition is by no means unwelcome, but it is not immediately obvious whose special needs it will serve.

It includes some minor errors: to begin with the list of abbreviations, the adjective *neueren* does not require an upper-case initial; Bede's *Historia Ecclesiastica* does not need to be listed in the accusative; and the Bolton revision of Wrenn's *Beowulf* does not need to be listed at all, since Fry never makes reference to it outside of the Abbreviations and Bibliography. In the Introduction, Fry's memorable phrase 'monsters have a habit of reappearing at the worse moment' (p. 13) involves a misprint for 'worst', and the discussion of, for example, vengeance (pp. 22–3) is, like so much else in his Introduction, based wholly on Germanic materials, overlooking contemporary Latin such as Alcuin's letter to Charlemagne (ed. E. Dümmler, *MGH*, Ep. IV, pp. 351–2) that would cast a somewhat different light on the topic. In the text, it is probably inadvisable to begin a new sentence with *ac* when it follows an overt or implied negative (e.g. *Fragment*, lines 5, 10; *Beowulf*, 1085); the half-line space is missing in *Fragment*, line 12; two different forms of upper-case *thorn* appear in *Beowulf*, lines 1075, 1079. In the Bibliography, bold-face type is used for volume numbers in Grein's *Bibliothek* but not those in Krapp and Dobbie's *Anglo-Saxon Poetic Records*. All the same, the edition is fundamentally clear and accurate.

By contrast, the edition by Farrell is neither clear nor accurate. A multitude of internal inconsistencies bears witness to both failings. Farrell cites Bede's account of the poet Caedmon from '*Historia Ecclesiastica* 4: 24' on page 2 but '*HE* IV, 24' on page 11, the former with a quotation including the impossible *dulcedinae* for Bede's *dulcedine*, and with the footnote, 'ed. and trans. by B. Colgrave and R. A. B. Mynors' although the punctuation shows that the text is Plummer's. Other variations in citation: Bartlett's book is called *The Larger Rhetorical Patterns of Anglo-Saxon Poetry* on page 19 but *The Larger Rhetorical Patterns in Old English Verse* on page 28 (likewise Callaway's book, p. 51, note 76 and p. 67, note 320–4); Theodoret's commentary is located in 'Migne, Patres Graeci lxxxi' on page 24, note 64 but '*PL* lxxxi' on page 29, note 71; Farrell's own article is located in *NM* lxix on page 29, note 73, but lxvix in the Bibliography (compare Jerome, p. 29, note 71 and p. 30, note 78, and a similar conflict in the year of Small's article, p. 60, note 221 and p. 62, note 264). Other errors in the Latin: *ventem* for *ventum*, p. 28; *universa* for *universi*, p. 58, note 192a; *euis* for *eius*, p. 53, note 96–8; verb *es* omitted from quotation, p. 66, note 320–4 but duly included when the same source is quoted, p. 44, note 94; three errors in the Latin quotation, pp. 40–41, note 90, and the wrong title for the source (the wrong title is also given for a book in this series, Needham's *Ælfric*, p. 80, note 541–5). Errors in Old English: 'Of' for 'Oft', p. 27; *hleorðade* for *hleoðrade*, p. 137; on *brædo* for *on brædo*, p. 138. Literal errors in Modern English: 'and' missing, p. 31, line 9; 'plusss', p. 60, note 226; 'Intro., p. oo', p. 63, note 269; 'ound' for 'found' and 'in' for 'is', both p. 139. Otiose, missing, or errant punctuation: p. 28 after 'ahton'; p. 32 after 'mærost'; p. 62, note 260a–62a; p. 67, note 327; p. 79, note 518–24; p. 95, note 110b; p. 102 s.v. Napier; p. 138 word *omr*. Errors in German: *angelsachsischen* for *angelsächsischen*, p. ix; 'Gedichte' for 'Gedichtes', p. 136. Farrell fails to capitalize Old English words in his notes as they appear in his text (e.g. *Daniel*, 30, 35, 61) or even to spell them the same way (e.g. ed. *foran*, MS *faran*, note *foron*, *Daniel*, 53;

likewise line 73); he identifies Professor Fred C. Robinson as 'Professor F. N. Robinson', p. 56, note 149b–51; he uses 'edds.' for 'edd.' or 'eds.' throughout; and, when he writes 'in the quarter century preceding the year 1,000 [*sic*]', his footnote observes 'Robin Flower has made a case for a more precise date, 870–990' (p. 36, note 83). This list has been compiled with almost no checking of Farrell's references; it is nothing like exhaustive.

Farrell's expository technique is not up to his task. His constant failure to observe the difference between restrictive *that* and non-restrictive *which* is always distracting and especially so when he actually gets them backwards in a single sentence: 'there is a break in the sense and metre between line 177, that comes at the bottom of page 180, and the sentence which begins at the top of page 181' (p. 3). He uses many impersonal and passive constructions, often in combination: 'When the Vulgate is closely examined, it is evident that . . .'; 'When the overall structure of OE *Daniel* is considered, it is clear that . . .'; 'When the comments of the early Christian Fathers on *Dan.* 3: 21–4 are read, it is clear that . . .' (pp. 26, 27, 29). The result is sometimes baffling: 'it has been concluded', he assures us at the top of page 39, but we get no idea when or by whom. Does 'it has not suffered from interpolation' (p. 41) mean that it has not undergone interpolation, or that the interpolation has been beneficial? He combines absolute and passive: 'In view of the easy confusion of *ð* and *d* in the insular script, emendation is made necessary for sense' (p. 49, note 35). He admits vague antecedents of pronominal 'this': 'This is so because . . .'; 'this is generally identified . . .'; 'because of this . . .' (pp. 5, 13, 31). Finally, 'either . . . but' and 'more . . . rather than' are not English correlations (pp. 15, 33).

Farrell is both unclear and circular when he says 'The force of *unræd* is very strong, since in the context of *Daniel* such a term represents the totality of all that is most ill-advised' (p. 57, note 185b–86a). Farrell's lack of clarity extends to his section on metre, in which a rather lengthy listing of metrical features in the Old English *Daniel* never establishes which ones are distinctive of the poem, or whether any emendations *metri causa* appear to be necessary. While internal inconsistencies and failure of expository technique distract the scholar, such inability to focus directly and expediently on the thematic issues of *Daniel* and *Azarias* discourages the student. Farrell claims 'What is new here is the suggestion that these two versions of the same material have a rightful place in their respective contexts in the Junius MS. and the Exeter Book' (p. 45). However, Farrell never considers the relationship of *Daniel* to the other poems in the Junius Manuscript in any but a perfunctory manner. What themes does *Daniel* share with *Genesis*, *Exodus*, or *Christ and Satan*? A tedious argument may suggest that *Daniel* is complete but what function can such an argument serve, how can any argument place *Daniel* in its 'rightful place . . . in the Junius MS.', if not supported by a cohesive rendering of that entire manuscript? Lacking such a rendering, Farrell's hypothetical 'solution' to the problem of relationship between *Daniel* and *Azarias*, especially concerning the question of priority, is not helpful.

Unfortunately Farrell weakens his own argument with misleading generalizations. One case in point is the 'theme of the angel' (p. 28). While it is indeed 'possible to see the use of the angel as a reworking of the single mention of an angel in the later narrative portion of the Vulgate into a poetical theme' ('The Unity of Old English *Daniel*', *RES*, 18 (1967), 129), Farrell's evidence poses rather than resolves difficulties. Kennedy and others have translated *halige gastas* (*Daniel* 26) as 'prophets' rather than 'angels'. Farrell never considers the possibility that 'holy spirit' (singular) refers to the third person of the Trinity, and while Saint Jerome does indeed refer to the spirit in the furnace as an angel, that spirit is a type of Christ who shields the righteous from the fires and furnaces of Hell. A second generalization on 'the pleasures of the *burh*' (p. 32) needs qualification. What precisely are the pleasures of the *burh*? Are these the earthly joys of the city of Babylon or the eternal treasures of the *heahbyrig*, the Jerusalem now lost?

Farrell's stress on the narrative or historical quality in *Daniel*, and his suggestion that the poet may be employing an exegetical tradition where Daniel the prophet is replaced by Daniel the historical figure, neglects the poet's emphasis on the fulfilment of dreams and the future of God's people. In fact, by Farrell's own admission there is no exegetical tradition that totally divorces Daniel from his role as prophet of the coming kingdom of God. The use of narrative shows clearly, by types, exactly how prophecy is prefigured by history and will be fulfilled in the future. Furthermore, Farrell's sources for such an exegetical tradition, Theodoret of Cyrus and Hippolytus of Rome, are not mentioned by Ogilvy as 'known to the English'. While Ogilvy is far from complete, this omission casts serious doubt on their influence upon the Old English *Daniel*. Finally, Farrell's insistence that *Daniel* presents 'a struggle between good and evil, with Daniel and the Three as protagonists, and Nabuchodonosor and Baltassar as antagonists' (p. 31) is undermined by the poet's play with the Old English verb *hweorfan* (to turn or convert), often applied to Nabuchodonosor. The poem of *Daniel* is not about a struggle between good and evil alone, but about the conversion of evil to good through the manifestation of God's grace. The central action of the poem is not destruction of the wicked but salvation of the righteous.

For all these reasons, Farrell's edition fails to meet the objectives of Methuen's Old English Library as Professors Smith and Norman set them out in 1933, and as other scholars have met them in the decades since then.

M. S. ALLEN

PRINCETON UNIVERSITY

W. F. BOLTON

RUTGERS UNIVERSITY

Ælfric. By JAMES HURT. (Twayne's English Authors Series, 131) New York: Twayne. 1972. 152 pp. $4.95.

Ælfric: A New Study of His Life and Writings. By CAROLINE LOUISA WHITE. With a Supplementary Classified Bibliography Prepared by MALCOLM R. GODDEN. (Yale Studies in English, 2) Hamden, Connecticut: Archon Books. 1974. 244 pp. $9.50.

James Hurt's little book provides an up to date, readable, and generally sound account of the life and work of Ælfric, to whom he refers, with justice, as 'the most accomplished prose writer of the Old English period'. It is a well-produced book and it should be of interest to the general reader as well as of use to students. Like Ælfric himself, Professor Hurt lays no claim to originality, but presents a clear, well-informed, and balanced survey of existing scholarly work. It will be of particular value to students for its generous and judicious coverage of historical background in the introductory sections of Chapter 1, on political and cultural history, and the sections on literary history included in subsequent chapters, for example the excellent section in Chapter 3 on the Old English hagiographic tradition and Ælfric's place in it, or the similar brief survey in Chapter 5 of the history of the study of grammar in Europe up to the time of Ælfric.

The main body of the book consists of four chapters on four major works, or groups of works, by Ælfric: *The Catholic Homilies*, *The Lives of Saints*, the biblical translations, and the grammatical writings. Each chapter offers ample summaries of the contents of the various works with some more detailed analysis of individual pieces. Similar analyses form a prominent feature of the final chapter, which abandons the form of 'organisation by content' adopted for the preceding chapters, 'to consider Ælfric's prose style, the aspect of his work for which he is chiefly remembered'. The book tends to be slightly repetitious and this seems to be, in part at least, due to its plan. The plan of the book may also be responsible for the somewhat unsatisfactory nature of Chapter 4, particularly in its rather uncertain, and occasionally confusing, treatment of Ælfric's methods of translation. These would have been better discussed, as Ælfric's style is, in the final chapter, with a wider range of reference to Ælfric's work, not limited to the translations and paraphrases of biblical texts (which in any case do not form a separate category of Ælfric's work of the same standing as the *Catholic Homilies* or the grammatical works). In contrast to these sections in Chapter 4 the corresponding general sections in Chapters 2 and 3 on Ælfric's homilies and hagiographical writings are excellent, especially the sections of Chapter 3 on the general characteristics of lives of saints and martyrs. Throughout the book the passages of Old English which are quoted have not been so well corrected by the exemplar as Ælfric would have wished and there are some inadequacies in the modern English translations which accompany them. There is, I think, nothing likely seriously to mislead; but the book in general deserves better and they should be set right when a second edition affords the opportunity, as one hopes it will.

Caroline White's book, first published in 1898 and here reprinted, rendered very much the same service in its time as Professor Hurt aims to render for the present day. Dr Godden's valuable bibliography, twenty-five pages in length and containing close on two hundred items, also includes brief but useful summaries of the more important developments in Ælfric studies in the last three-quarters of a century. Opinions will no doubt differ as to whether this is the best way to make such a very useful piece of work available, as they will also differ (though perhaps to a lesser extent) as to the need for a reprint of Caroline White's book. There can surely, however, be little room for doubt as to the propriety of retaining its old subtitle or, at least, of displaying it so prominently on the dustwrapper.

UNIVERSITY COLLEGE, LONDON   G. I. NEEDHAM

The Middle English 'Genesis and Exodus': A Running Commentary on the Text of the Poem. By PHILIP G. BUEHLER. (De Proprietatibus Litterarum, Series Practica, 74) The Hague: Mouton. 1974. 85 pp. fl 24.

The first part of this work contains a brief introduction describing and evaluating previous work on the Middle English *Genesis and Exodus*, followed by a detailed bibliography the arrangement of which involves a certain amount of duplication. Then come fifty pages of commentary on the text of the poem as edited by O. Arngart for Lund Studies in English in 1968. The notes deal with the interpretation of this difficult work and range in length from a single line to more than a page. They vary just as much in importance; some are fairly obvious glosses, some provide evidence to support the suggestions of other scholars, others suggest ingenious and convincing emendations and renderings, while in other cases the ingenuity is more evident than the plausibility. Future scholars interested in the poem must take account of this book, but the important material in it could equally well have been presented in one or two articles in a relevant periodical.   R. M. WILSON

UNIVERSITY OF SHEFFIELD

The Influence of Richard Rolle and of Julian of Norwich on the Middle English Lyrics.
By Sister MARY ARTHUR KNOWLTON. (De Proprietatibus Litterarum, Series
Practica, 51) The Hague: Mouton. 1973. 208 pp. fl 28.

Sister Mary Arthur Knowlton's purpose in this work is to demonstrate Richard
Rolle's considerable influence on religious lyrics written in the 150 years after his
death; and that Julian of Norwich, though as great a writer, contributed comparatively little to subsequent mystical and devotional poetry. Painstaking scholarship,
religious sympathy, and enthusiasm for the subject are apparent throughout.
Sister Knowlton gives brief descriptive accounts of Rolle's and Julian's principal
works, and then subdivides the lyrics into five categories (those on the Holy Name,
the Passion, Divine Love, the Virgin Mary, and Penitence, Mercy, and Death)
each of which is given a chapter. Within the categories an impressive number of
lyrics, taken from relatively inaccessible sources as well as from the well known
collections of Carleton Brown, are juxtaposed with comparable passages and lines
from the two major writers. Entire poems are set beside line references to their
'sources', and we are thus enabled to see how certain popular devotional formulae
echo and re-echo through two centuries of poetry.

It is a demonstration tending to confirm the suspicion (sometimes entertained
by the devout as well as by unbelievers) that religious poetry necessarily operates
within narrow limits. Piety is not, however, the same as religious belief; the former
expresses itself in stances, the latter in imaginative and intellectual engagement
with theological concepts. This study might lead us to conclude that a great deal
of medieval religious verse is *merely* repetitive, but this, I think, is a function of the
author's preoccupation with the affective aspect of her subject. This preoccupation
is reflected in both her methods and terminology.

Compilation of 'parallels' thus becomes sufficient demonstration of influence:
the particular power and subtlety of *Quia Amore Langueo* is disregarded in the
assertion that 'the languishing, the ardent gaze and yearning for everlasting association, bear a resemblance to Rolle's spirit and manner and diction', and that the
'alliteration and the reference to "sitting" ' in 'Now wol I syt and sey nomore |
Loue and loke with grete longyng' are 'further bonds with Rolle's work'. Audelay's
De Amore Dei reflects the influence of both Julian and Rolle because 'Fore loue is
loue, and euer schal be | And loue has been or we were bore' is 'close in wording and
idea' to part of the ending of the *Revelations of Divine Love* ('the loue wher in he
made vs was in hym fro with out begynnyng'), and also because 'Fore loue he
askys nonoþer fe | But loue aȝayn; he kepis no more' has a 'counterpart' in the
Incendium Amoris ('Si ergo queris amari, ama: quia amor vicem rependit'). That
the slightest verbal similarity constitutes a parallel for Sister Knowlton is indicated
at the outset of the book where she tries to show the way in which St Bernard is a
'literary source' for Rolle: ' "Mel in ore, in aure melos, in corde jubilus" (are)
sentiments that we find repeated in almost identical words in Rolle's commentary
on the same text of the Canticle, "Est autem Jesus in mente mea cantus iubilaeus,
in aure mea sonus coelicus, in ore meo dulcor mellifluus" '.

'In almost identical words': that *almost* has implications not only for this study,
but for the condition of medieval criticism in general. The analysis and evaluation
of the literature of the Middle Ages does indeed demand scholarly discipline, an
obvious fact which does not imply (as some modernists dismissively believe) that
scholarship can function as a mechanical *pis aller* for literary acuity. The extent
to which learning can be dissipated by critical naïveté and imprecision has a
melancholy demonstration in this book. The unhelpful organization of the bibliography, the laborious and repetitive footnotes are not simply scholarship heavily
worn, but indices of the author's (and presumably the publishers') assumption that
accumulation equals analysis and argument. Similarly, the fervid vocabulary

signals confusion between the literary expression of religious emotion with the particular effect that may have on the reader, and the presence of emotion. For example, 'The intimacy of love which now floods the soul of the lover pours itself out in repeated tender invocations to the Holy Name'; Rolle's writings 'are infused with a spirit of abounding joy . . . ardent love-longing . . . [and] intensely personal feeling'.

No one with any pretentions to understanding European intellectual history can ignore the variety of forms in which the religious imagination is articulated. Rolle contributed to the devotional by animating the commonplace with a terse festiveness: 'Loke þow lede þi lyf in lyghtsumnes; and hevynes, helde it away. Sarynes, lat it noght sytt wyth þe: bot in gladnes of God evermare make þow þi gle'. It is regrettable that knowledge should here contribute so little to the appreciation either of two talented writers or of an important tradition.

GAY CLIFFORD

UNIVERSITY OF WARWICK

Middle English Lyrics: Authoritative Texts, Critical and Historical Backgrounds, Perspectives on Six Poems. Selected and edited by MAXWELL S. LURIA and RICHARD L. HOFFMAN. (Norton Critical Editions) New York: Norton. 1974. xiv + 360 pp. $10.00.

This edition, for students, is 'larger, by nearly sixty poems, than any other' such anthology (p. x). It comprises two hundred and forty-five poems, 'spanning four centuries' (p. xi), including all the English lyrics in MS Harley 2253 and all Friar William Herebert's in Brown's *Lyrics of the Thirteenth Century*, but it does not include ' "representative" selections' from such poets as Lydgate, Audelay, or Skelton, and, with regard to Dunbar, Henryson, and Chaucer, it has 'a thinner sheaf . . . than they deserve'. When so much has been included I, personally, regret the omission of the macaronic Marian hymn 'Of on þat is so fayr and briȝt' (Brown, No. 17B), the Nativity lullaby carol, 'I saw a fayr maydyn syttyn *and* synge' (Greene's *Carols*, No. 143), the Agincourt carol (Greene, No. 426), and, particularly because their music is extant and recorded on Argo RG 443, the Marian hymn, 'Edi beo þu, heuene quene' (Brown, No. 60), and that of the Annunciation, 'Gabriel, fram evene-king', which is the 'Angelus ad virginem' of Chaucer's *Miller's Tale* (Brown, No. 44). On the other hand, there are included 'virtually all the poems of any consequence' in Robbins's *Secular Lyrics*, which are very attractive.

The editors rightly look forward to a new edition of all the medieval English lyrics but gratefully acknowledge that it is the current standard editions of Brook, Brown, Robbins, and Greene that have 'indispensably provided us with the texts offered here' (p. ix). They tell us they 'have made silently a very few textual emendations' (p. xi): I should, myself, have preferred them to have told us, for example (and there would be no need for elaborate apparatus) that *fast* at the end of 'Mirie it is' (No. 5) is not in MS, that their *winne* in line 11 of 'Lenten is come' (No. 4) is *wynter* in MS, and that their *ic* in the last line of 'Whanne mine eyhnen misten' (No. 234) is read by Brown in MS as *ihic* but is probably a scribe's misunderstanding of *I hit* ('*I* do not care a bean *for it*'). And even though, understandably, one may accept the texts in standard editions, for the most part, I wonder if one ought not to take into account the latest work, for example, the rearrangement of No. 163, 'D . . . dronken', proposed by Dronke after a fresh reading of MS, in *Notes and Queries* (July 1961) page 246?

The editors have done some selective adjustment of spelling: 'We have regularly modernized ð, þ, ȝ, ƿ; and, wherever necessary, we have sought to make our text readable by substituting genuine but recognizable Middle English spellings for unrecognizable or grotesque ones' (p. x).

Glosses are generally full and good: they are in the right-hand margin, or, if too long for there, at the foot of the page. This is very convenient though it gives the text a work-a-day look, somewhat increased by the large number which heads each poem and the absence of titles ('Nearly all of them are untitled in the manuscripts, and it makes a difference whether one apprehends a short literary composition directly or through the prism of a title' (p. xi), which is true). On the other hand, some teachers and students may regret that lines are not numbered. With regard to the select bibliography, I think that too much honour is done my own anthology of *Medieval English Lyrics* by its generous inclusion in the same category as such standard editions as Brook's *Harley Lyrics* and the collections of Brown, Robbins, and Greene; and I wonder if, in such a short list, there should be any place for Bowra's *Mediaeval Love-song* or Chambers's essay of 1907 from *Early English Lyrics*?

Poems have no individual annotation. Where the author is known, or (for an unexplained reason) if the poem comes from MS Harley 2253 or John of Grimestone's Commonplace Book, this is indicated at the end of the lyric. A table at the end of the section of poems gives, for all of them, in numerical order, the Brown and Robbins *Index* number, the manuscript in which the text is written, the source of the text, and a date. At the end of the brief preface (there is no introduction), some twenty-five poems are listed with page references to their discussion in the section of critical materials which occupy just under a third of the book. This means not only that over two hundred poems have no specific commentary but also that some general topics relevant to some or all of them receive little or no attention; for example, metre and stanza form, how poems have been transmitted, the various kinds.

The first section of critical materials, 'Critical and historical backgrounds', comprises substantial extracts from Dronke's *The Medieval Lyric* (on performers and performance), Manning's *Game and Earnest*, Oliver's *Poems Without Names* (on three levels of style), and Woolf's *English Religious Lyric* (on poems about death). It is unfortunate that the contribution from what the bibliography rightly calls 'the most distinguished' of these books, that of Miss Rosemary Woolf, magisterial, ample, original, having the clarity of mature learning, should reprint perhaps the only error I have ever found in her: the lines '[H]owe cometh al ye That ben y-brought' (p. 292 in this anthology, her p. 69) are a rough translation of Boethius's *Consolatio*, III, m. 10, where they refer to God or good or blessedness, not death and are not, in content therefore, rather of the Renaissance than medieval; whereas, in form, they need not be seen as peculiarly medieval (as is claimed) since they are rather reminiscent of, for example, the rhetorical pattern of George Herbert's 'Prayer the Churches banquet'.

The second section of critical materials, 'Perspectives on six poems', comprises characteristic extracts from Moore, Reiss, Robertson, Donaldson, Speirs, Dronke, Manning, Spitzer, Jemielity, and Halliburton. Reiss reads 'Foweles in the frith' (to my mind unbelievably) as a 'religious' poem, suggesting that '*beste* as "best" may be a more pointed reference to Christ, to him who was the best of living beings' (p. 320). With regard to 'Maiden in the mor lay', there had not been published in time for inclusion the article of S. Wenzel in *Speculum*, 49 (1974), 69–74, which resolves to my satisfaction that this is not a poem of Christian allegory; but more emphasis could have been put, than in a footnote to Dronke's extract, on Greene's case against allegorization in *Speculum*, 27 (1952), 504–6, and there could have been mention of Harris's different interpretation of the same evidence in the Red Book of Ossory in *Journal of Medieval and Renaissance Studies*, 1 (1971), 59–87.

Finally, the arrangement of the poems is 'by subject' and, within those divisions, regardless of chronology. The 'subjects' are broad and indicated by titles for the sections which are attractive by being anything but ponderous and formidable but are perhaps a bit whimsical. 'All for Love' (the inclusion of several poems for or against women can just about be defended); 'Thirty dayes hath November' (which comprises chiefly, for example, riddling, or gnomic or mnemonic verses but also (and why it does is a puzzle in itself) 'Mon in the mone' (No. 142) and 'Swarte smeked smethes' (No. 140); and 'Worldes bliss' in which No. 1 is in contempt of the world, No. 2 is a prayer to Jesus in his passion, No. 4 is 'Lenten is come with love to toune', No. 11 is Chaucer's 'To yow, my purse' — to give some examples why here, too, I am puzzled by the categorization. One section of delightfully bawdy poems or poems of sexual innuendo is called 'I have a gentil cok' which is the first line of the first poem in it (No. 77). But is it my culpable innocence that I have never until this edition suspected the 'cock' of this poem to be anything other than a bird?

R. T. DAVIES

UNIVERSITY OF LIVERPOOL

Did the 'Pearl Poet' write 'Pearl'? By GÖRAN KJELLMER. (Gothenburg Studies in English, 30) Gothenburg, Sweden: Acta Universitatis Gothoburgensis. 1975. 105 pp. 30 Kr.

This book would hardly merit a review if it were not that, to judge by the references in its notes and bibliography, there is at the moment something of a fashion for the application of linguistic analysis of this kind to the problems of authorship. Since it is just possible that its many tables and statistics might induce a welcome feeling of certainty in an uncertain world, it may be worth commenting briefly on the fundamental unsoundness of the method.

We are told that 'in order to find the constant features of an author's style we ought to look for his unconscious or subconscious linguistic habits and disregard conscious and deliberate rhetorical figures' (p. 19). This statement seems dubious in itself: other linguistic and stylistic criteria should surely not be excluded, and it would also seem ill-suited to poets who, of all people, are least unconscious in their use even of the minutiae of language. However, let us set these doubts aside and look at some of the 'unconscious or subconscious criteria' chosen by the author in the case of *Pearl*.

Seven categories are discussed, and the figures derived from counting the occurrences of the specific type of linguistic behaviour in a sample of the four poems of Cotton Nero AX and *St Erkenwald* are arranged on a scale. If one poem is consistently separated from the others on this scale (as *Pearl* is) this is taken as evidence of separate authorship.

The author is careful to point out that this conclusion cannot be regarded as absolutely certain, and also warns us that no single linguistic criterion of this type is sufficient to prove anything: it is the agreement of a number together which constitutes evidence. But, however weak they are individually, the separate criteria must actually exist as evidence of some sort, and this they do not do, or at least not as evidence of what the author is trying to prove. For example, one category is 'lexical frequency'. Here, the ten most frequent words are counted. These are 'he', 'his' etc., 'I', 'hit' etc., 'watz' etc., 'hym' etc., 'thou' etc., 'thay' etc., 'me' 'is'. But it is hard to say where the unconscious or subconscious choice comes in with most of these. The *Pearl* poet, like other users of English does not 'choose' pronouns, but must use a masculine one if he refers to a male, a feminine if he refers to a female; plural if there are many involved, singular if only one, and so on.

Moreover, a female character is overwhelmingly important in *Pearl*, while in the other poems the main character or characters are male. Is it surprising that *Pearl* uses all forms of the masculine pronoun fewer times than the other poems do? It seems, too, dubious practice to count the forms of the same pronouns as separate words, but if they are taken together the list becomes very short.

Another criterion is the 'choice' of the initial alliterating letters. Here, indeed, unconscious idiosyncrasy might assert itself; if, for example, a particular sound were consistently avoided, or if consonant groups were differently treated. In fact (Table, p. 92) this doesn't seem to happen. Each poem shows some kind of idiosyncrasy: *Gawain* is odd man out over *st*: *Purity* over *f* and *k*: *Patience* over *h* and *Pearl* (surely not surprisingly?) has a preference for *p*. The sample is small, only 300 lines from each, and the author has failed to allow for the fact that *Pearl* is not written in the alliterative line and is freer in its use of alliteration than the others.

Sentence length is another trap: what is the length of any given sentence in *Pearl*? We do not know until we have provided it with modern punctuation. Looking (at random) at the first stanza of Section II (ll. 61–72) in four editions, I find four different punctuations and thus four different sets of sentence lengths; and I could easily supply a fifth version. The present study does not give its actual evidence, only the figures derived from it, so that we have no means of judging how sentence length was determined. The surprising omission (among many other omissions) of any reference to either of the Gordons, to Tolkien, or to Davis in the bibliography suggests that only Gollancz's editions, which are fully listed, were used.

Types of clause and their connectors are now the only criteria left. Here again *Pearl* is found to differ from the others. It has, for example, numerous clauses with the connector omitted. Now, *Pearl* differs from the other three poems of its group in its frequent lyrical passages with their compressed, passionate utterance. Here we do find omission of connectives, for example: 'And, quen we departed, we wern at on; | God forbede we be now wrothe, | We meten so selden by stok other ston' (378–80). But, in contrast, *Pearl* also contains much tough argument. Section XII, for example, on grace and innocence, is laid out in a great variety of clauses, carefully introduced and connected by plenty of 'buts', 'thats', and 'thoughs'. Both the lyrical passion and the intellectual virtuosity of *Pearl* are unique to it in the group. In fact, as everyone knows, it differs from the others in content; a type of difference which, if we are to judge from the work of other known poets, is not necessarily indicative of different authorship. Content, however, and the relation of language to what it has to express are largely ignored in this study; although, ironically, these are the very features which the method has picked out, and which determine *Pearl's* position on the scale.

The problem of authorship thus remains where it was. In the absence of conclusive external evidence it will never be settled beyond possibility of dispute, but the only way to approach it will always be through sensitive and experienced study of the poems as poems and of their language as the language of poetry.

LADY MARGARET HALL, OXFORD   P. M. KEAN

Narrative Possibilities of the Tail-Rime Romance. By URS DÜRMÜLLER. (Swiss Studies in English, 83) Bern: Francke. 1975. viii + 245 pp. 28 Sw.F.

The Middle English tail-rhyme romances have, generally, enjoyed little scholarly respect. Chaucer's brilliant parody of inane romance clichés in *Sir Thopas* has often been taken as a well-deserved verdict on the genre as a whole, although editors of individual poems have often discovered poetic merits where others saw only

unimaginative drabness and hackwork. Dr Dürmüller's study is a welcome attempt
to provide a more thorough and substantiated appraisal of the tail-rhyme stanza as
a narrative medium and to point out some of its specific qualities. He is disarmingly
modest in admitting that 'the ME romances constitute no great documents of the
human mind' (p. 2) and in warning us against approaching the tail-rhyme
romances 'with too many expectations' (p. 114), but he believes (and I think
rightly) that these poems deserve more critical attention than they have received
so far.

About two-thirds of the book consists of a very close analysis of *The Erl of Tolous*
which, Dr Dürmüller claims, is a very competently narrated poem and a particularly successful example of the various possibilities of the tail-rhyme stanza. He
illustrates at great length the structure of the individual stanzas, the function of each
stanza-section and of the tail-lines, the use of direct speech, and the poet's adaptation of the metre to his subject. He demonstrates, on the whole convincingly, that
the poet makes conscious and skilful use of variation and that the tail-rhyme stanza
is far less monotonous than is often assumed. His approach is formal in a rather
limited sense and, I feel, tends to become at times a little mechanical. At least it
seems doubtful whether a meticulously detailed study of the function of each section
of a stanza, of minor variations in the introduction of direct speech or the linking of
stanzas will be enough to convince sceptics. Large stretches of the book are no more
than an almost statistical presentation of not very inspiring evidence, supported
by some even more detailed appendices. It is certainly well done and, perhaps,
needed doing, but the author's nearly exclusive concern with formal details prevents
him from dealing with many questions which might be more rewarding, such as
authorship, transmission, and audience of these romances and their relationship
with other types of narrative. Dr Dürmüller generally refers to the authors as
minstrels (whoever they were) and, in his conclusion, divides the romances into
those that were composed 'at the desk' and those 'composed in public' (p. 226);
this is, of course, much too vague to be very useful and only indicates the direction
in which further enquiries should be made. It would, naturally, be very unjust to
blame the author for not doing something he never claims to do, but his few
remarks on some more general aspects of his subject suggest that a purely formal
approach does not bring us very much nearer to a real understanding of these poems
and their purpose, much as we may be impressed by unsuspected variations in the
handling of the tail-rhyme stanza. At least these formal observations would have
to be more thoroughly related to other aspects of the poet's style and narrative art;
but Dr Dürmüller's attempts to link strictly formal and more thematic considerations are few and mostly superficial, as, for instance, his remarks on the subject
matter of the romances or on the 'sociohistorical background' (pp. 161–2).

Dr Dürmüller's almost pedantic interest in formal details is all the more regrettable because his conclusions are so convincing and the tail-rhyme stanza certainly
deserves some vindication. I agree with his high estimate of the narrative qualities
of *The Erl of Tolous*. I also think that his method proves more rewarding when he
comes to compare the poem with other tail-rhyme romances. Though stylistic
variation and avoidance of repetition is not an indiscriminately valid proof of
poetic competence, a convincing case is made for the inferior quality of *Emaré*
and (not quite so convincing because other qualities might have been taken into
consideration) *Athelstone*. Dr Dürmüller is quite successful in demonstrating the
originality of Thomas Chestre, whose *Sir Launfal* has often been compared unfavourably with the earlier couplet version of the same story, *Sir Landevale*. He also
makes an interesting point about *Sir Thopas* which, he believes, makes fun of silly
romances, but not of the tail-rhyme stanza as such, which Chaucer uses with
particular skill. This is certainly worth considering, even though the fact remains

that Chaucer never uses the tail-rhyme stanza when he is more in earnest. This, however, is part of a larger question which Dr Dürmüller does not attempt to answer; but he does supply much useful material for comparison and evaluation and should, I hope, provoke further scholarly interest in the tail-rhyme romances.

UNIVERSITY OF BONN   DIETER MEHL

The English Morality Play: Origins, History and Influence of a Dramatic Tradition. By ROBERT POTTER. London and Boston: Routledge. 1975. x + 286 pp. £6.95.

The English Morality Play raises high expectations. Dr Potter takes the pre-Shakespearian drama seriously, seeing it as 'a dramatic tradition which attempts to objectify theatrically the human predicament' (p. ix). He finds its origin in primitive ritual and argues that Mankind's fall and repentance is a Christian transformation of the death and regeneration of the folk hero of the mummers' play. He traces the development of the morality tradition itself and then goes on to consider its repercussions in Marlowe, Shakespeare, and Jonson. This way of treating the moralities is fairly familiar, though Dr Potter has much to say which is new in detail; but the book breaks fresh ground by extending its analysis both geographically and chronologically, surveying the morality tradition in Europe and tracing the history of the idea of the moralities into the twentieth century. A final chapter argues for the influence of Poel's 1901 production of *Everyman* directly and indirectly on Shaw, T. S. Eliot, and others, and finally on Brecht.

Such scope is very welcome but it brings its own problems. The second half of the book, from Marlowe onwards, contains many extraordinarily refreshing insights (the accounts of *Lear* as a political morality and of *Hamlet* as an ironic version of the traditional agent of repentance are particularly stimulating) but all in all one has a sense of a breathless rush through five countries and nearly as many centuries. Brecht in particular seems well worth more than the four pages he gets. Once the analogy has been proposed a great many parallels begin to suggest themselves. In *The Good Person of Szechwan*, for instance, Brecht is using allergory very like that of the morality writers, and for a similar purpose. When Shen Teh adopts the disguise of the tough, authoritarian Mr Shui Ta she might well evoke Anima temporarily disfigured by worldly values, or Wit unrecognizable after succumbing to sin. Brecht wants his audience to understand how capitalism inevitably superimposes a mask of false consciousness on 'good' humanity: the morality writers equally want their audiences to understand how sin transforms mankind's true nature. A number of moralities (Medwall's *Nature* in particular) emphasize the inevitability of man's loss of innocence in a fallen world: he needs the world's gifts and yet its values are the source of his corruption. In the sixteenth century the prevailing sin is increasingly seen as avarice, and Brecht might have been amused to know that in Wager's *Enough is as Good as a Feast* (c. 1560–70) the hero, exactly like Shen Teh, finally agrees to make money specifically in order to be charitable. He subsequently exploits his employees much in the manner of Mr Shui Ta. These connexions almost certainly owe little or nothing to direct influence but they may perhaps reflect a common concern with the use of the stage to encourage reasoned popular recognition of moral and social problems.

The first part of the book, dealing with the moralities themselves, presents problems of a different kind. The morality tradition is difficult to write about in a way which consistently compels the reader's interest. The plays are mostly relatively unfamiliar: some account of each is therefore necessary; but the plots of morality plays are rarely enlivening, and the reader finds that the monster Tediousness all too frequently blocks his hopeful path to Science. The solution (found, for instance, by Bernard Spivack and D. M. Bevington) is less matter with more argument, but Dr Potter's argument is not always strong enough to bear the weight of his analysis.

His central thesis is that the medieval moralities are 'about' repentance, and that in the Renaissance the repentance theme is diminished as the plays become more political. This evolutionary model ignores a good many Elizabethan plays which are political only in the most comprehensive sense of the word. It also, I suggest, distorts the emphasis of the medieval plays. Dr Potter argues that in the medieval moralities 'repentance is the climactic theatrical act' (p. 49). It is often (though not always) the last event of the play, but I wonder whether it is ever climactic. In *The Castle of Perseverance* it forms an interlude between Mankind's more spectacular falls from grace. (In a production by the Riverside Players in 1974 the most obvious theatrical climaxes were the hero's first surrender to temptation, the battle, and the coming of Death.) In *Wisdom* and *Mankind*, which conclude with repentance, the final episode works by reversing the temptation processes analysed in much greater detail earlier in each play. Even in *Everyman*, where the repentance theme is treated at length (250 lines in a total of 921), this is only a part of the play's analysis of the human predicament. The dramatists are concerned with the ways in which man deviates from the good as well as with the means by which he may return to it.

Dr Potter's emphasis is misleading to the extent that it ignores the morality analysis of the temptation processes and so allows such statements as this: 'the lures and snares of bad advice are demonstrated . . . fully by the quick-witted Ambidexter . . . For all its crudeness, then, *Cambises* looks ahead theatrically. Ambidexter the tempter functions as an ambiguous moral force, foreshadowing such complex figures of the late stage as Mephistophilis, Bosola and Iago. These Elizabethan and Jacobean tempters have their antecedents in the discoveries of a transitional play like *Cambises*, with its dawning comprehensions of the true ambiguity of evil' (p. 116). Mephistophilis, Bosola, and Iago are ambiguous in very different ways from each other, and of the three probably only Iago is a thoroughgoing descendant of the double-dealing Ambidexter. But, much more important, *Cambises* is a relatively late play (*c.* 1558–69), and its moralizing Vice is only one of a long line of quick-witted moralizing tempters whose common ancestor is the traditional Christian concept of the Devil, simultaneously ingenious tempter and exemplum, and thus a paradigm of the true ambiguity of evil.

University College, Cardiff   Catherine Belsey

John Mirk's 'Instructions for Parish Priests'. Edited from MS Cotton Claudius A.ii and Six Other Manuscripts with Introduction, Notes, and Glossary by Gillis Kristensson. (Lund Studies in English, 49) Lund:Gleerup. 1974. 277 pp. 65 Kr.

Mirk's *Instructions* has for long been a well known example of the many handbooks of rudimentary knowledge for priests that in the ensuing three hundred years followed the exhortations of the 1215 Lateran Council. It is somewhat hard to account for the text's fame, since the platitudinous doggerel offers only a digest of a longer, more explicit and enlightening Latin original; presumably early critics were attracted by the attribution of the vernacular work to a named and localized author, which, added to the fact that the text is in verse, made it the subject of analysis for dialectal features. The Early English Text Society edition by Peacock in 1868 (revised by F. J. Furnivall in 1902) was made from MS Cotton Claudius

A.ii; MSS Douce 60 and 103 were known to the editor but not systematically used; the notes are a mixture of relevant and anachronistic material characteristic of antiquarian study of the time. A new edition, now that four more manuscripts are known, seems timely. Dr Kristensson uses the same base text as Peacock, though he also prints separately MS Royal 17 C.xvii; presumably this latter is not collated, as are the other manuscripts, because of the degree of linguistic difference between it and Cotton. The text and variants appear accurate, although, since the editor has introduced modern punctuation, it seems perverse to retain manuscript capitalization.

Dr Kristensson's chief interest would appear to be the language of the text. His analysis is conventional, if not impeccable (for example, the rhyme *feynt*: *iweynt*, ll. 1101–2 is not explained by a reference to Jordan §103, since the second word did not originally contain the group *enct* which could give rise to *eint*). In other respects the edition is somewhat perfunctory. Emendations in the text are made for the sake of rhyme, but not for the sake of metre (for example, l. 1559 where variants cited show the obviously correct reading), nor for the sake of sense (for example, l. 923 where the base text gives the sense opposite to that required). Descriptions of the manuscripts are not altogether helpful. The quiring of MS Douce 60, for instance, is ascertainable at least as far as folio 187, and is nothing like so eccentric as is suggested (p. 21): all quires were originally of six, or more frequently of eight, leaves and the irregularity of the catchwords is the result of the excision of leaves, a loss which is immediately apprehensible if the contents are read consecutively. The editor appears to have made no study of the relationship of the *Instructions* to Mirk's source, though he cites an article by Dr L. E. Boyle which would have provided him with a starting point. Indeed Dr Boyle's paper (*Transactions of the Royal Historical Society*, 5th series, Volume 5 (1955), p. 87) would itself have given elucidation of the obscurity at lines 88–9 of the excommunication section (a section for which, oddly, the editor provides no notes): Mirk is here drastically compressing his source, the *Oculus Sacerdotis*, which includes the terms of the *charter of Forest* and the *gret charter* (Magna Carta) amongst the offences incurring excommunication. It is clear from the notes that the editor had no interest in the subject matter of the text. Regretfully one can only conclude that although it provides a text, a serviceable analysis of the language, and a comprehensive glossary, in other respects this edition offers sadly little advance on the edition produced over a hundred years ago.

ANNE HUDSON

LADY MARGARET HALL, OXFORD

The Earlier Version of the Wycliffite Bible: Volume 6: Baruch 3.20 — End of OT, edited from *MS Christ Church 145.* By CONRAD LINDBERG (Stockholm Studies in English, 29) Stockholm: Almqvist and Wiksell. 1973. vi + 393 pp.

Dr Lindberg's editorial work on the Earlier Version (EV) of the Wycliffite Bible (WB) goes steadily on, though with the change in basic text from Bodley 959 (*E*) to Christ Church 145 (*X*), shown by Dr Fristedt's pioneering study of 1953 to be probably the closest to the original for this part of EV (EV II), a change in emphasis has become necessary as well as a change of title. Since *X* lacks the many erasures, corrections, and additions which attest 'the high degree of originality' of *E*, the editor is able to concentrate on the relationships between the ten surviving manuscripts of EV II here, and their relationship to the later version (LV). The sections of his Introduction dealing with these points are painstakingly detailed, but not, I fear, completely accurate. To evaluate all variants, the reader must use simultaneously Introduction, footnotes, and end-notes; it is as well also that he have the standard edition of WB by Forshall and Madden (FM). When dealing with 'Corrections in *X*' in §9 the editor misrepresents the reading of the Later Version (LV) some twenty times on pages 48–9. To take four instances from a single chapter, Baruch 6: he gives '30 . . . torn *or kut*: V scissas (gloss = LV); . . . 42 3ouen aboute *or bounden*: V circumdatae (gloss = LV); . . . 53 discriuen *or iugen* a dome: V iudicium discernent (gloss = LV); . . . 69, place where kukumeris *pat ben bitter erbis* waxen: V cucumerario (gloss = LV). But the LV readings given in FM are not identical with the gloss or with the original in *X* for any one of the four, but are respectively 'torent', 'gird', 'deme', 'gourdis'. Exactly parallel inaccuracies are made for Ez. 1. 24, 8. 14; rather similar ones: (a) where the Introduction says 'no gloss LV', but there is a textual gloss given in FM, for Ez. 2. 3, 10. 13, 23. 10; (b) where LV differs from EV text and gloss, but the Introduction says simply 'no gloss LV' Ez. 3. 26, 5. 7, 7. 22, 14. 7, 16. 31, 20. 28; (c) where some other inaccuracy is found Ez. 1. 4 (electre), 45. 8, 45. 11.

In the course of the Introduction Dr Lindberg throws out some interesting suggestions, on the reason for the curious selection of verses in *Z* and *Ro*, on the importance of vocabulary study, but some of his conclusions arouse misgivings. The penultimate sentence in §12 sums up his impression of his basic text: 'Considering its date (beg. of the 15th c.) and its revised character, we can safely say that *X* is an example of WB in the finished form of EV (with minor modifications) from the stage when EV and LV were both current, largely influencing each other' (p. 66). The last three words are repeated on p. 71: 'The two versions of WB influenced each other, as is seen by collateral evidence. They may both contain original readings, at times corrected in either of them, though, by and large, LV is the revision of EV and not vice versa.' But they indicate some confusion. Independent versions can properly be said to influence each other, but if one version is a revision of another it must by definition be largely dependent on it, not merely influenced; and although readings from a revision may contaminate or be introduced into an earlier version, they influence not that version but our ability to identify it. The point has some importance, for a passage in §13 indicates that the confusion is affecting some of Dr Lindberg's datings. When he writes, 'If my conjecture in volume 5 is correct, Hereford left his work to be finished by Purvey in the London area about the year 1400. The date would fit the date of *X* (1400–1410) and the other MSS . . . Whether NT in EV and the whole of LV were finished by the time OT in EV was finished (and by whom) remains to be seen' (p. 70), a flood of objections springs to mind. It is not impossible that a modern palaeographer, relying on a battery of careful tests, would commit his dating to a specific decade; but Dr Lindberg accepts his on the opinion of FM in 1850 and the Christ Church catalogue of 1867. Caution should leave open the possibility of a date ten or fifteen years on either side of that decade. If LV is a revision of EV, EV must clearly have been finished some time before LV and therefore before the General Prologue to OT in LV, which can be dated specifically to 1395–6. It is difficult to believe that any group of translators who had worked out acceptable principles for an authoritative text would thereafter revert to an extreme literalism for another part of the Bible; and EV in NT had been revised into an acceptably idiomatic form and used as the basis of extensive commentaries (the Glossed Gospels) in time for these to have been approved by Archbishop Arundel while Anne of Bohemia was still alive, before 1394. Allowing time for all these processes, one must put the production of EV well back into the 1380s. One should not assume that when a manuscript of EV contains as a gloss a reading found also in LV it is necessarily evidence of contamination; an alternative hypothesis explains more economically both this phenomenon and others. When the first full draft was complete, its authors started to suggest alternative renderings for numerous 'equivok' words, and these appear first in the manuscripts as glosses. Later, in the full-scale revision that produced LV, the revisers sometimes accepted the alternative and rejected the original (Bar 6. 27, Ez. 1. 4 whirlewind, 3. 17, 4. 3, 7. 5, etc.), sometimes rejected the alternative and retained the original (Ez. 2. 4, 6. 14, 8. 17, etc.) and sometimes rejected both original and alternative, preferring a third word (Bar 6. 30, 6. 42, 6. 53, etc.).

Dr Lindberg promises to continue with his work on WB by editing NT in EV 'within this decade'. His problems will be greater as the number of manuscripts he has to deal with increases: it will be interesting to see if his views on this revision/contamination *crux* need to be modified.

H. HARGREAVES

UNIVERSITY OF ABERDEEN

Geoffrey Chaucer. The Tales of Canterbury Complete. Edited by ROBERT A. PRATT. Boston: Houghton Mifflin Company. 1974. xlvi + 587 pp. $10.95.

The present edition seems to be designed for undergraduates and has a very pleasant and useful format, with marginal glossing plus a few footnotes. The illustrations are fresh and interesting. This hardback edition is pleasantly printed on good paper and sturdily bound (apart from the fact that in the review copy pages 321–4 are not bound at all), so that its price seems reasonable for a new book. The important question for such a book is whether it can satisfactorily replace Robinson's famous edition, or such other text books as Professor Baugh's *Chaucer's Major Poetry*, or those of Professors E. T. Donaldson and A. C. Cawley.

The Introduction surveys Chaucer's life and works briskly, compactly, sensibly, and with the authoritative quality earned by a lifetime of distinguished Chaucer scholarship; though there are also some doubtful or unlikely matters confidently referred to as certainties, such as Chaucer's knowledge of *Sir Gawain and the Green Knight*; of the *Decameron*; of Beauvau's translation of *Il Filostrato*; of Chaucer's hearing of the Auchinleck MS read aloud (why should he not have read it?). In Professor Pratt's critical remarks there is some unnecessary summarizing: the main critical point is the liveliness of Chaucer's characterization, including the way that, for example, *The Knight's Tale* and *The Nun's Priest's Tale* characterize their own fictional tellers, a point which might be thought both over-familiar and questionable.

There are two and a half pages on Chaucer's language and pronunciation, naturally much simplified, with no treatment of open and close *e* and *o*, but only a reference to Robinson's introduction in his second edition. The short Bibliography, which yet contains an entry for A. Seton's novel *Katherine* (1954) lacks any reference whatever to studies in Chaucer's language. There is only a brief and general paragraph on metre. This is rough and ready indeed, and a serious handicap to a real grasp of Chaucer's meaning and music. Robinson, Donaldson (*Chaucer's Poetry*), and Baugh are fuller and more helpful.

The order of the *Tales* is the so-called '1400 order', built on internal references rather than MS sequence. It is almost identical with that of Skeat in his edition of 1894, except that Skeat's fragment C (*Physician's* and *Pardoner's Prologues* and *Tales*) is placed after Skeat's fragment F (as in Robinson). Robinson's line numbering is retained, as are Skeat's and Robinson's labels of each of the fragments, in the running headline on each page of the present edition, but since the actual position of this section of text in relation to the rest of *The Canterbury Tales* differs from both

Skeat and Robinson (VI(C) coming between V(F) and VIII(G), there is some little inconvenience. It is a pity that Skeat's order was not retained *in toto*, since the subtleties of the sequence are little likely to be noticed by the reader for whom the edition appears to be designed. In itself, however, the sequence is an improvement on the Ellesmere order adopted by Robinson and others.

The text is perhaps the most satisfactory so far produced for undergraduates. Unlike the editions of Baugh and Donaldson it is complete, and Professor Pratt has accepted a number of emendations recently suggested. His chief method has been the pragmatic one, as he explains, of taking Robinson's text as a base and emending it mainly in the light of the Manly–Rickert *Text of the Canterbury Tales* (M–R). This continues a process begun by Robinson himself, who similarly touched up his original 1933 text in his second edition of 1957. Pratt gives a list of his variations from Robinson but a random test shows that this is not very full or consistent. Thus pages 6 to 7 of Pratt, (*CT* I(A), ll. 131–206) are listed as having one substantial variant, plus two changes of punctuation in lines 171–2 leading to a change of syntax. But *writen* (l. 161) and *wroght* (l. 196) are M–R, not Robinson; they change the metre, and are not recorded. They are more substantial than some of the variants listed, and are probably improvements. Pratt rightly does not intend to record mere spelling variations, but one wonders why *greene* (l. 159) is so spelt, since Robinson, Baugh, and M–R have *grene*. Donaldson has *greene* (it rhymes with *sheene*, so spelt in all editions), but Donaldson confessedly changes spelling to help the reader.

A random check of Pratt's list of variants was made by examining page 574. On this page is a total list of forty-eight changes from Robinson covering 1,796 lines: forty-six changes derive from M–R. The two that do not are quite interesting from the point of view of textual criticism, though they show the dangers of pragmatic tinkering without principle, and show how wise Professor Pratt was to lean so heavily on M–R. The first is *The Pardoner's Tale* (VI, l. 532) where Robinson begins the line *That they*, and Pratt, *They*. M–R reads *Ther*. All three possibilities appear among the manuscripts and the line gives a splendid example of editorial variation over the centuries. Caxton's first edition has *That they*, not subsequently found until Urry (1721), which Tyrwhitt (1775), despite his contempt for Urry, did not disdain to repeat, and which was adopted by Skeat, Globe, and Robinson. It makes a regularly metrical line. *There* was printed by Thynne (1532) and subsequent editions to Speght (1598), but not subsequently until Morris (1845), and not again until M–R. Speght (1602) interestingly substitutes *They* (showing that Speght did really do some editing, as he claimed) and this was repeated in the 1687 reprint, not to be resumed until Professor Pratt. Of the three variants *They* seems least preferable, though of course defensible.

Pratt's second variant independent of M–R in this section is in *The Canon's Yeoman's Tale* VIII, l. 621, *ye may nat wite of me*. It is found thus in many manuscripts and so printed by all editions until Skeat, who substituted *at* for *of*, as all editors have done since. In view of Mustanoja's remarks (*A Middle English Syntax*, Part I, p. 350), on the interchangeability of *at* and *of*, where *of* is said usually to be the encroacher at the end of the Middle English period, it would seem that *at*, rather than *of*, is more likely to be Chaucer's form. It will however be clear that in general Professor Pratt has brought Robinson's text closer to M–R. There are more 'headless' lines in consequence but we seem to be nearer Chaucer's own feeling for verse.

The text has marginal glossing and a few footnotes on the page, clearly set out. The only way to judge this seems to be by comparison, and page 241 of Professor Baugh's edition, *General Prologue* I(A), ll. 152–93, was chosen at random as a basis. Baugh gets forty-two lines on the page, glossing and commenting only in footnotes;

Pratt's average is thirty-eight. In the passage selected Baugh glosses or comments on thirty-eight different words or phrases, with brief references to some of Chaucer's contemporaries, and also to modern books and articles. Pratt has no such references but glosses or occasionally comments very briefly forty-two times. This includes one of the extremely rare textual comments, arising out of Pratt's unique rejection in line 164 of *and preestes thre*, claiming that Chaucer left the line unfinished. For good measure we may further compare Professor A. C. Cawley's glossed and footnoted edition in Everyman's Library (1958) which uses Robinson's text unchanged. For the same passage Cawley has sixteen glosses and sixteen lines translated or explained, without references.

Baugh glosses or comments on, but Pratt and Cawley do not, *smal coral* (l. 158), *heng* (l. 160), *Another Nonne* (l. 163), *that text* (l. 177), *a fissh that is waterlees* (l. 180).

Pratt glosses, as Baugh, and in almost every case Cawley, do not, *therto* (l. 153), *spanne* (l. 155), *bar* (l. 158, also glossed at l. 105). Pratt alone adds the meaning 'pursuit of sexual pleasure' to *venerie* (l. 166), and glosses *able* (l. 167) as 'suited'. He alone glosses *eek* (l. 171, having also glossed it at lines 5, 41, 56), *reule* (l. 173), *ilke* (l. 175, also glossed at l. 64), *ben* (l. 178, though it was not glossed at l. 141), *thilke* (l. 182, also glossed by Cawley), *nat* (l. 182, though it was not glossed at l. 177), *poure* (l. 185), *swink* (l. 188), *fowel* (l. 190). Pratt glosses *deyntee* (l. 168) as 'elegant', Baugh and Cawley as 'valuable', which seems preferable. Pratt glosses *chapeleyne* (l. 164) as 'secretary and assistant' which seems, rather like cooks, to confuse substance with accidence.

If this sample is representative, and there seems no reason why it should not be, Pratt aims at a less intelligent audience, who cannot, for example, be expected to guess that *spanne* means 'span', than do Baugh and Cawley, but Baugh gives more information than either (though he does not include the prose of *The Canterbury Tales*).

In addition to glossing, Professor Pratt gives a basic glossary at the end of the book of commonly recurring words (though one wonders why, for example, *laurer* figures there). No grammatical descriptions are given and the meanings are mostly single-word equivalents, or several single-word equivalents without distinction.

The labour of producing a text book such as Professor Pratt's is very great, and the book deserves serious consideration. It has many virtues, but they do not seem to give it preference over works already in the field. Robinson is still much the best general value, and even his glossary seems preferable to those of his rivals. For students who cannot look up a word in the back of the book but need all information on the same page Baugh's annotation is fuller (and has a fuller glossary for those with strength to reach it); and though Baugh omits the prose works, will the student whom Professor Pratt seems to aim to serve really read, for example, *The Parson's Tale*? Even if he will, he will find Cawley's Everyman's Edition of *The Canterbury Tales* very soundly glossed, and far cheaper, though without pictures. Donaldson's edition, though very selective, has the advantage of very penetrating critical comments.

DEREK BREWER

EMMANUEL COLLEGE, CAMBRIDGE

*Geoffrey Chaucer. The Wife of Bath's Prologue and Tale and the Clerk's Prologue and Tale
from 'The Canterbury Tales'.* Edited by GLORIA CIGMAN. (The London Medieval and Renaissance Series, 2) London: University of London Press. 1975.
vi + 194 pp. £3.80 (£1.95 paperbound).

Geoffrey Chaucer. The Friar's, Summoner's and Pardoner's Tales from 'The Canterbury Tales'.
Edited by N. R. HAVELY. (The London Medieval and Renaissance Series, 3)
London: University of London Press. 1975. vi + 165 pp. £3.65 (£1.85
paperbound).

In preparing their groups of Canterbury Tales for the reader new to Chaucer, Mrs
Cigman and Mr Havely conform to editorial policies by which they are not uniformly well served. Both provide lexical and explanatory notes on the same page as
the text, reserving longer notes for an appended commentary, and both place the
main emphasis in their introductions on the communication of information. The
general editor, A. V. C. Schmidt, contributes a biography of Chaucer and a guide
to pronunciation but, surprisingly, there is no general note on Chaucer's language
nor is there an alphabetical glossary. Mrs Cigman gives summaries of each of her
tales but has no textual note: Mr Havely has a textual note and a selection of
critics' opinions for discussion, but no summaries.

To place copious notes on the same page as the text is a cumbersome device, for
the area cannot contain the total critical apparatus of a scholarly edition and there
must still be reference to the commentary. Very light glossing on the page can assist
rapid reading with immediate literary pleasure but undoubted loss of fine detail.
The present series, however, throws away the advantage of speed by filling more
than a third of every page with footnotes which, while removing 'the need for
constant reference to a glossary', do not greatly reduce the amount of thumbing
through end-pages. Even so, the disadvantages of incomplete glossing remain. A
reader who fails to guess the meaning of *viker or persoun* (*Summoner's Tale*, line 344)
will find a footnote referring him to 45 lines of comment on three separate pages,
but no solution of his language problem. And sometimes editorial idiom obscures
Chaucer's syntax. Thus, in the *Pardoner's Tale* (lines 176–7), the consecutive words
haunteden folye, | *As ryot, hasard, stewes and tavernes* are divided between two footnotes
of different construction: 'indulged themselves recklessly' and 'Such as extravagance and gambling and [frequented] brothels and taverns'. Without a glossary,
the reader has no way of finding out that *haunt* can be both 'practise habitually'
and 'resort to frequently' and that here the two meanings coincide.

Mrs Cigman, with her eye firmly on the inexperienced reader of Chaucer,
assembles in her introduction much useful information about gentillesse, poverty,
and the medieval church's attitude to women. She is wise to warn against using
critical approaches based on reading modern novels, but disregards her own advice
when she treats the conflict of experience with authority not as a great medieval
theme but exclusively as an expression of the Wife of Bath's character. At Mrs
Cigman's chosen level of simplification it is impossible to do justice to such complexities as the endings of the Wife's *Prologue* and *Tale* and the Clerk's *Envoy*. Moreover the reductive style subdues Dame Alice, whose 'cynical insistence on mastery
in marriage is a damp squib' and minimizes Grisilde's need for patient endurance
in 'a marriage in which the wife achieves happiness and fulfilment by acknowledging the *sovereyntee* of her husband'. There are several inaccuracies: the Marquis
Walter had no apparent heir at the late stage when he is credited with 'pretending
that the people openly resent having a peasant's child as heir-apparent' (p. 15);
'He has her stripped of her splendid clothes and turned out of the palace' (p. 15)
violates the characterization in lines 890–96; the note to line 450 of the Wife's
portrait has the people offering bread and wine to the priest in the Mass.

Mr Havely is an editor of a different order, who carries his learning lightly. He neatly summarizes the theory of indulgences, touches on problems of critical interpretation without dogmatizing, and has a pleasing turn of phrase. He is particularly good at recreating the living narrator's changes of tone and voice as he picks up cues to Chaucer's dramatic presentation of the Friar's and Summoner's Tales. A reader of Mr Havely's introductions will proceed to the texts well prepared to enjoy them and to take an informed part in critical discussion.

It is a pity that a series which serves the reader so well in providing a background of medieval thought does not have a more systematic approach to the language.

UNIVERSITY OF ADELAIDE   DOROTHY COLMER

Literary Monographs. Volume 6. *Medieval and Renaissance Literature.* Edited by ERIC ROTHSTEIN and JOSEPH ANTHONY WITTREICH, JR. Madison, Wisconsin and London: University of Wisconsin Press. 1975. 182 pp. $13.75.

The critics represented in this volume are all American scholars of high calibre. The four studies included, on Langland, Spenser, Crashaw, and the subject of Christmas in (mainly) seventeenth-century English verse, have been thoroughly 'researched' and minutely documented. Here, one is aware, we have a powerful concentration of intellectual competence served by articulateness of an enviable kind. Yet much of the commentary offered exhibits a depressing degree of erudite aridity which hardly seems compatible with the spontaneous enjoyment of literature and arouses some misgivings as to the ultimate usefulness of intensive research. Take the case of the third essay by R. V. Le Clercq on 'Crashaw's *Epithalamium*: Pattern and Vision'. In thirty-five pages the author embarks on a 'contextual' interpretation of the poem ('Come virgin Tapers of pure waxe...') which is so intricate and allusive that in the course of his analysis the hundred and forty-odd lines of Crashaw's work are entirely swamped in exegetical subtlety. The *Epithalamium*, we are told, 'requires a knowledge of various "readings" of marriage, including generic, typological, mystical (spiritual), and mythic (archetypal). These traditions inform the imaginative situation of the poem' (p. 73). But even if this is so, it is questionable whether these elements in the 'background' of the *Epithalamium* require to be followed through with the dogged deliberateness that Professor Le Clercq has made part and parcel of his idiom. Any appreciation of 'meaning', as we know, depends to a large extent on an awareness of conventions both literary and ideational: but in this instance the critic has surely elicited from Crashaw's poem far too much in the way of 'symbolic potential' and advanced excessive claims for the relevance of the theological implications he discusses at such length. To add to the complexity of the exercise, the structure of the *Epithalamium* is explained in terms of numerological associations, which are extended to stanza forms and metre in formidable detail (see pp. 83 and 172). There are also charts and diagrams.

In varying degrees the other essays here collected adopt the contextual approach. The virtue of A. Joan Bowers's much less taxing essay on 'The Tree of Charity in *Piers Plowman* ...' is that it relates arboreal symbolism to the cyclical nature of the B Text, and shows how variants on the one major image appear throughout the poem in a number of different relationships. William V. Nestrick's study of 'Spenser and the Renaissance Mythology of Love' strikes me as less happy; his coverage of the subject is wide and backed up by an impressive freedom of reference, yet the central thesis is far from clear, and in general the mode of presentation resembles a 'write-up' rather than a closely-argued synthesis. The objective is to 'reveal and define the mythopoetic imagination behind Book Three of *The Faerie Queene*'

(p. 37). This takes in 'The Hue and Cry after Cupid', 'Venus and Adonis', 'Cupid and Psyche', and the 'Triumph of Cupid'. Professor Nestrick enlarges on the provenance of the material Spenser draws upon and compares his use of myth with that of other poets. Yet the highly sophisticated explanation of Spenser's procedure is at times quite baffling; much of the essay is couched in tediously ambulatory prose and disfigured by critical jargon ('strategy', 'almost built-in feature of the form', 'basic narrative structure', 'higher didactic potential' and so on). In the finish, it seems to me doubtful whether Spenser's ability to discover and disclose the 'human essences contained in the myths' he utilizes is actually proved.

In some respects A. B. Chambers's account of 'Christmas: The Liturgy of the Church and English Verse of the Renaissance' is the most satisfactory section of the book. Mr Chambers points out that traditionally Christmas refers not to one day but to a cycle in the liturgical year, a cycle which 'possesses structural unity and internal coherence along with complex inter-relationships among its parts', this encouraging 'an exploration of any one of its parts not only for local meanings . . . but also for larger values of which the part can be a comprehensive symbol . . .' (p. 118). At this point one is perhaps justified in asking whether 'latent symbolism' is not in danger of becoming something of a fetish among those who are preoccupied with the religious 'dimension' of literature. But a perusal of what Mr Chambers has to say about the manner in which Donne, Herbert, Jonson, and Milton work through the variety of topics associated with the Christmas season proves to be reassuring: here, certainly, we have contextual evidence used with a kind of tact and restraint unfortunately absent from some other items included in *Literary Monographs*. I am not sure that now and again the analysis of Milton's 'Nativity' Ode does not gloss the obvious a little too artlessly. But the essay as a whole convinces by its lucidity and freedom from surplussage. It contains one particularly informative section on Henry Vaughan (pp. 131–9) in which a judicious balance is struck between careful textual explication and genuinely illustrative commentary.

UNIVERSITY OF SHEFFIELD

E. D. MACKERNESS

Renaissance Papers 1974. Edited by DENNIS G. DONOVAN and A. LEIGH DENEEF. Durham, North Carolina: The Southeastern Renaissance Conference. 1975. viii + 85 pp.

The seven essays that make up this volume are, it is indicated, a selection of papers presented at the thirty-first annual meeting of the Southeastern Renaissance Conference in April 1974. The principle of selection was, presumably, that of merit: there seems otherwise no common ground between them. An essay on Spenser is followed by one on *A Woman Killed with Kindness*; then come two on Shakespeare, one on Milton, one on Marvell's 'Bermudas', and one on Titian's Pesaro Madonna, which is accompanied by several plates. All the essays are competent and readable, pleasing examples of professionalism at work, and collectively suggest an academic version of the *divertissement* at the end of a ballet. Most of them are contributions to an already existent debate. Thus Professor Andrews disposes gracefully and thoroughly of Professor Eleanor Prosser's argument that the Ghost in *Hamlet* is an evil spirit, and endeavours to strangle at birth the 'growing concensus' of opinion in favour of this belief before it gets a stranglehold itself on *Hamlet* studies. Professor Bergeron reopens the question of the deposition scene in *Richard II*, suggesting that the passage missing from the early quartos was not in fact written until after 1601. He argues, quite persuasively, that had we not known the passage was there, we should not have missed it (good as it is). His argument is not, however, much strengthened by the suggestion that 'the abbreviated Act IV would serve the Essex rebels quite nicely', since this would apply equally well to abbreviation by omission. Nor (and this is a weakness) does he offer any suggestions as to why, if the play was good enough before, Shakespeare decided to expand it. His case remains therefore not proven. The debate, no doubt, will continue.

In '*Paradise Lost*, Book III: The Dialogue in Heaven Reconsidered', Professor Michael Lieb indicates at the outset the article by a fellow-critic that has been the initial inspiration to his own essay, just as his allusion towards the end to 'the balanced structure of *Paradise Lost*' shows again the critical camp to which he belongs. His argument itself, using certain passages from the early books of the Bible to demonstrate the dramatic nature of the Son's interchange with the Father in Book III, is nicely worked out.

As for Book VI of *The Faerie Queene*, Spenser critics have recently been drawn to this as irresistibly as iron filings to a magnet. The image of the Graces on Mount Acidale appears to be one of those images that 'tease us out of thought as doth Eternity'. Professor Snare's essay adds its ray of light to the rest, with its suggestion of a Calidore unable to comprehend the vision of a courtesy whose quest he has neglected, contrasted with a Colin to whom, having fulfilled his poetic 'travel', the vision is granted.

The final essay of the volume is Professor Philipp Fehl's examination of Titian's Pesaro Madonna, in which he invites and indeed persuades us to doubt the evidence of our senses which suggest that this is a purely worldly representation, and to see in it instead a mysticism created largely through the relationship and postures of the figures, the human ones being seen only in profile and so placed that they do not see the divine figures although the divine figures see them. Professor Fehl identifies the figures and the occasion. Altogether it is an absorbing essay, but one wonders what it is doing in this otherwise entirely literary collection. No literary parallels are drawn, and we are told disconcertingly in an editorial note that the editors have refused to print an extensively modified and expanded version of the paper here presented.

No explanation of this editorial decision is offered, nor is there any statement of the editorial policy governing the selection of essays in general. The essays are left to speak for themselves, which they do on the whole very well, although some editorial or authorial attention to expression and to proof-reading would have removed some blemishes, as in Professor Fehl's clumsily constructed sentence, 'He did not pose for himself, in so many words, the problems I have touched upon, and then went ahead to solve them'; the reading 'Diety' for 'Deity' on page 8; or the intriguing variant reading of 'th' Oceans besome' (for 'bosome') in Marvell's 'Bermudas' (page 52).

ROYAL HOLLOWAY COLLEGE, LONDON

JOAN GRUNDY

Discoveries and Reviews: From Renaissance to Restoration. By A. L. ROWSE. London: Macmillan. 1975. xii + 283 pp. £6.95.

The academic profession, Christopher Ricks once remarked, has its *young* fogeys. It has its old whippersnappers, too. Dr Rowse is one of them. In some moods he writes for all the world as if he were not old and famous. His easy scoffs at other scholars, many of them indeed those whose work has made his own possible, clearly meet some shabbier need than that of downright commonsense, accuracy, or good taste, such as he claims. At times the falsity is evident for all to see and hear in the writing style itself: sentences lumber and stumble along, clutching at clichés, bits of démodé slang and colloquialism, sketching vague gestures and throwing sideways many a broad wink. It is this unbuttoned drollness that the blurb-writer mistakes for vivacity. Actually, one suspects there is behind it all little real heat or humour.

Dr Rowse does not always (in his favourite phrase) 'get it right'. He must have read his friend Bowers to very little effect (p. 100) to understand him to have shown 'convincingly' that a collaborator wrote the comic scenes in *Doctor Faustus*. It was not Robert Parsons (p. 186) who 'wrote that Marlowe was reported as thinking Moses but a juggler and saying that Hariot, "Sir Walter Ralegh's man, can do more than he" ': it was Richard Baines. There are more serious, if less incontestable, faults. Even an 'Eng. Lit. person' must be disconcerted by some of the swingeing generalizations made about the character of the Elizabethan Age — with its inevitably crowded and noisy life (why are Elizabethan crowds and noises so much more fun than ours?). We are told, several times over indeed, and with a boisterousness purely academic, that the Elizabethans were much more free-and-easy in their sexual activity than we are. And there were great artistic impulses in the Renaissance. And there was great passion for place and power. Of John Stow Dr Rowse writes: 'Something very Elizabethan about him was the ambition, the sheer scale of his intended enterprise — it is so like the grandeur of their aims, the expanding horizons that led them on. How inspiring it must have been to live then! — everything bore one up, everything encouraged effort, instead of dragging one down, nothing to inspire one, nothing to encourage, nothing but what calls for contempt on every hand' (p. 171). Sentences of this kind condemn themselves, whichever way you hold them up.

Yet along with the old whippersnappery goes a remarkable depth of learning and width of interests, a genuine enjoyment of hard facts, and above all a special ability to tell a plain tale well; or rather, to manufacture from the frustrating bits and pieces of historical evidence an apparently plain tale when there was none before. His short accounts of Simon Forman, Mary Fitton, Thomas Hariot, and Pepys, make good, instructive reading. And there is no question but that Dr Rowse's original research work has been of great value; 'first-rate' would be his word. Here, considering the publicity that surrounded his *Shakespeare the Man* (1973), one would have expected to find some further argument about the personages in Shakespeare's Sonnets. Instead, Dr Rowse goes over his previous assertions as though mere brow-beating will carry conviction in the absence of solid proof. It is noticeable that Emilia Bassano is no longer said, on the strength of a misreading in the Forman papers, to have been brown in her youth; on the other hand, she is now regularly described as 'Italianate', so the retraction is not great. Her husband has quietly been re-named 'Alfonso' (instead of 'William'), with some unlamented loss to Sonnets 135 and 136.

On the whole this book is a trivial collection of papers, most of which are reprints of shortish reviews. They have some interest (and possibly, here and there, impor-tance), but it is rather as *The Reader's Digest* has interest (and importance). Con-cerning Brian Vickers's edition of *Shakespeare: The Critical Heritage*, Dr Rowse expostulates: 'Is it fair on a bankrupt country to waste so much paper and print on such a project, when what these writers wrote about each other is in print already, even assuming that it is worth reading?' (p. 96). Physician, heal thyself.

UNIVERSITY OF BRISTOL   E. D. PENDRY

Das Historiengedicht in der englischen Literaturtheorie: Die Rezeption von Lucans 'Pharsalia' von der Renaissance bis zum Ausgang des achtzehnten Jahrhunderts. By HEINZ-DIETER LEIDIG. (Europäische Hochschulschriften, Reihe XIV Angelsächsische Sprache und Literatur, 26) Bern: Herbert Lang; Frankfurt am Main: Peter Lang. 1975. 200 pp. 52 SwF.

Between the Renaissance and 1800, British literary critics were much preoccupied with what constituted epic and what place in literature historical epic occupied. Embodying the target of these criticisms was Lucan's *De bello civili*: the title *Pharsalia*, always used then, is poorly attested (though to speak of the field of Pharsalia, marked 'sic' on p. 153, is perfectly correct). 'Some', says an epigram of Martial's on Lucan, 'say I am no poet, but my bookseller thinks I am.' H.-D. Leidig's book examines the development of such criticism and links it with contemporary historical epic, whose writers themselves often touched on the question. Sir Philip Sidney groups Lucan among 'them that deal with matters philosophical', subdivided into moral, natural, astronomical, and (as Lucan) historical. Although William Webbe commends Lucan, he links him with Silius, inferior to the 'princelie' Homer and Virgil. A recurring objection is that Lucan's theme was too close to his times. Sir William Davenant wrote in the preface to his *Gondibert*: '*Lucan* who chose to write the greatest actions that ever were allow'd to be true ... did not observe that such an enterprize rather beseem'd an Historian then a Poet; for wise Poets think it more worthy to seeke out truth in the passions, then to record the truth of actions'.

The two historical epics of the Renaissance period which, like Lucan's, had a civil war theme were Samuel Daniel's *Civile Wars* and Michael Drayton's *Barrons Warres*. Daniel proclaims: 'I have carefully followed that truth which is deliuered in the Historie; without adding to, or subtracting from, the general receiu'd opinion of things as we finde them in our common Annalles'. Everard (not Edward) Guilpin comments: '*Daniel* (as some holds [sic]) might mount if he list, | But others say that he's a Lucanist.' This, implying that Lucan's style is pedestrian, is typical of the period. Whereas Daniel is content to be called an annalist, Drayton comments: 'The *Barrons Warres* ... were surely as well for their length in continuance, as for their manifold bloud-shed, and multitude of horrid accidents, meete matter for Trumpet or Tragedie', where, as Mr Leidig remarks, Trumpet stands for epic. The influence of the Cromwellian civil war is apparent: Thomas May, the poet and Long Parliament historian, was a most successful translator of Lucan.

Hostile criticism continues with Dryden, who regarded Lucan as a verse historian, not a poet, and a historical poem as inferior to an epic. Lucan, he claims, is 'wanting both in design and subject'; his main complaint seems to be that the work lacks a hero. Patriotism is also involved, since writers planning a national epic turned to Virgil, not to one who bemoaned the Empire's tyranny and extolled the past glories of the Republic. Some critics exaggerated the historical element in what we should consider mythological epic: John Harvey wrote that the *Iliad* and *Aeneid* were 'built upon certain fact, upon true and Undeniable History'! Mr Leidig rightly gives prominence to Dr James Welwood (mis-spelt Wellwood in most places), who in his introduction to Nicholas Rowe's translation (1718) wrote: 'I hate to oblige a certain set of men, that read the ancients only to find fault with them ... The Pharsalia is properly a historical heroic poem'. Welwood's commonsense approach, disapproving only of Lucan's characterization of Caesar, represented the view prevailing by that time. Hugh Blair, following Voltaire, extended the name 'epic' to a diversity of poems. He looked for taste in poetry, an eighteenth-century preoccupation. After admitting the poet's faults, he wrote: 'The subject of the Pharsalia carries, undoubtedly, all the Epic Grandeur and Dignity; neither does it want unity of object, viz. the Triumph of Caesar over the Roman Liberty'.

The volume concludes with a chapter on the supernatural in historical epic. The first to criticize Lucan, by implication, for avoiding the traditional epic machinery of divine interference was Petronius. William Hayley (1782) drew attention to Petronius's remarks and to his specimen of a civil war poem, interpreted as designed to injure Lucan. Dryden sneered at our poet for this too, complaining that 'he treats you more like a philosopher than a poet . . . In one word, he walks soberly afoot, when he might fly'. John Dennis (1701) commented: 'Virgil's Greatness and his Enthusiasm comes from his Machines, and the Ministry of the Gods, and the other Parts of his Religion; and *Lucan's* Littleness, from his want of those Machines, and that Ministry'. But Voltaire commended Lucan for having laid the gods aside, and his judgement on this issue prevailed.

The chronological limits of the title are strictly adhered to; thus Macaulay's views on Lucan are not included. More investigation into the indebtedness of individual poets to Lucan might have been helpful, and what is given on this is not always accurate. Thus it is wrong to say that Daniel's opening lines are typical of his borrowing from Lucan, since in fact they follow Book 1, lines 1–66 far more closely than the remainder follows other passages of Lucan. The dramatist Thomas Hughes deserves more than a footnote (p. 68, n. 2) with the phrase 'nicht ohne Einfluss', since he borrowed sections of Lucan's poem wholesale. The author has made a judicious assortment of his primary sources, which are well documented and helpfully paraphrased. His use of secondary sources, however, is not extensive enough; thus, although he has consulted G. M. Logan's Harvard thesis (1967), he does not know the present reviewer's 'Lucan and English Literature' in *Neronians and Flavians: Silver Latin I*, edited by D. R. Dudley, Greek and Latin Studies, Classical Literature and its Influence (London, 1972). There is still, no doubt, too much of a gap between the classicist and what this German series quaintly translates as 'Anglo-Saxon language and literature'. Studies such as the present one which may help to fill this gap are most welcome.   O. A. W. DILKE

UNIVERSITY OF LEEDS

Sonnets of the English Renaissance. Selected and edited by J. W. LEVER. (Athlone Renaissance Library) London: University of London, Athlone Press. 1974. iv + 186 pp. £4.00 (£1.50 paperbound).

If it is true that there is no such thing as Shakespearian tragedy (but instead there are the individual tragedies of Shakespeare), it may be at least equally true that there is no such thing as the Renaissance sonnet. Professor Lever was wise to choose the non-committal 'sonnets' rather than 'the sonnet' for his title but 'Renaissance' is also a difficult word. The Preface makes haste to define and justify it: 'These sonnets range over about a hundred years of English history, from the Reformation to the Civil War. Culturally the period had such underlying continuity and such close links with contemporary Europe that it may best be described as the English Renaissance'. In spite of these precautions, however, 'the Renaissance sonnet', running from Petrarch to Donne, appears in the Introduction and becomes the subject of generalization.

Professor Lever has selected from eleven poets: Wyatt, Surrey, Sidney, Spenser, Daniel, Drayton, Shakespeare, Greville, Drummond of Hawthornden, Alabaster, and Donne. This roll-call of names is a pointer to the nature of the anthology. An alternative possibility would have been to print gleanings from lesser known poets, and such a gathering of unfamiliar specimens would have had its own attraction and usefulness. The poets represented in this volume, however, are nearly all well known and most of them are readily accessible. Why then reprint handfuls of their sonnets here?

There are two answers to this question, one given by the editor himself in the Preface. The aim has been, he says, to show 'diversity in unity': to show, that is, by bringing examples of several poets' work together in one volume, what varieties of material, or of approach to the same material, were included within sonnet form. This is a limited and precise objective and its accomplishment makes the book a useful aid to teaching and reading. The second purpose of the anthology is a more ambitious one, not stated explicitly but to be deduced from the style of the Introduction. There the generalizations about 'the Renaissance sonnet' appear to offer the selection as a distillation of the essence of a genre. In that guise the volume is inevitably open to criticism both on the score of the critical attitudes it assumes and also on the grounds that the students who will be attracted by a relatively cheap anthology of this kind may be misled into believing that they need read no further in the sonnets of Shakespeare, say, or of Sidney, because all that they need to know is here.

Professor Lever's selection of poems and his commentary on them are firmly in line with the modern reappraisal of the Elizabethans. Once upon a time, not very long ago, these poets were a nest of singing birds: now they are tough dealers in paradox, intellectually probing, emotionally tense. 'The Renaissance sonnet', as the Introduction tells us, was initiated by Petrarch whose poetry 'involved every level of personality'. Then, much later, in the sixteenth century, Englishmen became aware that boundaries of all kinds could be pushed back, and they developed an interest in, among other areas of exploration, the 'hidden recesses of personality'. 'The Renaissance sonnet' has its function in this context: 'to chart the intimacies of personal experience', to choose 'internal landscapes and penetrate the moment'. Though the poems are not personal as the Romantics understood the word, they are 'preoccupied with an over-riding, all-important engagement of the self with an other, hence with the exploration of a polarity'. It may be thought that these terms are somewhat overweight when applied to many sonnets and sonneteers who are *not* represented here; they seem, moreover, to be only partially true of those that are. The purely literary impulse, the desire to create beautiful, witty, ingenious, skilful structures of words, the ambition also to master and extend the range of expressiveness of the contemporary language in order to create a modern vernacular literature comparable with that of Italy; these impulses, strong certainly in Sidney and Spenser, are given scant attention in this volume. Like the modern approach as a whole, Professor Lever's anthology tells a good deal of truth about the Elizabethans, but not the whole truth. A student who uses the volume will learn much but will still have surprises in store if he ventures to read for himself unselected poems or poets.

The fairly extensive notes include indications of sources and analogues. This is useful, especially as the point has been firmly made in the Introduction that imitation, as the Elizabethans practised it, in no way precluded originality. Altogether, a few slips apart, this is a very efficient production. Those who know the field will appreciate the skill with which the editor has presented his material. Those who do not may be overpersuaded on some points but will find themselves in possession of some splendid poems for their admiration and delight.

UNIVERSITY OF BIRMINGHAM   JOAN REES

Elizabethan Prisons and Prison Scenes. By E. D. PENDRY. (Salzburg Studies in English
Literature, Elizabethan and Renaissance Studies, 17) Salzburg: Institut für
Englische Sprache und Literatur, Universität Salzburg. 1974.   Two volumes.
vi + 385 pp.   £4.60.

Of the Elizabethan and Jacobean playwrights, Professor Pendry reminds us,
'Jonson, Chapman, Dekker, Lyly, Tourneur, Chettle, Daborne and Haughton —
and probably Middleton, Massinger and Field' had spent periods in gaol. And to
their audiences the prison, visible or off stage, was a familiar element in contemporary drama. Professor Pendry has searched beyond the theatre to the realities
of prison life. The result is a wide ranging study which explores the great variety
of London penal institutions and sets them in the framework of the social and
literary context. Within the limited compass of a modestly sized work, he has used
the historical sources to good effect to explain and illustrate the harsh facts of
London prison life, scarcely removed from the squalid episodes of theatrical fiction.
But not all prisons were alike. In their organizations and practices, and in their
internal divisions, they reflected the gradations of social hierarchy. The prisoners
themselves ranged from hardened criminals through to unfortunate debtors trapped
in their innocence or caught in the downward swing of an economic depression,
on to state prisoners, and prisoners for conscience, the Catholic recusants who both
flourished and were persecuted in the capital. Their conditions varied; the Clink
offered the greatest measure of comfort. With duplicate keys the Catholics could
let themselves in and out of gaol, hold services in their private chapel and, under
the leadership of a skilful priest, they became the brain centre for underground
work throughout London. Holding, no doubt, that missionary work, like charity,
should begin at home, they converted the gaoler to their faith. But not all Catholic
prisoners were so well served.
   Ludgate, too, providing for delinquent freemen of the City, had its attractive
features with prisoner participation, through a self-governing committee system,
and with accompanied outings for trusted inmates for pleasure or business. It was,
however, the Fleet which was a five-star establishment for those who could afford
to pay for their comforts; but it contained also foul dungeons for poor prisoners
and was the frequent scene of disorders. Newgate conditions could be ghastly except
that the prison officers could be incompetent in their duties: squalor tempered by
inefficiency.
   The latter part of the volume turns specifically to the literary sources. There is a
very interesting chapter which examines the notions aroused in the contemporary
mind by the idea of a prison, as well as the metaphors it provoked; but the last
chapters, concerned with dramatic productions themselves, extend over too many
examples and we cannot see the theatre for the plays. That apart, Professor Pendry
has made a useful and realistic contribution to our understanding of the social and
theatrical scene. An uncovenanted consequence is that it provides one more
antidote to the 'Merrie England' school of history of G. M. Trevelyan and his
successors. The illustrations and reproductions of texts are well chosen; but one
can only deplore that so scholarly a work appears without an index.

UNIVERSITY COLLEGE, LONDON   JOEL HURSTFIELD

The Frame Structure in Tudor and Stuart Drama. By STEVEN C. YOUNG. (Salzburg
Studies in English Literature, Elizabethan and Renaissance Studies, 6)
Salzburg: Institut für Englische Sprache und Literatur, Universität Salzburg.
1974. vi + 189 pp.

This book attempts to describe the relationship between a frame plot and the play
within it, and then assesses the effect of that relationship on the completed play.

In Mr Young's definition, the frame plot exists on a different narrative plane from that of the central play, has at least two speaking roles, and is a complete dramatic action. A list of frame plays before 1642 is supplied, which surprisingly omits Beaumont (or Field) and Fletcher's *Four Plays, or Moral Representations, in One* and Greene's *Alphonsus, King of Aragon*. It is puzzling, too, that on page 6 Mr Young should have miscounted his own earlier check list of induction plays (*PQ*, 48, No. 1 (January 1969), 131–4). There are, unfortunately, twenty-five misquotations, and a dozen slips in the text (including, on page 8, a reference to 'Vendici [*sic*], holding the skull of his murdered financé'). Other mistakes include the assertion on page 31 that the ghosts in Jasper Fisher's *Fuimus Troes* remain separate from the central narrative: in fact, they urge Nennius and Caesar into battle (II.7). But the argument of the book is cogent, illuminating of the plays discussed, and intelligent about the frame structure itself. Mr Young considers the frame a limited form (dramatists other than Ben Jonson tended to use it once and once only) but considers that it provides a unique opportunity to control an audience's response. This response will be a double one, involving objectivity about the dramatic illusion and, simultaneously, identification with it.

Mr Young distinguishes three kinds of frame plot: 'supernatural', 'narrative', and 'extra-dramatic'. The first, and largest, group employs gods, ghosts, fairies, and personifications such as Truth or Fortune. Because of the powers invested in these characters the balance between frame and play is tricky. If the frame is too extensive (as in the anonymous *A Warning for Fair Women*) it can reduce the significance of the inner play; if the play is too complicated (as in Greene's *The Scottish History of James IV*) it can operate against the frame. In *The Spanish Tragedy*, however, Kyd successfully utilizes the determinism inherent in the 'supernatural frame' to create a unified play, not of revenge but of sin and retribution, with Andrea's predominantly silent presence reminding the audience of the first in a series of bloody deeds.

A 'narrative frame', such as the frame of Peele's *The Old Wives Tale*, involves ordinary mortals in an action which merely provides a context for the play within. But in *The Taming of the Shrew* induction and play proper operate as two units which, in combination, develop the central idea about marriage. A series of problematic 'supposes' in both units establishes the interdependence of illusion and reality which forms the basis of Shakespeare's idea; the abandonment of the frame structure is a function of the Sly story's inability to reflect the development of that interdependency.

In the third and final group, 'extra-dramatic frames', the characters appear to belong to the world of the audience. This can create a complex dramatic structure, and while Mr Young admires Jonson's handling of the problem in *Every Man out of his Humour* he admits that the inner play, for all the reinforcement of its truths by the realistic treatment of comparable elements in the frame, is 'flattened' in the process. The discussion of *The Staple of News*, whose frame is dismissed as redundant, might be read beside the relevant section in Richard Levin's *The Multiple Plot in English Renaissance Drama* (1971). There the analysis, involving as it does a more flexible interpretation of 'frame', suggests some limitation in Mr Young's approach, which is refreshingly strong on dramatic effect but sometimes weak on the analysis of ideas.

NEIL TAYLOR

LONDON

Swordplay and the Elizabethan and Jacobean Stage. By ROBERT E. MORSBERGER.
　　(Salzburg Studies in English Literature, Jacobean Drama Studies, 37) Salz-
　　burg: Institut für Englische Sprache und Literatur, Universität Salzburg.
　　1974. iv + 129 pp. £4.80.

This slight work is hardly more than a résumé of what has been written on the
subject in the past hundred years or so. In a sense such a product is unavoidable,
given the closed nature of the subject: closed, that is, to possibilities of new interpretation or fresh insight. Nevertheless, an impression of a certain perfunctoriness
in its composition is inescapable. Early chapters describe briefly the type of weapons
used in fencing and duelling, different techniques of the native and Italian schools
of fence, and the code of the duello which accompanied the rapier to England.
The rest of the book tells us in what ways the contemporary theatre and drama
reflected these interests. It is, however, in this area that the impression of perfunctoriness is felt most. Recognizing that 'it would be futile' to analyse the plots of all
the plays which contain swordfights, the author chooses eighteen plays (of widely
varying merit) to make these two points. The swordfights in four of these lend
support to those who hold the view that such displays were nothing more than
demonstrations of skill in fence of the actor-duellist. The remaining fourteen show
that such sword play was often 'made a focal point of plot and an integral part of
character'. We are not told though if this is the definitive list or a random sample of
such plays. There is a chapter on the duel in *Hamlet*.

ERNST DE CHICKERA

LA TROBE UNIVERSITY

*Renaissance Dramatic Bawdy (Exclusive of Shakespeare): An Annotated Glossary and
　　Critical Essays*. By JAMES T. HENKE. (Salzburg Studies in English Literature,
　　Jacobean Drama Studies, 39 and 40) Salzburg: Institut für Englische Sprache
　　und Literatur, Universität Salzburg. 1974. Two volumes. xxiv + 345 pp.
　　£9.60.

Volume 1 of this work contains accounts of glossarial procedure together with
essays on two plays, *The White Devil* and *A Trick to Catch the Old One*. These play-
discussions are complementary to the glossary which fills Volume 2 in giving some
idea of how the bawdy functions contextually. That on Middleton's play is particularly effective in establishing the equations of wit with sexual potency and
stupidity with impotence as a structural feature.

　　Professor Henke discusses the several classes of word with which he has to deal:
those with bawdy primary or secondary meanings, and those where the bawdy
may be 'entirely dependent upon dramatic context'. The texts subjected to
investigation on this basis are those twenty-eight anthologized by Hazelton
Spencer in his *Elizabethan Plays* (Boston, 1933). Generally, only 'the first use of a
bawdy term in the Spencer canon plus later significant variations' is given. This is
explained by the declaration that the glossary 'aims to assist the reader. It does not
intend to do his job for him. With the reader rests the primary responsibility of
making his own interpretations'.

　　But things are not quite so straightforward as this latter statement suggests.
Professor Henke's own use of predecessors well illustrates how the veriest specula-
tion or idiosyncratic usage is apt to harden into unassailable authority. The entry
on *Pinch'd ware*, for instance, is a too facile assumption via Eric Partridge. Because
Falstaff's pox pinches we can scarcely claim a syphilitic link with *pinching* in
Bartholomew Fair. There is more merit to the suggestion that *White leprosy* = 'pox';
but both a tentative Partridge and unwitting Van Fossen are mustered in support.
Again resting on Partridge, Professor Henke mistakenly suggests that *What* =

'vagina' when Pride remarks to Faustus, 'indeed I do — what do I not'; and his glossing of *Pox* as both 'syphilis' and 'plague' stems from a careless misreading of Partridge. Grose, too, defining *Stranger* as 'a guinea' is alleged to mean not the coin but a prostitute.

Errors of this sort (another is the view that *Making ducks and drakes with shillings* alludes to the proverbial evacuating of ducks) are easily detected and avoided. Other areas can be more difficult to assess. These include over-enthusiastic following of Kökeritz, and a tendency to find more puns on *cunt* than can be readily countenanced. Jonson's Ursula, for instance, yields 'a man of rec*kon*ing'. Likewise, innuendos of oragenitalism are too often proposed without basis. The suggestion that the *O* of the Bridewell whores (*2 Honest Whore*) refers beyond a cry of pain to 'the shaping of the lips' in fellatio is absurd. And cunnilingus in *The White Devil* (III.1.31–5) or *A Trick to Catch the Old One* (*Tongue with a great T*) is extremely doubtful. Certainly primacy should have been given to a glance at ithyphallic shape in the latter instance. Again, in Jonson's 'Your fool he is your great man's darling, | And your ladies' sport and pleasure; | Tongue and bauble are his treasure', *tongue* casts back to the great man (no sexual implication), and only *bauble* to the ladies. What makes this area especially troublesome is that while four-letter words and oragenitalism feature in Elizabethan writings, they are very much a sub-surface phenomenon. They need the most careful excavation and provenance or the whole process becomes worse than futile, its excesses apt to disfigure the work of succeeding editors and lexicographers.

Bawdy punning on foreign words also requires circumspection. 'I am prest to give you succor' is thought to glance at cunnilingus through the French *succer*; though Cotgrave is even less help here than would be the English suck[er]. But this is *The Knight of the Burning Pestle*, a play of which Professor Henke remarks that 'in the light of Beaumont's affinity for sexual innuendo [no possibility] should be ruled out'. None is. Still less comprehensible is *See* meaning 'to lecher' by way of *soye* (Cotgrave); and this ramifies into a further entry, *Seen in it*. Yet such puns do occur so it is especially important that the idea should not be made disreputable. The same is true of Elizabethan uses which have survived into modern American slang. But *Pulses* won't yield 'pussy', nor will *Madam Suppository*, which means 'whore' by associations of filthiness (compare *common Shore*).

The bawdy permutations are heaped up vertiginously, with too little regard for function. There is some wild double-jumping: 'take 'em altogether' (see under *Playhouse poultry*) not only involves a play on 'take' but possibly *altogether* = 'as a whole', punning on 'hole' (vagina). The 'rare-witted gentlemen' in Marlowe's *Jew of Malta* become *rare-wetted*, the 'wet' being alcohol but also perhaps semen. Equally grotesque is *Wee'* [wi'] *yer daughter*, glossed as 'piss on your daughter'. Even if 'wee' in that sense had a pre-Victorian existence, the entry would still defy repair.

Professor Henke is largely concerned with areas where very fine discrimination is essential. He can be extremely erratic, so that his glossary needs using with the utmost caution. But he does have a good nose for sniffing out suspect passages, and often enough he has helpful things to say. There is some astute controversion at *Polecat*, for example; and he exposes the eunuch-reference in 'a king of spades' (*Shoemakers' Holiday*, see under *Delve*). Had he more conspicuously allied rigour with his enviable vigour, this contribution to a still thinly covered field could have been given a less qualified welcome.

GORDON WILLIAMS

ST DAVID'S UNIVERSITY COLLEGE, LAMPETER

Markets of Bawdrie: The Dramatic Criticism of Stephen Gosson. By ARTHUR F. KINNEY.
    (Salzburg Studies in English Literature, Elizabethan Studies, 4) Salzburg:
    Institut für Englische Sprache und Literatur, Universität Salzburg. 1974.
    viii + 291 pp. £4.60.

In these days one should be grateful for any modern edition of works by an author
such as Stephen Gosson (1554–1624), who is more often referred to at second hand
than actually read; so the fact that this contribution to the Salzburg Studies has
been produced by the offset method need cause no misgivings. What does provoke
surprise, however, is that such exhaustive scholarly effort has been expended on
the compilation of a book which, considered as a 'working' text, is almost as
confusing as some of the manuals of programmed instruction in current use in some
quarters. Considering the scale of the undertaking, Professor Kinney has perhaps
placed on offer a trifle too much. Not only has he supplied a life of Gosson and an
account of the author's critical position: he has given us *The Schoole of Abuse* (1579)
in full, together with two other related pamphlets (*An Apologie of the Schoole of Abuse*
and *Playes Confuted in Five Actions*) and subsidiary material. There is also some
elaborate bibliographical commentary, and accounts of textual variants as well as
textual and explanatory notes. It is always helpful to have reliable explications of
works so seldom submitted to editorial attention, but Professor Kinney's apparatus
is top-heavy and the layout of the book as a whole is something of an impediment to
straightforward reading.

    The Introduction, which makes an attempt 'through tracing Gosson's life and
writings in humanistic terms, to understand his success in his own time' (p. 3),
forms a useful background to *The Schoole of Abuse* and its sequels. The various
elements of Gosson's thought are followed up, and the nature of his attack on
'Poets, and Pipers, and such peevish cattel' studied in detail. The ground is not
unfamiliar: but the contrast with Sidney is neatly set out on page 36, where it is
explained that the two men differed in their conception of the imagination:
Gosson remaining true to the teachings of Plato, Cicero, and Augustine; Sidney
adopting a more recognizably 'Renaissance' viewpoint. Professor Kinney argues
that although the *Defence of Poesie* is in many ways a response to *The Schoole of
Abuse*, Sidney did in fact misinterpret Gosson in some important particulars. Yet
after the massive footnote 78 (pp. 44–6) little more need be said about the Gosson–
Sidney relationship, and it is useful to have the authoritative discussion of Gosson's
rhetorical schemata. In this analytical section Professor Kinney has possibly forced
his advocacy of Gosson's versatility a little too far; for in spite of what he tells us
about the 'structuring' of Gosson's style, few would contend that *The Schoole of
Abuse* now comes to life in the way Sidney's *Apologie* does. His mode of address is,
indeed, 'wavering', eclectic, or (some would say) plain patchy. In this edition Gosson
has not been helped by the decision to use old-style spelling. The Explanatory
Notes refer not to the editor's own pagination but to the signature letters and figures
of the original texts. As a 'finding device' this is simply infuriating. Also irritating
is the editor's practice of loading explanations upon us while at the same time withholding information that would be genuinely illuminating. Thus in the notes
(p. 270) applicable to page 140 we are given the STC numbers of ten 'other works'
dedicated to Sir Francis Walsingham between 1579 and 1582 (gratuitous, surely,
even if it does indicate Walsingham's generous patronage): yet the incident involving Callicratides (recorded, we are told, in Cicero and Xenophon) is not set in its
context at all. Elsewhere opportunities for meaningful annotation are missed,
though some quite trivial matters are given excessive explanation, and the abbreviation 'cf.' is much in evidence! The note on 'Torpedo', for example (p. 235) is
largely *de trop* since Gosson's own reduction of what he found in Plutarch's *Moralia*

is self-explanatory. And was it really necessary to trace every proverbial expression Gosson uses to its location in M. P. Tilley's *Dictionary*?

Despite the fact that *Markets of Bawdrie* has now made available some important examples of Elizabethan pamphleteering, I find Professor Kinneys' work less enlightening than William Ringler's *Stephen Gosson* (1942), mainly because in Ringler's book Gosson's essential idiom is more sharply focused. It is, of course, easy enough to complain when the dull duties of an editor have not been discharged altogether to one's liking. In this case there was indeed much to be said for attempting 'to render a text accessible to a wide spectrum of readers' (p. 70). I cannot feel, however, that the present edition is likely to do this. Perhaps an approach in which unquestionable erudition had been less deliberately obtruded would have served the author's interest rather better.

E. D. MACKERNESS

UNIVERSITY OF SHEFFIELD

The Chronicle of King Edward the First, Surnamed Longshanks with The Life of Lluellen, Rebel in Wales. By GEORGE PEELE. Edited by G. K. DREHER. Chicago, Illinois: Adams. 1974. xlvi + 96 pp. $5.95.

On the verso of the frontispiece, Mr Dreher announces: 'The aim of this edition is to provide a retroform, a few unriddles in the text, modern spelling and punctuation, and an introduction for readers who are not familiar with the play'. The introduction does indeed seem aimed at arousing interest. The text has no apparatus, notes, or line numbers (line numbers and scene numbers below are from the Yale edition). Scholars will be interested only in the 'retroform' and some of the 'unriddles'. Mr Dreher accepts the argument, advanced in the Yale edition, that an original version containing more historical episodes than survive in the quarto was altered to include material derived from two ballads, most of which is incorporated into the scenes leading to the spectacular sinking of Queen Elinor at Charing Cross, her subsequent resurrection at Queenhithe, and her deathbed confession of adultery. 'The retroform . . . is simply a search for Peele's version before the redrafting' (p. xviii).

The retroform is arrived at mainly by cutting and rearranging, generally along the lines suggested in the Yale edition. Except for the omission of twenty-one lines in Scene 3, Mr Dreher's text and the Yale text are substantially the same until midway through Scene 10 (l. 1630). From that point on the alterations are drastic. Scenes 11 and 12 are reversed. The material villifying Queen Elinor is excised: the last half of Scene 10, all of Scenes 15, 18, 20, the last two-thirds of Scene 21, and all of Scene 23 except the last seventy-five lines, which are divided between two earlier scenes. There are a number of smaller cuts and rearrangements. The retroform concludes with Scene 22 of the Yale edition.

One would hardly maintain that the result is a masterpiece. Elinor and Joan die offstage; the cause of death is never made known. Despite Mr Dreher's claim that his version provides a 'good curtain', the ending seems lamentably lame. But since Peele's revision undoubtedly necessitated cutting a number of scenes (including the original death scene for Queen Elinor) which, short of some miracle, cannot be recovered, any effort to remake the original from extant material is doomed to failure. Yet it is interesting to read a version in which the effort is made to recover what can be recovered. What he presents justifies Mr Dreher's claim that the original 'centers on the passionate duel between the king and a rebel' and might very well have eventually had its title shortened to 'Longshanks and Lluellen' (p. xix).

In a modernized version which sets itself a goal that necessitates a good deal of textual tinkering, there is not much point in cavilling about details. Since there is no textual apparatus it is not always easy to decide what is emendation and what is error. Clearly, though, 'honore' at line 78 is an error. Modernizing is hardly adequate reason for altering 'bide' to 'abide' (l. 435), 'thee' to 'that' (l. 442), 'have' to 'be' (l. 884). In a modernized text one might expect 'Aegeus' (l. 570), even though it is a dissyllable, and 'that's' for 'that' (l. 1183).

Some of the 'unriddles' are interesting. At line 1193, 'in deserts with Onophrius ever dwell' is very likely correct (though 'with' should have been bracketed to conform with the editorial procedure elsewhere in the volume). Inserting a full stop after 'yield' and adding 'band' at the end of line 1234 gives sense to an otherwise incomprehensible line, though I would not wish to defend the reading on any other ground. At line 1239 'To see Mnemosyne in disguise' is the best effort yet at correcting an obviously erroneous passage. 'Thee' for 'thine' in line 1257 is less satisfactory. 'See thou' for the impossible 'we there' in l. 1435 is the best of many attempts to remedy that line. Between ll. 1046 and 1047 something is obviously missing in the quarto text, and it must have referred to England. Mr Dreher tries to fill the gap by adding 'England for me, madam, while you are there', which is adapted from l. 1051. Given Peele's penchant for rhetorical devices based on repetition and parallelism, this is not a bad idea, but, unfortunately, it still leaves a solecism (no verb for 'England').

Since this volume may be difficult to locate, would-be readers may be interested in the note on the verso of the title page: 'Copies of this book may be obtained by sending $5.95 check or m.o. to Longshanks Book, 20 Church St., Mystic, Conn. 06355'.

Frank S. Hook

Lehigh University

George Chapman: Action and Contemplation in his Tragedies. By Peter Bement. (Salzburg Studies in English Literature, Jacobean Drama Studies, 8) Salzburg: Institut für Englische Sprache und Literatur, Universität Salzburg. 1974. ii + 292 pp.

Character in Relation to Action in the Tragedies of George Chapman. By Derek Crawley. (Salzburg Studies in English Literature, Jacobean Drama Studies, 16) Salzburg: Institut für Englische Sprache und Literatur, Universität Salzburg. 1974. iv + 202 pp.

These two books are of very different kinds despite their superficially similar titles. 'Character in Relation to Action' is one of those topics which seem to have been dreamed up (or, in this case, borrowed) to give a gratuitous new twist to a fairly well-worn subject; and I must say that I find it a very difficult concept to grasp. Luckily it is only in the brief Introduction and Conclusion that we are asked to focus closely on this issue. The rest of Dr Crawley's book offers a straightforward reading of Chapman's six tragedies and a fairly conventional account of the changing philosophical views which they evince; and if a single theme dominates at all it is a slightly different (and more manageable) one, which might be defined as 'Didacticism Versus Drama'.

Dr Bement's 'Action and Contemplation' has a much more authentic ring to it; and he is in fact sometimes a little too painstaking in his efforts to establish the historical validity of his terms of reference. But his study is afflicted by problems of a different kind. We are asked to see in Chapman's tragedies a development from Contemplation to Action which is at the same time a development from Neo-Platonism to Stoicism. Yet these two sets of concepts would seem to be related only tenuously, if at all: to Chapman at any rate Neo-Platonism could be a philosophy of Action, and Stoicism could be (and usually was, I should have thought) a philosophy of Contemplation. The business of Action and Contemplation would have been better treated at a greater distance (if not in total isolation) from the more conventional issue of Chapman's philosophical development.

Still there can be no doubt that Dr Bement's is the better book. Dr Crawley's is pedestrian in style and content. Its shortcomings are to some extent epitomized in the discussion of 'The Order of Chapman's Tragedies' in Chapter 1: no new points are made (and at least one important old one is omitted) so that the whole business might have been reduced to a bare chronological table. The point omitted, incidentally, is Norma Dobie Solve's persuasive case for dating *Chabot* later than 1621; and Dr Crawley's neglect of this bedevils his argument once again in Chapter 7, where he spends most of his time discussing the authorship of *Chabot* and assigning to Shirley passages in which 'Stoic doctrine . . . has been undermined in ways which Chapman would never have approved'. If Mrs Solve is right, of course, *Chabot* belongs a good ten years after Chapman's Stoic phase and, as G. de Forest Lord has suggested in his study of Chapman's *Odyssey*, he was himself quite capable of undermining Stoic doctrine by then.

Dr Bement is much more sensitive as a critic and stylist. His readings of the two *Bussy* plays are particularly stimulating (though I cannot agree that the darkness in which Bussy himself moves is a 'stepdame night of mind', or that he is anything less than ideal); and his brief treatment of Chapman's comedies in Chapter 2 warrants expansion. Other sections of the book, however, are thin, repetitious, and often poorly arranged. The frequent digressions into the intellectual background of the age are particularly annoying: all this material should have been collected together early in the book.

Thus Dr Crawley's study seems to me to have very little value at all, while Dr Bement's is valuable only in parts; and it is a little disconcerting to find that these parts have already appeared in the shape of periodical articles. I cannot see that anything has been gained by reproducing them in the company of lesser material, and I must confess to a sinking feeling that the Salzburg Studies in English Literature are (by their very nature) likely to incur the same sort of charge fairly frequently.

R. P. CORBALLIS

UNIVERSITY OF CANTERBURY
New Zealand

The Widow's Tears. By GEORGE CHAPMAN. Edited by AKIHIRO YAMADA. (The Revels Plays) London: Methuen. 1975. lxxxvi + 152 pp. £9.50.

This edition, which is not available in paperback, is more than ten times as dear as the paperback form of E. M. Smeak's Regents edition; so it has to have pretty substantial advantages to offer. It is, of course, much fuller, but it would be idle to pretend that more than a handful of students will find what it adds essential for their purposes. (Sales, one imagines, will be almost entirely to libraries.) However, it is the sort of edition Professor Yamada was commissioned to produce, and I do not wish to pursue the subject of the economics of publishing, though it is hard to banish it from one's mind.

The lengthy Introduction explores fully almost every topic that one could think of, in a scholarly and intelligent fashion. In the 'Survey of Critical Opinions', two dates need to be corrected. Langbaine first noted the Petronius source not in the *Account* of 1691 but in the *Momus Triumphans* of 1687; and John Palmer's *Comedy* was published not '*c.* 1923?' but in May 1914 (*English Catalogue*), which makes it a more strikingly early tribute to the play. The staging is interestingly discussed, but the 'out' of 'take out' (iii.2.108.1) has no relation to a stage 'out' or 'in', but is simply OED 85c (whose first quotation, from *Henry VIII*, it antedates). In the discussion of the source, quotations from Petronius are given only in Latin. Though the whole story is given in translation in an Appendix, the reader completely without Latin will find this inconvenient. On page xxvii, 'far more superior' should be 'far superior'. On page liii, note 7, there are a few slips in Greek. In the Introduction and in the notes on the Dramatis Personae, Professor Yamada is too ready to treat names as significant; Tharsalio certainly, and there may be a play on opposed meanings of Argus, but I doubt if anything can plausibly be made etymologically of Lysander (though the Spartan commander may be glanced at) or of Arsace.

Apart from a few probably insoluble muddles attributable to the foul papers, the text presents few difficulties, and I seldom quarrel with the editor's choices. At v.4.45, I still prefer (see *N & Q*, 219 (1974), 290) my 'Truth paces' (Q 'Truth pace is') to his 'Truth-pace is': an unnatural compound, and not such an appropriate subject for 'sets' in the next line as the simple 'Truth'. A few lines below this, 'Lycus — his' for 'Lycus his' can only be explained as the result of unfamiliarity with a common form of expression. Another passage involving punctuation is iv.1.69–70: 'My mind misgave me. | They might be mountaineers.' Most editors retain this rather breathless construction. Smeak reduces the full stop to a semi-colon. But surely 'They . . . mountaineers' is a subordinate clause: probably a comma in the manuscript, no stop in a modernized text. The only substantive emendation I should be inclined to propose is 'got' for 'get' at ii.2.68 (supported by l. 33, 'How came she by such a jewel?'). At iv.2.78, 'Good, hear him, this is a rare soldier' is unobjectionable in metre and idiom, as Smeak recognizes. There is no need to read 'Good mistress'. At iv.2.186, Reed's 'fast'st' for 'fasts' is unaccountably accepted. At ii.3.193, 'grudges.' for 'grudges,' must be a mere misprint; so, probably, the unrecorded (and certainly unnecessary) 'That' for 'The' at v.5.8. At i.1.155, the construction is clearer if we retain the Q comma after 'palace'. There is an infelicitous metrical emendation at iv.2.129. 'Than th'' [Q the] racked value of thy entire body', which, in the usage of this edition, should be 'rackèd'. The source of the trouble is failure to see that 'entire' is stressed on the first syllable. At iii.2.40, Professor Yamada does well not to follow Smeak and Ornstein in accepting Parrott's 'What ails [Q aile] you'. But he ought not to concede that it 'may be defended'; it cannot, if we consult OED *ail* v. 4. Ironically, it may even be a misprint, not an emendation, in Parrott, who introduces it silently.

One failure in modernization is at ii.4.266, where 'past' is retained, though 'passed' is required, as Smeak saw.

It is noted (p. lxxxv) that the critical apparatus 'is not a historical collation'. But it is too close to being one: it is cluttered up with trivial errors from earlier editions. At v.5.292, it gives 'from', which Parrott conjectured though he did not read it, to Ornstein (who duly credited it to Parrott).

The commentary errs on the side of fullness, but is generally careful and accurate. But a few remarks may be made. i.2.14–15: The idea of Ulysses stopping his own ears against the Sirens, which Parrott traced back to Ascham, is in no less a scholar than Erasmus (*Pietas Puerilis*). i.2.25–6: no doubt the brackets here indicate an aside, but that is no reason for so interpreting them at lines 43, 50–51, and 60–61 where no other editor has suspected an aside. i.3.151–2: the 'ass charged with crowns to make way to the fort' has nothing to do with the Trojan Horse: see, rather, Tilley A356. ii.3.22: 'sciatica', as in Shakespeare, has strong venereal connotations. ii.4.109: to refer to OED's '1588' for *Love's Labour's Lost* as 'an error for 1598' might suggest a misprint, whereas it is a deliberate, though erroneous, dating. III.1.38: 'wrapped in careless cloak' is from the opening line in Surrey's poem in *Tottel's Miscellany*, No. 26 (noted by Rollins in his 1965 Additional Notes). IV.2.115: in 'And do thou eat', 'And' cannot possibly mean 'if'; 'eat' is inoperative. IV.2.158: 'spinners' seems to mean 'daddy-long-legs', not 'spiders', as at *Romeo and Juliet*, 1.4.60, on which see A. S. Cairncross, *N & Q*, 220 (1975), 166. IV.3.38: 'God's me' (Q Gods me) — editors are silent, but OED identifies as an abbreviation of 'God save me': *God* 8b. V.5.130: 'replenished' is simply 'filled', not 'filled up again'.

†J. C. Maxwell

Balliol College, Oxford

A Critical Edition of Robert Greene's 'Ciceronis Amor: Tullies Love'. Edited by Charles Howard Larson. (Salzburg Studies in English Literature, Elizabethan and Renaissance Studies, 36) Salzburg: Institut für Englische Sprache und Literatur, Universität Salzburg. 1974. lxi + 156 pp.

This is the first critical edition of Greene's 'novel' since A. B. Grosart's in 1881–7. Clearly Mr Larson's aim has been (1) to present the reader with a correct text, arrived at by the employment of the bibliographical techniques developed since Grosart's time; and (2) to equip it with a literary introduction which discusses the work as an example of Elizabethan prose fiction rather than as a document in the early development of the English novel proper. He has performed these tasks with limited success.

First, the text. Mr Larson establishes the relationship between the nine early editions convincingly; and, basing his edition correctly on the 1589 Quarto, is wisely conservative in his emendations, most of which are confined to changes in punctuation. Among his substantive alterations, those adopting the readings of Quartos 2 to 9 on pages 104 and 112 are unnecessary; the acceptance of Grosart's reading on page 51 is debatable; and those on pages 36, 44, 81, 82, and 93 are excellent, with notes giving sound arguments for their adoption. The most puzzling point in the text (p. 119, ll. 22–3), which the editor deals with intelligently in his commentary, is perhaps susceptible to solution by simple re-punctuation, as '*Terentia* the daughter of *Flaminius*. That firebrand that set *Troy* to cinders, Beauty, is like to bring *Roome* to confusion'. The appendices recording the Emendations of Accidentals, the Historical Collation, and the Changes in Paragraphing are useful and accurate; but those detailing the first Quarto's type faces and signature divisions should more properly appear in accepted codified form in the description of the copy-text given on pages xlv and xlvi.

The textual work is of a high order generally, which makes it surprising that the analysis of the skeleton formes is rendered unusable, without a good deal of extra work by the reader, by the editor's decision to follow the 1589 Quarto's erroneous pagination rather than its signatures for the setting out of his evidence. In his analysis of the distribution of the formes, Mr Larson accurately detects the printing breaks in Sheets B, H, I, and K; but makes rather heavy going of the imposition peculiarities in Sheets H and K. In Sheet H, the inner skeleton has simply been turned to set the outer forme, which is a common enough occurrence in books of the period; and in Sheet K, the formes of Sheet I have been exchanged and turned.

The footnotes are sensible and adequate, with some of them showing a real success in clarifying the occasional murk of Greene's prose. The introductory sections on the author, date, sources, and popularity of the work are a succinct and judicious digest of the work of earlier scholars; though perhaps some setting of the piece in the context of Greene's prose canon would have been helpful.

In the critical evaluation, the opening paragraphs promise much, as they rightly point out that, owing largely to the influence of Northrop Frye, 'Greene and most of the other Elizabethan authors of prose fiction are no longer seen as novelists *manqués*, but are instead considered to be writers working in quite a separate form'. However, the promise is not fulfilled. The characterization and plot are discussed using much the same critical vocabulary as that appropriate for, say, Hardy or Dickens. For example, we find this on Terentia: 'She too is a stylised character, but not so much as she has no human warmth' (p. xxvii); or this on the plot: 'There are, to be sure, some improbabilities in the plot but they are not without human causes' (p. xxx). It is only in the section dealing with the style that we find a few fruitful suggestions and some evidence of the kind of modern reappraisal of Greene's writing that Mr Larson obviously wished to offer.

NORMAN SANDERS

UNIVERSITY OF TENNESSEE

The Poetry of Robert Southwell, S.J. By JOSEPH D. SCALLON, S. J. (Salzburg Studies in English Literature, Elizabethan and Renaissance Studies, 11) Salzburg: Institut für Englische Sprache und Literatur, Universität Salzburg. 1975. xiv + 235 pp.

This book, prepared evidently some eight years ago though published only recently, is in effect a résumé of what is already known about Southwell's life and poetry. Father Scallon has given thought and care to the materials, however, and the fruit of his work is a modest contribution to sympathetic understanding. No major reassessment of Southwell emerges but comments on, and some modifications of, the work of Nancy Pollard Brown and others are suggested. Father Scallon himself pays particular attention to the influence of Counter-Reformation thinking on Southwell's poetry and to the connexions between Southwell's activities as poet and as mission priest. The poetry of repentance, for example, is studied as derivative from a contemporary continental interest and also as relevant to the schismatics and other backsliders whom Southwell as priest hoped to bring to repent.

'Readers', writes Father Scallon, 'will agree or disagree that "Of the Blessed Sacrament" is poetry in accordance with their convictions concerning that mystery'. To some extent this comment holds true of much of Southwell's poetry and, after an interesting discussion of the long passage in 'St Peter's Complaint' about the eyes of Christ, the author acknowledges that 'a recognition of the theological and ascetical background of these stanzas . . . may not justify them as literature'. Yet Southwell wrote more than 'The Burning Babe' which deserves to be known and the analyses in this book of the poems on Christ and the Virgin Mary, and of that remarkable nature poem called 'A Vale of Tears', are contributions to this end.

Southwell's ambition, to persuade poets by his example to renounce the lusts of the flesh as their material, and to adopt instead 'solemne and devout matter', makes an interesting point in literary history. Greater poets were to take up the task, although Father Scallon's claim, that the divine poems of Donne, Herbert, Crashawe, Milton, and (surprisingly in this list) Dryden, testify to the efficacy of Southwell's efforts, is hardly convincing. Southwell's own attempts to convert the themes and styles of his contemporaries to religious uses are not very good but the cross-references from poem to poem hold some fascination for a student of late sixteenth-century poetry. 'What joy to live?', for instance, is based on a much handled poem of Petrarch's. 'Content and rich' is a version of Dyer's 'My mind to me a kingdom is' and 'A Phansie turned to a sinner's complaint' is closely modelled on another Dyer poem, 'A Fancy'. Father Scallon does not notice that Fulke Greville also wrote a companion piece to this second Dyer poem, *Caelica*, 83.

Greville's strenuous and subtle intelligence charges the ostensible plea of a discarded lover with an extraordinary range of meaning and this example is typical of his 'love' poetry. Even in the earliest written of the *Caelica* poems, the handling of conventional images and themes is edged with awareness that the objects of secular love poetry are over-prized by their lovers' adoration. Greville had no sympathy with Roman Catholicism and his whole cast of mind was different from Southwell's but, in their ultimate dedication of poetry to the service of religious truth, it is a somewhat ironic fact that these two very different men make common cause. The tough statesman, however, with his sharper wit and his many-layered treatment of human experience, is a greater poet than the gentle Jesuit priest.

UNIVERSITY OF BIRMINGHAM   JOAN REES

The Evolution of Michael Drayton's 'Idea'. By LOUISE HUTCHINGS WESTLING. (Salzburg Studies in English Literature, Elizabethan and Renaissance Studies, 37) Salzburg: Institut für Englische Sprache und Literatur, Universität Salzburg. 1974. viii + 187 pp.

Michael Drayton was an indefatigable reviser of his own poetry, and though the revisions in his sonnets were not so conspicuous as the transformation of *Mortimeriados* to *The Barons Warres* (from rhyme royal to *ottava rima*), or of *Endimion and Phoebe* to *The Man in the Moone* (from epyllion to satire), they deserve investigation. There were, in effect, six editions of the sonnets, from *Ideas Mirrour* of 1594 to *Idea* of 1619, a period of twenty-five years during which the sonnet passed from the height of its popularity to obsolescence. In 1619 twenty of the fifty-one sonnets of *Ideas Mirrour* remained, together with forty-three that had been added at various dates, ten of them as late as 1619. Of these last ten poems two (No. 6, 'How many paltry, foolish, painted things', and No. 61, 'Since there's no help, come, let us kiss and part') are probably Drayton's best known sonnets. It was characteristic of Drayton to continue striving to perfect a form once taken up, even after his contemporaries had abandoned it.

Miss Westling's thesis is that 'Drayton's avowed libertinism' (it is avowed in the sonnet which was first introduced into the sequence in 1599 and which, in the final version, is placed in the position of preface) became 'the key-note of the sequence'. 'This persona (of the libertine) becomes the structural principle unifying the collection of sonnets and determining the whole impact of the work.' What is this pose, this persona? What did Drayton imply by the word 'libertine'? In this prefatory sonnet he wrote, 'My verse is the true image of my Mind, | Ever in motion, still desiring change;' but behind the ironic mask there is a genuine romantic devotion, and in the final sonnets the pose is abandoned. There, in the celebrated sixty-first sonnet, Drayton sums up the whole sequence: 'What began with almost "libertine" practicality and lack of sentiment has . . . become an ironic plea for the renewal of love.' In the early sonnets of 1594 Drayton had not always been fully in control of syntax or diction, but here he has achieved a mastery which enables him to match the contrasted theme of octave and sestet with a stylistic contrast, and in so doing to make full use of the elegant form. 'Libertins' was the name applied to the followers of Montaigne, and Miss Westling refers to the *Apology for Raymond Sebond*, written under the influence of Sextus Empiricus, though whether Drayton would have known this before the publication of Florio's translation may be questioned. However, he would have known Florio when he was at work on the translation, and certainly 'the complex of assumptions which Montaigne expressed . . . inform much of the imaginative literature of late

Elizabethan and early Jacobean England'. To such movements of thought Drayton
was certain to respond.

Drayton must have known Donne through the Gooderes, and his disparaging
comments on those poets who refused to publish their poems and would only allow
them to circulate in manuscript must surely have been directed at Donne and his
friends. (Miss Westling's observation that Drayton never wrote any commendatory
verses to Donne is beside the point: Donne gave no opportunity for such things.
And Drayton, who died in the same year as Donne, could not contribute to the
Elegies on the Author's Death which were appended to the first publication of Donne's
Poems two years later.) Nevertheless there are certain analogies between the
development of Drayton's poetry and Donne's: 'Cynicism; morbidity; verbal
roughness; images drawn from the everyday world of commerce, taverns, the
bustling streets of London, science and medicine — these are the qualities which
make some of Drayton's sonnets seem metaphysical'. But it would be vain to seek
any influence of Donne on Drayton: their whole attitude to the art of poetry was
opposed. Yet Drayton was always sensitive to contemporary fashions in poetry; not
a pioneer, like Spenser, but a man of lesser gifts who was quick to follow a lead,
and always ready to learn. He was a man who strove to perfect his art in most
contemporary forms, even if this meant, as with the sonnet, persisting long after the
form had gone out of fashion.

JOHN BUXTON

NEW COLLEGE, OXFORD

The Marlovian World Picture. By W. L. GODSHALK. (Studies in English Literature,
    93) The Hague: Mouton.   1974.   244 pp.   fl 48.
Christopher Marlowe. By GERALD M. PINCISS. (World Dramatists) New York:
    Frederick Ungar.   1975.   vi + 138 pp. $8.50.

Professor Godshalk must have felt a degree of kinship with Tamburlaine when he
published this contribution to Marlowe studies, for he dedicates it to a friend 'who
encouraged my daring'. The daring is in the dating. Recognizing in Marlowe's
opus a 'thrust . . . away from the drama of unnatural conflict and towards mono-
drama', he settles *Dido Queen of Carthage, Edward II,* and *The Massacre at Paris* at the
beginning of Marlowe's career; places *Tamburlaine* in the centre; and allows
Dr Faustus to lead us on to *The Jew of Malta.* By reading the plays in this order we
get the 'true line' (no longer 'mighty', it seems) of Marlowe's development. The
separation of *The Massacre at Paris* and *The Jew of Malta* seems, to my mind, a
wilful denial of the similarities of humour and style which the plays share: in both
the comedy is so black that it is the murderers and not their innocent (and multiple)
victims who enlist our sympathies and applause; and, allowing for the fragmentary
nature of *The Massacre at Paris,* it is possible to see in both plays a verse line which
remains regular yet is flexible enough to adapt to the movements of natural speech
and thought in the many asides. To proceed from the shapely buckets-in-a-well
form of *Edward II* to the almost picaresque sequence of events in *Tamburlaine* sounds
like too great a perversion even for Mr Godshalk's Marlowe.

Mr Godshalk's idea of the critic as one who 'helps his reader more fully to
respond' to the work under consideration is sensible enough, although he (perhaps
in modesty) omits to add that the critic should himself be possessed of some peculiar
sensibility to fit him for this task. Mr Godshalk's own sensibility seems to have
been in part formed by the psychologists, Jung and Freud among them. Writing
about *Dido Queen of Carthage* he is obsessed by its symbolism. It is Jung, I believe,
who is dominant when we are told that in the disappearance of Dido and Aeneas
into the cave, to shelter from the storm and to consummate their passion, 'one might

see . . . a symbol . . . of reabsorption into the maternal womb' (p. 47). On the next page Freud takes over in the identification of Dido with Venus when Mr Godshalk, although admitting that Marlowe 'does not dwell on the incestuous implications of the identification', still asserts that 'Dido-Venus attempts to emasculate or pacify her lover'. He points out that the most powerful image in the play is of fire: the flames that burned the topless towers in Aeneas's narrative become fact at the end of Act v, with Dido's funeral pyre. The flame motif can, it is true, be seen through-out the play and, together with references to Dido as 'a second *Helena*', allows a *limited* identification; but I think it is going too far to attribute pyromaniac ten-dencies to the hero: 'One of the first things that Aeneas does after his arrival in Libya is to start a fire'. The line, 'Gentle *Achates*, reach the Tinder boxe', has caused some trouble in the past, but while Francis Cunningham in 1870 wanted to give it to Nashe on the grounds that it was too bathetic for Marlowe, Mr Godshalk is now proud to claim it as Marlowe's adumbrating hand: 'Metaphorically, Aeneas starts a larger fire in Libya than he is initially aware of' (p. 54).

Having identified Oedipal elements in *Dido Queen of Carthage*, Mr Godshalk proceeds, as one would expect, to the homosexual ones in *Edward II*. With a delicacy that verges on the prurient, he analyses the relationship between Edward and Gaveston, finding ambiguity where there is none in the 'lovelie boye' who hides with an olive branch 'those parts which men desire to see', and almost reluctantly concludes that 'the act is related to the modern fan dance' (p. 62). But in this play, too, nothing is allowed to exist in itself: all is symbolic. Thus Edward's homosexual 'fecklessness' is 'symptomatic rather than precipitative of the civil strife England undergoes' (p. 69); the shaving in puddle water is taken from Stow (in a departure from Holinshed) 'for symbolic purposes . . . [it] points to the loss of his royal identity' (p. 75). And of course the murder is not only the parody of the homosexual act that William Empson first suggested; it 'symbolizes the moral perversion which accompanies the political upheaval' (p. 76). Where all is symbolism, there is little pain. In Mr Godshalk's hands, *Edward II* is no more than 'a critique of a society which allows selfishness and ambition to destroy itself utterly' (p. 77). Had he seen the 1969 production of the play, I very much doubt whether Mr Godshalk's intel-lectual symbols would have protected him from emotions which must be desperately outraged by the human agony which lurks behind every single action and culminates in the nightmare torture of the final scenes.

Tamburlaine, like its eponymous hero, withstands all attempts at manipulation, but *Dr Faustus* is at any man's mercy. A slow plod through the events of the B Text is enlivened from time to time by the pointing out of symbols on the roadside. 'Faustus is an anti-type of the Biblical "suffering servant", who gives himself for others' (p. 182). Of all the Deadly Sins, Mr Godshalk seems to think that Faustus is most prone to Gluttony; of the Doctor's urbane dinner invitation to Valdes and Cornelius he remarks, 'one cannot help observing that with Faustus food comes before magic'. Of course this is symbolic too, for Faustus finally gives his body to be torn to pieces by the devils, just as Christ 'symbolically distributes himself to his disciples' (p. 188).

It might seem that so immense a task as the creation of an anti-Christ would set a crown upon any man's lifetime's effort, but (as in the best Greek tradition, perhaps, of the satyr-play that followed the tragic trilogy) there is yet *The Jew of Malta*. Certainly Barabas is a parody, of the popular conception of the Jew and, on a different level for a short time, of Job; but Mr Godshalk also permits us to 'toy' with a contrast between Christ's salutary death on the cross, and Barabas's cursing in the cauldron. 'It is Marlowe's method', we are told, 'to suggest such com-parisons' (p. 218). True, but not as wholesale as this. At one point, early in the play, Barabas *might* be compared to Christ by the Governor of Malta: 'better one want for a common good, | Than many perish for a private man' (1.2.98); but when his death comes at last it is in the form of the accepted Elizabethan punishment for poisoners. I think Mr Godshalk tries to see *The Jew of Malta* as a *greater* play, handling universal abstractions of Good and Evil, Love and Greed, than I do; but to me it is a *better* play than he allows it to be, precisely because it does not proceed in the abstract, schematized manner he suggests. Wherever Marlowe got his knowledge of Malta and the Knights from, he presents a remarkably topical and accurate play which shows a strange awareness of the politics which made the island a strategic base during the Anglo–Spanish hostilities of the 1580s.

'Marlowe's vision', Mr Godshalk concludes, 'is of a world of human evil', which he contemplates 'not with the optimistic eyes of Shakespeare, but with the savage indignation of Swift' (p. 222). Although the comparison is not unfair to either writer, it is a dangerous one, for it seems to confuse two kinds of irony. A long essay would be needed to explain the difference; all that can be said here is that whereas Swift's 'indignation' seems to have expressed his disgust and revulsion, Marlowe's is more compounded with fear and identification. Mephistophilis's description of the deprivation which for him is hell suggests that Marlow felt, imaginatively and profoundly, that last pain for the damned which Empson's 'Fathers' had found: 'They knew the bliss with which they were not crowned'. *The Marlovian World Picture* is a pretentious little book. Its author tries to rearrange the plays on a procrustean scheme of his own making, but he fails in his efforts. The plays are not dead; and they certainly will not lie down.

Mr Pinciss makes no great claims for his book, merely suggesting on the fly-leaf that 'it will be invaluable to the student tracing theme, structure and character in each play'. Glossing easily over difficulties of text and ambiguities of reading, and offering only a few elementary and pedestrian critical comments (on 'dramatic irony' in *Dr Faustus*, for instance), Mr Pinciss's highly derivative account of the plays would never tempt me to make further acquaintance with them or their author.

Roma Gill

University of Sheffield

A Selective Bibliography of Shakespeare: Editions, Textual Studies, Commentary. By James G. McManaway and Jeanne Addison Roberts. Charlottesville: Published for the Folger Shakespeare Library by the University Press of Virginia. 1975. xx + 309 pp. $12.50 ($3.95 paperbound).

Gordon Ross Smith's unselective bibliography of Shakespeare is indispensable for some purposes; and Stanley Wells's austerely selective *Reading Guide* is valuable too: but the editors of this new bibliography are doubtless right in thinking that a compromise between the two extremes will serve the needs of many scholars. It contains some 4,500 titles, some appearing more than once, published between 1930 and 1970, and thus serving as a supplement to Ebisch and Schücking. The editors say that 'a scattering of representative works of earlier date is given to serve as a background'. There is, however, some inconsistency in the application of this principle. In the sections on individual plays, few earlier works are listed; but in more general sections the proportion of early works is considerable. Of the first 28 titles, 12 were published before 1930; and in a strangely inflated section on the authorship question, nearly half the books listed were published before 1930, and nearly all of them belong to the lunatic fringe. Is it really necessary to list the works of Delia Bacon, Ignatius Donnelly, and Durning-Lawrence?

Another inconsistency is that we are often informed that an essay has been included in a later book, but by no means always. Two of Kirschbaum's essays, for example (841, 1746), were reprinted in 3122. Indeed, the list of collections of essays (2759–825) would be more useful to the reader if some indication were given of the contents of each. Nor are we told much about the contents of books in other sections. Ungerer's *Anglo-Spanish Relations*, for example, is chiefly interesting to Shakespearians for his attempt to identify the model for Armado; and Una Ellis-Fermor's *The Frontiers of Drama* contains a well-known essay on *Troilus and Cressida*, not otherwise listed.

The actual selection of titles is generally sound and is evidence of the compilers' catholicity of taste and breadth of knowledge. But a few items hardly deserve a place and we may regret the absence of Peter Quennell's biography, of Arthur Sewell's undervalued *Character and Society in Shakespeare*, of Eleanor Prosser's article on *The Tempest*, and of Pasternak's essay on translating Shakespeare, which is available in English.

There are a few slips. John Bayley's book, *The Characters of Love*, contains a section on Chaucer's *Troilus and Criseyde*, not on Shakespeare's play. The annotation to *Sixteen Plays* was by Kittredge himself, apart from textual notes and glossaries to two of them, which were added by A. C. Sprague. Several essays (606, 1160, 2453) are said to be included in 2813 (*Eighteenth-Century Essays on Shakespeare*) instead of in 2815, essays edited by Gordon R. Smith. The shadow Minister of Education appears as St John-Stevens.

Lastly, it may be worth considering the sixty-four items relating to the *Sonnets*. The first ten of these are editions, and of these the 1862 facsimile should, I think, have been omitted. Martin Seymour-Smith's edition is modest and admirable, but not listed, whereas A. L. Rowse's edition, which cannot be so described, is included. Some excellent editions of the Poems are omitted, none being listed between 1710 and 1938. Brents Stirling's essay (2328) is incorporated in 2375 and could therefore have been omitted. Wilson Knight's own poems, interesting to students of Knight, do not seem relevant to this section. L. C. Knights's *Explorations* is listed under 'Comprehensive Works and Single Studies', but no mention is made of his essay on the *Sonnets*.

In view of these criticisms, it is necessary to emphasize that the book as a whole will be a valuable addition to nearly all libraries, public and private.

UNIVERSITY OF LIVERPOOL   KENNETH MUIR

Shakespeare's Lusty Punning in 'Love's Labour's Lost': With Contemporary Analogues. By HERBERT A. ELLIS. (Studies in English Literature, 81) The Hague: Mouton. 1973. 239 pp. fl 44.

'Lusty' is an ambiguous word to use in the title of a book devoted to *double entendres*. To the Elizabethans it meant 'pleasurable' with reference to a great variety of pleasures, but Mr Ellis narrows it down to the kind of wit which elicits in *Love's Labour's Lost* the reproach: 'Come, come, you talk greasily.' There is plenty of this kind of punning in Shakespeare. He and his audience liked a good dirty joke; we still do. Mr Ellis hunts down the innuendoes in *Love's Labour's Lost* with great vigour, and I am afraid that in so doing he rides roughshod over other and possibly more important pleasures that the play can give. An example from the first scene illustrates this:

> *Ferdinand.* Will you heare this Letter with attention?
> *Berowne.*   As we would heare an Oracle.
> *Costard.*   Such is the simplicitie of man to harken after the flesh.

'Oracle' is glossed 'means of divine communication / pudendum' on the grounds that there is contextual wordplay; that the word has a bawdy significance in the slang dictionary of Farmer and Henley; and that it is used elsewhere in Shakespeare in scenes involving witches, who were associated with harlotry, as when Banquo asks: 'May they not be my oracles as well and set me up in hope?' Now it is not inconceivable that Shakespeare subconsciously associated the word 'oracle' with a woman's sex (always provided this meaning was current three hundred years before Farmer and Henley) and so was led on to Costard's phrase 'hearken after the flesh' in which 'hearken' is a *double-entendre*, as it is in Donne's famous compass image. But Shakespeare's uppermost and conscious purpose in using the awesome 'oracle' is surely to make the stage listeners and the audience doubly attentive to the absurdities of Armado's letter. The obligation to keep words in their context and so respond to the pleasure of the particular dramatic moment, to maintain decorum in the Horatian sense, is underlined by the sheer impossibility of our recognizing sexual innuendoes in Banquo's tragic soliloquy as we listen to it in the theatre.

I quote this example to show that my misgivings about Mr Ellis's explanations of Shakespeare's meaning (a word he uses rather rashly) are not due to his finding innuendoes everywhere in the play; they certainly are all over the place, and I am one up on him here, as 'hearken' is not in his list. What really worries me is that his method of isolating, listing, and glossing the rude puns (alongside a few 'modest' ones) reduces the pleasure of this entrancing play to little more than a salacious giggle from start to finish. The start is memorable: splendid rhetoric from a romantically royal figure. But here it is suggested that the audience would hear 'Our late edict shall strongly stand in force' as 'Our lated dick . . .' and instantly take this nonsensical phrase to mean what Mr Ellis requires several pages to argue that it might mean, an unsatisfied penis. I see that I have written against this explanation 'Oh God! Oh Montreal!' The follies of broadmindedness are every bit as catastrophic as those of prudery.

One great 'lustiness', one major pleasure of *Love's Labour's Lost*, resides, as Gladys Willcock showed us long ago, in its portrayal of a society inebriated through all its ranks with the yeast of language. Mr Ellis's explanations have a way of obscuring our pleasure in the comedy's many forms of wordplay other than puns. The pleasure to be gained from the formal patterning of such a phrase as 'Well fitted in artes, glorious in armes' is lost if we have to busy our wits with three possible meanings of 'arms'. The over-use of *amplificatio* is a source of laughter for Shakespeare and his audience throughout the play; but Armado's verbosity is robbed of its rightful effect if 'Anthony Dull, a man of good repute, carriage[,] bearing, and estimation' has to yield obscene meanings for 'carriage' and 'bearing'. 'For Armado to praise his messenger to the King for attributes which the latter could see at a glance seems manifestly unlikely' (p. 40). But what the theatrical audience sees at a glance is that Dull's carriage and bearing are somewhat less than courtly, and they innocently enjoy the smile of self-satisfaction that spreads across his face as the King reads Armado's letter. And the bumpkins of the play should surely be allowed their wordgames without lexicographic interference. When Armado promises to tell Jaquenetta wonders and gets the retort: 'With that face', the catchphrase needs to be as pert and empty as the current 'You must be joking'; a lightness of effect lost if we have to notice that 'tell' can mean 'count' and 'face' could mean 'money'. Generations of playgoers have enjoyed Costard's comparison of Armado's three-farthing 'remuneration' with Berowne's shilling 'guerdon' as an honest, homespun attempt to grapple with the disparity of words and things, but for Mr Ellis 'Costard's insistent repetition of *gardon* would be absurd even for him unless he were punning, which he most probably is, on the perennial association . . . between the human body, especially woman's, and a garden' (p. 137). In such comments the author of this book appears not so much to have stolen the scraps from Shakespeare's great feast of languages as to have brought to it some pretty musty crumbs.

It must be plain that I do not like Mr Ellis's procedures. Yet I wish very much I could like them, because he prefaces his glossaries of the semantic and homophonic puns in *Love's Labour's Lost* with kind references to my own interest in Shakespeare's wordplay, and his concluding chapter states that his count of puns in the play confirms my rough estimate that they total over two hundred. He has done carefully what I had previously done only casually with regard to this play, and moreover he has the advantage of a 'wide collateral reading' in Elizabethan literature. Not only does this reading lead him to the interesting conclusion that Shakespeare's innuendoes are more deft, more easily side-stepped, than the forthright bawdy of his contemporaries, but it also helps him to list upward of twenty puns that I am cross with myself for having missed. Adding these to our common stock, we seem to agree about some hundred puns in the play. But there remain well over a hundred places in the play where Mr Ellis detects a quibbling which would in my view be intrusive, and even sometimes downright destructive of the effects that I dare to think Shakespeare is seeking. For this reason I hope directors, who have tended to work puns rather too hard of late, will treat the book with caution. For future editors of the play it will be required reading, and it will be interesting to watch how many of these handily listed ambiguities they will accept and incorporate into their commentaries.

M. M. Mahood

University of Kent

Denmark, 'Hamlet', and Shakespeare: A Study of Englishmen's Knowledge of Denmark towards the End of the Sixteenth Century with Special Reference to 'Hamlet'. By Cay Dollerup. (Salzburg Studies in English Literature, Elizabethan and Renaissance Studies, 47). Salzburg: Institut für Englische Sprache und Literatur, Universität Salzburg. 1975. Two volumes. ix + 338 pp.

One sign and consequence of the extraordinary fascination exercised by Shakespeare's tragedy of the 'Prince of Denmark' is the curiosity it has excited as to precisely how Danish the prince and his Denmark are. In the most comprehensive inquiry there has been or is perhaps likely to be Cay Dollerup seeks answers to two questions: what features of the play are specifically Danish and how did Shakespeare know of them? The first question is the more tractable: one can at least work through the details of the play, from the dumbshow to the wager of Barbary horses, attempting to discover whether or not they correspond with Danish custom. This Mr Dollerup does, if more incidentally than systematically. But he has chosen to organize his book round the second question. So we have surveys of the sources of the Hamlet legend, of historical and literary works on Denmark, of plays (including lost plays), travel books, and maps, followed by accounts of English–Danish contacts by way of trade and diplomatic missions. All this yields interesting information on a variety of topics, from the Sound dues to King James's marriage and the composer Dowland's stay at the Danish court, but much of it at best tangential to the main inquiry. On that we are left with a series of negative replies, which have, I suppose, the use that an unrewarding search need not be repeated, and beyond them little more than a range of vague possibilities. 'The notion that the Poles were inveterate warriors could . . . derive from Abbot, though it was, really, widespread'; Shakespeare could have got those quintessentially Danish names Rosencrantz and Guildenstern 'from a diplomat (or his servants)'. So indeed he could; but the attempt to identify a particular informant for each detail of 'local colour' perhaps misrepresents the creative process which, while ready to make use of anything conveniently to hand (like Nashe's attack on Danish manners in *Pierce Penilesse*), sets the hero concretely in his milieu by the very intensity with which his story is imagined.

That Shakespeare nevertheless purposed to give his play an authentically Danish setting hardly admits of question. The opening salutations of the 'liegemen to the Dane' in the 'bitter cold', their talk of feats against Norway and of 'sledded Polacks on the ice', transport us to a northern region, where presently we find students from the University of Wittenberg amid a court accustomed to 'drink deep' to the sound of 'kettle-drum and trumpet' and reverberating cannon. Mr Dollerup, though not the first to authenticate these Danish 'cannon-healths' by citing notable instances, amply confirms them. He can supply facts about the drummers in the royal Trompeterkorps, statistics of the 'Rhenish' drunk in Denmark, chapter and verse for Danes at Wittenberg. He can show how even items not strictly Danish could contribute to the play by seeming to be so: the name Cornelius, borne by several Dutchmen at the court in Copenhagen, was presumably mistaken for a Danish one; and though the King's guard were not 'Switzers', they were sometimes described as such by those who apparently confused them with the Pope's similarly clad Swiss guard.

A hunt for evidence of things Danish brings a temptation to exaggerate, to claim more than firm evidence can warrant; and the danger is one that Mr Dollerup does not entirely escape. That the names Yaughan and Yorick held a joke for actors who had been in Denmark is mere conjecture. One can accept Osric, with its characteristic suffix, as a Danish-sounding name (though not its derivation from Alricus in Saxo); but Osric's fertile lands and affected style might belong to a gentleman anywhere. The joke of the hat he declines to put on also transcends nationality; and though it might be enhanced by something *outré* when the hat gets at length to his head, the Danish sugarloaf hat this book so confidently assumes finds no reference in the text. It is hardly a plausible supposition that Nashe's charge against the Danes that they 'naturally hate learning' is reflected in Hamlet's contempt for penmanship as a 'learning' he laboured to forget. Mr Dollerup is justly sceptical of that fantasy of some earlier scholars that the pictures Hamlet shows his mother were suggested by the royal portraits at Kronborg, but only to replace it with another that these 'counterfeit presentments' derive from the 'contrafej', or medals, which Danish kings were in the habit of bestowing. It seems doubtful whether the vocabulary of *Hamlet*, as distinct from the manners it denotes, is meant to strike us as Danish. The strongest case put forward is for the drinker's 'rouse'. But though Dekker speaks of 'the Danish *rowsa*' the chance that Shakespeare may have chosen the word for the sake of its Danish aura is countered by its occurrence in *Othello* and indeed in *Hamlet* itself when it refers to Laertes's doings in Paris. A proposal to explain the 'dram of eale' as Shakespeare's attempt at the Danish *øl* (ale) is one of the author's aberrations.

What is perhaps more characteristic than such lapses of judgement, though not incompatible with them, is a careful weighing of the possibilities. Between the desire to identify something as Danish and the honest recognition that the evidence falls short there is often an uneasy balance. The discussion of the players at Elsinore may be taken as fairly typical. An account of Kronborg castle which refers to its facilities for stage plays prompts the comment, 'This passage is interesting, because it could have given Shakespeare the idea of having itinerant players come to Elsinore to act'. Yet a knowledge of the travels of English actors makes it necessary to add at once, 'But this need not be so'. A reluctance none the less to relinquish the idea leads on to 'And yet the players' appearance in *Hamlet* would add local colour'; and even in the final summing-up 'we cannot completely disregard the possibility', though we come at length to the decision that it is 'more likely to be . . . coincidence'. In another instance, evidence from topography and painting, sailors and actors, is allowed to point to Cape Kullen as Horatio's 'eastward hill' before we accept the anticlimactic but eminently sane conclusion that 'the odds are still that Shakespeare had no specific hill in mind'. Such verdicts seem inevitable: the book, I think, would have gained from a readier recognition of what the questions are which are really worth pursuing.

An example of a question that seems to be misconceived concerns Fortinbras's journey through Denmark. What engages the dramatist's imagination is what affects Hamlet's story, and for that the essential about Fortinbras is that in marching to Poland across Denmark he encounters Hamlet on the way. The exact route that he takes is no more to be mapped than Lear's route to Dover, or for that matter Falstaff's in going from London to Yorkshire by way of Gloucestershire. Whether Fortinbras came by 'the main road down through Jutland' belongs with that other famous problem about the children of Lady Macbeth.

Why Shakespeare changed the venue of his story from Jutland to Elsinore is of course another matter, since it concerns the creator not the creature, the process of imagining a world rather than the world imagined. It is reasonable to presume that it had to do with the status that Elsinore and its fine new castle of Kronborg had in the English mind. Whatever we learn about this has therefore its relevance to the genesis of the play. But all that the dramatist need have known of Elsinore was that it had a royal residence and a position by the sea. The castle, never so much as mentioned in the text, is evoked for us not by the historic details of its courtyard and its portraits but by 'the platform' where the sentries watch, 'the lobby' where Hamlet walks, the 'closet' with its 'arras' where Polonius is killed, and the 'stairs' where the body is hidden. It comes to life in the rouses and the Rhenish and the kettle-drums contributed by a real Denmark, but also, and compatibly, in the beetling 'cliff' and the 'eastward hill' which by the actual geography of Denmark it could never have had at all. The quality of imagination in *Hamlet* is a little hard to reconcile with the account of 'a conscientious writer who took meticulous care to be correct' (p. 3).

All that is or might be Danish about *Hamlet* seems to be covered in this book. The inferences it draws from the evidence may often provoke dissent, and there is too much unprofitable speculation. But the evidence is fairly presented and an excellent index enables it to be quickly turned up.

HAROLD JENKINS

LONDON

Shakespeare: 'Measure for Measure'. By NIGEL ALEXANDER. (Studies in English Literature, 57) London: Edward Arnold. 1975. 64 pp. £2.20.

Beginning by asking whether *Measure for Measure* is a problem play, Professor Alexander answers that it is at any rate 'a difficult play'. And it is difficult in ways that make it hard for a brief survey to be satisfactory; it calls for leisurely examination of individual problems. Moreover, the purpose of this series demands that there should be sections in such topics as Text, Sources, Historical Settings, and the Legal Question. The last and longest chapter, 'The Play', is not reached until page 37, out of 61 pages of text.

The chapter on the Text draws hazardous numerological conclusions from the division of the play into sixteen scenes; all the more hazardous because, while a cleared stage is taken as the criterion for the end of a scene, the figure of sixteen is only arrived at by confessedly treating 1.2 and 1.3 as two scenes, though Lucio remains on stage.

A chapter on 'Shakespeare's Comic Method' notes the departures from the technique normal in the earlier comedies of placing the audience in a position of superior awareness to the characters. It is perhaps going too far to say that the audience watches Isabella's interview with Angelo 'without any awareness that the compromise he asks is impossible since Angelo will execute him in any case'. Certainly the audience has no *knowledge* that he will, but it surely comes as no surprise that, when he thinks that Isabella has paid the price, he fails to keep his side of the bargain. In III.1, the question whether he would or would not just fails to arise. When in a later chapter Professor Alexander writes that the Duke 'assures Isabella that Angelo's offer is not genuine' (p. 55), the incautious reader might take this to mean that he will not keep his word if she yields, when in fact what the Duke tells her is that Angelo was not serious in his attempt to seduce her.

There is some lack of proportion in the chapter on 'The Historical Setting'. I agree (though not with utter conviction) that it is probable that the play is in some degree angled at James I, but very little would be lost if we were in ignorance of this. Since Professor Alexander still has to insist that the Duke is in no way a portrait of James, there is just too much of him, in this chapter and elsewhere, for a brief study.

The chapter on the Sources is adequate though brief; that on 'The Legal Question' is less satisfactory. Unlike Schanzer, whose account he justly cites as the most accurate, Alexander does not make fully clear the distinction between *sponsalia de futuro* and *de praesenti*; nor that, though the latter brought into existence a valid marriage, consummation before a formal ceremony was fornication in the eyes of the Church: 'a strong feeling . . . that the church ceremony should precede co-habitation' (p. 33) is an understatement. On one related point where Professor Alexander follows Schanzer, I am not convinced that they are right. They would have it that Isabella is ignorant of the contract, and that this explains the nature of her plea to Angelo. But Angelo has made it clear that, contract or no contract, he proposes to consider Claudio's act as fornication (legally, as Schanzer admits, though tyranically), and, this being so, Isabella, whether or not she knows of the contract, has no alternative but to accept that what she is pleading for is 'a vice that most I do abhor'. There is also a curious sentence in the later discussion of this scene: 'Since he is her brother, Isabella does not regard Claudio as a hardened fornicator properly deserving death' (p. 46), as if it needed any such *parti pris* to hold that he was not; and Angelo, in any case, treats any fornicator, even if not hardened, as deserving death.

In the chapter on 'The Play', I could have done with more close following of the action, at the expense of such claims as that 'it is the structure of Renaissance philosophic images . . . which dramatically transmutes the old material of story' (p. 56). The whole 'justice and mercy' question I have discussed elsewhere, and do not wish to repeat myself. But what I cannot resist once more quoting is a sentence of Marco Mincoff: 'The very word mercy becomes slightly absurd when we are so constantly reminded that what is needed for Claudio is not mercy but a modicum of common sense.' Mincoff, and another of the play's best critics, Rossiter, are among those absent from a bibliography that is overloaded with more peripheral material.

†J. C. Maxwell

'Barnardine' is throughout spelt 'Barnadine'.

Balliol College, Oxford

The Tragedy of Othello, the Moor of Venice. By WILLIAM SHAKESPEARE. Edited by
LAWRENCE J. ROSS. (The Bobbs-Merrill Shakespeare Series) Indianapolis
and New York: Bobbs-Merrill. 1974. xl + 304 pp. $8.95 ($4.95 paperbound).

The aims of the Bobbs-Merrill Shakespeare Series are twofold: to eschew the
practice of presenting the reader with 'an approved response' to Shakespeare's
works in favour of furnishing him with 'whatever aids' may promote a 'fuller
understanding' of the plays, and to supply the student with reliable texts free from
the 'accretions and distortions' of earlier editions.

Mr Ross's *Othello* very neatly demonstrates the pitfalls attendant upon the
first, theoretically laudable, objective. While meticulously avoiding the conventional areas of critical analysis and scrupulously attempting to limit his attention to
background information, the editor has failed to recognize that his very choice of
'relevant' materials itself implies an interpretation, and that in discussing the way
in which Shakespeare has 'ennobled the Moor of the source', for example, or in
pointing out the relationship between Iago and the medieval Vice, he has already
trespassed beyond his brief, tantalizing his readers with glimpses of a response that
is never permitted to emerge. A similar failure to think through the policy of the
series betrays itself in the hesitancy the editor exhibits over the audience to which his
work is addressed. The provision of an elementary account of the structure of the
Elizabethan play-house, for example, forces us to postulate a student of this play
who is sophisticated enough to grapple with Mr Ross's exceedingly complex
critical vocabulary, and sufficiently erudite to follow a detailed account of the
problems presented by the Quarto and Folio texts, while being in total ignorance
of the most obvious characteristics of Shakespeare's theatre. Moreover, the 'aids'
themselves occasionally lack the accuracy and relevancy which this series demands.
The statement that 'The Elizabethan playwright customarily sold the manuscript
of his play . . . directly to the players for cash' (xxxiii) is misleading to say the least,
Appendix E on Shakespeare's English displays disturbing naivety (compare the
easy equation of the language of the play with colloquial usage), while it seems
unnecessary to inform us that the Elizabethan stage was furnished with a trap when
none is used in the play.

The second aim of the series, to present a reliable text cleansed, as far as possible,
from corruption, is clearly an unexceptional objective in line with modern editorial
principles, but again Mr Ross fails to fulfil the claims made on the cover of his
book. Textual variants and emendations are *not* 'given only where they affect the
possible meaning', every variation between the Folio and Quarto texts being
recorded in the conventional manner. The 'accretions and distortions' of earlier
editions are *not* swept away in favour of Folio readings; at 1.1.30, for example, the
Folio 'Christen'd' and Quarto 'Christian', both of which make sense, are discarded for a conjectural 'Christen' which, arguably, does not. Annotation goes
far beyond the merely 'explanatory', reducing the text to the now proverbial
'trickle' by such scholarly exhibitionism as 'the match with a "barb" or Arab — a
horse much prized for its running — suggests the not uncommon Elizabethan
cross between a stallion of this breed and an English mare' (explaining 1.1.112).
Some glosses are manifestly wrong (compare 'parts' at 1.2.31 which is clearly
'qualities, personal merits' (see Kermode, *The Riverside Shakespeare*) not 'past
deeds') while the editor shows a regrettable reluctance to explain Shakespeare's
bawdy.

Mr Ross's style, too, stands in the way of that straightforward relationship between
the reader and the text that the designers of this series clearly had in mind. Confronted by such remarks as 'as the passage itself suggests, moreover, much of the
enlargement of significance in the action is dependent on the symbolic capacities of
literal theme' (p. xv) or 'the Quarto's text is adjudged on the whole more reliably

to represent a less authoritative manuscript of the play, and the Folio's less reliably to represent a more authoritative one' (p. xxxvi), the reader might well feel on safer ground with a conventional edition.

However, it should not be overlooked that Mr Ross does propose a new theory of the relationship between Quarto and Folio texts which, while incapable of proof, is worthy of serious attention and that his edition does offer the reader a mass of information which, if not as 'thoroughly digested' as the background materials to the Bobbs-Merrill edition of *King Lear* (see Richard Proudfoot in *Shakespeare Survey 27*) at least rewards the patience of the scholar by a number of insights into the density of the language of the play.

LEAH SCRAGG

UNIVERSITY OF MANCHESTER

Lyric Forms in the Sonnet Sequences of Barnabe Barnes. By PHILIP E. BLANK, JR. (De Proprietatibus Litterarum, Series Practica, 18) The Hague: Mouton. 1974. 162 pp. fl 30.

As Professor Blank points out in his Introduction, the extreme differences of opinion among critics regarding the merit, and in some cases even the metrical classification, of Barnes's verse, highlight the need for a detailed study of his sonnet sequences. While Dowden praised him as 'one of the exquisites' of the Elizabethans, Courthope dismissed him as 'an idiot' who wrote nonsense (p. 27). The fact that, after Sidney and Spenser, Barnes is one of the most experimental of sixteenth-century poets in his use of prosody, gives his verse considerable interest to the student of Renaissance literature. Now that Victor A. Doyno's edition of *Parthenophil and Parthenophe* (1971) has made Barnes's love sonnets easily accessible to the reader, Professor Blank's study is especially opportune.

In his discussion of the sonnet sequences Professor Blank concentrates on analysing, and attempting to vindicate, their lyric forms. He aims 'to demonstrate that they are not amorphous, irregular, or even just servilely imitative, but that they make fresh use of conventional models and that they are diversely patterned in structure' (p. 31). In order to carry out this task he devotes admirable care to defining the conventional literary models which Barnes manipulates and adapts. As well as providing a yardstick for measuring Barnes's experiments and innovations, Professor Blank's concise definitions of the lyric genres adopted by the poet incidentally afford a useful guide to Elizabethan verse conventions.

Professor Blanks' analysis of the various verse forms employed in the sonnet sequences is at all times scholarly and precise. However, his examination of the love sonnets is perhaps the most illuminating chapter of his study. It is this particular section of Barnes's verse which has suffered most at the hands of ill-informed critics. Failing to appreciate the range and flexibility which the sonnet form contained for the Elizabethans, authors such as Lever and Prince have tended to dismiss Barnes's legitimate experimentation as betraying either ignorance of, or wanton disregard for, convention (p. 72). In his discussion of the love sonnets Professor Blank convincingly demonstrates that the frequent liberties which Barnes takes with convention are seldom random, but represent carefully contrived innovations. One of the reasons why Professor Blank's analysis of the love sonnets constitutes the most rewarding chapter of his study is that here he succeeds in illustrating not only the variety of Barnes's experiments with structure, metre, and syntax, but also their functional relation to the content of his verse. The demonstration of the way in which Barnes separates patterns of rhyme and sense in order to mirror the tensions of emotional conflict and debate is especially interesting (pp. 77–9). Professor Blank also successfully vindicates the introduction of a

fifteenth line in some sonnets, a practice condemned by previous critics. He comes
to the conclusion that Barnes uses this device for purposes of emotional emphasis,
and to do away with the effect of a final summary, conventionally provided by the
concluding couplet. On occasion Professor Blank's analysis of the relation between
form and content is a little simplistic. Although he is alert to complexities of
syntax and rhetorical ornament, he ignores the effects achieved by contrasts of
diction. He certainly cannot be accused of being over-subjective in his interpretation, or of inventing ambiguities where none exist. On the contrary, his analysis
would profit from being a little more adventurous.

In his examination of the other lyric genres which Barnes adopts, Professor
Blank pays less attention to establishing the aim of Barnes's experiments, or attempting to define the function they perform. As Professor Blank rightly insists, many
of the innovations of metre and syntax which Barnes introduces appear to be
chiefly decorative in purpose, employed to contribute to displays of wit and
stylistic ingenuity. However, since in the love sonnets they also appear to perform a
more complex function, and to be closely related to the emotional content of the
verse, there is every reason to look closely at the uses to which Barnes puts them in
the other genres he adopts. All too often Professor Blank treats the reader to a list
of rhetorical devices, or syntactical and metrical details, carefully illustrating their
use with textual references, but fails to make any mention of their intellectual or
imaginative significance. It could be argued that, since he has chosen to limit his
aims to examining the formal characteristics of Barnes's verse, any deeper analysis
lies beyond his scope. However, Professor Blank's exclusive attention to features of
style makes for rather arid reading. Since Barnes's devotional verse is not easily
accessible to the modern reader, a fuller use of quotations from the poems would be
helpful.

The limitations of this study are evidently not due to the author's lack of insight
into the intellectual content of the sonnets. Some of his most interesting comments
on *A Divine Centurie* are briefly incorporated in the final pages of his concluding
chapter. Here he tries to fathom the significance of Barnes's celebration of God's
mercies in terms of their numerousness, and his general emphasis on concepts of
number. Professor Blank points out the possible connexion between Barnes's
allusion to the theory of divine harmony, contained in his exhortation to his fellow
poets to praise God in 'sacred numbers', and his varied experiments with metrical
and structural patterns. It is a pity that these ideas are not expanded in the
preceding chapter on the divine sonnets.

Although Professor Blank aims to vindicate the intelligence of Barnes's metrical
and stylistic experiments, he steers clear of attempting to evaluate the literary merit
of his verse, or of making some kind of critical comparison between his poems.
Since Barnes is a notoriously uneven poet, and since the question of his stylistic skill
cannot be divorced from that of his general literary achievement, the lack of critical
appraisal makes the study seem incomplete. However, judged in terms of Professor
Blank's clearly defined aims, it constitutes a useful contribution to the appreciation
of Barnes's verse, preparing the ground for further critical discussion. The excellent
bibliography with which the book concludes encourages the reader to make his
own investigations into the literary and stylistic aspects of Barnes's verse.

UNIVERSITY OF WARWICK   PAULINA PALMER

John Donne's Poetry. By WILBUR SANDERS. London and New York: Cambridge University Press. 1971. Reprinted 1974. viii + 160 pp. £2.60 (£1.60 paperbound).

The appearance of Dr Sanders's book in a paperback edition could suggest that it is becoming a standard work on Donne. This would be unfortunate: although the book has important virtues, it is also seriously flawed.

Dr Sanders's study is a critical examination of the major poetry in the canon. Throughout the volume he takes issue with the tendency of many previous readers to emphasize what he terms the 'pyrotechnics' of Donne. His witty metaphysical conceits and his tricks and games with logic are not, Dr Sanders argues, characteristic of the poet at his best. In Donne's greatest poetry, the author suggests, he does not play games, does not rely on personae to distance himself from the experience he evokes.

These theories shape a consistent, though debatable, evaluation of the poems. Dr Sanders tends to respect those *Songs and Sonets* that affirm a joyous and contented relationship; indeed, he argues that in Donne the 'main creative impetus ran to affirmation' (p. 61). He finds those *Songs and Sonets* whose tone is more ironic (such as 'The Ecstasie') and the elegies far less successful. He sees in the satires warmth and good humour; he argues that the satire is 'participatory', for the protagonist is often laughing at himself and laughing with his audience. Differing from many readers in considering the religious poetry at its best equal to the love poetry, Dr Sanders admires the hymns far more than most of the *Holy Sonnets*.

Dr Sanders's approach, which is clearly deeply indebted to Dr Leavis, carries with it certain advantages. It is salutary for us to qualify the conventional wisdom about Donne's game-playing with Dr Sanders's insistence that we find little evidence of it in some of the greatest passages that the monarch of wit ever wrote. Dr Sanders's concern for making careful discriminations among and within the poems leads him to devote a great deal of space to detailed close readings; a few of them, such as his commentary on 'A Valediction: forbidding mourning' are quite illuminating. His emphasis on the way tones vary within a given poem provides a useful corrective to the very destructive and very pervasive tendency to divide Donne's poems rigidly into categories, such as serious versus light-hearted, Platonic versus Petrarchan, and so forth.

One difficulty is, however, inherent in Dr Sanders's very approach. His dislike of the type of metaphysical wit that he labels 'Clevelandism' and his respect for that difficult critical concept sincerity lead him to dismiss or denigrate many of the real achievements of the canon. For instance, he is consistently offended by one of the poet's favourite ways of yoking together disparates, the use of imagery that links love and religion. But such images often express deep truths about both spheres. Nor does Dr Sanders appreciate how often the heavy, self-conscious irony that he deplores leads to moments of real illumination. Donne's hesitation to commit himself fully to any one idea is probably ultimately a limitation in his sensibility, but it is not nearly as deep a limitation as Dr Sanders suggests, and it is not without its compensations.

Most of the problems of the study are not, however, inherent in its author's critical method; they stem not from his Leavisite principles but rather from an insensitive application of those principles. At several points he distorts a poem to make it fit his theories. A conflict between his general admiration for 'A Feaver' on other grounds and his distrust of the use of a persona apparently explains his very unpersuasive comment on the role of the mask at the end of that poem: 'The mask is now a matter of tact — Donne not wishing to expose the woman to an intrusive emotion she may not choose to entertain or reciprocate' (p. 49). Surely an odd response to a poem that ends 'For I had rather owner bee | Of thee one houre, than all else ever'. Similarly, he finds in 'The Sunne Rising' primarily an 'extreme sensitivity to the solipsistic, egocentric blasphemy against the *common* reality, which lovers are prone to fall into' (p. 71), rather than a joyous exclusion of any outside reality; thus, for example, in 'I could eclipse and cloud them with a winke | But that I would not lose her sight so long' he discerns a serious hesitation about shutting out the sun.

Dr Sanders frequently offers insensitive readings even when his thesis does not seem to be encouraging such misinterpretations. He tends to denigrate a number of justly renowned poems on the basis of responses that bear little relation to the text. Though one respects his determination to examine poems like Holy Sonnet 14 ('Batter my heart') and 'The Canonization' freshly rather than repeating the praises that they usually inspire, the results of this re-examination are often unfortunate. For instance, he sees in 'The Canonization' 'wit stumbling from a daring joke into uneasy impropriety' (p. 53); he finds 'a faint impression of bad taste' (p. 54) in its final couplet. Donne deserves, and has received, better readings.

UNIVERSITY OF MARYLAND, COLLEGE PARK   HEATHER DUBROW OUSBY

Thomas Heywood's 'The Fair Maid of the West, Part I': A Critical Edition. Edited by BROWNELL SALOMON. (Salzburg Studies in English, Jacobean Drama Studies, 36) Salzburg: Institut für Englische Sprache und Literatur, Universität Salzburg. 1975. iv + 209 pp.

When asked what he thought of *Love Story*, someone (Vonnegut perhaps) replied to the effect that one does not criticize an ice-cream sundae. *1 The Fair Maid*, similarly has been regarded as a confection rather than as a literary effort to be taken very seriously, and it is easy to see why. The play is about Bess Bridges, a beautiful and virtuous Elizabethan barmaid, who, having repulsed several unsuitable suitors and done very well in the tavern business, buys a ship, gathers a loyal crew (including the inevitable low-comedy clown), dresses as a sea-captain, and sails for the Azores to bring home the body of her true love Spencer, killed there during the Islands voyage. Because they have burned Spenser's heretical corpse, Bess declares a private war upon the Spaniards — shells their island, captures their ships (but spares the crews with, typically, 'Pray for *Besse Bridges*, and speake well o'th English'), and does very well once more by confiscating cargoes. Meanwhile, Spencer, who is not dead after all, is having his own excitement. Less successful than Bess, he is captured at sea by Spaniards, rescued by Bess (he does not quite recognize her nor she him), separated from her, and finally landed in Barbary by an English merchant. Bess has happened to put into the same place, and there the lovers are reunited under the splendidly barbaric auspices of Mullisheg, King of Fez, whose lust for gorgeous Bess is transformed into a heroic and generous spirit by the example of so much English virtue and constancy in love.

All this derring-do is good natured, high spirited, and unpretentious, as full of clichés of language and of action as Anthony Hope and Rafael Sabatini put together. Heywood was clearly interested in broadly simple effects, and to get them he let subtleties of characterization, complexities of theme, and intricacies of style go by the board in favour of rapidity of movement and direct appeals to sentiment and patriotism. Versimilitude was among the least of his worries, and so, according to most commentators, was a coherent organization of the narrative. Not that *1 The Fair Maid* has been extensively criticized or unduly disparaged. What Heywood was doing is too obvious to require much explanation, and evaluation of such an effort is uncharitably beside the point.

However, the scheme upon which most modern editions of old plays are laid out requires as part of the introduction a critical assessment of the work, and the editor's strategy often is to show that his play is a worthier piece of literature than anyone previously thought. In the most original part of his edition Professor Salomon argues that *1 The Fair Maid* 'is no casually episodic play, but rather one that is highly integrated, formally and thematically'. The integration is achieved by a reconciliation of realism and romanticism both in the leading character and in the structure of the narrative. As for the former, Bess changes during the course of the play from a 'real' girl of humble origins to a heroic paragon of valour and prestige. This proposition no one would doubt, although Professor Salomon says some strange things by way of proving it, as, for example, that Bess's adventures are superficially 'a credible account of an Elizabethan citizen's travels on the high seas to faraway lands', a 'matter-of-fact' travel narrative. As for the events of the plot, they are held together by 'an underlying organic substructure — a symbolic, archetypal frame-work' which confers upon them 'a coherent, holistic unity'. Through structuralist analysis this underlying form is shown to be Joseph Campbell's monomyth, the adventure-quest archetype, to the constituent parts of which Bess's adventures, like those of Prometheus, Jason, and Beowulf, correspond. She too has her Call to Adventure (she leaves Plymouth to become mistress of a tavern in Fowey); her Defeat or Conciliation of an Adverse Power (she tames a bully and wins over a friend of Spencer's who doubts her virtue); her Journey (with Tests) and Gaining of Helpers (she gathers a crew of gentlemen-adventurers and faithful underlings and goes to sea); her Supreme Ordeal (she also tames Mullisheg, 'the AntiChrist'); her Triumph and Reward (she marries Spencer); and her Return (omitted but implied). Once one has persuaded oneself to take this discussion seriously and examine these fragments of the butterfly broken upon the structuralist wheel, the remote correspondence must be granted, but unity of plot in the sense of a logical and credible articulation of the narrative events remains to be shown.

Professor Salomon's introduction also includes capable surveys of previous investigations into the date, sources, stage history, and literary influences of the play, but to these subjects little that is new is added. As for the text itself, there is only one early version of *1 The Fair Maid* with authority (Q 1631). It is a clean print evidently of a scribal transcript and, although the lineation and punctuation occasionally need adjustment, only a handful of verbal readings is suspect. There is not much an editor can or should do to the text except to render it correctly. Here some errors of transcription or judgement have slipped in: 'Now' should be 'Nor' (II.1.63), 'May' should be 'Nay' (II.1.134), 'self' should be 'selfe' (III.2.28), '*upon them*‸' should be '*upon them*,' (III.4.0.2), and 'Spencer' should be '*Spencer*' (III.5.96). At V.1.153 Collier's reading 'sit' is printed for Q's 'fit' without notice, perhaps because Q's ligature was misread. At I.5.12 Q probably reads 'accounts' rather than 'account,' and at II.2.55 'Gentlemen,' rather than 'Gentlemen.' (in both instances the last piece of type prints imperfectly). There is some looseness in recording emended accidentals (for example, at IV.2.109 Q is properly rendered as 'aboard,' but a note shows emendation from 'aboard‸'). Regarding the verbal changes introduced, I like Professor Salomon's emendations or his refusals to emend at I.1.4 and V.1.59, but his changes to II.2.43, II.3.55, III.5.10, IV.4.47, IV.4.124, and IV.4.156 strike me as unnecessary. At IV.1.20 Q is retained and the reading 'once' is defended, but the problem is rather with 'stay'; and at I.4.44 I believe more drastic surgery than P. A. Daniel's 'Within' is required, for this emendation makes the next line suspiciously unidiomatic. At V.2.114–15 Q seems to need emendation rather than explanation. By collating several copies of Q unexamined by previous editors, Professor Salomon picked up two hitherto-unknown press variants; neither matters in the establishment of the text, although their discovery is a minor technical triumph. He is unaware, however, that the change of 'Furner' to 'Turner' (Dramatis Personae, 11) was also a press correction in Q.

The *Dissertationsdruck* which manufactures these paperbound publications does a miserable job of binding them. My review copy was a heap of loose sheets after one reading.

ROBERT K. TURNER, JR

UNIVERSITY OF WISCONSIN, MILWAUKEE

Philaster. By FRANCIS BEAUMONT and JOHN FLETCHER. Edited by DORA JEAN ASHE. (Regents Renaissance Drama Series) London: Edward Arnold. 1975. xxxii + 152 pp. £4.00 (£1.95 paperbound).

The Regents Renaissance Drama Series has a lot to commend it: a well-spaced text, notes at the foot of the page, ample space for a helpful introduction, a reasonably unobtrusive system of modernization, and a large number of good titles in print. Unfortunately the *Philaster* is not quite so well served as some of the other texts in the series. It looks as if the editor completed her work in 1967 or 1968, since the most recent publication cited is from 1966, and no note has been made of any later material such as the 1969 edition of the play in the more substantial Revels series. This edition first appeared in 1974, and one could wish that some of the intervening years had been employed if not to up-date it at least to check the text a little more carefully.

One of the basic requirements of any edition is consistency, in general principles and in detail. Professor Ashe is not quite as thoroughgoing in either as she should be. Although she sensibly chooses to follow Turner's theory of the relationship between Q1 and Q2, she doesn't always stand by its implications. Lines appearing in Q1 and omitted from Q2, for instance, which one would expect on this theory to carry some authority, she provides only in the notes. Q1's alternative readings are made available only occasionally, tucked away in Appendix B. Even when Q2 is ungrammatical (for example III.1.49 'or known') she clings to her copy text. In view, too, of her own theory of Q1 as a reported text she could have made more use of Q1's stage directions. No distinction is made between editorial stage directions (for example, II.4.29) and Q1 stage directions (for example, II.4.49). Colloquially contracted forms are treated inconsistently. Q2 'Has' becomes 'He's' at I.1.208, but 'H'as' at III.2.27 and IV.5.116; 'th'art' becomes 'thou'rt' but 'y'have' stands where we might expect 'you've' at IV.4.41, and 'y'are' stands at IV.4.68. Pronouns seem generally to have been troublesome, notably Q2 'theile' at II.4.6, which is remarkably translated into 'thee'll', where 'they'll' (since the subject is eyes) would be appropriate. Pronouns are gratuitously changed also at II.4.148 where Q2 'ye' is modernized to 'you', and at 153 where 'my own' gets changed in the opposite direction to 'mine own'.

Stage directions need a little more care too. The directions at I.1.83, 281; IV.1.1; IV.5.143; and V.5.1 present some characters' names in roman and some in italic for no reason that I can fathom. Some editorial directions of the explanatory kind are inserted, but directions confirming actions called for by the text are omitted at I.1.168 (*kneels*); II.4.15 (*to* Bellario); III.1.273 (*kneels*), 252 (*draws his sword*); and V.5.9 (*embraces him*). In IV.4. Dion's comments are recorded as asides at lines 72 and 75, but not, where it is more important, at line 60. In IV.5. two speeches by Philaster at lines 19 and 28 are unnecessarily registered as asides.

The old problem of modernizing old spellings has given some trouble, too, as it always does (the General Editor's examples, 'murther' into murder and 'burthen' into burden, are too simple: few instances are as straightforward as that). In this edition I think 'Whootings' (II.4.117); 'lime-hound' (lyam-hound) (IV.1.15);

'troul' (v.3.134); and 'murrions' (v.4.82) would not have suffered unduly from modernization. Q2's 'soops' (a dialect form of modern 'sweeps') is probably rightly left unaltered. I cannot see why Q2 'bug words' should be altered to 'bug's-words' though, and two words, 'pursue' (iv.1.16) and 'track'd' (iv.5.51) are modern forms which obscure the distinct sense of the original 'persue' and 'traced', both of them recognized by OED as distinct in etymology as well as meaning from the modern words. The contracted form of the latter, incidentally (trac'd?) would be called for under the Regents editorial rubric.

The explanatory footnotes on the whole are well done, and as full as the format allows, although in places they lean perhaps too heavily on Dyce, who was not always precise in attributing meanings. One could have wished for a note explaining the historical link of the name Dion to Sicily; the notes on v.3.77 'prologue', v.4.37 'broadside', and 62 'kit' are misleading, and the one on iv.5.90 'Neptune' is wrong.

Straightforward transcriptional errors occur at 1.2.168 where 'forbear' should be 'forbore' (it is glossed as a past tense in the note); at 1.2.177 'gone' should be 'done'; at ii.2.8 'Madam' is added, as Turner suggests, but it is not then deleted as his theory requires from line 111; at ii.3.21 'you' is intrusive; at v.3.38 'awhile' should read 'a while'; at v.5.36 a full stop has been lost; and at v.5.95 'things' should be in the singular.

ANDREW GURR

UNIVERSITY OF LEEDS

Massinger's Imagery. By FRANCIS D. EVENHUIS. (Salzburg Studies in English Literature, Jacobean Drama Studies, 14) Salzburg: Institut für Englische Sprache und Literatur, Universität Salzburg. 1973. vi + 170 pp. £4.60.

In this study, based on a doctoral thesis completed in 1959, Professor Evenhuis has set out to catalogue and offer practical criticism of Massinger's figurative imagery according to its type and subject matter, using the categories developed by Henry Wells in his book *Poetic Imagery* (1924) for the first, and those employed by Caroline Spurgeon in her 1928 study of Shakespeare's imagery for the second. Drawing on a collection of some 1,900 images from sixteen plays, he first gives a short critical account of each type of image (the decorative, the violent, the intensive, the exuberant, the sunken, the expansive, the radical, and the humorous) then offers a statistical analysis of images grouped by subject matter, drawing comparisons with the patterns of imagery found in Marlowe and Shakespeare.

Wisely perhaps, in view of the uncertainties of attribution, no use is made of Massinger's collaborated work, other than *A Very Woman*. (From that play Professor Evenhuis quotes sixteen passages by way of illustration of Massinger's imagery; twelve of them are in fact Fletcher's work, including (ironically) one passage praised as the most genuinely imaginative lines in Massinger's drama.) However, Professor Evenhuis might well have given attention to the images in Massinger's non-dramatic poems (amounting to nearly 600 lines of verse), and it is surprising that he gives no consideration to what may be learned of his author's own poetic theory and strategy by an examination of the remarks about style and poetic imagery to be found in the poems, the dedications, the prologues and epilogues, and in the mouths of characters in the plays.

The critical discussion of Massinger's imagery is uneven in quality. In general, Professor Evenhuis is better at detecting deficiencies in poetic sensibility than he is at recognizing functional strengths. He reminds us, for instance, that many of the images are commonplace and repeated with little variation from play to play, that Massinger is inclined to label his images to clarify their meaning ('heaven's bright eye, the sun'), that he prefers an accumulation of simple comparisons to the sustained and organic development of one image, that he is over-inclined to abstraction and generalization, and that there is little evidence of sensuous feeling or close observation of nature in his imagery.

It is hardly necessary to draw the frequent and unflattering comparisons made with Spenser, Marlowe, and Shakespeare, particularly when the critic displays his own preferences as frankly as he does: 'Marlowe's zest for beauty, his gigantic ambition for knowledge and power, his pagan animism that rejuvenates ancient mythology are watered wine in Massinger. The power and beauty of Marlowe's verse subdue the rational faculties as we listen with awed imagination to his youthful enthusiasms' (p. 45).

In both sections of this study Professor Evenhuis multiplies quotations and illustrations, without subjecting enough of them to the intensive analysis which might have taken his inquiry beyond its somewhat conventional conclusions. In particular, insufficient attention is given to the poetic character and dramatic context of the passages, so that the intrinsic life of the lines often escapes notice.

For instance, the following passage from *The Unnatural Combat* is offered as an example of Massinger's frequent use of textiles in the form of metonymy:

> Nay, if a velvet petticoat move in front,
> Buff jerkins must to the rear.

Professor Evenhuis only observes that ' "velvet petticoat" represents the ladies of the court, "buff jerkins" the lower class' (p. 132). In the play these lines are spoken by the unemployed soldier Belgarde, whose application to Beaufort for relief and position is swept aside when the young man's attention is caught by a beautiful woman kneeling in petition to him. 'Velvet petticoat' refers to Belgarde's competitor, not to the generality of court ladies, and expresses exactly the speaker's scorn for melting female influence as well as his awareness of Theocrine's sexual attractiveness. (Compare the saucy courtier Ricardo's remark, 'I dare not aime at | The petticoate royall, that is still excepted' in *The Picture*, 1.2.53–4.) The phrase 'buff jerkins' means 'soldiers', and is nicely calculated to appeal to hearty masculine toughness and military sentiment. Appropriately for a professional soldier, these textile images are combined with the military phrases 'move in front' and 'to the rear', and the verse is constructed to provide a rough and emphatic stress pattern. In such lines, Massinger's poetic imagery is wholly suited to its stage context, but more than cataloguing is needed if its quality is to be recognized.

Elsewhere Professor Evenhuis observes that 'occasionally Massinger uses bird-imagery to criticize the financial ills of his period. In *A New Way to Pay Old Debts* Overreach is called a cormorant, and in *The Guardian* appears a similar image:

> The cormorant that lives in expectation
> Of a long wish'd for dearth, and smiling, grinds
> The faces of the poor.'
>
> (p. 122)

Massinger actually uses a cormorant image five times in his uncollaborated plays (in *The City Madam* and *The Unnatural Combat*, as well as in the two named plays), and in most of these contexts 'financial ills' are the subject. (In *The Unnatural Combat*, for instance, Belgarde complains that 'the citie cormorants, my monie-mongers, | Have swallow'd downe' his pay.) But there is a world of difference between the quality of the passage cited from the late play *The Guardian* (1633), with its overt social criticism in a romance setting (a group of nobly-minded *banditti* are being reminded of the types of criminals on whom alone they may prey) and its flabby writing (the tautology of 'lives in expectation | Of a long wish'd for dearth', the cliché 'grinds the faces of the poor', and the enervated sense of the vehicle of the cormorant metaphor leading to the comically confused image of the smiling bird grinding faces), and the two earlier uses of the same metaphor in *A New Way* (1625). There the wretched Welborn tauntingly asks his friend Alworth, 'what thinke you of | Faire *Margaret* the only child, and heyre | Of *Cormorant Ouerreach*? does it blush?' (1.1.129–31). The speaker's bitterness is conveyed by the sheer terseness of the phrase, as well as by its sound and position in the lines. Later, Massinger puts the same image into Overreach's own mouth, with still richer results:

> Now, for these other pidling complaints
> Breath'd out in bitterness, as when they call me
> Extortioner, Tyrant, Cormorant, or Intruder
> On my poore Neighbours right . . .
> I only thinke what 'tis to haue my daughter
> Right honorable.
>
> (IV.1.121–9)

Here there is more than criticism of the financial evils of the period. Massinger's dramatic poetry creates a strong impression of explosive energy and vulgarity (how Overreach raps out the second last line and rests lovingly on 'Right honorable'!); the texture of the verse invests Sir Giles with an authentic 'life' of his own, a vitality which has little to do with the narrow purpose of the moralist and which escapes the scrutiny of the cataloguer.

Professor Evenhuis's own style does not encourage confidence in his judgement of Massinger's. We are told that a character 'says turgidly his pedantic eroticism' (p. 40), another 'suffers revulsion in the possibility of being seduced' (p. 27), a third 'turbidly . . . rationalizes in stock-imagery to clarify his incestuous love' (p. 22). A Massinger expression 'fits into the uninventive pattern of his facilely whetting the emotions' (p. 11), his flame images 'resemble a febrile portrayal of love' (p. 131), images of torture express 'the sombre mental torment of Kyd's style' (p. 23), while the dramatist's 'artificiality echoes at times an effete use of the decorative images' of earlier writers (p. 8).

The standard of proof correction is poor. The errors left standing range from mis-spellings (subtelty, meager, diamongs, climatic [i.e. climactic] episodes) to mistakes concerning the titles of plays (*The Bordman*) and the names of characters (Cuculo, Eubulus, and Manto appear as Cucolo, Zubulus, and Minto), and of authors and writers (Lucius Annaleus Seneca). Indications of title are often omitted, and in scene references there is much confusion of case, letter, and number. Substantive errors are common in quotations from Massinger; the worst instance is an eight-line passage from *A Very Woman* in which two lines and a preposition are omitted and there are three punctuation and spelling errors. Quotations from Tucker Brooke's Marlowe appear to be erratically altered, leaving them half-modernized. The text used for quotation from Shakespeare is not listed in the bibliography.

These faults aside, this study accumulates an amount of useful information about Massinger's imagery, while it leaves ample room for more detailed and more exact studies in this field. The sources of Massinger's images have yet to be comprehensively explored, as has their distribution in individual plays. (Does Massinger exploit a particular group of images in a play, or associate particular characters and registers of action with distinctive kinds of imagery?) Massinger's ability to vary the texture of his verse and the density and complexity of images is worth closer examination. The rationale which governs his employment of imagery of any kind is still to be studied.

It may be true that, as Professor Evenhuis says, 'For want of a perceptive and sensitive poetic imagery Massinger falls short of the greatness that was beckoning him', but it is equally true that a perceptive and sensitive analysis of Massinger's dramatic language is still needed to demonstrate his actual achievement.

UNIVERSITY OF OTAGO   C. A. GIBSON
New Zealand

Silver Poets of the Seventeenth Century. Edited, with an Introduction, by G. A. E. PARFITT. (Everyman's University Library) London: Dent; Totowa, New Jersey: Rowman and Littlefield. Second Edition. 1975. xxii + 266 pp. £1.25 (hardback £2.95).

The five poets included in this anthology include two devotional poets, Vaughan and Crashaw, to whom much attention has been given in the last fifty years, and three secular poets, Waller, Denham, and Cowley, who have been undeservedly neglected. The editor says that he would have included Charles Cotton if space had allowed, but since the criteria for inclusion were that the poet's work should not be 'available in bulk in annotated and reasonably inexpensive form' the omission of Cotton is justified. The work of Vaughan and Crashaw is available, but not inexpensive; T. H. (not T. W.) Banks's edition of Denham, first published in 1928, was reprinted in 1969; but there has been no edition of Waller since 1893, nor of Cowley since 1905–6 (and that was without annotation). The most valuable contribution of this anthology therefore is in the selections from Waller and Cowley, and it so happens that of the five poets included these two, with Denham, had by far the greatest reputation in their own time. Our present neglect shows more than a post-Romantic disregard for Augustan taste; and only a fool would dismiss out of hand Dryden's praise of Denham, Waller, and Cowley — ' 'Tis the utmost of my ambition', he said, 'to be thought their equal, or not to be much inferior to them', or deride Milton's association of Cowley with Spenser and Shakespeare as his favourites among the English poets.

The selections are generous and well chosen, and they cover the whole range of each poet's work. 'I have included selections from the secular verse of Vaughan and Crashaw', Mr Parfitt says, 'to help make the point that both were competent verse-technicians rather than merely devotional versifiers'. (The last phrase would not have occurred to most of us as an adequate description of either.) And Waller, whose devotional verse prompted Dr Johnson's well known strictures on so presumptuous an undertaking, is shown to be much more than a purveyor of elegant compliment. Of Denham it is especially valuable to have *The Progress of Learning*, since it is the first (and one of the best) of those 'progress pieces' which were to form a separate genre throughout the eighteenth century and beyond, for Shelley's *Ode to Liberty* continued the tradition. It seems slightly odd not to include Cowley's sensitive and judicious poem *On the Death of Mr Crashaw* in a book which presents most of Crashaw's best poetry, and the *Ode upon Dr Harvey* would have been welcome, as would Waller's delightful *Battle of the Summer Islands*; but no two persons would ever agree about any selection of poems, and it is enough to commend Mr Parfitt's comprehensive and discriminating taste, which allows so good a choice of the poems of Waller, Denham, and Cowley.

One serious criticism must, however, be made: the texts provided are far from reliable, and this, in a volume intended to make accessible to students a selection of poems for the most part not easy to possess, is more than unfortunate, though it is capable of correction. In the first half of the volume alone I have noted some twenty substantive errors, including such major misrepresentations as 'headless' for 'heedless' ('To Van Dyck', l. 5, pp. 14–15), 'died' for 'dyed' ('Instructions to a

Painter', l. 148, p. 37), 'so our' for 'sour' ('The World', l. 11, p. 76), 'designs' for 'desires' ('Cooper's Hill', l. 94, p. 101), and 'taught' for 'first' ('The Progress of Learning', l. 37, p. 116). *Sat superest.*

JOHN BUXTON

NEW COLLEGE, OXFORD

The Benevolence of Laughter: Comic Poetry of the Commonwealth and Restoration. By DAVID FARLEY-HILLS. London: Macmillan. 1974. viii + 212 pp. £5.95.

In his Conclusion Mr Farley-Hills advances the view that Rochester is the greatest writer of comic satire of the Restoration, that his temper and his art exhibit in a pre-eminent degree those qualities necessary for high achievement in his kind (seriousness, moral consistency, detachment), and that his particular success was to judge the world as he found it

not like Marvell and Dryden by the idealistic standards of the past but by the less dogmatic, more relativistic standards of a kind of sceptical rationality. Clearly much of his satirical technique was learnt from Marvell, but he uses these techniques less to reflect an inherent order, as Marvell had done, than to create an order out of the material of actuality. In Rochester's satires man is seen on his own. Unable to rely on a god-given order, he uses his rational faculties not to solve the problem of his being, for that is insoluble, but to come to terms with the fact of its insolubility. (p. 189)

This is a good instance of the author's way of analysing satire. The satirist is considered as thinker and moralist and his poems as growing from his intellectual and moral convictions; much place is given to his formulation and artistic use of a moral standard that allows him to place the objects of his satire in a telling critical perspective.

This is the constant critical preoccupation of a book that is essentially a study of four Restoration satirists, Butler, Marvell, Dryden, and Rochester, through an examination of (mainly) *Hudibras, Last Instructions to a Painter, Mac Flecknoe, Absalom and Achitophel*, and Rochester's *Timon, Tunbridge Wells, The Satyr Against Mankind*, and *Artemisia to Chloe* within the broader context of seventeenth-century comic and satirical poetry and comic theory. It is Mr Farley-Hills's contention that the comic poetry of the Elizabethan and Jacobean ages was celebratory and its satire non-comic, that during the Civil Wars and Commonwealth burlesque, a confused and uncertain form, was typical, and that it was the distinctive achievement of the Restoration to fuse in some of its greatest verse the disinterestedness of true comedy with the faith in order or the consistent scepticism of the satirist. The first chapter surveys attitudes to comedy, laughter, and humour in the late seventeenth and early eighteenth centuries, and the second analyses the contents of such popular collections or 'drolleries' as *The Academy of Complements, Wit's Recreations*, and *Musarum Deliciae*. There is much here to recommend to the attention of students of the period as a preliminary to study of the great authors. These chapters are a useful guide to an abundance of unfamiliar, interesting, and generally neglected material, vigorously and often skilfully written, incorporating survivals from earlier comic tradition and, as Mr Farley-Hills points out, showing the beginnings of Augustan sophistication and scepticism.

Of the chapters devoted to individual authors the most original and interesting are those on Rochester, in which a strong case is put, with enthusiasm and subtlety, for the importance of his accomplishment in a difficult and demanding form. Chapter 3, on *Hudibras*, is the least satisfactory, for *Hudibras* fits awkwardly into the plan of the book. No more than a dozen pages are given to direct analysis of a long, dense, and allusive poem deeply rooted in the political and intellectual life of its time and addressed to sensibilities amply formed on religious controversy and polemic, popular literature, and classical burlesque; so that when Mr Farley-Hills concludes with George Gilfillian's remark that *Hudibras* is 'more a problem than a poem', we are entitled to feel that more attention might have made it less problematical.

Some minor matters: the translations from Saint-Évremond (p. 157) and from Boileau (p. 162) contain inaccuracies and the sense of Butler's famous

> Compound for Sins, they are inclin'd to,
> By damning those they have no mind to

is somewhat altered by a misquotation on page 50.

UNIVERSITY OF YORK   J. DONOVAN

Milton and the Literary Satan. By FRANK S. KASTOR. Amsterdam: Rodopi. 1974. 119 pp. fl 20.

Professor Kastor's book re-examines the anti-hero of *Paradise Lost* against the background of literary (as contrasted with theological or quasi-historical) tradition, stressing the persistence of the image of a 'trimorphic Satan': archangel, prince of hell, and tempter. Noting the failure of recent scholarship to explain satisfactorily the principle 'controlling the "*characterization*" of Milton's Satan' or to 'project an historical prototype which is consistent, convincing, circumscribable, and historically valid against which Milton's portrait can be understood, as well as measured and criticized', Professor Kastor attributes this failure, in part, to inconsistencies and contradictions in traditional discussions of Satan's 'character, appearance, and attributes' from patristic times to the present. The Satan of learned and popular traditions alike possesses 'a unique and multifarious nature: angel, devil, spirit, manlike shape, mythic entity, theological principle, and . . . philosophic concept'. Because of the paucity of scriptural details concerning Satan and his character, authoritative doctrine has been limited, whereas 'theological speculation has been voluminous' and widely varied. 'Historically . . . Satan is a multifarious complex, an . . . accretion of many ages, which cannot in any literary sense be called "a" character at all.'

A more stable and consistent 'model or prototype' (Professor Kastor maintains) is to be found in a tradition which offers an essentially 'literary Satan'. Against this model Milton's portrait can be effectively 'understood, measured, and criticized', as can the 'Satanic portraits of Dante, Marlowe, Vondel, Blake, Goethe, and many more'. The 'Christian Story of Divine History' (as Professor Kastor terms it) provided 'a narrative framework for the cosmic drama of God, Man, and Satan; and, in terms of myth, an explanation and genesis of evil in the character of Satan'. A study of Satan's character through a large number of literary versions of the story reveals a pattern that 'explains the controlling and artistic principles of Milton's Satan' and 'innumerable other satanic portraits in the tradition'.

The first chapter ('The Satanic Pattern') examines the three roles corresponding to the three 'main events' in which Satan participates: 'the war or apostasy in heaven, the council and subsequent scenes in hell, and the temptation in the garden'. Each 'involves a different role'; each role is 'established in a very different world'; each involves 'very different functions and types of actions and, ultimately, characterization'. Satan, in short, is 'a trimorph, or three related but distinguishable personages: a highly placed Archangel, the grisly Prince of Hell, and the deceitful, serpentine Tempter'. Though these roles are usually 'unified by a single consciousness', they are sometimes divided among 'distinctly separate characters'.

The 'methods of differentiating (and subsequently characterizing) the roles vary', ranging from 'overt statements about changed roles' and alterations in motivation to the division of these roles into three separate parts played by three distinct persons under three different names.

The second chapter ('The Satanic Pattern in Action') examines the trimorphic scheme as it occurs in 'representative single works': Avitus's poem on Mosaic history, the Old English 'Genesis-B', medieval religious drama, and the dramatic poems of Salandra and Vondel. The remaining chapters explore Milton's adaptation of the trimorphic pattern in *Paradise Lost*, where (as 'in other accounts of the story') the 'trimorph stems from a separation of the three roles in accordance with the demands made by three different places or settings'. In Milton's Satan, Professor Kastor finds 'one name, one consciousness', but also 'three roles, three characters'. The 'special literary problem' (he believes) that confronted Milton in casting this 'religious story in the mold of a classical epic' is reflected in the two principal functions of the Satanic figure in *Paradise Lost*; as epic antagonist and as exemplar of evil. These require contradictory rather than complementary rhetorical strategies: generally 'the epic antagonist demands aggrandizement, the exemplar of evil diminishment'. Milton 'diminishes the apostates' (and their leader) 'by showing a loss and change which is essentially inward and moral, while simultaneously creating a massive external force for his epic conflict'.

Observing that 'the perception of different levels and kinds of characterization in Milton's Satan by Waldock and . . . others seems entirely accurate', Professor Kastor emphasizes the flexibility which 'three different Satans rather than one' allowed the poet in structuring the major action in his epic, and the 'richness' of his presentation of these Satanic roles as 'exemplars of evil'. Appendix A ('Factor Analysis in the Genesis and Development of the Satanic Pattern') discusses the 'formative factors' that conditioned the basic trimorph. Appendix B ('Many Another Literary Satan') re-examines the role of the tempter in Milton's epyllion on the Gunpowder Plot (*In quintum Novembris*) and in *Comus* and *Paradise Regained*. After briefly discussing the devils of Marlowe, Marino, and Dante, the author suggests that 'the trimorphic pattern, the three different roles and characterizations, appear to form the foundation . . . of Satan's literary characterization generally'. This volume also contains a selected bibliography (6 pp.) and an index of names (9 pp.).

This is an interesting study, and one hopes that the author will continue his researches in this field. The variable relationships between theological or exegetical tradition and literary representations of Satan, and, in particular, the influence of Augustine and other patristic writers on the formation of the Satanic 'trimorph' and on its literary exploitation might be re-examined in detail. It might also be profitable to consider divergences among Protestant and Catholic commentators conerning the relevance of Isaiah 14. 12–15 and Ezekiel 28. 13–19 to Revelation 12. 9 and 20. 2 and to Genesis 3. 1–5, 14–15, and the extent to which these exegetical divergencies influenced literary representations of Satan. (Aspects of these problems have been examined by J. M. Evans, *Paradise Lost and the Genesis Tradition* (Oxford, 1968), pp. 81–8, 95, 134, 152; by C. A. Patrides, *Milton and the Christian Tradition* (Oxford, 1966), pp. 91–7, 106–7; and by Robert H. West, *Milton and the Angels* (Athens, Georgia, 1955), pp. 49, 59–60, 69, 76, 91.)

Professor Kastor's monograph is a welcome addition to the large body of criticism centred on Milton's characterization of Satan. His approach is potentially fruitful (though one should not draw too sharp a line between literary and theological treatments of the devil) and throws light on the literary problems faced by other poets in relating the fall of the angels and the fall of man, especially the problem of achieving consistency and continuity in characterization and of making the transitions between the traditional Satanic roles consistent with verisimilitude and probability. The book contains a large number of misprints.

HENRY E. HUNTINGTON LIBRARY, SAN MARINO   JOHN M. STEADMAN
California

Wedges and Wings: The Patterning of 'Paradise Regained'. By BURTON JASPER WEBER. Carbondale and Edwardsville: Southern Illinois University Press. 1975. xiv + 130 pp. $10.00.

In his preface Mr Weber describes his method as 'slightly unorthodox' and his interest in John Milton as 'a little unfashionable' (p. xi). While he does not define unorthodoxy or the unfashionable, he does explicitly describe his study of *Paradise Regained* as a formal analysis. He proposes to reveal the orderliness and coherence of Milton's poem. A formal analysis 'does not provide a total account of a piece' (p. xii), but it provides clarity by increasing the comprehensibility of the parts.

Mr Weber's study reflects the ideas of many scholars who have written on *Paradise Regained*. He has not only read Milton's poem carefully, but also he reveals a familiarity with the studies of Barbara Lewalski, Elizabeth Pope, Arnold Stein, Dick Taylor, Jr, Don Cameron Allen, A. S. P. Woodhouse, and others. Mr Weber's results are based on his pitting the views of one critic against another, his own interpretations against the various readings, and all views against textual evidence. Unfortunately, in his quest for consistency and a fair evaluation of other interpretations, he sometimes strays into bypaths which detract from his discussion, as in the following sample: 'the litotes indicates that the "wonted shape" in which he [Satan] appears is, as Mrs. Lewalski says, a fallen angel's shape, not, as Miss Pope suggests, the human form used on the preceding days ... Moreover, the elimination of hunger may be viewed in exactly the opposite way from the way that Mrs. Lewalski views it' (p. 11). The passage seems litigious and distracting.

Wedges and Wings is organized around the structure of Milton's poem. The book contains an introductory discussion of the overall structure of *Paradise Regained*, individual chapters on the major divisions of the poem, and a final section which integrates theme, character, and genre. Chapter 1, 'Wedges', reviews major critical interpretations of the poem's structure. Mr Weber does not take sides with exclusively schematic or dramatic interpretations; he finds non-dramatic and dramatic elements in the poem, with the argumentative materials predominating. The poem is divided according to each day's trial and subdivided into a triple trial within each day. The basis for the tripartite division is the Neo-Platonic conception of the soul. Each trial emphasizes sense, reason, and intellect. In each of the encounters Jesus demonstrates temperance, justice, and holiness. Because of Mr Weber's method of close textual analysis, it is difficult to do justice to the intricacies of interpretation. The reader would do well in using *Wedges and Wings* to have a copy of the poem nearby and to interweave his reading with close attention to Milton's text. Mr Weber leads the reader through the individual trials as they test Jesus's reason, passion, and intellect. He also moves backward and forward through the poem, indicating crucial connexions and integrating individual sections with the total poem.

He is particularly eager to correct controversial interpretations. He finds, for example, that the storm scene is not an example of Satan's regression, as some critics have asserted, but rather a powerful presentation of Satan's 'last awesome resource, the perverted will' (p. 56). He interprets the famous tower scene as a 'sudden epiphany' rather than as a manifestation of Jesus's divinity or as a joint act by God and Jesus. Jesus thus avoids Satan's invitation 'to display his glorious status or to test God's works' (p. 68). God's miracle is also an affirmation of Jesus's values and a reward for his moral fortitude. The focus remains on Jesus's humanity.

In Chapter 6, 'Wings', Mr Weber explores further the problem of Jesus's dual nature. He argues that since the poem is an epic, the action and character portrayal must be developmental; but a developmental view is contingent on seeing Jesus as human. The action in the poem hinges on the strengthening of Jesus through moral trial. Milton's statement of the poem's subject corroborates that Jesus is 'a man of wisdom ready for trial' (p. 74). If Jesus is divine, the sincerity of the temptations is called into question. Mr Weber reminds the reader that Jesus's actions are balanced against 'man's initial lapse' (p. 85). Where Adam failed, Jesus, the second Adam, succeeds. Mr Weber's interpretation thus integrates theme, dramatic action, and argument.

The final chapter treats the relationship between Satan and Jesus. Mr Weber charts Satan's decline. He finds that the three sections of Jesus's trials 'coincide with the three stages of Satan's decline' (p. 91). Satan's fall is triple. He falls like Antaeus, like the Sphinx, and does so while Jesus rises. His fall reveals multiple ironies. He has brought on himself the fate he had intended for Jesus; he learns, not that Jesus was supernatural, but that 'a mere man can defeat him as thoroughly as the heavenly Son once did' (p. 107). He becomes an instrument of God though he intended the reverse.

Mr Weber does not give a radically new interpretation of the poem. He does not concern himself with recent developments in Milton criticism; Milton's rhetorical strategies, his uses of myth and language, the role of the reader, or Milton's social milieu. He has limited his scope to an examination of the poem's structure. He succeeds in his intricate analysis of the text, in his exposure of a logical structure, and in his integration of existing interpretations of the poem. Both beginning readers of Milton and specialists will find *Wedges and Wings* useful.

UNIVERSITY OF PITTSBURGH   MARCIA LANDY

Studies in Dryden's Dramatic Technique: The Use of Scenes Depicting Persuasion and Accusation. By RICHARD LESLIE LARSON. (Salzburg Studies in English Literature, Poetic Drama and Poetic Theory, 9) Salzburg: Institut für Englische Sprache und Literatur, Universität Salzburg. 1975. viii + 317 pp.

'Professor Larson's present duties', a postscript to his book informs us, 'have prevented him from updating his Harvard thesis, presented in 1963' (p. 317). The author, then, has left his work for nine years and more, and we must regret that he did not use the interval to correct the many errors of punctuation, spelling, and syntax that disfigure his work and try the reader's patience. An undeviating commitment to 'ecstacy', for example, irritating enough in an undergraduate essay, is wholly unacceptable in a work of scholarship.

For all its age, however, Professor Larson's book springs from ambitions that are still timely and commendable. Now, as in 1963, it is largely true that studies of Dryden's plays have addressed themselves not to his dramaturgy but to his 'political and sociological assumptions' and 'philosophical or ethical doctrines' (p. i). Professor Larson's aim is to redress the balance: after tracing the preoccupation with audience 'concernment' that persists throughout Dryden's Protean critical career (pp. 1–28), he attempts to show how Dryden sustained the emotional appeal of his plays as he outgrew an initial dependence on crowded incident and arbitrary *peripeteia*. Dryden succeeds, according to Professor Larson, by increasing his subtlety and skill in depicting scenes of persuasion and accusation: the easy titillation of labyrinthine incident gives way to the excitement of intricately portrayed psychomachia.

Dryden's attitude towards the heart and pulse of his audience was, however, more ambivalent than Professor Larson allows. He certainly sought to delight and instruct by arousing emotional involvement; he also felt, nevertheless, that an informed response to his plays should comprehend arcana, 'secret beauties', inaccessible to the average spectator. (See, for example, 'A Defence of *An Essay of Dramatic Poesy*' and the Preface to *Don Sebastian*.) In concentrating on the manipulation of audience emotion, Professor Larson oversimplifies Dryden's artistic intelligence and dramatic practice, and at his worst dissolves finely integrated works into collections of discrete and superficial emotional effects.

Professor Larson oversimplifies because he reacts to excess against the heavily exegetical approach of his predecessors. Ideas, after all, form an integral part of drama: to excise them from the organism that they animate is certainly foolish; it is no less foolish, however, to consider plays largely as undulations of emotional stimuli and to ignore the 'secret beauties' and meanings that lie in the intricate coherence of image, motif, and antiphonal symmetry. Professor Larson does attempt to define the heroic values urged during the scenes of persuasion and accusation (though in doing so he says nothing new). Too often, however, he invites us to an ignorant rapture, sailing close to the freshman assumption that an 'emotional response' need have no basis in an intelligent and analytic reading. In the reconciliation of Dorax and Sebastian, for example, he sees no release from the Fall and resurrection of an identity lost through sin: instead, he gives us plot summary, a chart of emotional decibels, and a final verdict that the scene is 'heart-warming' (p. 285).

He has, furthermore, a formidable vein of pedestrianism and insensitivity. His account of Dryden's antecedents, for example, is tedious and uninformative: the analyses of scenes of persuasion, etc., are little more than factual synopses, telling us nothing about the assumptions that govern the portrayal of psychological manipulation and change. His discussions of the early heroic plays, moreover, are marred by oversimplification and inaccuracy, since he shares with other commentators a Procrustean readiness to see inconsistent, wavering, and human characters as rigid moral stereotypes. It is not true, for example, that 'Acacis' ability to adhere to his moral standards is never seriously threatened' (p. 93): Acacis duels with Montezuma in an attempt to usurp Orazia's hand. The accounts of persuasion often fail because the roles of the persuaders are often misrepresented.

Professor Larson does far better, however, in his commentaries on *The Conquest of Granada*, *Aureng-Zebe*, and *All for Love*. His account of Almanzor's development (which he sees as imperfect, erratic, and inconclusive) is the best to date, and in all three analyses he displays a welcome responsiveness to the complexity of psychological experience with which Dryden endows his characters. Only, however, in the discussion of *All for Love* (by far the best part of the book) does any sense of total dramatic unity emerge. The thematic links postulated in the section on *The Conquest of Granada*, for example, are too imprecise and limited to convey any sense of the play's linear and contrapuntal coherence.

Throughout the book, furthermore, Professor Larson is hampered by his habit of dwelling on emotional accident without deriving it from dramatic meaning: 'Aureng-Zebe', he states baldly, 'instantly censures himself and repents his jealousy — thereby pleasing the spectator with joyful feelings' (p. 193). As the analyses proceed, moreover, we become increasingly aware that the author's areas of enquiry do not adequately encompass Dryden's range and priorities as a dramatist: Professor Larson is too ready to censure scenes as irrelevant when their sole fault is to fall outside his blinkered and restrictive concerns. The duel between Gonsalvo and Rodorick in *The Rival Ladies* is dismissed for creating insufficient 'emotional involvement' (p. 153). Yet the comic deflation of Gonsalvo's romantic self-denial admirably sustains one of the play's principal concerns: the conflict between the expectations of conventional idealism and the bathos of human reality. The serious plot of *Marriage à la Mode* is presented as a sequence of self-contained emotional climaxes, lacking a developing dramatic logic (pp. 159–64). Nourmahal, we learn, has no importance in the design of *Aureng-Zebe*, serving merely to add some 'violent excitement' (p. 214). *Don Sebastian* fares worst of all: events in the first three and a half acts 'cohere but tenuously, if at all, about a moral theme' (p. 278); the scene of *anagnorisis* is 'tedious because it is insignificant' (p. 289); and 'Dryden does not repeat in subsidiary characters the moral themes of the principal "serious" plot' (p. 296). Judgements of such outrageous impercipience cannot be countered in the brief space of a review. Rebuttal, however, need not be attempted here. In the years since 1963 Alssid, King, Rothstein, Newman, and Myers have published work which exposes the worthlessness of such assertions. In choosing to ignore twelve years of Dryden scholarship, Professor Larson has shown little regard for the time and patience of his readers. Had he excerpted the best parts of his work (and these are by no means inconsiderable), he could have produced some valuable articles. Had he been prepared to 'update' his work, he might have removed many glaring defects. As it is, he has produced the least distinguished book on Dryden's plays since that of Professor Selma Assir Zebouni.

DEREK HUGHES

UNIVERSITY OF WARWICK

The American Puritan Imagination: Essays in Revaluation. Edited by SACVAN BERCO-VITCH. London: Cambridge University Press. 1974. viii + 265 pp. £4.50 (£2.00 paperbound).

It is worth recalling from time to time that America was settled not only by the English Puritans who landed in Massachusetts, but by Dutch Calvinists, English Anglicans and Catholics, French and Spanish Catholics, and many other cultural groups, apart from the mass immigrations of the nineteenth century. Like the Puritans, they too contributed to American political theory, wrote history, personal recollection, and a little poetry and, unlike the Puritans, they excelled at travel accounts and natural description.

Within the Puritan community too, the importance of ideological dialogue can be over-emphasized. Sumner Chilton Powell's *Puritan Village* (Middletown: Wesleyan University Press, 1963) is a reminder that the distribution of land and power could loom as large in everyday affairs as disputes over the efficacy of works or even the tests of church membership. Yet we are right to urge an understanding of the Puritans as a basis for the study of American history and literature, if only because everything the Puritans did and wrote flowed from the conviction of their unique-ness; their one accurate prophecy (because in the self-conscious atmosphere of Massachusetts it was, and is, self-fulfilling) turned out to be that of their own importance.

But taking the Puritans at their own valuation, the American literary historian has always had some difficulty relating the Puritans to the later literature. Studying their abstract theology did not help much; it was difficult to describe, extremely fluid, and connected only with the greatest ingenuity with the interests, say, of Melville and Mark Twain. (Even Hawthorne seems uninterested in, or ignorant of, the *theological* issues of Massachusetts Puritanism.) Various aesthetic conclusions were drawn, by Perry Miller, Charles Feidelson, and Harry Levin, from the Puritans' preference for Ramist over Aristotelian logic and from their meditative practice of scrutinizing minute occurrences for major abstract implications. But all of this, however intelligent as a system in itself, seemed powerless to describe more than a small amount of later American writing.

The most recent generalization about the Puritans is not strictly theological or psychological, but incorporates elements of both: it is that the Massachusetts Puritans were English Puritans frozen into the millennial expectations so widespread at the time they left the mother country and so soon to be thwarted there; that they were aware of enacting an imperfect physical antitype of the flight from Egypt and the settlement of the Promised Land; that they looked forward, where their English brethren could not after the Restoration, to the establishment of a spiritual millennium through a perfected polity in the new world. This account has the virtue of explaining not only the 'Americanness' of the American Puritans themselves, but also the preoccupation of Emerson, Whitman, and even Wallace Stevens with a poetics (always projected into the future) that will be the perfect, natural expression of ordinary things. More obviously, it also suggests a source for that persistent, perhaps too potent, evocation of the promised land in American novels: the territory that Huck Finn 'lights out' for, Hemingway's 'Clean, Well-Lighted Place', Fitzgerald's 'green breast of the new world'. Two recent books, Loren Baritz's *City on a Hill* (New York: John Wiley, 1964) and Ursula Brumm's *American Thought and Religious Typology* (New Brunswick: Rutgers University Press, 1970) have done much to establish the millennial habit of mind as appropriate to the American Puritans.

The value of *The American Puritan Imagination* is that it presents the current state of thinking on the subject. It makes no pretence to originality; all the essays have been published elsewhere, and three of them have appeared as chapters of books as early as 1963. The collection is divided into three sections: 'Approaches, Themes and Genres'; 'Four Major Figures' (William Bradford, Anne Bradstreet, Edward Taylor, and Cotton Mather); and 'Continuities', which attempts to trace the effects of the Puritan imagination on later American writing. Mr Bercovitch's introduction surveys the field and draws useful conclusions. There is very little in the collection that is not sophisticated and judicious, even though the high-powered scholarship can lead, at times, to unsurprising conclusions, as when Ursula Brumm ('Christ and Adam as "Figures" in American Literature') reveals that Faulkner's Joe Christmas is a Christ figure.

Three essays stand out from a background of a generally high standard. In the first section, Larzer Ziff, himself the author of the excellent *Puritanism in America* (London: Oxford University Press, 1973), disposes finally of the old problem of how the Puritans, with their taste for the plain style, could have written such ingenious poems and sermons. Through a study of William Wright, who wrote both 'Anglican-style' and Puritan sermons, Mr Ziff shows that 'plain style and passionate allegorizing are related elements of Puritanism'. Karl Keller convinces me of something I have not believed before: that Edward Taylor's modesty about his poetry is more than the conventional inability *topos*. Taylor was more interested in the process of writing than in its product. This makes his poetry 'one more example of what John A. Kouwenhoven [in an essay in *American Literary Essays*, edited by Lewis Leary (New York, 1960)] calls "the national preoccupation with process"' and connects Taylor's poetry with skyscrapers, gridiron town plans, jazz, and even the Constitution. This brief summary makes Mr Keller's analysis sound absurd; in fact, it is stimulating and convincing, and it deserves, perhaps more than the essays already there, a place in the 'Continuities' section of the collection. Jesper Rosenmeier, in the most extended integration of scholarship and critical acumen represented here, shows that William Bradford's history of the Plymouth Colony was entirely retrospective, and related to what Bradford saw as spiritual crises of the settlement. The essay is central to the theme of millennial literature, that hazy dividing line between history and fiction which so characterizes American Puritan prose.   STEPHEN FENDER

UNIVERSITY COLLEGE, LONDON

Increase Mather. By MASON I. LOWANCE, JR. (Twayne's United States Authors Series, 246) New York: Twayne. 1974. 185 pp. $7.50.

We should begin by disposing of the irreverent thought that having reached American author No. 246, it is only natural that the Twayne series should have had to winkle out an obscure Puritan divine who sounds like a fugitive from *The Alchemist*. In fact, the Twayne series did not begin with major authors and work its way down to minor scribblers, but has always included a certain number of representative men, an account of whose lives illuminates their setting. One of the best of these is Herbert Smith's study of Richard Watson Gilder, editor of the *Century* magazine (TUSAS, 166), which conveys a great deal of information, otherwise unobtainable, about the conditions of commercial publishing at the end of the nineteenth century.

Increase Mather certainly qualifies as a man of his time. For most of his long life he was involved with the civil government and spiritual guidance of the Massachusetts Bay Colony. He was born only nine years after the colony was founded as a tight, self-defined, millennarian community, and he lived well into the more liberal, cosmopolitan milieu of eighteenth-century Boston. His public activities reflected the opposing moods touched by the termini of his life. He supported scientific studies while president of Harvard, but allowed no doctrinal variation on the strict Congregationalism represented there. In the face of the prejudice of his more fundamentalist contemporaries, he urged innoculation against smallpox, but he opposed the progressive relaxation of criteria for admission to the membership and sacraments of the church. He supported the Salem witch trials, but argued against some of the more superstitious procedures of the court, especially the admission as evidence against the supposed witch the victim's claim to have been visited and tormented by the 'spectre' of the accused. He corresponded with the Royal Society, not only about the phenomena of New England natural history, but also about supernatural occurrences there.

Mason Lowance is well equipped to discuss these and other matters, being a Colonial Literature man at the University of Massachusetts, and having published widely in the field. His problem is that Increase Mather and his son, Cotton, wrote so much about themselves, and others have written so much about them since, that a simple biography is no longer newsworthy. Mr Lowance has settled instead for an account of Mather's ideas and, to a certain extent, the shape he gave to them. The difficulty with this approach is that Mather was such a faithful reflection of his times that his ideas, too, have already been accounted for in the numerous books on the thought of the period. Thus a chapter on Mather's sermons draws heavily on a well-known general description of the subject, Babette Levy's *Preaching in the First Half-Century of New England History* (New York, 1945), and another chapter, on his doctrine, owes a good deal to Ursula Brumm's *American Thought and Religious Typology* (English translation, New Brunswick, 1970). There is nothing wrong with building on established work in a field, but the question is, in what direction is Mr Lowance building? Presumably a student interested in Increase Mather would turn first to the standard biography, Kenneth Murdock's *Increase Mather: The Foremost American Puritan* (Cambridge, Massachusetts, 1925), and would anyone interested in him not already have absorbed most of the general information on American Puritan thought outlined here?

But even the general account, so carefully reiterated by Mr Lowance, needs qualifying. The Puritans' belief in typology is a case in point. The standard view is that typological thinking in New England underwent a degeneration from the purity of Increase Mather and his brother Samuel, who believed that the only appropriate exegesis of a text (say, in a commentary or a sermon) was a typological connexion between the Old and New Testaments established by God himself, through Cotton Mather, whose *Magnalia Christi Americana* extends the practice loosely to classical and historical parallels, down to Hawthorne, who, according to Ursula Brumm could not make up his mind if his figures were types in the old Puritan sense or in the nineteenth-century sense of a consciously applied symbol. More recently, Frank Kermode, in *The Classic* (London, 1975), has placed a quite different value on Hawthorne's 'shimmering' typology.

The difficulty with this view is that Samuel Mather's rigorous rejection of allegorical and figurative exegesis was not followed by all, even of his contemporaries. Puritan commentaries like James Durham's *Clavis Cantici* (Edinburgh, 1668) and Henry Ainsworth's *Annotations upon the Five Books of Moses, . . . the Psalmes and the Song of Songs . . .* (London, 1627), while stressing the distinction between type and allegory, followed the catholic tradition of 'spiritualising' the song of Solomon as the love song sung to Christ by his bride, the Church. The American Puritan poet, Edward Taylor, taking this interpretation from his own copies of Durham and Ainsworth, made rich use of the tradition in his *Preparatory Meditations*. Even Increase Mather extends his typology far beyond the scriptural province allowed by his brother, retrospectively recuperating disappointments as 'providences' foretold in scripture and interpreting contemporary events as types of things to come.

It is another question, though, whether in New England the typological habit was extended beyond the authority of Holy Writ with an easy conscience and without the sense of reacting to immense pressures. *Mourt's Relation*, the first account of Plymouth Plantation, written by William Bradford, Edward Winslow, and others, explicitly discourages even that famous reading of the Puritan emigration as antitypical of the Israelites' errand into the wilderness: 'Neither is there any land or possession now, like unto the possession which the Jews had in Canaan, being legally holy and appropriated unto a holy people . . . and a type of eternal rest in heaven . . . no land so appropriated, none typical, much less any that can be said to be given of God to any nation as was Canaan . . . But now we are all in all places strangers and pilgrims, travellers and sojourners, most properly, having no dwelling but in this earthen tabernacle.'

Yet only ten years later Bradford started to write *Of Plymouth Plantation* as though he had half forgotten the warning, recasting the often disappointing, and certainly short, 'history' of Plymouth into an antitypical, providential plan, focused on a specific place. What made him do it: the certainty that their common history was divinely ordered, and therefore properly subject to a typological reading? Or the suspicion that their enterprise might not, after all, be the chosen path to the Millennium? In an acute essay collected in *Typology and Early American Literature* (Amherst, 1972) and reprinted in *The American Puritan Imagination* (London, 1974), Jesper Rosenmeier suggests that the establishment of the relatively prosperous and well-connected Massachusetts Bay Colony, ten years after the arrival of the Plymouth separatists, may have prompted Bradford to start his history, as if to assert the primacy of Plymouth in the work of building the holy commonwealth. In that case, Bradford's typological assertions were the result not of certainty but of doubt.

When Increase Mather came to write his version of New England history, *A Relation of the Troubles . . . in New-England*, he drew, as Mr Lowance shows in a good chapter called 'The Shaping of History', on *Mourt's Relation*, interpolating, as had Bradford, his own *post facto* interpretation of events as part of God's plan. Was his typology, and his retrospective discovery of 'providences', also the result of uncertainty? The question should at least be asked.

This is one direction in which Mr Lowance might have gone further. What fascinates a modern reader of Mather is not only that he thought of himself as standing between the concentrated energy of an earlier generation and the easy complacency of a later, but also that the instability of his prose style often reflects that feeling. Even his *Essay for the Recording of Illustrious Providences* reflects his transitional status, written as it is in the clear, concrete descriptive style of the Royal Society, yet insisting, sometimes nervously, as though it had been forgotten for a moment, the immanence of God in the natural phenomena he seeks to record so faithfully.

To put it another way, it may be that the life of Increase Mather, in his discourse as distinct from his ideas, remains to be written. In any case the conventional view of the evolution, or degeneration, of New England typology needs now to be modified. The types began to 'shimmer' long before Hawthorne; before Cotton Mather, even. Mr Lowance might have been more critical of the secondary sources he so fairly summarizes, and he might have had more to say about why Mather wrote the way he did. It is this failure to exploit his opportunities that makes his book, for all its scholarly meticulousness, something of a disappointment.

UNIVERSITY COLLEGE, LONDON   STEPHEN FENDER

Two English Novelists: Aphra Behn and Anthony Trollope. By GEORGE GUFFEY and ANDREW WRIGHT. Los Angeles: William Andrews Clark Memorial Library, University of California. 1975. vi + 76 pp.

This short and readable book makes available two papers given at a Clark Library Seminar in 1974: the reader can well believe that they provoked lively discussion. In a closely documented argument, Professor George Guffey adds a new dimension to interpretation of Mrs Aphra Behn's vivid novel *Oronooko* (1688), an ostensibly realistic story of an African prince who misguidedly accepts a dinner invitation aboard an English ship and is sold into slavery in the West Indian colony, Surinam. Comparing contemporary descriptions of the Gold Coast and Surinam with the novelist's idealized pictures, Professor Guffey suggests that Mrs Behn intentionally distorted facts not merely in the interests of narrative colour but as a way of raising sympathy for James II, who was to be supplanted by William of Orange in 1689, a takeover to which Mrs Behn may have been alerting her readers by heightening the glories of Surinam, which England had lost to the Dutch in 1667. Professor Guffey wisely resists the temptation to exaggerate parallels between Mrs Behn's exotic settings and Restoration England into a case for *Oronooko* as a full-blown political allegory; he presents her Royalist bias more as a pressure behind the novel than as its main rationale. The chief value of his paper is that it reinforces recent critical emphasis on *Oronooko*'s thematic and structural unity, giving Mrs Behn her due as a skilful writer without overpraising her as an artist — or as a Women's Liberationist. By placing her firmly in her own unsettled century, Professor Guffey persuasively shows that *Oronooko*, like *Gulliver's Travels*, can sustain a political reading and be none the worse (or necessarily the better) as imaginative literature.

Trollope said that he had never read 'more detestable trash than the stories written by Mrs Aphra Behn'. But then, as Professor Andrew Wright's paper on

Trollope's reading demonstrates, this most prolific of Victorian novelists rated fiction puzzlingly low, reserving his highest praise, and most of his energies as a reader, for poetry and drama. Professor Wright draws on little-known evidence to present a survey of Trollope's reading preferences which opens up intriguing questions about the novelist's commitment to the literary form that earned him his fame and fortune. One possible solution to many anomalies is Professor Wright's opinion that for Trollope the reading of novels was harmless entertainment and the writing of them equally harmless building of castles in the air. It all seems very simple: yet the fact that when he wrote *An Autobiography*, which includes most of his pronouncements on fiction, Trollope had a public just as much in mind as when he was writing novels does not license a clear separation of his persona from his private poetry-loving self. The unpublished material mentioned by Professor Wright (p. 53) may be the notebooks kept by Trollope from 1835 to 1840 and containing copious notes on Bulwer as well as on Pope. Anyway, there are other reasons to believe that Trollope was not uttering ritualistic pieties but was in deadly earnest when he wrote that characterization was a matter of 'deep conscience' to the novelist, who must, like the clergyman, 'make virtue alluring and vice ugly, while he charms his reader instead of wearying him'. The reasons lie mostly in the novels themselves, where dazzling virtue and dark vice are all too often juxta-posed in Trollope's attempts to meet the demands of the Horatian recipe for mixed pleasure and profit.

Professor Wright justly points out that Trollope was more interested in his characters' private lives than in their public careers, particularly in the so-called political novels. But again Trollope's aim was to harmonize, not divide: the men and women he admires are the ones whose public activities reflect their private virtues, and who can (like the novelist himself perhaps) combine their own pleasure with the nation's profit. Critics have yet to explore satisfactorily the suggestion, made here by Professor Wright, that the genial Trollopian narrator is a mask, but the impressive realism of Trollope's best work makes it seem likely that the impulse to engage directly with contemporary reality was stronger than the need to escape from a hauntingly unhappy childhood.

VALERIE SHAW

UNIVERSITY OF EDINBURGH

From Heroics to Sentimentalism: A Study of Thomas Otway's Tragedies. By HAZEL M. BATZER POLLARD. (Salzburg Studies in English Literature, Poetic Drama and Poetic Theory, 10) Salzburg: Institut für Englische Sprache und Literatur, Universität Salzburg. 1974. iv + 301 pp.

Hazel Batzer Pollard's study of Otway is based on a doctoral dissertation of 1956. In an 'introductory preface' Professor Richard Pollard states that it 'owes nothing' to subsequent work, and the introduction makes it plain that only 'minor revisions' have been made to the dissertation. A selective bibliographical supplement lists works which have appeared relevant to the topic since 1956, and 'significant materials' have been added to the footnotes, especially from Pollard and Pollard, *From Human Sentience to Drama*.

The thesis is that 'Otway's position in Restoration tragedy is transitional; he grows surely and persistently away from the heroic drama into the drama of sensibility'. Close analysis of the tragedies shows Otway from an early stage responding to elements of potential sentimentality in the heroic material he inherited, and developing in the direction of a domestic tragedy which 'provides prototypes for the representative "Man of Feeling" of the eighteenth century'. The focus is mainly upon the seventeenth-century theatre, especially Racine and

Dryden, and the implications of Otway's work for the eighteenth century are not explored.

Considered as an academic thesis for the degree of doctor of philosophy, the book is typical of the kind. The bibliographical material is useful, although clumsily updated, the analysis of details of the text is thorough, if pedestrian, and the conclusion well substantiated by the evidence, but predictable. Pertinent amendments are suggested here and there to current scholarly views of Otway, and some of the close analysis, for instance of Otway as translator and adaptor of Racine, broadens the scope of the argument. Sentimentalism itself is seen, in the main, as an unnatural affectation, and Otway is shown as making a transition from one defective literary mode, heroic tragedy, to another, domestic melodrama. The prefatory introduction states that 'Dr. Batzer gives us insight into the conditions that give Otway's drama its immediately contemporaneous validity, but she also demonstrates those qualities of that drama that vitiate against its consideration as monumental expression of universal artistic merit'. Put more simply, for Dr Batzer, Otway is dead.

Perhaps that is true. The Stuart Restoration was in some respects an attempt to bring back life to a body already putrescent, and the Restoration theatre, so intimately related to the Court, was infected. Many have found a strange phosphorescence about this diseased body of drama, however, which persists in providing some theatrical illumination: witness *Venice Preserved*. The danger in doctoral anatomizing of the history of ideas is that it dissects the living with the dead. This thesis never grapples with the question of whether Otway is more than a phenomenon in the transition from Dryden to Rowe. But is there not a case to be argued that he was working out his own path to a vital drama when his career was so unfortunately terminated? What Otway discovered in *Venice Preserved* was not so much sentimentalism as his authentic dramatic power.

Critical sensitivity to unique qualities and the special case needs to be refined in this thesis. The term 'sentimentalism' is used as though it were descriptive of a specific malady like chicken pox. The doctoral exercise frequently leads candidates to play safe in this way, but it is by no means clear that the fundamental term on which this study is based has any precise meaning separated from evaluative judgement of specific instances, nor that the term is always the right generalization. There are qualities in Otway's writing which, to sympathetic judgement, seem to be peculiarly his, and which, hence, obstinately refuse to be reduced to documentary evidence in the history of an idea. Belvidera's reference to 'physical love' in the following lines, for example, is not exactly 'domestic' sentiment:

> when thy hands,
> Charg'd with my fate, come trembling to the deed,
> As thou hast done a thousand thousand dear times,
> To this poor breast, when kinder rage has brought thee,
> When our sting'd hearts have leap'd to meet each other,
> And melting kisses seal'd our lips together,
> When joyes have left me gasping in thy armes,
> So let my death come now, and I'll not shrink from't.

> (cited p. 244)

This morbid sensuality and psychotic sexual violence is something Otway learned to exploit, just as the creation of a true style here ('When our sting'd hearts have leap'd') is a development from his earlier bombastic huffing. This discovery of an effective poetic language, and its direction to the creation of this kind of sick and uneasy theatricality, demands explanation through critical exploration which is inward-looking to the craft and personality of a unique artistic talent, whereas this thesis absorbs Otway into the age, a convention, a movement, even a bibliography.

This depersonalization is one way of achieving that neutrality which can pass as objectivity in the writing of theses which, according to the rules of the game, must add to knowledge. *From Heroics to Sentimentalism* is a very respectable example of its kind. It is a thorough treatment of its subject, sensibly argued, and this reviewer concurs with the examiners back in 1956. He also concurs with Stanislavski. This sort of intellectual analysis undertaken for its own sake is harmful to art.

UNIVERSITY COLLEGE, CARDIFF   MALCOLM KELSALL

Short Fiction in 'The Spectator'. By DONALD KAY. (Studies in the Humanities No. 8, Literature) Alabama: University of Alabama Press. 1975. xii + 145 pp. $6.50.

The establishment of the literary periodical coincides with the emergence of the novel in the eighteenth century. With the success of the *Tatler* and *Spectator* the serial essay preceded the novel in popular favour and it was the essayists, purveyors of fiction as a mode of social commentary at once comic and serious, who pointed the way to the novel. The essays of Addison and Steele, it has been said, represent perhaps the finest achievement in English fiction before Richardson. Mr Kay's project 'to remedy the lack of incisive and thorough examination' of the fictional components of the *Spectator* was therefore well conceived. His method of proceeding is to classify the hundred pieces of short fiction that he identifies among the original papers of that periodical in nine groups: '(1) the Character, (2) the dream vision-cum-allegory, (3) the fable, (4) the domestic apologue, (5) the satirical adventure tale, (6) the oriental tale and rogue literature, (7) the fabliau, (8) the exemplum, and (9) the mock-sentimental tale'.

Necessarily these were short pieces of fiction, seemingly incidental to the larger design but, in the view of Mr Kay, basic to the role of the *Spectator* as an instrument for promoting social and moral instruction and reform. In writing of them he uses the terms 'short fiction', 'short narrative', 'short story' interchangeably, thereby obscuring the issue of their contribution to the evolution of the short story as a distinct genre. Though he recognizes that the latter did not emerge until the nineteenth century (p. 10), and twice offers a definition of the short story proper, he too readily slips into the assumption that the *Spectator* fictions were at times achieved short stories rather than, on his own admission, only 'ingredients for the short story' (p. 66). At most they are constructive approaches to the genre, important for the conscious craftsmanship they applied to the techniques of characterization, compression, and unity of mood, all essentials of the short story.

About the no less interesting question of the contribution the *Spectator* made to the emerging novel, which was to become the more dominant, pervasive, and enduring species of fiction, the book has disappointingly little to say. What is said of the function of Mr Spectator as narrator, concerned yet detached, could have been extended to a consideration of the role of the novelist in his kind of fiction. The blending of realistic and fictional accounts of London life achieved in the *Spectator* is equally a feature of the novel. The papers on Sir Roger de Coverley might usefully have been investigated as a suggestive early example of serial fiction approximating to one form of the novel. More generally, the opportunity is missed to emphasize that the continuing prestige of the *Spectator* assisted the novel by steadily promoting the acceptability and serious import of fiction among new classes of reader in a period when many of them were still inclined to regard the novel as frivolous and untruthful.

Both genres have certain antecedents in common. These are traced in the first chapter of the book without bringing anything particularly new to light, as is tacitly acknowleged by the frequent quotation from scholars who have already surveyed this field. Overlooked are the seventeenth-century biographies and collections of table-talk as precursors in the anecdotal mode that so intriguingly hovers between fact and fiction in the *Spectator*. The chapter on the Character neglects the tradition of the embodied 'humours' and their rendering to the life in Will Honeycomb and Sir Roger, who in turn lead on to the enlargement of the 'humour' in action in certain characters of Fielding and Smollett.

The book is a useful compendium in which each category of short fiction is treated separately, instances listed, and chosen examples analysed both for their intrinsic appeal as pieces of fiction and for their contribution to the larger aim of the *Spectator*. On the whole it is not particularly enlightening in its criticisms, which are frequently superficial and too often subside into such deflated conclusions as that 'Addison fits the narrator to the nature of the subject matter — one of the essential gifts of a successful writer of fiction' (p. 75). The instructive analysis of one of the best known of the dream allegories, 'The Vision of Mirzah', expires unworthily with the trite remark that Addison's technique 'gives it a freshness that still remains' (p. 73). A surprising omission is the no less famous tale of Inkle and Yarico, especially as it was the *Spectator* version of this story that remained the most admired instance of the sentimental tale throughout the eighteenth century.

The style of the book is unattractive, at times jejune. This is scarcely the way to write about Addison, a sensitive stylist who took care to avoid 'flat Expressions'. Not so Mr Kay, who writes of the 'smashing success' of the *Spectator* and observes that a particular essay 'contains some excellent indications of how Steele elasticized the Character in the direction of realism and believability' (p. 34).

Despite its shortcomings the book leaves a firm impression of the variety and artistry of the short fictions in the *Spectator*. Their qualities as narrative art are nevertheless overrated. One cannot agree that Mr Spectator 'is first and last a storyteller', even less (not even 'possibly') that the success of his essays was due to their 'striking and wondrous narratives'.

COLIN J. HORNE

UNIVERSITY OF ADELAIDE

Gulliver's Travels. By JONATHAN SWIFT. Introduction by CLIVE T. PROBYN. (Everyman's Library) London: Dent; New York: Dutton. 1975. xxx + 318 pp. £1.50 (95p paperbound).

Reissues of major texts in editions suitable for students are always welcome, especially in paperbacks which do not fall apart as one wrestles with small print or over-narrow margins. The Everyman edition dates from 1906, was last reprinted in 1970, and appears now with additional material to justify an inevitable price increase. Among new features is a considerably extended bibliography, three pages long, selective but up to date, adequately annotated, and to be commended not least for giving volume-numbers along with titles in the Herbert Davis standard edition of the prose works. Clive Probyn's introduction is also new. It summarizes, in a properly introductory way, contextual aspects of the work (the travel-book genre, the social, political, and philosophical backgrounds) and discusses the separate worlds of Swift and Gulliver concisely and helpfully. A textual note brings, as extra bonus, the suppressed passage on the suppressed Lindalinians.

The most obviously comparable among available paperbacks is the Penguin edition. That has notes, and Michael Foot's memorable essay, but virtually no bibliography: this has no notes. The Penguin text is based on Motte's 1726 edition, and the policy by which later corrections are incorporated is explained so that the reader is at least aware that choices have been made (the Lindalinian passage is incorporated in the text with an explanatory note). Spellings and typography are both modernized. The Everyman text is from Faulkner 1735–8, though we are told this only on the back cover without further discussion. I do not much care for the combination of modernized typography (no capitalized initials for nouns) with unusual spellings ('aukward' for 'awkward' is not from 1735 but may appear in the reset of 1738 which I have not seen). The 'Contents' page has evidently been reprinted without regard to the addition of new prefatory material. This paper-back is more expensive than the Penguin, but the print is larger and the paper is of better quality.

JENNY MEZCIEMS

UNIVERSITY OF WARWICK

Poems by Allan Ramsay and Robert Fergusson. Edited by ALEXANDER MANSON KING-HORN and ALEXANDER LAW. (Association for Scottish Literary Studies, 4) Edinburgh and London: Scottish Academic Press. 1974. xxxiv + 225 pp. £3.75.

Ramsay (1684–1758) and Fergusson (1750–1774) were the only significant poets writing in Scots in the eighteenth century before Burns published his Kilmarnock *Poems* in 1786. Although their historical importance is in large measure as revivers of the Scotch literary language and as precursors of Burns (who in emulation of Ramsay and Fergusson was to take the vernacular tradition in poetry to its climax), they would anyhow, had Burns not occurred, stand as two of the best minor poets of the century: in familiar epistolary verse, lyric, comic pastoral, social commentary, and satire. Their complete works have been made available in the scholarly editions of the Scottish Text Society (reviewed in *MLR*); Ramsay in six volumes by J. B. Martin, J. W. Oliver, A. M. Kinghorn, and Alexander Law (1953–74), and Fergusson in two volumes by M. P. McDiarmid (1954–6). Now Dr Kinghorn and Dr Law (the ageless doyen of Scottish eighteenth-century studies in Edinburgh) have increased our debt by bringing together, in a single inexpensive but elegant volume, the best work of these two poets; nineteen poems and *The Gentle Shepherd* by Ramsay, and twenty-eight poems by Fergusson. The texts, from the STS editions, are superior to anything hitherto available to students; they are introduced with the critical good sense and learning that are characteristic of both editors; and they are elucidated in concise notes and a sound glossary. All that the general student of eighteenth-century poetry needs, and likely to prove an excellent class-book.

JAMES KINSLEY

UNIVERSITY OF NOTTINGHAM

Marriage: Fielding's Mirror of Morality. By MURIAL BRITTAIN WILLIAMS. (Studies in the Humanities, Literature) Alabama: University of Alabama Press. 1973. vi + 168 pp. $6.50 ($2.95 paperbound).

This is a very disappointing study to have been produced at a time when, now that feminism has made us all more self-aware, one has every right to expect an enlightened and illuminating approach to marriage in general and, as here, to its function in a specific author as an almost symbolic expression of his moral values. My main objection to the book is that it is too limited in range of reference. Fielding himself was really only incidentally interested in courtship and marriage; and even as a lawyer, as Murial Williams points out (p. 132), he makes scarcely any use of the technicalities of marriage law in his plays or novels. What was needed (and still is) was a study of attitudes to women and marriage in eighteenth-century literature which possesses historical, sociological, and psychological awareness. The present book is as thin on ideas as it is slim physically.

In her Introduction Murial Williams fills in the background to her study: 'The marriage debate resolved itself around two fundamental concepts of morality: Should marriage be based on romantic love or on prudential considerations; should the parent or the child have the right of picking the marriage partner. These questions are actually outward expressions of more fundamental forces at work — the emergence of the middle class and the changing status of women' (p. 1). She draws attention to the cynical attitude to love and marriage in Restoration comedy and the corrective reaction in sentimental comedy and (with the publication of *Pamela* in 1740) in the novel, which 'served as the literary outlet for the marriage debate' (p. 3). As for Fielding himself, 'he faces the basic questions involved in the marriage debate by resorting to the classic conflict between parent and child over marriage'. But he 'never makes the choice one of romantic considerations alone. The chosen mate is characteristically morally superior, and on the issue of morality Fielding constructs his tales. The solving of external difficulties hinges upon the hero's arrival at a state of moral maturity' (p. 5). All this is fair enough. What is not so good is the biographical first chapter; a very brief survey of Fielding's background and what little is known about his own courtship and marriages (almost a whole page is given over to quoting unnecessarily the description of Sophia-Charlotte in *Tom Jones*, IV.2); and the chapter on 'Marriage in the Plays', which does little except mention the two basic plot types (arranged marriages, marital infidelity), tell the boring stories of some of the plays, and draw attention to *The Modern Husband* and its similarities to *Amelia*. We are told that Fielding insists in his comedies that 'the only satisfactory basis for marriage is love and merit' (p. 30), but we are not told how far this attitude was shared by contemporaries. Moreover, nearly all the genuinely critical points in this chapter are taken from J. H. Smith's *The Gay Couple* (1948), just as most of the sociological points are from Watt's *Rise of the Novel* and Utter and Needham's *Pamela's Daughters*.

Chapter 3 deals with the early novels. *Joseph Andrews* is approached by way of an orthodox Fielding's-defenders' discussion of *Pamela* which tells us that 'mercenary motives and lust are the foundations of the marriage between Pamela and Mr. B.' (p. 44) and gives no hint of awareness of complexities of motive, either of the characters within the novel or within Richardson himself. And there is a strange logic operating in this sentence: 'Fielding was not by birth of the middle class; hence he did not share the aspirations of this group for social elevation by marriage' (p. 47). Strangely for a book with this title there is nothing, except for a mention on page 95, of *Pamela*, Part II. On *Joseph Andrews* itself we go over old ground with Joseph's chastity; there is no hint here or anywhere else that the beauty of Fielding's heroines might be Platonic in origin; there is no consideration of the literary problems raised by didacticism and Fielding's choice of an alternative, comic, mode (despite a discussion of Adams's sermon to Joseph in IV.8); and, most noticeable of all, in the page or two devoted to the interpolated tales, the story of the two friends in IV.10 is omitted entirely, a curious oversight, since here Fielding raises a question that was to occupy him also in *Amelia*, the relationship between male friendship and married love. Fielding's satire at received Platonic notions on this subject, common enough in the eighteenth century, is something that Murial Williams should have gone into.

There is little to comment on in the chapter on *Tom Jones*. The following quotation embodies Murial Williams's conclusions: 'From the array of ill-assorted marriages presented in the novel in contrast with that of Tom and Sophia, it is the unavoidable conclusion that Fielding considered ideal marriages exceedingly rare.

Such a marriage would require two worthy partners who base their marriage on the highest concept of Christian love and merit; consent of the parents or guardians is desirable; and a comfortable income to provide adequately for the family is necessary. Significantly, class structure is maintained' (p. 93).

I had really lost patience by the time I started to read the *Amelia* chapter, but I recall reading nothing that was not obvious. The book concludes with three appendixes: on marriage law to 1753 (interesting but clearly too brief for its subject and mainly irrelevant to the book's actual, as opposed to ideal, argument); on divorce law (again mostly irrelevant); and on 'popular attitudes toward marriage and women', mostly quoting well known passages from the *Spectator* and *Tatler*. There is a bibliography, of what, I am not quite sure: there are items in it not mentioned in the book itself, so it is not a bibliography of references cited; neither is it even vaguely complete as a bibliography of Fielding and marriage matters. Murial Williams also is sometimes reluctant to give references for quotations, as at the top of page 36, on page 40, and in connexion with the *Pamela* quotation on pages 47–8; and she has a compulsive habit of quoting at second hand; for example, Dr Johnson quoted from Utter and Needham, page 46, Claudian quoted via Sherburn with no other reference given, page 112, and Fuller on pages 125–6. This is an insignificant book which says virtually nothing about an important topic. I have read much better work in third-year student dissertations.

UNIVERSITY OF MANCHESTER   DOUGLAS BROOKS

Oliver Goldsmith: Poems and Plays. Edited by TOM DAVIS. London: Dent; Totowa, New Jersey: Rowan and Littlefield. 1975. xxx + 258 pp. £4.95.

In the past decade, Goldsmith has been fortunate in his editors. The definitive edition of the *Collected Works* produced by Arthur Friedman in 1966 was followed by the highly competent editing of the poems by Roger Lonsdale in 1969. It is now appropriate that the Everyman series should offer a completely new edition of the *Poems and Plays*, first issued in 1910 and last reprinted in 1964.

The present editor has arrived at an independent text from his own collation of copies of editions nearest to Goldsmith's manuscript, at the same time not refraining from legitimate use of antecedent contemporary scholarship. A rearrangement of the contents places the plays first (omitting the negligible scene from *The Grumbler*) and prints the poetry in chronological order. Moreover, the light punctuation and the spelling that seem to be closest to Goldsmith's intentions are both restored. Since the edition is intended for the undergraduate and the general reader rather than for the specialist, the editor has wisely dropped from the old edition five poems considered to be of doubtful authenticity, including the Swiftian imitation, 'The Logicians Refuted', seriously questioned by Friedman and Lonsdale, and the 'Translation of Vida's Game of Chess', first published by Cunningham in the *Works* in 1854, reprinted in the Aldine edition in 1866, as well as in Austin Dobson's Oxford edition, but included by neither Friedman nor Lonsdale.

The scanty introduction by Sir Sydney Roberts has been expanded to include a compact and useful treatment of recent scholarship, regarding not only the plays and poems but also *The Vicar of Wakefield*, about which provocative new issues have been raised. One should not be inclined to argue too seriously with the editor's general conclusion about the *œuvre* that, though Goldsmith's ironic stance is one of the sources of his greatness, the works in which this stance is replaced by directness and sincerity are those that are most to be admired.

Since much of the nineteenth-century scholarship has been superseded, only two titles (the biographies of Prior and Forster) remain from the old bibliography, the emphasis in the brief new one being on work done in the present century. (The omission of the recent critical biography by A. Lytton Sells is in no sense a serious fault.) Though the annotation is not so rich as Lonsdale's, it is far richer than that of Roberts. An interesting bonus is a glossary from Johnson's *Dictionary*. In short, the whole is a workmanlike and a useful volume, the best of its kind now available for its purpose.

LODWICK HARTLEY

NORTH CAROLINA STATE UNIVERSITY, RALEIGH

This Singular Tale: A Study of 'The Vicar of Wakefield' and its Literary Background. By SVEN BÄCKMAN. (Lund Studies in English, 40) Lund: Gleerup. 1971. 281 pp.

In a review in *Eighteenth-Century Studies* (Summer 1972) G. S. Rousseau, commenting on the depressed state of Goldsmith's reputation, asks 'is not another kind of revaluation than a microscopic examination of his irony in order?' Sven Bäckman's book is at least in part an attempt to correct this excessive concern with the ironic aspects of Goldsmith's writings, and to place criticism of *The Vicar of Wakefield* on a more comprehensive and rational basis. It is, therefore, all the more disappointing to have to say that he merely repeats the opinions of earlier commentators and adds very little that is new.

This Singular Tale is in part a study of *The Vicar of Wakefield* 'in its natural context, as a literary product of the mid-eighteenth century' (p. 15), an exercise which has led Mr Bäckman to investigate works in all fictional genres from the sixteenth century to 1760. In terms of specific analogues for *The Vicar of Wakefield* his findings are sparse, and easily summarized in a few paragraphs at the end of the book. His larger purpose, however, is to use the literary background to provide a critical defence and 'to decide the position of Goldsmith's novel in the literary tradition' (p. 15). The opening sections of the book, however, show a rather simplistic view of this 'literary tradition': Richardson is excluded, and the remaining eighteenth-century novels are divided into two camps; the Fielding and the Smollett, the structured and the unstructured; in short, the good and the bad. Goldsmith's reticence about his intentions in writing *The Vicar of Wakefield* and his silence on the theoretical aspects of prose fiction (amounting, one feels, to lack of interest), afford Mr Bäckman *carte blanche* to make his own conjectures. Despite Goldsmith's stated preference for episodic, baggy Smollett (see, for example, *The Bee*, Nos. 5 and 6), we are given a Goldsmith of the Fielding kind (structured and good), who has assumed Fielding's fictional mantle to produce, in *The Vicar of Wakefield*, a lesser form of *Tom Jones*: 'the same underlying endeavour as in Fielding's novels, to create a neatly balanced and symmetrical composition, reflected in the chapter division, is indubitably there' (p. 52). When Mr Bäckman attempts to substantiate this claim by means of a ground plan (p. 43) one can only see his thesis as a lesser variant of Hilles's procedure in 'Art and Artifice in *Tom Jones*' (*Imagined Worlds: Essays . . . in Honour of John Butt*, edited by Maynard Mack and Ian Gregor (London, 1968), pp. 91–110). But *The Vicar of Wakefield* will not conform to these ambitious plans for it except in the most superficial way. *This Singular Tale*, despite its author's disclaimers, is largely a Procrustean exercise in fitting the book that Goldsmith wrote to the book that Mr Bäckman thinks Goldsmith was trying to write (or wishes he had written). Goldsmith comes off worse in this struggle.

Logic is sacrificed in the process. It is, for example, part of Mr Bäckman's case that *The Vicar of Wakefield* displays 'unity of tone' in the first-person narration of Dr Primrose. But if this is so, one cannot logically speak of *Goldsmith's* intrusions in the book, as Mr Bäckman frequently does; his discussions of what he sees as digressions can be made only with reference to the character of Primrose. Indeed, how can he refer to 'extraneous, interpolated material' at all, if the entire narrative is made by Primrose? In his concern to detect the intrusive hand of Goldsmith in the novel, Mr Bäckman fails to consider the possibility that such 'digressions' might be *dramatically* relevant.

Determined to impute Fieldingesque intentions to Goldsmith, however, Mr Bäckman doggedly reworks Ernest Baker's argument (that *The Vicar of Wakefield* is broken-backed because Goldsmith lost control of his narrative in the second half). Instead, we are told that Goldsmith deliberately 'allows the narrative to take another direction' so that 'there emerges another pattern, based on quite different principles' (p. 45). Yet, on page 209, we find Mr Bäckman talking about 'the scrappiness of the second half . . . largely due to the fact that Goldsmith lost some of the artistic control of the narrative'.

Something similar might be said of Mr Bäckman's control of his 'unity and coherence' thesis. In an attempt to have it both (or all three) ways, he turns (with relief?) from Goldsmith the frequently inept novelist to Goldsmith the successful essayist and future dramatist. Thus, he argues in Sections II and III, those features which seemed to be undermining Goldsmith's novel *as a novel* can be explained and excused by reference to his work as essayist and, later, as dramatist. If parts of *The Vicar of Wakefield* are reminiscent in style and subject of the periodical essay (for example, the unfortunate 'digressions'), that is because Goldsmith was a practising essayist at the time he was writing his novel. Similarly, Goldsmith's plays are invoked when Mr Bäckman feels them necessary to his argument. On these occasions he is never content merely to draw parallels: he constructs a conscious intention on the part of Goldsmith, who 'deliberately did his best to infuse as much as possible of the spirit and manner of the periodical essay into it' (p. 142) and who wrote a novel 'conceived and organized according to the rules and conventions which governed stage comedy', which is to be 'approached with the expectations and demands with which one sits down to read a comedy from the period' (p. 168).

Some of Mr Bäckman's interpretations, too, are open to question. He makes much of contrast as a structural principle in *The Vicar of Wakefield*, but sometimes gets the emphases wrong. Surely 'the main contrast among the older characters' (p. 92) is between the Vicar and Flamborough, not between the Vicar and Mr Wilmot, as Mr Bäckman suggests. There is, in fact, a running contrast between the two families — the Primroses patronize the Flamboroughs, and the Vicar's opinion of Flamborough's story-telling is an ironic comment upon himself: 'his manner of telling stories was not quite so well. They were very long, and very dull, and all about himself' (*The Vicar of Wakefield*, Chapter 11). In failing to appreciate the Flamboroughs' important normative function, Mr Bäckman's study greatly exaggerates the ambivalence of Goldsmith's attitude towards the rural idyll. (And incidentally, it is surely wrong to suggest that Thornhill is a neutral or 'realistic' name compared with the symbolic Primrose surname. Indeed, the lines from 'The Deserted Village' quoted on page 95 indicate a deliberate contrast.)

But these are trifles compared to the confusion apparently caused by the effort of seeing *The Vicar of Wakefield* as novel, essay, and play simultaneously. On page 153 we are told that 'there are a number of digressions and insets in the novel, but they are not allowed to take up a disproportionate amount of space'. Earlier, however, the opposite has been stated: 'Insets . . . become more numerous after the reversal, and some of them are allowed to grow to disproportionate length' (p. 45). Sometimes Goldsmith's handling of minor characters is praised: 'Mrs Primrose provides a good example of Goldsmith's ability to create vivid characters with a minimum of description' (p. 207). At other times, Mr Bäckman is less than satisfied: 'the other people apart from Dr Primrose tend to be "flat", "two-dimensional" ' (p. 97). The many repetitions (without which the book would shrink to a third of its length) sometimes result from lack of organization (for example, the comments on literary and theatrical topics on pages 188–9 merely repeat pages 63–4); more often repetition is local, with the same point being made in substantially the same language two or three times on each page. Grammatical and stylistic infelicities add to the reader's difficulties. The first sentence of the first part of the study is not an auspicious beginning: 'It is difficult to get a more definite idea concerning the extent of Goldsmith's reading in the field of the novel' (p. 21).

There are good things in *This Singular Tale*, but for the most part these are lost by dispersal among the various divisions and sub-divisions of this diffuse book. The genealogy of Dr Primrose is a useful and interesting idea, but its force is lost because it is scattered over three sections. The comments on Dr Primrose as first-person narrator (pp. 103–13) might be more aptly introduced alongside the placing of the Vicar in the amiable humorist tradition (pp. 189 ff.), while the section on names (pp. 94–6) might have been saved for the general discussion of Primrose's literary antecedents.

It is hard to see how this study of *The Vicar of Wakefield* 'will add to our knowledge of the formative period in the development of the English novel' (p. 17), since it applies a formula (of 'structural symmetry') irrelevant to the majority of eighteenth-century novels. While Mr Bäckman is correct in seeing the eighteenth-century novel as a point of generic confluence, the way in which he applies this notion vitiates its usefulness as a critical tool. Instead of indicating an approach to an eighteenth-century reading of *The Vicar of Wakefield*, Mr Bäckman's study forces us to agree with John Preston (*Essays in Criticism*, 21 (1971), p. 93) not only that 'the Eighteenth Century did not know what to say about novels', but that twentieth-century critics are little better. Although it claims to be a study of the literary background, *This Singular Tale* is ultimately an unhistorical book which imposes its own values and takes little real account of contemporary aims. Its idea of the nature and scope of the eighteenth-century concept of literature is confused: lip service is paid to the combining of instruction and entertainment, but Goldsmith is criticized for betraying the 'aesthetic function of fiction' by crossing 'the borderline between art and overt, direct propaganda' (p. 66). There is no perception of the close interrelationship between fiction and non-fiction in the period: exemplary tales in essay-journals have less to do with the (extinct) medieval tradition cited (p. 66) than with the *exempla* common in historical and biographical works in the early part of the century. Again, the discussion of themes in *The Vicar of Wakefield* overlooks an important political dimension: far from being 'an obtrusive excrescence' (p. 66), Primrose's political harangue (Chapter 19) is an integral part of the book's concern with problems of power and government in the family, in the parish, and in the state. Perhaps most unfortunate of all, the vexed critical question of Goldsmith's 'tone' is totally evaded: 'Whatever the exact quality of this tone, it is undeniably there, and contributes to our experience of the book as a coherent, unified whole' (p. 50). As far as this study of it is concerned, Goldsmith's 'very singular tale' remains as enigmatic as ever.

LEICESTER   ROSALIND NICOL

R. B. Sheridan: personnalité, carrière politique. By FRANÇOISE CHATEL DE BRANÇION. (Études Anglaises, 56) Paris: Didier. 1974. 502 pp. 65 F.

Dr Chatel de Brançion is descended from the Sheridans, and her book is something of an act of family piety. She recalls hearing from her aunt an amusing remark made by the playwright when he saw a rich heiress entering a room: 'Is her poundage equal to her tonnage?'. She also quotes her grandmother's paraphrase of Beaumarchais as a comment on Sheridan's volatility: 'Gens d'esprit, fichues bêtes'. Touches like these give animation to her narrative, and suggest her warm sympathy with her subject.

The first section of the book considers Sheridan's development before he entered the Commons in 1780; the second deals with his political career, and the third with his political ideas. Sheridan's essay on Chesterfield's *Letters to his Son* yields the conclusion, 'il est intéressant car il nous livre de la démarche de sa pensée, son indépendance d'esprit vis-à-vis des problèmes que pose l'instruction, son désir de liberté'. Certainly independence for himself and other people filled his thoughts. His attacks on Hastings, Pitt, and Buonaparte demonstrate his hatred for what he considered to be oppression. His speeches against Warren Hastings were given when Sheridan was at the height of his political popularity; his work on behalf of Muir and Palmer was the nobler because it showed his own courage in adversity. Buonaparte, he thought, would soon extirpate Jacobinism and become a real menace. 'My alarms begin when the alarms of some persons cease.'

This general theme is an interesting one, though perhaps some of the judgements that follow need to be qualified. It is true that 'Charles Fox incarnait pour lui cette générosité du cœur et ce plaisir de vivre qui formaient le fond de sa philosophie', but it also seems likely that Sheridan was more sentimental about Fox than Fox was about him: generosity of spirit is not always extended to the man who wants to go his own way. Again, there is something to be said for the notion that 'la hautaine réticence des aristocrates whigs et les caprices du Prince l'atteignirent et engendrèrent sa ruine', but Sheridan's own infirmities of character contributed much. Byron's ascribing Sheridan's 'wreck' to 'bad pilotage' is nearer the mark.

Dr Chatel de Brançion's work will be useful to French readers for the many quotations from Sheridan's speeches that are printed in English in the footnotes and in French in the body of the text. Even allowing for the element of rhetoric, do we not again see something of Sheridan's humanity when (in a speech of 21 January 1794) he wondered that people in high rank 'should seek to thrive on the spoils of misery and fatten on the meals wrested from industrious poverty'? There appears to be an error, however, in the translation reading 'd'une nation pleine d'opulence' (p. 233, l. 26), because it does not give the sense of merit to be found in Sheridan's phrase 'a nation full of private worth'.

English usage is not followed in 'Sir Romilly' (p. 200), 'Sir Hood' (p. 304), and 'Hon. Percival' (p. 329). 'Lord Fitzgerald' (p. 86, n. 22) should read 'Percy Fitzgerald'. 'Darrington' (p. 260, n. 8) is surely 'Donnington'. There are also far too many minor printing errors. Fortunately two of them are rather comic, 'Lord Putty' and a 'high-melted horse'.

CECIL PRICE

UNIVERSITY COLLEGE, SWANSEA

The Illuminated Blake. Annotated by DAVID V. ERDMAN. New York: Anchor Press/ Doubleday; London: Oxford University Press. 1974. 416 pp. £10.00 (£4.75 paperbound).

The relative inaccessibility of Blake's graphic works has for a long time been the greatest practical handicap to a wider appreciation of his achievements: even the masterly Trianon Press reproductions, published over the last twenty years in order to meet this need, were too expensive for most readers and indeed for most libraries to acquire. Many Blake enthusiasts have therefore concentrated largely upon printed editions of the poetry, neglecting the illustrations and the vital link between word and image. Blake scholarship has suffered as a result.

The Illuminated Blake, which contains black-and-white reproductions of all of Blake's illuminated plates (that is, of almost all of his poetry in the form in which it was originally published) together with a plate-by-plate commentary and index by David Erdman, and which is published at a reasonably competitive price, will fill a significant place in the Blake handbook field. The quality of its reproductions is on the whole adequate for reference purposes though an examination of the volume will not serve, and cannot have been intended to serve, as a substitute for the imaginative experience of viewing the original plates — or indeed the Trianon Press facsimiles. It is a pity that a few carefully selected colour plates were not included in order to highlight the terrain and to give the student an insight into Blake's world of colour. Reproduction in black-and-white tends to blur the outline and hence the significance of some of the designs. The format of the book has made it possible for commentaries to be included alongside the plates to which they refer; a convenient arrangement, though perhaps a lengthways design with commentaries *below* the plates would have been easier to handle and (especially in the case of the paperback) to preserve.

Professor Erdman's commentary is a ground-breaking exercise of admirable thoroughness. It is particularly commendable for its recording of 'minute particulars' and of the details of colour and style that differ from version to version, and for its ability to co-ordinate apparently separate aspects of individual plates; for example, its suggestion that the tiny, hovering figures on the frontispiece to the *Songs of Innocence & of Experience* are the spiritual forms of the boy and girl below, and its progressive, 'cartoon' reading of details above and below the text of *America*, plate 5. The style of the commentary has the virtues and the defects of its form. It is succinct and precise but it is also sometimes abrupt, unpolished, or over-abbreviated. It also tends to employ the jargon-ridden and almost cabalistic style unfortunately now fashionable among Blake specialists.

The amount of interpretation and of received knowledge which an annotated volume should contain is clearly a matter for personal discretion, though it is perhaps regrettable that Professor Erdman does not seem to have adopted a consistent policy towards the inclusion of such information. Given that he does sometimes include it, I was disappointed to find no reference in his discussion of *The Gates of Paradise*, plate 9, which depicts a ladder reaching to the moon, to the source which it parodies, James Gillray's ladder of Libertas which is too short to reach the moon; nor any reference to the ironic flavour of word and of design in the 'Holy Thursday' of *Songs of Innocence*. (Both are points made by Erdman himself in his *Blake: Prophet Against Empire*.)

Classical and artistic references are sometimes neglected. The traditional nature of the serpent-eagle motif in *The Marriage of Heaven & Hell*, plate 15, is ignored. The punishment of Tityos and his crime are not mentioned in the discussions of *Visions of the Daughters of Albion*, plate 3, nor of *America*, plate 13, both of which depict a victim (here female) with a bird of prey gnawing at her vitals. The supposed traditional significance of the winged and serpent-enclosed globe (the Egyptian equivalent of the Holy Trinity with the globe representing God, the serpents Christ, and the wings the Holy Ghost) is not referred to although it is a favourite motif of Blake's and is of particular relevance to *Jerusalem*, plate 33, which shows Albion collapsing on to a winged globe but supported by a humanized Christ. The reference to 'Jerusalem with eagle wings' (in the commentary on *Jerusalem*, plate 23) overlooks the evidence of the other plates, in which Jerusalem is portrayed as a butterfly, and the significance of the butterfly as a traditional emblem for the soul (or psyche). And the nearly naked woman with diaphanous veil who stands between two humanized harvest figures in *Milton*, plate 50, is surely Blake's nature goddess Vala or the classical Ceres, and not simply 'the female Human Form Divine, a combination of Oothoon and Ololon'.

Sometimes Professor Erdman overinterprets. His observations on the nature of the projected twelve-Book *Milton* must be conjectural; his references in discussions of *Milton* to the conversion on the road to Damascus on the ground that a falling star enters Blake's left foot 'on the tarsus', are ingenious; and it is not clear why the winged figure of *Europe*, plate 3, should be identified as Cassandra.

There are also errors of interpretation. In his analysis of *The Marriage of Heaven & Hell*, plate 11, Professor Erdman has overlooked the fact that text and illustrations are not always to be found on the same page: the figures at the top of the plate are not the animated 'sensible objects' beheld by a fresh pristine imagination (see plate 11, lines 1–5) but the products of a fallen and hence 'caverned' perception (see bottom of plate 14). The winged and manacled figure with bowed head and prominent knees, who is shown squatting on a block of stone in the frontispiece to *America*, is more likely to be the Urizen-surrogate Albion's Angel of the 'jealous wings' than he is to be Orc. Similarly, the figure on plate 37 of *Jerusalem*, who is also represented with bowed head and prominent knees, is more likely to be Urizen than Blake's Eternal Man. Erdman's speculation that it is Jerusalem (see *Jerusalem*, plate 18) who is wearing the crown of roses and Vala the crown of lilies is surely wrong: Blake consistently uses lilies to suggest the purity of the spirit, and roses to suggest the vulnerable and therefore fortified beauty of the natural world. The 'traveller's hat' shown behind the embracing figures in *Jerusalem*, plate 99, is surely a shared halo, similar to those found in several other Blake illustrations.

It would be surprising if it had not been possible to identify errors and omissions in a pioneering work of this magnitude, and it would be churlish to end on a critical note; for in editing this volume Professor Erdman has performed a 'labour of ages' with skill and with scholarly devotion, and has undoubtedly made a major contribution to Blake studies.

P. M. Dunbar

University of Warwick

The Permanent Pleasure: Essays on Classics of Romanticism. By Richard Harter Fogle. Athens, Georgia: University of Georgia Press. 1974. xvi + 225 pp. $8.50.

The fifteen essays collected here have appeared in various journals over the last twenty or so years. Although they cover a wide range of topics there is sufficient thematic and critical connexion to impart a satisfying unity to the volume as a whole. In general, they seek to explore 'the integrity and artistic responsibility of nineteenth-century romantic poetry and theory' (p. ix). Nine focus on some of the major texts of English romanticism, while the remainder examine the works of Hawthorne and Melville in relation to romantic tradition. Underlying most is a serious but unobtrusive concern with critical method. As the first essay makes clear, Professor Fogle wishes to resolve the conflicting claims of criticism and literary history. Although the essay is disappointing as a contribution to a major twentieth-century critical debate, it serves as a suitable introduction to the explications that follow. Accepting Coleridge's dictum that 'nothing can permanently please, which does not contain in itself the reason why it is so, and not otherwise', and consciously avoiding the high-principled myopia and anti-historicism of the New Critics, Professor Fogle offers practical proof that close criticism is not incompatible with biographical and historical scholarship.

A flexible idea of genre provides both the starting point and the framework of reference for most of the excellent explications. In an essay on 'Coleridge's Conversation Poems', Professor Fogle remarks that nothing could be more mistaken than the notion that 'Coleridge banished the idea of genre with his theory of organic unity'. He goes on to point out that the first duty of the critic in Coleridge's theory 'is not to judge, but to find out what he is dealing with, to determine what principles are genuinely applicable to the object'. This becomes Fogle's own method. In applying it he derives his idea of genre freely from his knowledge of literary history and from his sensitive response to the structure of each work. Once he has defined the Conversation Poems as 'romantic efforts to combine naturalness with dignity and significance' or the peculiar function of Shelley's *Prometheus Unbound* as reconciling 'ideal truth and sensuous reality by the agency of poetic imagination', everything seems to fall into place. The essay called 'The Imaginal Design of Shelley's "Ode to the West Wind" ', reinforces the truth that imagery analysis requires to be controlled by an informing sense of genre if it is not to be misleading. It demonstrates that the much criticized subjective stanzas are a necessary part of 'the absorption of the individual ego into a larger unity' and therefore proper both to the subjective lyric genre and to the master theme of the Ode. What is especially admirable about the essays in this collection is the tact and skill with which the author refers differences of interpretation back to first principles. They are inspired by a single-minded desire to reveal meanings, not to triumph over others.

Two essays offer contrasted reflections on the romantic ideal of wholeness. In the essay on Keats's 'Ode to a Nightingale', Professor Fogle draws most valuable distinctions between the romantic ideal of wholeness and the New Critics' ideal of wholeness, based on a poetry 'armed at all points, invulnerable to irony'. As he points out, the modern critic emphasizes 'the number and diversity of the elements to be synthesized, and gives correspondingly less attention to the synthesizing agent', while for the romantic poet, and for the poet of the Nightingale Ode, in particular, 'the agent of synthesis comes first, the unity and harmony, not the complexity and discordance' (p. 111). By contrast, in a timely reassessment of John Middleton Murry's work on Keats, it is precisely Murry's emphasis on unity and his disregard for the opposites that have to be reconciled that limits his approach and carries it dangerously near to absolute monism. A comparison of these two essays reveals the flexibility of mind and lack of dogmatism that characterize the volume as a whole.

Of the pieces on American literature only two fail to come up to the high standard set earlier in the volume. The expository essay on the themes of Melville's later poetry is thorough but dull, and the analysis of the same poet's massive poem *Clarel* has the single merit of drawing attention to a neglected Victorian poem on doubt and belief. In contrast to these routine critical exercises are the fine analysis of 'weird mockery' in Hawthorne's style and the cogently argued interpretation of *Billy Budd*, a fine essay that combines scrupulous regard for the nuances of the text with broader references to Melville's vision of life, as reflected in his other works. All in all, this collection doubly justifies its title. It provides practical illustration of Coleridge's belief that only works that obey an internal logic can please permanently. And the collection, with its compact strength and delicacy of discrimination, is itself likely to prove a source of permanent pleasure.

UNIVERSITY OF ADELAIDE   JOHN COLMER

Imitatio und Realisation: Funktionen poetischer Sprache von Pope bis Wordsworth. By
JÜRGEN SCHLAEGER. (Theorie und Geschichte der Literatur und der Schönen
Künste, 30) München: Werner Fink. 1974. 144 pp. DM 38.00.

This German study of Wordsworth's poetic development diverges considerably
from the standard kind of English criticism on the same subject typified by, say,
P. W. K. Stone's *The Art of Poetry 1750–1820*, published in 1967, a book not listed
in Dr Schlaeger's bibliography. Stone's enumerative, self-effacing, often pedestrian
approach provides for no more than a slight shift of emphasis as against those who
had worked before him in this field. It is up to the reader to decide where he will
have to revise his own position and where to maintain it in the light of the new
presentation of facts. Dr Schlaeger's study, on the other hand, draws the reader's
attention away from the facts as it becomes, itself, the artefact where presentation
has precedence over information. It is not the reader's consent, but his ideological
conformity, which is required in a metacritical exercise of this kind.

Dr Schlaeger's study of the resources ('Funktionen'?) of poetic language opens
with an extensive exposition of a poetics of 'realization' (words are 'incarnation of
thought') which succeeded theories based upon 'imitation' (where language is
'dress of thought'). Much is made of the evolutionary symmetry of the historical
forces at work. Pope, for instance, was successfully true to reality because his
poetics were in harmony with the assumptions of contemporary deism. His sincerity cannot be questioned, either, because his firm belief in the truth of these
assumptions explains his recourse to elaborate conventionality and the rhetorical
pose: the poet was eager to provide ideological support. Thomson, on the other
hand, failed on both scores. He was artistically incompetent: although increasingly
aware of the predominance of the factual, he failed to find the appropriately new
words for the new experience. He continued to employ a language which could be
truthful only within the context of a view of things where metaphysical principles
are paramount. Thomson could also be faulted for being insincere: terrified by the
approach of the new he escaped into the comforting refuge of 'poetic diction'
and the intellectual cliché. Wordsworth assimilated both the success and failure of
his two predecessors. He was authentic because his programme of poetic realism
properly reflected the contemporary triumph of inductive reasoning and the
empirical method. However, the poet's subjective truthfulness in making the thing
become incarnate in words was as valid and revealing a procedure as the scientist's
more objective methods. But Wordsworth failed because he did not adhere to his
own precepts, something which virtually every critic has found regrettable,
attributing it to premature imaginative senility. Yet one could justifiably maintain
that Wordsworth had no other choice if he wanted to remain truthful to himself.
Once he realized that a temperamental predisposition forced him to seek com-
municable certitude and that therefore a return to conventionality was needful,
he did so by giving a very personal definition of the metaphysical principles to
which his language and his poetic conventions were to refer. His contemporaries
misunderstood and assumed that the poet had allowed himself to be overtaken
and cast aside by the progress of history.

After this measured introduction Dr Schlaeger quickens the pace with a neatly
subdivided discussion of the *Lyrical Ballads*. These remain residually indebted to
past developments but also anticipate the climax of Wordsworth's achievement in
'Tintern Abbey'. This poem, successful in so many senses, nonetheless includes a
premonition of the poet's ultimate failure. And Dr Schlaeger uses twenty pages to
prove his point. The language of the opening lines of the poem is densely informa-
tional giving an almost empirical view of reality. But the poetic imagination
'realizes' truth as 'sentiment of Being' where words do not merely convey or
express truth but serve to substantiate it. They do so, however, at the price of

semantic clarity. Visionary intensity ('We see into the life of things') leads to abstraction. Abstractions from reality can only achieve meaning if, as Dr Schlaeger puts it, they are supported *vertically* by a publicly valid ideological context external to the poem. Wordsworth's 'realizations' are unique, personal, momentary; their 'truth-content' vanishes with their manifestation and so does the meaningfulness of words which, in theory at least, are identical with the truth of the thing 'realized', being, in fact, its very incarnation. So, almost in spite of himself, and in order to communicate, Wordsworth finds himself engaged in a process of universalizing his utterances: the poet not only 'realizes' spontaneously, he also thinks long and deeply. The experiencing self which lives only in the moment, or in a series of non-successive moments, is subdued. It is made historical, communicable by a reflective self which supplies a *horizontal* context: the moment is measurable in terms of the continuity of the self's memory, or tradition, of many moments. When the poet in 'Tintern Abbey' turns to the landscape a second time it has become more than what it appears to be: its uniqueness has been superseded by its exemplary significance which will sustain '. . . life and force | For future years'. The poet's 'I' becomes 'we', description becomes suggestion in support of the poet's argument, insight into self becomes sheer self-approbation. Thus monumentalized the self becomes the origin of its own convention, its own universal context, its own tradition and ideology. With these abstractions the necessary supportive rhetorical apparatus must also make its appearance in the form of a poetic diction where words are once again 'dress of thought': and it is this self which has the concluding say in 'Tintern Abbey'.

A brief survey of his later works supplies the coda to this study. No more is needed once the logicality of a development from 'realized' experience of self to dogmatically sustained selfhood has been established. The epic intent of the *Prelude* derives from the need to provide further support for the contextual self by means of the grand rhetorical gesture. In the *Excursion* the personal ideology's effectiveness is tested in relation to the perennially relevant problems of religion and morality. At this point the need to 'realize' has become dispensable, words no longer incarnate truth, they serve to 'announce a system'. However, Wordsworth's personal consistency runs counter to the inexorably operative purposefulness of what Dr Schlaeger calls 'poesiegeschichtliche Kontext'. Some of Dr Schlaeger's more cryptic Hegelianisms sound good in German but translated threaten to collapse into jargon. The Wordsworthian who stands aloof from these linguistic and intellectual traditions might feel perturbed by the aesthetic self-sufficiency of this study. He might pertinently ask whether Dr Schlaeger does not reduce Wordsworth's poetry to the status of supplying props for his metacritical argument. Does he not regard it as Pound's W. B. Yeats does the cathedral in Canto 83: '. . . Uncle William dawdling around Notre Dame | in search of whatever | paused to admire the symbol | with Notre Dame standing inside it . . .'?

UNIVERSITY OF WARWICK   R. H. LASS

The Confessional Imagination: A Reading of Wordsworth's 'Prelude'. By FRANK D. McCONNELL. Baltimore and London: Johns Hopkins University Press. 1974. xii + 211 pp. £5.50.

While 'confessional' has become an overworked term of late, there is at least a *prima facie* case for its application to *The Prelude*. Regrettably, this book does not advance that case beyond the point already suggested, parenthetically but more elegantly, elsewhere. Despite a useful discussion of the role of Coleridge as auditor of and in Wordsworth's poem, Professor McConnell's book does not evoke the sense of human reality and spiritual compulsion implied in that evocative term 'the confessional imagination'. Nor does his second theme, an often skilful discussion of how Wordsworth's poetry subdues the 'daemonic' thirst for sublimity, and 'channels the sublime into the quotidian' quite amount to 'a reading of *The Prelude*'. The title, and a suggestive introduction, promise more in human and aesthetic breadth than is realized.

The failure lies in the lack of critical conviction in pursuance of the central theme. The author suggests that 'the distinctive art form of these men (the Friends and the Methodists), the art of confession founded upon the ideal of Augustinian piety' is a 'vital force in the genesis of the Romantic imagination'. But too much is assumed. There is no demonstration that the confessional writings he adduces are an 'art form', or that Wordsworth is related in an essential way to the radical protestant tradition which produced them. While numerous parallels are claimed, between lines of Wordsworth and passages of confessional prose, Professor McConnell relies upon his reader's common sense, unaided by phrases much more analytical than 'of course' and 'the same', to provide the critical glue by which discrete modes and dissimilar matter (and radically dissimilar degrees of genius) are to be yoked together.

The most interesting questions, though latent in the material, are not raised to essentiality: they do not articulate the book. What is the paradigmatic confessional form? What are the parameters of confessional poetry? and if the thesis is a contribution to discussion of the Romantic imagination, what are its applications to other Romantic poems? *Is* Wordsworth's *Prelude* a confessional poem? Is it relevant that it is a poem? What are the formal consequences of its status as confession? Does the ascription solve any critical problems — of shape, of the process of composition, of meaning?

A book about the way language shapes consciousness should itself possess a feeling for words, but words appear to be a stumbling-block to an author who typifies 'sunrise' as 'an artificial fixation of process', and who asks the single term 'daemonic' to bear so many meanings, page after page, that it ceases to bear any meaning at all. A straining after significance (surely the daemonism of professional criticism) leads to obfuscation of simple poetic syntax, and to extravagant appreciation of modestly elegant lines which happen to support the thesis. A linguistically conscious critic, especially one who expounds the significance of pronominal displacement in Wordsworth's poetry, ought also to make sure that in his final sentence his own prepositional displacement ('within' for 'above') does not subvert the meaning of the poet he is quoting. After a reference to the closing words of Augustine's *Confessions*, 'it shall be opened', he concludes: 'And the poetic confession we have been exploring here, heralding an epoch more resolutely secular and fiercely aspiring than any which had gone before, ends with another opening, characteristically the linguistically compact and complex opening of the comparative adverb, in the assurance that the unaided human spirit is, within the physical universe which is its home and its heritage:

> In beauty exalted, as it is itself
> Of quality and fabric more divine.'

THE BRITISH COUNCIL, LONDON   RICHARD GRAVIL

Walter Scott. By ROBIN MAYHEAD. (British Authors, Introductory Critical Studies)
Cambridge: Cambridge University Press. 1973. x + 132 pp. £2.30 (£1.10
paperbound).

Mr Mayhead has set himself a most difficult task, to write an introductory volume
which examines Scott in the light of 'the literary criticism of the last thirty years,
and especially the methods associated with Cambridge', at the same time as it
positively innovates in analysis and judgement. Two full chapters on *Waverley* and
The Heart of Midlothian are followed by a third devoted to *Guy Mannering*, *Redgauntlet*, and *The Antiquary*; another to *Rob Roy*, *Old Mortality*, and *The Abbott*; a short
treatment of the Poems; and a note on Scott as a critic which originally appeared
as a review of Ioan Williams's *Sir Walter Scott on Novelists and Fiction*. The result is a
book like a tadpole, with a big head (the initial chapters on the two major novels)
and an ever thinning tail (six lesser novels, and the poetry and criticism, each less
important than the other). True to his Cambridge methods, Mr Mayhead proceeds
from illustrative examples to a general entity, his author's literary personality, and
even what characterizes him as a man, 'his complex make-up' (p. 93). The words
on the page point beyond self-contained works of art to a man speaking to men,
which puts the Leavisite, ultimately, in the same camp as Saintsbury, Grierson,
Buchan, and Edgar Johnson.

Mr Mayhead is deeply interested in the problems of coherence and 'mixture' in
the work of art: indeed, 'mixture' is the critical term which occurs most frequently
throughout this study. In his view, *Waverley* is of all the novels the most fully
coherent; its unity proceeds from Scott's simultaneous Romanticism and anti-
Romanticism, and it manages to include other but related mixtures (for example,
'ironic comedy with the grimly serious' or 'the shudder of the supernatural with a
rational explanation of it', pp. 26, 40). *The Heart of Midlothian* too is a 'mixture', of a
coherent and concentrated first half where various strands of interest interweave
in the justice preoccupation 'to give one a sense of texture rather than a chronicle'
(p. 70), with a second half which presents at its best an interesting narrative, at its
worst a moralizing tract (p. 65). Yet his use of the concept is not always clear:
sometimes it is a combination of good and bad, the original and the hurriedly
conventional that he is concerned with (*Guy Mannering*, *Redgauntlet*, where he feels
that the mixture is due to some uncertainty on Scott's part); at others, an inter-
mingling of genres; and at others still a deliberate strategic deployment, as when
he finds that *The Antiquary* is 'a very conscious compilation of incongruities',
deliberately using Johnsonian and other styles for 'mannerist' effects. These are
important perceptions: and his exposition of them would have been improved if he
had admitted, quite clearly and unequivocally, that Romantic narrative art
developed in a direction that was not novelistic in the twentieth-century sense
(compare Hogg's *Confessions of a Justified Sinner* and, even more, *The Three Perils of
Man*); that two of its cardinal principles were 'framing' and 'mixture', the latter
including, quite deliberately, genre mixture; and that it employed allegory, symbolism, and other poetic devices, even in prose, for aesthetic effect. A consideration
of the narrative style of Scott's longer poems (even if only in one summary paragraph) would have illuminated Scott's general narrative technique.

If Mr Mayhead had allowed himself to give full weight to the non-novelistic
features in Scott's work, to let not just the inferior historical fantasias speak to him
'in their own terms', but the major Scottish novels themselves, he might have
improved even on his treatment of *The Heart of Midlothian*, with which, in Scott
criticism, his name will always be associated. Before his present book appeared,
three formidable defences of the novel's unity were published by David Daiches
(1948), Francis Hart (1966), and Avrom Fleishman (1971); yet Mr Mayhead still
insists that the last half of the novel is inferior. It is surely impossible now to ignore

Fleishman's analysis of the main movement of the novel as an allegory of Scottish history (repeated, on a very different plane, by Lewis Grassic Gibbon in *A Scots Quair* during the present century), or to feel unconvinced that the 'mixture' in *The Heart of Midlothian* is both intentional (a piece of highly conscious artistry) and successful.

Mr Mayhead excels at practical criticism, and it is for his many demonstrations of what can be done with particular passages that this book will be valued by other teachers of literature. Though he refuses altogether to take the longer poems seriously as narratives, he provides us with sensitive readings of five lyrics (including 'Proud Maisie'); and his analysis of key scenes and paragraphs in the novels is generally better than we have had from previous critics. The detailed commentary on Waverley's education, or on Flora MacIvor's 'gardening' (Chapter 22), could hardly be bettered, while his character analysis of Fergus MacIvor and the Baron of Bradwardine can only be described as brilliant: these reveal new subtleties even in a work which has been subjected to closer scrutiny than most of Scott's novels. Despite certain inadequacies, this book is a 'must' for the professional teacher. For the beginning student, it needs to be supplemented by an introduction which pays some attention to Scott's biography, and to his work as editor, historian, poet, and antiquarian.

THOMAS CRAWFORD

UNIVERSITY OF ABERDEEN

Southey. By KENNETH CURRY. (Routledge Author Guides) London and Boston: Routledge. 1975. xii + 191 pp. £4.95.

The writer of a brief guide to Southey faces the double difficulty of encompassing his voluminous works and of persuading the modern reader that some of them are still worth reading. By allotting a few pages to each, Professor Curry succeeds in giving a comprehensive picture of Southey's prodigious output, but his cautious and defensive critical comments are unlikely to attract new readers. This is a pity, as there is much to be discovered in Southey by the student of literature and society, as Jack Simmons, Geoffrey Carnall, and Geoffrey Grigson have shown in recent years. An altogether more selective approach than the one adopted by Professor Curry could have revealed more clearly Southey's positive achievements as a poet, literary journalist, and critic of society.

The tripartite division into Life, Prose, and Poetry seems at first sight logical and sensible; in fact, it produces some tiresome repetition and makes it difficult for the author to give a coherent account of Southey's political development, since the political verse is dealt with in a separate chapter from the political prose and both are artificially separated from the account of Southey's life and times. Those who wish to know how much truth is contained in Hazlitt's famous taunt, that Southey 'wooed Liberty as a youthful lover', but 'has since wedded with an elderly and not very reputable lady, Legitimacy', will find little help from this guide. Professor Curry makes good use of material in the *New Letters* that he earlier edited to build up a picture of Southey's early life and he rightly stresses the crucial importance of his visits to Spain and Portugal both for supplying him with future subject matter and for fixing his anti-Catholic bias. Yet, in general, there is a striking contrast between the brisk up-to-date account of Southey's life and the outdated and inert summaries of the literary and historical situation, couched in the passive voice.

The first part of the study ends appropriately with a section on 'Literary Friendships'. As the author remarks, 'Southey either met or had some kind of interesting connection with almost every literary man of his time'. Of the connexions, in many ways the most important were those with Landor and Coleridge. It was Landor who encouraged Southey to go on writing his long poems in 1808 and offered to pay for their publication: 'His friendship is the main glory of my life', Landor wrote. Southey's relationship with Coleridge was more varied and tortuous; it was also more revealing, bringing out his strength as a man and his limitations as a writer. 'Is it not extraordinary', he wrote to a correspondent in 1810, 'that Coleridge, who is fond of logic and who has an actual love and passion for close, hard thinking, should write in so rambling and inconclusive a manner, while I who am utterly incapable of that toil of thought in which he delights, never fail to express myself perspicuously, and to the point'. Curry quotes contemporary praise of Southey's clarity and notes his highly valued services as a journalist, but he does not quote or explore the implications of this piece of puzzled self-revelation that helps us to explain why Southey always remained the workmanlike journalist and never became a writer of genious like Coleridge. He never saw the connexion between profundity of thought and complexity of language and all his work suffers in consequence.

In the third part of this study the author pays just tribute to Southey's amazing facility and range as a poet; but, as his contemporaries and as later critics have noted, these qualities were not matched by sufficient creative energy or craftsmanship; consequently there is little that today stands up to close critical scrutiny. When, in his youth, he courted the revolutionary and democratic muse, he produced nothing comparable to Wordsworth's 'Female Vagrant', while his later long narrative poems contain a strange combination of heroic morality and fanciful exoticism. In 1808 Mrs Thrale prophesied that 'the fashionable Poetry of Southey & Scott' would 'fall into decay, because all their long poems depend too much on their Colouring', adding 'In a hundred Years People will wonder why they were so admired'. Although Professor Curry neither quotes this passage nor fully explains what readers found to admire in *Thalaba the Destroyer* and *Madoc*, he does make it clear that Southey's long poems never enjoyed the same kind of success as those of Scott or Byron, even in his own day. A year after his death, Wordsworth noted that Southey's poems were read once but were rarely recurred to, and exclaimed 'how seldom quoted, and how few passages, notwithstanding the great merit of the works in many respects, are gotten by heart'. His explanation was a just one, 'that no man can write verses that will live in the hearts of his Fellow creatures, but through an over powering impulse'. In the absence of such a creative impulse, Southey's poems are now mainly of historical or political importance.

There can be few scholars as well qualified to write an authoritative guide on Southey as Professor Curry and he has much to say that is wise and temperate, but the overwhelming impression is of a well-informed specialist confined within uncongenial bounds.

JOHN COLMER

UNIVERSITY OF ADELAIDE

Sanditon: An Unfinished Novel. By JANE AUSTEN. Reproduced in Facsimile from the Manuscript in the Possession of King's College, Cambridge. With an Introduction by B. C. SOUTHAM. Oxford: Clarendon Press; London: Oxford University Press. 1975. xviii + 120 pp. £5.50.

Sanditon is Jane Austen's last work, begun in January and abandoned in March 1817. The unfinished manuscript is apparently the first draft. In some places it is heavily revised, in others there are only slight retouchings. In 1925 R. W. Chapman edited a diplomatic text, with notes recording the cancelled readings. But a transcript is no substitute for a good facsimile, and this is an excellent one. The manuscript is rarely illegible and with the facsimile we can follow Jane Austen's neatly interlined second and third thoughts. These revisions are of great critical interest.

In *Sanditon* we can see Jane Austen making the small adjustments to phrasing, diction, and syntax that reveal the extent of her conscious artistry. The door of her workshop stands ajar. Mr Parker's 'My Plantations astonish everybody by their Growth' becomes 'The Growth of my Plantations is a general astonishment' (p. 35). The second version creates a ludicrous Jack-and-the-beanstalk image of visible growth in front of a spellbound audience. Speaking of her brother Arthur, Diana Parker says at first that he 'is much more likely to eat too much than too little' (p. 89). Sensing the flatness of this, Jane Austen changed it to 'eats enormously'. But this did not satisfy her either: finally Arthur is 'only too much disposed for Food'. The last version is more economical, catches the tone of Diana's crusading self-righteousness, and conveys an image of Arthur's reluctant abstemiousness. There are many other examples throughout the manuscript.

The collective evidence of the revisions is of even greater importance. For critics have disagreed about the interpretation of *Sanditon*'s stylistic innovations. R. W. Chapman thought that the 'coarse strokes' of *Sanditon* (as he saw them) would have been 'smoothed' in revision (*Jane Austen: Facts and Problems* (Oxford, 1948), p. 208). But in *Jane Austen's Literary Manuscripts* (Oxford, 1964), Mr B. C. Southam concluded that 'Jane Austen was moving into a new, experimental style' (p. 125). Mr Southam repeats this view in his introduction to the facsimile, and the evidence of the manuscript supports it. Perhaps the best example is the first page, which is heavily revised. The difficulty of the syntax is not the result of haste or confusion, but a carefully worked-for effect. Mr Southam is surely correct in inferring that, although a first draft, the manuscript is 'not a rough sketch but a version that only requires continuation and minor changes (such as the expansion of abbreviations and paragraphing) to be ready for the printer' (p. ix). The corollary seems to me that we need a new edition of the work. In 1925 Chapman was certainly right to reject normalization as an editorial procedure: but now that we have the facsimile of the manuscript there is a strong case for producing a normalized text. We need an edition of *Sanditon* in which the genuinely innovative aspects of the work are preserved without being obscured by the retention of accidental orthographic idiosyncrasies. For example, Jane Austen often uses a dash as well as a full stop to close a period, apparently as a semi-automatic flourish. These dashes would surely have been eliminated in the printed version. But elsewhere she uses the dash Shandy-style, to punctuate the speech of asyntactic gushers. This deliberate use would obviously have been retained.

Scholars will still need to consult the original occasionally, but for almost all purposes the facsimile is an excellent working substitute. Its publication is sure to stimulate work on a fascinating fragment that has not yet received the attention it deserves. Mr Southam rightly styles it 'the most precious, poignant, and tantalizing of all Jane Austen's literary remains' (p. viii).

I noticed two slips in the introduction: Chapman's book is dated 1958 instead of 1948 (p. ix), and a line or two has dropped out, confusing the examples quoted from Lady Denham's speeches (p. xi). On the evidence of the facsimile, I would propose the following corrections to the text of *Sanditon* in the *Minor Works* (London, 1969): p. 368, l. 3, 'with' is not in the MS (p. 10); p. 393, l. 7, the MS has 'a odd' not 'an odd' (p. 56); p. 393, l. 35, the word is 'Chamber-House' not 'Chamber-Horse', whatever the thing may be; p. 395, l. 34, the MS has 'glances' not 'glance' (p. 61); p. 404, l. 18, 'since' appears to have been deleted in the MS (p. 75); p. 404, l. 25, I read 'Ingenuity' instead of 'Sagacity' (p. 75); p. 413, l. 18, 'one' is underlined in the MS (p. 92); p. 426, l. 19, MS has 'was a something' (p. 117); p. 427, l. 13, I take the insertion transcribed as 'order and the' to be a single word, but it is illegible in the facsimile.

F. P. Lock

University of Queensland

Charles Robert Maturin (1780–1824): L'Homme et l'Œuvre. By CLAUDE FIEROBE. (Centre d'Études et de Recherches Irlandaises de L'Université de Lille III, Etudes Irlandaises, 2) Paris: Université de Lille III, Éditions Universitaires. 1974. 754 pp. 97 F.

This is the first full length study of Maturin since W. Scholten's somewhat superficial study of Maturin as a novelist of terror was published in Amsterdam in 1933, itself preceded by N. Idman's more useful *C. R. Maturin: His Life and Works* (Helsingfors and London, 1923). M. Fierobe indicates some indebtedness to the eighty-five pages in Maurice Levy's *Le Roman Gothique Anglais (1764–1824)* (Toulouse, 1968) which deal with Maturin, albeit in a patchy way. The fact that the main works mentioned have been written by European rather than British scholars may indicate that Maturin causes some unease to islanders, and that he may be too easily labelled and almost forgotten as a Gothic novelist, known only for that apogee of the kind, *Melmoth the Wanderer.* Yet Maturin is worth attention, primarily for his innovation. He is probably the first author to write a novel dealing with an undergraduate's love affairs; and he blended Wordsworthianism with nationalism. Following upon Maria Edgeworth and Sydney Owenson, he was a regionalist, important in the beginnings of the Irish novel; in part shaping some of the self-consciousness which appeared after the Act of Union in 1800; in part reflecting a cultural pattern which developed out of the interest taken in Irish music, antiquities, and traditions in the latter part of the eighteenth century; and in part showing the divided attitude of the intelligent members of the Protestant ascendancy foreshadowed by Molyneux and Swift, anti-colonial, yet also anti-Presbyterian and anti-Catholic, and, particularly, anti-Methodist. What is most useful in M. Fierobe's study is the balance he holds between Maturin as novelist, as dramatist, and as Church of Ireland clergyman whose eloquence informs his published sermons. The old stories of Maturin the man are delightful: his habit of wearing a red cockade when composing his works, as a sign he was not to be disturbed; his sticking a wafer across his mouth to prevent his irresistible inclination to talk from stopping his writing; and his exuberant delight in dancing.

The first part of M. Fierobe's study (eight chapters and a conclusion) deals with Maturin's life, what we know of it. A minor point here; the oldest debating society still flourishing, at one time known as Mr Burke's debating club, should be known as the College Historical Society, not the Dublin Historical Society. The College Historical Society sprang from the 'Club' founded by Edmund Burke in April 1747 and from the 'Historical Club' instituted in October 1753. The College Historical Society was founded in 1770. The second part consists of three sections, the first discussing in three chapters the novels, the drama and poetry, and the sermons. The second section examines the themes of Maturin's work, in chapters treating Ireland, nature, dreams and visions, fantasy, the human condition and the problem of evil, and religious problems. The third section examines structure and style, its chapters discussing the art of the novels, the drama, and the preaching, with a final chapter on Maturin's style. There is a conclusion, and a full bibliography and index are supplied.

This, then, is a book in the French academic manner: thorough, penetrating, and exhaustive. What a pity the technocrats of the *hexagon* cannot extol the virtues of economy in academic expression, for M. Fierobe's work deserves a wider audience than that which its length and format is likely to give him. A book two-thirds the length would have drawn attention more effectively to Maturin and his strange work.

M. Fierobe is generally good on the background. He is surprised by the reading of an imaginary fifteen year old boy in one of the novels (but this was not yet the days of Victoria, and the Brontë childrens' reading was nearly as 'advanced');

but he does realize the effect of, say, Joseph Cooper Walker's *Historical Remains of the Irish Bards* (1786) upon Maturin himself. It might perhaps be useful to see Maturin as part of the general movement of Anglo-Irish thought in the late eighteenth and early nineteenth centuries. There was a shift in cultural attitudes which came about through the publication of such general works as Sylvester O'Halloran's *Introduction to the Study of the History and Antiquities of Ireland* (1772) and his subsequent *General History of Ireland* (1778). There were the specialized studies, such as Charlotte Brooke's *Reliques of Irish Poetry* (1789) and Edward Bunting's *General Collection of the Ancient Irish Music* (1796). Lady Morgan published *Twelve Original Hibernian Melodies with English Words, Imitated and Translated, from the Works of the Ancient Irish Bards* (1808), and Thomas Moore thought of including them in his own influential *Irish Melodies* (1808). Such travellers as Arthur Young and Charles Topham Bowden wrote of Ireland with fresh eyes at the end of the eighteenth century; and Maturin's own move westward, as curate, to Loughrea in 1804, may probably, as M. Fierobe suggests, have given him knowledge of an ancient Irish family's mode of life at Cloghan Castle as well as showing him the depressing rural poverty of the west.

There were, of course, many outside literary influences and those of the sensational novelists are fully examined by the author. But while there is a discussion of Maturin's delight in nature and the use to which he puts it in his novels, the sources may not be fully treated. For instance, what is unusual in *Fatal Revenge or, The Family of Montario* is its treatment of nationalism. The *Lyrical Ballads*, and its preface, gave Maturin's variety of highly romantic nationalism much of its peculiar flavour. He saw Irish resistance to English rule as part of a clash between two cultures, one nationalist and romantic, based on a Gaelic folk tradition and the 'natural' emotion of a native population living, perforce, in close contact with nature, the other cosmopolitan and neoclassical, making nature conform to the tastes and the habits of society. In *Fatal Revenge* this theme is admittedly incidental to the Gothic plot; but Cyprian (the name of one of the heroines) has disguised herself as a young man to be near Ippolito, the object of her affections. To 'his' comment that poetry must deal with nature 'modified and conformed to the existing habits and tastes of society' Ippolito (there are hints of homosexuality and unhallowed passions in Maturin's work) replies with the romantic view that the influence of prevailing manners would be admitted into her strains 'so far as they were conformable to Nature'. Ippolito suggests the need to study the poesy of the heretic English, alluding fairly obviously to *Lyrical Ballads*, and then claiming 'Irish poetry is richer in harmony and more melting than English'. This hint suggests that Maturin's own ballad of Bruno-Lin the outlaw, interposed not very successfully into the novel, depends not only on Scott's example but on the earlier cited interest in Gaelic poetry and music.

Again, while M. Fierobe asserts the influence of the heroes created by Godwin, Rousseau, and Voltaire upon Maturin's creation of Ormsby Bethel, the hero of that unsuccessful pot-boiler *The Wild Irish Boy*, he ignores the effect of Wordsworthianism upon him, even though he is placed in Cumberland and there profoundly affected by nature.

Few people can recently have read *Women, or Pour et Contre*, since very few copies of it survive. M. Fierobe calls it 'un roman d'analyse psychologique', rightly showing Maturin's 'compréhension du cœur feminin': he regards the novel as a triumph of purity. But he might also have extended his view of the novel by seeing de Courcy as a very young and immature undergraduate; it is not, perhaps, altogether a case of regarding Zaira as being, like Eva, *prise sous le joug masculin*, but one to which we might in charity apply Yeats's lines: 'Young | We loved each other and were ignorant.' And while M. Fierobe's analysis is sensitive and sympathetic, a modern reader must also take into account some of the accidental absurdities into which Maturin's pioneering led him: the hilarious effect caused by his somewhat primitive use of symbolism, in the incident where de Courcy clasps Eva to his bosom: 'Her long, light hair (of a different colour from Zaira's) diffused its golden luxuriance over his bosom; her white slender fingers grasped his with the fondling helplessness of infancy, and twined their waxen softness round and round them; her pure hyacinth breath trembled over his cheeks and lips. In clasping her closer to his heart, he felt something within his vest; he drew it out; it was the flower Zaira had given him the night before, and which he had placed there; *it was withered*; he flung it away.' And perhaps there is also a touch of extravagance in the violet odours exuded when his volatile heroes and heroines embraced. Against these extravagancies we should set the atmospheric achievement of his thunderstorms and the fire scenes (a new development in urban Gothic).

M. Fierobe's book is a very useful, intelligent piece of critical scholarship which takes Maturin seriously and adds to our understanding of his aims as well as offering a sympathetic view of his achievement.

A. NORMAN JEFFARES

UNIVERSITY OF STIRLING

Shelley and Nonviolence. By ART YOUNG. (Studies in English Literature, 103) The Hague: Mouton. 1975. 172 pp. fl 38.

Mr Young maintains that Shelley held a coherent philosophy of nonviolence, and that his opinions on this remained substantially unchanged from his early 'Address to the Irish People' to *The Triumph of Life*. He succeeds in general in showing that Shelley's thought, as expressed in the prose pamphlets, was more coherent, consistent, and sensible than has sometimes been allowed; and he compares it quite interestingly with that of Gandhi. More important, and more controversial, is his treatment of some of the poems. He shows himself capable of sensitive and intelligent reading, and honestly confronts the difficulties that he sees, but he does not altogether escape the dangers that beset anyone who approaches imaginative works from an interest in the author's opinions. Such a person wishes to find the opinions he believes the author to have consciously held, but sometimes what is there, the product of feeling more than thought, is different; perhaps more profound, perhaps more confused.

A difficult passage to interpret, as Mr Young honestly acknowledges, is that on the 'rude pikes' incident in *The Revolt of Islam*. When the tyrant supported by foreign armies returns to put down the revolution Laon organizes his followers to offer nonviolent resistance. They are mercilessly hewn down until they find, with a joy apparently shared by Laon, 'a bundle of rude pikes' in a cave. With this slight armament they almost put their foes to flight, but are in the end defeated, all but Laon himself being killed. This use of violence is surely either too little and too late (by a controlled use of force earlier Laon might have consolidated and defended the revolution) or too much (if the use of violence necessarily corrupts one's cause). Mr Young perceives the difficulty and tries to deal with it, though to my mind not very convincingly. The charge against Shelley is that he does not seem to, either in the 'rude pikes' incident or in the following one, where the supposedly nonviolent Cythna arrives on a huge black steed waving a sword, terrifying the foe, and rescuing Laon. If it is proper now to use terror to rescue a single individual would it not have been proper to use force earlier to rescue a whole people from the horrors of the counter-revolution? I am not saying that the question is unanswerable; my objection to Shelley is that he does not seem to ask it, but allows himself to float on varying currents of feeling, to delight in the picture of the giant steed and the sword-waving Cythna without reflecting on its implications.

In *Prometheus Unbound* Shelley, by transferring the contest to the realm of myth, largely avoids the problems of how to bring into being and maintain a better society in the actual world. Prometheus's hands are unsullied by violence. He casts out hatred from his mind; Jupiter is overthrown, and Utopia comes into existence. The poetry is so powerful that we normally accept this without asking awkward questions; but there is an awkward question that can be asked. Jupiter does not simply disappear as a result of Prometheus's change of heart. Demogorgon, a mighty power associated with volcanoes, rises and after a violent, if brief, struggle drags Jupiter down into the abyss. Is the implication of this that the revolutionary must in the end be willing to use force to accomplish his ends?

Mr Young puts up a spirited defence of *The Cenci*. The difficulty here for many readers is that, though Shelley clearly does not intend to condone Beatrice's use of violence, his sympathy for the victim of tyranny so overbalances his theoretical condemnation of violence that the actual effect of the second half of the play is confused, and different from what he may be supposed to have meant. Mr Young replies that Beatrice is shown to be indeed the daughter of her father. In the first half of the play her purity is contrasted with his evil; but in the second half Shelley 'ironically underscores the similarities of their personalities — their pride, determination, ruthless courage, and their delusions fostered by the religious superstitions of established orthodoxy'. Her flaw is her pride. I think this may well be a correct interpretation, but whether it is adequately embodied in the play could be shown only by a fine stage performance.

In his treatment of *The Cenci* Mr Young does genuinely and interestingly engage with the words on the page, but in his brief passage on *The Triumph of Life* he succumbs to the temptation to find what his thesis disposes him to find. The implied answer to the question 'what is life?' is, he says, that 'life for the misdirected few is a selfish searching after the things of another world; and that life for the sacred few is self-mastery through brotherly love. The state of existence for the sacred few is not static but creative — it is a dynamic struggle against the corrupting and degrading life of the world in a continuous attempt to fully realize the sacredness of humanity'. This is surely not what is actually embodied in the fragment, where all we are told about the sacred few is that they

> . . . could not tame
> Their spirits to the Conqueror, but as soon
> As they had touched the world with living flame
> Fled back like eagles to their native noon.

Their native noon was presumably another world; they look more like Mr Young's misdirected few than his sacred few. Shelley's feelings, probably even his opinions, were more unstable than Mr Young allows.

P. H. BUTTER

UNIVERSITY OF GLASGOW

Keats as a Narrative Poet: A Test of Invention. By JUDY LITTLE. Lincoln, Nebraska: University of Nebraska Press. 1975. viii + 107 pp. $8.50.

John Keats: The Complete Poems. Edited by JOHN BARNARD. (Penguin English Poets) Harmondsworth: Penguin Books. 1973. 731 pp. £1.00.

Dr Judy Little comes close to reducing the art of the narrative poet to the deployment of imagery. She thinks that Keats's early verse epistles and 'I stood tip-toe' take their shape not from processes of discourse but from patterns of repeated images; and that similar thematic recurrences make his first long narrative poem, *Endymion*, 'quite coherent' and perhaps 'better than the sum of its parts' (p. 63). A sceptical reader will reflect that *Endymion* does not seem like that as one reads it.

Acquaintance with Hazlitt's criticism, and in particular with his doctrines of 'gusto' and 'intensity', apparently influenced Keats's methods in 'Isabella'. Dr Little finds this story of real people in real distress remarkable for the full development and careful control of the imagery, which varies in power and vividness as the action rises and falls. Imagery employed in this fashion as a main structural support remains central in her view to the subsequent narrative poems. In 'The Eve of St Agnes' it serves the purposes of characterization and evaluation. Naturally sparse in the brief ballad 'La Belle Dame sans Merci', it nevertheless subtly reinforces the distinction between the suffering mortal and the mysterious lady. Thematic recurrences resume an important place in 'Lamia', but Keats continues to modulate the imagery with a view to revealing above all the ambiguities of his main character.

'Hyperion' and 'The Fall of Hyperion', finally, testify to the persisting influence of Hazlitt. These two fragments show Keats working towards a new kind of epic composed not of great actions but of huge, static, monumental images.

Dr Little sketches thoughtfully and judiciously the interpretations of particular poems to which her study of the imagery leads. She conducts her general argument clearly, concisely, and purposefully. Presumably out of a sense of duty, she encumbers it from time to time by ushering in Professors Bill Brewer, Jan Stewer, Peter Gurney, and the rest to deliver their divergent pronouncements. But she is level headed enough to dissociate herself from them when they talk rubbish: for example, when one of them moralizes 'The Eve of St Agnes' by making the Beadsman stand for spirit, the revellers for flesh, and the lovers for a synthesis of the two. Yet she herself surprises us by asking how the knight-at-arms knew that the Belle Dame said, 'I love thee true', since she spoke 'in language strange'. When in the history of the world did 'language strange' ever impede the understanding of that particular avowal?

What she has given us is an interesting and cogent study of Keats's structural use of imagery in his narrative poems. Surely the art of a narrative poet can comprise much more than this. Several of Keats's finest poems happen to be narrative poems, but did he really have everything it takes to be a successful storyteller? Even *The Lay of the Last Minstrel* has an *élan* Keats nowhere achieves; and Keats nowhere tantalizes his reader, intrigues him, and holds him in suspense, as does Byron in *The Giaour*. I feel some embarrassment at placing these tales alongside the best of Keats's. But they do possess certain humble virtues as narratives that are conspicuously absent from 'The Eve of St Agnes' and 'Lamia'.

No doubt Dr Little would retort, with the backing of some members of Uncle Tom Cobley's team, that these traditional virtues were passing out of reach during Keats's lifetime and that his only possible line of advance was by lyricizing his narrative. But were they as far out of reach as all that? Was not the nineteenth century one of the great ages of precisely the kind of narrative that is in question? We are surely not going to make the merely formal distinction between verse and prose an excuse for excluding the novel from our consideration.

Mr John Barnard's useful edition of Keats conforms in arrangement with earlier volumes in the same series. His notes give particulars of each poem's composition and early publication, report interesting textual variants, supply helpful explanations, and record what Mr Barnard considers 'major critical attitudes to the poetry' (p. 17). He is too generous in his recognition of major status. Why preserve the daft suggestion that two of the 'kisses four' which shut the 'wild wild eyes' of the Belle Dame are the 'pennies laid on the eyes of death' (p. 639)? A few misprints appear to have crept into a text that has evidently been prepared with care: 'To Charles Cowden Clarke', l. 61; 'Hither, hither, love —', l. 2; *Endymion*, IV.326; 'Isabella', l. 140; 'Why did I laugh tonight?', l. 5; *Otho the Great*, V.3.16; 'Lamia', 1.238, II.98; and 'The Cap and Bells', l. 223. In an explanatory note to 'The Cap and Bells', l. 429, Mr Barnard follows Professor Miriam Allott in deriving 'Candy wine' from Ceylon. Crete (Candia) seems more likely.

†JOHN D. JUMP

UNIVERSITY OF MANCHESTER

Der amerikanische Roman im 19. und 20. Jahrhundert: Interpretationen. Edited by EDGAR LOHNER. Berlin: Schmidt. 1974. 383 pp.

This is a useful collection of essays, mainly by German and American scholars, on American novels and novelists from Cooper to Bellow and Updike. With all but four of the essays appearing in German (a number of them specially translated), it is clearly intended primarily for German-speaking students of literature, and seeks to provide them with a comprehensive introduction to this field of study. The editor introduces the collection with a brief but lucid historical survey of the development of the novel in America and appends to it a select bibliography of general works on American fiction, together with short bibliographies of critical writings on the individual novelists under discussion. In selecting or commissioning contributions he has sought essays which, while presenting in most cases an interpretation of a specific novel, also serve as an introduction to the particular novelist's work as a whole, and go beyond what he terms the 'purely academic' by relating the work to its wider literary and socio-historical context. Thus Dietmar Haack focuses on the juxtaposition of incongruous elements and the stylistic unevenness to be found in *The Red Badge of Courage*, and relates them not simply to Crane's youthfulness but to the general uncertainty and experimentalism of a time of literary transition. Michael Hoenisch analyses the function of the first-person narrator in *The Great Gatsby*, stressing the relationship between the narrative device and the historical reality of a world which Fitzgerald saw to be beyond the individual's capacity fully to comprehend or control. Martha A. Woodmansee, in an essay (in English) on Melville which concentrates refreshingly on the relatively neglected last novel, interprets *The Confidence Man* as a bitter, if comic, criticism of nineteenth-century American life, using a technique of 'fictitious estrangement' to 'prod the reader out of his gullibility in relation to the conventions and clichés of fiction and society', and to 'demonstrate the untruth of those forms and institutions that claim to be the voice of truth'. Ursula Brumm on *Absalom, Absalom!* is less concerned with the wider context of the novel, its relationship to Faulkner's other works and to the culture of the American South, and more with its complexities as a novel about history, which she analyses in terms of a dialectic of history as 'happening' ('Geschehen') and history as 'understanding' ('Verstehen'). On the whole it is the American contributions, such as Mark Schorer's on *Babbitt*, that throw most light on the wider socio-historical and cultural dimensions of specific works. Most of these American essays have already appeared elsewhere, and the editor has chosen wisely: Robert Penn Warren on Dreiser's *An American Tragedy*, Richard Poirier on Hawthorne and James, and, translated into German, E. D. Lowry on *Manhattan Transfer*, Albert Guerard on 'Saul Bellow and the Activists', and Lionel Trilling on 'William Dean Howells and the Roots of Modern Taste'. One weakness of the collection is its thin coverage of the post-war period, which perhaps reflects the teaching habits of German universities: only Wilder, Salinger, Bellow, and Updike are discussed here. It is difficult to see why an essay on Wilder's *The Eighth Day* should be included when writers such as Mailer, Ellison, Burroughs,

Nabokov, Barth, and Pynchon are neglected. However, with this reservation, Professor Lohner's volume can be said to serve its purpose very well.

UNIVERSITY OF WARWICK   J. M. RIGNALL

Modern Fantasy: Five Studies. By C. N. MANLOVE. Cambridge, London and New York: Cambridge University Press. 1975. viii + 308 pp. £6.50.

C. N. Manlove has written a sensible and informative analysis of five modern fantasists: Charles Kingsley, George MacDonald, C. S. Lewis, J. R. R. Tolkien, and Mervyn Peake. He gives us biography, describes particular stories, and analyses the ideologies implicit in their works. He defines fantasy as *a fiction evoking wonder and containing a substantial and irreducible element of the supernatural with which the mortal characters in the story or the readers become on at least partly familiar terms* (p. 1). Science fiction is excluded because its other worlds are accepted as technically possible; ghost stories fail to qualify because of the unremitting alienness of the supernatural. Mr Manlove also rejects those fantasies which are the product of fancy rather than imagination, stories using fantasy gimmicks without being able to infuse them with 'potent' meanings. The elimination of so many works generally labelled fantasy is justifiable for the purposes of defining a uniform group, but is nonetheless disappointing, since the discarded works also embrace the impossible, and we may well be curious about what they gain by departing from empirical reality.

Mr Manlove makes genuine contributions to our understanding of each of the five authors, although the sameness of his approach makes his conclusions predictable. All five authors are shown to be intellectually inconsistent. In Kingsley's *Water Babies*, the hero's ethical progress is contradicted by his behaviour; Tom does not demonstrate serious moral improvement although he receives its assigned rewards. MacDonald claimed that fantasy should not be directed and organized by the conscious mind; in practice, however, he imposes order to such a degree that 'once he lets his — and our — organizing intellect into part of his tale, we begin to wonder why it has its disconnected form at all' (p. 77). Of Lewis's works, Manlove discusses only *Perelandra*, a questionable decision. *Perelandra* is Lewis's most ambitious and original fantasy, but there is not sufficient justification for letting the contradiction at its heart indict Lewis generally. The issues raised by the temptation and *agon* are mutually invalidating; for example, Tinidril would have fallen, like Eve, had Ransom not intervened, and yet she is rewarded as if she had successfully withstood temptation. The contradiction weakening Peake's *Gormenghast* trilogy is found in Titus's motives: he craves freedom from the Gormenghast ritual, but we do not see him particularly oppressed by the servitude it imposes. Nor do we see any person or experience which might have led Titus to realize that other lifestyles were possible. Peake announces spiritual changes in Titus but, as in *The Water Babies*, the hero's behaviour and statements do not support such assertions.

The discussion of Tolkien is particularly rewarding in its balance of admiration and criticism. The charge that Tolkien failed in his exaltation of the heroic will by not being 'prepared to allow any really telling loss or vicissitude into the book' is unarguable. Mr Manlove's critique of the prose is likewise cogent. I cannot, however, altogether accept his judgement that Sauron is so 'fascinating' and imaginatively presented as to make Tolkien unwittingly of the devil's party, though this is a personal disagreement. I do feel that Manlove takes a wrong turning in his analysis of the myth at the story's core:

There does seem to be a glimmer in Tolkien's book of a myth which is more definitely at the back of *Paradise Lost*: the idea of the minute yet enormously powerful Ring with its frail bearer, the long and difficult journey to enclosed Mordor and the casting of the Ring into the mountain suggests a process of fertilization. Of course there are inconsistencies: throwing the Ring into Orodruin results in destruction, not creation, and unless we are to grant an incest motif, a spermatozoon does not return to its ultimate point of origin. Nevertheless the basic pattern of the story does hint at this image. (pp. 205–6)

This extravagance does not detract significantly from Mr Manlove's overall reading of *The Lord of the Rings*.

Mr Manlove has done his authors the courtesy of taking them seriously, for which he deserves high praise. He studies their thought as one studies that of 'major' writers. He concludes, however, that all are logically deficient. This failure he ultimately attributes to fantasy itself:

The basic problem seems to be one of *distance*, distance between the 'real' and fantastic worlds, or between nature and supernature. However fantasists try to surmount it, it mutilates their aims. If they try to choose the fantastic world to the exclusion of their own — Gormenghast, the Muspel of David Lindsay's *A Voyage to Arcturus* (1920), or the unconscious or mystic mind — the natural order pulls them back. If on the other hand they attempt, as Kingsley or, say, Charles Williams (and, in other senses, MacDonald and Lewis) do, to join the worlds, one side comes to dominate the other. (p. 258)

Mr Manlove is correct in pointing out the difference between modern scepticism and the belief that a medieval audience would have felt in the verities of *Sir Gawain and the Green Knight*. He sees in our lack of faith a serious impediment to the success of modern fantasy, but this pessimistic conclusion, that modern fantasy cannot be written without damaging inconsistencies, seems unduly influenced by his choice of authors. Scepticism is no hindrance to the enjoyment of Kafka, Calvino, or Borges. Reservations notwithstanding, this book is an important step in the study of English fantasy. Mr Manlove's enquiry into the writers' intellectual concerns is one of the most interesting approaches to such fantasies that I have read, and all of his analyses contribute to our enjoyment of the stories themselves.

CORNELL UNIVERSITY   KATHRYN HUME

The Finer Optic: The Aesthetic of Particularity in Victorian Poetry. By CAROL T. CHRIST. New Haven and London: Yale University Press. 1975. xii + 171 pp. £4.75.

The title of this study is doubly appropriate, for by taking the Victorian poets' relation with the visible world as her theme, Dr Christ clarifies the blurred vision which still too often characterizes readings of the period's poetry. Firmly, but without ostentation, she first of all places the Victorians in the illuminating context of the long debate on the imagination's duties to general and particular, ideal and real, subject and object. There was, she shows, a marked shift of emphasis in the mid-nineteenth century towards seeing the object as in itself it really is, a discovery of 'the world's multitudinousness' which was both enriching and daunting; her book then goes on to explore very sensitively the poetic rewards, tensions, and implications of this assent to the 'plain and leafy fact' of the primrose by the river's brim. Perhaps Dr Christ tends to overstress a little the elements of panic at the expense of the delight which was also part of the response to the new vision of particularity. I cannot for example agree with her that the Ruskin of *Modern Painters* is reacting almost with 'desperation in the face of the world of objects', and I think that Tennyson's use of detail should be more positively distinguished as an imaginative tactic of great resource before it is identified with morbidity of outlook in the persons, such as Mariana, he is portraying. Undoubtedly, however, Dr Christ is right to point to the links between particularity and atomism, and to discern the fears of the age in the poets' problems of reconciling an appreciation of multiplicity with any sense of unity and order in (or beyond) a universe so constituted.

At the same time as she develops this theme, Dr Christ scrupulously resists the temptation to impose a common response to the particular on the four poets she selects for detailed discussion. Tennyson, Rossetti, Browning, and Hopkins are allowed their full individuality, and one of the chief pleasures of this study is its acute discriminatory readings, where Dr Christ presents her thesis in terms of the technical practice of each poet, yet never subordinates poem to theory. Out of much excellent close commentary, I would single out that on Hopkins for its fine demonstration of how the energy of 'instress' is poetically embodied through a correspondingly dynamic use of language, syntax, and structure. Brought together by Dr Christ's argument are Browning's depiction of people creating their own highly personal worlds; Tennyson's efforts to correlate extraneous objects and inner emotions; Rossetti exalting the moment's sensation for its own sake; Hopkins leaping from intensities of observation to the grandeur of God. This range of discussion stimulates a fresh awareness of cross-currents and affinities in the work of the period, so that Victorian poetry takes on a new coherence even as its variety and the independent vitality of its leading exponents is confirmed and honoured.

The same keen recognition of significant connexion underlying divergence distinguishes Dr Christ's view of the critical theory of the period; Pater, for instance, emerges as centrally Victorian in his stress on the separate moments of experience, differing from his contemporaries not in the mode of apprehension but in his readiness to accept the moment as his unit of value. Arnold too as theorist is illuminated by Dr Christ's approach, and it is therefore a minor regret that the poet of the signal-elm is not included in her study. Ruskin, on the other hand, is less well served. To my mind, his role in helping to form the sensibility of the age is reduced: *Modern Painters*, both as a direct influence (notably on Hopkins) and as a general landmark for the literary imagination deserves more acknowledgement and analysis than it receives here. But this deficiency in no way modifies gratitude and admiration for a book as well written as it is perceptive in its understanding of the Victorian attraction to and fear of the world's particulars.

UNIVERSITY OF LEEDS   PATRICIA M. BALL

Literary Monographs. Volume 7. *Thackeray, Hawthorne and Melville, and Dreiser.* Edited by ERIC ROTHSTEIN and JOSEPH ANTHONY WITTREICH, JR. Madison, Wisconsin and London: University of Wisconsin Press. 1975. viii + 164 pp. $13.75.

This volume includes three monographs all of which are of a high standard. The first, 'The Rookery at Castlewood' by Elaine Scarry, is certainly interesting. It takes up the matter of the contradictions and inaccuracies which abound in *Henry Esmond* and very clearly brings out how 'Esmond's narrative' differs from 'Thackeray's novel'. Esmond himself is devoted to truth, the subjective truth of autobiography, whereas Thackeray appears to devote himself to showing how even this is impossible to establish. In briefly commenting on this two points may be made. The first is that Elaine Scarry's study is thorough, teasing, clear, and ingenious; no one, however previously satisfied with a more superficial reading, will follow it through without having to reconsider his views. Yet the second may allow some disagreement.

Her whole argument rests on the fact that, since Thackeray is certainly arguing against a reliance on historical (objective) truth, and in favour of the subjective, then the truth of an autobiographical novel can only be conveyed by its internal consistency. And evidently *Henry Esmond* is highly inconsistent. Now Elaine Scarry asserts that 'most critics' readings . . . have not taken note of these contradictions'. Yet, true as this is, it does not follow that they have not attracted comment before. She may allow only three exceptions, including John Sutherland of *Thackeray at Work* (1974) and other studies, but the present obscurity (or past modesty) of T. W. and W. Snow, editors of *Henry Esmond* (Oxford, 1909) introduced by Saintsbury, ought not to mean that they are completely disregarded. Many such 'inconsistencies' were recorded there; and, though Saintsbury took the limelight, the Snows agreed with Sutherland in offering evidence that such contradictions were often plain mistakes. The evidence is good. The first two chapter headings, for example, are obviously transposed, and we are not asked (even now) to believe that Thackeray did this deliberately in order to undermine our confidence from the start. Places in the novel do move about England, but the manuscript makes it appear that Thackeray found it easier to change his mind than to make a thorough textual revision. It is true that Frank is said, on one occasion, to have been wounded at Ramillies (Signet 225) and, on another, to have been unharmed (267); but shouldn't we be told that the contradiction arises because, in the first reference, Thackeray seems to have confused Ramillies with Oudenarde (284)? We may be told that the novel offers two differing accounts of the reception of Esmond's comedy, *The Faithful Fool*, but it is the Snows who show that they are about two different occasions. Many more examples could be given.

There is, of course, a difference between those who seek for internal consistency in *Henry Esmond*, and those who are concerned about the way Thackeray wrote. But this is not the whole story. For if we are to believe in a Thackeray who planted these 'contradictions' intentionally (and I would not deny that this is likely of some of them) then how do we think of him as intentionally characterizing Esmond? If he meant them, then Esmond is more than elusive, he was extremely confused. In fact, the reason why such contradictions have received so little critical attention is because they were taken to be plain mistakes. But if they were deliberate, then we can hardly escape other internal implications just by insisting on the vital but elementary distinction between author and narrator. Of course they are distinct, but they are certainly not independent; and though it makes Thackeray interesting to suggest that he may have been writing like Samuel Beckett, it is not easy to see what manner of man he can have supposed his chief character to be. There are other problems and questions raised which are equally hard to answer. It is the virtue of this clever and intricate study that, as well as presenting a case which is partly convincing, it provokes further discussion.

The second and third monographs are by Sidney Moss, 'Hawthorne and Melville: An Inquiry into Their Art and the Mystery of Their Friendship', and Philip L. Gerber, 'Dreiser's *Stoic*: A Study in Literary Frustration'. Mr Gerber's study is an authoritative account, from manuscript sources, of the long-delayed composition of the third volume of the trilogy which it formed with *The Financier* and *The Titan*. Mr Moss's is persuasively thoughtful. All three monographs are well argued, and make a valuable contribution to our understanding of fiction.

K. J. FIELDING

UNIVERSITY OF EDINBURGH

Elizabeth Barrett Browning's Letters to Mrs. David Ogilvy, 1849–1861. With Recollections by Mrs. Ogilvy. Edited by PETER N. HEYDON and PHILIP KELLEY. New York: Quadrangle/The New York Times Book Co. and The Browning Institute; London: John Murray. 1973. xxxviii + 220 pp. £3.75.

This is a book that only a mother could love. Snippets of what Elizabeth calls 'babyology' (p. 82) are filled out with a great deal of what may as well be called babyography. The main subject is Robert Wiedeman Browning, self-named (as an infant) 'Penini', 'Peni', and 'Pen', whom Elizabeth tried to keep a baby as long as possible. 'You', she admitted to Mrs Ogilvy, 'have a relay of babies. I have but one, & must keep him as long as I can . . . the child [then six] with all his cleverness is peculiarly infantine still, thank God' (p. 132). There is much detailed description of Pen's baby talk and fancy clothes, both of which persist long into his childhood. Evidently Pen would have liked to grow up, if only so as to displace his father. But Elizabeth would have none of it. 'He cries out every now & then that he ought to be called "Robert" — but I cant afford two Roberts — and then Peni is grown so dear' (p. 161).

Pen is not the only literary baby in this book. Aside from frequent references to Mrs Ogilvy's own children (and Mrs Olgivy wrote 'verses', as Elizabeth guardedly calls them) there is often mention of other poetic children, and always the nursery overshadows the writer's study. 'Tennyson's child I have not seen, but it is said to be a nice baby' (p. 85). 'Mrs. Trollope has a little girl. She cant nurse' (p. 100). There is this remarkable résumé of sentimental Victorian literary topics, prompted by the death in Rome, of 'gastric fever', of Joseph Story (son of a sculptor and poet), aged six: 'nothing should induce me to remain here two winters together — and, for the rest, the feeling of *Rome* is lost to me . . . the mountains & great campagna slurred over by ghastly death-fingers smelling of fresh mould . . . not Caesarean dust. Think! My first drive was with that desolated mother to the gate of the cemetery. There's the Coliseum! — that's the temple of Vesta! — and that's little Joe's grave! — Ancient gods, renowned emperors, tumbled into the new grave & forgotten!! He's buried close by the heart of Shelley & away from his mother's . . . poor, good, dear, little Joe!' (p. 111). Another grotesque child-moment in this book has Pen 'making a little kissing sound with his mouth' to summon either his father, or his dog, or 'the horse on the tapestry' (p. 33) — the same animal that, a year later, his father would make into the most hideous horse in English literature: 'One stiff blind horse, his every bone a-stare, | . . . | Thrust out past service from the devil's stud!'

There is surprisingly little discussion of literary *adults* in these letters. Elizabeth seems to have thought silence to be the better part of criticism as regards Mrs Ogilvy's own poems. (A selection is printed in the appendix; they make even Elizabeth's weaker verses seem good. There is also a prefatory memoir by Mrs Ogilvy, notable mainly for its account of the Brownings' joint defence of their right to speak over the heads of the English common reader.) Elizabeth's own poetry hardly figures here at all, nor Robert's, although Robert's prosaic side is neatly caught from time to time. As regards money Robert has a 'superhuman prudence (for a human poet)' (p. 35). His views on the aesthetic education of children are of the cautious, Platonic sort, he holding 'rightly that it was quite wrong to expose a young child to the shows of grief [in the theatre], before he could possibly discern the meaning of the imitation of Art' (p. 39). There is one glimpse of Robert with his defences down, in a brief account of his return to England after his mother's death: 'I was perfectly unhappy about Robert, who lost his spirits from the moment of crossing the Alps & grew so unwell in Paris, fell into such a state of morbid nervousness, that at last I resolved on persuading him against going to England at all. The idea of taking his wife & child to New

Cross & putting them into the place of his mother, was haunting him day & night, & I was afraid to think how it might end' (p. 45).

The major literary opinions remarked in this correspondence were that Elizabeth preferred Tennyson's *Maud* to his *Idylls* and Bailey's *Festus* to the poems of Arnold, who 'wants vital heat, passion & imagination [which are] great wants!' (pp. 147, 117).

Although the Ogilvys spent much time in Italy, often travelling with the Brownings, they did not share Elizabeth's fondness for Napoleon III, and therefore many of Elizabeth's letters include partisan lectures on the intricate progress of Italian current events. 'Try to understand what the situation is', she pleads at one point; a plea that time has made into a *double entendre*.

The editors supply concise headnotes which make the political background as clear as possible. However, their desire to confine editorial annotation 'to a minimum (p. xxiv) means that some other details go unnoticed. For example, they do not note that the painting Robert discovered and bought, later supposed to be by Ghirlandaio (p. 8), was finally sold by Sotheby's *as* a Ghirlandaio, in the 1913 sale of the Browning estate; nor (and this is more pertinent) that it can be seen in the background of the frontispiece to their edition, a handsome colour reproduction of Mignaty's painting *Salon at Casa Guidi*, which they publish with no reference to the key given for it in the Sotheby catalogue. Nor do they identify certain magazine extracts from a 'new book' by Tennyson on which Elizabeth comments, reporting Robert's praise (p. 20).

MICHAEL HANCHER

UNIVERSITY OF MINNESOTA, MINNEAPOLIS

Robert Browning. By ROBERT BRAINARD PEARSALL. (Twayne's English Authors Series, 168) New York: Twayne. 1974. 193 pp. $6.95.

Browning's Lyrics: An Exploration. By ELEANOR COOK. Toronto and Buffalo: University of Toronto Press. 1974. xvi + 317 pp. £7.50.

Professor Pearsall has courageously attempted to provide a complete survey of Browning's work in fewer than two hundred pages. Not surprisingly he has failed, partly through over-compression, partly, I am afraid, because his accounts of specific poems are frequently inaccurate and his general view of Browning limited in the extreme. In addition the book is peppered with misprints and minor errors: I could not recommend it on any level. The brief authoritative profile of Browning which is so often called for seems as unattainable as ever. Meanwhile we must continue to profit from a number of more specialized accounts, such as those with which the University of Toronto Press is particularly associated: of recent publications from this source Professor Cook's extended discussion of Browning's lyric poems is by no means the least interesting.

The general framework of the book is chronological, with the obligatory visit to *Pauline, Paracelsus,* and *Sordello* in Chapter 1, *Bells and Pomegranates, Men and Women,* and *Dramatis Personae* in the central place, and *Pacchiarotto* and *Asolando* bringing up the rear. Professor Cook writes helpfully and sensibly, and there is no doubt that many readers will be grateful to use her book as a handbook to the lyrics. It is right to say at once that such readers are in excellent hands and will encounter many passages of admirably close criticism. Browning's lyrics are often taken very much for granted and deserve a careful and sensitive reading such as this. The reservations which follow are to be set in the context of this generally favourable response.

First, Professor Cook seems uneasy whenever she confronts the notion of the dramatic lyric. She very properly insists on the importance of maintaining the integrity of the dramatic viewpoint in Browning's poems and that 'Browning's dramatis personae are by no means simple masks' (p. 293), yet in practice she seems to me to give too little weight to the immediate context and too much to the situation of the lyric in the life and works of Robert Browning.

This is closely connected with my second and major reservation. *Browning's Lyrics* is built on the premiss that 'imagery and theme are often so intimately associated that it is impossible to comprehend some lyrics without comprehending their imagery'. Accordingly Professor Cook devotes most of her book to an exploration of the operation of imagery in the major lyrics. She makes good use of parallel passages from *Aristophanes' Apology, Fifine at the Fair,* and *Red Cotton Night-Cap Country,* and there is a certain fascination in watching such an accomplished detective at work. Yet she does not tackle the question of the critical value of such parallels. What can a passage written thirty years later in *Apollo and the Fates* tell us about *Two in the Campagna*? Again Professor Cook, and this is her main endeavour in the book, tries to demonstrate certain sets and patterns of images which Browning consistently used. If this is to be of value it must, I think, be so by virtue of an argument which assumes at some point that poems are not self-contained works of art but that an image in one poem is associated with and defined by a similar image in another. As Professor Cook says, 'With care, Browning's images can be made to elucidate each other'. This claim can be substantiated in two ways, either by a rigorous general argument, which Professor Cook does not offer and which I do not believe can be sustained, or by a conclusive demonstration in the particular case of Browning that such a procedure is both legitimate and helpful. On the whole I must record that I was not convinced by the examples she provides.

The core of the book is the extended accounts of *Two in the Campagna, Love Among the Ruins, Women and Roses, By the Fireside,* and *James Lee's Wife.* On all of these poems Professor Cook has some illuminating remarks, but the doubts about the validity of the basic procedure are not dispelled. The images are noticed, related, and formed into groups (often in new and surprising patterns) yet the individual poem remains obstinately itself and its own central organizing principle unaffected and unexposed by reference to other poems. Perhaps the issue can be most simply illustrated by an example. Talking about *Two in the Campagna* she draws attention to Browning's fondness for referring to the closed circle of the natural cycle: that the spirit of man is not subject to this cycle of birth, maturity, and death can be a source of human hope. Yet when she deals with *Love Among the Ruins* she suggests that the persistence of the natural cycle is a source of agitation similar to the passion in the *Lament for Bion.* I cannot resist here the common-sense view that the bearing of an image is determined by its context in the poem (and often in Browning's case by his imaginary *persona*). But to admit this would undermine Professor Cook's position. Again in *St Martin's Summer* and the *Epilogue* to *Pacchiarotto* the imagery is most interestingly used, as an extended and richly developed conceit which sustains the entire argument of the poem, yet Professor Cook's regard is almost always, it seems to me, away from what the images are doing in the poem and directed to similar images elsewhere in Browning. This is done, as I say, with great sensitivity and brings its unexpected incidental pleasures, especially in Professor Cook's discussion of Browning's images of houses and enclosures.

My other reservations are on points of detail. It is notable that Professor Cook does not make much use of the work of other writers on Browning. This gives her book its freshness and independence, but also means that she does not test her account of the way Browning's lyrics operate against different views. In particular she ignores William Cadbury's 'Lyric and Anti-Lyric Forms' (*UTQ,* 34), on which it would have been particularly interesting to have her comments, since it not only tries to establish a procedure for the criticism of Browning's lyrics but deals at length with one of her own special poems, *Love Among the Ruins*. Careful reader though Professor Cook normally is there are one or two minor oversights. She misses the reference to *Fidelio* in *By the Fireside* and therefore assumes that the poem is addressed to a woman called Leonor: she takes *Popularity* to be addressed to Keats, whereas the case for Domett is much stronger: she misses the allusion in the *Epilogue* to *Fifine* to a popular verse of Victorian obituary columns.

A final word about the printing. It is entirely unjustified, a style which I hope will not become general unless it is really a great deal cheaper than orthodox practice. The credit for the design of the book is claimed by Robert Macdonald: for the most part it is admirable, but for the running titles and list of contents Mr Macdonald has devised a combination of italic lower case and small Roman upper which looks like a series of unhappy misprints. In his favour I must add that titles of individual poems are italicized throughout the book, as they are in this review: the value of doing this is evident when you follow up a page-reference.

I hope that among all these qualifications my original favourable judgement has not become submerged. In case it has let me conclude with a compact example of Professor Cook at her best, when she comments, 'There is something in Browning that wants the corroborative deed, and that not so much mistrusts as views with detachment, waiting for the test of action, the man of words'.

PHILIP DREW

UNIVERSITY OF GLASGOW

Robert Browning: 'Men and Women' and Other Poems. Edited, with an Introduction and Notes, by J. W. HARPER. (Everyman's University Library) London: Dent. 1975. xx + 244 pp. £3.00 (£1.40 paperbound).

One of the difficulties which confront those beginning the study of Browning is that of deciding the best place to start. The most suitable single work is *Men and Women*, but Browning rearranged his poems so radically in his later years that it is seldom easy to identify from a collected edition the fifty-one poems which were originally published under that title in 1855. A reprint in one volume is thus always welcome: Mr Harper adds to the usefulness of his edition by including a further dozen poems, some earlier and some later than *Men and Women*, among them 'My Last Duchess', 'Pictor Ignotus', and 'Caliban upon Setebos'. He has a short but sensible introduction which will, I think, be particularly helpful to those encountering Browning for the first time.

I am less happy about other features of this edition. The presentation on the page is cramped and unattractive. There are a number of misprints, some in the text, such as 'convey' for 'convoy' in 'A Grammarian's Funeral' and 'hand's-breath' for 'hand's-breadth' in 'Memorabilia'. If the book is intended primarily for the use of students I think that the notes should be fuller. They do not compare in width of reference or range of interest with the excellent notes in Paul Turner's edition of *Men and Women* (Oxford, 1972), which is admirably presented and would be my recommendation for those who require a reprint of *Men and Women* only.

One final word. The publishers say that Mr Harper's book 'replaces' the five-volume Everyman's Library edition. It does nothing of the sort. With all its qualities it can be no substitute for what was one of the very few complete editions of Browning and is now presumably lost.

PHILIP DREW

UNIVERSITY OF GLASGOW

Loss and Gain: An Essay on Browning's 'Dramatis Personae'. By LAWRENCE POSTON III.
    (University of Nebraska Studies, new series 48) Lincoln, Nebraska: University
    of Nebraska. 1974. xii + 65 pp.

Professor Poston's monograph makes a modest but useful contribution to criticism
of *Dramatis Personae*. Critics have tended to discuss the volume as a document of
Victorian intellectual history or as a statement of Browning's religious beliefs.
Professor Poston has clearly benefited from the results of these approaches, but his
own focus is critical and his method is close analysis. His study produces no
strikingly original interpretations and provokes no major revaluation of Browning's
achievement, but it is consistently workmanlike and sensitive.

The main contention is that *Dramatis Personae* is 'a unified collection of poems,
meant to be read from start to finish' (p. vii). Coming after the heterogeneous
abundance of *Men and Women* and before the controlled dramatic unity of *The
Ring and the Book*, it effects a transition between these modes. Professor Poston's
account of the volume's recurrent preoccupations tells a familiar Victorian story.
Beginning *Dramatis Personae* after his wife's death, Browning moves from poems like
'James Lee's Wife', which deal with loss on the personal level, to poems like 'Abt
Vogler' and 'A Death in the Desert', which place loss in a larger religious context.
The unifying note of the volume, Professor Poston suggests, is 'the attempt to make
sense out of loss, thus converting it into gain' (p. xi).

In its main lines this is a sensible, though hardly striking, interpretation. Much
of its value obviously depends on the way it is applied, and here Professor Poston is
usually successful. The one occasion where he succumbs to the temptation to ride
his thesis too hard is in the discussion of 'Mr. Sludge, "the Medium" ', where the
poem's meaning is narrowed and sometimes distorted to fit the critic's argument.

Far more typical of Professor Poston's good sense is his account of Browning's
use of the persona. He is certainly right to reject that older interpretation which
saw many of the poems as personal statements: his own cautious suggestion is
that Browning 'speaks unequivocally in his own voice at most twice' (p. viii)
in the volume, in 'Deaf and Dumb: A Group by Woolner' and in the third section
of 'Epilogue'. He explains the poet's diminishing interest in individualizing his
speakers and their situations as the result of a desire to create a drama or debate of
ideas: 'The speakers of *Dramatis Personae* do tend to say in somewhat greater
measure what Browning himself might have said; their views, however, are likely
to reflect only a part of the truth, and the perspective of one speaker is not so much
disproven as it is enlarged or corrected by that of another' (p. viii).

It is disappointing that a work otherwise so careful should contain typographical
flaws. Professor Poston (or his printer) is uncertain about whether to italicize the
titles of individual poems or to put them in inverted commas. There are also
several annoying proof errors: pages 7, 20, and 26 all have mistakes in the use of
inverted commas around quotations.

IAN OUSBY

UNIVERSITY OF MARYLAND, COLLEGE PARK

Dickens Studies Annual. Volume 4. Edited by ROBERT B. PARTLOW, JR. Carbon-
    dale and Edwardsville: Southern Illinois University Press; London and
    Amsterdam: Feffer and Simons. 1975. xviii + 189 pp. $15.00.

The two most valuable essays in this volume are those in which Dickens's novels
are placed in an historical context. In 'Sir Leicester Dedlock, Wat Tyler, and the
Chartists: The Role of the Ironmaster in *Bleak House*', Professor Harvey Peter
Sucksmith makes a contribution to the controversy about Dickens's attitude to
Rouncewell, who is seen as socially responsible, pointing towards Daniel Doyce

rather than Bounderby; and in 'Dickens and Mayhew on the London Poor', Professor Anne Humphreys offers some comparisons between Dickens and Mayhew in their treatment of the poor: Dickens's approach is generalized, whereas Mayhew's is particularized. There are two straightforward, if rather plodding, character studies: the development of Mr Pickwick is analysed by Professor Steven V. Daniels in 'Pickwick and Dickens: Stages of Development' and that of Esther in ' "Through a Glass Darkly": Esther Summerson and *Bleak House*' by Professor Lawrence Frank; and Professor Margaret Ganz offers some sensible comments on the ways in which humour transcends moral and didactic responses in '*Pickwick Papers*: Humor and the Refashioning of Reality'. Somewhat less sensible, however, and divorced from historical reality, are the psychoanalytical approaches of the other essays. Mr Edward Heatley is right, in 'The Redeemed Feminine of *Little Dorrit*', in supposing that there is room for a discussion of Dickens's attitude towards the radical religious ethic of the mid-nineteenth century; but such a discussion might be more valuably conducted by a social historian than by a critic's invoking the concept of the Father-Religion and Jung's description of religion as an integrated psychotherapeutic system, notions which Mr Heatley seems to assume have won universal assent. For assent, too, to the psychoanalytical concepts used by Professor Gordon D. Hirsch in 'The Mysteries in *Bleak House*: A Psychoanalytic Study', faith of medieval proportions is required; in Miss Flite, for example (whose madness, like Esther's blindness, 'is a common dream-symbol for castration', a comment of obscure significance), 'one finds all the degenerative and incapacitating consequences one might expect to accompany a child's guilty wish connected here with an obsessive looking at the activities of Chancery. Viewed psychoanalytically, such scoptophilia usually derives from the child's need compulsively to repeat his observation of or speculations about parental sexuality — his "primal scene" memory or fantasy' (p. 142). But perhaps part of the point of reading a writer like Dickens is in not finding what one so triumphantly expects. Equally eccentric is Professor Stephen L. Franklin's 'Dickens and Time: The Clock without Hands', in which a main moral criterion applied by Dickens to his characters is said to be their acceptance of a Christian attitude towards time, a thesis on behalf of which Dickens's most casual humorous inventions are bulldozed flat, so that when Dick Swiveller is miscalled 'Mister Snivelling' and 'Mr. Liverer' this fits in with the thesis about time, since it 'depicts his development from Mr. Snivelling — snivelling before destiny, incapable of using time — to Mr. Liverer — the "good gentleman" who has learned to act in time and, hence, truly to live' (p. 13). There *are* a lot of clocks in Dickens, though.

P. F. FAIRCLOUGH

UNIVERSITY OF WARWICK

Charles Dickens' 'Sketches by Boz': End in the Beginning. By VIRGIL GRILLO. Boulder, Colorado: Colorado Associated University Press. 1974. xvi + 240 pp. $11.00.

The point of this new study of *Sketches by Boz* lies in the sub-title, 'End in the Beginning'. One might well approach it hoping that it would provide the first full and sound study of the *Sketches*, well rooted in an understanding of how they were conceived, first published, and received. It is this in part, but it is also much more ambitious. It takes this first work by young Dickens, which some of its earliest readers felt was written with 'great' or even 'terrible power', and uses it to enter that strange territory for which we have still no better term than the cliché 'Dickens's world of the imagination'. In many ways it is modestly written, but its aims are wide reaching; and though they are not all achieved, the work as a whole is a considerable achievement.

Yet if we are not to condescend to it as a minor work on a minor work, some criticisms have to be made. There are a few too many misprints, the sense of the actual world of 'Boz' is occasionally remote, and there are some critical comments of an all too familiar sort that one can only strain at: 'In any realistic sense Nell's moral perfection exists at the expense of any carnal forces that are represented in Quilp.' *Realistic?* — 'The name for one of the more charming acrobats of *Hard Times*, "Kidderminster" (apparently one who along with Childers "ministers" to the fancies of "kids") shows its origins in Boz's first coining of the word as an allusion to the high-quality, mass-produced carpets of Axminster: "And such a parlour. . . . Beautiful Kidderminster carpet" . . . explains the narrator of "The Vocal Dressmaker" (*Sketches*, p. 252).' *First coining?* — And what does either comment *mean?*

Yet the main line of critical approach is still an interesting one, with intelligently developed comments. It begins by showing how contemporary readers were right in immediately perceiving that the stories and sketches expressed powerful insights of a kind lacking in the journalism and fiction of the day. They were the work of an 'accomplished ironist' who had found for himself ways of presenting a 'complicated picture of reality'. So much is convincingly shown in the first part of this study. Then, in the second part, it goes on to examine the progress towards the mature novels through the development of a rhetoric of paradox. The simplest form this takes is the now familiar one in which Dickens's initial irony becomes involved with sympathy; yet the many other stratagems by which Dickens permits himself to have almost everything both ways are acutely observed and explained, so that we are shown how 'through a variety of devices Dickens tells us that human beings are as generous as they are petty, as fluid and spontaneous as they are mechanical, as complex and impenetrable as they are simple, as sane and rational as they are crazy'. There is much in this that is new and rewarding. The reader will be wrong who thinks he has read all this before, unless he has learned to understand it as well as the author from the *Sketches* themselves.

K. J. FIELDING

UNIVERSITY OF EDINBURGH

Myths of Power: A Marxist Study of the Brontës. By TERRY EAGLETON. London: Macmillan. 1975. x + 148 pp. £6.95.

The dust jacket of Dr Eagleton's book shows a large portrait of Karl Marx in a dominating position above three smaller sketches of the three Brontë sisters, and this may well frighten genteel Brontë readers. Such alarm is needless because there is a great deal more about the Brontës than about Marx in this short book. The introduction does both boldly assert that Marxist literary criticism must be accepted as something fundamental rather than ancillary to other kinds of criticism, and give a brief political history of nineteenth-century Yorkshire, but our confidence in the relevance of this is reduced by repeated questions about how far social history affected the Brontës. The rest of the book follows a more conventional pattern; there is a discussion of each Brontë novel with a vaguely, but not exclusively, sociological bias. The Brontës' poetry and juvenilia are not mentioned, and there is not much biographical discussion. On biographical matters Dr Eagleton shows little finesse: in his confident statements that Ellen Nussey's family had been landowners for centuries, and that Miss Branwell fastidiously regretted the superior Cornish stock from which she came, he seems to be following secondary authorities who take as evidence for the Brontës' lives the testimony of their novels.

Charlotte Brontë occupies five chapters in *Myths of Power*, and Dr Eagleton certainly makes some valid points about her, stressing her ambivalent attitude to the problem of class, and linking this ambivalence with Charlotte's ambiguous views on religion, feminism, and the relationship between realism and romance. The social views are seen as being of prime importance, just as in recent feminist books on the Brontës Charlotte's worries about the role of women are regarded as central. But, since not enough notice has been taken of the social tensions within Charlotte's novels, Dr Eagleton's approach is refreshing. *Shirley* is an obvious candidate for political discussion, and though Dr Eagleton is a little rash in assuming that Charlotte was necessarily thinking about the Chartists when writing about the Luddites, he makes some telling comparisons with contemporary novels dealing with social problems. Disraeli is too bold, and Mrs Gaskell is too mild when trying to find a political solution, but Charlotte Brontë, with one Disraeli heroine in Shirley Keeldar and one Mrs Gaskell heroine in Caroline Helstone, has the worst of both worlds.

Moving to Emily Dr Eagleton is aware that he is dealing with a different kind of ambivalence. Charlotte veers between two contradictory positions: Emily holds them both simultaneously. Heathcliff is both capitalist and worker, oppressed and oppressor, hero and villain, vanquished and victorious. There is a sensible if not very original discussion of the ending of *Wuthering Heights*, with the useful comment that Lockwood's coy sentimentality about the courtship of Hareton and the younger Catherine reduces their stature. On the other hand there is a fruitless discussion of the significance of Cathy and Hareton digging up the blackcurrants and replacing them with flowers. This is seen by both Mrs Leavis, in *Lectures in America*, and Dr Eagleton as the victory of capitalism over old fashioned yeomanry, but it is not a very impressive victory, as Hareton is compelled to replant the blackcurrants and put the 'surplus value' of the flowers in another place. This example shows the absurdity of treating *Wuthering Heights* as a sociological treatise, and Dr Eagleton would have done better to spend more time on Anne, whose two novels are treated in a single chapter. The clear sociological message of Anne Brontë's novels is as obvious as their literary inadequacy, but Dr Eagleton blurs the clarity of Anne's social treatise, by finding for example unexpected faults in the Markham household, and he seems to find unexpected virtues in Anne's work. Presumably if he admitted that a good sociological treatise was a bad novel, Dr Eagleton would be negating his thesis that Marxist literary criticism is fundamental and not ancillary; perhaps Anne's novels perform a useful function in casting doubts on this thesis.

T. J. WINNIFRITH

UNIVERSITY OF WARWICK

The Language of Truth: Charlotte Brontë, the Woman Question and the Novel. By HARRIET BJÖRK. (Lund Studies in English, 47) Lund: Gleerup. 1974. 152 pp.

Dr Björk's work is a welcome contrast to recent feminist studies of the Brontës. It is not gossipy, or biographical, or filled with rancour against the male sex, or dominated by the single wish to prove Charlotte a feminist writer to the exclusion of every other consideration. Instead we have here a scholarly examination of Charlotte Brontë's ideas on the position of women in the light of contemporary discussions of the subject. The scholarship is certainly formidable if not a little forbidding; Dr Björk seems to have read everything that has been written on the Brontës, and cites some unpublished material as well. She is also exceptionally well informed on nineteenth-century writings on woman's role, and casts a cautious eye on modern feminist thinking.

This approach has its disadvantages. The book with its battery of footnotes is difficult to read, and we are not helped by the proof-reader's occasional lapses into Swedish. More worrying is the discrepancy between Dr Björk's scholarship and that of Charlotte Brontë. In her lonely parsonage, unable to buy or even to borrow books, Charlotte would not have been aware of, and certainly would not have read, many of the feminist tracts which are quoted in the chapter, 'The Female Sphere'. There is an odd gap between this chapter and the previous one, entitled a little ponderously, 'Charlotte Brontë's Views on the Woman Question and the Novel as Reflected in her Letters'. The fact that there are only eleven footnotes in the chapter on Charlotte's letters and fifty-three in 'The Female Sphere' is an indication that Charlotte's letters are unpromising feminist material. Ellen Nussey was of course an unpromising correspondent, but Charlotte is as much to blame as Ellen for these letters full of trivial gossip about husband-hunting rather than deep reflections about woman's lot.

When we turn to the later chapters on the novels Dr Björk is able to turn her wide reading to better use. By an examination of the symbols as well as the story of the novels, she is able to show that as much unconsciously as consciously Charlotte was working her way towards a vision of woman rejecting the fashionable role of a mindless sex object and rejecting the alternative of being a sexless old maid in the hope of becoming a fully equal partner to her husband. It is of course true that the rejection makes better sense than the visionary hope. Many of the outstanding scenes in the novels are clear portraits of the two rejected alternatives; Dr Björk gives an illuminating account of Jane Eyre's visit to the two Reed sisters, and the contrast in *Villette* between the portrait of Cleopatra and the four portraits entitled 'La Vie d'Une Femme'. Charlotte is often accused of being ambivalent, but she is in fact fairly clear-cut in her rejection of silly flirtatious behaviour on the one hand and a dreary passionless existence on the other; the conduct of Jane Eyre in being nearly overwhelmed by her initial love for Rochester and in nearly accepting her missionary role as St John Rivers's unpaid curate is shown to be wrong because it approaches these two extremes. A similar explanation is true of Lucy Snowe's infatuation for John Bretton and her lapses into loneliness. What is not clear is whether there is any satisfactory compromise; a maimed Mr Rochester and a dead Paul Emanuel suggest that Charlotte Brontë is better at posing questions about woman's role than at giving answers. Perhaps the same is true of *The Language of Truth*, but we should be grateful to Dr Björk, as to Charlotte Brontë, for posing the questions so clearly.

T. J. WINNIFRITH

UNIVERSITY OF WARWICK

The Foreign Vision of Charlotte Brontë. By ENID L. DUTHIE. London: Macmillan. 1975. xiv + 237 pp. £7.50.

The influence of France on Charlotte Brontë is obvious, but it has been obscured by the eagerness of critics to eschew any approach that smacked of biography and by the eagerness of biographers to write the story of Charlotte's life from the pages of Charlotte's novels. Miss Duthie's story is therefore welcome, and it is doubly welcome that she avoids the weakness of similar specialist studies on one aspect of the Brontës, which seem to feel obliged to fit everything into their particular straitjacket. At times, it is true, she does seem to be trying to turn an article into a book, as in her first chapter, where she goes through references to France in the juvenilia, and in her penultimate chapter, where she tries to prove against the comments of previous critics that Charlotte's lapses into French in her novels all serve a useful purpose. Such chapters, and the careful analysis of trivial mentions of France in novels like *Jane Eyre*, are not really relevant to the central thesis of Miss Duthie's work: that Charlotte's stay in Belgium was the catalyst which turned her into a great novelist.

Such a thesis may not seem a very original one. Generations of Brontë students, noting that Charlotte's heroes are schoolmasters or married men or Belgians or Belgian schoolmasters who are nearly married to someone else, have concluded that M. Heger, a married Belgian schoolmaster, was the source of Charlotte's inspiration. It is greatly to Miss Duthie's credit that by a careful examination of Charlotte's French devoirs and M. Heger's comments on them, and by her study of the Romantic authors which M. Heger recommended Charlotte to read, she is able to put the Belgian influence into its proper perspective. She is able to distinguish M. Heger from Paul Emanuel, thus clearing up the biographical confusion between fiction and fact. She is able also to show that M. Heger was a real influence on the novels, thus avoiding the critical tendency to underestimate biographical influence. The heroes of Charlotte's novels are an odd mixture of Angrian supermen and real life Belgian schoolmasters. It is Miss Duthie's achievement to show us that M. Heger was responsible for this mixture, not because he was an Angrian hero with pedagogic tendencies, but because he taught Charlotte to moderate her romanticism into realistic novels. M. Heger was happily married, an excellent father, and a brilliant teacher; such qualities, though admirable, are not the qualities we expect in Angrian heroes or find in Charlotte Brontë's heroes, but they are the qualities which persuaded Charlotte to water down the preposterous figures of Angria into the more palatable heroes of the novels.

Miss Duthie's scholarship is not impeccable; she accepts without question the text, dates, and attributions of authorship provided by the editors of the Shakespeare Head Brontë. Biographically, apart from a realistic picture of Charlotte's life at Brussels, she has little to offer, and critically her work is obvious and unexciting. Nevertheless, because of its central sanity this book is an important one for Brontë students, and perhaps it will deter scholars from combing the libraries for more unreadable juvenilia, critics from combing the novels for new and improbable sexual images, and biographers from combing the heather for real-life Mr Rochesters.

T. J. WINNIFRITH

UNIVERSITY OF WARWICK

George Eliot and Judasim. By WILLIAM BAKER. (Salzburg Studies in English Literature, Romantic Reassessment, 45) Salzburg: Institut für Englische Sprache und Literatur, Universität Salzburg. 1975. iv + 270 pp.

Whereas Henry James and F. R. Leavis deny the credibility of George Eliot's Jews in *Daniel Deronda*, Sigmund Freud for one was amazed at her knowledge of Jewish intimate ways. Certainly most non-Jewish readers seem to find her presentation of the Cohen household as authentic and generous as that of Mrs Davilow. The 'Cohen's very ordinariness ensures a kind of cultural continuation', which, as William Baker points out, is one of George Eliot's most important themes. He demonstrates also how her account of Lapidoth's life, based partly on Solomon Maimon's *Lebensgesichte*, is carefully related to the break-up of traditional Jewish settlements and occupations and that three other characters in particular reveal the scope of her rendering of nineteenth-century Jewish experience: Kalonymos, descendant of medieval scholars, who combined his international business interests with pride in his role as protector of the Jewish inheritance; Klesmer, the only unaffectedly funny portrait of authentic genius in our literature, whose idealism provides 'a patent contrast to the entrepreneurial metaphors' of Kalonymos, and whose name is Yiddish for travelling musician; and Daniel's mother, trapped in the feeling of *Hass-Liebe* described by Heine and experienced also by the actress Rachel Levin, whose gentile husband the Leweses met frequently in Berlin in 1854. This book also documents the knowledge of Jewish cultural history evident in *Daniel Deronda*, how the 'Hand and Banner' debate reflects the different responses of Jewish historians to the modern world. Of particular interest is the account of those scholars whose work proved relevant to George Eliot's technique as well as to her subject. Thus the literary historian Zunz distinguished between prophetic exhortations based on an invocation of the past, and penitential prayers 'expressing the anguish of the people amid great suffering' and Sachs emphasized the role of Jewish poets in general and the poet Halevi in particular in preparing the Jewish people for the Return from Exile. Halevi's 'quasi-biological explanations of Jewish existence' and Christian David Ginsberg's book *The Kabbalah* prove to be the main sources of Mordecai's vision and of Daniel's place in it. In addition it would seem that Mordecai is a portrait of the scholar Emmanuel Deutsch, whom the British Museum treated so disgracefully. And yet, in spite of all that is said and shown in this book, one still feels that James and Leavis are largely right.

The problem is the integrity with which George Eliot handles her material. Like Methodism and Catholicism in earlier works, Judaism in *Daniel Deronda* is accorded a positive value which a sincere believer would find offensive. This is fair enough. A religious system can be valuable and meaningful precisely as the expression of psychological or social tensions which believers cannot directly acknowledge, but for George Eliot religion is validated on rather different grounds: 'an emotional intellect', she writes, 'may have absorbed into its passionate vision of possibilities some truth of what will be'. It is this prophetic emphasis, necessarily dim, abstracted, and idealized, which destroys the individuality of her major religious characters: in the end Mr Tryan, Savonarola, Mr Lyon, and Mordecai are too like each other for comfort, ours or theirs. The theme of prophecy also raises important questions about the nature of reality in *Daniel Deronda*. Robert F. Preyer has suggested that there is a break with realism in the novel, and U. D. Knoepflmacher that, in asserting 'the need for righteousness', its Jewish sections 'flaunt the causality of the "real" world'. It is just possible that George Eliot does abandon naturalism in *Daniel Deronda*, but she does not do so flauntingly. Thus, in spite of Mr Baker's apparent approval of Preyer and Knoepflmacher, he notes how rarely Mordecai refers to the Pentateuch, how he presents Moses and Ezra as earthly leaders, and plays down Halevi's reference to the Divine Power. Moreover George Eliot herself insists that it 'is a part of probability that many improbable things will happen', a view endorsed by as rigorous a determinist as Jacques Monod. She is clearly anxious about abandoning naturalism, yet she clings to it with notable evasiveness. Halevi's reliance on physiological metaphors helps her, as similar metaphors did in her earlier work, to avoid precise analysis of intuition and motivation. Images of the seed bringing forth fruit after its own kind conveniently blend the natural and the wonderful, obviating the necessity for detailed specification of process. As Mr Baker notes, Mordecai's sexuality is not placed, and there is a notable failure also to indicate either what kind of Christian Daniel was or what kind of Jew he became.

This book is valuable chiefly for the scope of its documentation. From the young evangelical's reading of the Old Testament to the writing of the last Theophrastus Such essay it traces every tenuous link between George Eliot and things Jewish. Perhaps some details are uncalled for. Nevertheless it is remarkable how the Jewish theme bears on all the acknowledged 'influences', Hennel, Strauss, Heine, Spinoza, Feuerbach, Comte, Spencer, and Riehl. The influence of the latter has recently been given much attention. It is useful to note, therefore, that in choosing Gypsies and Jews for her two major explorations of naturalism, George Eliot was departing from Riehl's emphasis on rootedness as a vital aspect of Volk experience. For her, a common ancestry and culture were of far greater importance than a common soil.

W. F. MYERS

UNIVERSITY OF LEICESTER

Melville's Use of Classical Mythology. By GERARD M. SWEENEY. (Melville Studies in American Culture, 5) Amsterdam: Rodopi. 1975. 159 pp. fl 20 ($8.00).

The previous offering in this series was a weak dissertation belatedly turned into a weaker book; Joseph Flibbert's *Melville and the Art of Burlesque.* Professor Sweeney's 1971 Wisconsin dissertation is much superior; indeed, some pages have the genuine Melvillean savour of Mrs Hussey's smoking chowder.

Professor Sweeney's starting point is the fact that 'most of the critics who refer to Melville's allusive use of classical mythic heroes are really not focusing on the heroes Melville had in mind'. As Professor Sweeney shows, since Richard Chase's *Herman Melville* (1949) popularized discussion of the 'true' and the 'false' Prometheus, many critics have followed him in treating Prometheus 'as a *concept*, not as a specific mythological or literary figure located in particular sources'. Here is the heart of Professor Sweeney's corrective argument:

Underlying the several faults and contradictions of the criticism cited above [that by Chase and his followers] seems to be a preliminary assumption which critics frequently make and which is patently wrong: namely that Prometheus is a single character (such as the 'true Prometheus') to whom a single interpretation can be affixed. This is simply not the case. For whereas there is only one Lear, one Manfred, and at the most a few Satans, Cains, and Fausts, there are literally dozens of Prometheuses. The references to the Titan in classical literature alone are legion, and the number of references in Renaissance, neo-classical, and Romantic writing is similarly great. It is, therefore, really impossible for a scholar to speak accurately of Prometheus in Melville's work without first identifying the source of the specific Prometheus, without describing *what* Prometheus is being cited.

By focusing on the 'specific sources that Melville is known to have read', Professor Sweeney shows that Melville 'employs a number of complementary mythic patterns in shaping the highly original, highly complex character of Ahab'. Aware that the limits of his study may make him seem to constrict knowledge about Melville and to reduce *Moby-Dick* to a book about Ahab, he makes a decent attempt at keeping perspective on his own arguments.

Professor Sweeney's first chapter is a survey of the 'random knowledge of the ancient fables' which Melville possessed before 1849, the year he bought the 37-volume set of Harper's Classical Library. The next three chapters are devoted to Ahab. In the first, 'Ahab and the Classical Prometheus', Professor Sweeney gradually loses a sense of proportion and comes to see far too much of *Moby-Dick* in dubious relationship to classical tragedy. 'Ahab and the Renaissance Prometheus', a genuinely informative chapter, deals with the ways in which Melville's knowledge of the Prometheus myth was indebted to Bacon and Burton, both of whom 'interiorized the vulture of Prometheus', Bacon seeing the vulture as Prometheus's deep thinking and Burton as his secret grief. 'Ahab, Oedipus, and Narcissus' is also useful on Ahab, though marred by Professor Sweeney's failure to see anything either Oedipal or Narcissus-like in Ishmael. The reader's uneasiness becomes even keener in Chapter 5, 'Ishmael: The Revolutions of Ixion', which crucially ignores the ways in which Ishmael is *like* Ahab, not merely unlike him. Chapter 6, '*Pierre* and the Myth of Orestes', and Chapter 7, 'Oracular Silence: Melville, Euripides, and the Meaning of *Pierre*', are even less interesting, since classical mythology is not nearly so important to the characterization of Pierre as it is to that of Ahab. Two final anticlimactic chapters chart the post-*Pierre* dwindling of Melville's interest in Prometheus.

Traces of dissertation amateurishness survive. Sometimes Professor Sweeney fails to listen to himself talk, as when he uses 'becoming' in this context: 'Stasis — becoming, like Ahab, ossified in a single, unswervable view of the world — inevitably means battling the currents of the vortex, and this means death as much as does reaching the center'. Frequently Professor Sweeney chooses to cite later reprints of works Melville read rather than the editions which he certainly or very likely read, a practice out of keeping with the prevailing scholarly rigour of this book. Amateurishness is most obvious in the author's failure to make use of the textual sections of the Norton Critical Edition of *Moby-Dick*, the edition he cites. Professor Sweeney blithely says that Ahab 'dallies with the question of his own identity' in ' "Is Ahab, Ahab? Is it I, God, or who, that lifts this arm?" ', even though the Norton editors point out that the English variant, ' "Is it Ahab, Ahab?" ' fits better into the pattern of the paragraph and may well be Melville's own correction. (Here Sweeney miscopied 'his arm' for 'this arm'.) Professor Sweeney also ignores the Norton suggestion that quotation marks should be put around the long and much-quoted 'Ifs' paragraph in 'The Gilder', making Ahab the speaker, an emendation supported by the fact that the chapter is built, like 'The Doubloon', around a series of responses to the same thing, in this case a mood of the Pacific. Indeed, Professor Sweeney innocently applauds a critic who had called the 'Ifs' passage 'the crown of Ishmael's [as opposed to Ahab's] wisdom'. The author's self-entrapment in this small textual snare points up his more pervasive mistake of reducing Ahab and Ishmael to a pair of opposites rather than perceiving that in profound ways they are akin, and that Ahab may well be to some extent Ishmael's projection of some of his own impulses. But for all the minor flaws and more serious distortions, this is a book from which almost any Melvillean will learn something. How long has it been since you could say that about a book on Melville?

HERSHEL PARKER

UNIVERSITY OF SOUTHERN CALIFORNIA

Ruskin and Gandhi. By ELIZABETH T. MCLAUGHLIN. Lewisburg: Bucknell University Press; London: Associated University Presses. 1974. 202 pp. £4.50.

To Gandhi, *Unto This Last* came as a transforming influence, a 'great book' in which he found some of his 'deepest convictions reflected'. Immediately after reading it in 1904 he established the first of his experimental settlements for simple living, and four years later his Gujarati paraphrase was published under the title, *The Welfare of All*, so propagating Ruskin's message as part of his own. He thus proved himself one reader who fulfilled Ruskin's hope that his books would do some good to those who admired them.

Starting from this evidence of a close affinity between the two, fundamentally a common approach to society and economics based on a religious world-view, Dr McLaughlin scrutinizes its political, educational, ethical, and other ramifications. She examines the nature of Gandhi's debt to Ruskin, the inspiration he found in both his understanding and his misinterpretations of *Unto This Last*, and she illuminates Ruskin's reading of society by showing it in the comparatively unfamiliar context of this Indian attempt to apply his principles as a way of life. Her book is therefore of value whether the reader's interests are primarily Ruskinian and Western or centred on Gandhi and the East.

Some suggestive and unexpected cross-references arise out of the convictions they shared. Both Gandhi and Ruskin saw society as a family structure, and their views on economic relationships in particular, and community life as a whole, depend on this organic conception. Here Ruskin's enthusiasm for medieval guilds meets Gandhi's awareness of caste and Hindu family values, and this is one example of the interesting connexions Dr McLaughlin demonstrates. She is, however, forced to admit at times the need to appreciate the gulf between Victorian England and Gandhi's India, and her book would be more secure and substantial, and her two heroes more firmly assessed in their social aims and remedies, if more space were given to some consideration of the two societies and philosophies of life in their separate nature; a glossary offering brief explanations of key concepts, names, and other general information is not an adequate substitute for such a background study and is, moreover, awkward to use profitably.

Where Dr McLaughlin turns to relate not the ideas but the characters of her prophets, her judgement of priorities again seems unsure. The question of whether Ruskin's illness should be classified as schizophrenic rather than manic-depressive obtrudes into the social preoccupations previously emphasized, while the argument that his failure to become a Gandhi was the real cause of his breakdown leaves aside too much biographical and social matter to be convincing. The attempt to draw psychological parallels is also somewhat strained, whereas when Dr McLaughlin observes that together they have much to contribute to our own concern with the welfare of all she offers a much stronger justification for her joint study. She clearly shows that, in the context of modern western relations with the developing world, 'Ruskin and Gandhi challenge us to substitute idealism for materialism'.

UNIVERSITY OF LEEDS   PATRICIA M. BALL

Walt Whitman and Wallace Stevens. By DIANE WOOD MIDDLEBROOK. Ithaca and London: Cornell University Press. 1975. 238 pp. £5.50.

References to Whitman by Wallace Stevens are relatively few. They tend to come late in Stevens's career. Of the two recorded in the index to the *Letters*, the first is a disparaging remark of 1942, in which Stevens calls Whitman a 'poseur', acting out a caricature of the typical poet, but belonging in reality 'in the same category of eccentrics to which queer looking actors belong'. The second is a whole letter of February 1955, written a few months before Stevens's death. It is of great interest, and shows Stevens trying to give praise where it is due, despite a temperamental antipathy towards Whitman. Stevens says that 'The elan of the essential Whitman is still deeply moving in the things in which he was himself deeply moved', but insists, in a pregnant comment, that much of Whitman's work 'exhibits little or none of his specific power. He seems often to have driven himself to write like himself.' Professor Middlebrook's book begins by quoting from this letter.

Outside the *Letters*, Whitman is referred to in the late essay 'Effects of Analogy', in what Professor Middlebrook calls an 'allusion . . . trivial in itself' but from which she seeks to extract more capital than it is capable of yielding. The earliest known reference, by no means 'trivial in itself', is the poem about Whitman which is the first item in 'Like Decorations in a Nigger Cemetery', the only explicit mention of Whitman in Stevens's poems. Whitman is imagined 'walking along a ruddy shore . . . singing and chanting the things that are part of him. . . . His beard is of fire and his staff is a leaping flame'. The poem, which shows an elated reverence tinged with a hint of derision, crystallizes Stevens's feelings more accurately and more completely than the prose statements, interesting though these are (especially that of 1955). Like Pound, Stevens needed to dissociate himself from Whitman,

Europeanizing himself in the process (in what might, incidentally, be felt to be a peculiarly American way), but was also strangely drawn to Whitman as an inescapable part of the American poetic inheritance, and therefore felt impelled to make his 'pact' with him. The poem from 'Like Decorations in a Nigger Cemetery' occupies perhaps the same place in Stevens's *œuvre* as 'A Pact' does in Pound's.

This is not primarily what Professor Middlebrook is interested in. Nor is she very interested in a number of specific analogies and continuities between the two poets: the connexion for example between Whitman's *eleves* [*sic*] and Stevens's *ephebe*, both separately discussed but not seriously brought together, and, related to this, between the pedagogic postures adopted by both poets; or Stevens's many intimations of mortality, which resemble, in sentiment and sometimes in verbal detail, Whitman's 'Whispers of heavenly death murmur'd I hear, | Labial gossip of night, sibilant chorals' (although the sentiments and even the vocabulary of Whitman's poem are not exclusive to Whitman but are parts of a larger Romantic and post-Romantic tradition). She may be right in tacitly assuming that such things are inessential. A more radical analogy, which she does capture well, is that of Whitman and Stevens as examples of that 'turn of mind which views the everyday man as "a figure of heroic innocence and vast potentialities, poised at the start of a new history" ', which R. W. B. Lewis wrote about in *The American Adam*.

Professor Middlebrook's main preoccupation is with analogy and common bonds rather than with influence, and the last-quoted example is given in that spirit. She finds the principal resemblance between the two poets to lie in a conception of the imagination, shared by both, which is derived from Coleridge and was Americanized by Emerson. It is described thus:

this theory assumes that there are two mental conditions: an ordinary, workaday state of mind and a creative state of mind; when the mind ascends to its creative mode, the man transcends his own ego and can utter universal truths: he becomes a poet. 'In a century, in a millenium, one or two men; that is to say, one or two approximations to the right state of every man,' writes Emerson. 'All the rest behold in the hero or the poet their own green and crude being — ripened.' On the basis of this concept of the potential poet in the ordinary man, Whitman and Stevens formulate what Stevens called 'supreme fictions': myths in which the human imagination is personified and given a heroic role in new epics of American culture.

Whitman's Real Me, Stevens's I, and the many variants on the theme of the hero or major man in Stevens's work are examined in the light of this. This 'noble, affirmative, solitary, central man' is 'metaphorically identified with the sun'. One of the forms this hero takes in Stevens is that of 'the ancestor or "bearded peer" ' (*Collected Poems*, p. 494), and Professor Middlebrook aptly notes that the Whitman described in Stevens's 'Nigger Cemetery' is an early example of this type.

The manner of proceeding is to give separate accounts of Whitman and of Stevens, in the light of the Coleridgeian and Emersonian model, with an attempt at synthesis at the end. How far the accounts are true to Coleridge, and to what extent the Coleridgeian elements are specific to Coleridge rather than common among Romantic theorists of literature, I am not qualified to say. On pages 142, 181, and elsewhere, my feeling is that the use made of Coleridge's primary and secondary imaginations is somewhat strained. In the separate accounts of Whitman and of Stevens, and in the exploration of the theme of the major man, this book has useful information to offer. But it amounts to less, in the way of fruitful confrontation between the two poets, than would justify a study of book length (much of what Professor Middlebrook has to say about the strong man and the sun is said in a single paragraph of Northrop Frye's essay of 1957, 'The Realistic Oriole', for example), and perhaps less than the material itself seems to make possible.

I close this review with a series of observations on individual passages in the book, in order of appearance. On page 20, the figure of 'the son who bears upon his back | The father that he loves, and bears him from | The ruins of the past' (*Opus Posthumous*, p. 87) is deliberately Virgilian, and recalls Aeneas carrying his father out of Troy (*Aeneid*, II.707 ff.). Professor Middlebrook touches on Virgil's significance in Stevens elsewhere in her book (p. 167), and Stevens, who in the same poem mentions 'Aeneas seen, perhaps, | By Nicholas Poussin', also speaks about Virgil in an essay she discusses, 'Effects of Analogy' (*Necessary Angel*, pp. 116 f.), as well as in other poems. On page 21 Dowden is hardly so obscure as to need to be referred to (rather misleadingly) as 'Edward Dowden, an English reviewer'. On pages 73 and 86, it is one thing to speak of the epic ambitions of *Song of Myself*, but quite another (and quite wrong) to say that 'its formal structure resembles epic'. On page 77, the stanza from 'A Primitive Like an Orb', about how 'the used-to earth and sky . . . the used-to tree and used-to cloud' come to 'Lose the old uses' in the 'sharp, | Free knowledges' of the 'central poem', looks back, directly or otherwise, to the passage in *Biographia Literaria*, XIV, in which Coleridge speaks of 'awakening the mind's attention from the lethargy of custom' and showing 'things of every day' without the 'film of familiarity' which we interpose between ourselves and them. On page 134 Professor Middlebrook says of the invocation to the One of Fictive Music ('sister and mother and diviner love') that it has 'suggestions of the medieval worship of the Virgin as patroness of the arts and of the Renaissance worship of her human counterpart in, for example, Beatrice and Laura'. Most of this seems garbled and uninformed. The echo of addresses to the Virgin is there, and has not been unnoticed. It is also present in Stevens's half-mocking address to his Imagination/Muse at the beginning of 'Le Monocle de Mon Oncle': 'Mother of heaven, regina of the clouds'. But there is no need to suppose that these things involve anything more elaborate or recondite than 'Hail Mary . . . Mother of God', together with the *Regina Coeli* and perhaps *Salve Regina*. I do not know of any widespread medieval worship of the Virgin as a 'patroness of the arts', and the description of Beatrice and Laura as 'her human counterparts' is so variously crude and question-begging as to seem oddly sub-literate: it is not so much true or untrue as embarrassingly confused on many fronts. And Beatrice is not a Renaissance figure: Dante died in 1321, before Chaucer was born. But some of the other things Professor Middlebrook says about the One of Fictive Music are useful.

C. J. RAWSON

UNIVERSITY OF WARWICK

The Woman in White. By WILLIAM WILKIE COLLINS. Edited with an Introduction by HARVEY PETER SUCKSMITH. (Oxford English Novels) London: Oxford University Press. xxxviii + 624 pp. £7.50.

The Oxford English Novels have performed a valuable service by providing largely inaccessible eighteenth-century and early nineteenth-century texts in a reliably edited form. The policy of the series on mid-nineteenth-century fiction seems more conservative; so far we have had *Jane Eyre*, *Alice's Adventures in Wonderland*, *Cranford*, *North and South*. As the Collins offering we have not had *Antonina* or *The Dead Secret* but *The Woman in White*. Professor Kinsley's practice, as General Editor, of choosing popular, much reprinted Victorian novels makes comparisons inevitable. There is not much room for a newcomer. Dr Sucksmith's *Woman in White* has to compete with the authoritative edition by Anthea Trodd and Kathleen Tillotson (1969), Julian Symons's *Penguin English Library* edition which preceded this latest edition by only a few months, and the serviceable *Everyman's Library* edition.

The OEN version aims at distinguishing itself from such competitors by virtue of editorial rigour and accuracy. To a large extent Dr Sucksmith's *Woman in White* achieves this superiority. His text is thoughtfully different from previous texts; his introduction is a convincing defence of melodrama and plot; there is an excellent note on the printing history of the novel; finally there is annotation more impressive in density and erudition than what Julian Symons offers, to take his nearest rival in the field.

Having welcomed this *Woman in White* as a respectable addition to an excellent series one must register some misgivings. First, and most important, the accuracy of the copytext. Dr Sucksmith adopts the *All the Year Round* serialization of the novel as 'not only being closer to the manuscript and strikingly illustrating the superiority in accidentals postulated by Sir Walter Greg's theory of copy-text but also as following the original spirit of the novel' (p. xxiv). In line with this editorial decision examination of any surviving manuscript of the novel is essential. Dr Sucksmith reports: 'The manuscript of *The Woman in White* was sold after Collins's death in 1899 for £320 but I have been unable to locate its present whereabouts or those of any surviving proofs' (p. xxiii). In fact the manuscript resides at the Pierpont Morgan Library (the proofs, according to Collins, were not kept). Locating literary remains involves a degree of luck, and occasionally inevitable bad luck. Nonetheless in this case the editor should have enquired of a library whose nineteenth-century holdings are world-famous. As it is *The Woman in White* will have one day to be re-edited to meet the standards which Dr Sucksmith sets himself. One may also note, in passing, that the manuscript is accompanied by a calendar of composition which is more reliable than the accounts which the novelist offered to journalists a quarter of a century later (reprinted here as Appendixes C and D). There is no editorial enlightenment as to whether we are to believe the assertion on page 593 that the title eluded the novelist until one third of the work was written or the flatly contradictory assertion on page 597 that the work was complete before the title was hit upon. In fact the second of these assertions, with its corollary that the novel was wholly written before any part of it was serialized, is grossly misleading. According to the note he made on the manuscript and letters, which are well enough known, Collins composed the novel from 15 August 1859 to 26 July 1860 and it was published from 26 November 1859 to 25 August 1860. Although he offers us a two-and-a-half page chronology of Collins's life Dr Sucksmith nowhere gives us any reliable chronological information as to the writing of the work.

Dr Sucksmith bases his text on the *All the Year Round* version. In fact this is what Trodd and Tillotson did in their 1969 edition. They, however, kept faithfully to the serialized narrative, adopting only the corrections in chronology which Collins made to his later book-form issues of the novel. Dr Sucksmith has incorporated certain 'substantive' alterations from the 1860 and 1861 editions 'which Collins might reasonably be supposed to have made' (p. xxv; what these are, incidentally, he does not anywhere tell us). Editorial decisions which produce synthetic or composite texts are open to cavil. A hostile reviewer might say of this *Woman in White* that it compromises the fluidity of the serial yet does not do justice to the three-decker structure which Collins superimposed on the book. Particularly, Collins altered chapter divisions and separated the narrative into three equivalent 'epochs', congruent with the three-volume division. As it stood in *All the Year Round* and stands here the work is often split mid-chapter by number breaks and consists of three asymmetrical 'parts'; the first 379 pages, the second 136 pages, and the third a diminutive 67 pages. In her book *Mudie's Circulating Library* (Indiana, 1970) Guinevere Griest argues strongly for the three-volume form being a pre-existing pattern for the novel in Collins's mind. Dr Sucksmith has taken his stand on a quite different notion of the novel's 'original spirit'; hence his text is fragmented into the forty *All the Year Round* sections. His *Woman in White* is a serial, first and last.

With some slight regret that he does not indicate in the notes where it was that he made his substantive incorporations one can approve Dr Sucksmith's stand. Taking all the evidence (including the manuscript) into consideration there is little doubt that *The Woman in White* was conceived as a weekly serial and modified for issue as a book. The text which Dr Sucksmith provides should take its place as a standard edition for any critical discussion of Collins's fiction.

UNIVERSITY COLLEGE, LONDON   J. A. SUTHERLAND

'The Ordeal of Richard Feverel' and the Traditions of Realism. By SVEN-JOHAN
    SPÅNBERG. (Acta Universitatis Upsaliensis, Studia Anglistica Upsaliensia, 20)
    Uppsala: Institutionen för Engelska Språket, Uppsala Universitet. 1974.
    110 pp.

This slight but sometimes useful book, based on a Doctoral Dissertation (which shows), argues that Meredith's kind of realism in *The Ordeal of Richard Feverel* belongs less to contemporary mimetic theory in England, typified by George Eliot and G. H. Lewes, than to an ironic and parodistic tradition of realism which begins with Cervantes, is exemplified by Stendhal, and which offers 'a mode peculiarly suited to the modern sensibility'. In this tradition the nature of reality is problematical, and is approached through a critical, although not necessarily unsympathetic, impersonation of false models. The bulk of the book attempts to show, mainly by internal evidence, Meredith's 'technique of allusion' to Richardson's *Sir Charles Grandison*, Rousseau's *Emile*, and Goethe's *Wilhelm Meister* and the tradition of the *Bildungsroman*. It ends by comparing Meredith's practice with that of the French realists, notably Stendhal, and with a brief and rather dismissive discussion of the rest of Meredith's novels.

Mr Spånberg has put Meredith in stimulating company, 'insolent works, which require and compel the reader to think' (Stendhal), and at times writes well of the kind of fiction *Richard Feverel* embodies. But much of the book is tentative and unconvincing. There are the usual problems of 'influence' and 'tradition', and in particular an uncertainty about whether this kind of fiction always depends on models and how many it can accommodate. Indeed the notion of the English 'contemporary theory of reality' and of other kinds of realism is much too simple. The idea of *Richard Feverel* as an anti-novel is less of a shock than Mr Spånberg seems to think, now that we are all, under the pressures of the new orthodoxy which has come from all directions, finding all major novels, even 'solid' nineteenth-century English ones, problematic in this way. To be reminded of other books is often to forget the book at hand, and in fact Mr Spånberg has very little of interest to say directly about this novel. Nevertheless there are interesting attempts to sketch the contemporary presence of Richardson, Rousseau, Goethe, and Stendhal, although Carlyle's *Sartor Resartus* looks an important omission, and the discussion of Stendhal disappointingly focuses on character. Indeed, eventually this comparison becomes biographical; they have similar 'divided natures', their novels are attempted 'therapy'. This is characteristically reductive. Compare these remarks in the final glance at the other fiction: 'misdirected energy and unfocused brilliance . . . absence of a firm clear structure. Proliferation of incident and character is used as an unsuccessful substitute for plot and action . . . a jumble of aperçus . . . a novel of missed opportunities' (on *Sandra Belloni*). What was positive is now negative. Back to square one: biographical explanation, with a touch of 'modern' despair, and orthodox distaste.

But there is interest and stimulation too; perhaps in this respect the book successfully mimes its subject.

DAVID HOWARD

UNIVERSITY OF YORK

An 'Idle Singer' and His Audience: A Study of William Morris's Poetic Reputation in England, 1858–1900. By DELBERT R. GARDNER. (Studies in English Literature, 42) The Hague: Mouton. 1975. vi + 135 pp. fl 30.00.

It is not altogether easy for the author of the Critical Heritage volume on William Morris's reputation, published in 1973, to review a book on an aspect of the same subject, published two years later, which shows no awareness of the earlier publication. But it can hardly be claimed that Mr Goodwin's book opens up any new perspectives.

An 'Idle Singer' and His Audience is a thorough piece of work which still bears many marks of the thesis from which it obviously emerged. The statistical emphasis is disconcertingly overt, for example in the statement that 'more than three fourths of the commentary freely admitted *Guenevere* into the charmed circle of true poetry, worthy of honor. About a fourth of the whole even ranked the book above all Morris's other works.' (p. 31). To be so emphatically quantitative tends to give every review equal status, regardless of length or quality. But perhaps in a study of taste this can hardly be avoided; the quotation also illustrates the oddness of Mr Delbert's literary style. We might feel that he was parodying the reviewers in his phrase 'the charmed circle', but alas! there is no evidence of irony. There is a particularly muddled and strident phrase in the book's blurb: 'when he resumed his poetic calling in 1883, his Muse had folded her wings and become a marcher in the ranks of the Socialist faithful'. One is prepared to ignore this as blurb-writer's baroque, until one discovers that in fact it is quoted from the book itself (p. 81).

Apart from these lapses of style, however, the book can be recognized as an accurate account of its subject. The opening chapter, 'Truth or Beauty?', gives a rapid survey of Victorian attitudes to literature, arguing that these moved from the stress on Truth, exemplified by Henry Taylor's Preface to *Philip Van Artevelde* in 1834, in a fairly consistent way, towards the belief in pure Beauty. This is of course roughly true, but Mr Gardner allows for no qualifications or subtleties. He writes, for instance, of the Aesthetic Movement with capital letters that give it a coherence and substance that it never possessed, and credits it with more importance than it deserves, if one can follow him in his use of metaphor: 'whereas earlier devotees of Beauty had seemed to be little side-eddies away from the main stream, the Aesthetes formed one of the main currents of creative literature, one with its own tributaries extending back into the earlier part of the century' (p. 6). The footnote reference to Rosenblatt hardly closes the case.

The chapters focusing on Morris's various books are thorough and well balanced, and the account of *Sigurd the Volsung* is particularly sound. Mr Gardner was prevented by his definition from using American criticism, which seems a pity as it would have added weight to the discussions of Morris and Chaucer, and allowed such a curiosity as Henry James's review of *Jason* to be considered. But the main English critics are accurately reported. The only omissions seem to be of those who knew Morris politically but also commented on his literary work, mainly in some of the obituaries, including those of Robert Blatchford, Kropotkin, Edward Carpenter, and Walter Crane. These are not significant as literary criticism, but they do show an important aspect of Morris's achievement; his ability to communicate with a different kind of audience than that to which the 'idle singer' had originally made himself appealing.

The book is free from misprints, although E. D. A. Morshead, who appears correctly in the index, appears as Morehead twice on page 70.

UNIVERSITY OF EXETER   PETER FAULKNER

The Pastoral Vision of William Morris: 'The Earthly Paradise'. By BLUE CALHOUN. (South Atlantic Modern Language Award Study) Athens, Georgia: University of Georgia Press. 1975. viii + 263 pp. $11.00.

It is unlikely that many modern readers follow George Eliot's advice to John Blackwood, 'If ever you have an idle afternoon, bestow it on *The Earthly Paradise*'. Critics of Morris, too, as Blue Calhoun says in her Introduction, have tended to find the poem dull, to attach the label 'escapist' to it, and pass on. The value of this study is that it looks with some care at this neglected poem.

Professor Calhoun's argument is that *The Earthly Paradise* should be considered not as a document of late-romantic escapism, but within the tradition of pastoral. The seasonal arrangement of the poem supports this approach, as do the themes of many of the individual poems. The pastoral is seen as a literary form which holds in tension the rustic and the civilized forms of life. What is not so persuasive is the assumption that Morris's use of the pastoral precludes an escapist emphasis; but it is certainly a suggestion worth exploring. (Incidentally, it is strange that the Bibliography does not include J. R. Wahl's article 'The Mood of Energy and the Mood of Idleness' of 1959, since the approach to pastoral here is related to this antithesis).

The book is convincing in its general understanding of important Victorian issues, like that of machinery; and in placing the poem within Morris's overall development. And the consideration of how the different stories are related to the months to which they are allocated is interesting, even if one feels that sufficient ingenuity would enable one to find different links if these were felt to be relevant. More attention might usefully have been given, though, to the linking passages concerning the reception of the stories by the listeners and their general attitudes, which occur at the end of each story and also after the introductory poem for each month. The most striking passage of this kind occurs after the story of 'The Proud King', a moral fable about the need for humility. The listeners then start talking about kings and how their fathers had felt 'the death of kings' to be 'a glory and a gain', and enjoy those emotions aroused by the minstrels' 'high heroic strain'. Professor Calhoun is keen to emphasize the unity of Morris's achievement and to suggest that the pastoral antitheses of *The Earthly Paradise* point forward to the socialist vision of *News from Nowhere*: reference to this passage would have strengthened her case. Although she is well aware of Morris's later writings, she states that Morris 'claimed not to have read' Marx (p. 25); the sentence would be more accurate if it included a clause like 'at the time when he made his first criticisms of the industrial system', since Morris certainly read Marx later.

There is a sensitive and thoughtful account of the poems for the months in the final chapter, but one or two points fail to convince. Thus the description of both 'March' and 'April' as investing the months with 'a paradisal quality of perfect independent loveliness' (p. 223) cannot really apply to such references as those in 'March' to the 'bitter wind' and the 'faint blue sky'. The account of 'November', too, seems inexact. To say that the poet wishes away the complexities of civilization and so becomes involved with 'romantic illusion' is to ignore the matter-of-factness of the central stanza: the changelessness is certainly there, in the 'dead midnight' of November. The poet's puzzle is how to relate this to his own uncontrollable restlessness.

However, these are relatively small matters. Perhaps more serious is Professor Calhoun's tendency to drop into academic jargon when considering the larger issues, and there is something uncomfortably stilted in the opening description of Morris as 'a man of complex dimensions' (p. 1). I feel also that the influence of Northrop Frye results in too easy a belief in the presence of archetypal patterns. The climax of *News from Nowhere* certainly occurs when the narrator fades back into the present moment as the harvest-feast gets under way in the old church, but it is unilluminating to say of this, 'the lonely observer cannot cross the threshold; he is denied access to the "sacred" mysteries. His prototype is Satan' (pp. 218–19). Nevertheless, despite these reservations, I believe that this book does contribute to one's understanding of Morris by giving full recognition to a poem which, whatever its limitations, was undoubtedly significant in its author's development. The crucial question which remains is how Morris managed to rouse himself from the melancholy which saw suffering as the fundamental human experience to a greater belief in the capacity of man to create positive values within the 'steely sea' of life.

University of Exeter   Peter Faulkner

Thomas Hardy and the Modern World: Papers Presented at the 1973 Summer School. Edited by F. B. Pinion. Dorchester: The Thomas Hardy Society. 1974. x + 161 pp. £2.50.

This collection of essays examines three of the major novels in chronological sequence: '*Far from the Madding Crowd*: A Reassessment', by Dr C. J. P. Beatty; '*The Return of the Native*: Thomas Hardy and the Evolution of Consciousness', by Professor F. R. Southerington; '*Tess of the d'Urbervilles*: The Move towards Existentialism', by Mrs Jean Brooks. Then follow discussions of Hardy's philosophy and treatment of history; of textual problems in editing the poetry; and of aspects of Hardy's biography. Professor J. O. Bailey provides a framework for the discussions by examining 'Hardy and the Modern World' in the first essay, and by concluding the volume with 'Changing Fashions in Hardy Scholarship', a survey of the major critical work on Hardy since the first decade of the twentieth century. A helpful bibliography is included.

All the papers suffer from being tailored to meet the demands of summer school sessions; most would benefit from expansion and better documentation. But, in general, they are lively and varied. Lord David Cecil's 'The Hardy Mood', on the poetry, is slight, despite some sensitive evaluations; he misses the strength and technical surety of the best poems, and is too much given to using the words 'naive' and 'prosaic'. Dr Desmond Hawkins's 'Thomas Hardy and Radio' is somewhat superficial; and C. J. P. Beatty's essay on *Far from the Madding Crowd* is a strained application of Hardy's expertise as an architect to the techniques of the novel. But Professor Harold Orel has a substantial essay, 'Hardy, War, and the Years of *Pax Britannica*', on Hardy's changing attitude to war, his reaction to the Great War, and its effect on his art. Dr Robert Gittings, in 'Emma Hardy and the Giffords', takes a new look at Hardy's first wife to scotch rumours of her insanity, material which has since appeared in *The Young Thomas Hardy*. 'The Poetic Text', by Mr James Gibson, reveals some of the difficulties in establishing a definitive text of

Hardy's poems and demonstrates the poet's habit of constant revision; this essay is tantalizingly brief.

The papers do not really add up to a thorough examination of a daunting subject, 'Thomas Hardy and the Modern World', but they give the impression of many enthusiastic and well-informed people enjoying and discussing Hardy; plain proof that Hardy still has something to say to 'the modern world'.

UNIVERSITY OF NOTTINGHAM   SHEILA M. SMITH

Six Dramatists in Search of a Language: Studies in Dramatic Language. By ANDREW
   KENNEDY. London: Cambridge University Press. 1975. xiv + 271 pp.
   £5.00.

Academic criticism of drama has in the last few years become increasingly aware of the need to think of plays as theatrical rather than literary events; the term 'total theatre' is a household word now, and with every new play by Edward Bond or David Hare or any of today's playwrights who make stunningly imaginative use of stage materials, it becomes less possible to think of studying a play from the page alone or through focusing on any one of its elements in isolation. Dr Kennedy is well aware of these trends, but he has chosen, as he says in his preface, to isolate language as a subject of special study, in the belief that this need not involve losing the sense of the drama as a whole. And on the whole it does not: his critical judgements of individual plays are sometimes a little blurred by his angle of vision, but criticism is not his main business: essentially he is concerned with the ideas and theories on dramatic language of his six playwrights and this is certainly a subject rich enough to justify the exclusive approach he takes to their drama.

Dr Kennedy's *Les Six* are all, as he sees it, self-conscious about language in a peculiarly modern way. All are seeking to create a 'new' language through invention, borrowings, parodies; it is their virtuosity as mimics that especially fascinates him. He does not have to search for his illustrations: from Shaw to Arden his six can be seen continually trying out different voices and allowing their characters an unusually high degree of self-consciousness about their ways of speaking. How to be lifelike without falling into the restrictions which naturalism for so long imposed on modern playwrights; how to explore those regions where words fail or are felt to be inadequate; these are not exactly unfamiliar problems, as Dr Kennedy takes pains to indicate. What gives his study its special value, apart from its wealth of documentation (there are one or two embryonic books in the footnotes alone) is the grouping of his playwrights and the cross-reference from one to another which highlights unfamiliar features and often puts a new gloss on the more well-worn. It is lively, for instance, to have Eliot following fast on the heels of Shaw, making an astringent comparison between Shaw's drama and Maeterlinck's, both hybrids to Eliot, falling short of the pure, intense formalism he required of a poetic drama. Of course Eliot had some very wrong ideas about Maeterlinck, but Dr Kennedy has not the time to pursue that particular notion, nor many others thrown out in the course of the dazzling mental display his playwrights put on. It is for us to gather up the careless scatterings of all their intellectual vivacity and one of the greatest attractions of this book is the stimulus it gives us to do just that.

The account of Eliot is in a way an acid test, the ground being so familiar, and Dr Kennedy survives it by bringing out sharply the radicalism of Eliot's dramatic position, expressed from the start of his dramatic career, both practically, as in the jazz rhythms of *Sweeney Agonistes*, and theoretically, in essays like 'The Possibility of Poetic Drama', where he suggestively touches on the dramatic potentiality of ballet and opera and even envisages a 'mute' theatre. Dr Kennedy refers interestingly to the impact on Eliot of speculations of other thinkers (Cornford on ritual, Hulme on the organic nature of conventions) and establishes how his 'powerful pull towards the past' worked both for and against him as a revitalizer of language, giving him many voices to mimic, as he mimics the style of *Everyman* in *Murder in the Cathedral*, but also increasing a tendency to polarize (dead/living, sacred/profane) which results in the theoretical rightness but actual thinness of the language in late comedies like *The Confidential Clerk*. Of course there are other ways of looking at the effect the plays make in production, and I should have liked to have heard Dr Kennedy's view on some of these, but the range he is attempting does not allow him much time for consideration of plays in performance.

If Eliot is the most predictable choice, Shaw is in some ways the least so. That robust rhetoric, that bravura confidence, how can these be thought of in the same way as the intense self-consciousness of Eliot and Beckett, the histrionic uneasiness of Pinter and Osborne, the restless improvization of John Arden? Dr Kennedy's answer to that question provides him with one of his most interesting and also most controversial chapters. Shaw, too, he shows, was attempting the flight from naturalism to a more ritualistic drama, was searching out appropriate styles and voices, including non-verbal forms of expression, particularly musical. But Shaw, he claims, stands out in this group as a 'naif', critically only half-conscious of what he was doing with language, wanting, impossibly, to have the best of both worlds, to keep a kind of naturalism going along with a great range of imitated styles and his own brand of rhetoric. He could not distinguish, says Dr Kennedy, between naturalism as a style and naturalism as a philosophy; and this he connects with a deep split in Shaw's mind between his puritanical and romantic impulses, an unresolved art/anti-art tension.

We may want to agree that Shaw's style falters when he drops his protective irony and tries for straight poetry or pathos, as in some of the rhetoric of *Candida* or *St Joan*. And there is force in the idea that he was held back from more radical experiment in near-Brechtian vein by his commitment to naturalism as an ideology. But Dr Kennedy surely misses something special about Shaw's drama when he faults his exuberant mix of styles and use of quotation. We can laugh at the deflation of all those compulsive talkers, from Tanner to Aubrey, without necessarily feeling that they are suffering from 'ego-mania — Shaw's complaint'. And as the current production of *Too True to be Good* at the Aldwych shows (or indeed as the previous production of the play, with Alastair Sim and Dora Bryan, showed), the quotations from Bunyan and the Bible in the magnificent final scene cannot possibly be thought of as mere pastiche or 'fossil' style. That insistent question, 'What shall we do to be saved?' gains a totally new life in the Shavian context of disillusionment and uncertainty, a vexed and poignant irony, in contrast with the buoyant tones in which it was once asked. It is pleasing however, for those of us who admire Shaw particularly for his skill in mixing unlike styles, to find Dr Kennedy in a footnote admitting that when he saw the National Theatre productions of *Major Barbara* and *Mrs Warren's Profession* he was not after all worried by these Shavian inconsistencies: unity was achieved, and even that real fossil style, melodrama, actually worked.

There is plenty to take issue with in the chapter on Shaw; and plenty also to stimulate one into thinking freshly about Shaw's use of language and about his relation to other playwrights in the modern movement. With the more recent playwrights a different approach has to be taken; they none of them have speculated so much about dramatic language and the emphasis has to fall more on what has been said about them than on what they have said themselves, with the result that rather less critical excitement is generated. Beckett in particular is chary of offering theories about his own work and the more concrete criticism which Dr Kennedy offers instead of a discussion of ideas does tend to suffer from his exclusive focus on language: a play such as *Words and Music* can hardly be appreciated without some attention to what the effect of the music might be. With Pinter, Osborne, and John Arden, however, the discussion gains greatly from being set in the context of *Les Six*. It is interesting to see Arden emerging as a most highly conscious worker of the vein opened up by Eliot, his 'pastiche' of primitive styles lapsing sometimes into antiquarianism but achieving genuine re-creation in a masterpiece such as *Serjeant Musgrave's Dance*. And it is a good highlight on Pinter to have him set in contrast with the others as the master of naturalism, the one who really makes use of that 'minimal language', with its disconnectedness and illogicalities, to express the exact nature of the relationship among his characters, their alienation and incomprehension of each other. It is naturalism without tears for Pinter; almost too easy a process, Dr Kennedy hazards. Osborne in contrast suffers from the same kind of split consciousness as Shaw, to whom he is indeed close in many ways. He, too, it is argued, wants to be clear and committed, a 'public' playwright, but is also restlessly trying all the time for a strange mixture of styles to express the private as well as the public self. Though dubious about his achievement, Dr Kennedy would agree with other critics that he can bring off remarkable blends of inner and outer idiom, as in the 'self-alienated monologue' at the start of *Inadmissible Evidence*; he achieves in that a texture of 'ordinary despair' which is characteristic of his language at its best. At such times he moves away from Shaw towards Beckett, although, Dr Kennedy remarks, in a coarse grain of his own: he has the kind of linguistic vitality which makes him seem to be acting out in his own person the line from *Too True to be Good*, 'since the war the lower centres have become vocal'.

Humorous touches like this are welcome in a study which sometimes seems to undervalue the playwrights' humour, especially Shaw's, which can so marvellously dissolve dissonant and unlike things into striking and poignant harmony. But the sweep of the discussion, the illuminating and suggestive comparisons it puts forward and provokes us to pursue for ourselves, make this book a valuable addition to the criticism that is most truly modern on the modern drama.

ROYAL HOLLOWAY COLLEGE, LONDON   KATHARINE J. WORTH

This Our Caesar: A Study of Bernard Shaw's Caesar and Cleopatra. By GORDON W. COUCHMAN. The Hague: Mouton. 1973. 183 pp. fl 32.

Caesar and Cleopatra. By BERNARD SHAW. Edited by GALE K. LARSON. New York: Bobbs-Merrill. 1974. xxxii + 192 pp. 95c.

'I am a crow who have followed many ploughs', wrote Bernard Shaw towards the end of his Preface to *Three Plays for Puritans*, a preface in which he acknowledged numerous debts of positive and negative inspiration for the volume's three plays. Tracking down his admitted obligations and adding to the list has now become such a popular activity among Shavian biographers, critics, commentators, and Ph.D. students that the Shaw industry will soon bid fair to rival the Shakespeare one in a competition that must appal as well as amuse the ghost of G.B.S.

Now Professor Couchman has opened up frightening new vistas by broaching a new avenue for exploration: what Shaw *may* have thought of works produced before and during his lifetime, although he made no public comments, and what he probably *would* have thought of works produced since his death. Professor Couchman's text abounds in such passages as: 'If Shaw had included Lucan's *Pharsalia* (*The Civil War*) in his list of sources, we might surmise . . .' (p. 67), and 'supposing

he read them at all, Shaw must have read Bergson's words with the keenest attention' (p. 133), and (of Arthur Weigall's *The Life and Times of Cleopatra, Queen of
Egypt*) 'This should have been grist for Shaw's mill if unfortunately it had not
appeared a quarter of a century too late' (pp. 45–6).

Ostensibly this discursive and sometimes turgid book is, as its subtitle declares, a
study of a major Shaw play, and the titles of its first three parts, 'Origins', 'Sources',
and 'Appraisals', support the claim. But the text remains almost constantly at a
remove from Shaw's play. The 'Origins' chapters focus upon Shaw's Puritan concept of human greatness and his evident, probable, and possible reactions to
predecessors' treatments of great men, principally Shakespeare's portrayals. The
'Sources' chapters discuss Shaw's likely and conceivable historical sources without
much specific reference to the play to back up bald assertions. (In fact, Professor
Couchman is given to accepting opinion as proof; for example, 'W. W. Tarn . . .
quietly dissolves the Cleopatra legend with the simple assertion that "the keynote
of her character was not sex at all, but ambition" ' (p. 46).) The 'Appraisals'
chapters do occasionally come to grips with particular features of *Caesar and
Cleopatra*, but the direct and specific passages are heavily interspersed with long,
somewhat incoherent discussions of Puritanism, the essence and modes of comedy,
and (the subject that seems to trouble Couchman most sorely) Shaw's attitudes
towards democracy, dictatorship, and the elimination of dissidents, especially as he
evinced them in the 1930s. This last subject receives climactic emphasis in Professor
Couchman's brief 'Conclusion': 'If Caesar, as Shaw himself said, is the "greatest
of all protagonists", and if, as Hesketh Pearson contends, Caesar is Shaw's greatest
self-portrait, then it follows that although Caesar himself is not a study of a
dictator, in his portrayal lies the germ of that Caesarism which eventually led
Shaw down the political primrose path' (p. 168).

Ultimately it is difficult to identify Professor Couchman's intended audience.
Non-Shavians will find much of his book frustratingly allusive rather than informative. Shavian specialists will find it unfocused, eccentrically selective in its choice of
subjects and authorities, and often wrong by omission of available facts. In treating
the impact of Theodor Mommsen's *History of Rome* upon Shaw, Professor Couchman talks of Mommsen's idealization of Caesar but fails to note the Mommsen
paradoxes that must have been irresistible to Shaw. Caesar, says Mommsen, was
unique in being utterly normal (Shaw was delighted by a similar verdict on his
own eyes), and of a practicality that approached mysticism. And Couchman has
apparently not consulted some of Shaw's acknowledged sources, notably St George
Stock's Introduction to the Clarendon Press 1898 edition of *Caesar: De Bello Gallico:
Books I-VIII* and John Murray's *Handbook for Travellers in Lower and Upper Egypt*.
These books specifically depreciate the usefulness to Caesar researchers of several
works which Shaw whimsically recommended to critics in a list that Couchman is
half-inclined to take seriously. Nor does Professor Couchman appear to know of the
notes from Suetonius's *The Twelve Caesars* in Charlotte Shaw's hand, or Shaw's
autograph notes on Mommsen (both sets are in the Hanley Collection, University
of Texas), or a 1916 letter (in the L.S.E. 'Shaw Material') in which Shaw names
Luc Olivier Merson's painting *Le Repos en Egypte* as his inspiration for the 'Sphinx
scene'. In short, although Professor Couchman has clearly read widely, his homework
was deficient on materials directly pertinent to the play.

By contrast, Gale K. Larson's annotated edition of *Caesar and Cleopatra* contains a
cogent, well-organized introduction to the play which is admirably thorough for
its length. The editor does know the Shaw notes on Mommsen, which include
Shaw's mistaken calculation that in 58 B.C. 'Cl was then 6'. This note to himself,
together with Shaw's defensive opening to his 'Notes' on Cleopatra, 'but in Egypt
sixteen is a riper age than it is in England', would seem to obviate the Introduction's

passage on whether or not Shaw believed he was misrepresenting Cleopatra's age. And in one or two places the Larson edition follows the Standard edition of the play into error. For instance, in the first authorized editions punctuation makes it plain that the Centurion of Act III addresses his peremptory 'Peace there' to his subordinate and Apollodorus before saying, 'Cleopatra: I must abide by my orders'. The Standard edition's less logical 'Peace there' directs his rebuke to Cleopatra. But these are small lapses in what is generally a good edition of the play supplemented by an informative introduction, a useful annotated bibliography, and an illuminating collection of relevant Shaw reviews, letters, and interviews. Despite Shaw's well-documented aversion to 'school editions' of his plays, one feels that he might at least have forgiven this one.

FRANCES M. FRAZER

UNIVERSITY OF PRINCE EDWARD ISLAND

Gissing in Context. By ADRIAN POOLE. London: Macmillan. 1975. xii + 231 pp. £7.95.

There have been several critical biographies of Gissing (the latest is Gillian Tindall's *The Born Exile*, 1974) but Dr Poole has written the first full-length study of his major novels. The word 'major' is, of course, a bugbear to students of this writer; it is what George Gissing continually just refuses to be. Dr Poole takes the line that, regardless of his artistic inferiority to Hardy, Meredith, and James, he was their equal in responding to the central issues and experiences of his age. To do him justice we must study him 'in context'. The result is an ambitious and penetrating book, of much more than specialist interest.

Gissing is notorious for the deterministic traps in which virtually all his characters are shown to be caught. But this pessimism is an index of the extreme frustration of his characters, and of the volume of their desires which remain unsatisfied. Dr Poole sees him primarily as a novelist of desire and deprivation, and of the social maladjustments to which this leads. The advantage of such an approach is that it recognizes the inevitability of the formal imperfections of the novels, whose perpetual attraction and disappointment the author concedes. He honours Gissing, rather than condescending to him, for the 'grim energy' with which he responded to the state of privation.

Gissing in Context falls into three sections. The first explores Gissing's position as a late Victorian writer and the portrayal of urban poverty in the novels up to *The Nether World*. Then there is a section on *New Grub Street*, introduced by a survey of the literary world of the 1880s and 1890s which ranges from the experiences of Hardy and James to Marie Corelli, Walter Besant, and the *Bookman* magazine. In discussing *New Grub Street* itself, Dr Poole turns from Gissing's failed writers to stress the centrality of Marian Yule, whose tragedy is that of the thwarted intelligent woman. This is a provocative shift of emphasis, suggesting some dissatisfaction with the novel Gissing actually wrote; but it follows the direction in which his interests were turning, looking towards novels like *The Odd Women* and *The Whirlpool*, which balance the frustrated hero against some of the finest literary realizations of the New Woman. Dr Poole's discussion of these late novels, under the heading 'Desire, Autonomy and Women', is among the best things in the book.

The weakest part, I think, is the first section, where the author's slightly ponderous style makes some difficulties for the reader. We begin with a schematic contrast of 'early-Victorian' and 'late-Victorian' fictional structures, useful in itself but cavalier in its treatment of Dickens, who is fitted unhesitatingly into the former category. Dr Poole even implies (perhaps inadvertently) that *Great Expectations* is an example of the early Victorian convention of culmination in marriage.

He then proceeds to a survey of 'The Writer and the City', which has its acknowledged precedent in Raymond Williams's work. This chapter offers a striking collection of images of the writer's loneliness and detachment from metropolitan life. The use of quotations taken out of context, however, imposes a literary and historical unity which is at best questionable. Morris and Wells, for example, are cited here as witnesses to the 'intransigence' and 'immoveability' of the city, yet this was an attitude that both men vehemently rejected. (Wells was astonished by the stolidity of Fabianism in the mid-eighties, while Morris in the period before Bloody Sunday believed the revolution would come in his lifetime.) Part of the problem in this chapter is the author's uncritical use of the term 'image', which blots out crucial distinctions between different modes of discourse and levels of metaphor. While this may be legitimate for some purposes, it becomes a hindrance to the close scrutiny of literary contexts. Here the book lays claim to a methodological precision in establishing Gissing's 'centrality' which it does not really possess.

This is a local embarrassment, however, which is transcended by Dr Poole's later handling of contextual material. I felt that *Gissing in Context* got better and better as it proceeded. The concluding endorsement of the 'fierce, tenacious endurance' of so much of Gissing's work seemed just and authoritative. And the pages on Meredith, Hardy, James, and other contemporaries scattered throughout the text remind one of how much Dr Poole has managed to cram into this stimulating book.

PATRICK PARRINDER

UNIVERSITY OF READING

Conrad, the Later Moralist. By JOHN E. SAVESON. Amsterdam: Rodopi. 1974. 129 pp. fl 125.

Professor Saveson, a frequent contributor to Conrad scholarship, has followed up his previous book (*Joseph Conrad: The Making of a Moralist*) with this volume, which attempts, among other things, to show the influence of Nietzsche on the moral focus of what he calls the 'later Conrad'. In so doing he allies himself to a recent critical shift in Conrad studies, which has increasingly dealt with the fiction in its European intellectual context. The fact that Conrad nowhere indicates any profound interest in Nietzsche (though he does mention him in the letters), makes the topic a surprising one; though, as Professor Delavenay has shown in the case of D. H. Lawrence and Edward Carpenter, it is possible for such apparently improbable influences to be made convincingly concrete.

The major part of *Conrad, the Later Moralist* is devoted to critical analysis of *Under Western Eyes, Chance*, and *Victory*, which seek to show the 'Nietzschean' elements at work. The case, however, is far from convincing. It is based largely on similarities of vocabulary between the two writers, but the connexions made are insubstantial. The following is typical: 'what convinces the reader that Conrad's conception is Nietzschean is the fact that Marlow uses Nietzschean words and phrases to set it forth. Words such as ideal and idealism, expletives such as mad (Anthony's renunciation is a "mad" action; his is the "madness of generosity") (p. 388) are common to both Conrad and Nietzsche and, when applied to the same object, establish a broad similarity' (p. 97). Even less satisfactory, because more ambitious, is the reading of *Victory*, an unconvincing account designed to answer (though it never does) Guerard's well known dismissal of that novel. Professor Saveson's thesis is that the novel's flaws — minor inconsistencies and illogical juxtapositions (he fails to mention what Guerard calls 'tired' writing) — are there intentionally, and that a 'percipient reader' (a category that seems to me to include only Professor Saveson) will recognize the novel's apparent flaws as its hidden virtues.

These are, of course, matters of interpretation; perhaps I can only say that Professor Saveson's readings do not enrich my understanding of Conrad's works. The fact is that no amount of work on the background to, or influences on, Conrad's work (and certainly Professor Saveson is very good on the extent to which *The Times* dispatches from Chile influenced the writing of *Nostromo*) can help us to decide how good the novels are. In this case, such material even seems to cloud critical judgement: thus we are told that *Nostromo* and *The Secret Agent* are a 'desperate' (though salutary) immersion in the derivative. It is also Professor Saveson's opinion that *Lord Jim* is a more 'massive' novel than *Nostromo*, and that, from the point of view of this work, *Victory* is the greatest of Conrad's novels. Even more shocking than these failures of judgement are a series of errors of fact: the Assistant Commissioner of *The Secret Agent* is wrongly identified as an aristocrat; Marlow, amazingly, is cited as the narrator of *Victory*; *Under Western Eyes*, *Chance*, and *Victory* are twice cited as Conrad's last novels.

The book has neither an index nor a bibliography, thereby underlining the fact that it is an uneasy amalgam of previously published articles. Some of the articles are quite interesting, but the whole does not justify its publication in book form.

UNIVERSITY OF WARWICK   R. A. GEKOSKI

Charles W. Chesnutt: America's First Great Black Novelist. By J. NOEL HEERMANCE. Hamden, Connecticut: Archon Books, The Shoe String Press. 1974. xiv + 258 pp. $12.50.

Charles Chesnutt (1858–1932) is a beneficiary of Black Study programmes that have lately proliferated in the United States. He deserves his posthumous luck. For, previously remembered, if at all, for his Negro dialect stories from the Old South, *The Conjure Woman* (1899) and a second collection, *The Wife of His Youth* (1899), he was too readily patronized as a black equivocator in the 'Uncle Remus' tradition. His less successful novels, *The House behind the Cedars* (1900), *The Marrow of Tradition* (1901), and *The Colonel's Dream* (1905), were quite neglected.

Yet he was one of the few outstanding Black intellectuals of the Reconstruction generation. Both Booker T. Washington and Chesnutt wrote biographies of Frederick Douglass. Both saw themselves as isolated Moses figures to lead their race, if not to a promised land exactly, through the snares and complexities of White supremacy, White sexuality, White cultural hegemony.

As a distinctly prosperous, bourgeois figure of a light-toned skin colour, holding himself aloof from most civil rights organizations, he has always proved difficult to fit into the hurly-burly radical tradition of Black protest. He felt himself to be doubly isolated: first, as the son of 'free colored' parents who had fled North Carolina in 1856 to settle in Cleveland; secondly, by his complexion. If his 'free issue' and pale skin made him seem uppity to local Blacks, he was too dark for local Whites. As a sensitive Negro intellectual he was cut off from just about everyone in the nineteenth-century South.

Nevertheless Chesnutt was an early member of the National Association for the Advancement of Colored People as it developed in 1909 and 1910, though always on his own terms. He constantly differed with Booker T. Washington, even if he never went over to the public attack. He operated independently as a liberal Black spokesman, protesting against 'Jim Crow' railway cases, working for a Social Settlement house in Cleveland, denouncing Thomas Dixon's *The Birth of a Nation* to the Governor of Ohio, attacking Harvard University for attempting to exclude Black students from its dormitories and dining halls.

He might have passed for White, that is, but he never tried to duck his racial responsibilities. William Dean Howells's warm review of his stories, in any case, made his 'African descent' wholly explicit. In fact, as early as 1891 he had been conscious of his opportunity as a pioneer Black writer. In writing to Houghton Mifflin, he emphasized:

There is one fact which would give this volume distinction. It is the first contribution by an American of acknowledged African descent to purely imaginative literature.

In this case, the infusion of African blood is very small — is not in fact a visible admixture — but it is enough, combined with the fact that the writer was practically brought up in the South, to give him knowledge of the people whose description is attempted.

It had taken many years of teaching in rural Black communities (near Spartanburg, South Carolina) and of business ventures as stenographer on his return to Cleveland, before he could launch on that proud boast.

J. Noel Heermance, in this first full-length study of 'America's first great Black novelist', takes a good deal for granted from his readers. Above all, he appears to take for granted an easy acquaintance with Helen Chesnutt's (his daughter's) memoir, *Charles Waddell Chesnutt*. For most of the biographical facts are suggested, rather than stated. What Professor Heermance supplies is a series of forays into that *fin de siècle* period of White militancy and Black disfranchisement, culminating in the Wilmington 'massacre' of 1898. It reads more like a kind of alibi, or apologia, for this Black author unable, at first sight, to live up to the more radical expectation of his heirs. So the opening decades of the Klu Klux Klan are rapidly sketched to reveal what 'Chesnutt Was Pitted Against'; followed by explorations of the author as a Black Horatio Alger, as cultural Isolato and Social Crusader. By 1900, with that salute from Howells, Chesnutt was recognized as a major spokesman of 'the Color Line', corresponding on equal terms with W. E. B. DuBois, George Washington Cable, and Albion W. Tourgée.

What Professor Heermance makes admirably clear is the high moral vision that drove Charles Chesnutt to authorship. His was to be 'a moral revolution' to elevate the conscience of Whites and support the Blacks. As he wrote of *The Marrow of Tradition*: 'The book was written, as all my books have been, with a purpose . . . the hope that it might create sympathy for the colored people of the South in the very difficult position they now occupy' (1905). But his dream, like that of the Colonel of his last novel, failed. The progressive reconstruction of the South had dramatically failed. The Colonel, acknowledging defeat, moved back North, even if his creator could still insist: 'I have faith in humanity, and if that faith is justifiable, the problems involved in the Southern situation will in time be worked out in a number for the best happiness of all concerned'. Yet he too was to give up. He gave up fiction altogether in 1905, acknowledging final defeat.

His clearly stated aim had been to stem the sentimental stereotypes of the Plantation Nigger School, led by Thomas Nelson Page, with the creation of genuine Blacks and genuine Mulattos. Page himself was generously quick to recognize the achievement. But the ultimate target was none other than the White press, North and South, that fostered such stereotypes. Torn between his professional White (invariably Northern) narrators and Black (usually Southern) actors, the literary stance no doubt often seemed ambiguous. But only from the shallow view that equated the sly Uncle Julius of *The Conjure Woman*, for example, with Uncle Remus rather than Brer Rabbit. For Chesnutt was deeply committed to the Black man's rightful place in American society. Professor Heermance makes out a strong case for the revival of *The Marrow of Tradition* as a major achievement. If the social and biographical settings are useful, even more so are the parallels he suggests with his literary contemporaries, Henry James, Sarah Orne Jewett, and Mark Twain. On sketching in the whole range of his Black characters, poor farmers and labourers, wharf workers and convicts, lawyers and tricksters, a further suggestion is raised that these are far more than protest novels; that it is time, in fact, that they were recognized beyond the closed circles of Chesnutt's racially conscious readers. Such were the readers, of course, he wanted and invited. But such were the very readers whom, in life as well as in art, as a spokesman and as a novelist, he had also consistently and self-consciously transcended.

HAROLD BEAVER

UNIVERSITY OF WARWICK

A Concordance to the Complete Poetry of Stephen Crane. Compiled by ANDREW T. CROSLAND. (A Bruccoli Clark Book) Detroit: Gale Research. 1975. xx + 189 pp. $40.00.

The compiling of concordances is an obvious area for the application of labour-saving computer techniques to literary and linguistic study. SNOBOL 4 is the programming language employed in the preparation of this concordance to the poetry of Stephen Crane, and the text upon which it is based is Fredson Bowers's edition of Crane's *Poems and Literary Remains* in the University of Virginia Edition of the Works of Stephen Crane. (Inevitably, the Virginia edition is itself produced under the auspices of the Center for Editions of American Authors, that somewhat grandiose monument to American literary scholarship.) A difficulty with this concordance is that, since most of Crane's poems are untitled, it can only be used in conjunction with the Bowers edition of the poems: a full line of poetry is provided for each word entry, but context is identified only by page and line reference to the Bowers volume. Nonetheless, critics and scholars of Crane are sure to find much to interest them here. As well as the basic concordance, Andrew Crosland has included, thanks to his computer, word-frequency lists in alphabetical and numerical order. From the latter one notices that the noun most frequently used in Crane's poetry is 'God' (71 references), with 'man' (59) as runner-up. Other interesting figures are 'love' (44), 'heart' (24), 'black' (22), 'sea' (19). Contrary to expectations, perhaps, 'death' and 'blood' occur only 14 and 11 times respectively.

At more than twenty pounds this book is very expensive even at current prices.

UNIVERSITY OF ABERDEEN   ANDREW HOOK

J. M. Synge: A Bibliography of Criticism. By E. K. MIKHAIL. Foreword by ROBIN SKELTON. London and Basingstoke: Macmillan. 1975. xiii + 214 pp. £7.50.

Professor Mikhail has now been working for some years in the field of Anglo-Irish drama bibliography, and this book on Synge follows a bibliography of O'Casey criticism and a general bibliography of modern Irish drama. As one would expect, therefore, his work is accurate and sensibly organized. After sections listing 'Bibliographies' and 'Books by J. M. Synge and their Reviews' he divides his main 'Criticism' section into books, periodicals, reviews of play productions, unpublished material, recordings, and background. The background section is inadequate and might have been better omitted, but the rest of the work is solid and meticulous, and the listing of the reviews of individual plays is potentially very helpful. There are, inevitably, occasional gaps. Professor Mikhail has missed some interesting oddities, as, for example, the editorial on the *Playboy* riot in *An Claidheam Soluis*, the organ of the Gaelic League (9 February 1907), most probably written by Padraig Pearse. Pearse there denounced Synge for 'railing obscenely against light, and sweetness', but he was later to change his mind and see him as a misunderstood Irish nationalist. Or again there is a review unlisted by Mikhail of a French production of the *Playboy* in 1914 by A. V. Lunacharsky, who was to become a well known Soviet writer, in which he links Synge's humour with that of Swift and Shaw. A more serious deficiency in Professor Mikhail's claim to comprehensiveness is his failure to include many theatre and book reviews from Irish newspapers in the period from 1920 onwards. This, by contrast with his diligent coverage of English and American papers, stands out as a weakness which will impair the usefulness of the book for any researcher interested in Synge's reputation within Ireland.

It is unfortunate that Professor Mikhail should have been forestalled in this field by Paul Levitt's *J. M. Synge: A Bibliography of Published Criticism* published in 1974. A third projected Synge bibliography which is to appear as Volume v of the Oxford Synge *Collected Works* necessarily arouses questions as to the value and importance of this sort of work. Clearly Professor Mikhail's volume will be useful to research students writing on Synge, and they may even find assistance here which they would not get from Professor Levitt's book, which is organized along slightly different lines. But does a bibliography of criticism have a significance beyond its usefulness as a work of reference? Professor Robin Skelton in his Foreword argues that it has. He claims that 'even a brief scrutiny of the titles of the various articles and critical works reveals the way in which Synge's work has aroused an extraordinary variety of reactions' (p. ix). Comparing Synge with Shakespeare, Professor Skelton implies that by the very bulk and diversity of the critical reaction registered in such a listing we have a measure of Synge's greatness and enduring value.

This view has become so much a commonplace of modern literary criticism that it is perhaps worth contesting. A writer whom critics disagree about, whose work can be approached from a variety of angles; this, the argument goes, is an important writer. Our casebooks and our anthologies of criticism all insist on divergence of opinion and approach as a criterion of merit. But when we come to examine the material which accumulates to fill a work like Professor Mikhail's, much of it appears utterly insignificant. We learn, for example, that the text of *Riders to the Sea* has been included, with or without commentary, in some fifty-four anthologies, most of them intended for undergraduates; we find that in the month following the *Playboy* riot over one hundred and fifty items about it appeared in the newspapers. The conclusions to be drawn from many of the entries are at this level of triviality. Even with more substantial critical articles (and they make up only a small proportion of the total bulk), many of the controversies which they debate are factitious. They testify not so much to the many-sidedness of Synge, but to the intense pressure on university teachers to say something in print, however fatuous or perverse.

Synge is not at all the sort of Protean problematic figure that Professor Skelton implies. He is not, like Yeats, a 'centrifugal' writer with whom peripheral study may be justified by the complexity of his life and art. Instead he requires only steady attention to a handful of works, unified in theme and setting, which impress us not by their diversity, but by the depth and intensity they achieve within such narrow bounds. With such a writer a wealth of widely varying critical approaches may not be especially significant or even relevant to our understanding of his work. Professor Mikhail's book fulfils its purpose conscientiously and well, but it is unlikely to alter in any way our evaluation of Synge's gifts, nor is there any reason why it should.

NICHOLAS GRENE

UNIVERSITY OF LIVERPOOL

Orage as Critic. Edited by WALLACE MARTIN. (The Routledge Critics Series)
London and Boston: Routledge. 1974. xii + 218 pp. £5.95.

Orage as critic, in the same breath, or at least the same series, as Swinburne, De
Quincey, Wordsworth, Johnson, gives us pause; and one can readily agree with the
first part of the claim on the dust wrapper that Orage 'is almost certainly the least
known of those critics who warrant consideration as major critics of the twentieth
century'. The company is heady and in truth above his head, in spite of quotations
such as that from Professor John Holloway that 'when his work is better known,
Orage may prove to be one of the decisive figures in the continuity of criticism over
the last century'. Orage's 'work' was not just his critical writing, and to be a decisive
figure in the continuity of criticism is not to be a great critic.

Perhaps it is the shortness of breath of Orage's writing which makes his limitations so evident. None of the pieces here reprinted is longer than four pages and
many are selections of a few lines or a few paragraphs. This is in some ways a
consequence of their source; most of the pieces come from the necessarily brief
essays in *The New Age* which Orage edited from 1907 to 1922, and particularly
from the literary column that he wrote from 1913 to 1922; but even then many are
abbreviated, selected from those brief articles. There is no convincing sense, as one
would expect in a great critic, of a thorough exploration of a subject and the
accompanying depth of perception, nor is there, *pace* the editor's claims, evidence
of remarkable originality.

Orage is limited also by his idea of the role and style of the causerie. One can
gain a sense of his views from his letters to Herbert Read, whom he was grooming
to succeed him, which Wallace Martin quoted in his earlier book *The New Age
under Orage*: 'You have the causerie style', he wrote, 'and a good sense of what can
and cannot be said in brilliant talk at leisure'. Or later: 'the causerie style . . .
requires the urge of some fresh enthusiasm to carry it along rapidly. Pace is an
essential of the causerie; but it can only be developed by the whip of a keen interest.
You like Moby Dick immensely, and become lyrical about it, — lyrically critical,
of course, for otherwise it would be gush. Critical lyricism! Voilà the causerie!'
Orage certainly had this causerie ability, a geniality, a capacity to entertain, to
keep an audience stimulated week by week and give them a sense of being in the
current literary swim. A glance at the dates of the articles always gives an added
interest to their comments; yet a criticism that counts with Johnson and Coleridge
does not need a date to prove its pressure of ideas.

The accident of its appearance in a series, however, should not blind us to the
real value of the book. It may be, as Wallace Martin wrote of Orage in the earlier
book, that 'it is as an editor that he will be best remembered' and that Orage was
most remarkable for the way he gathered and influenced a large group of writers.
It may be that the emphasis on literary criticism here does not fully represent
Orage's editorial objective of embracing politics, economics, and philosophy as
well as the arts. And it may be that there are curiously few examples of Orage's
writing before or after *The New Age* period, as if to emphasize that his influence
was exercised through the review as a whole. But the book does give us an insight
into the thought of an intelligent and alert observer of the artistic scene in a formative period for modern writing. If the series had allowed us to have Orage the
Essayist, or Orage the Editor, he would have been placed in a more appropriate
mode and in more appropriate company, and his place in the continuity of criticism
perhaps would have been more clearly seen.

R. K. R. THORNTON

UNIVERSITY OF NEWCASTLE UPON TYNE

Sean O'Casey: Das dramatische Werk. By HEINZ KOSOK. Berlin: Schmidt. 1972.
   419 pp. DM 58.00.

Comprehensiveness and empiricism seem to be Heinz Kosok's two guiding values
in this dissertation-based study of O'Casey's dramatic work. All the relevant
material is brought in: the corpus of plays, including the short plays and the seldom
discussed last three plays; the autobiographical writings, sifted for the scattered
critical remarks that point to O'Casey's improvised poetics; and recent critical
literature, especially studies by Hogan and Krause, is used with frequent but
questioning reference. There is no central thesis or interpretation; if anything,
Professor Kosok's method of play-by-play revaluation is intended to bear witness
to the vitality and variety of O'Casey's drama, without forcing any category or
overall pattern on the works themselves. The plays are grouped in five carefully
documented chapters in the order of O'Casey's main creative periods, and even
within the particular studies the approach is many-angled, each play's genesis,
theme(s), structure, and value system are in turn examined in meticulous detail.
   The book's 'empirical' plan goes with a healthy avoidance of snap judgements
and schematization. Although the general student of drama may at times feel that
Kosok's patient map drawing entails so much circumspection and cross-reference
that there is a certain loss of critical energy, there is no loss of direction.
   Professor Kosok's scholarly moderation is underscored by an ideological detachment which, as he himself claims, owes something to his geographical distance
from the Anglo-Irish battlegrounds, physical and verbal. At the same time, the
book bears witness to a genuine sympathy with the Irish causes, passions, and absurdities dramatized by O'Casey. Indeed the recurrent discussion of values within and
across the plays is among the best things in the book, particularly in the sections on
Juno and the Paycock and *The Plough and the Stars* where O'Casey's shrewdly compassionate humanity is illuminated in terms of character and action.
   It seems clear that the book will be found useful primarily by the university
student who, after reading or seeing a particular play, would find concentrated
here nearly all the material he needs for further discussion. The book almost
invites a section-by-section or *ad hoc* reading; it could even become a kind of
Reader's Guide to Sean O'Casey if translated into English.
   An attempt is made to widen the insights drawn from the practical criticism of
individual plays in something like a strategic overview in Chapter 6: a sustained
survey of form, theme(s), and influence. As a survey this is masterly, with a good
deal of new material; as criticism it is rather modest, because here the reluctance to
conceptualize becomes a limitation. Thus the section on dramatic form (which I
found particularly interesting) does succeed in giving a clear account of O'Casey's
restless shifts of style between the extreme poles of naturalistic imitation and
expressive (not Expressionistic, in the narrow sense) inventiveness. It illuminates
changes in the structure of plays; it sees O'Casey's whole development as a move
from the action-centred play-form of the Dublin period, through a more complex
design of scenic contrast (*Within the Gates* and after), to the joyous use of the
elements of festive drama, fantasy, and fairy tale in the late plays. And the right
connexions are made with mutations of genre. However, at this point Professor
Kosok is content to list O'Casey's genre categories (given in the subtitles), to point
to the tension between tragic form and non-tragic vision, and then hand over the
very interesting question of tragi-comedy to the potential research student. Peda-
gogically, this may be quite sound: here are your references (Karl Guthke, Styan,
Cyrus Hoy, and others), and here are the problems of tragi-comedy to be studied.
Critically, it passes the buck. And since there is no discussion of O'Casey's dramatic
language either (on the grounds that it has already been done by Thomas Metscher
in *Sean O'Caseys dramatischer Stil*) one misses a testing of two of the most 'problematic'

areas in O'Casey criticism. There is a lack of sustained generic or stylistic criticism; and so, in the end, the detailed criticism of the plays does not seem to be gathered and judged adequately.

In the end one also misses evaluative criticism of the kind that would underpin Professor Kosok's high regard for O'Casey's work through a scaling of the plays within the total work. Nor is it quite clear, after we have pondered the 'uniqueness' of O'Casey, how his drama is to be related to the movements in modern drama as a whole.

Perhaps one should not expect that kind of criticism from a thoroughgoing description. And if such an expectation is dropped, then the surveys of O'Casey's major themes and of data relating to influence (influences on O'Casey and his influence on others) will be appreciated for what they are — carefully researched compilations. The list of influences certainly has documentary value, but the data will have to be stored in very different kinds of memory before they are transmuted into further research or criticism. I am not sure, for example, what to make of the expressions of mutual admiration between O'Casey and Arden. Perhaps this is another invitation to someone to write a comparative article on the two dramatists' work. Elsewhere we are given a detailed description of Joseph Tomelty's *The End House* (Dublin, 1944 and 1962) as the clearest example of a play derived from *Juno and the Paycock*; this information will probably go into the files of some centre for Abbey Theatre studies. The general argument from influence itself looks a little unsteady when it is claimed that while the influence of the early plays on later dramatists shows O'Casey's significance, the lack of such influence, when we come to the later plays, probably shows that his originality has not yet been grasped.

These reservations about the critical method of some of the final sections should not, and do not, make one forget the real strength of the book. The plays are re-examined with a scholarly integrity that runs right through the book and gains further support from the admirable bibliography.

ANDREW K. KENNEDY

BERGEN UNIVERSITY

George Kelly. By FOSTER HIRSCH. (Twayne's United States Authors Series, 259) Boston: Twayne. 1975. viii + 138 pp. $7.50.

Like a decent unpretentious plot in a suburban graveyard this brief biography serves its memorialist function without much faith in the proposed resurrection. Dr Hirsch offers the obligatory pieties and concludes 'Kelly's position in American drama is unique and high', but his essential fairmindedness ensures that he does more to bury Kelly than to praise him. A Kelly play, said Mary McCarthy, 'is not like anything else while on the surface it resembles every play one has ever been to'. Mr Hirsch does justice to the famous Kelly predilection for conventional stage 'business': the glasses of water, pocket books, trivial conversation, and attention to details of stage furnishing that make his plays a parody of 'every play one has ever been to'; unfortunately for Kelly he also does justice to the way in which the Kelly play is not like anything else: it being unswervingly concerned with the demonstration of banal moral dicta in the manner of a severe Thornton Wilder. George Kelly is an unfortunate choice for a biographer in one respect; his unwillingness to divulge details of his personal life. This explains the lack until now of any full-length study of his life and indeed the slightness of Mr Hirsch's volume, which offers hardly any account of Kelly the man. Mr Hirsch is forced to rely largely upon his interpretations of the plays for his account of Kelly and out of these he constructs a picture of a puritanical, cold, and overbearing personality, a man who insisted on devotion to one's vocation, domestic order (the repression of females) and a respect for the demands of the community; a man who won fame early in vaudeville but 'aspired toward higher levels and refused to capitalize on his clearly established ability to entertain', and thus became an odd combination of vaudeville and Ibsen.

Mr Hirsch explains how Kelly, after *The Torch-Bearers*, *The Show-Off*, and *Craig's Wife*, turned away from popular humour towards idiosyncratic or personally obsessive themes, treating the sending of flowers with the solemnity due to matters of great social significance. He says that Kelly 'is simply not interested in social implications or in large socio-cultural generalizations', thereby justifying his own failure to analyse either the complex implications of Kelly's depiction of his society as bound up in material objects and microcosmic speculation, or the implications of the immense popularity, for a time, of a drama obsessed by surfaces. Though Kelly was not, thankfully, another Eugene O'Neil, these considerations make it necessary to go beyond the scope of American Drama 100 in drawing attention to this neglected American playwright.

ALLAN SMITH

UNIVERSITY OF EAST ANGLIA

George S. Kaufman and his Friends. By SCOTT MEREDITH. New York: Doubleday. 1974. xviii + 723 pp. $12.95.

This massive compendium of gags from one of the most successful of Broadway comedy writers, George Kaufman, and his friends (who include Moss Hart, Alexander Woolcott, Edna Ferber, the Marx Brothers, Irving Berlin, and Dorothy Parker) offered Mr Meredith the opportunity to be witty, entertaining, and irreverent as well as instructive. Unfortunately it is an opportunity which he has missed. Mr Meredith has relied too mechanically on Kaufman's witticisms and the *bon mots* of the Algonquin Round Table in recognition of the likely interests of his audience, and he becomes pompous in his effort to make this study the definitive version of Kaufman's life. Mr Meredith's method is simple and perhaps, given the collection of ten thousand clippings and the massive bibliography of his researches, irresistible: Kaufman figures under such headings as 'The Hit', 'The Growth', 'The Continued Growth', and other personalities are introduced by a collection of their memorable sayings or anecdotal experiences. Thus Mr Meredith manages to establish the true provenance of some well worn jokes and to trace the progress of his writer/director from hit to hit, but he manages also to submerge their lively humour in his own pedestrian prose and to organize Kaufman's life into a succession of disconnected themes.

Mr Meredith's book suffers from major failures; in organization, in impartiality, in critical intelligence. His chronology is sometimes most confusing, as when in Chapter 19 he returns abruptly from the 1940s to the 1920s, and his changes of direction within chapters are as frequently inexplicable. In Chapter 26, for example, 'The Diary', Mr Meredith begins (as the reader expects) by giving a brief account of the celebrated misadventure with Miss Astor and her infamous diary which catapulted Kaufman to an unwelcome fame as America's Number 1 lover. Mr Meredith then detours to include some theatrical activities on Broadway and moves aside in order to recount Woolcott's joke about Moss Hart's mansion ('it just goes to show what God could do if he had money') before concluding with a poem by Kaufman for the *New Yorker*, 'Lines upon looking through a pile of old checks'. The chronicler then remembers that this chapter is about Kaufman's sexual behaviour and suggests that 'the pleasantly conventional tone of the poem may seem difficult to reconcile with Kaufman's torrid record as a Don Juan, but the fact is that, aside from all the extramarital sex, Kaufman's attitudes were essentially orthodox'.

Mr Meredith displays a personal commitment unfortunate in one who proposes to discuss Kaufman's friends and family as well as his professional life; he seems, in fact, to be carrying on a vendetta against Kaufman's adopted daughter, Anne Schneider. Howard Teichmann, writer of a biography of Kaufman which was published in 1972, *George S. Kaufman: An Intimate Portrait*, and collaborator with Kaufman on 'The Solid Gold Cadillac', is portrayed as a nuisance whom Kaufman attempted to drop, and the success of the Kaufman–Teichman collaboration is accounted as exactly proportionate to the attention G.S.K. gave it.

The third failure is perhaps more significant than these two. It is that in a full-length study of one of America's greatest humourists Mr Meredith never attempts to analyse the nature of Kaufman's wit nor, except for some laudatory remarks about craftsmanship, does he establish the basis of Kaufman's success as a playwright. Mr Meredith is impressed chiefly by his subject's commercial success and his ultimate accolade is that a play was 'a distinguished hit'. His book offers no improvement on Teichmann's biography, except in length.

ALLAN SMITH

UNIVERSITY OF EAST ANGLIA

Twelve Modern Anglo-Welsh Poets. Edited by DON DALE-JONES and RANDAL JENKINS. London: University of London Press. 1975. 208 pp. £3.50 (£1.50 paperbound).

The twelve poets the editors chose are: Idris Davies, Vernon Watkins, R. S. Thomas, Dylan Thomas, Alun Lewis, Roland Mathias, Harri Webb, Leslie Norris, Harri Jones, John Ormond, Dannie Abse, and Raymond Garlick. The choice was not absolutely free: the editors lament the exclusion of Emyr Humphreys who does not accept the label 'Anglo-Welsh'. But the choice was sufficiently free in that respect to include Vernon Watkins who just as insistently used to refuse the description. And in two other respects the editors *chose* not to be free: firstly by deciding to consider only poets born after 1900; in this, they regret the exclusion of Edward Thomas, W. H. Davies, and A. G. Prys-Jones, but oddly do not mention the more surprising avoidance of David Jones. The latter is not easily anthologized of course, but the policy had to do with time, not difficulty. And so has the second decision, not to include any poet younger than Raymond Garlick (born 1926): the editors explain, 'this is not a *contemporary* anthology (though we think that there ought to be such an anthology)'.

I feel that the 'Modern' of the title and the emphasized 'contemporary' of the above disclaimer were not as fully considered as they might have been. One can glimpse the ghost-presence of an alternative, perhaps more challenging, anthology in the implications of the present one. It would not have to superannuate the main virtue of what we have here, namely, the generous and generally well chosen representation of the poets from Roland Mathias to Raymond Garlick. But it would more decisively challenge our response. For example, the inclusion of David Jones would have set the 'modern' in relationship to the 'Modernist' possibilities available for exploring in English the more-than-English experience. Perhaps Philip Larkin's recent *Oxford Book of Twentieth Century English Verse* (1973) could differently afford to omit David Jones because Eliot and MacDiarmid (though not Pound) were there to illustrate the larger assaults made by works elaborately allusive, impersonal, and mythic. The present anthology is certainly not misleading in this respect: modern Anglo-Welsh poetry is largely as depicted here, essentially lyric and occasional. But we are not forced to consider anew what, in respect of wider possibilities, we think of it. David Jones's presence would have done this, and, just to give one possible example, a passage from the end of 'The Sleeping Lord' would have been a rich addition.

Or one might imagine the word 'contemporary' being involved less narrowly. From two of the first five poets, Idris Davies and R. S. Thomas, a very real continuity (suitably both urban and rural in its emphasis) runs through to the main concerns shown in the work of the other seven. It involves what the editors, though referring to all twelve poets, call an understanding of 'what it means to be a Welshman in the twentieth century'. But more specifically it involves a decidedly *self-conscious* awareness of a Wales culturally and linguistically disinherited, ill-used, viewed across a gap only apparently bridged by that hyphen in 'Anglo-Welsh' and only really closed by an ability to speak the Welsh language itself. All the poets of course reveal involuntarily a wider unity involving certain modes of thought and association. But it is this painful awareness of the role of conscience that has flowered most importantly in the later poets, and which best defines 'contemporary'. It makes it less pressing to re-introduce poets like Vernon Watkins, Dylan Thomas, and Alun Lewis with poems which would make the same impact in a purely 'English' anthology. Incidentally, it also makes the twentieth century the only period in which the term 'Anglo-Welsh' is more than a comment about language, nationality, or simple location. And in this sense the present anthology is better conceived than *This World of Wales* (University of Wales Press, 1968) which included Vaughan, Dyer, and Hopkins (though also, to good effect, David Jones). But one could imagine it presenting its seven later poets much as it does, excellently, now, and then introducing some of the best poems by younger poets. To allow this, the editors could have afforded to be more, and sometimes differently, selective of the earlier established poets. For example, though Idris Davies's 'I Was Born in Rhymney' is reduced from 112 to 34 stanzas, it perhaps still unnecessarily takes four pages. It was also unnecessary to have three poems on Dylan Thomas. And in Thomas's own case, it is a poem like 'After the funeral' (not included) which we would most interestingly remember on coming to the poems of personal-cultural relationship that are amongst the best in the later part of the volume.

The poets are introduced individually, and annotated for the general reader and for use in schools. I felt that the Notes did not need to replace a dictionary quite so often. Both Notes and Introductions are generally reliable on facts, which makes the occasional lapse, through error or exaggeration, mysterious. Vernon Watkins, for example, was born in Maesteg, not Swansea; Dylan Thomas did not draw on his Notebooks 'virtually to the end of his life', unless 1941 can be said to be 'virtually' 1953; and it is curious to find Auden described as 'the most "modern" and experimental of British twentieth-century poets'.

But within its own accepted limits, the book is generous and helpful. It will find new readers for the warmly intelligent verse of Harri Jones, whose life in New South Wales literally compounded the theme of exile so variously given emphasis in these pages generally. And new readers will be introduced to the excellent John Ormond, whose sturdily sensitive qualities are perhaps most nearly matched elsewhere by Seamus Heaney: both achieve symbols without damage to the ordinary integrity of things. The book remains a valuable introduction to these and many others.

UNIVERSITY COLLEGE OF WALES, ABERYSTWYTH   WALFORD DAVIES

L'Inquiétude religieuse dans le roman américain moderne. By ROBERT ROUGÉ. Librairie
C. Klincksieck. 1974. 479 pp. 68 F.

This is a long, elaborately organized study, a large part of which covers ground that
has been well trodden by numerous other critics. The familiarity of the theme, the
crisis of religious identity in the twentieth-century American novel, and the slightly
misleading use of the term 'modern' in the title (used to describe works of major
importance in the first half of the century rather than post World War II fiction)
combine to give the whole study a somewhat dated quality. No new theories to
explain the crisis are advanced and the choice of writers such as West, Hemingway,
Anderson, and Faulkner is only following a well-established stereotyped view of
American literature.

The involved structure of M. Rougé's study is both his greatest strength and his
greatest weakness. The first four chapters, grouped under the heading 'La tradition
et les temps modernes', attempt to place the crisis of religious uncertainty in a
historical context, tracing the Puritan vision of life as a dichotomy between good
and evil through the stages of its development in the nineteenth century and
examining the problem of finding a suitable language and style to act as a vehicle
for the expression of that duality.

After this rather general introductory survey, M. Rougé moves on to a close
analysis of various authors, gathered under separate headings. The first group,
examined under the heading of 'Le Monde brisé et la sensibilité religieuse', consists of West, Fitzgerald, and Hemingway, all writers whose questing protagonists
strive to make some kind of sense out of an apocalyptic world. From this first stage,
where M. Rougé sees the writer as concerned with showing the crisis of the individual in a fragmented universe, in a language heavy with ironic symbolism and
double meanings, he moves to his second group of writers, Dreiser, Anderson,
Frank, Miller, and Steinbeck, under the heading 'La recherche de la Vie Sacrée'.

Whereas M. Rougé feels that the central motif of the first group is the quest, the
motif of the second group is *communion*, and the *Vie Sacrée* is presented as the point
where the inner imaginative experience and the outer reality coincide. The writers
in this second group, he feels, are searching for a way to shape and describe the
split between the desire for spiritual transcendence and the blocks which existence
imposes on that desire. The interior world of these writers is presented through their
portrayal of a universe of memories, frustrations, and latent ambitions and their
works provide an account of the search for an adequate stylistic expression of their
sense of alienation.

M. Rougé's study of the first two groups of writers builds towards his examination of the last group, made up of Robert Penn Warren and Faulkner, who 'clearly
face up to the problem of God, whether he exists and has a place in the modern
world from whence he seems to have been cast out'. In this final section M. Rougé
considers those two writers who, he believes, investigate the crisis of religious
uncertainty in a form which adequately reflects that crisis. What exists in Warren
and Faulkner is a discussion of negation, where life itself becomes a statement of the
unknowable. Both these writers, examined under the heading 'Du discours
mythique à la vie comme passion', tackle the problem of man's rediscovery of his
own spiritual uncertainty, which can no longer be solved by traditional religious
formulas or mysticism because the crisis of uncertainty lies in the truth that,
although religion may be dead, atheism cannot be a substitute. Summing up his
whole thesis in a conclusion aptly entitled 'La dimension théologique', M. Rougé
explains that 'the God who is dead is therefore the God who is *necessary* to any
culture that defines itself in relation to him. He is the God of man's *dependence*.
But beyond this dead God, the *inevitable* God still haunts the soul of man, and he is
also the God of man's *Freedom*, not of his dependence'.

M. Rougé's organization attempts to formulate certain patterns and in so far as it shows the contrasts between the philosophies of the writers considered it is useful and, on occasions, very penetrating indeed. But the extent of this structural organization tends to take over the subject and become clumsy rather than clarifying. It is this same organization which forces him to run through a cursory examination of several writers as a preamble where he does no more than repeat long held general views. Even his truly excellent analysis of Warren and Faulkner, the climax of his study, does not altogether compensate for the lack of originality in the first part of the book.

SUSAN E. BASSNETT-McGUIRE

UNIVERSITY OF WARWICK

Die moderne amerikanische Literatur: Eine Einführung. By IHAB HASSAN. (Kröners Taschenausgabe, 444) Stuttgart: Kröner. 1974. 262 pp. DM 17.50.

Amerikanische Erzählliteratur, 1950–1970. Edited by FRIEDER BUSCH and RENATE SCHMIDT-v. BARDELEBEN. München: Fink. 1975. 260 pp. DM 19.80.

Ihab Hassan's *Contemporary American Literature, 1945–1972* first appeared in 1973. It was a useful compendium of *idées reçues* with sometimes trenchant, sometimes trite, always partial annotations; a concise literary encyclopedia, as it were, with listings by genre rather than alphabet or date. As a guide to contemporary stock-market quotations, for provoking and forming responses in schools and colleges, it met a need. Here was quarter of a century of recent history from Riesman and Kinsey to Norman O. Brown's *Love's Body* and Jerry Rubin's *Do it!*.

To this German edition is appended a useful survey by Brigitte Scheer-Schäzler of Ihab Hassan's personal contribution to the debate, particularly in *The Literature of Silence* (1967) and *Paracriticisms* (1974). Yet such a critical frame puts rather too portentous a weight on this wholly pedagogical excursion with its starring of major novelists (Saul Bellow, Norman Mailer) and important novelists, who turn out to be Wright Morris, Bernard Malamud, J. D. Salinger, Kurt Vonnegut Jr, James Purdy, Truman Capote, John Hawkes, William Styron, John Barth, and John Updike. Nabokov's American offspring, with the exception of Barth, it is revealed to German readers, are not 'bedeutende Autoren', though room is made in the text for Joseph Heller, Thomas Berger, Thomas Pynchon, Terry Southern, and Donald Barthelme. And if Updike and Styron, why not Ellison and Baldwin? Nor do Jack Kerouac or William Burroughs attract star billing.

Fortunately 'Amerikanistik' in Germany, as the Festschrift dedicated to Professor Hans Galinsky on his sixty-fifth birthday testifies, is well able to take care of such questions and correct such imbalances. Here are seventeen essays by young critics, whose academic enthusiasm for American literature was first prompted and promoted by Professor Galinsky while they were students at Mainz. It is a remarkable achievement. All are now teaching in German High Schools. The full impact such enthusiasm must have on a national scale is yet to be seen. For these are not trifling, descriptive panegyrics of quixotic new culture heroes, but detailed *explications de textes* in a rigorous, old-fashioned mode which has much to offer transatlantic readers, whose professional magazines now seldom print such academic exercises and whose critical prophets prefer more radical thematic keys to reveal the mysterious braille of a whole cultural predicament. The painstaking exploration of a single short story by J. D. Salinger, to take but one example, with its exact weighting of Zen Buddhist and Catholic and Lutheran elements, achieves a far closer understanding of 'Ichhaftigkeit' (egocentricity) and enlightenment in an archetypal American context than yet another paracriticism on the Ishmael

theme of self and cosmic consciousness from Melville to Vonnegut Jr. With such an
offering Professor Galinsky had good reason to congratulate himself on his birthday.

UNIVERSITY OF WARWICK   HAROLD BEAVER

P. H. Newby. By E. C. BUFKIN. (Twayne's English Authors Series, 176) Boston:
    Twayne. 1975. 144 pp. $6.95.
C. P. Snow. By DAVID SHUSTERMAN. (Twayne's English Authors Series, 179)
    Boston: Twayne. 1975. 161 pp. $7.95.
Michael Arlen. By HARRY KEYISHIAN. (Twayne's English Authors Series, 174)
    Boston: Twayne. 1975. 150 pp. $6.95.

Twayne's World, United States, and English Authors series are steadily providing
critical studies of major, middling, and minor figures in world literature. Designed
primarily for institutional libraries, the series cater to that need for the feeling of
security that somewhere, sometime, someone has written something on everyone.
You might never want to read or even refer to the study, but at least it is there.
But this impulse to provide comprehensive coverage has too often taken precedence
over any sense of a need to provide engaging and stimulating commentary.

Professor Bufkin notes that 'only scant serious, extensive critical attention' has
been devoted to P. H. Newby; but his own study never makes a persuasive case of
why any attention is worth giving. He singles out Newby's 'five best novels' that
have gained him 'a secure and eminent place in contemporary letters' (*The Young
May Moon, The Retreat, The Picnic at Sakkara, The Barbary Light, Something to Answer
For*) but his admirable refusal to make excessive claims for them leaves the rationale
of this critical study somewhat mysterious. The books are dealt with one by one and
inevitably, for a study of a writer not especially well known, the plots are summarized. This results in a dutiful, pedestrian approach, noting rebirth images,
quest myths, the significance of characters' names, but rarely moving to a wider
critical context. The faults of the lesser works are indicated ('occasionally failing
to focus a novel clearly . . . becoming burdened down with detail almost to the
point of narrative immobility . . . overreliance on the mythic pattern') but no
striking sense of Newby's work emerges. Professor Bufkin gestures at associating
him with 'the comic tradition in the modern English novel with such predecessors
as Forster, Aldous Huxley, Joyce Carey, and Henry Green and with such a contemporary as Kingsley Amis' but he makes no further, detailed explorations of
these specific connexions. Instead he is content to leave Newby drifting in a very
wide category. 'Despite the unique individuality of his writing, Newby's lineage
from the great tradition of the English novel is easy to trace'; he cites Dickens 'in
his creation of humorous, eccentric, and grotesque characters', George Eliot and
James in his 'constant concern with moral behaviour', and Lawrence, Forster,
and Conrad for other influences.

With C. P. Snow Professor Shusterman has a somewhat easier task, since a
critical debate exists around Snow's work. Yet Professor Shusterman never pene-
trates deeply into the issues that have been raised; and his summary of Snow's
qualities and limitations offers so limited a case that the rationale for offering a
critical study once again seems obscure.

His writing, however, will probably never appeal to young romantic rebels (except as a
curiosity piece: an interesting example of how Establishment people supposedly live) or to
those who have a predilection for experimental fiction; it will never have an audience among
those who demand violent action and erotic, deviant, or unusual behaviour that stimulates
the sense; it will probably never be acceptable to the proletariat of any country.

Ultimately Professor Shusterman rests the case on Jerome Thale's claim that Snow is 'one of the most tolerant novelists in generations because he is "a great deal more interested in studying and understanding character than in judging it" '. And it is this acceptance of the reduction of the novel to a study of character that leads Professor Shusterman into some of his more naive critical pronouncements. 'Most of us tend to forget many of our experiences, whereas [Lewis] Eliot apparently has forgotten very little, though it is problematical as to whether he tells his readers everything he knows: there are long lapses of time within each story — in some cases, several years — and surely things must have happened that are not revealed.' These speculations about the documentary reality of fictional creations, and the commonsense approach, readily lead us into the banal. Professor Shusterman laments that we see so little of Jago's rival Crawford in *The Masters*, but concludes: 'we feel that the dons have probably elected the right man after all because Jago has been shown to possess great flaws of character and because Crawford has not been sufficiently characterized. If we had seen Crawford as intensively, he too might have revealed serious flaws'. With *The Malcontents* Professor Shusterman moves from character to more structural and linguistic points, noting that there are 'in this novel several new departures for Snow. One is that he has abandoned the chapter titles and uses only numbers. Perhaps he did so because so many of his critics in the past had mentioned that chapter titles were old fashioned, but no advantage is to be found in the new method'. And yet overall in his low key way Professor Shusterman is able to make some useful comments and gives a final assessment of Snow that seems a fair one. 'Snow's influence has, in the main, not been artistic but intellectual and moral; he is being read, for the most part, by those of the middle and older generations who have found some approximation in their own lives to his indeterminate and balanced outlook . . . Many find these novels quite unexciting; probably fewer are stimulated by them.'

With Michael Arlen Professor Keyishian produces the most interesting of these three studies, succeeding to a large extent because he establishes a sociological context in which to view Arlen's development. He traces Arlen's career from its earliest stages when, as Dikran Koyoumdkian, he was writing polemical articles in the emigré Armenian journal, *Ararat*; he touches on Arlen's associations with such literary figures as George Moore and D. H. Lawrence and such artistic hangers-on as Nancy Cunard; and he examines Arlen's contributions to Orage's *New Age* that collected together formed his first book, *The London Venture*, a volume that provoked Scott Fitzgerald to give 'a profound bow to my successor, Arlen'. The transformation from Dikran Koyoumdkian to Michael Arlen, the burying of his Armenian identity beneath that of 'Englishness', the plunging into the literary-bohemian-Mayfair milieu of the 1920s; all this is valuably sketched in to provide an interpretative background for the short stories in *These Charming People* and the novel for which he is now solely remembered, *The Green Hat*. Professor Keyishian creates a sense of the 1920s, and implicitly makes the case for seeing Arlen's role as that of an English Scott Fitzgerald, someone worth further reading and investigation. Engagingly, he has the rare ability of the appropriate use of anecdote to capture a sense of the period and to encapsulate critical points. Whereas the refusal to make high claims for their authors in the studies of Newby and Snow resulted in an impression of dutiful studies of the uninterestingly mediocre, Professor Keyishian's tactful discriminations between the successful and unsuccessful works of Arlen contribute to his picture of the writer: the lesser work illuminates the better, and illuminates, too, the man, with his need for acceptance, with his fascination for the glamorously rich, and yet with his inescapable alienation, his sense of standing to one side, of seeing the ephemerality and illusoriness of it all. Professor Keyishian preserves the right balance between the critical and the biographical, and the final judicious assessment captures both the achievement of Arlen in the extraordinarily successful *The Green Hat* and in the novel Professor Keyishian thinks his best, *Man's Mortality*, and at the same time the sense of a wasted potential. Arlen began his career as 'spokesman for an uprooted scattered people' but from 'personal inclination and the advice of his mentors' abandoned the polemical role he was uncomfortable in and became a romancer. 'He could and did occasionally pursue serious themes, as in "The Romance of Iris Poole" and *The Green Hat*, but he usually chose not to probe the issues these works raised.' And yet a part of him still wanted to be a 'serious' author, and in his later books 'he was honestly coping with the problems to which he had in the past given only conventional answers'. Professor Keyishian sees him finally and regretfully as 'a man of passion who settled for being a man of style; but he remained, in his books as in life, supremely good company'.

UNIVERSITY OF SYDNEY   MICHAEL WILDING

The Literature of Exhaustion: Borges, Nabokov, and Barth. By JOHN O. STARK. Durham, North Carolina: Duke University Press. 1974. viii + 196 pp. $7.95.

According to Mr Stark, the word 'exhaustion' in John Barth's 1967 *Atlantic* essay, 'The Literature of Exhaustion', has two meanings: 'one, that literature is, or is nearly, used up; the other, that, given its current condition, writers should invent and exhaust possibilities and thus create for literature an infinite scope'. The book which Mr Stark offers us is a very useful annotated catalogue of certain literary devices (the Chinese box, the infinite regress pattern) and strategies (the methodical undercutting of characterization and plot, and the explicit and mannerized inflation of the authorial presence), favoured variations on popular themes (concerning time, memory, space, love, the fixation on process rather than product, and the fascination with symmetry and with narrative constructs based on the principle of opposites), and central images (the labyrinth, the mirror, the circle) that recur in the fiction of Borges, Nabokov, and Barth. The book's purpose is in this way to expose in the work of three writers what Stark believes to be a new and integral literary movement expressive of the outlook Barth had in mind.

Mr Stark does neglect the tantalizing opportunity to view his trio in the larger perspective, but perhaps it would be unwarranted in the present setting to challenge his disregard for the fact, for example, that most of their compositional devices were part of the repertoire as early as Sterne and Diderot and that his authors' use of imagery is strikingly and revealingly reminiscent of the unnatural-natural history of the generations of Lyly and Browne. Moreover, the crucial issue of the dual existence of a fiction, both as object and as representation of the world in which it is an object, has been an essential and persistent theme throughout the history of human ritual behaviour. It was fundamental to Vico's and Bacon's notions of hieroglyphs, to the ideas behind Swedenborg's (and the Symbolistes') correspondences, Flaubert's *livre* and Mallarmé's *livre*, Poe's codes, Breton's *coupures*, and Pound's ideograms. It is intriguing, in fact, that when any intellectual discipline, in theology, mathematics, experimental science, the occult sciences, the arts, becomes highly self-conscious with regard to its relationship to 'external reality' (at the time of the nominalist-universalist crisis, at the time of the emergence of the uncertainty principle and the conjoint formulation of wave and particle mechanics), it seems almost certain at some stage to display a 'literature' or a system of '*ficciones*' characterized by traits comparable to those singled out in this volume. Mr Stark *has*, perhaps not altogether consciously, observed a trend of a widespread and classic sort. The condition which he posits at the bottom of it all, the exhaustion paradox, is one that Thomas Mann prefigured for the novel half a century ago. But his hypothesis is marred by its failure to register fully the difference between the descriptive and the prescriptive functions of the word 'exhaustion', between 'being exhausted' as a stimulus and 'being exhaustive' as a response. So far as Borges and Nabokov are concerned, he simply does not manage to bring sufficient evidence that the repletion motive which they share with Barth stems from any depletion theory.

'Nabokov', Mr Stark says, 'manipulates genres to attack realism, thereby again exemplifying the Literature of Exhaustion. His most daring imitation of forms . . . imply [sic] that the form of the novel has indeed been exhausted'. The first of these statements is surely the point; the second sentence illustrates neatly the kind of *non sequitur* that vitiates his thesis. As he says in concluding his Introduction, 'All these themes form part of one, over-arching theme: the relation between literature and reality'; and the rest of the book indeed establishes effectively, however inadvertently, that what unifies the work of Barth, Borges, and Nabokov is not the exhaustion dilemma but what Stark himself calls the 'anti-realist' impulse. They join in a conviction not that fiction is dead but that that special constellation of conventions is false by which novelists have represented (a) the universe as a fixed, finite, and positivistically definable entity, and (b) themselves as slaves bound over to the labour of mimicking such a vision, sacrificing imagination to the rhetoric of probability, and abdicating the role of creator in the name of the determinist fallacy of the spontaneous generation of the work of art.

Mr Stark describes usefully how literature (traditionally an instrument for the propagation of external truths), feeling itself to be growing impotent in the mixed company of a multi-media world, multi-disciplined, and mass-educated, can turn autoerotic. Thus, without saying it, he provides us with a salutary distinction between his cluster of authors (which might also include a Queneau, a Beckett, a Hawkes) and two other branches of writers in an anti-realist genealogy; those (such as Bosco, Tolkien, Buzzati, Barrios) who wish us to 'believe' their fables, and those (such as Burroughs, Charles Williams, Grass, Vittorini) who wish us in some way to 'act' in reaction to their fables, whether we 'believe' them or not. Further, he attempts cursorily to link his group to a philosophical tradition, notably to idealism. In this he is unsuccessful partly because, while he does try to explain the esoteric aspect of their work, he does not seem ready to notice its real source, and one of the most remarkable features shared by these writers, their *eclecticism*. It *is* sometimes to their theoretical advantage to exclude certain kinds of readership, just as it suits them from time to time to show ostensible allegiance to one familiar philosophical lineage or another. But what finally makes them (with Joyce, Queneau, and perhaps Calvino) among the initially most obscure of modern fictionalists is the free-ranging heterogeneity of their allusions, of the lodes they mine. And this in turn springs from their determination (so forcefully evoked by Mr Stark in other contexts) to demonstrate that there is no 'matter' which they would exclude, 'no limit' to what they may create or recreate, whether their readers can follow them or not. What more appropriate rejoinder to its own condition, they might say, can a culture rich in information and poor in resolution produce? In this fashion, of course, these writers become precisely what they most abhor in the realist tradition, a mirror of their times. Such is the one paradox which even they cannot accommodate, except through silence. *The Literature of Exhaustion*, as its author freely confesses, is not the deeply thoughtful book we need. But it is a good index to some of the things we ought to think about.

University of Warwick   Cristopher Nash

Number and Nightmare: Forms of Fantasy in Contemporary Fiction. By JEAN E.
KENNARD. Hamden, Connecticut: Shoe String Press. 1975. 244 pp. $10.00.

Taking her lead from a distinction between literary types made by Elizabeth
Sewell and applied by Ihab Hassan to Beckett and Joyce respectively, Professor
Kennard considers Joseph Heller, John Barth, James Purdy, and Kurt Vonnegut,
Jr, as 'novelists of number' and Anthony Burgess, Iris Murdoch, and William
Golding as 'novelists of nightmare'. For her, 'number . . . is a dramatization of the
Post-existentialist view of the human condition'; it 'takes the reader systematically
and logically towards nothing, towards the void, by breaking down one by one his
expectations of realism'. Meanwhile, 'nightmare is the form used by writers who
offer answers to the Post-existential dilemma, or rather deny its existence' and who
'all believe that the world has order even if man cannot discover its meaning'. It
'is basically a constructive form; each of these writers creates myths. They move the
reader towards recognition of an all-inclusive world, a puzzle in which all the
pieces fit'. Her book, then, is a companion piece to John O. Stark's *The Literature
of Exhaustion,* reviewed here (p. 331). While Mr Stark's study glosses the stylistic
devices by which the novel now addresses those epistemological and esthetic problems which its own traditions have generated for it, Professor Kennard charts a
variety of contemporary novelists' technical responses to man's external metaphysical
and psychological condition.

Professor Kennard has caught the spirit of the modes she has in mind, and
contributes sizeably to the ongoing effort to single out and compare the members of
several 'breeds' of fictionalists writing today. Where she seems to falter is in her
approach to her two immediate objectives, the aim of setting her types in their
historical context, and the 'attempt to define two major forms of fantasy in
contemporary fiction'.

What do we mean by fantasy? Professor Kennard bypasses this axial question.
She asserts that her seven authors 'are all writers of fantasy'. Subsequently, without
method, she alludes to fantasy variously as a quality characteristic of certain
objective events in our physical world; as an aspect of events that may take place
in other (e.g. 'future') worlds but not in ours; as any phenomenon that is incredible
or improbable; as a literary instrument serving 'to undermine the reader's expectations of realism' and/or to 'draw the reader's notice to the pattern of the book by
separating him from the experience of the characters'; as a process of mind (e.g.
'our own sexual fantasies', 'fantasy worlds which [Murdoch's] characters weave
around themselves', or 'a fantasy world where everything is spun from one consciousness' which is Murdoch's); as a function of our failure to understand events;
as a form of 'supra-realism . . . exaggerating certain aspects of realistic techniques',
acting 'to suggest the mysteriousness, the enchantment of reality' and/or to 'suggest
that the real world is stranger than [the reader] had thought' and/or to reveal to
us some 'darker and more mysterious world'; as a technique which 'makes us see
substantive action' in a way that realism does not; and so forth. Whereas in none
of her chapters on the novelists of number does she make it clear how we are to
see them as writers of or about fantasy (why should it be equated with the frustration of one's expectations of realism?), in her single sequence on Murdoch she
precipitates us into a forest of such notional 'forms of fantasy', whose radically
diverse qualities she herself seems unprepared critically to discern. This is fertile
terrain. It must be rigorously tilled before it can yield 'digestible' fruit. We desperately need a lucid, workable definition for something, or several things, currently
occurring in fiction which many writers persist in covering enthusiastically and
vaguely with the term fantasy. More gifted and disciplined critics, like Scholes,
thrust the word uneasily aside or, like Todorov, garrotte it with strictures. The
thing itself meantime stands alone in the arena, flailing and spitting.

Two difficulties arise with regard to the historicist aspect of *Number and Nightmare*. (When the author speaks of 'Post-existential' writing, she means roughly 'absurdist' fiction which she believes to follow directly from the early Sartre and Camus of *L'Etranger*, *La Nausée*, *Le Mythe de Sisyphe*, *L'Être et le Néant*, and parts of *L'Homme révolté*.) The first is that Professor Kennard neglects the essential question as to why novelists of number write so *differently* from Sartre and Camus. Setting aside the matter of fantasy, she has little to say, for instance, about the centrality of the comic among them. Without due attention to the vast (if feckless) body of theoretical literature on the operation of humour, she accepts outright Bergson's explanation of laughter in terms of incongruity (the 'frustration of our expectations') and over-looks that this may as readily apply, for example, to some of the most horrifically un-funny passages in Kafka. Some unaccounted new scruple is in the balance.

The other difficulty concerns a certain historical myopia which this author shares with Mr Stark. Starting with the disturbingly insubstantial and non-sequential premise that 'few would deny that the postwar atmosphere has been permeated with Existentialist concepts since [?] the notion of the absurd seems to define the contemporary situation so well', she proceeds, without further cogent documentation of it, to insist on this French connexion. It remains to be seen just to what extent her authors are indeed second-generation, secondhand sensibilities living in a world whose givens are more or less purely literary. But were she inclined to place her literary categories in a fuller perspective, Professor Kennard would probably agree that the impulse of the novel of number, however pessimistic its outcome, ensues from the rationalist tradition whose procedure (like that in the mathematics, say, of Church and Gödel) is to dissolve or dismember specious relationships ('temporal', 'spatial', 'causal', 'logical', 'associational', etc.) whereas the motive of the novel of nightmare is symbolist, in its endeavour to multiply and amplify the sense of hitherto undetected relationships. Now in so far as she might accept this, it would seem reasonable to consider her authors in the context of the very long and broad double intellectual tradition (rationalist and symbolist) from which they have drawn so much of what she deems to be solely a 'Post-existentialist' strategy. With the 'novelists of number' in mind, one might think, for a start, of the comic and deliberate simultaneous fabrication and dissolution of standard narrative relationships in Rabelais, Sterne, and Diderot. Regarding the 'novelists of nightmare', Professor Kennard would have done well to study their processes (as 'myths of total explanation' by way of the principle of *correspondances*) against the ideological background of the family of Bacon–Vico–Swedenborg–Blake–Baudelaire and the Symbolistes. As I have suggested in connexion with Mr Stark's work, in the matter of the process by which her writers believe the novel may unmake itself and thereby reveal its ultimate inner nullity (a poetic conceit which she fails to ascribe intelligibly to a descent from Sartre and Camus), a comparison with the speculations of Flaubert and Mallarmé (with Blanchot) on 'le livre' would have helped enormously.

A further problem is that Professor Kennard, like many writing today, may be somewhat mesmerized by her authors' own publicity into overplaying the extent to which any novel is in fact in a position to 'frustrate our expectations of the novel'. The *concept* is so attractive. Even the best novelists have themselves sometimes grown oblivious of the fact that they and their critics are often the only people aware that such a monolithically 'expectable' thing as 'the novel', 'the Realist novel', is ever supposed to have existed. A peculiarity of literature, both creative and critical, whose initial interest is conceptual is that its writers tend to lose contact with the actualities of readership. Purdy describes the fall of a lady through a skylight as a casual event. 'This discrepancy between what and how events are described suggests, of course', says Professor Kennard, 'the impossibility of language's capturing reality'. Present criticism, like this book, is convulsed with leaps of that sort. Purdy (with Barth, and others) was right in his time to challenge the conventions of perception and communication. Professor Kennard and the rest of us are surely wrong to confuse the abstract general programme by which a book may explain itself in a unified way (particularly when this is paradoxically at odds with the author's anti-positivist attitude) with the actual sensual import of its individual moments. We may wish to beware of the allure of this new, cerebral brand of softmindedness.

The compensating insights in Professor Kennard's survey are numerous. Criticism will be infinitely more accurate and useful, for example, once it has taken into account the idea, so simply and effectively developed by her, that in contemporary hands (such as Vonnegut's) the satiric mode itself may often be intended as merely another naive convention, now resurrected and displayed in grotesque contexts with ironic purpose to test or to subvert the easy rhetoric of satire's more optimistic and credulous times.

CRISTOPHER NASH

UNIVERSITY OF WARWICK

Harriette Arnow. By WILTON ECKLEY. (Twayne United States Authors Series, 245) New York: Twayne. 1974. 138 pp. $6.50.

The work of Harriette Arnow is, perhaps, largely unknown in Britain; her reputation in the United States is similarly thin, although her third novel *The Dollmaker* (1954) did enjoy a certain critical and popular success and came very close to winning the National Book Award for 1955. Professor Eckley's short critical and biographical study of Mrs Arnow may be taken, therefore, as an attempt to bring a wider audience to her work.

Mrs Arnow is a novelist (and social historian) in an essentially Southern literary tradition, one that looks back, as Professor Eckley notes, to the mountain stories of William Gilmore Simms, but other fruitful comparisons can be made with the Kentucky novelist James Lane Allen, with Mary N. Murfree, the chronicler of Tennessee mountain life at the end of the nineteenth century, and with Constance Fenimore Woolson. Mrs Arnow's studies of the Cumberland Valley of Kentucky are firmly rooted in the tradition of literary regionalism, or 'local-color', a tradition that has generally, and incorrectly, been characterized as a sentimental, melodramatic, and politically regressive treatment of backwater communities in America, isolated by their poverty, manners, and archaic social rituals. Indeed, in contrast to this description, Mrs Arnow's fiction contains much of the realistic hardness of Mary Murfree's Tennessee stories, with a similar precision in her attention to dialect. Moreover, in *The Dollmaker* Mrs Arnow successfully handled a theme that had belonged almost exclusively to the negro urban realists of the 1930s, that is, the migration of agrarian, peasant communities from the rural South to the industrial North, in this case Detroit, and the manner in which the members of these communities collectively assume a new status as an urban proletariat. In this novel Mrs Arnow bleakly charts the disintegration of her migrant family and the inevitable 'teacup' tragedies of city life.

Professor Eckley justly finds *The Dollmaker* to be Mrs Arnow's best novel to date and his commentary on it is competent if not entirely exhaustive. He rather underplays the propagandist tone of the novel and ignores those elements of literary populism that, perhaps, betray the influence of another regionalist, Hamlin Garland. Moreover, when Professor Eckley shifts to a more general perspective on Mrs Arnow's work he makes some curious observations, particularly on her current standing in American letters. He feels that she has been penalized for her realism and her 'lean prose style', and that success has not been possible for her at a time when contemporary American fiction is obsessed with 'the pyrotechnics of sex' and a 'mania for neurotic protagonists'. This is a strangely one-sided view of recent American fiction, to say the least, and detracts from the soundness of Professor Eckley's other judgements.

These criticisms aside, however, Professor Eckley has written a useful book on one of the minor figures of American literature whose work is evidence of a continuing tradition of regionalism in Southern writing today. Unfortunately this study appeared shortly before the publication of Mrs Arnow's most recent novel *Kentucky Trace* (1974) and therefore takes no account of this new work which sees her exploring, in fictional terms, some of the themes of her best work of social history, *Flowering of the Cumberland* (1963).

HENRY CLARIDGE

UNIVERSITY OF KENT

William Golding: The Dark Fields of Discovery. By VIRGINIA TIGER. (Critical Appraisals) London: Calder & Boyars. 1974. 244 pp. £4.95.

Doris Lessing: Critical Studies. Edited by ANNIS PRATT and L. S. DEMBO. Madison, Wisconsin: University of Wisconsin Press. 1974. xii + 172 pp. $13.75 ($4.35 paperbound).

'I must admit to a certain degree of concern that this book is adding to the proliferating burden of some twenty years' commentary' says Mrs Tiger in her Introduction. I wish I could say that her misgivings were unfounded, for she is an intelligent, sensitive reader of Golding's fiction. The trouble is that there is really very little left to say that is both new and significant about Golding's major fiction, at least along the lines of interpretative explication followed by Mrs Tiger. Too many other critics have trodden that path before her, and the effort to be both scrupulously fair to their endeavours and to claim some originality for her own imparts a sense of strain to her discourse which gradually communicates itself to the reader.

Mrs Tiger's general view of Golding is that he is essentially a religious but non-dogmatic writer (no surprise there). Her method is closely to examine the novels in chronological order and with special attention to the following topics: their initial critical reception, the thematic use of darkness, and certain characteristic technical features: 'point of view'; the inversion of literary models; the confrontation scene; the 'ideographic structure'. This last phrase turns out to refer to the device, characterestic of Golding's fiction, of abruptly presenting the action in a new light and compelling the reader to a reappraisal of its meaning; as at the end of *Lord of the Flies*, with its sudden switch to the point of view of the naval officer. 'The meaning of *Lord of the Flies* is not, then, allegorically simple but instead ideographically suggestive ... The moral operation on the reader of the fable's ideographic structure — when the two patterns clash — makes such a symbolic density possible.' Fair enough; but I found I had to translate this comment into more ordinary English in order to test its validity, and I am not convinced that the coinage of a new jargon term, 'ideographic structure', is either necessary or useful.

This is not a book to send the reader back, or on, to Golding's novels with a quickened appetite. It will be more appreciated by readers coming in the opposite direction, fresh from a second or third reading of the canon. They will derive some profit and pleasure from testing their responses against Mrs Tiger's and will find incidental illumination in her frequent quotation of Golding's own *obiter dicta*.

The collection of essays on Doris Lessing edited by Annis Pratt and L. S. Dembo, originally published as a special issue of *Contemporary Literature*, Autumn, 1973, and now reissued as a paperback book, does not suffer from the same disadvantages as Mrs Tiger's book. Doris Lessing's reputation as a major contemporary novelist is of more recent date than Golding's and she has not yet attracted the same weight of critical attention. Of the two monographs in existence, one is critically feeble and the other very much out of date. Despite the unevenness of its contents, therefore, this collection can be said to supply a 'need', at least until something better comes along. It is to be hoped that the latter will be of British origin: all credit to the Americans for being the first to give Doris Lessing due recognition, but one would welcome a serious appraisal of her work written from within the culture, British and Colonial, that she is concerned with.

It was *The Golden Notebook* which first suggested to this reviewer that Doris Lessing was a novelist of real consequence, and this seems to have been a common experience. Annis Pratt describes the book as 'one of the novels that seemed to speak directly to a whole generation's experience'. Just because it was such a complex and multifaceted book, however, it interested different readers in different ways. To many of the contributors to this volume it was clearly an early manifestation of contemporary feminist sentiment, and just as clearly they have been somewhat disconcerted by Doris Lessing's subsequent playing down of the novel's 'women's lib' element and her emphasis on its formal questioning of the novel as a genre. Likewise, some readers mainly interested in *The Golden Notebook* as a study of neurosis and psychosis have been disconcerted by the increasingly polemical Laingian emphasis of her subsequent work, and still more by its Sufist religious mysticism. The essays on *Briefing for a Descent into Hell* and on Sufism, with which this collection ends, are respectful but somewhat non-commital compared to the more engaged studies of *The Golden Notebook*. The ability to surprise and disconcert one's admirers is, however, one of the signs of a major writer, though not, of course an infallible one.

Both these books have valuable bibliographies or checklists of primary and secondary sources.

DAVID LODGE

UNIVERSITY OF BIRMINGHAM

The Ray Bradbury Companion: A Life and Career History, Photolog, and Comprehensive Checklist of Writings with Facsimiles from Ray Bradbury's Unpublished and Uncollected Work in all Media. By WILLIAM F. NOLAN. Detroit, Michigan: Gale Research. 1975. xiv + 339 pp. $28.50.

Let a thing be appraised in the spirit in which it was made. Once, in a shop in Southern California where he sold books to the Doris Days of the world by the yard and hue, and Pelican *Coriolanus*es to Olivier by the handful (garnished with sprays of fresh-sharpened pencils), the reviewer in his nonage encountered author Ray Bradbury poised before a massive bibliography of editions of Shakespeare. 'Ah!' he was saying with a wistful smile.

The present extravagantly boxed large volume vividly expresses an ethos and a man whose vigour comes to flower with the unflagging cultivation of a homespunness of manner, naive freshness of imagination and invention, and an unstoppable pragmatic 'thrust'. Thus the text itself, while irreplaceable for those who will study him, has a certain enthusiastic quirkiness characteristic of a *vade mecum* for fans and collectors. For example, its compiler cannot always cite volume or page numbers of periodicals because his data are based on his own private collection of his friend Bradbury's publications, which consists in part of tearsheets. Taken as such, it amounts both to a lavish record and to a prodigal celebration, a Pop monument to the mammoth energies of a writer who follows Faulkner, Steinbeck, and

Hemingway as Russia's fourth favourite American writer; who has appeared in perhaps four or five times as many anthologies as Hemingway himself; whose titles have served as the names for at least eight rock groups and a section of the moon; and who has been represented in every printed and performed medium in existence in his era. Interspersed amid the chronologies, tables, and bibliographies of his work (comic books, operas, the lot), and of the work of others about him, are lists of his many pseudonyms, photographs of himself with family and friends, reproductions of nearly a hundred dust covers (including those of twenty-seven foreign language publications), and some eighty full-page facsimiles of printed title pages (undoubtedly to protect the Bradbury speculator from pirate editions) and of leaves from his manuscripts (largely revealing his typing skills). There are line drawings and halftones of paintings, doodles, high-school newspaper clippings, and a sketch map of his home-town neighbourhood, all by Bradbury himself. The Bradbury ana and arcana overflow here; what more can one say? Ah! And it couldn't happen to a nicer guy.

CRISTOPHER NASH

UNIVERSITY OF WARWICK

Zur Lyrik von Ted Hughes: Eine Interpretation nach Leitmotiven. By WALTRAUD MIT-GUTSCH. (Salzburg Studies in English Literature, Poetic Drama and Poetic Theory, 22) Salzburg: Institut für Englische Sprache und Literatur, Universität Salzburg. 1974. xiv + 282 pp. £4.80.

It is hard to know for what audience this book was intended. As an introduction to Hughes's poetry for the German reader it fails because it provides too little information about the poet's life and the background of his work; the earlier poetry, moreover, receives very little attention because the focus is on *Crow*. As a new interpretation of Hughes's lyric, on the other hand, it is too superficial a study to be useful. In her opening chapter Waltraud Mitgutsch argues that, contrary to the general view, Hughes is less the heir of Blake, Lawrence, and Dylan Thomas, than he is a metaphysical poet in the Donne tradition, although she later admits that he is ultimately 'ein Metaphysiker ohne Metaphysik' (p. 29), and that his poetry was also strongly influenced by Expressionism. But these labels are soon discarded, and the bulk of the book deals with Hughes's central themes: his longing for and fascination with death, his search for a centre of Being, his conviction that human civilization is worthless and nature wholly indifferent to man, and his growing faith in the primitivistic, chaotic animal energy, the indomitable and heroic vitality symbolized by the non-human Crow.

All this is well worn ground, and the organization of the book according to leitmotifs does not help. The three central chapters deal respectively with Hughes's cult of violence, his response to nature (for example, water, blood, stone imagery), and his treatment of the animal world. Such division necessarily leads to a great deal of overlap: Hughes's conception of the natural world and the animal world (and the violence of both) are, of course, all part of the same thing. In her fourth and last chapter, Waltraud Mitgutsch turns to an interpretation of *Crow*, based on her previous generalizations. Here we find some useful, if somewhat laboured, analyses of individual poems, for example, 'Crow Improvises'. But one wishes the author had given more citations from the poems themselves (there are precious few; evidently the author was not given permission to cite more than short passages) and fewer from secondary sources; she relies very heavily on previous Hughes criticism. *Zur Lyrik von Ted Hughes* reads like a dissertation that might have been condensed into a short review essay on the critical reception of Hughes in English;

as such, it would have helped German readers new to Hughes's work. Those who want to know what British and American critics through 1971 have said about Hughes's poetry will find ample reference throughout this study.

UNIVERSITY OF SOUTHERN CALIFORNIA   MARJORIE G. PERLOFF

An Uncommon Poet for the Common Man: A Study of Philip Larkin's Poetry. By LOLETTE
    KUBY. (De Proprietatibus Litterarum, Series Practica, 60) The Hague:
    Mouton. 1974. 190 pp. fl 28.

Philip Larkin's poem 'Broadcast' opens with a description of a concert:

> Giant whispering and coughing from
> Vast Sunday-full and organ-frowned-on spaces
> Precedes a sudden scuttle on the drum,
> 'The Queen' and huge resettling. Then begins
> A snivel on the violins:
> I think of your face among all those faces,
>
> Beautiful and devout before
> Cascades of monumental slithering

Dr Kuby takes this poem to be Larkin's comment on the stubborn refusal of the British to relinquish feudal habits of mind: 'The entrance of the queen, heralded by "a snivel on the violins", is the important one. Before her the audience "slithers" in mass rote obsequiousness, historically inbred by centuries of proclaimed divine right and power' (p. 54). Besides exhibiting beliefs about the British monarchy that went out of date in 1642, this comment illustrates some of the outstanding features of *An Uncommon Poet for the Common Man*. It is written in ignorance of English idiom (' "The Queen" ' is of course the National Anthem, not Her Majesty in person, as the quotation marks clearly indicate). It adopts misreadings, not merely through unfamiliarity with the language, but through insufficient attention to what is literally being said (it is of course the strings that are 'slithering', not the audience). It shows lack of awareness of the attitudes of the subject of the book (Larkin is a monarchist, not the reverse) that, even if they were missed in reading the poems, might have been gained from more thorough scholarship in secondary sources. Unfortunately, this is merely a conveniently succinct demonstration of the faults of the book as a whole, and does not exhaust them.

An Uncommon Poet for the Common Man is a mine of misinformation. It is inaccurate on dates of publication. It often misquotes Larkin's poems. It gets titles wrong (the substitution of an 'i' for an 'e' in 'The Blinding of Betjeman' provides a provocative new slant on Larkin's opinion of the Poet Laureate). 'An Arundel Tomb' suffers particularly in these regards. Not only is it misinterpreted, its literal content is misunderstood, and it is called 'Arundel Tombs' throughout. In addition to the errors relating directly to Larkin, there are others of a more general nature. We are told that Larkin dispenses with 'the traditional interlocutor in dramatic monologue' (p. 95). D. H. Lawrence is called a 'Victorian' writer (p. 123), and the context indicates that the adjective is meant literally. The scholarship of the book is inadequate and presented in a slapdash fashion. Dr Kuby might have made more accurate estimates of some of the poems had she sought out more of the numerous prose pieces in which Larkin writes about his own and others' poetry. She presents a totally misguided picture of modern verse: the 'Movement', it is suggested, was a self-conscious literary school that began to flourish in the early forties. The select bibliography, which I assume to set out Dr Kuby's primary sources, does not include many important items, while it does include items that do not exist, and items that are given totally inadequate bibliographical detail, being distinguished neither by author nor by title.

The book is badly written. At times it sinks into the most depressing pseudo-academic jargon: 'Yet when Larkin's voices move from the idiosyncrasies of speech with maximal voice print into the lyrical endings of "The Whitsun Weddings", "Dublinesque", or "At Grass", the movement is felt by contrast to be of great weight and significance, inherently both a loss and a gain which the paradoxical life–death imagery of the closing of the poems reinforces' (p. 29). However, it does escape now and again into the purely unintelligible, as in this comment on 'Spring': 'The scene depicted in the first six lines is a confusion of humanity, artefacts, and nature. Propelled by verbals: "set", "awakened", "stands", "sings", "flashing", one image follows another with the speed of a kaleidoscope' (p. 59).

Bluntly, Dr Kuby's views are sometimes ridiculous. Of 'Maiden Name' we are told that 'the tone of the poem, the stress in the speaker's emotions between continued love and pretended unconcern, is contained in the sniping double meanings of such words as "confused", which means, of course, both mingled together and mixed up, i.e., confused about her choice of husbands; and "losing shape", which suggests her transition from virginity to pregnancy after she is "laden", a word that suggests "layed-on" with "luggage", a word that implies that her husband is a "big lug" and an encumbrance' (p. 143). 'Mingled together and mixed up' indeed. This statement confuses a desperate search for ambiguity, a classic misreading of both the tone and the literal significance of the poem, and, the corollary to ignorance of English idiom, an assumption that, hidden in the language of a poem by an English poet addressed primarily to an English audience, is a complex substructure of American slang.

Amid all this, there are some genuine insights. Dr Kuby makes some perceptive observations on Larkin's use of the impersonal pronoun, and draws an instructive parallel between 'Dover Beach' and Larkin's 'Talking in Bed'. Many of the elements she emphasizes, the dramatic nature of much of Larkin's work, the importance of nuances of tone in his poems, are rightly emphasized. But the good points make the faults all the more regrettable, since the major defects of the book derive not from straightforward lack of ability in the author, but from a quite mistaken notion of what the criticism of poetry demands. Dr Kuby takes it as a truth universally acknowledged that certain concepts are good — ambiguity, for instance, or the Absurd, or the Void, or (that all but meaningless abstraction) the Human Condition — and she also takes Larkin's poems to be good. Therefore, Larkin's poems must be ambiguous, or be aware of the Absurd, or look into the Void, or make statements relevant to the Human Condition. She cannot, in fact, let poems stand on their own terms. Larkin's 'Myxomatosis', for example, is about the feelings of a man who comes across a rabbit in the final stages of the disease indicated in the title. Dr Kuby ransacks the poem for statements about universals, as if it should be insignificant with a narrower range: but the poem's strength is in the very particularity of the situation. It is about *one* speaker's feelings and *that* rabbit; it is not about Man, nor about Rabbits.

An Uncommon Poet for the Common Man started life as a Ph.D. thesis. The fact that it has been little altered (or even corrected) for its new form may explain some of Dr Kuby's misdirections. She was ill-advised to publish.
DAVID TIMMS

UNIVERSITY OF MANCHESTER

The Modern Humanities Research Association

was founded at Cambridge in 1918 and has become an international organization with members in all parts of the world. Its main object is to encourage advanced studies in Modern and Medieval languages and literatures by its publications.

PUBLICATIONS

All volumes of the Association's major publications are available either in original issues or in reprint. Price lists for volumes held by the Association can be obtained from the Hon. Treasurer, MHRA, King's College, Strand, London WC2R 2LS, England. For reprinted volumes and back issues not held by the Association see foot of next page.

1. THE MODERN LANGUAGE REVIEW

The official journal of the Modern Humanities Research Association; it is received by all individual members. It is edited by Professor C. P. Brand, Professor G. K. Hunter, Professor C. J. Rawson, Professor A. J. Steele, Dr C. C. Smith, Professor H. B. Nisbet, and Professor R. Auty. Published in January, April, July, and October of each year, it contains original articles and reviews on medieval and modern languages and literatures (including English).

Volumes 70–72

2. THE YEARBOOK OF ENGLISH STUDIES

Edited by Professor G. K. Hunter and Professor C. J. Rawson, is an annual supplement to the *Modern Language Review* devoted to the language and literature of the English-speaking world. It contains both articles and reviews.

Volumes 1–7

3. THE YEAR'S WORK IN MODERN LANGUAGE STUDIES

Edited by Professor Glanville Price, is an annual critical bibliography of work done in the following languages and literatures: medieval Latin, neo-Latin, French, Provençal, Spanish, Catalan, Portuguese, Italian, Rumanian, German, Dutch, Danish, Norwegian, Swedish, Czech, Slovak, Polish, Russian, and Serbo-Croat.

Volumes 30–37

4. THE ANNUAL BIBLIOGRAPHY OF ENGLISH LANGUAGE & LITERATURE

The aim of the editors is to list annually all scholarly books and articles concerning English and American literature and language published anywhere in the world. Editor John Horden. American editor Professor James B. Misenheimer, Jr.

Volumes 40–48

5. THE PRESIDENTIAL ADDRESS

Published annually in Part 4 of the *Modern Language Review*.

6. PUBLICATIONS OF THE MHRA

Volume 1: *The Future of the Modern Humanities*. The papers delivered at the Jubilee Congress of the MHRA in August 1968. Edited by J. C. Laidlaw. 1969, x + 137 pp.

Volume 2: *Горски вијенац: A Garland of Essays for E. M. Hill*. Edited by R. Auty, L. R. Lewitter, and A. P. Vlasto. 1970, x + 321 pp.

Volume 3: D. J. A. Ross, *Illustrated Medieval Alexander-Books in Germany and the Netherlands: A Study in Comparative Iconography*. 1971, xx + 202 pp. + 157 pp. of illustrations.

Volume 4: *European Context: Studies in the History and Literature of the Netherlands. Presented to Theodoor Weevers*. Edited by P. K. King and P. F. Vincent. 1971, xiv + 421 pp. 1 plate.

PUBLICATIONS OF THE MHRA — *continued*

Volume 5: *Liber Apologeticus de Omni Statu Humanae Naturae: A Defence of Human Nature in Every State (c. 1460). A Moral Play by Thomas Chaundler*. Edited and translated by D. Enright-Clark Shoukri. 1974, x + 208 pp., with 15 plates. (Published in conjunction with the Renaissance Society of America.)

Volume 6: Frederick John Stopp, *The Emblems of the Altdorf Academy: Medals and Medal Orations 1577–1626*. 1974, xxii + 226 pp. + 23 plates.

Volume 7: Robert M. Flores, *The Compositors of the First and Second Madrid Editions of 'Don Quixote'*. 1975, x + 148 pp. + 2 plates.

Volume 8: *An Anglo-Norman Dictionary*. Edited by †Louise W. Stone and William Rothwell (in progress).

7. MHRA DISSERTATION SERIES

Edited by Dr F. J. Stopp and Professor R. A. Wisbey (Germanic); Professor W. H. Barber and Professor D. J. A. Ross (Romance).

Volume 1: T. J. Rogers, *Techniques of Solipsism. A Study of Theodor Storm's Narrative Fiction*, 1970.

Volume 2: D. A. Wells, *The Vorau 'Moses' and 'Balaam'. A Study of Their Relationship to Exegetical Tradition*, 1970.

Volume 3: H. B. Nisbet, *Herder and the Philosophy and History of Science*, 1970 (Part 1 of this volume is also available in paperback, under the title *Herder and Scientific Thought*).

Volume 4: Nicole Marzac, *Édition Critique du Sermon 'Qui Manducat Me' de Robert Ciboule (1403–58)*, 1971.

Volume 5: Rosemarie Jones, *The Theme of Love in the 'Romans d'Antiquité'*, 1972.

Volume 6: C. D. Rolfe, *Saint-Amant and the Theory of 'Ut Pictura Poesis'*, 1972.

Volume 7: C. Todd, *Voltaire's Disciple: Jean-François de La Harpe*, 1972.

Volume 8: A. Subiotto, *Bertolt Brecht's Adaptations for the Berliner Ensemble*, 1975.

Volume 9: V. Moleta, *The Early Poetry of Guittone d'Arezzo*, 1976.

8. MHRA STYLE BOOK: Notes for Authors and Editors

Edited by A. S. Maney and R. L. Smallwood. Notes for contributors to, and authors and editors of, the publications of the MHRA which are also designed to assist authors and editors of other academic publications and students preparing dissertations.

Available from W. S. Maney & Son Ltd, Hudson Road, Leeds LS9 7DL.

Price including postage, £0.40 (US-$1.00), payable in advance.

9. PROCEEDINGS OF CONGRESSES OF FILLM

Literature and Science. Proceedings of the Sixth Congress. Oxford, 1954.

Expression, Communication and Experience in Literature and Language. Edited by Dr R. G. Popperwell. Proceedings of the Twelfth Congress. Cambridge, 1972.

BACK VOLUMES

Modern Language Review, Volumes 1–69; General Indexes to Vols 11–20, 21–30, 31–50, and 51–60.
The Annual Bibliography of English Language and Literature, Volumes 1–39.
The Year's Work in Modern Language Studies, Volumes 1–29.
Presidential Addresses.

All are obtainable from Wm Dawson & Sons Ltd, Cannon House, Park Farm Road, Folkestone, England, and should be ordered from them direct.